THE HANDBOOK TO
THE BLOOMSBURY GROUP

ALSO PUBLISHED BY BLOOMSBURY

Katherine Mansfield and the Bloomsbury Group, edited by Todd Martin
Modernism's Print Cultures, Faye Hammill and Mark Hussey
Modernist Lives: Biography and Autobiography at Leonard and Virginia Woolf's Hogarth Press, Claire Battershill
Woolf: A Guide for the Perplexed, Kathryn Simpson

THE HANDBOOK TO
THE BLOOMSBURY GROUP

Edited by Derek Ryan and Stephen Ross

BLOOMSBURY ACADEMIC
LONDON • NEW YORK • OXFORD • NEW DELHI • SYDNEY

BLOOMSBURY ACADEMIC
Bloomsbury Publishing Plc
50 Bedford Square, London, WC1B 3DP, UK
1385 Broadway, New York, NY 10018, USA

BLOOMSBURY, BLOOMSBURY ACADEMIC and the Diana logo
are trademarks of Bloomsbury Publishing Plc

First published in Great Britain 2018
Paperback edition published 2020

Cover design: Eleanor Rose
Cover image: A Conversation, 1913–16, Bell, Vanessa (1879–1961) / Samuel Courtauld Trust,
The Courtauld Gallery, London, UK / Bridgeman Images © Estate of Vanessa Bell, courtesy
Henrietta Garnett

A catalogue record for this book is available from the British Library.

A catalog record for this book is available from the Library of Congress.

ISBN: HB: 978-1-3500-1491-6
PB: 978-1-3501-4365-4
ePDF: 978-1-3500-1493-0
eBook: 978-1-3500-1492-3

Series: Bloomsbury Handbook

Typeset by Newgen KnowledgeWorks Pvt. Ltd., Chennai, India
Printed and bound in Great Britain

To find out more about our authors and books visit
www.bloomsbury.com and sign up for our newsletters.

CONTENTS

FIGURES

CONTRIBUTORS

Peter Adkins is a PhD candidate at the University of Kent, where his thesis focuses on modernism, ecology, and the Anthropocene.

Todd Avery is associate professor of English at the University of Massachusetts Lowell. He is the author of *Radio Modernism: Literature, Ethics, and the BBC, 1922–1938* (2006) and a number of articles on British modernism and the Bloomsbury Group.

David Ayers is professor of modernism and critical theory at the University of Kent. He has published widely on modernist studies and the avant-garde, including *Wyndham Lewis and Western Man* (1992), *English Literature of the 1920s* (1999), *Modernism: A Short Introduction* (2004), and *Literary Theory: A Reintroduction* (2007).

Claire Battershill is a Banting Postdoctoral Fellow at Simon Fraser University. She has published various articles on modernism, the Bloomsbury Group, and life writing and works on the Modernist Archives Publishing Project. She also writes fiction and has published a book of short stories, *Circus* (2014).

Michaela Bronstein is assistant professor at Stanford University. She has published on modernism and literary transhistoricism, and her forthcoming monograph is titled *Out of Context: The Uses of Modernist Fiction*.

Lauren Elkin is a critic, translator, and writer. Her latest book is *Flâneuse: Women Walk the City* (2016).

J. Ashley Foster is assistant professor of twentieth- and twenty-first-century British literature with emphasis on digital humanities at California State University, Fresno. She is currently working on a book project, *Modernism's Impossible Witness: Peace Testimonies from the Spanish Civil War*.

Jane Goldman is reader in English literature at the University of Glasgow, and general editor of the Cambridge Edition of the Works of Virginia Woolf. She has published widely on Woolf, modernism, and the avant-garde, including *The Feminist Aesthetics of Virginia Woolf: Modernism, Post-Impressionism and the Politics of the Visual* (1998), *Modernism, 1910–1945: Image to Apocalypse* (2004), and *The Cambridge Introduction to Virginia Woolf* (2006).

Benjamin D. Hagen is assistant professor of English at the University of South Dakota. He has published articles in *Modernism/modernity* and *Twentieth-Century Literature* on Virginia Woolf and Wallace Stevens and is currently completing a monograph on the lives and works of Woolf and D. H. Lawrence.

Maggie Humm is emeritus professor in the School of Arts and Digital Industries at the University of East London. She has published numerous books on modernism, feminism, visual culture, and the Bloomsbury Group, including *Border Traffic* (1991), *Feminism and Film* (1997), *Modernist Women and Visual Cultures: Virginia Woolf, Vanessa Bell, Photography and Cinema* (2002), *Snapshots of Bloomsbury: The Private Lives of Virginia Woolf and Vanessa Bell* (2006), and *The Edinburgh Companion to Virginia Woolf and the Arts* (2010).

Mark Hussey is distinguished professor of English at Pace University, New York. He is editor of the *Woolf Studies Annual* and has dozens of publications on Virginia Woolf and the Bloomsbury Group, including scholarly editions, edited collections, monographs, and articles. Recently, he edited *Between the Acts* for the Cambridge Edition of the Works of Virginia Woolf and is currently writing a biography of Clive Bell.

Clara Jones is lecturer in modern literature at King's College, London. She has published research on Woolf, class, and feminism, and is author of *Virginia Woolf: Ambivalent Activist* (2016).

Laci Mattison is assistant professor of twentieth-century British literature at Florida Gulf Coast University. Her publications include essays and articles on H.D., Vladimir Nabokov, Elizabeth Bowen, and Virginia Woolf, and she is a series editor of *Understanding Philosophy, Understanding Modernism* (Bloomsbury), for which she has co-edited the volumes on Henri Bergson and Gilles Deleuze.

Steven Putzel is associate professor of English at Penn State University, Wilkes-Barre. He has published widely on various aspects of modernism, and his latest monograph is *Virginia Woolf and the Theatre* (2011).

Stephen Ross is professor of English and cultural, social, and political thought at the University of Victoria, Canada. He has published widely on modernism, including *Modernism and Theory: A Critical Debate* (2009) and *Conrad and Empire* (2004). He is past-president of the Modernist Studies Association (2015/16) and General Editor of *The Routledge Encyclopedia of Modernism*.

Derek Ryan is senior lecturer in modernist literature at the University of Kent. He is the author of *Virginia Woolf and the Materiality of Theory: Sex, Animal, Life* (2013) and *Animal Theory: A Critical Introduction* (2015). He is currently co-editing *Flush: A Biography* for the Cambridge Edition of the Works of Virginia Woolf.

Sonita Sarker is professor of women's, gender, and sexuality studies at Macalester College. She has published widely on imperialism, globalization, and modernism, including *Trans-Status Subjects: Gender in the Globalization of South and Southeast Asia* (2002) and *Sustainable Feminisms* (2007).

Kathryn Simpson is an independent scholar who has published widely on Virginia Woolf, Katherine Mansfield, and the Bloomsbury Group. She is author of *Gifts, Markets and Economies of Desire in Virginia Woolf* (2008) and *Woolf: A Guide for the Perplexed* (Bloomsbury, 2016).

Anna Snaith is professor of twentieth-century literature at King's College, London. She has published widely on modernism, empire, and women's writing, and is author of *Virginia Woolf: Public and Private Negotiations* (2000) and *Modernist Voyages: Colonial Women Writers in London 1890–1945* (2014). She recently edited *A Room of One's Own* and *Three Guineas* for Oxford World's Classics and *The Years* for the Cambridge Edition of the Works of Virginia Woolf.

Vicki Tromanhauser is associate professor of English at the State University of New York, New Paltz. She has published articles on modernist literature, animality, and the life sciences in *Twentieth-Century Literature*, *Woolf Studies Annual*, and *Journal of Modern Literature* and is completing a monograph on modernism and meat.

Susan Wegener is an instructor at Purdue University. She has published on Virginia Woolf, Bloomsbury, and antisemitism.

Jesse Wolfe is associate professor of English at California State University, Stanislaus. He is author of *Bloomsbury, Modernism and the Reinvention of Intimacy* (2011) and is currently writing a book about the legacies of Bloomsbury in contemporary literature.

Introduction

DEREK RYAN AND STEPHEN ROSS

Writing to Leonard Woolf from France in the summer of 1950, Vanessa Bell aimed to 'warn' him that yet another interested onlooker was descending on them in search of information about their lives and circle. In response to the request from a Miss Benson, Bell reports that she 'told her that the Friday Club was a small society which didn't last very long, and implied that it was quite unimportant and that there never was such a thing as the "Bloomsbury Group"' (*Letters* 527). This appears to be a disavowal of the idea of 'Bloomsbury' and its formation, of which the Friday Club played a role, having started in 1905 to exhibit and discuss art just as Thoby Stephen's 'Thursday evenings' created space for literary, philosophical, and often downright bawdy chat. Yet the letter betrays an awareness not only that there was such a group but also that its history was too important to fall into the hands of someone who was not part of it:

> I don't want to be brutal to the woman, but I simply cannot go on telling people about such things. They always and inevitably get it hopelessly wrong. It seems to me that if Bloomsbury is to be written about it must be by its own members (most of whom have done so). One can't tell the truth about living people and the world must wait till we're all dead. Don't you agree? I don't mind telling what I can about the past generation, but not about my own – except to my own family and friends. (527)

At the same time as Bell stresses her frustrations at the spreading of falsehoods by outsiders, the letter registers an anxiety about how, when, and with whom Bloomsbury can share its story. Versions may be told by its 'members' (and in Bell's case strictly only *to* them), though even then its truths are evasive and must be deferred for the next generation to grapple with. That a certain defensiveness can be detected in a private letter to a fellow member so many years after the group's peak activity indicates that Bell was keen to claim there was no such thing as Bloomsbury precisely because of how profoundly there was.

While wariness of critics leading to avoidance of them was by no means a uniform reaction among the Bloomsburians (Leonard's own response was more often than not to engage in an effort to shape their, and particularly Virginia Woolf's, reception), Clive Bell similarly bristles in his recollection of those he called the 'Bloomsbury-baiters' ('Bloomsbury' 137). Feeling that the critics were misguidedly characterizing the group as out of touch, he rhetorically wonders who they are actually referring to:

> Obviously not Roger Fry who introduced the modern movement in French painting to the British public, nor Maynard Keynes, who, I understand, revolutionised economics. Nor does it seem likely that the critics are thinking of Lytton Strachey who, far from being reactionary, went out of his way to help the cause of Women's Suffrage when

that cause was reckoned a dangerous fad, or of Leonard Woolf who was a Fabian long before British socialism had become what the Americans call the racket. Whom can these castigators of 'Bloomsbury' have in mind? Clearly not Virginia Woolf, who invented what amounts almost to a new prose form; nor, I hope, certain critics who, long before the 1920s, had appreciated and defended the then disconcerting works of Picasso and T. S. Eliot. (136–7)

This selection of Bloomsbury's achievements (including his own in the final sentence) ranges across literature, the visual arts, politics, and economics to make a mockery of the notion that the members of the group 'devoted themselves to stifling, or trying to stifle, at birth every vital movement that came to life' (136). Where Vanessa Bell's tactic was to dampen down the furore around Bloomsbury, Clive Bell shouts about its successes. He might have added to the list the innovative paintings of Vanessa herself, alongside those of Duncan Grant.

The group was never short of detractors to defend itself against. Among the contemporaries who sneered at their artistry and lifestyle were Wyndham Lewis, whose frequent personal jibes turned into savage satire in *The Apes of God* (1930), and D. H. Lawrence, who described them as 'beetles' in letters to both Ottoline Morrell and David Garnett when bemoaning the 'horror of little swarming selves' that left him with feelings of 'hostility and rage' (Garnett, *Flowers* 53–4).[1] A host of commentators followed in labelling Bloomsburians elitist, detached dilettantes. Cambridge critics F. R. Leavis and Queenie Leavis notoriously promoted this view of them, skewed as it was with a 'gendered' bias (Hussey 13–15), in 'unremitting attacks' that for a long time influenced the British education system to Bloomsbury's, and particularly Virginia Woolf's, detriment (Silver 154). This distinctly English reception was bound up in assumptions and judgements about class privilege (with the incomes of its individuals often exaggerated, though of upper-middle-class heritage they by and large were)[2] married to an underplaying of the extent to which Bloomsbury was 'engaged in a systematic, if playful and parodic, dismantling of the moral and aesthetic underpinnings of the class system that provided such privilege' (Piggford 84; see also Simpson in this volume). By the start of the 1960s, when the first volume of Leonard Woolf's autobiography appeared, a division was discernible between America and Britain in what would turn out to be the beginnings of a revival in Bloomsbury's fortunes. As Regina Marler underlines in her thorough and even-handed documentation of the group's reception in *Bloomsbury Pie* (1997), American critics were mostly immune to, or ignorant of, British class dynamics, meaning that they 'had never felt diminished by Bloomsbury's power and influence in the world of arts and letters'; though it also meant they could be seen 'to look mildly, even nostalgically' at the social privilege from which its members benefited (35). Reviewers on the other side of the Atlantic were, on the contrary, 'more severe, trotting out the old jibes against Bloomsbury as if answering a drill in cultural commonplaces' (35). As the four further volumes of Woolf's autobiography appeared over the course of the decade, the reception became far more generous (36).

The specific focus of the renewed interest in Bloomsbury was something neither Clive nor Vanessa Bell could have anticipated. With its frank portrayal of the group's lively and unconventional sexual relationships, Michael Holroyd's two-volume *Lytton Strachey: A Critical Biography* (1967, 1968) was to blast away some of the persistent stereotypes of Bloomsbury as confined to a world of high intellect and aristocratic taste. In doing so, it revealed just how much about the group had yet to be revealed, prompting new interest in their radical lifestyles. As Marler puts it, 'after *Lytton Strachey*, there were no more virgins' (92). When other significant Bloomsbury-related publications appeared – most notably E. M. Forster's long-delayed *Maurice* (1971), with its explicitly homosexual storyline, and Quentin Bell's *Virginia Woolf* (1972), with its revelations of sexual abuse and lesbianism (albeit any meaningful treatment of these was often overlooked in favour of depicting Woolf's 'madness' and 'frigidity')[3] – sex became an inextricable part of the group's biography and bibliography. In both their lives and their works, Bloomsbury's flexible and creative forms of domesticity and experiments with new models of intimacy have been celebrated as breaking from the strictures of the Victorian family and values and heralding their modernism (see Reed, *Bloomsbury Rooms* [2004]; Wolfe, *Bloomsbury, Modernism* [2011]). More recently, the landmark essay collection *Queer Bloomsbury* (2016) demonstrates how Bloomsbury's legacy has shaped and been shaped by queer studies to such an extent that the book's very title is in many ways 'redundant, implying that there could somehow be a neutral or "unqueer" Bloomsbury', when any separation of the terms – queer and Bloomsbury – is now 'impossible' (Helt and Detloff 5).

It is now almost equally as difficult to discuss Bloomsbury without invoking Virginia Woolf's account in 'Old Bloomsbury' of Lytton Strachey pointing at a stain on Vanessa Bell's white dress and asking 'Semen?' – an incident that marked a shift from the 'monastic' early Bloomsbury filled with 'barriers of reticence and reserve' and that opened the floodgates to endless talk about bodily fluids (56). How much artistic licence is at play in Woolf's account is up for debate, but the moral of the story is clear: the Bloomsburians would discuss and explore sexuality with the same openness and desire for truth that characterized their intellectual pursuits and aesthetic creations – and significantly with women at the centre of it all (see Caws; see also Elkin in this volume). Uncovering this side to Bloomsbury may not have halted criticism of the group, but queer scholarship has convincingly exposed the basis on which those attacks are often made. Christopher Reed, packing even more alliterative punch than Clive Bell's term for the group's detractors, refers to this criticism as 'Bloomsbury Bashing', in which Bloomsbury's centrality to modernist aesthetics and politics is 'violently disowned' by both 'academic Marxists' (primarily British) and 'academic feminists' (primarily American). The former have done so, he provocatively argues, by making 'homosexuality the badge of evil – in this case the decadent and effeminate bourgeoisie', and the latter by allying themselves with 'heterosexual privilege' so that 'homosexuality is denied all complexity as lived experience and is simply deployed to signify the oppression of women' (58). To take seriously Bloomsbury's queering of sex and relationships is to alter our impressions both of the group itself and its critical reception (see Avery and Wolfe in this volume).

Such defences of Bloomsbury, whether by its own members or by later critics, give a flavour of the controversies and commitments of a group that few would now doubt existed. If it could be stated over twenty years ago that 'Bloomsbury is the best-documented literary and artistic coterie in twentieth-century Britain' (Marler 7), then this has only become truer over time. However, the somewhat polarized reception of the group has often obscured the complexity of the question of *what* it was.[4] This is a question that can only be answered through considerations of its membership (*who* was it?), temporality (*when* was it?), and geography (*where* was it?). On the one hand, there is a fairly standard answer to these questions. The 'who' of Bloomsbury would consist of its inner core, without whom the term cannot be meaningfully invoked. In the absence of any official membership, this list would have to include as a minimum Clive Bell, Vanessa Bell, E. M. Forster, Roger Fry, Duncan Grant, Maynard Keynes, Desmond

MacCarthy, Molly MacCarthy, Lytton Strachey, Adrian Stephen, Saxon Sydney-Turner, Leonard Woolf, and Virginia Woolf. While not all those who gathered in Bloomsbury were based there – the MacCarthys, for example, were 'a most important ingredient of Bloomsbury' even though they lived in Chelsea (V. Bell, 'Notes' 107)[5] – the question of when it was can be tied to where it was. The decade 1904–14 saw regular gatherings first at 46 Gordon Square, where the Stephen children had moved after the death of their father Leslie Stephen; next at 29 Fitzroy Square in 1907, where Virginia and Adrian moved after the death of Thoby, and Vanessa's marriage to Clive; and then 38 Brunswick Square in 1911, when Leonard Woolf, the year before he married Virginia, entered the household alongside Maynard Keynes and Duncan Grant.

This period accounts for the 'Old Bloomsbury' whose origins lie in the Cambridge Apostles, the secret society of which Leonard Woolf, Lytton Strachey, and Maynard Keynes were a part, and which was 'dominated' by G. E. Moore's philosophy and presence (Keynes 13; L. Woolf, *Sowing* 130). What shines through in accounts of the Apostles is the manner in which Moore enabled them to interrogate ever more precisely the question of intrinsic goods which were considered to be, as Moore writes in *Principia Ethica* (1903), 'personal affection' and 'appreciation of what is beautiful in Art or Nature', all under the pursuit of truth (188). In 'My Early Beliefs' (1938), Keynes recollects how it was 'Moore's method' that allowed them 'to make essentially vague notions clear by using precise language about them and asking questions. It was a method of discovery by the instrument of impeccable grammar and an unambiguous dictionary. "What *exactly* do you mean?" was the phrase most frequently on our lips' (17). Leonard Woolf similarly recalls how Moore taught them 'to make quite certain that we knew what we meant when we made a statement', but adds that Keynes gives a 'distorted picture' by suggesting that they were concerned too much with analytic contemplation and not enough with action: 'He [Moore] and we were fascinated by questions of what was right and wrong, what one *ought* to do ... and argued interminably about the consequences of one's actions, both in actual and imaginary situations' (*Sowing* 147–9). Not everyone in what became the Bloomsbury Group would be as closely attuned to the finer details of Moorean philosophy as is often assumed (see Hagen in this volume), but that it had some influence on shaping their approach to one another and to life itself is undoubted.

The Bloomsbury of intimacy, irreverence, and innovation that grew out of the encounters between the Apostles and Stephen sisters can be characterized by two events that bookended 1910, the year in which 'human character changed', as Virginia Woolf would later famously write in 'Character in Fiction' (421).[6] On 7 February, Adrian Stephen, Virginia Woolf (then Stephen), and Duncan Grant were among a group who dressed up as Abyssinian royals and gained entry to the HMS *Dreadnought*, at the time the world's largest and most powerful warship, causing much embarrassment to the Navy and sparking public scandal when the truth was uncovered (thanks to Horace Cole, who with Adrian had been the driving force behind it). In his account of the hoax, Adrian Stephen writes of having to 'speak fluent gibberish impromptu' in order to fool the officials (10), and in the press it was reported that the expression 'Bunga-Bunga' was used, which would for some time become associated with the event (13; see also Stansky 33). The authorities were unsure how to react, and in a bizarre episode, officers seemingly satisfied themselves by visiting Duncan Grant, driving him to a field near Hendon, and subjecting him to 'two ceremonial taps' with a cane. He returned home via the tube while still wearing his slippers (Stephen 15). While comically proving their credentials as pranksters, the Dreadnought hoax also speaks to what Frances Spalding describes as the group's 'refusal to accept any authority without questioning the value on which it rested'; as 'a swaggering, ostentatious symbol of arrogant patriotism', this warship was an ideal target (*Duncan Grant* 85; see also Snaith in this volume).

By the end of the year, Bloomsbury was challenging authority in the world of art through Roger Fry's organization of 'Manet and the Post-Impressionists' at the Grafton Galleries in London, which ran from 8 November to 15 January. Here, the works of Paul Cézanne, Vincent Van Gogh, Paul Gauguin, Henri Matisse, and Pablo Picasso, among others, were on display, upsetting the conservative English critics and changing the course of art history. According to Vanessa Bell, 'it caused even more dismay and disapproval than Bloomsbury itself' ('Notes' 111), while it made Fry, in Quentin Bell's words, 'the best-hated man in the London art world' (*Bloomsbury* 50). This 'new movement' of 'Post-Impressionism', the term Fry was largely responsible for popularizing, is summarized by him as 'the re-establishment of purely aesthetic criteria in place of the criterion of conformity to appearance – the rediscovery of the principles of structural design and harmony' (*Vision and Design* 8), that was to become a reassessment of the relationship between art and 'nature' (see Adkins in this volume). Clive Bell in *Art* (1914) declared in quasi-religious language that it was 'the reassertion of the first commandment of art – Thou shalt create form' (43–4; see also Hussey in this volume). It was only in January 1910 that Fry became properly acquainted with Bloomsbury, due to a chance encounter with Vanessa Bell at a train station in Cambridge, and his inclusion very quickly added intellectual weight to the group: 'The old skeleton arguments of primitive Bloomsbury about art and beauty,' Virginia Woolf recalled, 'put on flesh and blood' ('Old Bloomsbury' 57). The group was well aware that the effects of the Post-Impressionist exhibition travelled much further than Bloomsbury: 'It is impossible I think that any other single exhibition can ever have had so much effect as did that on the rising generation', wrote Vanessa Bell, describing it as 'a sudden pointing to a possible path, a sudden liberation', an 'influx of new life' (qtd in Spalding, *Vanessa Bell* 92). These new creative energies would be evident in the Omega workshop that Fry, Vanessa Bell, and Duncan Grant established in Fitzroy Square in July 1913, producing furniture with vibrant colours and spontaneous design (see Humm in this volume).

But if the above people, period and places are unarguably crucial to any understanding of Bloomsbury, this story of the group throws up contradictions and tensions. If we foreground the Cambridge Apostles, then Bloomsbury's roots appear to be distinctly male and its intellectual heritage to be firmly within the British tradition. The approach of the Apostles is specifically distinguished by Leonard Woolf, for example, from the 'intricate, if not unintelligible, intellectual gymnastics of a Platonic, Aristotelian, Kantian, or Hegelian nature' (*Sowing* 147). Alternatively, the Dreadnought hoax and Post-Impressionist exhibition show them, respectively, sending up patriarchal, imperialist bombast associated with the British Empire and welcoming an influx of experimental aesthetics from the Continent to revivify the stale English art world (the French dimension being particularly important, as Mary Ann Caws and Sarah Bird Wright have comprehensively documented in *Bloomsbury and France* [2000]). Then again, just as many of the group played no part in the former event, the latter's impact on Bloomsbury was uneven, with Lytton Strachey reportedly of the view that the others 'were downright silly about Matisse and Picasso' (C. Bell, 'Bloomsbury' 134). And we might query how much this version of the story tells us about Bloomsbury's most famous writers, E. M. Forster and Virginia Woolf, who never actually met until 1910, by which time Forster was already an accomplished writer onto his fourth novel, *Howards End* (Stansky 149). As a Cambridge Apostle, Forster was in a sense rooted to the group's origins, and yet he did not see them regularly in the early years. He himself remarked 'I dont [sic] belong automatically' to Bloomsbury (80), while Vanessa Bell described him as an 'elusive visitor' ('Notes' 107). On the other hand, Woolf was, like her sister, excluded from that Cambridge heritage, though she is central to any version of Bloomsbury in the years that followed. These examples do not make the idea of 'The Bloomsbury Group' less tenable, but they do serve as reminders that, as Desmond MacCarthy emphasizes, 'in taste and judgement "Bloomsbury" from the start has been at variance with itself', containing 'enough difference of temperament and opinion to stimulate talk; enough intellectual honesty to enable them to learn from each other' (67).[7] From the group's inception, an open mind and open ears were among its principal values.

Fixing Bloomsbury to its founding members, philosophical origins, prewar gatherings or strict geographical location is also to emphasize certain elements and ignore more varied worlds they inhabited and influenced. Not mentioned in the above list of members are numerous figures for whom a serious claim could be made to be considered part of early Bloomsbury, such as Gerald Shove and James Strachey. Moreover, and despite Vanessa Bell's assertion in a 1931 letter to Clive Bell that 'Bloomsbury was killed by the War' (a comment that is once again provoked in response to critics 'sniping' about the group in the press; *Letters* 364), the list expands during the war to include Francis Birrell and Dora Carrington; into the 1920s and 1930s, it involves the likes of Frances Partridge and Lydia Lopokova Keynes, as well as the Bell children, Julian, Quentin and Angelica (see Rosenbaum xi). Sometimes figures who became integrated into the group are awkwardly positioned as not properly a part of it. David 'Bunny' Garnett, who in his autobiography records his ambivalent sense of both belonging to and being outside of the group during his first meetings with them (*Golden Echo* 252), is repeatedly described as one of the 'secondary' or 'fringe Bloomsberries' (Marler 10, 40), or in the case of Sarah Knight's magisterial recent biography, *Bloomsbury's Outsider*. Others who form associations with the group have been ignored or marginalized in histories of it. Mulk Raj Anand's *Conversations in Bloomsbury* (1981) is a fascinating, if not wholly reliable, account of the friendships he formed with the group's central figures after moving to London in 1925 (and working for a period at the Hogarth Press a couple of years later), but it is relatively recently that his life and work has been considered in the contexts of Bloomsbury and modernism (Marcus, Snaith, Berman; see also Mattison in this volume). One important consequence of considering figures such as Anand is that it opens up questions about the wider imperialist context of Bloomsbury. The anti-imperialist politics the group is often credited with remains complicated and problematic, where many of its members' backgrounds were 'firmly rooted in the Raj' (Gerzina 113) and where many of its writings retain, as Urmila Seshagiri argues of Virginia Woolf's novels, 'a wide range of assumptions about nonwhite otherness' (60; see also Sarker in this volume). It is significant, too, that one of Bloomsbury's most outspoken anti-imperialists, Leonard Woolf, did not develop his politics in Cambridge or Bloomsbury but in his time working as a civil servant in Ceylon (now Sri Lanka) between 1904 and 1911 (see, for example, *Growing* 25, 157, 224).[8] Similarly, E. M. Forster, whom Anand felt was 'perhaps the only Englishman of this century who came near enough to understanding Indian people' (qtd in Gerzina 125), derives his knowledge about, and critique of, empire primarily from his relationship with Syed Ross Masood and subsequent experience of visiting India.

If Bloomsbury did not come to an end due to the war, it had become dispersed, with Vanessa Bell and Duncan Grant moving to Charleston Farmhouse in Sussex in 1916 and the Woolfs to Hogarth House in Richmond in 1915, as well as their own Sussex retreats in Asheham, Beddingham and then, from 1919, Monk's House, Rodmell.[9] These moves would more accurately be considered a relocation of Bloomsbury than a break from it – this is especially true of Charleston, where the Woolfs were frequent visitors, and where Clive Bell, Keynes, Lytton Strachey and David Garnett all spent lengthy periods of time (see Jones in this volume). This continuation of Bloomsbury appears in other ways, too. While the Omega ended in 1919 due to financial difficulties, other initiatives with distinctly Bloomsbury origins that began around this time would flourish for decades. The Memoir Club was started in 1920 by Molly MacCarthy – who described herself as 'secretary and drudge of the club' on invitation cards (Rosenbaum, *Memoir Club* 54) – and included the majority of those who had been at the heart of 'Old Bloomsbury'; it had its last meeting in 1956, by which time a younger generation had joined.[10] Being aware when they started out 'that there was something absurd in an early-middle-aged group of people reading one another memoirs' (Rosenbaum, *Memoir Club* 15), the group's practice of writing biographical pieces about their own lives or those of their circle – Woolf's 'Old Bloomsbury' and Keynes's 'My Early Beliefs', mentioned above, are two of the best examples – spurred them on to produce longer works of autobiography. These range from Molly MacCarthy's *A Nineteenth-Century Childhood* (1924) to Leonard Woolf's five volumes, as well as playful experiments in biography such as Lytton Strachey's *Eminent Victorians* (1918), *Queen Victoria* (1921) and *Elizabeth and Essex* (1928), and Virginia Woolf's *Orlando* (1928) and *Flush* (1933) (Woolf returned to a more straightforward biographical mode, with much tribulation, for *Roger Fry* [1940]).

Leonard and Virginia Woolf's Hogarth Press, begun in 1917 at their home in Richmond (then from 1924 in 52 Tavistock Square) after they had taught themselves how to set type and print, opened Bloomsbury up to broader 'networks' of modernism over the decades that followed (Southworth 11; see also Battershill in this volume). In *Beginning Again*, Leonard recalls shopping with Virginia for a printing machine, 'star[ing] through the window at them rather like two hungry children gazing at buns and cakes in a baker shop window' (234). What started out with the excitement of amateurs grew to be a demanding and professional outfit. Together the Woolfs published some 450 titles before Virginia's death in 1941, including their own work and that of personal friends Katherine Mansfield and T. S. Eliot, but also a diverse list of numerous popular writers, nonfictional works, and translations of international writers, including the first English translations of Sigmund Freud.[11] Finally, Bloomsbury's longevity resides in the very fact that many of its members' most significant achievements came in the 1920s and 1930s, from Forster's *A Passage to India* (1924) to Virginia Woolf's *The Waves* (1931) to Keynes's *The General Theory of Employment, Interest and Money* (1936). It is within this longer timespan that Bloomsbury has been considered 'avant-garde' in both its aesthetics and its advancement of pacifist politics within the context of 'the postwar battle for Europe's future' (Froula 2; see also Foster and Goldman in this volume). There has been a resurgence of interest in later works by Woolf, published of course by the Hogarth Press, in particular *The Years* for its exploration of topics ranging from Jewishness to animality (see Wegener and Tromanhauser in this volume); in its very scope, this novel has even been called Woolf's 'most ambitious' (Snaith, 'Introduction' xl).

There are, then, many versions of Bloomsbury and various avenues through which to approach its figures and works. Yet the group has, it could be argued, been taken for granted in the rush to expand the parameters of modernist studies temporally, spatially and – in Douglas Mao and Rebecca Walkowitz's words – in 'vertical' ways, namely the elision of boundaries between high and low forms of culture, the critique and reorganization of canons to include previously marginalized figures and works, and the increased focus on 'matters of production, dissemination, and reception' (737–8). If modernist studies is, as Paul Saint-Amour has recently summarized, now 'a strong field – populous, varied, generative, self-reflexive' precisely because the 'theory of modernism has weakened and become less axiomatic, more conjectural, more conjunctural' (41), then the problem for the Bloomsbury Group is that in the eyes of many scholars it has remained too 'strong' a term. Scholars either fall into the trap of thinking that the group is a more or less totally known quantity or consider Bloomsbury to belong to the high modernist past with which the new modernist studies has broken. One consequence of this is that critics often overlook the manner in which Bloomsbury's own contours of expansion map onto modernism's new horizons along similar temporal, spatial and vertical lines. That is, to dispose of Bloomsbury as the outdated centre of modernism is to do a disservice to Bloomsbury's own expansive, transnational influences and reach (see Bronstein in this volume). And so, while the globalizing impulse of the new modernist studies has indeed been salutary for the discipline and its many fields, a truly 'planetary' (Friedman 2015) understanding of modernism requires that, as well as opening up hitherto ignored or marginalized figures, texts, and contexts, we return this new global apprehension of modernism to its foundations in what James and Seshagiri describe as 'historically conditioned and culturally specific clusters of artistic achievements between the late nineteenth and mid-twentieth centuries' (88). This effort in contextualizing also ensures that Bloomsbury is judged not only on its own terms but on those of the wider social and political landscape in which it sought to intervene (see Putzel and Ayers in this volume).

How to make sense of Bloomsbury's formation, reception and import for modernist studies is the aim of *The Handbook to the Bloomsbury Group*. Presenting Bloomsbury as historically and culturally rooted as well as exploring how its members' lives and works flow into the expanse of new approaches, the volume showcases Bloomsbury's ongoing vitality. The chapters are divided in a way that suits this purpose: each of the ten pairs of essays offers lucid, up-to-date overviews of topics central to understanding the group's activities and influences, followed by cutting-edge examinations of a more specific aspect of its figures, texts, and contexts. In focusing on the rubrics of sexuality, the arts, empire, feminism, philosophy, class, Jewishness, nature, politics, and war, Bloomsbury is situated in a broader context than is usual, while coverage ranges over its central figures, some of its key associates, and a wide variety of literary, artistic, political, economic, and biographical works. Taken together, the chapters attempt to both confront controversies directly and articulate nuanced analyses, with the aim of sparking new debates about the group and its legacies. Pairing the essays as we have done provides the uninitiated with sufficient context to understand the more concentrated 'case study' essays, while these essays in turn add detail and heft to the broader claims made in the overview chapters. We have also added cross-references in the essays themselves, following the same format as above, to point to connections across different sections of the volume. The end result is, we hope, a textured introduction to Bloomsbury that will also appeal to established scholars.

Readers working through the book will find that chapters have been organized thematically rather than to provide any sense of a linear history or development of the group. Across these essays, a range of affinities and dissonances emerge that showcase the multiplicity of the Bloomsbury Group. In terms of affinities, no one even passingly familiar with the group will be surprised to learn that friendship, sex, the Cambridge Apostles, visual and literary aesthetics, and the Hogarth Press all feature prominently. Conversation occupies a central place in the volume, too, with Vanessa Bell's *A Conversation* (1913–16) serving as something of a centrepiece. Lauren Elkin, Maggie Humm and Benjamin Hagen all use the painting as exemplary in their essays, and it features on our cover in recognition of the fundamental role played by conversation itself for the group. Likewise, war appears in many of the essays. The First World War naturally dominates such references, but Ashley Foster, Jane Goldman, Steven Putzel and Laci Mattison all note that certain key members of the group remained concerned with war through the Spanish Civil War into the Second World War, and even beyond (as in Leonard Woolf's efforts to influence British policy on Palestine [Putzel] and Mulk Raj Anand's determination to explain Bloomsbury's long shadow [Mattison]). Finally, there is general agreement, most fully explored by Humm and Clara Jones, that domestic interior spaces were also critically important for Bloomsbury. For Humm, homes such as Charleston and Durbins, as well as the Omega workshops, afford key aesthetic insights for the more public demonstrations of exhibition and publication. Jones details domestic life in Bloomsbury's rural outposts and their engagement with local communities and politics.

But these affinities are balanced by the dissonances or multiple perspectives taken on several overlapping areas of concern. For instance, many of our contributors note Moore's impact on the group's philosophy and ethos, with Todd Avery and Jesse Wolfe reminding us that *Principia Ethica* has long been seen as 'Bloomsbury's Bible'. But Hagen complicates that view in suggesting that the evidence of a direct philosophical link between Moore's philosophy and Bloomsbury's thought has been overstated, and that his influence may have been at least as much charismatic as it was conceptual. Instead, he argues that Bloomsbury must be understood to be *doing* philosophy through other nonphilosophical activities: painting, talking, decorating, writing. Goldman's thoughtful approach to the concept of peace and the responses of Woolf, Keynes, and John Rodker to the Armistice and the aftermath of war provides a case study in just such an understanding, reading the very fibre of Bloomsbury aesthetics as itself an act of peace.

Queerness and sexuality unsurprisingly provide lively terrain for a variety of views on Bloomsbury. Across Avery's discussion of Saxon Sydney-Turner, Vanessa Bell, Grant, Strachey, and Virginia Woolf, and Wolfe's focus on Forster and Edward Carpenter, there is a deep engagement with issues of intimacy and desire. Between them, Avery and Wolfe link queer sexuality to aesthetic experimentation and political activism, overlapping with Jones's treatment of the importance of rural settings, as well as Peter Adkins's tracing of Woolf's and Vita Sackville-West's queering of nature. Anna Snaith provides an unexpected twist on this tale by elaborating the role played by queer desire in David Garnett's involvement with Madan Lal Dhingra, Indian nationalism, and the plot to assassinate Sir William Curzon Wyllie. The metaphorical connections achieve concrete realization in Snaith's account, with queer desire motivating direct political action. In contrast, David Ayers offers a sobering insight into Keynes's queer characterizations of key diplomats and of his own political involvement. And so the challenges of thinking about a group which comprises so many deeply individual members surface yet again: not only was there no homogeneity of thought among them, individuals were more than capable of behaving in breathtakingly contradictory ways.

Such contradictoriness is nowhere more clearly in evidence than when it comes to questions of race. From Forster's passionate love for Masood, to Leonard Woolf's service in the former Ceylon, to the casual racism of the Dreadnought hoax (along with its piercingly critical intentions), through David Garnett's anti-imperialist conspiring, Anand's ambivalence about his time with Bloomsbury, and prejudicial attitudes of the group towards Jews and Jewishness, race is a livewire. No one seems to have touched it in quite the same way as the others, and what we learn is that often individual members openly behaved, spoke or wrote in ways that can only be understood as consummately human for their total lack of consistency. Sonita Sarker's essay notes the multifarious layers of group belonging and identity politics that complicate any attempt to characterize Bloomsbury's racial politics straightforwardly. Her essay adopts a meta-perspective that questions our ongoing scholarly investment in Bloomsbury. From this perspective, she reads the Dreadnought hoax as evidence of semiconscious racism in which the unmarked and privileged categories of 'English' and 'white' irrevocably frame the group's politics. Snaith, by contrast, reads the hoax in terms of its intended critique of British militarism and imperialism, linking it to the Curzon assassination as a mode of political intervention. From a different perspective still, antisemitism comes under scrutiny in essays by Susan Wegener and Putzel. Wegener takes the group to task for their recycling of Jewish stereotypes – with Leonard Woolf often personally on the receiving end – arguing that this allowed them to define their artistic philosophies in opposition to Jewishness. Putzel puts this antisemitism in a global political context by comparing Leonard's critique of Zionism with Keynes's support for it and for the Balfour Declaration, drawing out the paradoxes in both positions along the way.

For Sarker and Snaith, as we think for all our contributors, imperialism is the ultimate frame within which Bloomsbury must be understood. It shaped the lives and privileges of every single member of the group and determined much of what they undertook in sexual, aesthetic, activist, economic, and philosophical terms. Sarker's critique of how imperialism continues to inflect the reception and study of Bloomsbury today is compelling if not necessarily comfortable. Snaith's approach likewise challenges us to think through the complexities of what it meant and looked like to be a well-meaning intellectual in the last days of high imperialism. Foster and Goldman, in turn, illuminate the extent to which the Treaty of Versailles and its fallout were experienced by Keynes and others as implicated with imperialism. Leonard Woolf's and Keynes's ongoing involvement in British governmental policy-making with regard to Palestine, as outlined by Putzel, even after the Second World War in Leonard's case, extends this concern with imperialism well through the end of what we normally think of as the hey-day of Bloomsbury. As Mattison's essay shows, the topic remained important for Anand well into the last quarter of the twentieth century, as he sought to reconcile his experience of casual racism with genuine intellectual and artistic fellowship.

If they were far from coherent in their approach to imperialism, the Bloomsburians were nevertheless unafraid to engage with the question of religion. As Avery shows, religious experience was often very close to aesthetic experimentation and, of course, sex, in some members' thinking. For Avery, this nexus manifests in the linking of erotic paganized Christianity with aesthetic experience, most strikingly in Lytton Strachey's sadomasochistic crucifixion games with his lover Roger Senhouse. For Mark Hussey, the link is less salacious and partakes of a longer tradition going back at least to Charles Baudelaire (with important stops at Walter Pater and Arthur Symons) which treats aesthetic experience in secularized religious terms. Mattison provides a fascinating new perspective on this tendency to think the aesthetic in religious (and sometimes erotic) terms in her exploration of how Anand understood Hinduism as both a religion and a philosophy that anticipated, exceeded and remained consonant with Bergsonism. Extending Hagen's insights into the group's tendency to perform philosophically rather than doing philosophy per se, Mattison draws on Anand to suggest that Bloomsbury was capable of seeing religion as philosophy mediated through aesthetics and – this is crucial – affording political agency as a result.

This emphasis on politics is perhaps the broadest unifier of all the essays gathered here. Bloomsbury is consistently understood as a political entity whose enthusiasm is only matched, at times, by its clumsiness. Yet the kinds of politics on offer here vary widely – sexual, rural, (anti-)imperialist, feminist, class-based, and internationalist – but all are anchored in aesthetic experimentation and a genuine will to understand and then improve the world (unintended consequences and unconscious biases notwithstanding). Avery, Wolfe and Adkins outline the extent to which the group considered sex inseparable from politics, whether in the broadly democratic terms of the freedom to explore sexuality as roughly equivalent to the freedom to be a full individual (Avery) or in the more programmatically utopian vein of Edward Carpenter's influence on the rural eroticism of the farm at Milthorpe as a mode of pastoral liberation erotics (Wolfe and Adkins). This politics of the rural extends into Clara Jones's treatment of how local village politics influenced the Woolfs, Vanessa Bell, and other Bloomsburians in their periodic retreats from the neighbourhood that now so indelibly marks them. It includes, in this respect, Virginia Woolf's often ambivalent participation in the suffrage and women's rights movements, as Elkin discusses, or a similar ambivalence to questions of class, as Simpson and Ayers comprehensively explain. Claire Battershill outlines the history of how critics have gradually come to recognize Woolf's fundamentally feminist orientation and turns this topic in an archival direction. Focusing on what a handful of otherwise insignificant-seeming artefacts from the Hogarth Press can tell us, Battershill expands our understanding of how local politics are often the literal flipside of modernist prose experiments. Extending this engagement with the politics of publishing, Michaela Bronstein charts Constance Garnett's translation of Russian novels into English as a political endeavour. Motivated by the philosophy she saw enacted by writers such as Fyodor Dostoyevsky, Garnett equally sought to drum up popular support for the 1917 Russian revolution by making select Russian literary works widely available to the English-speaking world.

From an entirely different perspective, Humm links the group's 'relational aesthetics' to an internationalist (though with a distinctly Francophile flavour) aesthetico-political scene, in which context is all. Foster links Bloomsbury aesthetics to pacifism with a particularly activist bent, a view Goldman confirms in her reading of Woolf's prose as a mode of political engagement precisely when it seems least involved. Against such views of the group – or at least some of its members – as in some way of a revolutionary political persuasion, Ayers argues that the class politics on offer are deeply quietist. He provocatively asserts that the political valences assigned to Bloomsbury today are more a function of critics' wishes than of the realities to be found in the lives and works of the group. Then again, Vicki Tromanhauser's account of the politics of food in Virginia Woolf's writing suggests that Bloomsbury's class politics are complex and embedded at all levels of both representational and lived reality. What is abundantly clear is that the political dimensions of aesthetics were frequently a fraught and nonetheless essential feature of Bloomsbury's diverse works.

The Handbook to the Bloomsbury Group has sought to remain true to its subject by corralling into one place an exciting, provocative, lively assortment of perspectives on a wide array of topics. We have respected the original group's multiplicity by seeking to avoid the appearance of homogeneity or – even worse – a settled state of the field. Instead, we have variety, disparity, and contradiction to go along with our affinities, overlaps, and agreements. Even where things seem most settled, as you will see, there are yet questions unanswered and objections unmet. As a handbook, this volume aims only to set the table, lay some tantalizing new dishes alongside comforting favourites, and invite you to partake.

NOTES

1. In his long essay 'Bloomsbury', Quentin Bell provides an account of Lewis's brief time at the Omega and his falling out with the group (54–6) as well as Lawrence's fraught relationship with them (70–76).
2. Leonard Woolf is a notable exception, coming from a middle-class family that cannot be equated with what he calls the 'intellectual aristocracy of the middle class' of the Stephens and Stracheys (*Sowing* 186). In *Beginning Again*, Leonard records the modest income he and Virginia made in their first years together (see 88–93).
3. This language is evident from the start of both volumes of Quentin Bell's biography: Virginia is introduced to us as 'threatened by madness' 'from the outset' (35); volume 2 opens with her 'frigidity' in relation to Leonard (5) and later downplays the sexual element of her relationship with Vita: 'I think we may call it an affair of the heart, but so far as Virginia was concerned that was where it began and that was where it ended' (119).
4. The most comprehensive study of the history of the Bloomsbury Group's formation and first decade remains Rosenbaum's trilogy, *Victorian Bloomsbury* (1987), *Edwardian Bloomsbury* (1994) and *Georgian Bloomsbury* (2003).
5. The group's members were first referred to as 'Bloomsberries' by Molly McCarthy in a 1910 letter (Clive Bell 129). Rosenbaum suggests that Lytton Strachey's diary note that there was 'no Bloomby' at one of Lady Ottoline Morrell's gatherings earlier that year was the first recorded use of the location of Bloomsbury to stand for the group (*Collection* 17).
6. For a broader study of 1910 and its implications for Bloomsbury and modernism, see Stansky and Minow-Pinkney. Notable events that year included, in no particular order, the death of King Edward, marking the shift from the Edwardian to Georgian period; two general elections as a result of two political crises, the first over the budget, the second over the power of the House of Lords; the demise of the liberal party, whose last ever election win was in 1910, and the rise of the labour party; rallies and strike action of printing unions in disputes over working hours; the Irish Home Rule campaign; the appearance of Halley's comet; the popularization of non-Euclidean geometry and theories of the fourth dimension; and the performances of two of Richard Strauss's operas, *Salome* and *Elektra*.
7. One example of the group's 'variance with itself' is recorded in E. M. Forster's Rede Lecture on Virginia Woolf in 1942. At the same time as praising the innovative aesthetics in her novels, Forster notoriously takes issue with the 'spots' of feminism in her works, most problematically, in his view, in *Three Guineas* (see 22–3).
8. On Leonard Woolf's time in Ceylon, see also Ondaatje.
9. For a further discussion of east/west constellations in Bloomsbury, see Laurence, who focuses on Julian Bell's relationship with the writer and painter Ling Shuhua, whom he met when teaching in China in 1935, and connects them to modernist networks in both England and China.
10. For a full member list and details of readings, see Rosenbaum, *Memoir Club* 177–82, 184–5.
11. For an account of the setting up of the Hogarth Press, see L. Woolf, *Beginning Again* 231–54. As Leonard recounts, the Woolfs collaborated on some of the Russian translations with S. S. Koteliansky (see also Davison). Details of Hogarth Press publications can be found on the new Modernist Archives Publishing Project, http://www.modernistarchives.com/

WORKS CITED

Bell, Clive. *Art*. London: Chatto and Windus, 1914.

Bell, Clive. 'Bloomsbury'. *Old Friends*. Chicago, U of Chicago P, 1973 [1956]. 126–37.

Bell, Clive. *Civilization* and *Old Friends*. 1928, 1956. Chicago: U of Chicago P, 1973.

Bell, Quentin. *Bloomsbury*. London: Weidenfeld and Nicolson, 1986 [1968].

Bell, Quentin. *Virginia Woolf: A Biography*. 2 vols. London: Hogarth Press, 1982 [1972].

Bell, Vanessa. 'Notes on Bloomsbury'. *The Bloomsbury Group: A Collection of Memoirs and Commentary*. Rev. ed. Ed. S. P. Rosenbaum. Toronto: U of Toronto P, 1995. 102–13.

Bell, Vanessa. *Selected Letters*. Ed. Regina Marler. New York: Pantheon Books, 1993.

Berman, Jessica. *Modernist Commitments: Ethics, Politics, and Transnational Modernism*. New York: Columbia UP, 2011.

Caws, Mary Ann. *Women of Bloomsbury: Virginia, Vanessa, and Carrington*. London: Routledge, 1990.

Caws, Mary Ann and Sarah Bird Wright. *Bloomsbury and France: Art and Friends*. Oxford: Oxford UP, 2000.

Detloff, Madelyn and Brenda Helt. 'Introduction'. *Queer Bloomsbury*. Ed. Brenda Helt and Madelyn Detloff. Edinburgh: Edinburgh UP, 2016. 1–14.

Forster, E. M. 'Bloomsbury, An Early Note'. *The Bloomsbury Group: A Collection of Memoirs and Commentary*. Rev. ed. Ed. S. P. Rosenbaum. Toronto: U of Toronto P, 1995. 78–80.

Friedman, Susan Stanford. *Planetary Modernisms: Provocations on Modernity across Time*. New York: Columbia UP, 2015.

Froula, Christine. *Virginia Woolf and the Bloomsbury Avant-Garde: War, Civilization, Modernity*. New York: Columbia UP, 2005.

Fry, Roger. *Vision and Design*. London: Chatto and Windus, 1920.

Garnett, David. *The Familiar Faces*. London: Chatto and Windus, 1962.

Garnett, David. *The Flowers of the Forest*. London: Chatto and Windus, 1955.

Garnett, David. *The Golden Echo*. London: Chatto and Windus, 1970 [1953].

Gerzina, Gretchen Holbrook. 'Bloomsbury and Empure'. *The Cambridge Companion to the Bloomsbury Group*. Ed. Victoria Rosner. Cambridge: Cambridge UP., 2014. 112–30.

Helt, Brenda and Madelyn Detloff. Eds. *Queer Bloomsbury*. Edinburgh: Edinburgh UP, 2016.

Holroyd, Michael. *Lytton Strachey: The Unknown Years, 1880–1910*. London: William Heinemann, 1967.

Holroyd, Michael. *Lytton Strachey: The Years of Achievement, 1910–1932*. London: William Heinemann, 1968.

Hussey, Mark. 'Mrs. Thatcher and Mrs. Woolf'. *Modern Fiction Studies* 50.1 (2004): 8–30.

James, David and Urmila Seshagiri. 'Metamodernism: Narratives of Continuity and Revolution'. *PMLA* 129.1 (2014): 87–100.

Keynes, John Maynard. 'My Early Beliefs'. *The Essential Keynes*. Ed. Robert Skidelsky. London: Penguin, 2015. 13–25.

Knights, Sarah. *Bloomsbury's Outsider: A Life of David Garnett*. London: Bloomsbury, 2015.

Laurence, Patricia. *Lily Briscoe's Chinese Eyes: Bloomsbury, Modernism, and China*. Columbia: U of South Carolina P, 2003.

MacCarthy, Desmond. 'Bloomsbury: An Unfinished Memoir'. *The Bloomsbury Group: A Collection of Memoirs and Commentary*. Rev. ed. Ed. S. P. Rosenbaum. Toronto: U of Toronto P, 1995. 65–74.

Mao, Douglas and Rebecca L. Walkowitz. 'The New Modernist Studies'. *PMLA* 123.3 (2008): 737–48.

Marcus, Jane. *Hearts of Darkness: White Women Write Race*. New Brunswick: Rutgers UP, 2004.

Marler, Regina. *Bloomsbury Pie: The Making of the Bloomsbury Boom*. New York: Henry Holt, 1997.

Piggford, George. 'Camp Sites: Forster and the Biographies of Queer Bloomsbury'. *Queer Bloomsbury*. Ed. Brenda Helt and Madelyn Detloff. Edinburgh: Edinburgh UP, 2016. 64–88.

Reed, Christopher. 'Bloomsbury Bashing: Homophobia and the Politics of Criticism in the Eighties'. *Queer Bloomsbury*. Ed. Brenda Helt and Madelyn Detloff. Edinburgh: Edinburgh UP, 2016. 36–63.

Reed, Christopher. *Bloomsbury Rooms: Modernism, Subculture, and Domesticity*. New Haven: Yale UP, 2004.

Rosenbaum, S. P. *The Bloomsbury Group: A Collection of Memoirs and Commentary*. Rev. ed. Toronto: U of Toronto P, 1995.

Rosenbaum, S. P. *The Bloomsbury Group Memoir Club*. Ed. James M. Haule. Basingstoke: Palgrave Macmillan, 2014.

Rosenbaum, S. P. *Edwardian Bloomsbury: The Early Literary History of the Bloomsbury Group*. New York: St. Martin's Press, 1994.

Rosenbaum, S. P. *Georgian Bloomsbury: The Early Literary History of the Bloomsbury Group*. London: Palgrave Macmillan, 2003.

Rosenbaum, S. P. *Victorian Bloomsbury: The Early Literary History of the Bloomsbury Group*. New York: St. Martin's Press, 1987.

Rosner, Victoria. Ed. *The Cambridge Companion to the Bloomsbury Group*. Cambridge: Cambridge UP, 2014.

Saint-Amour, Paul. *Tense Future: Modernism, Total War, Encyclopaedic Form*. Oxford: Oxford UP, 2015.

Seshagiri, Urmila. 'Orienting Virginia Woolf: Race, Aesthetics, and Politics in *To the Lighthouse*'. *Modern Fiction Studies* 50.1 (2004): 58–83.

Silver, Brenda. *Virginia Woolf Icon*. Chicago: U of Chicago P, 1999.

Snaith, Anna. '*Conversations in Bloomsbury*: Colonial Writers and the Hogarth Press'. *Virginia Woolf's Bloomsbury: Volume 2: International Influence and Politics*. Ed. Lisa Shahriari and Gina Potts. Basingstoke: Palgrave Macmillan, 2010. 138–57.

Snaith, Anna. 'Introduction'. *The Years*. The Cambridge Edition of the Works of Virginia Woolf. Cambridge: Cambridge UP, 2012. xxxix–xcix.

Southworth, Helen. 'Introduction'. *Leonard and Virginia Woolf, the Hogarth Press and the Networks of Modernism*. Ed. Helen Southworth. Edinburgh: Edinburgh UP, 2010. 1–26.

Southworth, Helen. Ed. *Leonard and Virginia Woolf, the Hogarth Press and the Networks of Modernism*. Edinburgh: Edinburgh UP, 2010.

Spalding, Frances. *Duncan Grant: A Biography*. London: Pimlico, 1998 [1997].

Spalding, Frances. *Vanessa Bell: Portrait of the Bloomsbury Artist*. London: I. B. Taurus, 2016 [1983].

Stansky, Peter. *On or about December 1910: Early Bloomsbury and Its Intimate World*. Cambridge: Harvard UP, 1997.

Stephen, Adrian. 'The Dreadnought Hoax'. *The Bloomsbury Group: A Collection of Memoirs and Commentary*. Rev. ed. Ed. S. P. Rosenbaum. Toronto: U of Toronto P, 1995. 6–17.

Wolfe, Jesse. *Bloomsbury, Modernism and the Reinvention of Intimacy*. Cambridge: Cambridge UP, 2011.

Woolf, Leonard. *Beginning Again: An Autobiography of the Years 1911–1918*. London: Hogarth Press, 1968.

Woolf, Leonard. *Growing: An Autobiography of the Years 1904–1911*. New York: Harcourt Brace Jovanovich, 1961.

Woolf, Leonard. *Sowing: An Autobiography of the Years 1880–1904*. New York: Harcourt Brace Jovanovich, 1989 [1960].

Woolf, Virginia. 'Character in Fiction'. *The Essays of Virginia Woolf, Vol. 3*. Ed. Andrew McNeillie. London: Hogarth Press, 1988. 420–438.

Woolf, Virginia. 'Old Bloomsbury'. *Moments of Being: Autobiographical Writings*. New ed. Ed. Jeanne Schulkind. Intro. and revd. by Hermione Lee. London: Pimlico, 2002. 43–61.

CHAPTER ONE

Bloomsbury and Sexuality

TODD AVERY

Since the beginning of what Regina Marler has dubbed the 'Bloomsbury Boom' in the 1960s and 1970s, Bloomsbury's reflections on and creative representations of sexuality, together with the group's sexual habits and experiments, have given rise to an industry comprising popular and academic elements that tests the accuracy of the moniker 'cottage'. A recent contribution to the ongoing mass cultural fascination with Bloomsbury's intimate lives, the 2015 BBC television mini-series *Life in Squares*, written by Amanda Coe and directed by Simon Kaijser, also represents the reduction to absurdity of the proposition that, whatever else Bloomsbury may have done, the identity and significance of the group rests finally on its members' sexual predilections.

And yet, maybe Coe is right to place her emphasis squarely on the personal side of sexuality. Beyond the fact that sex is sexier on-screen than the private mental effort to find *le mot juste* or the perfect brush stroke, in the long run is it necessarily personally more satisfying or intrinsically socially more important to write *The Economic Consequences of the Peace*, or *A Passage to India*, or *Eminent Victorians*, or to paint the murals in Berwick Church or Lincoln Cathedral, or to reshape British feminism and expand the possibilities of the novel as a literary genre, than it is to achieve the bliss of intimate sexual and friendly communion with a lover, or loving intimacy with a friend? Sexuality was central to Bloomsbury's ways of being in the world. They possessed a rich, complex, passionate, humane, considered, and sustained interest in sexuality, both as a physical activity and as an ideological site and opportunity for challenging old artistic, economic, ethical, and political values, and crafting new ones.

FOUNDATIONS I: CAMBRIDGE

For Clive Bell, E. M. Forster, John Maynard Keynes, Lytton Strachey, Saxon Sydney-Turner, and Leonard Woolf, a recognizably Bloomsburian fascination both with sex as physical activity and with sexuality as a site of ideological contestation and transformation began to take shape at the turn of the twentieth century at Cambridge University, where many of them were also members of the notorious and secretive Cambridge Conversazione Society, or the Apostles. At that time, G. E. Moore's *Principia Ethica* (1903) inspired what these proto-Bloomsburians understood as a radical challenge to the supposed naturalness of their Victorian sexual-ethical inheritance – and to the ostensible unnaturalness of their predominantly homosexual preferences. Moore's book has come to be known as the 'Bloomsbury Bible', and Moore himself as, in Paul Levy's phrase, 'Bloomsbury's Prophet' (for an alternative view, see Hagen in this volume). The group's ethos owes its impetus to a pair of sentences in Moore's final chapter, on 'The Ideal':

> By far the most valuable things, which we know or can imagine, are certain states of consciousness, which may be roughly described as the pleasures of human intercourse and the enjoyment of beautiful objects. No one, probably, who has asked himself the question, has ever doubted that personal affection and the appreciation of what is beautiful in Art or Nature, are good in themselves; nor, if we consider strictly what things are worth having *purely for their own sakes*, does it appear probable that any one will think that anything else has *nearly* so great a value as the things which are included under these two heads. (188–9)

This claim 'carried away' Lytton Strachey, who 'date[d] from October 1903 the beginning of the Age of Reason' (*Letters* 17). In later years, Keynes would criticize his and his Cambridge friends' Moore-inspired unworldliness, their youthful conviction that 'Nothing mattered except states of mind' ('Early Beliefs' 86); but he would reaffirm his belief in the essential rightness of Moore's claim: 'It remains nearer the truth than any other [ethics] that I know' (91). Beyond a vigorous though generalized reasonableness, what Moore offered his Apostolic acolytes among the young men who would help to form Bloomsbury was an intellectual justification for ethical autonomy – for pursuing their aesthetic and sexual preferences where they might lead, regardless of convention, tradition, or external rules. Strictly speaking, when Moore wrote of 'the pleasures of human intercourse', he meant *conversation*; the phrase was ambiguous enough, though, to be read – as Bloomsbury read it – more suggestively.

FOUNDATIONS II: LONDON – ON THE THRESHOLD OF THE MODERN

Friendship and lust mingled for Strachey and his friends at Cambridge; the Bloomsbury Group formed when, visiting Thoby Stephen at home in London, they grew closer to Vanessa and Virginia Stephen. As Desmond MacCarthy writes in a short memoir, 'early Bloomsbury ... was an attempt to colonise the Spirit of the Apostles in London' (70–71). The presence of women was central to this attempt; together with the young men's commitment to sexual freedom, it speaks to Bloomsbury's original and fundamental sexual inclusiveness. MacCarthy explains, once 'transplanted' to Bloomsbury, contemporary Cambridge 'flourished in a company in which women were not excluded' (71). For MacCarthy, this flourishing represented, 'from the point of view of the social historian, a most important change' (71). According to Virginia Woolf in her 1928 memoir 'Old Bloomsbury', the death of Thoby Stephen in 1906 and the marriage between Clive Bell and Vanessa the next year marked the end of Bloomsbury's first chapter. During this first chapter, conversations and relations had been intellectual and conventionally chaste – even, as she recalled, 'monastic' (195). 'Moore's book', she writes, 'had set us all discussing philosophy, art, religion [and] the atmosphere ... was abstract in the extreme' (190–91). Over time, as 'Mr. Turner, Mr. Strachey, Mr. Bell' became 'Saxon, Lytton, Clive' (Leonard Woolf was at this time serving as a colonial administrator in Ceylon) (192), friendships deepened and identities particularized, and eventually Saxon's, Lytton's, Clive's, and Adrian Stephen's private conversations about love and sex spilled over into the drawing rooms of Gordon Square.

Bloomsbury's foundational, self-defining understanding of sexuality as a private psychophysical capacity with public implications – indeed, their understanding of sexuality as always and inevitably a socially and politically involved fact of human nature – takes shape here, in Bloomsbury Chapter Two. It finds its clearest mythographical expression in Woolf's recollection of the event that marked the transition into this chapter, an event in which conversational spilling achieved a new level of physicality. 'It was a spring evening', Woolf writes:

> Vanessa and I were sitting in the drawing room … Suddenly the door opened and the long and sinister figure of Mr. Lytton Strachey stood on the threshold. He pointed a finger at a stain on Vanessa's white dress.
>
> 'Semen?' he said.
>
> Can one really say it? I thought and we burst out laughing. With that one word all barriers of reticence and reserve went down. A flood of the sacred fluid seemed to overwhelm us. Sex permeated our conversation. The word bugger was never far from our lips. We discussed copulation with the same excitement and openness that we had discussed the nature of good. (195–6)

Woolf explains the significance of this moment for Bloomsbury as a group of friends committed to what Katherine Mullin calls 'revolutions in domesticity, intimacy, and sexuality' (22). 'So there was now nothing', Woolf writes:

> that one could not say, nothing that one could not do, at 46 Gordon Square. It was, I think, a great advance in civilization. It may be true that the loves of buggers are not – at least if one is of the other persuasion – of enthralling interest or paramount importance. But the fact that they can be mentioned openly leads to the fact that no one minds if they are practised privately. Thus many customs and beliefs were revised. Indeed the future of Bloomsbury was to prove that many variations can be played on the theme of sex, and with such happy results. (196–7)

Did Lytton Strachey actually stand in that doorway and point his finger at a real stain on Vanessa Bell's dress? Woolf, in the typically overlooked qualification with which she introduces her anecdote, admits, 'I do not know if I invented it or not' (195). Even if Woolf drew this 'now-notorious moment of transformation' out of thin air, it nevertheless gains its 'power', Mullin writes, 'from its creation of a foundational myth', one in which, speaking on behalf of all Bloomsbury, Virginia Woolf 'defined [the group] against a past identified with sexual repression' (22).

SEXUALITY, AESTHETICS, AND MORALS: FOUR CLASSES

More important, however, than defining Bloomsbury as a collection of sexual heretics who spent their time and energies in the negative (though necessary) work of social and moral critique, Woolf portrays herself and her Bloomsbury friends as a group committed to the expansion of sexual 'variations'. The energy of her anecdote proceeds not primarily from a desire to criticize the repressive sexual ethics of their parents' generation, but from her excitement about a freer, more various sexual future which would enrich 'civilization' by radiating outwards from the drawing rooms of Bloomsbury. Likewise, at about the same time that Woolf is remembering and mythologizing, Lytton Strachey himself, with an even more licentious glee, was not only gesturing suggestively at stains on dresses but defending what he forecast as the inevitable benefits to 'civilization' of a radical expansion of sexual freedom. In a paper delivered to the Cambridge Apostles around

1908 titled 'Will It Come Right in the End?' Strachey insists that 'the only hope of our ever getting a really beautiful and vigorous and charming civilization is to allow the whole world to fuck and bugger and abuse themselves in public and generally misbehave to their hearts' content' (80).

This paean to sexual liberty as a prerequisite to civilization occurs in the first of two essays in which Strachey applies Moore's notions of 'organic unities' and 'complex wholes' to what he calls in 'Art and Indecency' the 'partly aesthetic and partly moral' question of the proper place of 'lasciviousness' and 'indecency' in works of art (83). In *Principia Ethica*, Moore had argued that beautiful things possess a 'great complexity' and that the value of their contemplation (constituting a 'good' equal in value to the state of mind attendant on 'human intercourse') depends on the simultaneous apprehension of the value of the whole and of the parts that compose it (202). Strachey brings Moore's highly abstract reflections on the contemplation of beautiful things into the everyday artistic, personal, and social world of sexuality. He groups individuals interested in this subject into several 'classes', arranged on a spectrum according to their relative embrace of lasciviousness and indecency as valuable aspects of organic unities or complex wholes, either in art or in life. The 'official class', which 'includes the average Englishman', occupies one extreme end of the spectrum – for it, 'all lasciviousness is bad, and therefore indecent' and contributes nothing valuable to works of art or to the organic unities of social relationships ('Will' 74). The next class, comprising 'our leading writers and critics', is the 'advanced class', which seems to oppose the official class in denying the indecency of all lasciviousness but whose position actually remains 'vague' (74–5). The third class, that of the 'naturalists', is ideologically more flexible than the official or advanced classes but equally serious, even solemn, in its approach: it refuses 'to condemn what is natural' and denies the lasciviousness or indecency of bodies and their physical functions (75) – but in so doing the naturalist class eliminates not only untold aesthetic and ethical opportunities but also a great deal of fun, for according to Strachey lasciviousness can represent a positive good in art as in life, by celebrating the human need for humour and, seemingly paradoxically, spiritual enlightenment.

Strachey is 'proud to acknowledge myself a member' of the fourth and final class, the only class that heartily rejoices in the artistic, ethical, and even spiritual possibilities of the lascivious and the indecent. This is the 'bawdy class' (76), which alone acknowledges 'the value of [ethical-aesthetic] wholes [that] depends on some element of appropriateness between the parts' (79). As a *soi-disant* member of the bawdy class, Strachey wishes to 'giv[e] copulation a fair chance' (79). To do this is to escape the clutches of officialdom, the confused uncertainties of the advanced, and the seriousness of the naturalists; it is also, positively speaking, to accept that 'one must conjure up a whole world of strange excitements, gradually beginning and mysteriously deepening, one must imagine the shock and the pressure of bodies, and realize the revelation of an alien mind, one must find oneself familiar with miracles and, assuming an amazing triumph, swim in glory through a palpitating universe of heavenly and unimaginable lust' (79–80). Such miracles and universes and lusts composed, for Strachey, the *sine qua non* of any civilization worth the name.

Virginia Woolf's memoir and Lytton Strachey's Apostles papers typify Bloomsbury's interest in sexuality; they also capture various aspects and expressions of this interest, ranging from gleeful naughtiness to a commitment to social and cultural critique and a desire for mystical union. Their texts reveal that, from its very beginnings, Bloomsbury defined itself as a 'queer' subculture. As such, the group was committed to what Brenda

Helt and Madelyn Detloff, in their introduction to the collection *Queer Bloomsbury* (2016), call 'habits of intimate, sensual, artistic and philosophical conviviality [that] intentionally resist the heteronormative "logic of cultural intelligibility" that underpins western neoliberal ideals for social and familial organization' (5). Yes, Bloomsbury critiqued. They also created; and, as Helt and Detloff write, 'they arranged their intimate lives and kinship networks in ways that reinforced their ethical commitments' (6), as well as the social and political aims that arose from these commitments.

Strachey's analysis of late Victorian and Edwardian attitudes toward lasciviousness might serve as a rough model for a highly selective survey of Bloomsbury's engagements with sexuality. Such a survey of representative moments and creative expressions might usefully suggest some of the more significant aspects of these engagements. Bloomsbury's interests in, depictions of, and reflections on sexuality can be arranged along a continuum of the sacred and the profane, under heads that range from a jejune and irretrievably gratuitous profanity at one end to a tender and ennobling spirituality on the other, with additional categories devoted to playful bawdiness and to social and political critique.

THE PROFANE AND PERVERSE: SAXON SYDNEY-TURNER

The most profane of Bloomsbury's explorations of sexuality come from the group's most obscure member, Saxon Sydney-Turner, who, as the only one of Thoby Stephen's Cambridge friends to attend his inaugural Thursday evening 'at home' on 16 March 1905, was arguably the first non-Stephen member of Bloomsbury (Hussey 281). While a student at Cambridge, Sydney-Turner organized the publication of a volume of poems, *Euphrosyne: A Collection of Verse* (1905), whose contributors included himself, Clive Bell, Lytton Strachey, and Leonard Woolf, and which S. P. Rosenbaum dubs 'the first book of Bloomsbury' (388). Sydney-Turner's poems constitute for the most part pale imitations of tired aestheticist and decadent conventionalities. More interesting are the poems he regularly sent as birthday gifts to Lytton Strachey, which tantalize – 'And still for you the dying embers blaze' – in their suggestions of a sexual relationship (Avery, *Saxon* 16–20). Sydney-Turner's poems seldom, however, venture into the 'spiritual and moral perversity' of a proper 'decadence' (Symons 135).

His short stories are another matter entirely: they positively revel in the perverse. One of them, 'Eidolon', is a story of – to put it mildly – a peculiar relationship between a master, Pasquin, and his 'willing but puzzled pupil', Cecil, whom he dresses in long gowns and trains to adopt a feminine identity. Cecil eventually identifies as female. The story ends when they embrace, both of them lamenting their apparently fixed sexualities: 'Oh,' Cecil, now identified as 'she', cries, 'if I could only be both' (Avery, *Saxon* 25–7). From one perspective, 'Eidolon' is a disturbing tale of paedophilic violation and coercion, subjugation and submission. From another, it is a story of queer, and specifically hermaphroditic, longing, of a desire to inhabit multiple, shifting sexual identities. This story, which ends sadly and enigmatically in the twilight of dusk, sees both master and pupil, adult and regendered child, wishing for a dizzying sexual existence in which they could each be both male and female. In this way, 'Eidolon' explores the fluidity of gender performance in a way that anticipates by twenty-five years the sex change in Woolf's *Orlando* (1928). Another story, 'The Homecoming', which Sydney-Turner passed around to his Cambridge friends in manuscript in 1905, contains the perverse account of a young man's return to his unnamed British home town after eight years abroad and the perhaps innocent but more likely incestuous debauch that ensues. The most disturbingly perverse example of Sydney-Turner's prose-fancies is 'The Punishment', which harkens back to the dark religio-erotic fantasies of the Gothic. These stories of drunken incest and of aristocratic threesomes accompany tales of debauchery, defilement, paedophilia, and even necrophilia. As perverse as they are, they are also undergraduate exercises, circulated in manuscript among a select group of friends. They were meant, no doubt, to shock – or rather, as they were never intended to be seen outside that circle of friends, they were more likely meant to confirm not only their author but also their audience in a shared sense of moral antinomianism, sexual and ethical radicalism.

A BLOOMSBURY BAWD: VANESSA BELL

To turn from Sydney-Turner's short stories to other of Bloomsbury's private writings on sexuality from the group's early years is to escape from the perverse into the realm of the merely bawdy, and to witness how Bloomsbury often quite playfully spoke of sexual proclivities, desires, and habits as another way of cementing their developing and increasingly complex friendships and other intimate relationships. Through such sharing, the Bloomsbury Group forged the habit of morally unfettered discussion that, as Virginia Woolf recalled, led to the 'revision' of 'many customs and beliefs'. Such revision of course is part of the Bloomsbury Group's DNA; at Cambridge, it took a specific form of 'immoralism' remembered by Keynes in his 1938 memoir 'My Early Beliefs' which, despite his intention 'to introduce for once, mental or spiritual, instead of sexual adventures' into the group's proceedings (85), bears implicitly on the question of Bloomsbury's attitudes toward sexuality. Under the influence of Moore, Keynes writes:

> We entirely repudiated a personal liability on us to obey general rules. We claimed the right to judge every individual case on its merits, and the wisdom, experience and self-control to do so successfully ... We repudiated entirely customary morals, conventions and traditional wisdom. We were, that is to say, in the strict sense of the term, immoralists ... we recognised no moral obligation on us, no inner sanction, to conform or to obey. (94)

From a vantage of thirty-five years, Keynes affirms his allegiance to these fundamental beliefs: 'I remain, and always will remain, an immoralist' (94).

According to Keynes's definition of the term, Bloomsbury generally remained immoralists in refusing to acknowledge anything but inner sanction as the source of ethical legitimacy. Bloomsburians were also often bawdy, to boot. Vanessa Bell's letters reveal a natural bawd in the spirit of Strachey, just as her sexual relationships epitomize the complexities of the group's sexual entanglements. In 1911, she teasingly writes to Roger Fry, with whom she was embarking on an intense affair, of recent days spent in the company of the then exclusively homosexual Duncan Grant – with whom she was also beginning a creative partnership that would soon grow into a sexual and domestic intimacy of an even greater magnitude. She and Grant, she says:

> have decided to emulate [Eric] Gill and paint really indecent subjects. I suggest a series of copulations in strange attitudes and have offered to pose. Will you join? I mean in the painting. We think there should be more indecent pictures painted, and you shall show them at your show. (99–100)

Often flirtatious, naughty, and suggestive, three years later Vanessa Bell tells Grant of her awkward first attempt to throw clay pots, in a line that captures her sense of the Promethean eroticism of artistic creation: 'the feeling of the clay rising between one's fingers is like the keenest sexual joy' (162). A few weeks later, in one of Bloomsbury's most self-consciously bawdy letters, she sends Keynes a note of thanks for having hosted the evidently pimpish Bells over the Easter holiday. Noting her intention 'to make my letter so bawdy you will have to destroy it at once', she asks whether Keynes has spent 'a pleasant afternoon buggering one or more of the young men we left for you', and imagines a scene of public sex on the downs:

> It must have been delicious ... I imagine you ... with your bare limbs intertwined with him and all the ecstatic preliminaries of Sucking Sodomy – it sounds like the name of a station ... How divine it must have been ... Well, it was a very nice interlude and I felt singularly happy and free tongued ... one can talk of fucking and Sodomy and sucking and bushes and all without turning a hair. (163)

Despite – and no doubt precisely because of – Bloomsbury's commitment to honesty with respect to personal relationships, sexual life in Bloomsbury was never easy. Later, much hair-turning in Bloomsbury was caused by the conspiratorial silence with which Vanessa Bell, Clive Bell, and Duncan Grant, and indeed the rest of Bloomsbury, concealed from Angelica Bell, until her eighteenth birthday in 1937, the fact that Grant, and not Clive Bell, was her biological father. Angelica's memoir, *Deceived with Kindness: A Bloomsbury Childhood* (1985), details her efforts to come to grips with the emotionally fraught and sexually complex history of her immediate family, and of Bloomsbury as a whole. Further anxiety of a kind that bespoke Bloomsbury's not always successful commitment to sexual liberalism happened with Grant and Vanessa Bell when Angelica, a few months after learning of Clive's paternity, entered into an intimate relationship with David Garnett, who had once been Grant's lover and whom she would marry in 1942. Christopher Reed describes Bloomsbury as a richly 'queer' group – 'not simply as a social circle but as an ideology that combined aesthetic creativity with a profoundly inventive attitude toward relationships among children, parents, spouses; that refused to limit notions of family to those relationships; and that accepted the varieties of emotional and sensual intimacies characteristic of human experience' (86). With the notable exception of the deception of Angelica Bell, the Bell-Grant *ménage* and Bloomsbury in general pursued this combination of artistic creativity and domestic inventiveness with great vigour and honesty.

MAKING THE WORLD DANCE: VIRGINIA WOOLF

For Bloomsbury, sexuality represented an occasion for profane fantasy, as in the short stories of Saxon Sydney-Turner; it also offered an opportunity for earthy humour and playful naughtiness, as in the letters of Vanessa Bell, the letters and Apostles papers of Lytton Strachey, and in Strachey's epistolary novella, *Ermyntrude and Esmeralda*, posthumously published in *Playboy* in the late 1960s, and which details two adolescent girls' efforts to learn all they can about sex, love, and making babies. These examples and many others materialized Bloomsbury's ethical and aesthetic desire to expand the limits of permissible public discussion about sexuality. Bloomsbury also understood sexuality as a fact of life possessing a broader social significance; the politics of sexuality is a common theme in Bloomsbury's art and writing. Sexuality and gender were central fictional and discursive topoi for Virginia Woolf. To paraphrase Strachey, the very name of Virginia Woolf conjures up a palpitating personal and literary universe of sexual and gendered complexities, both biographical and literary. These complexities developed through Woolf's early adulthood with its inevitable courtships and then marriage. After considering numerous suitors of varying degrees of seriousness, including the seemingly asexual Saxon Sydney-Turner, and mutually ending the shortest possible engagement with the improbable Lytton Strachey – it began and ended in the course of a single conversation – in 1912 she married the exclusively heterosexual Leonard Woolf, who later accepted her physically intimate relationship with Vita Sackville-West (whose own sexually open relationship with her husband Harold Nicolson represents a further complexity in the sexual relationships of Bloomsbury's satellite figures).

The complexities of Woolf's engagements with sexuality and gender also evolved in her lesbianism and in her fictional and critical (not to mention many diaristic and epistolary) explorations of and reflections on sexuality and the politics of gender. Indeed, complexity is the keynote of Woolf's understanding of sexuality. In a remarkable August 1930 letter to Ethel Smyth filled with a series of 'disjected observations' and meant to reassure Smyth of her affection, Woolf admits tantalizingly that 'I am diverse enough to want Vita and Ethel and Leonard and Vanessa and oh some other people too' (*Letters* 4: 199). She then reflects, under the heading, 'Perversion', on the emotional and physiological grounds of her sexual preferences. 'Why did I tell you', Woolf writes:

> That I had only once felt physical feeling for a man [perhaps Lytton Strachey] when he felt nothing for me? I suppose in some opium trance of inaccuracy. No – had I felt physical feeling for him, then, no doubt, we should have married, or had a shot at something. But my feelings were all of the spiritual, intellectual, emotional kind. And when 2 or 3 times in all, I felt physically for a man, then he was so obtuse, gallant, foxhunting and dull that I – diverse as I am – could only wheel round and gallop the other way. Perhaps this shows why Clive [Bell], who had his reasons, always called me a fish. Vita also calls me fish. And I reply (I think often while holding their hands, and getting exquisite pleasure from contact with either male or female body) 'But what I want of you is illusion – to make the world dance'. (200)

Speaking again to her own sexual 'diversity', and her belief in the self-diversity and irreducible complexity of sexual desire, Woolf adds, 'Where people mistake, as I think, is in perpetually narrowing and naming these immensely composite and wide flung passions – driving stakes through them, herding them between screens. But how do you define 'Perversity'? What is the line between friendship and perversion?' (200). Refusing to simplify sexual identity and preference is one way that Woolf challenges what she calls 'a more fundamental tyranny – the tyranny of sex' ('Women' 15).

In Woolf's works, the exploration of the 'immensely composite' complexities of sexuality and gender, especially among women, ranges in tone from the ludic fantasy of the sex-changing, gender-bending love letter to Sackville-West, *Orlando*, to the melancholy intimacy, bursting into moments of joy, in her depictions of the imaginative worlds of such fictional characters as Mrs. Ramsay, the matriarch of *To the Lighthouse* (1927), and perhaps especially Clarissa Dalloway, whose inner life shapes the core of *Mrs. Dalloway* (1925). The latter example is particularly notable given Woolf's stated interest in 'telling the truth about my own experiences as a body' ('Professions' 8), for it represents one of the few works in which she strives to capture the felt experience of sexual arousal and climax, a 'something warm which broke up surfaces and rippled the cold contact of man and woman, or of women together' (*Mrs. Dalloway* 31). Clarissa, like Woolf herself, feels this 'something warm' almost exclusively with women:

> she could not resist sometimes yielding to the charm of a woman ... she did undoubtedly then feel what men felt. Only for a moment; but it was enough. It was a sudden revelation, a tinge like a blush which one tried to check and then, as it spread, one yielded to its expansion, and rushed to the farthest verge and there quivered and felt the world come closer, swollen with some astonishing significance, some pressure of rapture, which split its thin skin and gushed and poured with an extraordinary alleviation over the cracks and sores! Then, for that moment, she had seen an illumination; a match burning in a crocus; an inner meaning almost expressed. (31)

She feels it most intensely, in young adulthood, with her friend Sally Seton: 'the most exquisite moment of her whole life' happens when, as they are walking through a country house garden, 'Sally stopped; picked a flower; kissed her on the lips. The whole world might have turned upside down!' (35). These passages are regularly cited in discussions of Woolf's attitudes toward sexuality. Moreover, a concern for sexuality as a fundamental aspect of being human permeates Woolf's fiction. As Harold Fromm observed almost forty years ago, and as critics Eileen Barrett, Patricia Cramer, Madelyn Detloff, Susan Gubar, and many others have continued to show, in one of the richest areas of modernist literary and biographical studies, 'sex figures as a major or a subsidiary force' across Woolf's fiction, 'where it is a bright thread in the multithreaded tapestry of that complex [body of] work' (454).

SEXUALITY AND SPIRITUALITY: LYTTON STRACHEY AND DUNCAN GRANT

Bloomsbury's members did not always agree about the moral, social, or political – or personal – desirability of every type of intimate physical relationship. But they all, on principle, defended their pursuit, and grounded their judgments on reason and experience. Clive Bell, in a discussion of Plato's *Symposium*, and particularly of its 'praise of a form [of love] for which in England people are sent to prison', agrees with the common prejudice against what English law at the time labelled 'gross indecency': 'To this form my instinctive reaction resembles that of the bulk of my fellows; it is one of amazement and slight disgust' (97). Despite this reflexive aversion, though, Bell subdues his taste to a test of reason and tolerance, and appeals to a civilized ideal: 'No one has a right to call himself civilised who cannot listen to both sides of an argument; and he is no better than a brute who cannot tolerate many things which, to him, personally, are distasteful' (97). Ultimately Bell's idea of civilization may have been no more expansive than, as Virginia Woolf caustically remarked, 'a lunch-party at no. 50 Gordon Square' (qtd in Quentin Bell 137). And yet, according to her recollection, it was at just such gatherings – at 46 Gordon Square or 50 Gordon Square or in many nearby Bloomsbury houses over the years – that 'great advance[s] in civilization' were made by the open discussion and private practice of 'many variations ... on the theme of sex'.

Such advances were also made in even more intimate gatherings; such variations were also played in the most public of spaces. Any reasonable survey of sexuality in Bloomsbury must include those moments in which group members saw it as a vehicle for or an expression of religious experience. None of the Bloomsburians were in any way conventionally religious, or amenable to religion as an institutional expression of supernatural belief, which itself to them seemed at best a dubious intellectual proposition. Virginia Woolf acknowledged a certain 'mystical' longing, while writing *The Waves* (1931) (*Diary* 3: 203); and in *Mrs. Dalloway* Clarissa's 'most exquisite moment' of being kissed by Sally figures sexual arousal as 'the revelation, the religious feeling!' (35). But for the most part, she dismissed belief in God as unreasonable and criticized organized Christianity, as in *Three Guineas* (1938), as a mechanism of patriarchal coercion. E. M. Forster more consistently discovers, or presumes, a natural and historical connection between sexuality and spirituality; for him, as early as the short stories collected in *The Celestial Omnibus* (1911) and in common with many late Victorian and Edwardian writers, sexuality represents one expression of eternal natural forces, best exemplified in the ancient figure of Pan. In Pan, to borrow the definition of mysticism that Strachey devised while thinking of Forster's *The Longest Journey* (1907), and which would later inform the protagonist's experiences in his novel *Maurice*, Forster discovers 'an underlying secret divinity in things' (Strachey, 'Do Two' 121) – one to be recuperated and revered after centuries of Christian repression. Equally compelling examples of Bloomsbury's explorations of connections between sexuality and religion are to be found in Lytton Strachey's personal life, and in Duncan Grant's religious painting.

For Strachey, sexuality serves several purposes: it is a site of ideological contestation over social and ethical legitimacy; it is a complex psychophysical tendency that represents an occasion for biographical psychodrama – as in his *Elizabeth and Essex: A Tragic History* (1928), which Freud himself considered the first genuinely Freudian work of biography (Holroyd 615); it is an opportunity for experimentation in domestic arrangements and new 'convivialities;' and it is, at the most personal and the most intimately interpersonal level, a physical and emotional vehicle to spiritual transcendence.

In Bloomsbury's most sensational marriage of sexuality and religion, Strachey looks to the past for help in discovering a fresher air to dispel the 'atrocious fog of superstition that hangs over us and compresses our breathing and poisons our lives' (*Letters* 594). Ironically, given the formative influence on him of Plato's *Symposium* and of the equally non-Christian ethics of Moore, as well as his general loathing of Christianity and of organized religion in general, Strachey, like Forster, found a rich source of spiritual inspiration in Christianity's founder. Strachey devoted much of his writing career to the ethical and ideological critique of religion – as metaphysical system and as a type of social organization. And yet, at various times, he thought of sexuality in religious terms, sometimes confusing sexual and religious – or, more precisely, spiritual – sensation: 'I seem', he tells Leonard Woolf in 1904, 'to have a physical feeling in my abdomen of spiritual affection. But perhaps it's merely lust' (*Letters* 31). The next year, the beginning of an affair with Duncan Grant inspired thoughts of heaven and imaginations of himself in the role of a new St. John the Baptist as a prophet of love: 'I've managed … to catch a glimpse of Heaven. Incredible, quite – yet so it's happened. I want to go into the wilderness, or the world, and preach an infinitude of sermons on one text – Embrace one another!' (*Letters* 74–5). In later years, Strachey's conflation of sexual desire and religious ecstasy reached a climax when he embarked on a series of sadomasochistic crucifixion experiments with his last lover, Roger Senhouse (Avery, 'Nailed' 183–7). These experiments, with Senhouse playing the spear-thrusting Saint Longinus to Strachey's Christ, reveal Strachey's keen understanding of the symbolic power of the cross, and of how his adoption of the persona of the crucified Christ, besides resulting in his own orgasmic ecstasy, represented a symbolic challenge to and ironic fulfilment of St. Paul's political gloss on that world-historical event. Through the crucifixion, Paul writes, Jesus 'Blot[ted] out the handwriting of ordinances that was against us, which was contrary to us, and took it out of the way, nailing it to *his* cross' (Colossians 2: 14). So too Lytton Strachey, nineteen hundred years later, in a private sexual act with political resonances, challenges the moralism and heteronormativity of Section II of the Criminal Law Amendment Act of 1885 – the Labouchère Amendment, under which Oscar Wilde had been prosecuted – toward the performative articulation of a new sexual ethic that paradoxically shares a spiritual and political impetus with the event and the person in whose name so many adherents of that moralism and that heteronormativity ground their opposition to sexual difference.

Bloomsbury's creative engagements with sexuality and religion, and specifically with images and stories from the Judeo-Christian tradition, were not always so physically extreme as Strachey's. Many of Bloomsbury's forebears were religiously active, particularly in the Society of Friends and in the Clapham Sect of the Church of England. In common with many modern (and modernist) intellectuals, they jettisoned much of their religious heritage as part of their ideologically parricidal tendencies; they also, like many others, retained a sense of spirituality separate from organized religion. Bloomsbury's own most intimate connection to organized religion, and its visually most striking entwinements of sensuality, sexuality, and spirituality, took shape relatively late in the day, after the deaths of Lytton Strachey, Roger Fry, Virginia Woolf, and John Maynard Keynes in the 1930s and 1940s diminished its ranks. In the early 1940s, Duncan Grant and Vanessa Bell won a commission to decorate the interior of Berwick Church near Charleston in Sussex; their decorations included a large crucifixion painting, for which the bisexual painter Edward le Bas, Grant's occasional lover, posed tied to an easel. A few years later, Grant met Paul Roche, a Catholic priest wearing a sailor's outfit, with whom he quickly developed an intimate, if apparently one-sided, sexual relationship. Grant and Roche's friendship translated quickly into a mutual creative influence. Grant painted a growing number of religious subjects on canvas, and Roche was newly invigorated by the sensual reasonableness of Bloomsbury, including the writings of Virginia Woolf, which he credited with teaching him an important lesson in spiritual economics. As Roche writes in his semiautobiographical novel about his loss of vocation, *Vessel of Dishonor* (1963), *Mrs. Dalloway* reveals to the protagonist Father Martin Haversham that 'Life was the context of religion and not the other way round. Life was the only stuff of which religion could be made' (143). Shortly after meeting Grant, Roche left the priesthood, began writing poetry and fiction, and ultimately forged a career as a translator of classical Greek drama.

In the 1950s, Grant and Roche's personal relationship and professional interests – Grant's growing interest in religious subjects as well as Roche's unchained, self-proclaimedly pagan sensuality – would result in the creation of one of Bloomsbury's most beautiful visual testaments to the spiritual power of sexuality and the sexual potency of religious imagery. Just as Grant encouraged Roche to pursue a career as a writer, for his part Roche seems to have confirmed, and perhaps even enriched, Grant's sense of how Bloomsbury's ethics might be compatible with a flexible understanding of religion that affirms the fullness of bodily experience and sensual joy. Grant's murals in Lincoln Cathedral, completed in 1958, brought, Edward Mayor writes, 'the world of Charleston onto the walls of the Russell Chantry' (12); they brought 'Charleston's Queer Arcadia' into the precincts of Anglicanism (Clarke 159–61). Grant's Lincoln murals commemorate the city's historical wool trade: a Breughel-like depiction of the richness of everyday medieval life on the quays with Lincoln on a hill in the background occupies one wall. They also celebrate the spiritual joy of physicality and the embodiment of spiritual plenitude, for on the opposite wall, flanked by handsome shepherds amid a flock of sheep, a young, blonde, beardless, golden, glowing Christ with a lamb draped over his shoulders kindly surveys the scene. This reverential portrait of Christ the Good Shepherd, hearkening back in its features to early Christian (and earlier religious) iconography, is also a reverential portrait of Paul Roche, who posed as Jesus. Grant's is a reverence that suits the physicality and spirituality of the human subject; the homoeroticism of his Good Shepherd, as Frances Spalding observes, is a key ingredient in his transformation of Roche into Jesus, and recalls that of the Sistine Chapel (Spalding 428). Together with Strachey and Senhouse's crucifixion experiments, Grant's reverence for both the physicality and the spirituality of Christ embodies the harmonic compatibility of spiritual aspiration and sexual freedom; it also illustrates the persistence, deep into the twentieth century, of Bloomsbury's early-formed belief in the ethical, political, and artistic desirability of sexual liberty.

Bloomsbury remains a powerful cultural presence in the early twenty-first century for many reasons, not least because they helped significantly to shape our own attitudes toward sexuality, gender, and the erotic. In an obscure survey of orgies from ancient Greece and Rome to the twentieth century, Burgo Partridge, the son of Bloomsburians Ralph and Frances Partridge, writes of how 'the Greeks ... achieved an attitude towards sexual matters not since equalled in its realistic sanity' (16). Regardless of the accuracy of Partridge's claim about 'the Greeks', it applies well to the Bloomsbury Group, whose own many and vigorous efforts to achieve 'realistic sanity' toward sexuality include the creation of Burgo Partridge himself.

WORKS CITED

Avery, Todd. 'Nailed: The Crucifixion of Lytton Strachey.' *Queer Bloomsbury*. Ed. Brenda Helt and Madelyn Detloff. Edinburgh: Edinburgh UP, 2016. 172–88.

Avery, Todd. *Saxon Sydney-Turner: The Ghost of Bloomsbury*. London: Cecil Woolf, 2015.

Bell, Clive. *Civilization*. West Drayton: Penguin, 1947.

Bell, Quentin. *Virginia Woolf: A Biography*. Vol. II. New York: Harcourt Brace Jovanovich, 1972.

Bell, Vanessa. *Selected Letters of Vanessa Bell*. Ed. Regina Marler. New York: Pantheon Books, 1993.

Clarke, Darren. 'Duncan Grant and Charleston's Queer Arcadia'. *Queer Bloomsbury*. Ed. Brenda Helt and Madelyn Detloff. Edinburgh: Edinburgh UP, 2016. 152–71.

Fromm, Harold. 'Virginia Woolf: Art and Sexuality'. *Virginia Quarterly Review* 55:3 (Summer 1979): 441–59.

Helt, Brenda and Madelyn Detloff. 'Introduction'. *Queer Bloomsbury*. Ed. Helt and Detloff. Edinburgh: Edinburgh UP, 2016. 1–12.

Holroyd, Michael. *Lytton Strachey: The New Biography*. London: Vintage, 1995.

Hussey, Mark. *Virginia Woolf A to Z*. New York: Oxford UP, 1995.

Keynes, John Maynard. 'My Early Beliefs'. *The Bloomsbury Group: A Collection of Memoirs and Commentary*. Ed. S. P. Rosenbaum. Rev. ed. Toronto: U of Toronto P, 1995. 82–97.

MacCarthy, Desmond. 'Bloomsbury: An Unfinished Memoir'. *The Bloomsbury Group: A Collection of Memoirs and Commentary*. Ed. S. P. Rosenbaum. Rev. ed. Toronto: U of Toronto P, 1995. 65–73.

Marler, Regina. *Bloomsbury Pie: The Making of the Bloomsbury Boom*. New York: Henry Holt, 1997.

Mayor, Edward. *The Duncan Grant Murals in Lincoln Cathedral*. Lincoln: Lincoln Cathedral Publications, 2000.

Moore, G. E. *Principia Ethica*. Cambridge: Cambridge UP, 1966.

Mullin, Katherine. 'Victorian Bloomsbury'. *The Cambridge Companion to the Bloomsbury Group*. Ed. Victoria Rosner. Cambridge: Cambridge UP, 2014. 19–32.

Partridge, Burgo. *A History of Orgies*. New York: Bonanza Books, 1960.

Reed, Christopher. 'Bloomsbury as Queer Subculture'. *The Cambridge Companion to the Bloomsbury Group*. Ed. Victoria Rosner. Cambridge: Cambridge UP, 2014. 71–89.

Roche, Paul. *Vessel of Dishonor*. New York: Signet, 1963.

Rosenbaum, S. P. 'The First Book of Bloomsbury'. *Twentieth-Century Literature* 30:4 (Winter 1984): 388–403.

Spalding, Frances. *Duncan Grant: A Biography*. London: Pimlico, 1998.

Strachey, Lytton. 'Art and Indecency'. *The Really Interesting Question and Other Papers*. Ed. Paul Levy. New York: Capricorn Books, 1974. 82–90.

Strachey, Lytton. 'Do Two and Two Make Five?' *Unpublished Works of Lytton Strachey: Early Papers*. Ed. Todd Avery. London: Pickering & Chatto, 2011. 117–23.

Strachey, Lytton. *The Letters of Lytton Strachey*. Ed Paul Levy. London: Viking, 2005.

Strachey, Lytton. 'Will It Come Right in the End?' *The Really Interesting Question and Other Papers*. Ed. Paul Levy. New York: Capricorn Books, 1974. 71–81.

Symons, Arthur. 'The Decadent Movement in Literature'. *Aesthetes and Decadents of the 1890s: An Anthology of British Poetry and Prose*. Ed. Karl Beckson. Rev. ed. Chicago: Academy Chicago, 1981. 134–51.

Woolf, Virginia. *The Diary of Virginia Woolf, Vol. 3, 1925–1930*. Ed. Anne Olivier Bell. San Diego: Harcourt Brace, 1980.

Woolf, Virginia. *The Letters of Virginia Woolf, Vol. 4, 1929–1932*. Ed. Nigel Nicolson and Joanne Trautmann. San Diego: Harcourt Brace, 1978.

Woolf, Virginia. *Mrs. Dalloway*. Orlando: Harcourt, 2005.

Woolf, Virginia. 'Old Bloomsbury'. *Moments of Being*. Ed. Jeanne Schulkind. San Diego: Harcourt Brace, 1985. 179–201.

Woolf, Virginia. 'Professions for Women'. *Killing the Angel in the House*. Harmondsworth: Penguin, 1995. 1–9.

Woolf, Virginia. 'Women Novelists'. *Killing the Angel in the House*. Harmondsworth: Penguin, 1995. 13–18.

Case Study: Edward Carpenter's Radical Integrity and Its Influence on E. M. Forster

JESSE WOLFE

CARPENTER'S WRITINGS AND LIFE

In an outpouring of essays, pamphlets, and lectures written between 1870 and 1925, Edward Carpenter articulated – perhaps as fully as any thinker of his time – a radical-left sensibility. He was openly gay – or 'Intermediate', a term he popularized – and he championed Intermediate people, studied sexological literature to understand their characteristics, and traced the evolution of Intermediate sentiments from past through present times. An ardent feminist, Carpenter spurned Victorian misogyny and supported women's rights, birth control, and female sexual pleasure, among other progressive and/or taboo causes. A Ruskinian socialist, he saw industrial capitalism as a 'sickness'; he imagined that a precapitalist, agrarian past was freer and more sexually egalitarian than Victorian society; and he sought a 'cure' for modern maladies in a simple, back-to-nature lifestyle (*Civilization*). The social transformations he advocated in his half-century of writings extend beyond those mentioned, in dynamic, interconnected ways.

E. M. Forster's admiration for this pioneer of gay consciousness is well known, including the gentle irony with which he regarded Carpenter's more mystical and idealistic tendencies (*Two Cheers* 206). Less appreciated, though, is Carpenter's deep impact on Forster's writing, in part through his example as a man, but more through the forcefulness of his polemics. Sometimes Carpenter supplied models to emulate and other times he illustrated pure or extreme attitudes that Forster preferred to modulate. But in both situations, he helped to mould the content and the form of Forster's novels and essays, from how Forster imagined characters' psychosexual interrelations to how he constructed plots and envisioned the possibilities or impossibilities of future social change. Forster's intuitions about history, which respond to Carpenter's provocations, shape his novels' endings, from Margaret Schlegel's ruminations about the future in the midst of her questionable marriage, in *Howards End*, to Aziz's assertion, at the conclusion of *A Passage to India*, that only when India drives Britain 'into the sea' can men like Fielding and him be friends (312). The need for *Maurice* to have a happy ending, as that novel's Terminal Note explains; Forster's need to compose a Terminal Note at all; and his attempt to supply *Maurice* with an Epilogue (with which he was dissatisfied) all also bear likely traces of Carpenter's influence (*Maurice* 250, 254).

Carpenter's life – eventually – embodied the same principles as his writings, despite his conventional origins. He was born in 1844 to a respectable middle-class family: his father was governor at a Sussex boarding school. In 1867, when Leslie Stephen's scepticism led him to resign his Cambridge clerical fellowship, a comfortable establishment niche opened for Carpenter. He was appointed as Stephen's replacement in 1870, at the young age of twenty-six. But by 1874, Carpenter also resigned, for the same reason as Stephen. He entered an unsettled period, lecturing through University Extension, an adult education movement that aimed to bring learning to the masses (Rowbotham 24–64). This career choice brought Carpenter closer to living out his evolving socialist ideals. But ironically, his substantial inheritance upon his father's 1882 death enabled him to move more fully off the grid. In North England's remote Cordwell Valley, he constructed Millthorpe Cottage, his 'Thoreau ideal', where he lived until his 1929 death (Rowbotham 75). He pursued subsistence farming, often gardening in the nude, and he strove – with initial difficulty but eventual success – to forge alliances with the local working class. Increasingly as he embraced his dissident lifestyle, he came to see the interests of various oppressed groups – women, gays and lesbians, and manual labourers – as congruent. As Forster comments in an appreciative 1944 essay, Carpenter 'may not have got into another class', but by discarding his own, he 'gained happiness'. Moreover, Forster says that parting with inherited gentility was 'very revolutionary' for its time; 'it astonished people' (*Two Cheers* 205–6).

But the zenith of Carpenter's courageous individualism came in 1898, when his working-class lover, George Merrill, twenty-two years his junior, moved to Millthorpe, where he lived with Carpenter until he died in 1928. Carpenter has been mocked for his Whitmanesque belief that 'homogenic' love (another contemporary term for same-sex attachment) could bind class divisions, as a form of *democracy in action* (Tsuzuki 3). But his three decades of cohabitation with Merrill were a conspicuous example of durable love and a foundation for the friendships and political alliances he cultivated in his community.

Carpenter's self-assurance in the threatening context of post-Labouchere England, discussed further below, made Millthorpe into a pilgrimage site for gay men and radical thinkers. Siegfried Sassoon wrote to Carpenter as a 'leader' and a 'prophet' before visiting him in 1911 (Moeyes 25). Forster visited Millthorpe a year later 'as one approaches a saviour'. As *Maurice*'s Terminal Note testifies, the experience inspired Forster's only novel that treats same-sex love with the romantic frankness of a Carpenter essay (249–50). Nonetheless, *Maurice* – completed in 1914 but not published until 1971, the year after Forster's death – does not affirm such love in the here-and-now. Its two main lovers, the Cambridge-educated Maurice Hall and the gardener Alec Scudder, reproduce Carpenter and Merrill's cross-class partnership. But society will not tolerate their love, so in order to be together, they flee to somewhere in the English 'greenwood' that, says Forster, post-Second World War industrialization wiped away (254). Forster dedicated *Maurice* to a 'happier time'; between the novel's plot and its dedication, it displaces happy same-sex love to a fairytale nowhere or an unspecified future time, betraying its author's wariness.

By contrast, the Millthorpe community pursued its ideals actively. In 1913, Carpenter founded the British Society for the Study of Sex Psychology, which (à la Bloomsbury) promoted the open discussion of sexual and social topics including abortion, divorce, and sex education (Rowbotham 333). Forster and D. H. Lawrence joined the society, which exposed each to potential risk – especially Lawrence, given the wartime suspicion aroused by his German lover, Frieda. Despite such dangers, the society expanded, and within months of its founding Carpenter delivered a talk on the exclusion of homosexuality from cultural history, at the First International Congress for Sex Research, in Berlin (Moffat 121; Rowbotham 333–4).

But despite his prestige, Carpenter aroused scepticism even among fellow leftists. George Bernard Shaw saw Carpenter's circle as steeped in 'illusions' and the ex-clergyman as an 'impostor' (Rowbotham 8). In 1936, seven years after Carpenter's death, George Orwell lamented that Carpenterism, with its mystical strains, distracted from socialism's needed focus on economic justice. In a private correspondence, Orwell denounced with homophobic brio the 'eunuch type with a vegetarian smell ... readers of Edward Carpenter or some other pious sodomite' (see Orwell's April 1936 letter in Orwell and Angus 245). Forster did not share Orwell's homophobia, but he did share his wry perspective on the combination of 'socialism [and] mysticism' that left Carpenter 'not interested in efficiency or organisation, or party discipline, [or] industrialism' (*Two Cheers* 206).

Notwithstanding the harsh judgements of Shaw and Orwell, nor Forster's kinder self-differentiations, the 'sage of Millthorpe' inspired his peers, both in direct, personal ways and in more diffuse ways, through his writings. Admittedly, pinning down this latter influence can be difficult because Carpenter's polemics belong to a current of advanced opinion that was fed by multiple sources. Furthermore, Bloomsbury in general and Forster in particular found inspiration in numerous places: from classical Athens to the poetry of Constantin Cavafy in early twentieth-century Alexandria, from the Cambridge Apostles (which supplied the group's nucleus) to the poetry of Walt Whitman, and elsewhere.

These caveats aside, Carpenter's lines of inquiry shaped the questions Forster explored, even when Forster reached more ambivalent answers than Carpenter. This was true of Carpenter's critique of Victorian gender personalities, his exploration of human sexual nature, and his speculations into the shape of history, all of which were informed by his outsider's perspective, as an Intermediate, and by his utopian confidence in a future society in which everyone's varied natures would flourish, Intermediates included. In arguing this, I will build on previous scholarship that appreciates Carpenter's value to his time and ours. Sheila Rowbotham's biography asserts that, although Carpenter was largely forgotten when he died, he 'helped to prod the modern world into being' and has been a resource for social justice movements from feminism to gay rights since his passing (1). In conversation with Rowbotham and others,[1] I examine Carpenter's importance not for social history but for aesthetic history, in the ways his polemics feed Forster's belletrism.

LABOUCHERE, A CULTURE OF FEAR, AND THE COMPARATIVE VIRTUES OF SINGULAR AND DOUBLE SELVES

To understand why Carpenter was so suited to influence Forster – largely for reasons of self-recognition, but for other reasons too – it will help to review the legal and aesthetic predicaments that enmeshed Forster throughout his career. Prior to 1885, English law reacted to sodomy in the ghastliest way, punishing it with death (from 1533) or life imprisonment (from 1861).[2] But the difficulty of proving the act made prosecutions rare. This silver lining was erased when Section 11 of the Criminal Law Amendment Act, otherwise known as the Labouchere Amendment, made acts of 'gross indecency' in public or private punishable by up to two years in prison. In 1895, a decade after its passage, Oscar Wilde was convicted under Labouchere, and fear spread through Britain's gay communities. Many wealthy Englishmen fled for continental nations subject to the French Empire, under whose Napoleonic Penal Code sodomy was not a crime. Some who remained in Britain and were prosecuted under Labouchere killed themselves, including Alan Turing, whose oestrogen therapy punishment likely, in conjunction with his bipolar disorder, precipitated his 1954 suicide. This cruel legislation was not repealed until 1967, three years before Forster's death. It so frightened Forster that as late as 1953, when he was 74, his *New Statesman* article entitled 'A Magistrate's Figures' lamented how common it was for police officers to entrap gay men.

From a literary-historical point of view, however, the effect of this culture of fear on Forster's published and unpublished writings – from his short stories and novels to his essays, letters, diaries, and notebooks – was complex and not wholly negative. His short stories merit a study of their own, from the half dozen in *The Celestial Omnibus* (1911) and the additional half dozen in *The Eternal Moment* (1928) to the fourteen tales unpublished while he lived but collected posthumously in *The Life to Come* (1972). His opinions about these works varied: some letters express his pride in and fondness for some stories, but he also called stories a 'wrong channel for [his] pen' and in 1922 he even burned a number of them that he considered 'indecent' (Stallybrass xii). Whether he did so for aesthetic reasons or out of fear is debatable (many of his stories treat homosexuality with varying levels of obliqueness).

Whereas Forster's stories – both their content and publication history – dramatize his struggles as a gay writer in general, his novels and essays more clearly illustrate the Carpenterian issues of particular interest to this study, from questions of novelistic craft concerning the depictions of Intermediate protagonists in a heteronormative society to the question, broached in various essays, of how broad and radical a social critique is entailed in the cultural politics of Intermediacy. His novels negotiate his fear of exposure, on the one hand, and his compulsion to explore sexuality on the other, by crafting 'double narratives',[3] wherein surface plots of opposite-sex love disguise dramas of male–male desire. Philip Herriton, the protagonist of Forster's first novel, *Where Angels Fear to Tread* (1905), is attracted consciously to an Englishwoman, Caroline, and unconsciously to an Italian peasant, Gino. Just when Caroline seems ready to tell him, 'I love you', and he to respond, 'I love you too', instead she exclaims, 'I love him' (Gino), and Philip completes the ironic revelation by responding, 'I love him too' (145). Readers can then infer that Philip's passivity and habitual irony, and the awkwardness of his romance with Caroline, all stem from his repressed Intermediate longings.

Forster's second novel, *The Longest Journey* (1907), is also an Intermediate Bildungsroman. Its hero, Rickie Elliot, endures Philip's dilemma, but with an added twist. Rickie marries a woman, Agnes, while harbouring homogenic desires both for his Cambridge friend, Stuart, and for his unrefined half-brother, Stephen. Thus Forster contrasts not only opposite-sex with same-sex love, but also intraclass with interclass homoeroticism. Whitman's ideas about male 'comradeship's' transgressive power influenced Forster directly, but all the more richly because they also did so indirectly, enriched as they were by Carpenter's wide-ranging critiques of gender norms.

When *The Longest Journey* was published, Forster still had his three masterpieces ahead of him: *A Room with a View* (1908), *Howards End* (1910), and *A Passage to*

India (1924), two of which have disguised same-sex love plots. *Howards End* is the anomaly: it portrays no Intermediates sympathetically, but instead adopts a moralistic tone towards Tibby and Monica, its two characters with ambiguous sexual orientations. Upon completing *Howards End*, Forster vaulted to a position as one of England's elite authors, thanks largely to the disguises his Intermediate love themes were so cruelly compelled to assume.

Forster learned – even before conceiving his first novel – the art of indirection, that is, doubleness of various kinds. Even his use of double narratives had Bloomsburian precedents, of sorts. As I argue elsewhere, G. E. Moore's 1903 philosophical treatise, *Principia Ethica*, which has been called 'Bloomsbury's Bible' and which treasures friendship and art as life's two greatest goods, invoked – without explicitly naming – Wilde's illicit love (Wolfe 31–50). In *Principia*, the term 'friendship' is freighted. To uninitiated readers of this highly regarded work of analytic philosophy, the word carried no queer connotation. But to the Bloomsburians who knew and loved Moore, it bristled with suggestiveness. Bloomsbury emerged from the Apostles, a secret Cambridge undergraduate discussion society that dated to the 1820s and that Moore led until shortly before *Principia*'s publication. Its members – hovering on the verge of adulthood in a repressed and homophobic society – often harboured unspoken, or ambiguously spoken, erotic feelings for one another. Indirection and partial self-revelation were the DNA of Apostolic culture, and Bloomsbury, for all its celebrated frankness, also struggled against external and internal sexual restrictions (Levy 65–120). Forster's double narratives represent the aesthetic flourishing of a culture of internalized fear, self-repression, hard-won self-acceptance, and guarded self-expression – all the way through to *Passage*, in which Fielding and Aziz's 'friendship' recalls the sexual indeterminacy the word carries in *Principia*.

But this strategy of speaking to two audiences was not sustainable. Forster's 1911 diary entry confesses to weariness 'of the subject that I both can and may treat – the love of men for women and vice versa' (qtd in *Howards End* 275). Forster underrates his own artistry, for opposite-sex love is not the *only* subject his cagey novels treat. But his psychological and creative anguish is clear enough. It makes sense, then – notwithstanding his literary success – that Forster found a journey to Millthorpe necessary. Even before he met Carpenter, Forster shared his nostalgia for England's rural traditions, as expressed both in *Howards End*'s paean to the land and in *Maurice*'s mythical 'greenwoods'. But more importantly, Forster admired Carpenter's sexual self-understanding. Carpenter represented an entirely different way of being an Intermediate and an engaged citizen-author than Forster could summon the courage to be. Carpenter lived with Merrill: he was not closeted like Forster. Carpenter wrote about his sexual feelings unabashedly. Whereas Forster lived a double life (and made an aesthetic virtue of it), Carpenter shone with singularity of purpose. Forster's only openly gay novel would probably not have been possible had he never trekked to Carpenter's cottage.

Maurice dispenses with the 'screen' portion of *The Longest Journey*'s double narrative. The eponymous protagonist and his readers become aware of his homogenic tendencies early in the novel, which pursues a *single* narrative driven by a sequence of questions: Will Maurice and his Cambridge friend, Clive, acknowledge their attraction to one another? When they do so, will they act on it in more than chaste ways? When Clive renounces his Intermediacy, marries, and follows the life-script laid out by family tradition, he frees Maurice to couple with Alec, an under-gamekeeper and symbol of natural honesty in opposition to Clive's refined duplicity. But will Maurice and Alec find the lasting love that Philip cannot realize with Gino, nor Rickie enjoy with Stephen, but that Carpenter and

Merrill did achieve in real life? As compelling as these dramatic questions are, *Maurice*'s single narrative – its undisguised same-sex love plot – was as unsustainable a solution to Forster's predicament as double narratives were. Hence Forster, perpetually afraid of exposure, circulated its manuscript only among trusted friends, as he did with many short stories. After he finished *Maurice*, he took ten years to work *Passage* into satisfactory shape, then for the remaining forty-six years of his ninety-one-year life, this leading light of English letters produced no more novels.

The end of Forster's novel publishing, however, did not mean the end of his authorship. Just around the time Carpenter stopped writing, as though Carpenter had passed him a baton, Forster sprinted into a new phase of his career, the fruits of which are collected in *Abinger Harvest and England's Pleasant Land* (1936) and *Two Cheers for Democracy* (1951). As discussed, Forster's treatments of Carpenterian themes antedate his turn to essay writing. But after Forster met Carpenter in 1912, and especially after expository forms became his primary mediums in the 1920s, he took cues even more strongly from Carpenter's critiques of Victorian gender codes, his examinations of Intermediacy, and his historical speculations.

THE SICKNESS OF VICTORIAN GENDER ROLES

Carpenter loathed what middle-class Victorian gender roles did to both sexes. He was judgmental towards his sisters, whose 'dabbling in painting and music' and immersion in 'rituals of fashionable life' he saw as symptomatic of the domestic angel code (Rowbotham 20), and he associated muscular masculinity with oppressiveness in the home, national culture, and the British Empire. He developed these ideas in writings including *Love's Coming of Age* (1896). All my succeeding comments on Carpenter address this essay collection, whose title expresses its author's belief in a benign historical evolution towards a world in which each sex will realize its varied potential. Its second and third essays, 'Man, the Ungrown' and 'Woman, the Serf', diagnose the sexes' current stunted states. They trace Victorian repression to two main sources: first, the English public school system, and second, capitalism and private property. 'Man, the Ungrown' describes men of the 'well-to-do' class as 'half-baked' due to an education that prizes athletic skills and 'organizing capacity' and gives them a tolerable 'grip' on 'the practical and material side of life' but instils no 'conception of love'. After a boy glides on his parents' money into a predictable profession and marries whom he chooses, because his 'latent ... affection and tenderness of feeling' have not been developed, he degenerates from 'beefy self-satisfaction' into 'dreary cynicism'. His sex instinct still predominates, even as it wanes, because nothing in his 'sympathetic nature' balances it (20–21).

Forster works through these ideas in texts including *The Longest Journey*, *Howards End*, *Maurice*, and the 1926 essay 'Notes on the English Character'. Readers do not see Henry Wilcox during his school years, but otherwise he embodies Carpenter's argument to a tee. His organizing capacity manifests in large and small ways, some of which Margaret appreciates, others of which she resents. He arranges their wedding, including food and accommodations for the guests, an event in which Margaret is so emotionally invested that she resents Helen's intrusion with the Basts. (This is, of course, before Margaret learns that Jacky was once Henry's mistress.) Henry also demonstrates managerial wherewithal in running the Imperial and West African Rubber Company. This corporate name is highly suggestive. As mentioned, Carpenter analogized authoritarian men in various public and private contexts; *Howards End* develops the analogy in the Wilcox patriarch whose wife is 'thankful not to have [the right to] vote' and whose profits derive from empire (58). Lest readers fear the 'Imperial type' insufficiently, given that he is 'healthy, ever in motion', Forster's narrator explains that he is not the 'super-yeoman' he may appear to be, but 'a destroyer' (229).

Margaret, then, might raise an eyebrow at Henry's business. But Forster, unlike Carpenter, explores the seductive appeal of the authoritarian personality type before exposing its spiritual poverty. Hence Margaret, to her sister's incredulity, justifies her engagement by insisting that without people like the Wilcoxes, England would have 'no trains, no ships ... just savagery' (127). Helen had been similarly seduced, her love for Paul stemming from her sense that 'Wilcoxes were so competent, and seemed to have their hands on all the ropes' (22).[4] Helen's metaphor recalls Carpenter's observation about the 'ungrown' man's 'grip' on practical and material concerns. This supposed 'grip', however, can only endear either sister for so long. In Margaret's case, when Henry asks what she wants to order, then says that her choice – fish pie – is 'not a bit the thing to go for', she allows him to choose her food, all the while pretending to agree with him about the restaurant's 'Old English' ambience (110). When he insists on chaperoning her back to her hotel, she initially objects to his condescending protectiveness, but allows herself to be overruled (132). She imagines that she retains her independence of mind, but the narrator, wiser than she, observes that Henry 'did alter her character – a little' (126). In 'Woman, the Serf', Carpenter complains that Victorian gender roles encourage defects in each sex: the man's 'brutality and conceit' and the woman's 'finesse and subtlety' (34). Henry's interactions with his second wife-to-be add a novelist's deft touch to Carpenter's analysis of pathological gender personalities.

Eventually, what Carpenter calls the ungrown man's lack of a 'sympathetic nature' or 'conception of love' – in the broad sense, not specifically regarding Margaret – leads Margaret to a scathing verdict. After Leonard's death, she decides that Henry is 'rotten to the core' and will have to 'build up his life without hers' (235). Henry, of course, does have a heart, but in Carpenter's terms it is 'half-baked', and this has influenced his and his son Charles's actions leading to Leonard's death. When Henry proposes marriage to Margaret, he does so in the most awkward, unromantic way. His cruelty and hypocrisy enrage Margaret when he invokes his dead wife in refusing to grant the pregnant Helen one night's stay at Howards End (219). Margaret accuses him of canting with the memory of Ruth and insists that he see the connection between his having had a mistress (for which she forgave him) and Helen now carrying an illegitimate child. Margaret strains to appeal to Henry's sympathetic nature, but he can only read attempted blackmail in her allusion to Jacky. This scene shows how perspicacious Helen is in seeing 'panic and emptiness' behind the aggressive Wilcox exterior (21, 124, 168). In making this diagnosis, Helen speaks for Forster, who – following Carpenter's suggestions – uses Henry in a quasi-allegorical way to illustrate the impasse to which Victorian gender types have brought intimacy-seeking men and women.

The Longest Journey and *Maurice* complement the Carpenterian themes that Henry Wilcox helps Forster develop. Both Rickie Elliot and Maurice Hall graduate from public schools and predictably – given this training – behave like petty tyrants: Maurice to his conventional sisters and Rickie to his students. Each young protagonist, however, attends Cambridge (as Forster did), where each, prodded by his exposure to Plato and by the mentorship of a more sophisticated Intermediate friend, discovers his sexual identity. This process of self-discovery, fraught with reversals, self-deceptions, and torments, carves out the soul in each young man that the 'half-baked' Wilcox patriarch never develops. The process not only refines Rickie's and Maurice's introspective powers in general, it also leads each to recognize the injustices of bourgeois heteronormativity and to find both moral clarity and courage. Rickie's marriage to Agnes has been a sham, given his sexual orientation and her cruel, manipulative personality. Also to the hero's discredit, he has been shunning his half-brother ('brother', like 'friend', being a freighted term), since Stephen is illegitimate. But eventually, Stephen too discovers that they are half-brothers and reappears in Rickie's life. His rustic integrity – comparable to that of Gino from *Where Angels Fear to Tread* – helps to restore Rickie's better self, including his awareness of his marriage's hollowness and the cruelty of stigmatizing bastard children. The siblings become friends, though Rickie cannot save Stephen from his destructive drinking habit. He does, however, save Stephen's life: Rickie's legs are severed and he dies heroically when he pulls the larger man from an oncoming train. Maurice, for his part, does not die in the act of proving his loyalty to Alec, but he does sacrifice his job and social position – in essence, his life.

Even after Forster, in multiple novels, worked through his ideas about ungrown Englishmen – and about the humanizing power of a stigmatized sexual orientation – his dialogue with Carpenter continued. One of his earliest important essays, 'Notes on the English Character', though it doesn't address Intermediacy, does strike numerous Carpenterian themes and at times seems to recast Carpenter's ideas in Forster's words. Forster states that the 'heart' of England is the middle class and (*pace* Carpenter) that the heart of the middle class is the public school. He makes observations similar to Carpenter's about life scripts: whereas Carpenter describes boys gliding on parents' money into predictable professions, Forster explains that, on leaving school, 'the boy either sets to work at once' – in the army or business, or emigrating – then attends university, after which he 'becomes a barrister, doctor, civil servant, schoolmaster, or journalist' (4). Both authors regret the character type produced by these institutions: Forster transmutes Carpenter's 'half-baked' man (with his 'organizing capacity' but no 'sympathetic nature') into his celebrated litany of public school graduates' 'well-developed bodies, fairly developed minds, and undeveloped hearts' (4–5).

'Notes on the English Character' complicates this critique, however – in a manner that may or may not distinguish Forster's sensibility from Carpenter's. Forster's novels are famed for their 'double turns': their 'respect for two facts coexisting', though the facts might seem contradictory (Trilling 17). His essays perform similar manoeuvres; hence he explains that the Englishman has 'an undeveloped heart – not a cold one'. England's writers, including Romantics like Shelley, demonstrate that its people are anything but unfeeling: there is 'no real coldness' in them, Forster reiterates. In fact, he hopes and believes that in the next twenty years, the 'supremacy of the middle classes' will end and the national character will change, from what public schools have made it, into something 'more lovable' (13). As it happened, the next twenty years witnessed the Second World War and a dampening of Forster's faith in meliorism. But his historical optimism in 'Notes' is distinctly Carpenterian.

'Woman, the Serf', like its companion essay, 'Man, the Ungrown', illustrates both what distinguishes Carpenter from Forster and elements of Carpenter's thought that influenced his admirer. On the one hand, Forster's nostalgia was always qualified: he never shared Carpenter's belief in a sexually egalitarian, utopic past. In *Howards End*, when Margaret assumes Ruth's former role as the titular property's matriarch, this triumph of rural lyricism comes at a price. Not only does 'grey cosmopolitanism' threaten to swallow

Howards End, but as Margaret transforms into a domestic angel, her intellectual capacities wane. She loses her inclination for complex thinking: for understanding, for example, that her good fortune depends upon the misfortune of others, such as Leonard. The closing chapters' mottled picture of a vanishing rural world and their retrenchment in Victorian feminine psychology are a far cry from Carpenter's vision of a time 'far back in History' when 'the thought of inequality had hardly arisen' (Love's Coming 25).

'Woman, the Serf' also takes a more sharply defined stance than Forster with regard to present sexual inequality. Simultaneously targeting capitalism and Victorian separate spheres, Carpenter asserts that 'Man's craze for property and individual ownership ... culminated in the enslavement of woman – his most precious and beloved object' (29). Forster expressed socialist sentiments in various writings, including Howards End, where the Schlegel sisters' sincere (if ineffectual) concern for the poor contrasts favourably with the male Wilcoxes' callous superiority complex. But Forster never made such sweeping ideological gestures as to claim that the middle-class Victorian marriage paradigm expressed capitalism's inner logic.

These differences between the two writers, however, mask an array of similarities. Each detested Respectability and aimed much of his social critique at its hypocrisy and cruelty – not just to Intermediates, but to a range of nonconformists. Each believed that the gender code into which he was born had artificial ideas about maleness and femaleness, but each nonetheless used Victorian categories as launching pads for his questions and speculations. When Margaret wonders, 'Are the sexes really races, each with its own code of morality?' (Howards End 172), she reiterates the question around which much of Love's Coming of Age revolves. The thinkers also shared ideas about the psychological damage of artificial gender roles. In adapting to being treated as a cross between an 'angel and an idiot', says Carpenter, women become this way, combining 'weak and flabby sentiments' with an 'undeveloped' brain (29–30). Was Forster intentionally echoing Carpenter in 'Notes' when he assailed Englishmen's 'undeveloped' hearts? Does Margaret betray the 'flabby sentiments' of an 'angel-idiot' when she acquiesces to Henry's will, even while trying to convince herself that she's doing something else? In either case, regardless of Carpenter's demonstrable influence on Forster, their moral visions are deeply aligned.

This alignment is further evident in their combinations of gender and class analyses. Carpenter's critique of artificiality embraced not only the middle-class 'lady' and her counterpart, the 'gentleman'; he also decried the roles of household 'drudge' and 'prostitute' as common fates of working- and underclass women. His sympathy for people occupying various positions in his socioeconomic scheme anticipates Howards End, although the novel's categories differ somewhat from his. From the financially cushioned and culturally refined Schlegel sisters, to Charles Wilcox's philistine wife, Dolly, to the desperate and vulgar Jacky Bast, Howards End dramatizes how women's personalities are constructed by class and circumstance; how socially disparate women are all threatened by male privilege, despite their differences; and how many of them (though perhaps not Dolly) deserve sympathy.

SEXOLOGY, STRATEGIC ESSENTIALISM, AND THE IDEA OF A DISSIDENT

But if conservative Victorian thinking was wrong about human sexual nature, then what conceptual scheme could contest it? In 1908, twelve years after Love's Coming of Age appeared, Carpenter enlarged its penultimate chapter, 'The Intermediate Sex', into book form. This text, more than any other writing of Carpenter's, provides the theoretical foundation for Forster's double narratives. It also supplied Forster with questions that remained useful for years: do Intermediates share a secret understanding that generally passes unnoticed by their fellow men? And: when is it useful to speak in general terms about Intermediate men – or for that matter, about all men or all women – even though there are exceptions to every rule, and even though Intermediates themselves are often victims of crude generalizations?

Carpenter didn't generate these questions alone. His work rests largely on the labours of courageous Germans. Beginning in the 1860s, Karl Ulrichs 'came out', as we would now say, telling his family that he was an 'Urning' – a term of his coining for men who desire other men. His essays, published first pseudonymously and later under his name, asserted the naturalness of same-sex love. In 1867, he argued before the Congress of German Jurists against antihomosexual laws. In 1868, he received a private letter containing the first known use of the term 'homosexuality' (German *Homosexualität*), in place of his own *Urningtum*. The following year, the letter's author again referred to *Homosexualität* in an anonymous pamphlet containing the term's first known use in print (Takács 29). The discussion that Ulrichs broached took a scientific turn with the 1886 publication of Richard von Krafft-Ebing's *Psychopathia Sexualis* (translated as *Sexual Psychopathy: A Clinical-Forensic Study*). This reference book for judges and medical practitioners went through multiple editions and established the field of sexology with its 238 case studies and its range of terms, including 'heterosexual' and 'bisexuality', some of them appearing for the first time in medical literature. Sadly, authorities sometimes turned Krafft-Ebing's terms (such as 'paresthesia' – a perversion of the sexual instinct) against sexually nonconforming citizens. But in conjunction, the confessional Ulrichs and the scientific Krafft-Ebing spurred Carpenter's thought – as he would spur Forster's and Bloomsbury's – by delineating extensive continua of sexual orientations and behaviours, in opposition to the Victorian binary gender taxonomy.

In his role as an advocate, Carpenter explains that history, literature, and life combine to verify that *Urnings* (1) are a large class, (2) that they are not 'morbid', as commonly believed, and (3) that their orientation is ineradicable. (The importance of this third assertion is evident in the many men, including the fictional Maurice Hall, who endured hypnotherapy in attempts to 'cure' their pathology. The American Psychiatric Association did not remove homosexuality from the *Diagnostic and Statistical Manual of Mental Disorders* until 1973, where it had been listed as a 'sociopathic personality disorder'.) It is society's duty, Carpenter says, to understand 'homogenic' men and women and to help them understand themselves. Prejudice harms them: they suffer severely from how they're regarded. But they're unfairly feared: their orientation is often emotional, not sexual; and contrary to popular opinion, homogenic men *do* like women (*Love's Coming* 83–6).

To a large degree, sexological precursors pushed Carpenter's thought in antiessentialist directions. Their schemata – their version of the biologists' phylogenetic system of nomenclature – had the danger of pigeonholing people. But at the same time, by virtue of their sheer number, Krafft-Ebing's categories could dissolve fixities. For his part, Ulrichs defined *Urnings* as possessing a 'feminine soul enclosed in a male body' (*Love's Coming* 82). Just as Carpenter was sceptical enough, in another context, to remark that 'Nature' is a convenient shorthand – a 'personification' of human forces, not a metaphysical entity – likewise he mistrusted the essentialism of 'soul' and 'body' in Ulrichs's formulation, even as he praised Ulrichs for recognizing 'the existence of what might be called an Intermediate sex' (*Love's Coming* 3, 82–3). Carpenter says that the sexes are not, or shouldn't be, 'hopelessly isolated' from one another in thought and feeling. Their temperaments fall along a continuum (some men are very sensitive, some women are leaderly), and feelings ranging from love to friendship also form a continuum. The range of phenomena in each continuum, says Carpenter, have long existed but have only recently been studied. Carpenter was especially useful for Forster in suggesting that the continua do not map onto one another in predictable ways. One cannot deduce the nature of a man's affection – sexual, Platonic, or nonexistent – for women or for other men solely on the basis of his 'feminine' temperament. As Carpenter explains, 'Nature … in mixing the elements which go to compose each individual … often throws them crosswise in a somewhat baffling manner' (*Love's Coming* 80).

In spite of himself, though, Carpenter sometimes employed essentialist formulations. At one point he calls Intermediates a 'race' and acknowledges the existence of unattractive 'extreme specimens' in each sex. In language that could strike a twenty-first-century reader as unwittingly humorous or sadly stigmatizing, Carpenter describes the man who is 'mincing in gait and manner, something of a chatterbox, skilful at the needle', with a figure 'large at the hips', a voice 'inclining to be high-pitched', and affections 'clinging, dependent, and jealous'. Complementing this man, the 'extreme' homogenic woman possesses a 'muscular' figure, a voice 'rather low in pitch', and a 'dwelling room decorated with sporting-scenes, pistols, etc., and not without a suspicion of the fragrant weed' (*Love's Coming* 88–9).

An important scene in *Howards End* brings out both the comic possibilities and the ominous normative implications of Carpenter's marginalizations of 'extreme specimens'. When Leonard Bast turns up at Wickham Place looking for his umbrella, only to disappear promptly, the Schlegel siblings and Aunt Juley commence arguing. Helen calls her brother 'Auntie Tibby', says he's not a 'real boy', blames him for Leonard's discomfort, and calls their house a 'regular hen-coop'. Margaret, who sometimes disagrees with her sister, in this case backs her up, explaining that their house is irrevocably 'feminine', as it was even in their father's time. (This is, on the whole, a compliment to her father's sensitivity and dislike of empire.) 'All we can do', Margaret continues, 'is to see that it isn't effeminate'. She echoes Carpenter's disaffection for each gender 'extreme'. She adds that, based on Helen's description, the Wilcoxes' house 'sounded irrevocably masculine, and all that its inmates can do is to see that it isn't brutal'. As if this exchange isn't enough to recall Carpenter, Helen asks for a cigarette (i.e. a fragrant weed) and Margaret laments 'you do what you can' for the house's masculine flavour. 'The drawing-room reeks of smoke' (33–4).

The gender politics of this scene are complex but predominately reactionary in a way that is atypical for both Forster and Carpenter. The dead father seems to have been 'feminine' in a way the novel approves of, though perhaps not 'effeminate'. Tibby, by contrast, seems to be 'feminine' in a disappointing way – perhaps all too 'effeminate'. So there is some intimation of 'Nature' mixing the elements that make up a man 'crosswise in a somewhat baffling manner', to quote Carpenter. But for the most part, *Howards End* shores up gender differences and associates Tibby's effeminate masculinity with the cowardly self-indulgence of an aesthete. Other Forster novels employ more 'crosswise', 'baffling' combinations of personality traits, including *Maurice*, whose titular hero is thoroughly masculine in appearance and manner. The Intermediate men whom Maurice encounters illustrate a range of personality types, with the undergraduate Risley recalling Lytton Strachey's queenly performativity. Alec, whom Maurice chooses as his life's mate, has no noticeably 'feminine' traits – apart from the capacity for tenderness that their love brings out in both men – suggesting that a successful male–male couple needn't seek an artificial balance of masculine and feminine energy, with one partner playing the 'woman's' role.

Forster and Carpenter each sometimes found it useful to analogize sex, sexual orientation, and/or personality in essentialist ways, but at other times they each exploded false analogies. In service of his advocacy, for example, Carpenter says that, unlike 'extreme' male and female Intermediates, typically nonmaternal women and sensitive men are beacons of a better future. Their double nature makes them reconcilers and interpreters. The Intermediate man is 'complex' and has the 'emotional soul-nature of a woman'. While his 'logical faculty' might not be 'well developed', he has 'the artist-nature, with the artist's sensibility and perception' (*Love's Coming* 90). Thus Carpenter contributes, to a discourse of collective pride, a broad generalization that Forster was either too intellectually sceptical or too emotionally timid to espouse before a large audience. The pride sometimes led Carpenter to wonder whether Intermediates' double natures exalt them. On the one hand, he approvingly quotes an unnamed writer who says that Intermediates form 'a peculiar aristocracy of … good and refined habit, and in many masculine circles are the representatives of the higher mental and artistic element' (*Love's Coming* 91). On the other hand, his frequently espoused antiessentialism suggests that 'refined habits' and 'higher artistic elements' are thrown crosswise into all human subpopulations.

Forster entertained similar questions about whether Intermediacy, or nonconformism broadly construed, or some constellation of other traits, contributed to some people's being more perceptive or ethically admirable than others. Risley seems to intuit Maurice's Intermediacy before Maurice realizes this about himself, and Risley's competitive, ironic manner suggests that he and Maurice share a joke that goes over others' heads (31–3). But the novel refuses to endorse this attitude of Risley's, especially considering Maurice's limited self-knowledge by this point in the narrative. Forster strikes a different note in the essay 'What I Believe', when he touts an 'aristocracy of the sensitive, the considerate, and the plucky' among whom there exists a 'secret understanding' (70). He does not specify that this elect band has a particular sexual orientation, but nonetheless he may have had a double audience in mind. A broad readership drawn from the liberal-humanist intelligentsia would see itself in Forster's 'aristocracy', while Bloomsburians would see, in the adjectives 'sensitive', 'considerate', and 'plucky', their affections for one another in defiance of bourgeois love customs, their protests against the Great War, and their idealistic business ventures in the Hogarth Press and the Omega Workshops.

For that matter, Bloomsburians were both lay and intimate readers of Forster's works: they belonged, like he did, to a broad current of liberal sensibility. They were insiders (sons, daughters, and friends of cultural celebrities) and outsiders (sexual nonconformists and wartime pacifists). They were avant-garde artists and thoroughly bourgeois in their entrepreneurialism. The indeterminate meaning of 'aristocracy' in Forster's usage, in the wake of its narrower denotation in the passage that Carpenter quotes, encapsulates a question that animates each man's oeuvre: where do Intermediates fit into society?

CARPENTER'S HISTORICAL IDEALISM
AND FORSTER'S SCEPTICISM

This question about Intermediates is also a question about history. Bloomsburians shared Carpenter's utopian longings, though not his belief in the likelihood of their realization. Carpenter's optimism expressed itself in multiple (more or less implicit) theories of history. Predominant among them was a loosely deterministic meliorism common in nineteenth-century thought. He uses words like 'evolution', 'drift', and 'tendency' to describe the emergence of a benevolent form of monogamy, such as he enjoyed with Merrill. Marked by spiritual rather than physical motivations and free of coercion by Church and State, this form of partnership struck Carpenter – at moments – as 'natural' and therefore generally applicable.

At other times, though, Carpenter was determined not to banish the group marriage paradigm or other alternative forms of intimacy from a future worth welcoming. 'The Free Society', the final essay in *Love's Coming of Age*, argues that 'the practices of former races and times' express 'needs and desires' still present in 'human nature'. Thus, as all life evolves benignly 'from confusion to distinction', a 'rational' society will make room for radically different practices, from monkish asceticism to Bacchanalian festivals, from 'a woman's temporary alliance with a man for the sake of obtaining a much-needed child' to the ethically preferable 'permanent spiritual mating' of two people (98–9).

Even though Bloomsburians' optimism tended to be more guarded than Carpenter's, they loved envisioning a better time. What Carpenter calls, above, 'the Free Society' and elsewhere 'the Celestial City', Forster calls 'the millennium' and 'Love the Beloved Republic'. Carpenter convinced himself that his 'City' was 'ever through human history ... working unconsciously in the midst of mortal affairs and impelling towards an expression of itself' (*Two Cheers* 67; *Love's Coming* 103). But how far off did Bloomsburians think it was? Playfully, Strachey wrote in an April 1906 letter to John Maynard Keynes that 'our time will come about a hundred years hence, when preparations will have been made, and compromises come to, so that at the publication of our letters, everyone will be, finally, converted' (qtd In Holroyd 92). The conclusion of *A Passage to India* has a fuzzier view of the future. Fielding and Aziz debate the possibility of 'friendship', with all of that word's Moorean freight. Though Fielding wants friendship 'now', Aziz explains that it might take Indian nationalists 'fifty or five hundred' years to banish their colonizers and that only then can the men be 'friends' (312). *Howards End* begs yet more patience from its readers. When the Schlegel sisters dispute whether men will ever understand women, Helen votes for 'never', while Margaret asserts that 'In two thousand years they'll know' (211).

Without a doctrinaire Marxism to structure his anticipation of future change – or a doctrinaire Enlightenment liberalism, or Carpenter's sanguinity – Forster was consigned to playful speculations like these. But the hope that infused the philosophies of many Victorian progressives, including Carpenter, and that buoyed Bloomsburians through the dark times of Labouchere and two World Wars, lies behind these ludic 50, 500, and 2,000-year timeframes. And so suggestive was Carpenter to Forster that, even at gloomy moments, Forster could – with the help of a double turn – find cause for hope in the Millthorpe sage's ruminations. 'There are millions of people today', Carpenter laments in 'Marriage, a Forecast', 'who never could marry happily', lacking the capacity for 'loving surrender'. Sadly, 'short of the millennium', they will always be with us ... no institution of marriage alone, or absence of institution, will rid us of them' (*Love's Coming* 78).

The outbreak of the Second World War gave cause for gloom, hence Forster's 1938 'What I Believe' observed that 'No millennium seems likely to descend'; no better League of Nations; no 'form of Christianity [or] alternative to Christianity' will effect a 'change of heart'. Forster's vocabulary ('millennium') recalls Carpenter, though they were far from the only two Victorian and modernist writers to toss that term around. More tellingly, the cadence of Forster's sentence echoes that of Carpenter, whose 'institution of marriage ... or absence of institution' becomes Forster's 'form of Christianity [or] alternative to Christianity' (69). How, though, is Forster to buoy his spirits at a moment when, unlike Carpenter, he is so determinedly anti-'eschatological' (Trilling 21)? His crafty choice of a verb ('No millennium *seems* likely') sets up his quiet double turn: 'Certainly it is presumptuous to say that we *cannot* improve' (69).

NOTES

1. See Tsusuki and Copley.
2. In the Buggery Act 1533 and Offences Against the Person Act 1861, respectively.
3. I adapt this term from Martin, who analyses *Maurice* not in terms of a screen narrative but in terms of the contrasting versions of same-sex love represented, respectively, by Clive and Alec.
4. Ironically, Leonard repeats the same phrase in admiring the Schlegels (39, 42).

WORKS CITED

Carpenter, Edward. *Civilization, Its Cause and Cure. And Other Essays.* New York: Humboldt, 1891.

Carpenter, Edward. *Love's Coming of Age: A Series of Papers on the Relations between the Sexes.* Manchester: Labour, 1896.

Copley, Antony. *A Spiritual Bloomsbury: Hinduism and Homosexuality in the Lives and Writings of Edward Carpenter, E. M. Forster, and Christopher Isherwood.* Lanham: Lexington Books, 2006.

Forster, E. M. *Abinger Harvest and England's Pleasant Land.* Ed. Elizabeth Heine. Abinger edition of E. M. Forster 10. London: Andre Deutsch, 1996.

Forster, E. M. *Howards End.* Ed. Paul Armstrong. New York: Norton, 1998.

Forster, E. M. *The Longest Journey.* Ed. Elizabeth Heine. Abinger edition of E. M. Forster 2. London: Edward Arnold, 1984.

Forster, E. M. 'A Magistrate's Figures'. *New Statesman* 135 (4 December 2006): 62.

Forster, E. M. *Maurice.* New York: Norton: 1971.

Forster, E. M. *A Passage to India.* London: Harcourt, 1924.

Forster, E. M. *A Room with a View and Howards End.* New York: Signet, 1986.

Forster, E. M. *Two Cheers for Democracy.* Ed. Oliver Stallybrass. Abinger edition of E. M. Forster 11. London: Edward Arnold, 1972.

Forster, E. M. *Where Angels Fear to Tread.* Ed. Oliver Stallybrass. Abinger edition of E. M. Forster 1. London: Edward Arnold, 1975.

Holroyd, Michael. *Lytton Strachey: The New Biography.* New York: Farrar, Straus, and Giroux, 1994.

Levy, Paul. *Moore: G. E. Moore and the Cambridge Apostles.* New York: Holt, 1979.

Martin, Robert K. 'Edward Carpenter and the Double Structure of *Maurice*'. *E. M. Forster.* Ed. Jeremy Tambling. New York: St. Martin's, 1995.

Moeyes, Paul. *Siegfried Sassoon: Scorched Glory: A Critical Study*. New York: St. Martin's, 1997.

Moffat, Wendy. *A Great Unrecorded History: A New Life of E. M. Forster*. New York: Farrar, Straus, and Giroux, 2010.

Moore, G. E. *Principia Ethica*. New York: Cambridge University Press, 2000.

Orwell, Sonia and Ian Angus. Eds. *The Collected Essays, Journalism, and Letters of George Orwell, Vol. 1: An Age Like This, 1920–1940*. London: Penguin, 1970.

Rowbotham, Sheila. *Edward Carpenter: A Life of Liberty and Love*. London: Verso, 2008.

Stallybrass, Oliver. 'Introduction'. *The Life to Come and Other Stories*. Ed. Oliver Stallybrass. Abinger edition of E. M. Forster 8. London: Edward Arnold, 1972.

Takács, Judit. 'The Double Life of Kertbeny'. *Past and Present of Radical Sexual Politics*. Ed. Gert Hekma. Amsterdam: Mosse Foundation, 2004. 26–40.

Trilling, Lionel. *E. M. Forster*. London: Hogarth Press, 1962.

Tsuzuki, Chushichi. *Edward Carpenter, 1844–1929, Prophet of Human Fellowship*. New York: Cambridge University Press, 1980.

von Krafft-Ebing, Richard. *Psychopathia Sexualis*. Trans. Charles Gilbert. Philadelphia: F. A. Davis, 1894.

Wolfe, Jesse. *Bloomsbury, Modernism, and the Reinvention of Intimacy*. Cambridge: Cambridge UP, 2011.

CHAPTER TWO

Bloomsbury and the Arts

MAGGIE HUMM

Virginia Woolf remembers the Bloomsbury of October 1904 as 'the most beautiful, the most exciting, the most romantic place in the world' ('Old Bloomsbury' 184–5). The arts were not only central to this brave new world but determined Woolf's historical understanding: 'The Watts-Venetian tradition of red plush and black paint had been reversed; we had entered the Sargent-Furse era' (185). Virginia and Vanessa's first year in Bloomsbury reveals a dedication to the arts as they rushed 'off to a Mr Rutter's lecture on Impressionism at the Grafton Gallery … met an art critic called Nicholls [and] Nessa was in a state of great misery today waiting for Mr Tonks who came at one to criticise her pictures' (185). Although the arts were crucial to the Stephen sisters, Bloomsbury's contributions have often been side-lined in modernist art histories (Reed, *Bloomsbury Rooms* 2). Much of this undervaluation has to do with Bloomsbury's dedication to different genres: murals, textiles, pottery, book design, as well as paintings, and to collaborative, decorative projects. Art history typically focuses on individual artists, assessing their innovations chronologically within specific movements and genres. Bloomsbury's art was not about, or only about, creating singular objects but seeing art as a process, as a mode of being in the fullest sense: aesthetically, socially, even politically – for example, with John Maynard Keynes's key role in founding of the Arts Council, the UK government body responsible for arts funding.

This approach to the totality of art, as well as erroneous views of Bloomsbury's elitism, may account for the number of attacks on Bloomsbury until the last decades when their contribution has been more fully recognized. Even now the recent absurd claim by Michael Northen, unproblematically endorsed by Claire Warden, that between 1910 and 1920 'it is strange that at this period in Britain serious painters had not been asked to design for the theatre', ignores Bell and Duncan Grant's many ballet and theatre designs (228). Simon Watney's attacks on Roger Fry for having a private income and 'a frankly mandarin teleology of culture' and on Charleston for 'enshrining the view of Bloomsbury as a picturesque idyll for exotic Edwardian aesthetes' is particularly sad given Watney's support for, and pioneering account of, Grant ('The Connoisseur' 74, 82). Charles Harrison's claim that 'none of the inner circle of Bloomsbury were really very competent painters', that Bloomsbury, and specifically Clive Bell, had a 'self-certifying concept of aesthetics', and an 'areopagite simple-mindedness' is both ludicrous and elitist in itself in Harrison's choice of unnecessarily complex vocabulary (69, 56, 57).

The range of Bloomsbury's art sites including houses, gardens and churches as well as galleries, combined with Bloomsbury's dedication to mixed media, make issues of classification and summation difficult. Their techniques and subject matter are also very diverse, ranging from Grant's almost cubist abstractions in 1915–16, to collage in

Bell's *Triple Alliance*, with its attack on politics of the First World War, and the domestic interiors of her still lifes. There is also the issue of their debts to preceding arts which are equally diverse, for example, Bell's recasting of her great-aunt Julia Margaret Cameron's photographs in some paintings, and the impact of the Arts and Crafts Movement on Fry. Above all the issue of process continually interacted with art product and with their belief that aesthetics can be discovered anywhere. As Lytton Strachey said, 'we find satisfaction in curves and colours, and windows fascinate us, we are agitated by staircases, inspired by doors, disgusted by cornices' (Reed, *Bloomsbury Rooms* 19).

Any practices like Bloomsbury's, which expand beyond conventional art confines, face problems of definition. The transmedia and cooperative nature of Bloomsbury's art combined with Fry's refusal, in the Omega Workshop, to sign art works could best be defined as 'relational aesthetics'. While the term was in use before the English translation of Nicolas Bourriaud's *Relational Aesthetics* (2002), he brought the concept more centrally to attention. The focus of Bourriaud's work is on 1990s artists, for example, the gay artist Félix González-Torres, but his paradigm has applications to earlier art including Bloomsbury's. Bourriaud defines relational aesthetics as 'artistic practices which take as their theoretical and practical point of departure the whole of human relations and their social context, rather than an independent and private space' (112–13). Although Bourriaud's 'relational aesthetics' has been rightly attacked for its disregard of gender, race and class, the practice involves constructing 'social spaces' much like Charleston, Bell's and Grant's home (Reckitt 81; Bourriaud 46).

Christopher Reed convincingly argues that Bloomsbury 'made the condition of domesticity its standard for modernity' (*Bloomsbury Rooms* 5). Relational aesthetics would take this idea further into notions of cultural regeneration. The role of art, to Bourriaud, is not to form 'utopian realities' or an art object 'closed in on itself by the intervention of a style or a signature', but a 'social interstice' (45). As Jacques Rancière has noted, this idea of art as praxis was a crucial aspect of modernity in the early twentieth century (5). Relational aesthetics dispense with the utopian project of early modernism to focus on local and national artistic formations, refusing compartmentalization. Bloomsbury's art is exemplary of Bourriaud's new 'models of sociability' and art in Charleston's rhizomatic designs which were much more than a collection of art objects (28). As Bourriaud suggests, art should arise from the fabric of everyday life rather than being locked in a distinct realm. Charleston acts out that relation between art and life. The farmhouse, leased by Bell in 1916, was intended for Grant and his then lover David Garnett to avoid conscription by working on a neighbouring farm. Bell and Grant transformed the house creating wall illustrations, costumes, textiles and ceramic designs, furniture sketches and paintings which in their circular motifs and cross-hatching both reference past artists, including Michelangelo and Ingres, as well as art 'which exists in the encounter' (21). The eclectic mixtures with vivid colour schemes were as carefully constructed as their paintings, many of which referenced Charleston – *The French Window Charleston* (Grant) and *The Pond at Charleston* (Bell).

Charleston was not only a repository of their artistic work, but was art in process revealing changing pictorial styles and artistic experiments in interstice art. As Reed suggests, Charleston not only blurred boundaries between 'domestic existence and aesthetic creativity' but integrated history and modernity (*Bloomsbury Rooms* 184). The garden displayed the same aesthetics. Designed by Fry, it nodded to Gertrude Jeykll's Edwardian gardens while exemplifying modernity in Bell and Grant's bright, colour-clashing plants. As Nuala Hancock explains, Charleston is far from being 'auratic' but immersed 'in the materiality of paint' with Bell's 'repertoire of mark-making' (67). The influences on Charleston art were numerous: pointillism, abstraction, cubism, Byzantine, African, and Greek art. Notably Charleston generated more art than Monet's Giverny, as Shone points out (*Art of Bloomsbury* 32). Bell and Grant constantly repainted Charleston and other domestic interiors, including Keynes's Cambridge rooms. Family and friends became part of their art, for example, as with Bell's figure of Bacchus on a painted panel in Dorothy Wellesley's house in 1929 which models Bell's photographs of her son Quentin (Reed, *Bloomsbury Rooms* 257–8). This focus on art as praxis might seem at odds with Clive Bell's concept of significant form (see Hussey in this volume), but it best describes Bloomsbury's artistic innovations in producing art that was ethically as well as artistically compelling.

Vanessa Bell suggests that the term Bloomsbury was coined by the critic Desmond MacCarthy but, as he himself decided retrospectively about the arts, Bloomsbury 'never was a movement. In taste and judgement "Bloomsbury" from the start has been at variance with itself' (*Sketches* 103; MacCarthy, 'Bloomsbury' 67). However, Bloomsbury as a group did begin in discussions about art. Virginia's brother Thoby Stephen's Thursday evening 'parties were ... the germ from which sprang all'; it was Vanessa's account of a 'picture show' when she 'incautiously used the word "beauty"', which 'pricked' all their ears until it was 'two or three in the morning [before Virginia could] stumble off to bed feeling that something very important had happened' ('Old Bloomsbury' 186, 189–90). Although Woolf came to wonder 'where does Bloomsbury end? What is Bloomsbury? Does it for instance include Bedford Square?' she was not simply querying geographical boundaries but that larger sense of identity which was the group's major strength (199). By 1965 Leonard Woolf thought that, critically speaking, 'Bloomsbury was and is currently used as a term – usually of abuse – applied to a largely imaginary group of persons with largely imaginary objects and characteristics' (*Beginning Again* 21). Bloomsbury *was* imaginary as an art movement in the sense that it did not publish a manifesto as did Futurism, but like other avant-garde art, such as Vorticism and Cubism, it did have an innovative, radical aesthetics; and it was the arts, as Vanessa pointed out, which generated 'the great expansion' of Bloomsbury 'with a life full of interest and promise', particularly with the entrance of Fry and his 1910 Post-Impressionist Exhibition (*Sketches* 110).

In 1906 Fry had seen his first Cézanne and it changed his life. As Fry later said Cézanne was 'the great originator of the whole idea' of Post-Impressionism (*Vision and Design* 191). In turn, Fry's dedication to Cézanne in the 1910 exhibition impacted on Bell's and Grant's paintings, already receptive to European art. The group had a new and nonexclusionary sense of artistic truth. As Quentin Bell remembered ' "Why is it" asked my brother Julian "that you, Clive and Roger too, are so hard on what you call rhetoric in art?" "But surely, rhetoric leads to falsehood, to insincerity" ... "you have created an ideal artist who is anti-rhetorical; for Roger, he is a kind of saint" ... "and for Duncan?" We all looked at Duncan, who went on drawing and said nothing. The truth of the matter was that for him everyone was an ideal artist, everyone who painted, that is' (*Family Album* 14). Bloomsbury's dedication to this ideal of artistic life and expression is what underpinned their artistic innovations; and Bloomsbury's understandings dominated British visual arts between 1910 and 1930. In the two years between Fry's Post-Impressionist exhibitions (1910–12) London transformed into a major space of continental art. The Bloomsbury Group introduced the British public to modern French painting; influenced gallery acquisitions; shaped art publishing and journals;

and were themselves pioneering modernist and domestic artists. Early twentieth-century art was being propelled by a new cosmopolitanism, by new mobility, and by capitalist developments in the art trade with burgeoning publications, dealerships, collectors, and galleries, for example, Agnews, the Courtauld and the New English Art Club. There was a proliferation of new artistic 'isms': Post-Impressionism, Futurism, Vorticism, and Cubism. Cinema and photography offered a new, publicly embraced aesthetics. Connoisseurship was giving way to Fry's more 'scientific' art historical methods, inspired by Giovanni Morelli's scientific positivism, marking a transition in art history from an anecdotal nineteenth-century approach to a more methodological history (Humm, 'Woolf and the Arts' 4).

The introduction of modern art to the public was not always welcome. While dealers had exhibited French art, particularly Paul Durand-Ruel's major exhibition at the Grafton Gallery in 1905 (where Vanessa and Virginia heard Rutter's lecture), the focus on Cézanne in Fry's Post-Impressionist Exhibition of 1910 startled the art world as much as it startled London society. Bloomsbury was instrumental in introducing Cézanne and French art to a sceptical public. In Fry's studio Grant seized the catalogue of the 1918 sale of Degas's collection, persuaded Keynes to obtain a Treasury grant of £20,000 and, together with Charles Holmes Director of the National Gallery, to attend the sale and acquire French art (although Holmes baulked at Cézanne). Fry translated the painter-theorist Maurice Denis's 'Cezanne' for the *Burlington Magazine* ('Cézanne-1'). Gerald Duckworth, Woolf's half-brother, published illustrated monographs. Fry continued to champion French art in the Contemporary Art Society and, with Clive Bell and Grant, through the Allied Arts Association. Fry's summative account of these unprecedented decades 'What France Has Given to Art' was broadcast on the BBC.

During these years Bloomsbury art was esteemed. In 1922 Bell exhibited with the Fauve artist Othon Friesz at the Independent Gallery causing Fry to claim 'how high a place Vanessa Bell is entitled to in contemporary English art' (*Reader* 349). Nina Hamnett, Omega artist and one-time lover of Fry, had drawings in major modernist magazines including the *Transatlantic Review*, and Grant's stature was secured with the Contemporary Arts Society purchase of his major painting *The Queen of Sheba*. Bloomsbury's contribution was not limited to art galleries and magazines. Bell, Grant, and Fry participated in twentieth-century debates about gender, aesthetics, and the progress of modernity. In her Friday Club Bell encouraged nine women artists including Gwen Darwin (Raverat), Jessie Etchells and Helen Saunders. Although Bell left in 1913, the club continued to hold exhibitions at London galleries and Clifford's Inn Hall until 1922. Bell entitled one of her 1913 Omega textiles *White* after Amber Blanco-White a feminist artist, writer and activist, hinting at that larger world of gender relations. Blanco-White, one-time mistress of H. G. Wells with whom she had a daughter, was a suffragette whose novel *The Reward of Virtue* (1911), attacking the inadequacies of women's education, presages Woolf's *A Room of One's Own*. Blanco-White's daughter attended Bell's short-lived experimental school at Charleston. Women artists and art critics were also highly visible in art journals, exhibitions, and art schools. For example, Grant took classes with Louise Jopling who founded an art school and worked with the Artists' Suffrage League. Grant designed a poster for the National Union of Women's Suffrage Societies. Fry supported women's rights and included six women painters in the Second Post-Impressionist Exhibition (although exhibiting none in 1910).

ROGER FRY AND RELATIONAL AESTHETICS

While Bell and Grant's Charleston is pure relational aesthetics, Fry's personal trajectory is also exemplary of the concept. What became significant for twentieth-century art was Fry's development beyond the confines of gallery curatorship to a wider understanding of art practice. Fry was an expert on Renaissance art, particularly Florentine and Giovanni Bellini, and an influential critic and curator. Before the 1910 Post-Impressionist Exhibition, he advised the American collectors Henry Clay Frick and Joseph E. Widener and, as curator at New York's Metropolitan Museum of Art, he exhibited Derain, Persian pottery and African carvings together in a relational aesthetics. Fry's alliance of arts with crafts stemmed from his belief in the unity of the arts and the significance of art groups and this came to fruition in his later UK exhibitions, and his founding of the Omega Workshop, the Grafton Group and the Contemporary Art Society, as well as publishing. His output was prodigious. In one six-year period he wrote 491 articles including book and exhibition reviews and historically reflective pieces. Perhaps not surprisingly, what Fry appreciated in Picasso was that he was 'continually experimenting' (Robins 76).

Although Fry's first meeting with Bloomsbury was a 'violent quarrel about Sargent' with Vanessa Bell, Woolf realized that Fry had made them all 'think the whole thing over again. The old skeleton arguments of primitive Bloomsbury about art and beauty put on flesh and blood' (*Sketches* 118; 'Old Bloomsbury' 197). Christopher Reed points out that Fry's ideas were so radical they can 'be assessed by their *distance* from the assumptions of his own generation' (*Reader* 243). The range of his interests was vast. In the decorative arts alone, as well as organizing the famous murals for the Borough Polytechnic, he designed rooms for the art dealer Arthur Ruck focusing on London transport, for Adrian and Karen Stephen in 1921, for Beatrice Mayor, Clive Bell and Keynes, fireplaces for Margaret Bulley (1926), and the Sitwells's Chelsea home (including a portrait) among other interior designs (Shone, *Bloomsbury Portraits* 223). The relation between this decorative practice and his writing ensured that his art criticism had a deeper understanding of aesthetics. Like William Morris before him, Fry combined all these elements into a *Gesamtkunstwerk* – a complete work of art – in Durbins, the house he designed for his family.

The architecture critic Nikolaus Pevsner called Durbins 'one of the landmarks in the evolution of a contemporary style in English architecture', in a line from Arts and Crafts designs, although, as Reed points out, Durbins had many modern features including central steam heating and industrial sized windows ('Omega' 45–8; *Bloomsbury Rooms* 39). The colour scheme was modernist, light, and airy with personalized features to help his wife Helen recover from her mental breakdowns. Although Fry worked with Jekyll the Edwardian garden designer, he populated the garden with Bloomsbury murals, and modernist sculpture including Eric Gill's. Durbins, as Bourriaud suggests, could be described as 'the invention of a model of sociability in art' (28). Bell, in a relationship with Fry at the time, described the house in modernist terms: 'Every inch of house and garden were exposed to the sun . . . the floors were bare polished wood with rugs, the walls were pale greys and dull greens' (*Sketches* 122–3). Fry's architecture and painting were interrelated. As Shone points out, Fry's painting *South Downs* of 1913–14 with its 'increasing bareness' was stimulated by Fry's 'freedom of form' in Durbins and the Omega (*Art of Bloomsbury* 164).

THE POST-IMPRESSIONIST EXHIBITIONS
OF 1910 AND 1912

Fry's 1910 exhibition, 'Manet and the Post-Impressionists', presages Bourriaud's call for a relational art which 'can generate relationships with the world' (9). The exhibition and its 1912 successor were sites of multigeneric art and activities, and responses to the exhibitions were equally diverse. Although Frank Rutter the art critic, not Fry, first used the term Post-Impressionism in a review of October 1910, and Fry notoriously was unconfident saying 'oh let's just call them Post-Impressionists; at any rate they came after the Impressionists', Fry intended the title to show how painting had left behind an Impressionist visual recording of the world in favour of the emotional significance of art (Robins 116; MacCarthy, 'Bloomsbury' 76). Bell agreed: 'That autumn of 1910 was to me a time when everything seemed springing to new life – a time when all was a sizzle of excitement, new relationships, new ideas, different and intense emotions all seemed crowding into one's life' (*Sketches* 126). Fry retained among his papers MacCarthy's unpublished backward look (27 March 1913) at the exhibition. Wondering whether Post-Impressionists are 'mad, bad and dangerous to know', MacCarthy claims that Post-Impressionism is the desire for 'pure form and colour' but also 'emotional significance' and 'the primitive' ('Papers').

The mixture of art from differing periods and countries was a dramatic relational revision of conventional hangings. For example, Fry included African sculpture (placed in a prominent last room) with French art. The aesthetic cadence of the primitive was reinforced by the exhibition poster and a Slade student ball in 1910 where Bloomsbury wore Gauguin-like fancy dress although, as Peter Stansky points out, this was 'manufactured in Manchester' (211). Grant's personal scrapbook of newspaper cuttings (in the Tate Archive) belies the overdetermined focus of critics, writing about the exhibition, on the triumvirate of Cézanne, Gauguin and Van Gogh. Grant retained an essay by Lewis Hind, 'The Ideals of Post-Impressionism', in which Hind suggests that 'Matisse elates and stimulates me', although he disliked Picasso's portraits, 'unsympathetic as they are unintelligible' ('Ideals'). Similarly, among Fry's archive papers is a contemporary article 'The Art World, Post-Impressionism and Socialism' by Christine Walshe, who praises the artists as 'Socialists (with a capital letter) of art ... they know where to look for the elements of the greatest beauty in labour' (unpaginated). The artist David Bomberg claimed that Fry had brought 'the revolution ... to fruition', because he [Bomberg] had 'never hitherto seen a work by Cézanne' (Cork 16). Tony Pinkney points out that, at the other end of the artistic continuum, William Morris's daughter Mary visited the exhibition while 'engaged on the monumental task of editing her father's collected works' and found Gauguin's 'extraordinary experiments have wild snatches of poetry' (137). Along with these new publics and constituencies, including writers at *Vogue* and *Vanity Fair*, there were less favourable responses. The artist and Slade teacher Henry Tonks famously forbad his students to visit the exhibition. Fry suggested, however, that if spectators 'will look without preconception as to what a picture ought to be' then they 'will admit that there is a discretion and a harmony of colour, a force and completeness of pattern, about these pictures which creates a general sense of well being' (*Reader* 88). Woolf defended the exhibition in an ironic letter to Violet Dickinson asking 'why all the Duchesses are insulted by the post-impressionists, a modest sample of painters, innocent even of indecency, I cant conceive' (*Letters* 1: 440).

By the time of the Second Post-Impressionist Exhibition in 1912 the public response to Post-Impressionism had transformed. Fry delightedly reported that even 'Matisse has become a safe investment' (*Vision and Design* 228). The exhibition was a Bloomsbury collaboration. The poster was designed by Bell and Grant, Clive Bell selected works for the English section, Boris Anrep choose the Russian section, and Fry selected French art for the third. There were 50,000 visitors to see 257 works of art including those by Fry, Bell, and Grant. Along with encouraging new responses to art, Fry turned the exhibition into a relational experience, opening the galleries in the evenings, as Woolf described, 'to bring people together – people from many different worlds, ladies of fashion, painters, poets, musicians, business men ... young French poets were invited to read aloud from their work ... he arranged concerts ... Post-Impressionism had become, he noted, all the rage' (*Roger Fry* 145).

OMEGA WORKSHOPS

Immediately before founding the Omega in 1913 in Fitzroy Square, Fry wrote in 'Art and Socialism' that art must have links with society, history, and culture. The essay concluded with Fry's call for an art 'purified of its present unreality by a prolonged contact with the crafts', which would, Fry claimed, give society 'a new confidence in its collective artistic judgement' (*Vision and Design* 69). The Omega Workshops did just that. In his letter soliciting funds Fry argued that Omega would create 'objects for common life' with the 'spontaneous freshness of primitive or peasant work', attacking commercial products as 'dead mechanical exactitude and uniformity' (Stair 28). Art works were to be created without signatures (as Bourriaud says 'the signature implies a loss of polyphony'), and to deliberately eschew polished techniques (93). Quentin Bell remembers Fry using an inheritance from his chocolate-making family (Fry's Chocolates) and that the name Omega was chosen to suggest the last word in art ('Omega' 316). In *Roger Fry* Woolf claimed that Fry reported to Goldie Dickinson 'I've got £1,500 and am going ahead' (152). There were five shareholders: Fry £300, Sir Alexander Kay Muir £100, Vanessa Bell £50, Lady Ian Hamilton £50 and Grant £1.00 (*The Omega Workshops* 29).

The Omega gave Bell and Grant the opportunity to design in many media: clothes, textiles, rugs, pottery, furniture, as well as painting. Indeed the interrelations between Omega's applied and fine arts transformed Bloomsbury art. Bell's Omega abstract rug designs and painted screens are echoed in her design *Adam and Eve*. Similarly, Grant's rug designs shaped his abstract painting *In Memoriam: Rupert Brooke* (1915). Two large first floor studios were atop ground floor showrooms where Woolf, in 1915, bought 'stuff from a foolish young woman in a Post-Impressionist tunic' and seemed to see Omega designs wherever she turned (*Diary* 1: 11). Furniture was designed at the Omega but often made elsewhere in professional workshops. Artists included Frederick Etchells (before he left to join the Vorticists) and Paul Nash (until the requested candlestick painting become too onerous for him). The 'art work as social interstice', as Bourriaud later describes, could be Omega's theme (Bourriaud 45). International figures were drawn to the Omega, including the writer Gertrude Stein and, more amusingly, a German spy complete with camera in the guise of Dr Ahne from Norway, a specialist in new artistic movements ('Roger Fry and the Omega Idea' 19). Fry experimented successfully with pottery, woodcuts, stage scenery, stained glass, and children's toys. Non-Omega objects from a wider aesthetic world were sold, including African jars, Indian bedspreads and

Algerian pottery, as well as the work of younger painters. As Reed argues, this refreshing openness represented 'the exhortative rhetoric of the English Arts and Crafts movement with the visual vocabulary of the Parisian avant-garde' (*Bloomsbury Rooms* 113). In this Omega matched other European groups, particularly in Vienna, in its synthesis of original aesthetics with applied arts, but also art outside Europe. The Japanese poet Noguchi was attracted to Omega's use of Japanese compositional devices, possibly a nod to the 1910 Japan–British exhibition in London.

The range of media was startling including theatre designs by Grant, as well as hand-painted vases decorated by Bell, drawing on her *Studland Beach* (1912) and described by Fry as 'most intimately connected with life' (Collins 63). Designs were reused in several media, for example, 'Mechtilde' in linen and carpets. Omega fabrics, said by Paul Nash to instigate 'the modern movement in textile design', were the success story (83). In April 1915 Bell suggested to Fry she would 'make or at least superintend the making of several dresses' (*Letters* 173–4). Like other art/fashion interrelations in Paris and Vienna, Bell designed clothing incorporating a modernist aesthetic with international materials (Turkish silk) which she and Grant had acquired abroad. Bourriaud argues 'form only exists in the encounter' and Fry organized music evenings to support Belgian refugees, published four books on pacifism, and worked for the Friends War Victims Relief Mission (21). Although after the Vorticist attacks on Omega, Fry wrote 'I have come definitely to the conclusion that the painting of pictures is too difficult a job for human beings ... wherefore I rejoice in the Omega because it is not beyond the wit of man to make a decent plate', after the liquidation of Omega in July 1920 he returned to painting (Woolf, *Roger Fry* 155). Omega had however made its mark. As Shone points out, watered down versions of Omega were copied and sold more expensively by Heals, and in the late 1920s there was a 'craze' for unadorned pottery that resembled pottery that 'Roger Fry had pioneered fifteen years before' (*Bloomsbury Portraits* 190). There was talk of reviving Omega in France in the late 1920s, and in Sussex after an exhibition in Lewes (1946), but plans dissipated. Whatever else could be said about Omega, it had triumphed as an example of art as praxis in a durable community of relational aesthetics.

THE HOGARTH PRESS

The Hogarth Press was founded by the Woolfs in 1917 with a small hand-press, intended as therapy for Virginia to 'take her mind completely off her work' and named after their house in Richmond (L. Woolf 233) (see Battershill in this volume). Unlike other small presses in the first decades of the twentieth century, Hogarth did not claim to be an art publisher in the sense of producing beautiful, deluxe editions but did have a continuing commitment to the arts. As Laura Marcus points out, the Woolfs 'hand-printed thirty-four texts' including Virginia's own publications *Kew Gardens* (1919) and *On Being Ill* (1930), which was the last of her books to be hand-printed; T. S. Eliot's *The Waste Land* (1923); and Hope Mirrlees's *Paris: A Poem* (1918) utilizing experimental typography, graphic qualities, and 'cinematicity' (266–7, 271). In this way the press enacted Omega's ethic of 'expressing directly the artist's sensibility of proportion and surface' (Stair 30). From the age of nineteen Virginia was an active bookbinder: 'I have been making endless experiments and almost smelled my room out this afternoon trying to do gold lettering' (*L1* 56). She continued to be a 'lidder' throughout her life, sending covered books to friends, including twenty volumes of Georges Sand's *Histoire de ma vie* with marbled boards and green leather spines to Susan Buchan in 1938 (Bradshaw 281).

The Woolfs contributed to the arts both in their choice of subject matter for example, Fry's *Cézanne*, with paper quality and typefaces, and inviting a range of artist designers. Dora Carrington illustrated their first book *Two Stories* which involved, according to Leonard, months of difficult typesetting and was 'not bad' (235). The Woolfs 'took a great deal of trouble' to find Japanese papers for covers and 'beautiful, uncommon and sometimes cheerful paper for binding our books ... from all over the place, including some brilliantly patterned from Czechoslovakia' (236). *Kew Gardens*, particularly the third edition, with illustrations by Bell, is generally considered the most expert collaboration between the sisters. With hand-coloured covers, each of its pages carried a different design by Bell interacting with, and embracing, Woolf's text to such a degree that Woolf claimed 'God made our brains upon the same lines' (*Letters* 2: 289). Woolf's *Flush* has several illustrations by Bell who was intimately involved in the design. Illustrations have a larger space in *Flush* than in other of Woolf's books and incurred extra work for Bell and the Woolfs (Humm, '1930s' 11). The novel carries four line drawings by Bell who made the endpaper illustrations in the first issue. In a letter to Bell dated 12 June 1933, Woolf outlined in detail the artistic work required for a later edition – the drawings would be 'bound in separate pages' involving Bell in redrawing designs (Letter 1933). Bell agreed immediately and monitored the layout of the proofs which 'which had too much reduced the illustrations' but were 'better than being too large' (Letter 1933). The sisters' collaborations reveal how central were the arts to Woolf, and Bell's designs were the most significant contributions of the Hogarth Press to the arts.

VANESSA BELL

In her early years Bell said that she 'suffered from the effects of Tonks and Furse' studying at Cope's School and the Royal Academy Schools until seeing, at the New Gallery, 'a work by Cézanne, one that impressed me without knowing why' (*Sketches* 125, 129). Well before Fry's exhibitions, Bell had a burgeoning interest in French art, reading Camille Mauclair's *The French Impressionists* (1903) which had a tremendous impact on her: 'One's chief source of knowledge of all that was going on in France ... was Mauclair's tiny book ... how one poured over those absurd little reproductions ... something fundamental and permanent' (129). The book is an exemplary case study of the strengths and yet underlying issues involved in Bell's enthusiasm. At first glance the book matches Bell's and Bloomsbury's values, promoting women's art (two chapters), and apparently anti-establishment – 'Degas, Monet and Pissarro have achieved great fame and fortune without gaining access to the Salons' (xix). Mauclair attacks 'academic allegory, historical painting', and, like Bell, shows an interest in mural arts (10, 175). Bell's *The Tub* mirrors Mauclair's praise for Degas's 'awkwardness of the nude' (90). However, Bell fails to mention an explicit theme in the book for which Mauclair became notorious. He is overly keen to promote 'Frenchmen of pure blood' like the artist Simon Bussy; and his later attack on Jewish dealers, whom he claimed were eroding the purity of French culture, was codified in the Vichy government's antisemitic law of 23 June 1941, greatly influenced by Mauclair's work (196; Aukland 105).

As an emerging artist, Bell learned much from overseas trips: in 1904 thinking Tintoretto in Venice an absolute revelation; visiting the studios of Rodin and Picasso; as well as trips to Greece, Istanbul, and to Cologne for the 1912 Sonderbund exhibition. Her first exhibited work was a portrait of Lady Nelly Cecil (1905). Although she did not have a solo exhibition until 1922 at the Independent Gallery, she exhibited prolifically, for example, in 1912 showing several works at three exhibitions. The 1910 Post-Impressionist Exhibition had a great impact on Bell. 'No other single exhibition can ever have had so much effect', she claimed, and her most innovative decade was 1910–20 with abstracts, collage, experimental portraits and modernist still life and landscapes (*Sketches* 129). *Studland Beach*, with its abstract figuring in a restrained palette, Shone calls 'one of the most radical works produced at that time in Britain' (*Art of Bloomsbury* 74). It was followed by *Abstract Painting* and Bell's domestic interiors also had a formal, geometric language. Shone suggests a debt to Picasso's *Pots et Citron* owned by Clive and Vanessa (42). Bell's *Triple Alliance* is a ground-breaking collage that combines paint, newspaper and a cheque made out to her to make a political statement against war (see Foster in this volume). *The Tub* (1917–18) is also bold in its formal dimensions and colouration echoing Matisse.

Bell is Britain's pre-eminent colourist. Her control of tonal colour is consistent throughout her career but strongest in the decade 1910–20, and particular objects (flowers, fruit) are always stylized. *Still Life by a Window* (1912–13) has an almost cubist sense of solid colour which is not decorative but spatial. Bell's portrait *Lytton Strachey* (1913) has extraordinary contrasts of violet and yellow with Lytton's bright red beard. In *Iris Tree* (1915), two years later, the brilliant pinks and yellows of the face contrast with the solid black clothing. In her lecture at Leighton Park School, Bell explained that artists are 'so made that the world presents itself to one as form and colour instead of presenting itself as it does to most sane and respectable people' and that different 'artists have seen different things but what they have all seen is form and colour' (*Sketches* 151, 156). Bell's Omega work encouraged her incredibly controlled sense of colour, and to combine figurative with abstracts for example, in her transitional works painted screens (1913). This translated into her paintings such as *Landscape with Haystack, Asheham* which utilizes colour blocks. Bell's work also represents a new maternal modernism. *Nursery Tea* (1912), focusing on mothers and children, refuses a conventional viewpoint. As Reed suggests, it can be read 'as a feminine alternative to Augustus John's high masculine modernism' (*Bloomsbury Rooms* 83). Similarly, her portraits, particularly those of her sister, are far from conventional in Bell's refusal to paint Woolf's face, instead evoking associative spaces. In her early self-portraits, particularly Self-portrait (1915) Bell used dynamic poses to portray herself as an active artist.

The collaboration with the Woolfs' Hogarth Press, as argued above, represents Bell's major contribution to twentieth-century book design. Here let me mention how her designs interact with her paintings. Bell imagined *A Conversation* (1913–16) in relation to Woolf's *Kew Gardens* although, eventually, it was not used. The grouping explicitly celebrates female conversation with three women caught up in each other's lives (see front cover image and Elkin in this volume). Bell's woodcuts impact on her painting; for example, the woodcut *Nude* shapes Bell's *The Tub*. Bell's interior designs also reveal attentiveness to her historical location. For example, her 1916 designs for Mary Hutchinson's River house with its Omega furniture and pottery were undertaken in full knowledge of the house's former owner – an Arts and Crafts bookbinder – and connections with William Morris's nearby Kelmscott (*Bloomsbury Rooms* 200).

Much of Bell's decorative work was in collaboration with Grant – particularly Charleston – as well as murals for Nan Hudson and Ethel Sands at Château d'Auppegard

(1927), decorations for Keynes's Cambridge rooms (1920–22), and a Wedgewood dinner service of forty-eight pieces for Kenneth Clark, with plates depicting Greta Garbo and Virginia Woolf. A significant shared design of a whole room was a competition entry for the *Architectural Review*, and won third prize. In 1939 Bell and Grant were invited by the Bishop of Chichester to decorate Berwick church near Charleston and their work, together with Quentin Bell's, included murals and inset scenes. Bell focussed on Mary's annunciation and nativity (her mother Julia, while pregnant with Vanessa, was depicted as Mary in Burne-Jones's *Annunciation* of 1879) while Grant's focussed on Christ's life events (see Avery in this volume), but backgrounds and vegetation were of Charleston itself (*Art of Duncan Grant* 66). Grant's last major decoration was another church – the Russell Chantry, Lincoln Cathedral (1955–9).

DUNCAN GRANT

Like Bell, Grant worked in a multiplicity of styles and media. His Omega decorative work alone included costumes, ceramics, painted furniture, murals and textiles, drawing on a variety of artistic traditions: Byzantine and early Renaissance frescoes through to the paintings of Chardin and Poussin. Although his first solo exhibition was not until February 1920 at the Carfax Gallery, Grant began portraiture (often based on photographs) in 1908. Photographs taken in Greece and Turkey by Keynes, his one-time lover, were used for his dynamic, fluid group nudes of *Bathing* (1911); his numerous portraits of Bell, nude and as a mother and painter, draw on naked photos of Bell; and he used photographs of Fry's daughter for the details of *Pamela* (1911) (Humm, *Snapshots* 106). Grant's nude photographs of George Mallory, the Everest climber, were inspirational for his later homoerotic figures (100–101). Darren Clarke argues that *Two Bathers* is 'sexually charged … inverting physical space, inverting social protocol, opening up a space for behaviour outside the socially acceptable' (163). The process of painting *The Bathers* was a relational aesthetic – not of the men as commodified objects. The subjects Robert Medley and the ballet designer Rupert Doone would draw each other and Duncan during the making of the work as if in a social and queer interstice (166).

The 1910 Post-Impressionist Exhibition had as great an impact on Grant as on Bell, although there are influences on his work too of Romanesque art and African sculpture. *Abstract Kinetic Collage* (1914), a long painted scroll designed to be unwound to a music accompaniment, prefigures, as Simon Watney argues, the abstract films of Hans Richter and Fernand Léger in the 1920s: 'There is no other European work of art in this period that so imaginatively fulfils Apollinaire's Orphist dream of a modernist art that aspires to the condition of music' (*Duncan Grant* 39). Other contemporary abstractions include his *In Memoriam: Rupert Brooke*. The painting's coloured shapes are a modernist alternative to statuesque memorials. Grant also made collages with textiles and paper, like Picasso, while *The Glass* (1916) shows the influence of Cézanne's colouration. *The Tub* (1913) is inspired by Matisse but also draws on early Renaissance mosaics and African sculptures. In 1975 on *Desert Island Discs*, Grant chose this painting as the one he would most like to be remembered by (Shone, *Art of Bloomsbury* 150).

Visits of the Ballet Russes, pre- and post-First World War, were almost as great an artistic shock to Bloomsbury as the Post-Impressionist exhibitions, culminating with Keynes's marriage to the star ballerina Lydia Lopokova. The Russian choreography and costumes stimulated Grant's incipient interest in modernist costume and theatre design and he was to design for the theatre and Charleston theatricals all his life. A modernist *Macbeth* for Harley Granville-Barker in 1912 was followed by costumes (some painted at Charleston) for Jacques Copeau's *Twelfth Night* utilizing Omega textiles including *Mechtilde*. From *Juggler and Tightrope Walker* (1919) through to *Two Acrobats* (1966) performance art of any kind continued to fascinate Grant. This wide range of Grant's influences and subjects continued until his death. He painted London's river Thames; during the Second World War he was commissioned by Kenneth Clark to paint St Paul's surrounded by blitzed buildings; and he continued to paint through the war completing with Bell a mural *Cinderella* and, for a younger generation, decorations for Raymond Mortimer and John Lehmann. Grant is buried beside Bell in the churchyard of St. Peter's church near Charleston, where he and Vanessa had pioneered relational aesthetics.

ART INSTITUTIONS

Bloomsbury's continual involvement in art institutions is one way it diverges from Bourriaud's relational aesthetics. After his curatorship at New York's Metropolitan Museum of Art, Fry founded the National Art Collection Fund in 1903. In 1910, Fry, Clive Bell and D. S. MacColl, Keeper at the Tate and the Wallace Collection, established the Contemporary Art Society for public acquisitions, because the National Gallery Millbank (now Tate Britain) was barred from collecting non-British art (Humm, 'Woolf and the Arts' 6). Fry contributed to the Gorrell report of 1932 about industrial art, which led to the establishment of a Council for Art and Industry. In 1925 Keynes founded the London Artists' Association, which held exhibitions and supported regional art and artists' exhibits abroad. In 1936 Keynes contributed to a BBC series 'Art and the State'. Finding that 'the position today of artists of all sorts is disastrous', and that current political thinking about the arts was 'profoundly mistaken and that it may even, in the long run, undermine the solidity of our institutions', Keynes proposed the establishment of a Commission of Public Places to control development (373). His ambitious plan for London to demolish all the South Bank buildings and build anew was partially realized with the Festival of Britain in 1951 but, luckily, not realized in full since demolition then would have meant no Tate Modern today.

After the Second World War, the Attlee government asked Keynes for his ideas about national and regional arts which culminated in the founding of the Arts Council. Board meetings were initially held in Gordon Square, the heart of Bloomsbury. For Keynes, London had a special role in the arts 'as the new artistic capital of Europe', symbolized by the reopening of Covent Garden in 1946 with *The Sleeping Beauty* in which Keynes's wife Lydia had first starred (Mackrell 394–5). Throughout their lives Bell and Grant supported nascent art institutions and, after her death, Grant was advisor to the Arts Council and the Society of Industrial Artists and Designers (*Duncan Grant* 15).

SIGNIFICANCE

Bloomsbury was not elitist but a group of pioneering artists who were internationalists in every sense: aesthetically, politically, and personally. Fry's Omega glazes (particularly *Blue Tureen* 1915) echo Chinese Song dynasty ceramics. The Bells' collection of French art included the first Picasso (*Pots et Citron*) in an English private collection (Shone, *Art of Bloomsbury* 42). As soon as Vanessa Bell met Picasso she recognized immediately that he was 'probably one of the greatest geniuses who has ever lived' (Shone, *Bloomsbury Portraits* 136). Clive Bell's *Art*, always in print, sustained interest in Cézanne. The Grafton Group exhibited Wassily Kandinsky. Bloomsbury also actively supported younger artists. For example, Bell and Grant taught with William Coldstream and Victor Pasmore among others at the Euston Road School, and in the 1950s promoted Roger Hilton. With Tate acquisitions (nine works between 1971 and 1984); and gallery dealers' support, particularly Anthony d'Offay, as well as curators, including Frances Spalding, Bloomsbury arts are again central in English art. Celebrities and royalty have bought their art. Bryan Ferry, of the music group Roxy Music bought five Bloomsbury paintings from d'Offay, and the Queen Mother bought her fourth Grant *Still Life with Matisse* for £400 in 1973 (Marler 207). Pioneering books include *The Art of Duncan Grant* and *Bloomsbury Portraits*. Spalding's 2014 National Portrait Gallery exhibition *Virginia Woolf: Art, Life and Vision* revalued Vanessa's portraits of Woolf, as well as Woolf's own contribution to the arts. Dulwich Picture Gallery mounted an entire exhibition devoted to Bell (2017). Both exhibitions gained critical and public acclaim. In 2018 Tate St Ives exhibited works by eighty artists influenced by Woolf.

The wide-ranging impact of Bloomsbury's arts is no longer in doubt. The sculptor Henry Moore acknowledged that 'Roger Fry's *Vision and Design* was the most lucky discovery for me' (Harrison 219). Marion Dorn's rugs betray the influence of Bell's Omega designs. I would argue that the American abstract painter Lee Krasner's *Gothic Frieze* is in a direct line from Bell's Omega painted screens in their shared use of bold zigzag black lines. Even in his nineties Grant was open to new aesthetics, telling Watney that Jackson Pollock 'interests me', and painting Gilbert and George (*Duncan Grant* 87). The Angelica Garnett bequest to Charleston of over 8,000 largely unseen pieces, including paintings, sketches, and ephemera, are now being digitalized and will transform future understandings.

Any group which expands beyond its immediate circle faces issues of legacy and definition, a particular problem for Bloomsbury which worked in so many media. The term 'relational aesthetics' captures well Bloomsbury's uses of cultural materials of all kinds, its experimentation and attention to multiple art sites. Bloomsbury's unity of art and life never depended on particular works or styles and reshaped art practice. As Vanessa Bell said 'artists, in the opinion of many are little better than lunatics [but] besides being rather mad, artists are apt to be revolutionaries' (*Sketches* 150).

WORKS CITED

Aukland, Tobah J. *'Les juifs et nos chefs-d'oeuvre:* French Artistic Patrimony and the Jewish Art Collector 1840–1945'. Dissertation, Wesleyan University, 2013. http://citeseerx.ist. psu.edu/viewdoc/download?doi=10.1.1.343.3043&rep=rep1&type=pdf. Accessed 1 November 2016.

Bell, Quentin. 'The Omega Workshops'. *The Bloomsbury Group*. Ed. S. P. Rosenbaum. Toronto: Toronto UP, 1995. 316–19.

Bell, Quentin. *Vanessa Bell's Family Album*. Ed. Quentin Bell and Angelica Garnett. London: Jill Norman & Hobhouse, 1981.

Bell, Vanessa. A Handwritten Letter to Miss West, Manager of the Hogarth Press, 9 July 1933. Ms. Hogarth Press Archive, University of Reading.

Bell, Vanessa. *The Selected Letters of Vanessa Bell*. Ed. Regina Marler. London: Bloomsbury, 1998.

Bell, Vanessa. *Sketches in Pen and Ink*. Ed. Lia Giachero. London: Hogarth Press, 1997.

Bourriaud, Nicolas. *Relational Aesthetics*. Paris: Les presses du réel, 2002.

Bradshaw, Tony. 'Virginia Woolf and Book Design'. *The Edinburgh Companion to Virginia Woolf and the Arts*. Ed. Maggie Humm. Edinburgh: Edinburgh UP, 2010. 280–97.

Clarke, Darren. 'Duncan Grant and Charleston's Queer Arcadia'. *Queer Bloomsbury*. Ed. Brenda Helt and Madelyn Detloff. Edinburgh: Edinburgh UP, 2016. 152–71.

Collins, Judith. 'Ceramics'. *The Omega Workshops*. Ed. Judith Collins. London: Crafts Council, 1983. 63–9.

Cork, Richard. *David Bomberg*. New Haven: Yale UP, 1987.

Downey, Anthony. 'Towards a Politics of Relational Aesthetics'. *Third Text* 21:3 (May 2007): 267–75.

Fry, Roger. 'Cézanne-I'. *Burlington Magazine* (January 1910): 207–9.

Fry, Roger. *The Roger Fry Reader*. Ed. Christopher Reed. Chicago: U of Chicago P, 1996.

Fry, Roger. *Vision and Design*. Harmondsworth: Penguin, 1961.

Fry, Roger. 'What France Has Given to Art'. *The Listener* (30 December 1931): 1121–3.

Goldman, Jane. *The Feminist Aesthetics of Virginia Woolf*. Cambridge: Cambridge UP, 1998.

Green, Christopher. *Art Made Modern*. London: Merrell Holberton, 1999.

Hancock, Nuala. *Charleston and Monk's House*. Edinburgh: Edinburgh UP, 2012.

Harrison, Charles. *English Art and Modernism 1900–1939*. New Haven: Yale UP, 1981.

Hind, Lewis. 'Ideals of Post-Impressionism'. Tate Archive Duncan Grant 7243.15. 1912.

Humm, Maggie. 'The 1930s, Photographs and Virginia Woolf's *Flush*'. *Photography and Culture* 3.1 (March 2010): 7–17.

Humm, Maggie. *Snapshots of Bloomsbury: The Private Lives of Virginia Woolf and Vanessa Bell*. Brunswick, NJ: Rutgers UP, 2006.

Humm, Maggie. 'Virginia Woolf and the Arts'. *The Edinburgh Companion to Virginia Woolf and the Arts*. Ed. Maggie Humm. Edinburgh: Edinburgh UP, 2010. 1–16.

Keynes, John Maynard. 'Art and the State I'. *The Listener* (August 1936): 372–4.

MacCarthy, Desmond. 'The Art-Quake of 1910'. *The Listener* (February 1943): 6.

MacCarthy, Desmond. 'Bloomsbury an Unfinished Memoir'. *The Bloomsbury Group*. Ed. S. P. Rosenbaum. Toronto: U of Toronto P, 1995. 65–74.

MacCarthy, Desmond. The Papers of Roger Fry, King's College Cambridge Archive REF/10/5, 1913.

MacCarthy, Fiona. 'Roger Fry and the Omega Idea'. *The Omega Workshops*. Ed. Judith Collins. London: Crafts Council, 1983: 9–23.

Mackrell, Judith. *The Bloomsbury Ballerina*. London: Weidenfeld & Nicolson, 2008.

Marcus, Laura. 'Virginia Woolf as Publisher and Editor: The Hogarth Press'. *The Edinburgh Companion to Virginia Woolf and the Arts*. Ed. Maggie Humm. Edinburgh: Edinburgh UP, 2010. 263–79.

Marler, Regina. *Bloomsbury Pie*. London: Virago, 1997.

Mauclair, Camille. *The French Impressionists*. London: Duckworth, 1903.

Nash, Paul. 'Modern English Textiles'. *Artwork* (January/February 1926): 83.

Pevsner, Nikolaus. 'Omega'. *Architectural Review* 90 (August 1941): 45–8.

Pinkney, Tony. 'Modernism and the Gothic Utopia'. *Virginia Woolf and December 1910*. Ed. Makiko Minow-Pinkney. Grosmont: illuminate, 2014. 136–42.

Rancière, Jacques. *The Emancipated Spectator*. London: Verso, 2011.

Reckitt, Helena. 'Forgotten Relations, Feminist Artists and Relational Aesthetics', 2013. www.imprintgold.ac.uk. Accessed 1 November 2016.

Reed, Christopher. *Bloomsbury Rooms*. New Haven: Yale UP, 2004.

Reed, Christopher. Ed. *The Roger Fry Reader*. Chicago: U of Chicago P, 1996.

Robins, Anna G. *Modern Art in Britain 1910–1914*. London: Merrell Holberton, 1997.

Shone, Richard. *The Art of Bloomsbury*. London: Tate, 1999.

Shone, Richard. *Bloomsbury Portraits*. London: Phaidon Press, 1993.

Stair, Julian. 'The Employment of Matter'. *Beyond Bloomsbury*. Ed. Alexandra Gerstein. London: Courtauld, 2009. 27–34.

Stansky, Peter. *On or about December 1910*. Cambridge, MA: Harvard UP, 1996.

Walshe, Christine. 'The Art World, Post-Impressionism and Socialism'. The Papers of Roger Fry, King's College Cambridge Archive, REF/10/5. Undated.

Warden, Christine. 'John Piper's Modernist Scenography'. *Modernist Cultures* 11.2 (2016): 225–42.

Watney, Simon. *The Art of Duncan Grant*. London: John Murray, 1990.

Watney, Simon. 'The Connoisseur as Gourmet'. *Formations of Pleasure*. Ed. Formations Editorial Collective. London: Routledge/Kegan Paul, 1983. 66–83.

Woolf, Leonard. *Beginning Again*. London: Hogarth Press, 1964.

Woolf, Virginia. *The Collected Letters of Virginia Woolf*. Ed. N. Nicolson and J. Trautmann Banks. London: Hogarth Press, 1994.

Woolf, Virginia. *The Diary of Virginia Woolf, Vol 1, 1915–19*. Ed. A. O. Bell. Harmondsworth: Penguin, 1979.

Woolf, Virginia. Letter to Vanessa Bell headed 'WOOLF FLUSH', Dated June 12 1933 Hogarth Press Archive, University of Reading.

Woolf, Virginia. 'Old Bloomsbury'. *Moments of Being*. Ed. J. Schulkind. San Diego: Harcourt, 1985. 179–201.

Woolf, Virginia. *Roger Fry*. Ed. Diane F. Gillespie, Oxford: Blackwell, 1995.

Case Study: Clive Bell and the Legacies of Significant Form

MARK HUSSEY

> There are many people who appreciate the expression of sincere emotion in verse ... But very few know when there is an expression of *significant* emotion, emotion which has its life in the poem and not in the history of the poet. The emotion of art is impersonal.
>
> – T. S. Eliot, 'Tradition and the Individual Talent' (1919)

In 1958, William Kennick asked the readers of *Mind* to imagine a person asked to retrieve from a warehouse stocked with miscellaneous items all the works of art. For Kennick (writing several years before Arthur Danto insisted that it is the 'artworld' that defines art), this appeared to be a straightforward task. 'Now imagine the same person,' he continued, 'sent into the warehouse to bring out all the objects with Significant Form ... He would be rightly baffled; he knows a work of art when he sees one, but he has little or no idea what to look for when he is told to bring an object that possesses Significant Form' (322). Clive Bell, who popularized the term in his 1914 book *Art*, would not be much help for two reasons. The first is that Bell did not define significant form beyond saying that it consisted of 'lines and colours combined in a particular way, certain forms and relations of forms' which provoke an 'aesthetic emotion' in the viewer (*Art* 17). The second is that Bell emphasized that discerning significant form was an entirely subjective matter. He allowed that a critic could lead him to see significant form where before he had seen none, but also stated unequivocally that any system of aesthetics must rest on subjective experience (17). And subjective experience cannot be contradicted, although it can, obviously, be disagreed with.

When Clive Bell and his wife, Vanessa, encountered Roger Fry on a Cambridge railway platform early in 1910, all three had a familiarity with modern French painting that was somewhat unusual for most English people of the time. Those whose business it was to know (e.g. critics) were aware of the new art that was being shown in Paris, and since 1905 works by Cézanne, Matisse, Manet, Gauguin, Van Gogh and others had been exhibited in England from time to time, but these would not be grouped together as 'Post-Impressionists' until 1910 (see Humm in this volume). In 1908, Fry had written a letter to the *Burlington Magazine* in response to the review of an exhibition of the

International Society that characterized works by Matisse and his contemporaries as the exhausted fading of the Impressionist movement (Bullen 5). Fry suggested that painters such as Cézanne and Gauguin should in fact be regarded as 'proto-Byzantines', making an analogy with the changes that occurred between the end of the Roman Empire and Byzantium (Bullen 46). In 1909, Fry published his ground-shifting 'An Essay in Aesthetics' in which he began to articulate the terms and concepts that would frame the arguments in England around Post-Impressionist painting.

Clive Bell had gone to Paris in 1904, ostensibly to conduct research in the Archives Nationales for his Cambridge fellowship dissertation. A letter of introduction to the painter Gerald Kelly led Bell to the cafés and nightlife of artists' Paris, where he met Roderic O'Conor and J. W. Morrice. Kelly, O'Conor, and Morrice made Bell aware of the work of Cézanne and Gauguin, told him about the Pont-Aven group, and informed him about the Nabis, the Salon des Indépendants, and the Salon d'Automne. Already unusual among his Cambridge undergraduate cohort for his interest in visual art, Bell's time in Paris early in 1904 transformed his sensibility and changed the direction of his life. That spring, when his best friend Thoby Stephen visited with his two sisters, Vanessa and Virginia, Bell introduced them to the artists with whom he had become acquainted. On her return to London, Vanessa wrote to thank him, telling her future husband that she had been horrifying her half-brother George Duckworth with tales of their exploits abroad (Spalding, *Vanessa* 42). Virginia, meanwhile, wrote to Violet Dickinson of being taken by Kelly to visit Rodin's studio, and how they had dined with Clive Bell at 'a real Bohemian party' and stayed up late 'talking of Art, Sculpture and Music' (*Letters* 1: 140). In 1905, Vanessa enlisted Clive to help her set up the Friday Club through which young painters could exhibit their work and attend lectures (Shone).

Clive Bell recalled in his memoir *Old Friends* how on that journey from Cambridge up to London in early 1910 Fry told him that he 'proposed to show the British public the work of the newest French painters' (80), an endeavour in which Clive was pleased to help. (He and Ottoline Morrell would later accompany Fry on a visit to Paris dealers to select works for the exhibition [Robins 784n20]). Although Robert Dell had organized an exhibition of modern French painters in Brighton in the summer of 1910, it was Fry's 'Manet and the Post-Impressionists', which opened on 8 November at the Grafton Galleries in London, that became the focus of outrage and argument, and has served the historicization of modernism as a point of origin. The defence in England of Post-Impressionism's legitimacy as art in the face of establishment outrage reminiscent of Max Nordau's most dire warnings of degeneracy fell largely to Fry and Bell, with support from Desmond MacCarthy and other sympathetic critics. To change the way that people thought about visual art it was necessary both to demonstrate how these surprising new works related to the tradition, and also to provide a new vocabulary through which the public might come to terms with what it was looking at. As with the development of any new community of feeling, or in the pathways to a paradigm shift, it is possible retrospectively to see stirrings of these movements before they crystallize into a settled narrative.

For example, although Clive Bell has frequently been represented by hostile critics or biographers as taking most if not all of his ideas from others, most particularly from Fry, it is also possible to see him as at the confluence of number of currents that enabled him, given his fluency as a writer and his remarkable journalistic skill, to codify what was new about Post-Impressionist art in terms that resonated with people's experience. Frances Spalding has pointed out that Fry wrote in a *Fortnightly Review* article of 1911 that

Cézanne 'seems, as it were, to have touched a hidden spring whereby the whole structure of Impressionist design broke down, and a new world of significant and expressive form became apparent' (qtd in Spalding, *Fry* 164). Others have noticed that in his inaugural lecture as Professor of Poetry at Oxford in 1901, A. C. Bradley said that there was 'no such thing as a mere form in poetry. All form is expression'. Bradley argued that it would not be possible to maintain interest in a composition for the sake of its form alone; the form must be 'expressive also of a particular meaning, or rather is one aspect of that unity whose other aspect is meaning. So that what you apprehend may be called indifferently an expressed meaning or a significant form' (23). A month before the 1910 Grafton show opened, Elie Nadelman, who had moved to Paris in 1904, was quoted in *Camera Work* on the subject of his drawings: 'The subject of any work of art is for me nothing but a pretext for creating significant form, relations of forms which create a new life that has nothing to do with life in nature' ('Photo-Secession' 41).[1] Clive Bell popularized the term 'significant form', but, like 'Post-Impressionism', it served as a shorthand for concepts that were circulating throughout the first decade of the twentieth century. Indeed, as Hana Leaper has recently remarked, in Vanessa Bell's letters from around 1904–6 she 'foreshadow[s] Post-Impressionist concerns in precisely the language later used' by Clive Bell and Fry (44). A model of contagion would more accurately account for the circulation of ideas and terms than the usual model of influence, which implies their linear transmission.[2]

Fry's 'Essay in Aesthetics' was first published in the *New Quarterly* (edited by Desmond MacCarthy), but gained a far wider audience in 1920 when it was reprinted in his popular collection *Vision and Design*. Fry stressed the separation between 'imaginative life', which was expressed and stimulated by art, and 'actual life' (20). Art, he argued, expressed emotions as 'ends in themselves' (29), and required 'unity of some kind' for the restful contemplation of what he enumerated as 'emotional elements of design' (33).[3] The criterion of likeness to nature was to be abandoned as irrelevant to the evaluation of art. In the essay written for the catalogue accompanying 'Manet and the Post-Impressionists', MacCarthy, basing his remarks upon notes provided to him by Fry, described the paintings shown as rendering 'the emotional significance which lies in things'; unlike the Impressionists who had preceded them, these artists were conveying, for example, 'the "treeness" of the tree' (96). Perhaps the most often quoted line of MacCarthy's essay at the time was that the work of the Post-Impressionists 'may even appear ridiculous to those who do not recall the fact that a good rocking-horse often has more of the true horse about it than an instantaneous photograph of a Derby winner' (96–7).

Fry, Bell, and others continued to make a case for the artists who had been mocked in the press as lunatics, anarchists, and children.[4] In an article in the *Fortnightly Review* that was based upon a lecture he gave at the close of the Grafton exhibition, Fry explained that the Post-Impressionists were attempting 'to discover the visual language of the imagination. To discover, that is, what arrangements of form and colour are calculated to stir the imagination most deeply through the stimulus given to the sense of sight' (Reed, *Reader* 100). Freed from the 'incubus' of representation, the artist now creates 'particular rhythms of line and particular harmonies of colour' which have 'spiritual correspondence' (Reed, *Reader* 105). Throughout 1911, Bell, too, carried forward the doctrine in a number of reviews in the *Athenaeum* which hint at ideas he would disseminate widely in *Art*.

Even in a review of an edition of the letters of Edward John Trelawny, Bell noted that, 'as the catalogue of the Grafton Galleries might say, the Trelawniness of Trelawny is completely expressed' (7). There is less flippancy in his expression of a similar notion in his review the following month of Frank Rutter's *Revolution in Art*: 'he understands that the younger French painters are ... not trying to represent youths dancing, oak trees in a storm, or gardens on the banks of rivers, but rather to translate into line and colour such abstractions as the rhythm of the dance, the stir of trees, and the lush wetness of swampy places' (135). Reviewing Laurence Binyon's *The Flight of the Dragon*, Bell finds that it is 'the widespread consciousness of the universal in the particular that produces all great movements' (428). 'Primitives' are the artists who must express what they feel without regard for convention and tradition 'because they have perceived more clearly than others the reality that lies beneath the superficial' (428). In a review of C. Lewis Hind's *The Post-Impressionists*, Bell refers to the 'spiritual significance of the universe' being behind these artists' work. The 'spiritual significance of things' is troubling to critics used to 'materialistic art', but Bell notes that Hind has perceived a 'mysterious "something great"' in the post-impressionists' paintings (51). Visiting the Bells in Studland in September 1911, where Roger Fry, staying nearby, also visited as often as he could, Lytton Strachey wrote to his brother James that Clive was 'burgeoning out into inconceivable theories on art and life ... It is all the fault of Roger' (203).

By the time he chose the paintings for the English section of the Second Post-Impressionist Exhibition (5 October–31 December 1912), Bell could write confidently in its catalogue that 'the battle is won'. 'We all agree, now, that any form in which an artist can express himself is legitimate' (a line loudly echoed several years later in Woolf's 'Modern Novels' – 'Any method is right, every method is right, that expresses what we wish to express' [34]): 'they recognise no authority but the truth that is in them' (349). It is in this brief catalogue essay that Bell first deploys the term for which he is notorious: the Post-Impressionist *simplifies*, 'omits details, that is to say, to concentrate on something more important – on the significance of form' (350). Even so mundane an object as a coalscuttle, he continues, is regarded by the Post-Impressionist 'as an end in itself, as a significant form' (350). Desmond MacCarthy put Bell's term into the context of canonical aesthetic theory in an article published in *Eye Witness* just as the exhibition opened: 'What Mr. Bell means by "significant form" is what Kant meant by "free" beauty' (377). While the exhibition was going on, Bell made his first effort to codify his emerging theory in 'Post-Impressionism and Aesthetics' for the *Burlington Magazine* of January 1913.

Bell here outlined propositions that he would elaborate in *Art* the following year. First, the essential quality of a work of art is 'its power of raising a peculiar emotion, called aesthetic' (226). This emotion will be different for each person as a person's aesthetic depends upon their subjective experience: we can be certain of no one's feelings but our own. Second, although the emotions produced by different artworks are different, they are the same *kind* and can be produced by 'every kind of visual art, by pictures, sculpture, buildings, pots, carvings, textiles' (227). Third, the 'essential' quality that evokes aesthetic emotion is 'significant form'. The question of *why* significant form evokes aesthetic emotion is irrelevant, Bell claims. It is a question for metaphysics (i.e. philosophy) rather than aesthetics: 'For a discussion of aesthetics it need only be agreed that forms arranged and combined according to certain mysterious laws do move us profoundly, and that it is the business of an artist so to combine and arrange them that they shall move us' (227).

The plastic arts, then, are not for telling stories or conveying information: representation is not relevant to *aesthetic* emotion – a claim Bell would subsequently refine but which continues to be misunderstood or distorted. Fry wrote in 1910 that the Post-Impressionists 'have recognised that the forms which are most impressive to the imagination are not necessarily those which recall the objects of actual life most clearly to the mind' (Reed, *Reader* 98). In 'Post Impressionism' in 1911, Fry referred to the intense aesthetic pleasure to be derived 'from a mere pattern' (Reed, *Reader* 105). Fry more gingerly hinted at what Bell tended to state with assurance. These issues were all intensely discussed among the Bells, Fry, and other friends. In February 1913, Vanessa Bell wrote from Asheham to her sister that Fry had visited on Sunday 'and the air is teeming with discussion on Art. They think they are getting further. I don't know. Roger's views of course are more mature than ours. He is at one pole and Clive at the other and I come somewhere in between on a rather shaky foothold, but none of us really agree with Leonard' (137). She asks if Virginia will go to Leeds to hear Fry lecture the following week. Clive Bell had also written from Asheham to Molly MacCarthy and described the great arguments about aesthetics that were going on. He told Molly he had so persuaded Fry that the 'great doctrine of "significant form"' would appear in Fry's forthcoming lectures at Leeds and Leicester.[5]

The discussion at Asheham must have been prompted by Bell's *Burlington* article which had, he told Molly, exasperated Lytton Strachey. Leonard Woolf had sent an article of his own to Vanessa, which she shared with Clive and Duncan Grant. Whatever Leonard wrote can only be inferred from Vanessa's response as no trace of the article has come to light. Vanessa tried to explain to her brother-in-law what her husband had been trying to say: 'It seems to me clear that if the chief aim or if one of the principle [*sic*] aims of an artist is to imitate or represent *facts* accurately ... it is impossible that he should also produce significant form, or whatever you like to call it. Does Clive say any more than this?' (Marler 133). Vanessa took issue with Leonard's challenge to Clive's dismissal of mimesis: 'I often look at a picture ... without seeing in the least what things are ... The picture does convey the idea of form, of what you call secondary form I suppose, but not the idea of form associated with anything in life, but simply form, separated from life. As a matter of fact we do first feel the emotion and then look at the picture' (133). Vanessa told Leonard that when she had looked at one of the paintings in the Second Post-Impressionist Exhibition, she had identified 'trees, but never dreamt of a lake'. Her 'emotion' had been provoked by 'forms and colours', but when some weeks later it had been pointed out to her that 'the blue was a lake', this had not affected her initial response. Despite her ambivalence about formalism, she tried in this letter to explain to Leonard what she thought Clive was getting at.

At the conclusion of his 1913 article, Bell indulges briefly in a 'metaphysical question': '*why* do certain arrangements and combinations of forms move us so strangely?' (229). Despite saying the question is irrelevant to aesthetics, and in the absence of anything probative, Bell offers his 'dreams'. Significant form lifts us out of ordinary life into ecstasy, into 'the world of reality': 'Form is the boat in which artists ferry us to the shores of another world' (230). Significant form is how artists communicate *their* emotion to the viewer, how they enable the sharing of subjectivity. Bell concludes that when successful, 'for a moment the world has become a work of art, we see it as form: and behind form we catch a glimpse of reality' (230). As both S. P. Rosenbaum and Pierrette Jutras have argued, Bell is markedly different from Fry in his willingness to cross into a kind of mysticism. In 'Retrospect', the essay with which Fry closes *Vision and Design*, he had concluded that Bell's 'aesthetic emotion' provoked by significant form could not be explained in rational terms, and he did not want to fall into 'the depths of mysticism' by trying (302). Bell's use of a kind of secularized religious language is at odds with Fry's more rational and analytic approach, but it allies Bell more closely with Virginia Woolf, at least, insofar as she often struggled to find words for ineffable feelings about 'reality'.[6]

In the same month that Bell's *Burlington* article appeared, Fry had set another cat among the pigeons by mocking the popular Victorian painter Sir Lawrence Alma Tadema in *The Nation*, for which he was taken to task in a letter from George Bernard Shaw. Fry had described the existence of 'two absolutely separate cultures, so separate that those who possess one culture scarcely ever take notice of the other' (*Reader* 147). In coming to Fry's defence, Bell made the important point that the same language was being used in entirely different ways by adherents of two opposed views of art, one of which he called 'the official', the other 'the aesthetic'. Thus, 'well-drawn' in the official view meant 'anatomical correctness', whereas in the aesthetic view it meant 'that it is aesthetically moving' ('Mr Roger Fry's'). In March, Bell again expounded the 'fundamental critical proposition' behind the Post-Impressionist movement that 'a picture is a surface covered with lines and colours arranged in a certain order, and that it is this arrangement which inspires true aesthetic emotion' ('Post-Impressionism Again'). Detached from its specific origins as a term deployed to facilitate the acceptance of a radically new form of visual art, 'significant form' would go on surfacing in contexts as heterogeneous as a textbook on nervous diseases by Charles Loomis Dana in 1921, and on into the twenty-first century where it can be found in books on the films of Steven Spielberg (Buckland 43) or on Chinese theories of fiction (Ming 67). In 1913, recognizing an opportunity, Chatto & Windus invited Roger Fry to write a book explaining the new artistic movement. Being at the time absorbed in setting up the Omega Workshops, Fry declined and instead suggested Clive Bell.

Bell was well positioned to take on the task as not only had he been involved in the promulgation and defence of Post-Impressionism already for several years, he had also been for some time contemplating a book to be called *The New Renaissance*, a sweeping account of what he believed to be a threshold moment in western civilization.[7] In a 1917 article, 'Before the War', he would explain how August 1914 had destroyed that optimism. But although by 1913 Bell was already beginning to become deeply involved in public debate about the possibility of military conscription, his book *Art* was written quickly and published in February 1914.

When a third edition was prepared in 1949, Bell explained that he had let the text stand without revision as the record of a particular historical moment. It was a rebellious and intemperate book in which he made ridiculous generalizations about the history of art, and absurd judgments about particular painters. As he would write in *Since Cézanne*, 'the intemperate ferocity of the opposition drove us into Protestantism and Protestantism is unjust always' (18). Many of Bell's more sympathetic commentators have recognized that *Art* is a manifesto rather than a work of scholarship. Treatment of Bell's contributions to aesthetics, therefore, often depends upon the lens through which *Art*, in particular, is seen. Thus Nigel Warburton says of Bell's hypothesis that when *Art* is read 'as a manifesto for Cézanne and other Post-Impressionist painters, this theory is relatively uncontroversial. It suggests a way of approaching these artists' work which locates them within the great tradition of Western painting' (15–16). Kennick states that Bell found not the essence of art, 'but *a new way of looking at pictures* ... his dictum ... is a slogan, the epitome of a platform of aesthetic reform. It has work to do. Not the work which the philosophers assign it, but a work of teaching people a new way of looking at pictures' (324–5).

Bell described significant form as 'a combination of lines and colours (counting black and white as colours) that moves me aesthetically' (20), but has nothing to do with *beauty*, thus rejecting a hitherto unquestioned tradition of what was the proper object of visual art. To represent what is beautiful, or to evoke a pleasurable response to beauty, is not the purpose of art; beauty may be found in nature, certainly – the wings of a butterfly are beautiful, flowers are beautiful – but this is not the quality that for Bell identifies a work of art. He acknowledges that significant form is only a convenient term for something difficult or perhaps impossible to describe, and would have no quarrel if someone preferred instead to speak of the *rhythm* of 'significant relations of form' (22). Bell is concerned more with leading his readers to see in a new way than with imposing a doctrine. As William Bywater, perhaps Bell's most eloquent defender, put it, he is trying 'to convey a quality no idea of which is transmitted by language' (20). Indeed, to offer 'a purely verbal or linguistic characterisation of significant form would be to violate all our conclusions about the nature of this concept' (74).

Sometimes Bell proceeds by negative example, as when he uses the very popular 1862 painting by William Frith, usually called *The Railway Station* but called *Paddington Station* by Bell, to illustrate forms used to convey information: 'Forms and relations of forms were for Frith not objects of emotion, but means of suggesting emotion and conveying ideas' (23). It is, therefore, a *painting* but not a work of *art*. Fundamental to Bell's point is that artists – and by artist he means only those whose work embodies significant form – *create* form, they do not imitate it. His point, as Vanessa Bell tried to explain to Leonard Woolf, is not that representation is in itself bad, but that it is irrelevant to *aesthetic* emotion. The aesthetic emotion is not an emotion that derives from associations with either lived experience or objects in the natural world. This is, as Bell acknowledged, an austere doctrine; it ultimately constituted a notable tributary which flowed into the formalism of the mid-twentieth century exemplified by critics such as Clement Greenberg and Michael Fried.

Although Bell was always clear that he was presenting a hypothesis, and that his hypothesis was explicitly drawn from his own subjective experience, his vivid and direct style inevitably led to equally direct opposition. Sometimes this took the form of ridicule, as in an appendix devoted to significant form in Curt J. Ducasse's *Philosophy of Art* (1929), where it is described as a joke perpetrated by a man of devilish cunning. Sometimes the writer took a more sinister tone, as in Petronius Arbiter's article on Cézanne's 'degeneracy', where *Art* is described as 'pernicious poison' for its praise of art that is 'detached from all the concerns of life' (330). This objection to Bell's aesthetics' rejection of a moral or ethical dimension was also made more temperately by other reviewers, such as Charles Aitken who wrote in the *Burlington Magazine*: 'Surely the truth is that the ecstasy of art and "good actions" are closely interrelated, the one leading to the other in endless succession' (196).

Reviewing *Art* for *The Nation*, Fry drew particular attention to what Bell himself always stressed was a vital element of his theory – that significant form was not confined to painting and sculpture. *Art*'s first edition included six images which, as happens all too often, have been dropped from subsequent printings.[8] In the first chapter, 'The Aesthetic Hypothesis', Bell asks what quality is 'common to Sta. Sophia and the windows at Chartres, Mexican sculpture, a Persian bowl, Chinese carpets, Giotto's frescoes at Padua, and the masterpieces of Poussin, Piero della Francesca, and Cézanne?' (17). Fry pointed out that in their very heterogeneity Bell's catalogue of objects 'separated out the emotions aroused by certain formal relations from the emotions aroused by the events of life' (*Reader* 159). Nevertheless, Fry was sceptical about Bell's claim that significant form was a route to 'ultimate reality' (160). For Fry, something had to be fused with form in order to make the form significant.

Randall Davies, reviewing *Art* in the *New Statesman*, balked at the list: 'A carpet is one thing, a picture is another: and to apply the same test to one as to the other is about as reasonable as to multiply a cheese by a bottle of ink ... To look for the same qualities in a carpet and a picture would be ... absurd' (693). In the correspondence which ensued, Bell explained that if Davies could not understand that the 'emotion I feel for a carpet is of exactly the same kind as the emotion I feel for a picture, a statue, a cathedral, or a pot', there could be no point in their discussing the matter further ('Aesthetics' 756).[9] 'Significant Form' is merely a label for that quality he holds to be exclusive to works of art *that move him aesthetically*. Davies mocked Bell for saying that Frith's painting was not a work of art. But by what criteria does Davies establish that something is art? Bell simply said that *Paddington Station* does not move him aesthetically, but 'I may have looked at the picture stupidly and remained insensitive to the real significance of its forms' (757). Bell's key point here, and one often lost in subsequent discussion, is that 'we might all disagree about particular works of art and yet agree about aesthetics' (757). In a discussion about whether there could be a science of aesthetics, the philosopher A. E. Heath agreed, in referring to Bell's hypothesis, that while 'we may differ about the presence or absence of the quality x', we can differ about different works of art without denying that x exists. However, Heath noted that 'the sceptic might well accept this, but demand the instant production of x' (199).

Davies did not take up Bell's point, instead becoming involved in an argument about whether carpets could be said to be works of art given their utility ('Little'). But Bell raised another point that is often overlooked in response to his polemic: he consistently held that his response to an artwork could be modified by another's argument on its behalf. He asked Davies to provide his own criterion for deciding that something was 'art'. This remains an issue. For example, Noel Carroll describes Bell as 'one of the major forerunners of the twentieth century's philosophical obsession with discovering an essential definition of art' (87). Carroll agrees with Bell that representation is not a *necessary* condition for art: 'The bejeweled patterns on Islamic funeral monuments, Bach's fugues and Ellsworth Kelly's wall sculptures are all pertinent examples here. They are not representational but they are *undeniably* art' (89, emphasis added). The question 'what is art?' is not a particularly productive one. The philosopher's 'foolish preoccupation with definition' is the problem (Kennick 325); the critics grasp what the philosophers overlook.

Art's reception, particularly with regard to its concepts of aesthetic emotion and significant form, has been marked by a number of cruxes. One, as intimated above, concerns the extreme formalist position that the aesthetic should have nothing to do with lived experience, with the practical, everyday concerns of life. This objection usually centers on what is perceived to be Bell's banishing of representation from art, although this is not borne out by what he wrote. Another is the circularity of Bell's argument: aesthetic emotion is provoked by significant form, which is that which provokes aesthetic emotion. Yet another objection is to Bell's apparent detachment of art from history: he wrote that 'to appreciate a work of art we need bring with us nothing but a sense of form and colour and a knowledge of three-dimensional space' (*Art* 28).

I. A. Richards mounted a serious attack on Bell's contention that the 'aesthetic emotion' was separate from any other kind of human experience or activity. Richards denied there was any such thing as a purely 'aesthetic' emotion, writing in *Principles of Literary Criticism* (1922):

When we look at a picture, or read a poem, or listen to music, we are not doing something quite unlike what we were doing on our way to the Gallery or when we dressed in the morning. The fashion in which the experience is caused in us is different, and as a rule the experience is more complex and, if we are successful, more unified. But our activity is not of a fundamentally different kind. (10)

Richards also connected Bell and his acolytes to the 'art for art's sake' movement of the late nineteenth century, seeing in this heritage the influence 'of Continental and German aesthetics upon the English mind' (55). In the preface to *Landmarks in Nineteenth Century Painting* (1927), Bell breezily dismissed Richards's point: the eminent professor does not recognize an aesthetic emotion because he has not ever experienced one (viii).[10] In the following decade, Louis A. Reid also sidestepped Richards's objection: 'The obvious seems to me the only really tenable view. If we adopt it we need not trouble ourselves very much about whether there is a special aesthetic emotion or not. Of course there isn't and of course there is. There isn't, in that to have an aesthetic experience is not to cast off human nature, and there is, in that aesthetic experiences as a class are noticeably different in many ways from any others' (135). Bell's solution to the perennial question of why certain objects are classified as art and others are not was either elegantly or absurdly simple: art is that which possesses significant form, and we respond to it with aesthetic emotion.

Art was still being reprinted in the 1960s, leading Ruby Meager to remark in the year following Bell's death that despite philosophical objections, he 'has something to say that people still wish to hear' (124). Like Kant, Bell believed in the potential for responding to art with a 'peculiar' emotion to be an aspect of what makes us human. R. K. Elliott argued that Bell's ideas about significant form had changed by the time he published the essays that form *Since Cézanne* (1922). In 'Criticism', Bell acknowledges, for example, that most people will need assistance from critics to have even 'some fraction of pure aesthetic emotion' (Elliott 119). Elliott identified as phenomenological description the method by which Bell characteristically indicated his belief that a work possessed significant form, exemplified by a passage from Bell's essay on Bonnard:

> The first thing one gets from a picture by Bonnard is a sense of perplexed, delicious colour: tones of miraculous subtlety seem to be flowing into an enchanted pool and chasing one another there. From this pool emerge gradually forms which appear sometimes vaporous and sometimes tentative, but never vapid and never woolly. When we have realised that the pool of colour is, in fact, a design of extraordinary originality and perfect cohesion our aesthetic experiment is at its height. And not until this excitement begins to flag do we notice that the picture carries a delightful overtone – that it is witty, whimsical, fantastic. ('Bonnard' 100)

Bywater, too, adopts this phenomenological method to explain significant form: rather than offer definitions, there is a gradual accretion of descriptions of particular works from the point of view of subjective experience. In *Enjoying Pictures*, Bell fully embraced this approach when he set as his task 'to follow the vagaries of my mind through a tangled experience – an hour in the National Gallery' and then 'catch my reactions alive and pen them in phrases' (3). Even in 1934, twenty years after *Art*, Bell acknowledges that his ideas about what happens in the encounter with art remain difficult to explain. But he now believes that the 'unique aesthetic emotion' is a starting point for that encounter, not its terminus (11).

Following the publication of J. K. Johnstone's *The Bloomsbury Group* in 1954, renewed attention was given to the debt to G. E. Moore of Bloomsbury aesthetics. George

Dickie held that Bell's was an intuitionist aesthetics analogous to Moore's intuitionist ethics, and that Bell had been confused in his explanation of significant form as a quality common to all works of art. For Dickie, Monroe Beardsley's *Aesthetics* was a more sound approach as it thoroughly discussed the fusion of form and content that Dickie believed was necessary to aesthetic response (143n10), a point made by Fry in 1914. Rosalind Ekman took up Dickie's point to argue that 'when understood in terms of Moore's theory of value, the apparent paradoxes in Bell's theory, especially those generated by the form-content distinction, will be resolved' (351). In the 1970s, writers were able to see Bell's work within a broader perspective. Already, he had been placed by Solomon Fishman in a tradition of art theorists including Ruskin, Pater, Fry, and Herbert Read. Thomas McLaughlin, who noted how Bell's identification with the phrase 'significant form' had tended to overshadow everything else he had written, saw Bell's entire career as 'an attempt to educate the visual sensibilities of the public' (436).

Bell is usually represented in anthologies of art theory or aesthetics by an extract from chapter 1 of *Art*, 'The Aesthetic Hypothesis'. This is, after all, his claim to fame, but the consequence is to render less visible any subsequent refinement of his thinking. Carol Gould, noting Bell's presence in such anthologies, defends him against two often-repeated charges that 'aesthetic emotion' rests on either a falsehood or a 'fatal contradiction' ('Aesthetic Experience' 125). In line with other commentators, such as Dickie, Gould locates in his vocabulary some of the difficulties Bell's hypothesis has always encountered. For example, it was misleading for Bell to use 'emotion'. Dickie suggested 'experience' would better fit what Bell described, but Gould believes 'perception' clarifies what Bell was after: 'significant form is to aesthetic experience what yellow is to visual experience of yellow' (128). Bell himself several times stated that he was not too concerned about what people called the experience he was trying to describe as long as they understood it to be something that occurred solely and distinctively in the presence of art. (Richards's critique could be seen as the result of the word 'emotion', after all; Bell's rebuttal simply says he is unconcerned with 'psychology'). In a later article, Gould acknowledges Bell's 'central place in philosophical aesthetics' ('Clive Bell' 38), answering the frequent charge of circularity in his explanations of significant form by saying that 'his problem is that facing any philosophical theory moving from the subjectivity of experience to a world existing outside of that experience' (40). Although his theory has been surpassed, she finds that he remains a key figure in contemporary art theory owing to his 'insouciant erudition and passion for art' (42).

This is borne out by the number of contributions to the *Routledge Companion to Aesthetics* (Gaut and Lopes) that engage with Bell, albeit often to take issue with his hypothesis. However, there is still a tendency to embalm Bell in the Post-Impressionist moment of 1910–14. For example, Berys Gaut writes that someone who reacted to Picasso's *Guernica* 'merely as a set of lines and colors in cubist style would be missing out on a central item of aesthetic interest: namely, how Picasso *uses* cubist fragmentation to convey something of the horror of war and fascism' (296). While I agree with Gaut, her argument against Bell depends on the notion that he does not progress beyond the subjective shock of aesthetic emotion to any other considerations about a work of art, but this is not confirmed by his later writings. Furthermore, as Christopher Reed pointed out in his germinal article of 1992, the 'constantly evolving' formalism of Fry and Bell has too often been ignored in discussions about aesthetics, as if their ideas were static ('Through' 23). Reed makes the argument for an ethical component to a dynamic formalism that Virginia Woolf recognized in her long engagement with Fry's and Bell's theories. The 'disinterested' looking promoted by Bell, for example, 'is a rudimentary attempt to problematise seeing as vicarious possession, art that would serve desire' (27).[11] The point made by Nick Zangwill that Bell and Fry's 'eradication of specifically representational aesthetic properties' does not seem familiar to our 'ordinary aesthetic experience and thought' (616) again depends upon a rather static version of their ideas used to underpin a narrative of their work simply as inaugurating 'extreme formalism' (612). By 1922, Bell described the critic as someone who 'merely tells us what a book, a picture, or a piece of music makes him feel. This method can be intensely exciting: what is more, it has made vast additions to our aesthetic experience' ('Criticism' 175). Bywater enumerates three reasons why Bell should not even be considered a 'formalist': (1) 'It does not follow on Bell's theory that non-objective or non-representational art is to be preferred' (72); (2) 'Concepts such as empathy, an aesthetic attitude, and aesthetic distance are avoided by formalists because they feel that the use of such notions promotes an undesirable overemphasis upon the spectator' (72), but 'Recognition of significant form is not a totally 'intellectual' exercise. It is emotional, thrilling, a discovery of connections, not to a further goal, but with a song of their own' (73); (3) formalism tends to insist on specific paradigms for the production of art. Bell's is a 'theory of criticism, not of creativity' and as such is 'non-normative' (74).

It seems likely that Bell will continue to feature in discussions of the relations between ethics and aesthetics; of the ontology of the artwork; of the status of intention in art (see Cronan); and, more generally, in the ongoing debate about the historicization of modernism. Recent commentary has produced some surprising new characterizations of Clive Bell. Mark Foster Gage, for example, has allied Bell's insistence on the separateness of aesthetic emotion 'with the anti-formalist stances of Nietzsche's Dionysian states as well as Bataille's decisive and inexplicable state of mind, both of which call for a similar displacement from the world of common experiences' (162). In most discussions of Bloomsbury aesthetics, as well as in all biographical studies, Bell's ideas have usually been compared with or seen as derived from those of Fry. His sensibility, however, often aligns him closely with the efforts of Virginia Woolf to find a language for her ineffable sense of 'reality'. Rosenbaum highlights the mystical strain in Bell's writings on art (223–4), an interpretation reflected also in Banfield's discussion of Bertrand Russell's influence on Bell (41). If we agree with Banfield that, for Bloomsbury, art 'became an inquiry into the nature of reality akin to physics' (279), and that form is a ' "reality" beneath appearances' (280) – 'reality', as Rosenbaum says, being that 'crucial Bloomsbury term' (223) – then perhaps it is time to read Bell in relation to Woolf rather than only in relation to Fry.

NOTES

1. A show of Nadelman's drawings had been planned for Alfred Stieglitz's Photo-Secession Gallery, but they had to be unexpectedly returned for an exhibition in Europe before they could be shown in New York. *Camera Work* quoted from remarks Nadelman had prepared for the projected catalog. This instance of the term 'significant form' was noted in a 1982 *Art News* article by James Mellows cited by Beverly Twitchell in her unpublished dissertation (105).
2. Berel Lang discusses how the notion of 'intuitive knowledge' circulated among G. E. Moore, Fry, and J. M. Keynes because there existed 'a context in which such passage would have the opportunity to take place' (300).
3. Fry's elements are described by Johanna Drucker as 'the first uncompromising articulation of formalism' (73).

4. This story has been widely recounted, for example, by Bell, 'How'; Bullen; Nicolson; Spalding, *Fry*.

5. My thanks to Julian Bell, and to the Society of Authors as representatives of the Estate of Clive Bell, for permission to quote this letter.

6. The Tamil philosopher A. K. Coomaraswamy quoted from *Art* in 'Hindu View of Art: Theory of Beauty', pointing out that Bell restated a point of view which implied 'that through the false world of everyday experience may be seen by those of penetrating vision (artists, lovers and philosophers) glimpses of the real substrate' (36). Coomaraswamy's essay was in a collection published by Sunwise Turn, a bookshop founded in New York in 1916. Its founder, Madge Jenison, dedicated her memoir to 'Mr. Clive Bell, who, though I have never seen him, and he has never heard my name, founded this bookshop because he wrote a book'.

7. A sketchbook containing Bell's jottings on, among other matters, 'slopes' in art is dated 1912 (Tate Gallery Archive 8010/2/413).

8. The images accompanying *Art*'s text are: a fifth-century Wei sculpture; an eleventh-century Persian dish; a Peruvian pot; a detail from a sixth-century S. Vitale mosaic; a painting by Cézanne; a painting by Picasso (in fact, his 1907 *Pots et Citron*, purchased by Clive and Vanessa Bell in 1911).

9. Nigel Warburton assumes that what Bell refers to in his list 'are the finest examples of each of these' (22), but this misses the point that Bell's argument is *subjective* rather than *normative*. Bell makes no claim about the 'fineness' of the objects that move him: his point is that this disparate list is united by provoking in *him* an 'aesthetic emotion'.

10. Fry countered Richards much more methodically in 'Some Questions in Esthetics' (2–10).

11. In *Bloomsbury Rooms* Reed adds another nuance to this point: 'In a socio-political order structured around aggression and acquisition, this insistence on the aesthetic as a separate realm is not apolitical. On the contrary, it may be seen as another form of wartime "conscientious objection", deployed not just in response to military conscription but also against capitalist imperatives to commercialize all aspects of experience' (9).

WORKS CITED

Aitken, Charles. 'On Art and Aesthetics'. Review of *Art*. *Burlington Magazine* 26.143 (February 1915): 194–6.

Beardsley, Monroe C. *Aesthetics: Problems in the Philosophy of Criticism*. Indianapolis: Hacket, 1981 [1958].

Bell, Clive. 'Aesthetics: A Reply'. *New Statesman* (21 March 1914): 756–7.

Bell, Clive. *Art*. Perigee, 1981 [1914].

Bell, Clive. 'Before the War'. *Cambridge Magazine* (12 May 1917): 581–2.

Bell, Clive. 'Bonnard'. *Since Cézanne*. 98–104.

Bell, Clive. 'Criticism'. *Since Cézanne*. 154–79.

Bell, Clive. 'The English Group'. *Post-Impressionists in England: The Critical Reception*. Ed. J. B. Bullen. Routledge, 1988. 349–51.

Bell, Clive. *Enjoying Pictures*. New York: Harcourt, 1934.

Bell, Clive. 'How England Met Modern Art'. *Art News* 49.6 (October 1950): 24–7.

Bell, Clive. *Landmarks in Nineteenth Century Painting*. New York: Harcourt, 1927.

Bell, Clive. 'Mr. Roger Fry's Criticism'. *Nation* (22 February 1913): 853–4. Letter to the Editor.

Bell, Clive. *Old Friends*. New York: Harcourt, 1957 [1956].

Bell, Clive. 'Post-Impressionism Again'. *Nation* (29 March 1913): 1060–61.

Bell, Clive. Review of *The Flight of the Dragon: An Essay on the Theory and Practice of Art in China and Japan* by Laurence Binyon. *Athenaeum* (7 October 1911): 428–9.

Bell, Clive. Review of *The Letters of Edward John Trelawny*. Ed. H. Buxton. *Athenaeum* (7 January 1911): 7–8.

Bell, Clive. Review of *Revolution in Art* by Frank Rutter. *Athenaeum* (4 February 1911): 135.

Bell, Clive. *Since Cézanne*. Harcourt, 1922.

Bradley, A. C. *Poetry for Poetry's Sake*. Oxford: Clarendon Press, 1901.

Buckland, Warren. *Directed by Steven Spielberg: Poetics of the Contemporary Hollywood Blockbuster*. London: A&C Black, 2006.

Bullen, J. B. Ed. *Post-Impressionists in England: The Critical Reception*. New York: Routledge, 1988.

Bywater, William G. *Clive Bell's Eye*. Detroit: Wayne State UP, 1975.

Carroll, Noel. 'Formalism'. *The Routledge Companion to Aesthetics* (3rd ed.). Ed. Berys Gaut and Dominic McIver Lopes. New York: Routledge, 2013. 87–95.

Coomaraswamy, A. K. *The Dance of Śiva: Fourteen Indian Essays*. Sunwise Turn, 1918. Repr. Dover, 1985.

Cronan, Todd. *Against Affective Formalism: Matisse, Bergson, Modernism*. Minneapolis: U of Minnesota P, 2013.

Davies, Randall. 'Clive Bell'. *The New Statesman*, 7 March 1914, 692–3.

Davies, Randall. 'The Little Gallery'. *The New Statesman*, 28 March 1914, 789–90.

Dickie, George. 'Clive Bell and the Method of *Principia Ethica*'. *British Journal of Aesthetics* 5.2 (July 1965): 139–43.

Drucker, Johanna. *Theorizing Modernism: Visual Art and the Critical Tradition*. New York: Columbia UP, 1994.

Ducasse, Curt John. *The Philosophy of Art*. New York: Dover, 1966 [1929].

Ekman, Rosalind. 'The Paradoxes of Formalism'. *British Journal of Aesthetics* 10.4 (October 1970): 350–58.

Elliott, R. K. 'Clive Bell's Aesthetic Theory and His Critical practice'. *British Journal of Aesthetics* (April 1965): 111–22.

Fry, Roger. 'An Essay in Aesthetics'. *Vision and Design*. Phoenix, 1928 [1920].

Fry, Roger. 'A New Theory of Art'. Review of *Art*. *The Nation* (7 March 1914): 937–9. *A Roger Fry Reader*. Ed. Christopher Reed. Chicago: Chicago UP, 1996. 158–62.

Fry, Roger. 'Retrospect'. *Vision and Design*. Phoenix, 1928 [1920].

Fry, Roger. *A Roger Fry Reader*. Ed. Christopher Reed. Chicago: Chicago UP, 1996.

Fry, Roger. 'Some Questions in Esthetics'. *Transformations*. Brentano's, 1926. 1–43.

Fry, Roger. *Vision and Design*. Phoenix, 1928 [1920].

Gage, Mark Foster. Ed. *Aesthetic Theory: Essential Texts for Architecture and Design*. New York: W. W. Norton, 2011.

Gaut, Berys. 'Art and Ethics'. *The Routledge Companion to Aesthetics* (3rd ed.). Ed. Berys Gaut and Dominic McIver Lopes. New York: Routledge, 2013. 394–403.

Gaut, Berys and Dominic McIver Lopes. Eds. *The Routledge Companion to Aesthetics* (3rd ed.). London: Routledge, 2013.

Gould, Carol S. 'Clive Bell on Aesthetic Experience and Aesthetic Truth'. *British Journal of Aesthetics* 34.2 (1994): 124–33.

Gould, Carol S. 'Clive Bell (1881–1964) British Critic and Art Historian'. *Key Writers on Art: The Twentieth Century*. Ed. Chris Murray. New York: Routledge, 2003.

Heath, A. E. 'The Scope of the Scientific Method'. *Proceedings of the Aristotelian Society* (1919): 179–207.

Jenison, Madge. *Sunwise Turn: A Human Comedy of Bookselling*. New York: Dutton, 1918.

Jutras, Pierrette. 'Roger Fry et Clive Bell: Divergences fondamentales autour de la notion de "Significant Form"'. *Revue d'Art Canadienne/Canadian Art Review* 20 (1993): 98–115.

Kennick, William E. 'Does Traditional Aesthetics Rest in a Mistake?' *Mind* 67.267 (July 1958): 317–34.

Lang, Berel. 'Intuition in Bloomsbury'. *Journal of the History of Ideas* 25 (1964): 295–302.

Leaper, Hana. 'Between London and Paris'. *Vanessa Bell*. Ed. Sarah Milroy and Ian A. C. Dejardin. Philip Wilson/Dulwich Picture Gallery, 2017. 41–53.

MacCarthy, Desmond. 'Kant and Post-Impressionism'. *Post-Impressionists in England: The Critical Reception*. Ed. J. B. Bullen. New York: Routledge, 1988. 374–77.

MacCarthy, Desmond. 'The Post-Impressionists'. 1910. Bullen. 94–9.

Marler, Regina. Ed. *Selected Letters of Vanessa Bell*. New York: Pantheon, 1993.

McLaughlin, Thomas. 'Clive Bell's Aesthetic: Tradition and Significant Form', *Journal of Aesthetics and Art Criticism* 35 (Summer 1977): 433–43.

Meager, R. 'Clive Bell and the Aesthetic Emotion'. *British Journal of Aesthetics* 5 (1965): 123–31.

Ming, Gong Du. *Chinese Theories of Fiction: A Non-Western Narrative System*. New York: State U of New York P, 2006.

Nicolson, Benedict. 'Post-Impressionism and Roger Fry'. *Burlington Magazine* 93.574 (1951): 10–15.

Petronius Arbiter. 'A Degenerate Work: "The Bathers" by Cézanne'. *The Art World* (January 1918): 326–32.

'The Photo-Secession Gallery'. *Camera Work* (October 1910): 41. www.modjourn.org

Reed, Christopher. *Bloomsbury Rooms: Modernism, Subculture, and Domesticity*. New Haven: Yale, 2004.

Reed, Christopher. 'Through Formalism: Feminism and Virginia Woolf's Relation to Bloomsbury Aesthetics'. *Twentieth Century Literature* 38.1 (Spring 1992): 20–43.

Reid, Louis Arnaud. *A Study in Aesthetics*. New York: Macmillan, 1931.

Richards, I. A. *Principles of Literary Criticism*. New York: Routledge and Kegan Paul, 1976 [1924].

Rosenbaum, S. P. 'The Art of Clive Bell's *Art*'. *Contemporary Philosophy, Vol. 9: Aesthetics and Philosophy of Art*. Ed. G. Fløistad. Dordrecht: Springer, 2007.

Shone, Richard. 'The Friday Club'. *Burlington Magazine* 117.866 (May 1975): 278–84.

Spalding, Frances. *Roger Fry: Art and Life*. Berkeley: U of California P, 1980.

Spalding, Frances. *Vanessa Bell*. New Haven: Ticknor & Fields, 1983.

Strachey, Lytton. *The Letters of Lytton Strachey*. Ed. Paul Levy. New York: Farrar Straus & Giroux, 2005.

Twitchell, Beverly H. *Cézanne and Formalism in Bloomsbury*. Ann Arbor: UMI Research P, 1987. Rev. of 1983 PhD dissertation, SUNY Binghamton.

Warburton, Nigel. *The Art Question*. New York: Routledge, 2003.

Woolf, Virginia. *The Letters of Virginia Woolf*, Vol. 1. Ed. Nigel Nicolson. Hogarth, 1975.

Woolf, Virginia. 'Modern Novels'. *Essays*, Vol. 3. Harcourt, 1988 [1919].

Zangwill, Nick. 'Feasible Aesthetic Formalism'. *Noûs* 33 (1999): 610–29.

CHAPTER THREE

Bloomsbury and Empire

SONITA SARKER

In the title of this section, 'Bloomsbury' as signifier for 'the group' performs a metonymic sleight-of-hand that bestows a certain power on the latter, as if Bloomsbury can only be a reference to 'the group'. It also carries the risk of collapsing, or at least confusing, past, present, and future. While Bloomsbury (the place) still exists, the group (the people) and Empire (the system and structure) are physically no longer here. Bloomsbury, then as now ... is alive; it is a place that, in the past, generated and nurtured a group, and then becomes a concept. Empire is ... dead; it is a concept that is made manifest in places. To resuscitate a pastness may mean to some degree, almost unavoidably, to conjure up the aura around both group and Empire and, paradoxically, to render their significance timeless and thus transcendent.

More accurately, then, the section title would be 'The Bloomsbury Group and (the British) Empire'. This chapter reanimates the corpus of a group in/and empire by foregrounding historicity, that is, particular moments in their contexts, and through those instances, reveals certain key refractions that the members negotiated. The focus on historicity, in Section 1, makes possible an exploration of both group and Empire as dynamic organisms in their own time and as cultural artefacts in later eras. Historicity also enables particularity to counter the aura often ascribed to, or assumed about, the group. In addition, historicity ties the phenomenon of Bloomsbury to time and place, not to render it mundane but to anchor the reverence as well as to appreciate both the transience of the group and as its continued life.

With such a title as 'Bloomsbury and Empire' for this chapter, one temptation may be to present Empire as infusing and explaining all facets of the members' lives. As the last part of Section 1 briefly addresses, in actuality, the imperial permeates the quotidian and yet is obscured in the group members' accounts of their personal lives and in many of their work lives. Sections 2 and 3 stop at the word 'Empire' and reflect upon how white Britishness (translated as national identity) informs the Bloomsbury Group ethos and how that intersects with a correlative white-identified Englishness (cultural affiliation) to qualify their cosmopolitan reputation.

An ensuing temptation may be to present the group as a microcosmal reflection of the British Empire, as if the members were transparent subjects. This particular kind of cosmopolitanism camouflages the many political, racialized, and gendered disjunctures and unevennesses that characterize the group. One such disjuncture is that most of the male members, already adherents of exclusive societies at elite academic institutions (from which the female group members were excluded) were also pacifists, conscientious objectors, and former civil servants who were critics of their empire and of their nation at war. Section 4 takes a closer look at the ways in which opposition to war is not necessarily accompanied by a divestment from imperialism; Section 5 scrutinizes another disjuncture – the position of the group in an Empire that defines itself as a liberal democracy, a position in which the group's privileges and freedoms derive from their status as white natives and citizens, even as, internally, this status is differentially experienced. Section 6 illustrates how the resuscitations of the Bloomsbury Group in television mini-serials or in films hardly refer to Empire as a constitutive category of the group members' lives. British and other intellectual and media industries, as custodians of heritage, legislate insiders and outsiders, directly or indirectly. They constitute a cultural hegemony that, while more nebulous than the Empire of old, establishes normative values for the accidental visitor, the indifferent or curious tourist, and the academic specialist alike, but by largely absenting Empire.

SECTION 1: HISTORICITY, PARTICULARITY, LOCALITY

Britain births the Bloomsbury Group. Like the British Empire, the group comes into being gradually, but grows while the Empire wanes. At the turn of the twentieth century, the conditions that inform these counter-trajectories in early twentieth-century modernity are paradoxical: for one, democratic ideals and imperial rule generate both the conscription of colonial subjects in the two World Wars and rising resistance in Britain's colonies. For another, the expansion of nation-state based free market liberal capitalism is coterminous with the rise of international socialist and women's movements.

The workings of Empire and Nation as ecosystems within these coexisting counter-forces are reflected to some degree as well as refracted in the formation of the Bloomsbury Group. In the era of minoritized gender, class, and race struggle, perceived and received divisions between 'high' and 'low' culture and revolutionary art, the group issues manifestos on all these matters at the same time as it disavows its status as an entity with any social or political significance. Leonard Woolf recalls in *Beginning Again* that while there have been 'writers and artists, who were not only friends, but were consciously united by a common function ... or purpose ... [such as the] utilitarians, the Lake poets, the French impressionists, the English Pre-Raphaelites [were] ... [their] group was quite different. Its basis was friendship, which in some cases developed into love and marriage' (25). A deep influence upon the lives of others that the group actually comes to have, is simultaneous with this claim to an apolitical set of universal values (friendship, love and marriage), and this simulates a power akin to an imperial ideological tactic. In Leonard Woolf's observations, the frames of reference, English and French, reveal this particular member's standards of aesthetic and social value while, in turn, the group's own influence spans the globe. To take another horizon of references, the group's contemporaries that have 'a common function ... or purpose' include the Women's League, the Women's Cooperative Guild, and the Men's Association, dedicated to the political and economic rights of working-class British citizens. There are cultural and social groups such as the Neo-Pagans and the Memoir Club. Other labels also carry a particular kind of weight, words such as collective, set, tribe or 'clique, coterie, gang, clan, commune, and mafia' (Rosenbaum i). In comparison, 'group' does not indicate any loyalty explicitly and, in effect, masks any particular class identity or political affiliation or philosophical grounding.[1]

One way to negotiate this personal-local but also diffuse sense that Leonard Woolf depicts is to visualize the Bloomsbury Group as a cohering and also metamorphosing organism.

While cohesion ordinarily implies the accumulation of political and social power, so, in some cases and contexts, does fluidity. The ability to merge and transition across groups, absorbing and adjusting, gives the Bloomsbury Group the prolonged life that it has across eras of changes in imperial British power. Many of the most prominent male members had belonged to other groups before being 'Bloomsberries', as affectionately dubbed by Molly MacCarthy, around 1910 or 1911 (Bell, *Old Friends*). Many of the young men were at King's College and Trinity College, institutions that were often training grounds for future officials of the British Empire (Rich 1989). The Cambridge University's Conversazione Society (the Apostles) bonded around G. E. Moore's philosophy, and a lifestyle of free intellectual exchange and homosexual relationships (see Avery in this volume). John Maynard Keynes also belonged to the Pitt Club (Cambridge) and there was the Midnight Society (the origin of the Bloomsbury Group, according to Clive Bell), the X Society (Cambridge), and the 1917 Club, created by Leonard Woolf who was also part of the Fabian Society. The deep and broad network demonstrates the origins of the Bloomsbury Group that manifests homosociality, an aspect that is not exclusive to, but characterizes, the British Empire.

Altering, for a moment, the title of this chapter from 'Bloomsbury and Empire' to 'The Bloomsbury Group IN Empire' reminds us of these particularities as well as the mutually informed relationship between the place and the people. Where the British Empire converges with the English Nation, the Bloomsbury Group travels between urban and rural locales that ground their identities (see Jones in this volume). 'Bloomsbury in Empire' could read 'Bloomsbury in England' since England is the specific centre of Empire. It could furthermore read 'Bloomsbury in London' as an even more accurate signifier for the locale, emblematic of England's national urban-bohemian modern culture in which the group's members hold property as they do in the country. In these material ways, British nationalism claims both urban intellectual modernity as well as rural tradition as unique emblems of its imperial-democratic identity.

A visceral articulation that underscores the local nature of the Bloomsbury Group is their very manner of articulation, namely, their accent. Osbert Sitwell in *Laughter in the Next Room* (1949) describes the members' voice and phraseology as arising 'on a basis of clan ... that characteristic *regional* way of speaking ... as rare and ritualistic outside the bounds of West Central London as the state voice of the Emperor of China beyond his pleasances and palaces' (qtd in Rosenbaum 251; emphasis added). Sitwell imagines, referring to 'experts', that this accent, originating in the Strachey family, took many 'captive ... acclimatising itself first in the *haute vie intellectuelle* of King's College, Cambridge' and then having 'marched on London, prospering particularly in Gordon and Mecklenburgh Squares and in the neighbouring sooty piazzas, and possessing affiliations, too, in certain country districts' (qtd in Rosenbaum 251). It is at least of passing interest that Sitwell compares this local-made-universal English nativeness with local-made-imperial Chinese, and links it to both urban and rural English traditions, which are then universalized through imperial circuits in early twentieth-century globalization.

Much like Sitwell's analogies of the English urban-rural with the Chinese imperial, the title of Leonard Woolf's *The Village in the Jungle* (1913) carries a curious link between the topography and locality of the 'other' (Ceylon/Sri Lanka in this case) and the particularity of Bloomsbury, which becomes an English village-like community in the urban 'jungle' of London. Also in his *Beginning Again*, Woolf recollects that he finds, in Cambridge an 'unchanged and unchanging' set of values to which he had given 'the love or loyalty of youth' before leaving for Ceylon, and returns from Ceylon to Gordon Square, into 'a society which had completely changed since [he] left it seven years before, but in which [he] found [himself] immediately and completely at home' (26). In 1904, Leonard Woolf had taken the Civil Service examination and gone to Ceylon as a cadet in the Ceylon Civil Service; his resignation from the Civil Service came in 1912, and he visited Ceylon (independent Sri Lanka) much later, in the 1960s. Woolf frames these years in terms of his time before and after Ceylon – the distant colonial geography symbolizes and informs his work and identity as much as colonial Bloomsbury. Ceylon and Bloomsbury define each other, not only on a factual basis, but also in values such as love and loyalty. In contrast, the very physical attributes of locality shape an inalienably essential nature and intellect, the basis of absolute difference, as evident in his observations: 'The colour of our minds and thought had been given to us by the climate of Cambridge and Moore's philosophy, much as the climate of England gives one colour to the face of an Englishman while the climate of India [113] gives a quite different colour to the face of a Tamil' (qtd in Rosenbaum 25–6).

Bloomsbury, which signifies this national-local project as well as the place, becomes 'more than a local phenomenon, or even an international one in the uncontested modernist sense … [even] worldly in another sense – that is, global in its resonances, a site of cultural contact and contestation where both canonical high modernisms and an emergent anti-colonial modernism take shape' (Blair 814). Describing London as 'an exemplary global city' (Blair 817) at once underscores its imperial history (its 'global' identity rests upon its colonial past) and obscures its neocolonial/postimperial power that maintains an international reach. My emphasis in this discussion is rather on the idea that 'high modernism' and 'anti-colonial modernism' are not only simultaneous but actually constitutive of each other, and furthermore on Bloomsbury as emblematic of the Englishness of Empire, in ways that are analogous to the Left Bank as quintessentially Parisian and representatively French.

It is also possible to contemplate the Bloomsbury Group *sans* Empire. The 'and' in 'Bloomsbury and Empire' may imply an additive to Bloomsbury or it can be read as a signifier that the Bloomsbury Group and Empire cannot be extricated from each other. It is tempting indeed to assert that Bloomsburians cannot but be seen as imperial subjects. Then what would it mean to analyse it without Empire? The group's contributions in art, economics, literature, and politics differentially connect the Bloomsburians to imperialism; at the same time, being an imperial subject does not mean that each Bloomsbury Group member addresses every matter as grounded in imperial politics. Certainly Leonard Woolf as colonial officer in Ceylon, Maynard Keynes in the British Civil Service, and E. M. Forster as private secretary to an Indian feudal lord, Tukojirao III (Maharaja of Dewas), are most directly experienced in Empire. However, that politics is not fully and always present in their quotidian personal transactions (domestic matters, property ownership) or professional work, especially in art and art critique, as evident in Roger Fry's, Vanessa Bell's, and Duncan Grant's works.

SECTION 2: THE WHITE BRITISHNESS OF EMPIRE

Across the range of engagement, from deep and direct experience with the matters and milieux of the British Empire (in the colonies and in the centre) to lively curiosity towards those perceived as 'other' in empire, to an almost complete absence of address to empire, a differential experience but shared understanding of whiteness informs the various positions of the members of the Bloomsbury Group. Both the historicity and particularity of the moment (time) and situation (space) of the Bloomsbury Group illuminates the Britishness of this Empire, a concept that can only gain substance and meaning when compared with other competing Empires, such as the French or the Dutch or the Italian (Jarboe and Fogarty). The particularity also implies that the expressions of the members of the Bloomsbury Group formulate a certain experience of whiteness in/of the British Empire. Two features emerge in their social, artistic, literary, and political enactments: one, while 'race' refers to skin colour (e.g. 'black'), it also signifies civilizational-cultural identity (e.g. 'Chinese') and two, there is a distinction between the ways in which civilizations-cultures inside the British Empire (e.g. India) and those outside it are invoked (e.g. Abyssinia). In both features, the 'other' is marked explicitly by their colour in every encounter; this insistence itself consolidates an unmarked, and thus implicit, British whiteness.

This absent-but-always-present British whiteness informs the unique nature of the Bloomsbury Group's orientalism. For instance, when referring to Black identity in the United States, Virginia Woolf uses 'black' and the 'n' word to signify skin colour, but 'savage' and 'native' for (perceived lack of) the cultural histories of black peoples in Africa and brown peoples in Asia. Her use of the word 'jew'/'Jew' or 'jewess' carries connotations of inferiority when referring to the Portuguese but invokes an unlocated cultural difference in a condescending and familiar tone when referring to her husband Leonard Woolf and his family (see Wegener in this volume). Leena Kore Schröder comments: 'when Virginia Woolf writes about "the Jew", she is always also writing about her own self' (312). In each instance, including references to the 'jew', this 'self' is a British (Anglo-Saxon) whiteness that remains unmarked but is reasserted implicitly as the basis of her observations.[2] In comparison, China holds a unique place in the group's view – since China is not directly under British imperial rule and itself claims an imperial glory, its peoples are described only as Chinese, 'strange' in some social customs (as Virginia Woolf writes to Ling Shuhua, the Chinese writer who had an affair with Julian Bell), but not referred to in terms of skin colour. The word 'strange' directly underscores Chinese otherness and simultaneously but indirectly inscribes Woolf's own British difference, again not with reference to skin colour but to a normative cultural standard that is associated with (white) Britishness.[3]

British whiteness is instantiated *in absentia* not only in observation but also through participation. The Dreadnought hoax (1910), involving some members of what became the Bloomsbury Group (Adrian Stephen, then Virginia Stephen, and Duncan Grant), has been read primarily as making a mockery of what was then awe-inspiring and seemingly invincible British imperial naval power, and exposing its inefficiency and bumbling bureaucracy (see Snaith in this volume). There have been analyses of blackface, the scandalous prank that is the talk of the town, and their genteel apology that has no negative consequences; these analyses have also emphasized the young Virginia Stephen's anti-colonialist sentiments as well as gender- and race-awareness (see Kennard; Reid; Johnston; and Jones).[4] 'Race' is not only about locating the 'other' but also about the ways in which simulating otherness underscores the group's own whiteness, a national difference that is imbued with privilege.[5] Adrian Stephen, in his account, speaks matter-of-factly about having the faces of those playing the Emperor of Abyssinia and his entourage 'blackened … [wearing] fake beards and moustaches and elaborate Eastern robes … and a little sunburn powder' (qtd in Rosenbaum 34). While he expresses benign ignorance of where Swahili is spoken, he boasts that the newspapers recounted him talking 'fluent Abyssinian' while he also confesses that he did not find it easy to speak 'fluent gibberish impromptu' (qtd in Rosenbaum 36). 'Gibberish' is mixed with boyhood classical Greek grammar (derived from a British schooling) to pull off a prank; Adrian Stephen expresses relief that the one man who could catch them out was on leave and satisfaction that the national anthem of Zanzibar played because the 'band-master had been unable to get a copy of the Abyssinian National Anthem' (qtd in Rosenbaum 38). He says proudly that one of the published interviews quoted a shop assistant that 'Bunga-Bunga' 'became public catchwords for a time, and were introduced as tags into music-hall songs and so forth', and follows it with an apology about the entire incident since they had 'no wish to make anyone really uncomfortable' (qtd in Rosenbaum 40).

The target of the hoax is to expose the weakness of British authority but not to advocate for any cause related to the oppressed in Ethiopia. The 'other' is addressed in two ways: one, by conflating various cultural norms and languages from that region and substituting distinctly different forms for another (Zanzibar instead of Abyssinia!), thus homogenizing the 'other', and boasting of their English college education as providing a fake vocabulary. A second way is to create a negative space – the people they are mimicking are not addressed at all and become mere shells of costumes to don and discard. Their apology is made to the British officer, not the persons whom they imitate. There is also misrecognition of 'Abyssinia' (Ethiopia) in relation to Italian colonialism and of Italy itself an aspiring empire in this era. Much later, in 1940, Virginia Woolf reads a paper about the Dreadnought hoax to the Women's Institute in Rodmell and then at the Memoir Club, and writes the short story, 'A Society', thus translocating a potentially formative incident into a nostalgic narrative about a group of friends.

SECTION 3: NATIONALLY BRITISH, CULTURALLY ENGLISH

This section reveals another layer of whiteness beneath the one discussed above by addressing a question that further expands the chapter title: 'How is the Bloomsbury Group part of the British Empire?' This section also asks 'How does the Bloomsbury Group see itself as part of the British Empire?', drawing attention to their self-representations rather than only to their relationships with citizens/aliens and objects of the British Empire and beyond.

In the early twentieth-century British imperial capitalist modernity that forms the context for the Bloomsbury Group, whiteness is not a category but a series of relationships. The fault lines of race/ethnicity appear unevenly in the relationship with various 'others' – the otherness of Jewishness inside the world of Bloomsbury is distinct from the otherness of colonial subjects from Africa and Asia, and also discrete from the otherness from North America, South America, and Western Europe, as described briefly in the section above. Some 'others' are not aligned along the same lines or on the same basis (China or Egypt as ancient civilizations).[6] Among Bloomsburians, cultural Englishness is secured in relations of contradistinction from these various others. In this discussion, Britishness refers to the national and political identity in empire (implicitly white, as analysed above), and Englishness to the related cultural and social heritages of the Bloomsbury Group. Englishness is manifested not in an ineffable essence but rather through its materiality, namely in its rural and urban geography. Virginia Woolf often invokes the classic nature of these landscapes, invoking Thomas Hardy's quintessential descriptions of the English countryside. Even when away from England, on trips mostly to the European continent, she asserts an Englishness by marking out other English people, visible to her in their whiteness or in their manner or their accents (one assumes), or by comparing those foreign lands negatively to an England invoked with longing.

Englishness is generated also through gendered institutions such as the school, the army, and the civil service as it is through institutionalized structures of English literature and philosophy. The more-well-known male members of the Bloomsbury Group – Clive Bell, Lytton Strachey, Saxon Sydney-Turner, Leonard Woolf, E. M. Forster, Desmond MacCarthy, Roger Fry, and John Maynard Keynes – attend the most famed and traditionally English schools, like Eton and Harrow, Cambridge and Oxford, that send out officers to the colonies, and some of which Virginia Woolf calls 'the sausage machine' in a letter written on 10 June 1938 to Viscountess Rhondda (*Letters* 6: 236–7).[7] In that same letter, Woolf comments on a collective gendered position as outsiders, an exclusion that becomes an advantage in *Three Guineas* (also 1938). While there were some women's colleges, none of the prominent female Bloomsbury Group members attend such institutions of formal education. Woolf, for one, is able to range far and free and wide in her father's library at home instead, exploring English heritage.[8] Compare this gendered, classed, and racialized status with that of contemporary women from the colonies who attend institutions of higher education in England, such as Cornelia Sorabji (Burton; Boehmer).

This uneven sense of access and inclusion, based on gender difference, does not affect group members' individual sense of being culturally English; this sense of belonging, however, obscures some of the male Bloomsburians' lineages or early formative stages (Duncan Grant, Lytton Strachey) and casts professional experiences in the British colonies (Leonard Woolf) as not constitutive of their racial-cultural identity.[9] In both the assumed equivalences and actual schisms between nation and culture (I say more about this below), being English and British are coded white, economically independent, morally and intellectually virile, while also resistant to hegemonically heteromasculine sexual mores. Like imperialism, this code of cultural membership can be deciphered to a greater degree through contrast of their unqualified and uncontested citizenship with that of other imperial subjects.[10]

SECTION 4: OPPOSITION, INDEPENDENCE

English spells modern as it does white. In the group's literary, artistic, economic, and political manifestos, 'modern' (the new vs. the old) intersects with 'modernity' (especially in the concept of autonomy) most prominently in the notion of revolt and independence. Situating the group's revolt in context and scale, across concentric circles of family, fraternity, nation, and empire brings us to the feature that is crucial to the nature of their opposition – that antiwar dissidence does not also signify divestments of nation and empire.

Revolt begins in a living room. The Bloomsbury Group, as such, begins to meet on Thursday evenings in 1905 in the 'drawing room' of the Stephen siblings' new house in Gordon Square where they find freedom and self-determination in moving from the rigidly controlled patriarchal household in Hyde Park Gate. Vanessa Bell is described as 'a madonna with a sense of humour' who creates 'a feminine atmosphere without the false obligations created by convention', refreshingly different from the exclusively masculine society at college and the 'polite and inconsequential chatter of their mothers and sisters' (Noble 82–8). Raymond Mortimer's 1928 account as well as Leonard Woolf's autobiography both insist on the modest and apolitical origins of the familial (siblings, parents, wives, and husbands), the fraternal (college contemporaries) and the intimate (multiply crossing sexual relationships) that collect into a revolutionary force (Rosenbaum 242). This gathering hosted by two young, attractive, socially rebellious sisters renders modern the Western European Enlightenment legacy of the salon, through the inherited spaces of middle-class Victorian settings that were often the founts of cultural and political change. This urban domestic space of the Bloomsbury Group, bolstered by economic independence, straddles the private and the public, the former in the familial and domestic, and the latter in that they are formed by citizens who become the social as well as cultural draw of the metropolis; the living room/salon becomes the destination for the 'brightest minds', locals and cosmopolitans alike. These spaces and their inhabitants are formed by the material conditions of early twentieth-century modernity, of which globalization is the condition and colonialism is the vehicle.

The modernness of the Bloomsbury Group is also expressed through their rejection of their predecessors in culture, politics, and philosophy. In 'Hyde Park Gate', Virginia Woolf declares that 'everything was going to be new; everything was going to be different. Everything was on trial' (163–4). Leonard Woolf records in *Sowing* how, in the last days of Queen Victoria, they felt they were not only in revolt against 'bourgeois Victorianism', living in times of revolt against existing systems, but even that it was his 'right ... [his] duty to question the truth of everything and the authority of everyone, to regard nothing as sacred and to hold nothing in religious respect' (qtd in Rosenbaum 106–7). He attributes this attitude to the climate of scepticism and to G. E. Moore's philosophy. John Maynard Keynes similarly expresses a faith, 'violently and aggressively held, and for the outer world ... [their] most ... dangerous characteristic', in their uncompromising ability to repudiate 'customary morals, conventions and traditional wisdom', and describes the group members as 'immoralists' in taking this stand (qtd in Rosenbaum 61).[11] The group's newness and nowness, their modernness in this very rejection, reads quite differently when one takes into consideration their location within Empire. The intellectual and the philosophical legacies of the group have been mostly inserted into the frame of national literary-cultural politics, namely the Edwardian vs. Georgians in the movement from Victorian to Modern. However, in the wider context of imperial relations, Edwardian and Georgian, like Victorian, are monikers of imperial rule in the colonies, marking transition and change in those sites, as much as in London particularly or England generally. In short, Empire binds the Moderns to the Victorians.

The critique and repudiation of British cultural legacy by many members of the Bloomsbury Group actually expresses, I would argue, an irreducible Englishness, in the specific senses of belonging or birth right or cultural citizenship. Virginia Woolf's volumes of essays focus on major figures in English literature; in her evaluation, Joseph Conrad is recognized as influential, alongside Jane Austen and Thomas Hardy, but marked ultimately, as a Pole, an outsider. Bloomsburians variously disavow citizenship, based in political commitment, as Virginia Woolf does in *Three Guineas*; however neither she nor the others of the group suffer the risks or consequences of being stripped of it or denied it as might a colonial subject. Repudiation of the old (a feature of modernness) and assertion of autonomy (a crucial element of modernity) are actually shared by anti-colonial and proindependence subjects across the British Empire but with different consequences for them. When read in a larger context of revolt and rejection of tradition or hegemonic frameworks, the scale and nature of the Bloomsbury Group's revolutionary impetus can appear in perspective. When Clive Bell in *Civilization* says that the Englishman is 'less free than a Roman slave' (4), he uses 'slave' as a metaphor when slaves actually do exist in the British Empire during his time; second, he refers to a past empire with an analogy that cannot be proven; and third, 'less free' is relative, if one compares the outcomes for the group with the harsh consequences of dissent – incarceration, torture, death – for contemporary colonial subjects.

Members of the Bloomsbury Group, while rising up against the cultural and political regimes of their predecessors still benefit from both the moral and the material property, even in their disaffiliations. Economic independence, not economic disenfranchisement, allows for selective opposition as well as selective ownership of national politics and culture.[12] Their identity as reluctant inheritors of the heritage of literature and politics is counterbalanced by their ownership of property in the city and the country.[13] This basis of ownership supports their independent artistic and literary endeavours, including the ability to have space and decision-making powers, such as over the Hogarth Press (started in 1917). The power of the Hogarth Press extends across the British Empire and beyond, in a manner that depends upon imperial networks even as it publishes many anti-Imperial texts: for instance, it publishes members of the group, some American, Russian, and other British authors; South African William Plomer's *Sado* and *Paper Houses*, the Indian G. S. Dutt on Sarojini Naidu in 1929, the Caribbean C. L. R. James in 1933, Ahmed Ali (from then India, now Pakistan) in 1940, and the Chinese Ling Su Hua in 1953 (Snaith; Young).

Far from being ostracized or targeted or persecuted for their opposition to systems and values that made their very existence possible, the group gradually coheres in its public identity, becoming a particular barometer of the tumultuous times. It ultimately becomes a constellation of arbiters, even promoters, of social and cultural value. The range of connections between the group and the structures of Empire is significant – from the technical/administrative link (as evinced in Keynes's economic treatises and Leonard Woolf's political essays) to the sociocultural consumer/producer link (in many members' nonfiction social commentary and literary output) to the artistic, which is often tenuously and contingently linked to anti/imperialism, as in Fry's case. To take Keynes's case: in 1905, he joins the India Office and in 1908, he leaves the Civil Service. In 1913, he publishes *Indian Currency and Finance*; in 1919, *The Economic Consequences of the Peace'*, and leaves an indelible mark on theories and practices of liberal economies.

Leonard Woolf's administrative career in the British Empire reveals both commitment to and ambivalence about its values. In 1917, Woolf edits *The Framework of a Lasting Peace*, founds the 1917 Club, and starts as secretary to the Labour party advisory committees on International Affairs and Imperial Questions, a position he holds for more than twenty years, and shapes policies for African colonies. Could colonial administration be conducted with sympathy and humanity? It would seem that Leonard Woolf did not oppose the structure of empire but had rather a dispute with the means of delivering the structure; this sits interestingly in relation to other antiwar protests in which there is an opposition to the structure and mission itself. Leonard Woolf's part in creating the League of Nations ultimately signals the turn from Empire to colonies-as-nations.

At times, Bloomsbury Group members' opposition is defined by the separation of English culture from British nationalism, the latter in the country's participation in the World Wars; Roger Fry and Virginia Woolf do so, though for different reasons. At other times, as Leonard Woolf does, they tie the values of English culture to the political structure of the nation, the crucible for which is Empire. Various commentators on the Bloomsbury Group encountering the global conflicts of their times describe their collective journey from considering their lives 'au dessus de la melee [as] untenable' to participation as well as pacifism, from demonstrating solidarity with the working class to being disillusioned by the deception that their own governments commit (qtd in Rosenbaum 311).[14] Both World Wars change many things, but neither being a pacifist nor a conscientious objector connects or leads in a straight line to arguing for the dismantling of empire; theirs is not an advocacy of the rights to liberty of the colonized nor even a reference to the colonized as individuals, except through the sponsorship of the Hogarth Press or, individually, in Leonard Woolf's case because of his direct experience in the Civil Service, as secretary to the Labour party advisory committees on International Affairs and Imperial Questions, and in creating the League of Nations. Ultimately, their position is not a rejection of the structures of Empire itself, the structures from which they derive their identity and the benefits that support their self-fashioning.[15]

SECTION 5: POWER INSIDE AND ACROSS BORDERS

The Bloomsbury Group's liberal philosophy and casual social power camouflage the intangible borders created by belonging through English nativeness, borders that give the group an inside and an outside. Leonard Woolf, as cited above, distinguishes his group of friends from others in claiming that they had 'no common theory, system, or principles ... to convert the world to [and that they] were not proselytisers, missionaries, crusaders, or even propagandists' (25). However, he continues on to mention the impact of Keynes's economic theory and the Fry-Bells-Grant complex regarding Post-Impressionism; these examples cancel the disavowal of influence. Similarly, Virginia Woolf addresses the Memoir Club in 1922, musing: 'What is Bloomsbury? ... where does [it] end ... where does it begin? ... What are the qualities that admit one to it, what are the qualities that expel one from it?' ('Old Bloomsbury' 199). Once again, the very claim to diffuseness, contradicting the phrases 'admit one to' and 'expel one from', underscore this very inside-outside. Much later, in 1980, Leon Edel writes, 'Bloomsbury friends were linked by old ties, old sympathies, old loyalties, old habits of thought, common opinions' (284). This portrait of a seemingly accessible and familial crowd is still characterized by generations of social and political intimacy, barely concealing a national-racial kinship that could not have been shared by other imperial subjects, whether inside or outside England.

Despite these and other disavowals, borders also mean coherence, somewhat uneven as that coherence may be, given that, as I have mentioned above, natives/insiders are not positioned equally in all aspects to one another. The unevenness in the group's attitudes, I would argue, relates to contradictory sociopolitical forces. The formal waning of the British Empire is accompanied by the anxieties generated by both World Wars about English 'civilization' and is coterminous with England's prominence on the global stage of militarized relations as well as with the rise of global liberal capitalism, both derived from imperial power.[16] In this context, the group's self-presentation as a casual company of friends masks a philosophical lineage that moves from binding family to empire (from Virginia Woolf's grandfather, James Stephen), to dissociation between civilization and empire (in various members' writings), to an argument featured in Clive Bell's *Civilization* (1928) that 'slaves' or servants are necessary to produce 'the surplus time and energy' for the existence of a leisured class which is required to carry civilization through.[17]

Leonard Woolf's career and publications serve as a microcosm of some of the changes in position expressed by the group collectively. In his first anti-Imperial publications, the notion of political as well as economic hierarchy is intrinsic to his understanding of civilization. However, his anti-Imperialism remains ambivalent since he also expresses a refusal to bow to the colonial mission, showing both sympathy and distance from the Sinhalese 'native', while arguing for self-government in Asia and Africa.[18]

Through these internal and external asymmetries, the group relates unevenly to a range of classed and racialized 'others', whether they are the 'masses' or visitors to Bloomsbury or the cultures-civilizations of 'the Orient'.[19] To take the 'masses' first: early twentieth-century modernity generates the 'group' and also the very notion of the 'masses' in new ways (including the working class as well as peoples of the British colonies). Such simultaneous distinctions between 'high' and 'low' culture, and the elites and the commoners affect the boundaries that the group places around itself. Many members of the group are aware and also ambivalent about their class privilege, burdened as they are with an implicit understanding of the benefits of education and cultural difference; culture here could stand as code for racialized, classed, and differently gendered/sexualized identities. Many of the members of the group wrote for leading and diverse publications such as the *Times Literary Supplement* and *Good Housekeeping*, drawing in the highbrow and the middlebrow. Leonard Woolf's work with The Workers Educational Association and Virginia Woolf's teaching literature at Morley College in London and meeting with the Women's Cooperative Guild were efforts, as she put it, to reach 'a far wider circle than a little private circle of exquisite and cultivated people … to make *humanity in the mass* appreciate what they knew and saw' (italics added).[20]

In its relationships to yet other 'others', the group's selective and various conflations and separations of war, civilization, and empire inform their uneven orientalism regarding China, Japan, and Egypt (imperial civilizations in Asia and Africa not under British imperial rule), and parts of England's colonies in both those continents (overtaking previous indigenous imperial civilization). The 'Orient' as a racial/cultural signifier that carries difference is incorporated into the Bloomsbury Group's worldview through translation (language acquisition), cultural familiarity (public service, visits, and collaborations), and a consumerism that is also coloured by a respect for ancient and proud cultures. The work of translation draws in several languages that are part of as well as outside the British Empire: French, Chinese, Japanese, and Russian as directly taken on by members of the group, and Farsi, Urdu, Hindi, and Bengali, as spoken by colonial subjects. Virginia Woolf's correspondence and literary relationships with a range of writers – from Ling Shu-Hua (China), Victoria Ocampo (Argentina), and Katherine Mansfield (New Zealand) to name only a few – spans the globe. Cultural familiarity is built through work in foreign lands, participation in artistic collaboration inside the group, or through academic study – for instance, E. M. Forster's service in the Red Cross as a volunteer officer in Egypt produces his *Alexandria: A History and a Guide* (1922) and *Pharos and Pharillon* (1923); Duncan Grant, Vanessa Bell, and Roger Fry are involved in drawing the title page for Waley's translation of *Monkey* (1942), a Chinese work of fiction; and Roger Fry in his *Last Lectures* writes about Egyptian, Mesopotamian and Aegean, Negro, American, Chinese, Indian, and Greek art.

At times, Orientalism means a reference to what the English deem as savagery and primitivism. In the foreword to 'Recent Paintings by Vanessa Bell' (1930), Virginia Woolf includes both an unnamed woman and an anonymous native in her sardonic conjecture about the morally and sexually circumscribed life of a spinster in Victorian families, each of which

> has in its cupboard the skeleton of an aunt who was driven to convert the native because her father would have died rather than let her look upon a naked man. And so she went to Church; and so she went to China; and so she died unwed (qtd in Rosenbaum 170).

There are many offhand references to 'negroes' in America and 'savages' in Asia strewn across her letters to English women and men of letters. This approach extends to her record of objects in Roger Fry's room, chronicled in *Roger Fry: A Biography*; her eye scans

> the Derain picture ... the blue Matisse ... the negro masks and the Chinese statues ... the rare Persian china and the cheap peasant pottery that he had picked up for a farthing at a fair (qtd in Rosenbaum 134).

Virginia Woolf's comment on the range of European, rural English, African, and Asian objects flattens their relationships in the global economic and political circuits, and camouflages the power of the consumer/owner to possess objects from across the world, as happened in the Dreadnought hoax.

At other times, there is a dismissal or erasure of other cultures as valid or even comparable to British civilizational achievements and, in odd conjunction, an unqualified praise that romanticizes the 'native' and obscures the asymmetry of power. In *Old Friends: Personal Recollections*, Clive Bell prefaces his friend Roger Fry's dismissal of an entire corpus of 'oriental' art by emphasizing the latter's 'open-mindedness and integrity ... [in relation to] his slightly biased approach to works of art', adding at the same time that Fry had 'always . . . disliked Indian art: it offended his sense of reasonableness and his taste' (qtd in Rosenbaum 146). In contrast, Leonard Woolf, in *Beginning Again*, ties artistic and aesthetic appreciation to the colonized; he records how, while staffing Roger Fry's Post-Impressionist exhibition, he thinks longingly 'how much nicer were the Tamil or Sinhalese villagers who crowded into the veranda of my Ceylon kachcheri than these ... incorrigibly philistine ... smug, well dressed, ill-mannered, well-to-do Londoners ... [in their] rank stupidity and uncharitableness' (94).

To stand, for one moment, in the shoes of those 'others', not the Sinhalese villagers perhaps but those of various South Asian and South American cosmopolitans, provides the image in the mirror, that is, how the Bloomsbury Group is perceived by these 'others'. Victoria Ocampo (Argentina), Cornelia Sorabji (India), Mulk Raj Anand (also from India) are connected to the Bloomsbury Group through Virginia Woolf, Lydia Lopokova (Russia) is drawn in by marriage to John Maynard Keynes, and William Plomer (South Africa) and many others, British and foreign, are linked through the Hogarth Press. To depict the perspective of only one such 'other': Mulk Raj Anand self-consciously styles himself not merely as a 'Eur-Asian' from India, or a colonial subject in exile, but 'in effect – a Bloomsberry' (Blair 831). While he goes against Bloomsbury pacifism by joining the Republicans against Franco, he returns as BBC broadcaster and a writer of film scripts, 'sustaining his engagement with a cultural industry indebted to the legacy of Bloomsbury' (Blair 832). Anand writes in the 1980 preface to *Conversations in Bloomsbury*: 'Not only did I learn to indulge in dangerous thoughts in Bloomsbury, but I began a love affair with life which has lasted till today' (6).

When read by imperial subjects such as Mulk Raj Anand who claim a place in the Bloomsbury Group, the 'and' in 'Bloomsbury and Empire' appears redundant. To them,

Bloomsbury *is* Empire, that is to say, it represents imperial power; that perception appears to colour Anand's aspiration: to claim to be a Bloomsberry is also a claim to belonging in Empire. To Cornelia Sorabji, a Parsi-Christian student of law at Somerville (at the same time that Virginia Woolf was not allowed to attend similar institutions) and an ardent Anglophile, Bloomsbury Group members were part of her social circles which also included other litterateurs, lawyers, and government officials. Victoria Ocampo's literary relationship with Virginia Woolf is well documented; here, I note that her presence, in juxtaposition with those of Anand, Sorabji, Plomer, Lopokova, and many prominent and celebrated personages, illuminates the reality that 'others' were heterogeneous in their various privileges and marginalities. They view the Bloomsbury Group as a social group that is representatively English, as much an object of contemplation to them as they themselves are to the group.

SECTION 6: LIFE THEN. DEATH. LIFE NOW

Across the twentieth and twenty-first centuries, the Bloomsbury Group metamorphoses from familial and fraternal company to British cultural icon, through the global circulation of dominant knowledges across colonial and neocolonial routes of education and commerce. However, latter-day representations continue to frame the icon in terms of the family, maintaining the emphasis in the group's self-descriptions in which social, economic, cultural, and political exigencies fade from view, as discussed above.[21] In the macro-view of the early twentieth century, empire is structurally tangible; and in a postimperial condition (which I would term neocolonial), the tangible disappears and structures become diffuse in the cycles of cultural commodification.

Starting with Death. Vanessa Bell, in 'Notes on Bloomsbury', chronicles how war causes 'a dispersal and general scattering' of the group's members but also notes how they do reconvene and carry on through early twentieth-century turmoil (qtd in Rosenbaum 83). The actual demise of the group occurs through the successive deaths of its members – Clive Bell in 1964, Leonard Woolf in 1969, and E. M. Forster in 1970. The 'death' of the group can be read in relation to the organically evolving life and subsequent death of a metamorphosing Empire. The latter 'dies' in the sense that colonials experience the disappearance of structures of power integral to their identity, where newer structures take over but are not recognizable as 'empire'.

In 1969, David Garnett does refer to Britain's former colonial outposts but only to foreground his own professional and philanthropic efforts, under the sponsorship of E. M. Forster, a Bloomsbury Group member. In 'Forster and Bloomsbury', he reminisces about Forster's generosity in 'supplying the state of Hyderabad with educational books ... [and] equipping Palestine with terrestrial globes', and of himself benefiting from that generosity in acquiring a job at the *Daily Herald* as well as having his book translated by 'a Danish lady' to whom Forster recommends it (qtd in Rosenbaum 168). The range of Forster's power across continents and adoption of causes of the underprivileged speaks to a liberal-imperial reach and politics, but is smoothed over here in a personal homage. The influence of Bloomsbury continues in such later appearances as Forster's prefaces of Huthi Singh's *Maura* (1951) and G. V. Desani's *Hali* (1950). Forster continues his political commitments as president of the National Council on Civil Liberties during the Second World War, petitioning for the release of the Indian political figure J. P. Narayan, and protesting both Chinese aggression on India's borders and US involvement in Vietnam.

Do the iterations above confirm the past-ness of the Bloomsbury Group and simultaneously breathe new life into it? In 1970, Noel Annan attempts to render the group comprehensive and timeless in their influence by claiming that 'some of the credit goes to Russell and Woolf and their friends' (with an emphasis yet again on friendship) for having influenced 'British public opinion today' to be

> vastly more skeptical than it was [about] the necessity of hanging all murderers, enforcing monogamous sexual relations and imprisoning homosexuals, blasting colonial people with cordite, proclaiming as offensively as possible the superiority of the white to all other races, and, therefore, its inalienable right to treat them as second-class citizens (qtd in Rosenbaum 188).

Life now. The Bloomsbury Group is a cultural artefact as well as a dynamic organism – it is subject to insiders' (mostly white British cultural commentators') selective scorn and admiration, and to outsiders' alternating reverence or prurient curiosity that dislodges it from its ensconced position (as a jewel in the crown, if you will). The Bloomsbury Group, in postimperial England today, is part of a culture industry that includes a steady manufacture of movies, memoirs, and memorabilia. The aura of individual group members is re-produced across websites and print studies – each figure gathers a halo and lends its glow to the group. Ironically, those who thought of themselves as iconoclasts are ensconced in hagiographies, and those who took control of the means of production are launched into a machine of cultural commodification.

Popular media only intermittently feature the influential roles of members like Leonard Woolf and Keynes in politics and economics, respectively. The Bloomsburians distanced themselves from the notion of 'clique' or 'set', whereas media today (webpages, cultural commentators, etc.) continue to use those terms and focus instead on sexual revolutions, gossip, and fashion, and passingly on literature (including memoirs) and art.[22] BBC television presents itself as custodian of this British cultural heritage, in such productions as *Life in Squares* and movies such as *Mrs. Dalloway*, *The Hours*, *Orlando*, and *Carrington*. In *Life in Squares*, the posed photo simulates the original photo in the Tate Gallery, and the caption reads 'lived life in squares and loved in triangles'. As recently as 25 March 2016, the Oxford Art Online article on the Bloomsbury Group mentions the aspect of war but neglects to include colonialism and empire as part of the landscape of Western European art.[23] How many outlets in the last thirty years refer to empire when covering Bloomsbury? Should 'empire' be, in that case, a category of analysis in the other essays in this volume, if we contemplate for a moment, how it is constitutive of the Bloomsburians' selves? How does the Bloomsbury Group stand in relation to other cultural cliques that also enjoy power and status derived from economic, political, and cultural systems?

CONCLUSION: THE PLACE
WITHOUT THE PEOPLE

Bloomsbury ... and there was a group there. The significance of the bustling place, without the persons that were part of the Bloomsbury Group in the British Empire, both stands still and changes, in the lingering aura of empire, amidst the rush of human and machinic motion that is largely oblivious of that history today. Blue plaques, the heritage signs on buildings, remain as silent guides for those who might look up at the façade of an edifice to consult it. In the context of Britain's initiation of a process of disidentification from the European Union, the influence and reach of Bloomsbury becomes circumscribed in some ways and amplified in other ways. There was a time when the English men and women of the Bloomsbury Group travelled to Europe easily and frequently; that travel today is constrained, for some, by the possible pulling up of the ramparts, culturally speaking. Even in this limitation, or perhaps because of it, the Englishness (also coded whiteness) of the Bloomsbury Group is emphatically reasserted.

NOTES

This writer's positionality in relation to the focus in this chapter has a certain impact on the approach in the analysis. The author is a student of feminism, postmodernism, and postcolonialism, a former resident of independent India, a Bengali who is now an US citizen, and who has lived in South Asia, North America, and Western Europe. She is also a professor and researcher who has frequently stayed in the Bloomsbury district. The approach in this discussion relates additionally to her positionality in that she is alert to the processes by which aura and prestige accrue around people and objects, particularly through imperial circuits of knowledge export, as is the case with the Bloomsbury Group.

1. 'Tribe', as a label for a group, is most often associated with primitivism and premodern tradition. In relation to Bloomsbury, it can at best be used as metaphor; for example, 'a modern tribe' does not face the same consequences and risks as 'tribes' that are named as such by missionaries of modernity within the contexts of colonial or neocolonial conditions.
2. In this context, the institutionalization of Sanskritic and Vedic culture, an orientalism which is initiated under those monikers in British imperial eras, is a process of constructing and bestowing the status of 'civilization' that simultaneously inscribes white Anglo-European modernity. That legacy is still enshrined in the name of the University of London's School of Oriental and African Studies Department.
3. Virginia Woolf includes Arthur Waley, a Sinologist at the periphery of the Bloomsbury Group, in her preface to *Orlando* and acknowledges his influence on the turn she takes towards the 'Orient'.
4. Jean Kennard mentions how Woolf links Arab military costume and effeminacy, implying that they (Woolf and Arab masculinity) are on the same side, as oppositional to white British imperial maleness.
5. Members of the group dressed as figures from Gauguin paintings at the Chelsea Art Club ball for the Slade students' parody exhibition 'Septule and the Racinistes'. This bit of play-acting prank, presented as Virginia Woolf and her troupe's ingenuity, is described affectionately, admiringly, and nostalgically by various contemporaries. See Forster; Plomer; and Morrell.
6. Gretchen Gerzina focuses on racial prejudice and anti-Imperialism in her essay on Bloomsbury and Empire. In my analysis, I argue that whiteness and Englishness are constitutive of these issues, and in remaining implicit and uninvoked, have perpetuated their power.
7. Barbara Caine observes how the male Bloomsburians' rejection of stereotypical roles and behaviour did not lead them to support or celebrate women. For instance, Affable Hawk (pseudonym of Desmond MacCarthy) agrees with Arnold Bennett that women were intellectually inferior to men. Virginia Woolf writes 'The Intellectual Status of Women' (October 1920) in response.
8. E. M. Forster recounts fondly and nostalgically how Woolf loved Cambridge. I submit that Virginia Woolf's 'love' of Cambridge is based in her awareness of gender disparities, and that her self-schooling in English letters is her means of claiming it as heritage, through conscious and directed labour, and of eventually asserting her place in it.

9. See Barbara Caine and also Leonard Woolf's own autobiographies; see also the Bengali lineage for Virginia Woolf in William Dalrymple's account and research on Virginia Woolf's ancestry on RootsWeb.

10. Some exceptions of black and brown citizens, residing in England at that time, do exist. See Barbara Caine about male intellectual and moral strength and restraint as part of the imperial narratives of white male superiority over 'native' (Bengali) men. See also Raymond Mortimer's account of Duncan Grant's lineage that includes 'early years in India before an English prep-school' (qtd in Rosenbaum 230). Lytton Strachey's father, Lieutenant-General Sir Richard Strachey, served in various imperial administrative capacities, was an amateur botanist on Indian flora, and a member of the Royal Asiatic Society. One of Lytton Strachey's aunts was Indian, and he visited Egypt as well as wrote on the Chinese diplomat Li-Hung Chang. See footnote 9 for Virginia Woolf's Bengali lineage. These crucial aspects of the Bloomsbury persona of members of the group are not invoked in modernist studies scholarship at all.

11. Keynes curiously comments that this attitude of repudiation is 'perhaps, rather a Russian characteristic. It is certainly not an English one' (qtd in Rosenbaum 61).

12. Quentin Bell observes, 'Bloomsbury was attacked as part of a leisured class that cultivated its sensibilities while living on unearned income' (qtd in Rosenbaum 330). Did that income, even partially, derive from empire?

13. To what extent liberal capitalism, and Keynes' theories on it, informed 1930s imperialism and the Bloomsburians' anti-Imperialism is an issue that I cannot pursue here. Some related connections to Leonard Woolf's socialism and the many references to property in Virginia Woolf's letters also remain to be explored. Gretchen Gerzina often uses the term 'cosmopolitanism' to describe the group. I hold that the Bloomsburians' beliefs to be part of a kind of metropolitanism, rather than cosmopolitanism, for two reasons: one, that the members of the group, with a couple of exceptions, identified primarily with London and England, their engagement with the world being a benign desire to claim belonging without any material anchorings in places elsewhere; and second, that their migrations between urban and rural England tie them more strongly to a localized Englishness, based in property ownership, that is distinct from an unmoored cosmopolitanism. The Bloomsbury Group has been bestowed with a larger mantle ('cosmopolitanism' rather than 'metropolitanism' for example) by virtue of their status in imperial eras and in Anglophone-European modernist studies.

14. Noel Annan observes how H. G. Wells and Rupert Brooke 'responded emotionally ... only to be bitterly undeceived as the slaughter went on' (qtd in Rosenbaum 189). Annan also writes in defence of Bloomsbury politics and class-awareness, commenting that Bloomsburians were not 'political innocents engaged purely in contemplation of the eternal verities and of their own genitals when excited by the behaviour of other members of the group' (qtd in Rosenbaum 192).

15. See Virginia Woolf's The Waves, Leonard Woolf and Clive Bell's writings, and Lytton Strachey's essay on General Charles George Gordon in Eminent Victorians as critiques of Empire. Laura Gottlieb and others who analyse the 'European' War rarely mention that colonial subjects of various Western European empires were on the European battlefield.

16. John Maynard Keynes joined the India office in 1905 and left the civil service in 1908, and published seminal economic treatises on Indian currency and commerce in Africa, among others, that left an indelible mark on theories and practices of liberal economies. See Collected Writings of John Maynard Keynes.

17. In Virginia Woolf's To the Lighthouse, Mr Ramsay comes to the same conclusion but then rejects the idea as distasteful. The discussion here focuses on the actual group members themselves rather than on the ample anti-Imperial and antislavery accounts found in their fictional works. James Stephen describes the colonies as 'wretched burdens to this country ... which we have no right to lay down again. We emancipate our grown up

sons, but keep our unmarried daughters, and our children who may chance to be ricketty, in domestic bonds' (in 'Liberty, Equality, Fraternity', qtd in Marcus, *Patriarchy* 83). Interestingly, the analogy of family is both the basis of the core members of the Bloomsbury Group and a consistent trope in their self-descriptions. Regarding G. E. Moore's influence on the pre-Bloomsbury Group identity of the Cambridge Apostles, Noel Annan, in 'Keynes and the Bloomsbury Group', comments on how it helped to separate empire and civilization conceptually in espousing that 'civilisation meant trying to live the good life and that was to be found in love of friends and through art and literature' (21).

18. See Leonard Woolf's *Imperialism and Civilisation* (1928), *Empire and Commerce in Africa* and *Economic Imperialism* (both in 1920), and *Socialism and Cooperation* and *Stories of the East* (both in 1921). Gillian Workman describes him as a 'moral imperialist' (17). In a review of Leonard Woolf's *Autobiography*, Noel Annan comments that Leonard Woolf 'knew ... that the only way to get acceptable government was for the indigenous political leaders themselves to decide' (qtd in Rosenbaum 193).

19. Gretchen Gerzina ends her discussion with the observation that Bloomsburians did not worry what the empire thought of them. Does 'empire' refer to brown and black subjects or to imperial powers? In any case, the independence of the group from opinion underscores their privilege and protected status.

20. In this letter to Benedict Nicolson, dated 24 August 1940, Virginia Woolf marks her own gendered difference in terms of a 'very imperfect education' while chronicling the contributions of other group members to the larger society, such as those of Leonard Woolf, Maynard Keynes, Lytton Strachey and saying that each 'is [or was] Bloomsbury' (*Letters* 3: 419–20). Christine Froula quotes Raymond Williams' description (from his 1980 essay 'The Bloomsbury Fraction') of the group as 'an oppositional splinter' of England's ruling class; she herself describes the group as 'not a programmatic organisation but a contingent, indeterminate network' (95). Curiously, this image is also often used to describe 'the masses'.

21. See Clive Bell (*Old Friends*) and Nigel Nicolson for insistence on the use of 'friends' as an image of the Bloomsbury Group.

22. See, for example, Dayla Alberge or Emma Woolf.

23. See Susanna Rustin, and webpages such as 'Leonard Woolf's forgotten Sri Lankan novel' and 'Duncan Grant: The war and Charleston'.

WORKS CITED

Alberge, Dalya. 'How a Bearded Virginia Woolf and Her Band of "Jolly Savages" Hoaxed the Navy'. *The Guardian*, 4 February 2012. www.theguardian.com/books/2012/feb/05/bloomsbury-dreadnought-hoax-recalled-letter

Anand, Mulk Raj. *Conversations in Bloomsbury*. London: Wildwood House, 1982.

Annan, Noel. 'Keynes and the Bloomsbury Group'. *Biography* 22.1 (1999): 16–31.

Bell, Clive. *Civilization and Old Friends*. Chicago: U of Chicago P, 1973.

Bell, Clive. *Old Friends: Personal Recollections*. London: Chatto & Windus, 1956.

Blair, Sara. 'Local Modernity, Global Modernism: Bloomsbury and the Places of the Literary'. *ELH* 71.3 (2004): 813–38.

Boehmer, Elleke. *Indian Arrivals, 1870–1915: Networks of British Empire*. Oxford: Oxford UP, 2015.

Burton, Antoinette. *At the Heart of the Empire: Indians and the Colonial Encounter in Late-Victorian Britain*. Berkeley: U of California P, 1998.

Caine, Barbara. 'Bloomsbury Masculinity and Its Victorian antecedents'. *Journal of Men's Studies* 15.3 (2007): 271–81.

Caine, Barbara. *Bombay to Bloomsbury, A Biography of the Strachey Family*. Oxford: Oxford UP, 2005.

Dalrymple, William. 'Kolkata, My Ancestors, and Me'. BBC News, 22 October 2016. www.bbc. com/news/world-asia-india-37687562

'Duncan Grant: The War and Charleston'. www.tate.org.uk/learn/online-resources/bloomsbury-group/biographies/duncan-grant/war-years

Edel, Leon. *Bloomsbury: A House of Lions*. New York: Avon Books, 1980.

Forster, E. M. *Virginia Woolf*. Cambridge: Cambridge UP, 1942.

Froula, Christine. 'War, Peace, and Internationalism'. *The Cambridge Companion to the Bloomsbury Group*. Ed. Victoria Rosner. Cambridge: Cambridge UP, 2014. 93–111.

Gerzina, Gretchen Holbrook. 'Bloomsbury and Empire'. *The Cambridge Companion to the Bloomsbury Group*. Ed. Victoria Rosner. Cambridge: Cambridge UP, 2014. 112–27.

Gottlieb, Laura. 'The War between the Woolfs'. *Virginia Woolf and Bloomsbury: A Centenary Celebration*. Ed. Jane Marcus. Palgrave Macmillan, 1987. 242–52.

Jarboe, Andrew and Richard Fogarty. Eds. *Empires in World War I: Shifting Frontiers and Imperial Dynamics in a Global Conflict*. London: I. B. Tauris, 2014.

Johnston, Georgia. 'Virginia Woolf's Talk on the Dreadnought Hoax'. *Woolf Studies Annual* 15 (2009): 1–45.

Jones, Danell. 'The Dreadnought Hoax and the Theatres of War'. *Literature & History* 22.1 (2013): 80–95.

Kennard, Jean. 'Power and Sexuality in the Dreadnought Hoax, *The Voyage Out, Mrs. Dalloway* and *Orlando*'. *Journal of Modern Literature* 20.2 (1996): 149–64.

Keynes, John Maynard. *The Collected Writings of John Maynard Keynes*. London: Macmillan, 1971.

'Leonard Woolf's Forgotten Sri Lankan Novel'. BBC News, 23 May 2014. www.bbc.com/news/magazine-27518833

MacCarthy, Desmond. *Bloomsbury: An Unfinished Memoir in 1933*. London: MacGibbon & Kee, 1953.

Marcus, Jane. Ed. *Virginia Woolf and Bloomsbury: A Centenary Celebration*. London: Macmillan, 1987.

Marcus, Jane. *Virginia Woolf and the Languages of Patriarchy*. Bloomington: Indiana UP, 1987.

Morrell, Ottoline. *The Early Memoirs of Lady Ottoline Morrell*. Ed. Robert Gathorne-Hardy. London: Faber & Faber, 1964.

Nicolson, Nigel. 'Bloomsbury: The Myth and the Reality'. *Virginia Woolf and Bloomsbury: A Centenary Celebration*. Ed. Jane Marcus. Palgrave Macmillan, 1987. 7–22.

Noble, Joan Russell. Ed. *Recollections of Virginia Woolf*. London: Peter Owen, 1972.

Plomer, William. *At Home*. London: Jonathan Cape, 1958.

Reid, Panthea. 'Stephens, Fishers, and the Court of the "Sultan of Zanzibar": New Evidence from Virginia Stephen Woolf's Childhood'. *Biography* 21.3 (1998): 328–40.

Reid, Panthea. 'Virginia Woolf, Leslie Stephen, Julia Margaret Cameron, and the Prince of Abyssinia: An Inquiry into Certain Colonialist Representations'. *Biography* 22.3 (1999): 323–55.

Rich, P. J. *Elixir of Empire: The English Public Schools, Ritualism, Freemasonry, and Imperialism*. London: Regency Press, 1989.

RootsWeb: INDIA-L. Virginia Woolf's Indian Ancestor. n.p. n.d. http://newsarch.rootsweb.ancestry.com/th/read/INDIA/1999-04/0924161053

Rosenbaum, S. P. *The Bloomsbury Group: A Collection of Memoirs, Commentary and Criticism*. Toronto: U of Toronto P, 1975.

Rosner, Victoria. Ed. *The Cambridge Companion to the Bloomsbury Group*. Cambridge: Cambridge UP, 2014.

Rustin, Susanna. 'Boom Time for the Bloomsbury Group'. *The Guardian*, 5 June 2015. www.theguardian.com/books/2015/jun/05/bloomsbury-booming-legacy-celebrate-virginia-woolf

Schröder, Leena Kore. 'Tales of Abjection and Miscegenation: Virginia Woolf's and Leonard Woolf's "Jewish" Stories'. *Twentieth-Century Literature* 49.3 (2003): 298–327.

Shaffer, Brian. 'Civilization in Bloomsbury: Woolf's *Mrs. Dalloway* and Bell's "Theory of Civilization"'. *Journal of Modern Literature* 19.1 (1994): 73–87.

Sitwell, Osbert. *Laughter in the Next Room*. London: Macmillan, 1949.

Snaith, Anna. 'The Hogarth Press and Networks of Anti-Colonialism'. *Leonard and Virginia Woolf, the Hogarth Press and the Networks of Modernism*. Ed. Helen Southworth. Edinburgh: Edinburgh UP, 2012. 103–27.

Southworth, Helen. *Leonard and Virginia Woolf, the Hogarth Press and the Networks of Modernism*. Edinburgh: Edinburgh UP, 2012.

Woolf, Emma. 'The Joyful, Gossipy and Absurd Private Life of Virginia Woolf'. *Newsweek*, 16 March 2016. www.newsweek.com/2015/02/27/joyful-gossipy-and-absurd-private-life-virginia-woolf-306438.html)

Woolf, Leonard. *Beginning Again: An Autobiography of the Years 1911–1918*. London: Hogarth Press, 1964.

Woolf, Leonard. *Economic Imperialism*. New York: H. Fertig, 1970.

Woolf, Leonard. *Empire and Commerce in Africa*. London: Allen & Unwin, 1968.

Woolf, Virginia. '22 Hyde Park Gate'. *Moments of Being: Unpublished Autobiographical Writings*. Ed. Jeanne Schulkind. New York: Harcourt Brace Jovanovich, 1976. 162–77.

Woolf, Leonard. *Imperialism and Civilization*. New York: Garland, 1972.

Woolf, Virginia. *The Letters of Virginia Woolf*, 6 Vols. Ed. Nigel Nicolson and Joanne Trautmann. New York: Harcourt Brace Jovanovich, 1975.

Woolf, Virginia. 'Old Bloomsbury'. *Moments of Being: Unpublished Autobiographical Writings*. Ed. Jeanne Schulkind. New York: Harcourt Brace Jovanovich, 1976. 179–201.

Woolf, Leonard. *Socialism and Cooperation*. London: National Labour Press, 1921.

Woolf, Leonard. *A Tale Told by Midnight*. London: Hesperus, 2006.

Woolf, Virginia. *To the Lighthouse*. New York: Harcourt & Brace, 1927.

Workman, Gillian. 'Leonard Woolf and Imperialism'. *Ariel* 6 (1975): 5–21.

Young, John. 'William Plomer, Transnational Modernism and the Hogarth Press'. *Leonard and Virginia Woolf, the Hogarth Press and the Networks of Modernism*. Ed. Helen Southworth. Edinburgh: Edinburgh UP, 2012. 128–49.

Case Study: Race, Empire, and Performative Activism in Late Edwardian Bloomsbury

ANNA SNAITH

Early in the morning of 17 August 1909, Madan Lal Dhingra, a revolutionary Indian nationalist, was hanged at Pentonville Prison. Dhingra had assassinated Sir William Curzon Wyllie, the aide to the Secretary of State for India, Viscount Morley, at point blank range during a reception held by the National Indian Association at the Imperial Institute the month before. As the aftermath of this assassination was playing itself out, the famous *Dreadnought* hoax, during which members of the Bloomsbury Group dressed up as Abyssinian royalty and hoaxed the British Navy, took place on a warship docked on the south coast. This chapter explores different modes of anti-colonial and anti-imperial activity in late Edwardian London by discussing these events alongside one another, connecting as well as contrasting them via the surprising involvement of David Garnett in the aftermath of the assassination as documented in the first volume of his autobiography, *The Golden Echo* (1953). Juxtaposition of these events speaks to the complex and multifarious ways in which resistance operated in this prewar moment, but also the transnational lens required to fully investigate its import. Furthermore, their conjunction reminds us that attention to Bloomsbury and empire demands an intersectional approach. Garnett's involvement with Indian nationalism stems, by his own account, from a nexus of queer desire and transracial solidarity. The contours of subversion shift according to our critical paradigms and the hoax can, and does, read as a problematic act of imperialism from one vantage point and an act of feminist transgression from another. Only by rotating these events so that they, prism-like, catch the light from different angles will we attain a three-dimensional understanding of their signification.

THE ASSASSINATION OF SIR CURZON WYLLIE

Madan Lal Dhingra, an engineering student at University College London, had been training for the assassination for several months at a rifle range on the Tottenham Court Road. His target was, in fact, the colonial administrator Sir William Lee Warner, and more broadly the pro-empire stance of the National Indian Association and its attempts to subdue anti-colonial activism. A Parsi doctor, Cawas Lalcaca, who came to Sir Curzon Wyllie's assistance was also killed; Dhingra, attempting to turn the gun on himself, was restrained by guests until the police arrived to arrest him (Tickell 135–6).[1] At his trial he declared:

> I maintain that if it is patriotic in an Englishman to fight against the Germans if they were to occupy this country, it is much more justifiable and patriotic in my case to fight against the English. I hold the English responsible for the murder of 80 millions of Indian people in the last 50 years … Just as the Germans have no right to occupy this country, so the English people have no right to occupy India. (Waraich and Puri 62)

Dhingra was part of a group of revolutionaries who clustered around India House (or *Bharat Bhavan*) at 65 Cromwell Avenue in Highgate, set up as a hostel for Indian students by the Oxford scholar of Sanskrit turned freedom fighter, Shyamaji Krishnavarma. He founded the Indian Home Rule Society in London 1905, alongside a journal called the *Indian Sociologist*, which was published in London until its suppression in 1909 following Wyllie's assassination. Krishnavarma used his periodical to report on colonial violence in India as well as to set out his thoughts on the justification of violent resistance. The assassination, and nexus of radicalism at India House, speaks to London's position as a crucible of anti-colonialism, and also to the transnational networks of revolutionary nationalism in the Edwardian period. Particularly after 1905 when the British partitioned Bengal, London was a key site, perhaps *the* key site outside India, for nationalist activism. This was due, as Nicholas Owen has explored, to the relative freedoms of movement and the press in England as opposed to India before surveillance operations were stepped up following the assassination (Owen 63). Many revolutionaries made their way to London, where they could publish, exchange tactics and recruit young students.

Of particular resonance here, in relation to Garnett's later involvement, is the wider context of Russian anarchists and revolutionaries in London in this period. In Conrad's *The Secret Agent* (1907), for example, the central act of terrorism (based on the self-detonation of Martial Bourdin in 1894) is staged to foreground the leniency of British law in relation to terrorism and the harbouring of political fugitives. Conrad based Verloc's anarchist comrades on Russians such as Peter Kropotkin who was exiled in London during 1881. As many critics have explored, Conrad's novel teases out the various definitions, contexts and traditions of anarchism, terrorism and revolution, but of particular significance here is the perception of late nineteenth-century London as a facilitating site for revolutionary networks.[2]

By 1909, India House was being run by another émigré activist, Vinayak (Veer) Damodar Savarkar, who had founded a revolutionary organization, the Abhinav Bharat, in India before travelling to London in 1906 on one of the scholarships Krishnavarma offered to Indians studying abroad. Once in London, he set up the Free India Society, made contact with Irish, Turkish, and Egyptian revolutionaries in London and arranged the transport of arms and bomb-making manuals to India (Tickell 141). At India House he gathered and trained participants for 'an armed revolt against the British on return to India' (Owen 68).[3] In response to the 1907 fiftieth-anniversary celebrations of the suppression of the Indian 'Mutiny', Savarkar organized counter commemorations for India's martyrs at India House and on campuses across Britain. In 1909 he published his revisionist account of the event: *The Indian War of Independence*. It is likely that Savarkar masterminded the Wyllie assassination plot.

The reaction to the assassination and Dhingra's trial in the British media was immediate and hyperbolic. One of the first reports in *The Times* responded with 'indignation and with horror' to the enemy within, and noted Wyllie's dedication to the 'natives of India'; 'he is remembered there as one of their warmest friends' (*The Times*, 3 July 1909: 11). The article called for 'vigilance and alertness' 'even in the heart of Empire': 'it has long been thought not improbable that the Indian anarchist movement might be directed more and more from London and from Paris and less and less from Calcutta and from Poona' (3 July 1909: 11). Indians in London held meetings at which nationalist leaders like Bepin Chandra Pal denounced the event and distanced themselves from terrorist actions (*The Times*, 5 July 1909: 8). Quickly attention turned to the networks within which Dhingra worked: India House and the *Indian Sociologist*. In *Indian Unrest* (1910), a collection of *Times* articles by Valentine Chirol, India House is named as the 'most dangerous organisation outside India' (1910: 148). Chirol writes: 'it required nothing less than the shock of a murder perpetrated in the heart of London to open the eyes of those in authority at home to the nature of the revolutionary propaganda which has been, and is still being, carried on outside India' (1910: 145). Warnings had appeared as early as 1908, Chirol reports, but the authorities only belatedly realized the threat posed by India House: its connections with 'the Irish Fenian and Russian anarchist' and its role as a producer of 'incendiary literature' sent back to India (146, 149). As Alex Tickell has argued, the assassination 'revealed how the supposedly culturally assimilative process of migrant education in the universities of Edwardian Britain might expose young Indians to political ideas that would alienate them from, rather than binding them to the idea of empire' (Tickell 138). In fact, the Lee Warner committee, which included Curzon Wyllie, had been set up in 1907 to 'investigate the radicalisation of Indian students in Britain', but surveillance efforts were intensified following the assassination (Boehmer 209). Intelligence records indicate that concerns about Indian radicals prompted not only routine surveillance and the use of informers at India House but communications at the highest levels. In a letter to the Secretary of State, Viscount Morley, Viceroy Minto declared it 'intolerable that enemies of British rule ... should ... be permitted to use the headquarters of the Empire as the centre of a seditious and revolutionary campaign' (Visram 155).[4] King Edward VII became involved, writing to Minto calling for 'serious steps' 'to prevent these men coming over to England with no fixed occupation, and falling into bad hands ... they only learn sedition and treason' (Datta 74).

But not all the collaborators were Indian. David Garnett was present at India House meetings prior to the assassination and masterminded a plot to free Savarkar from jail in the aftermath of the event. This immediately predates Garnett's introduction to the Bloomsbury Group members with whom he was to form such close relations. It also predates his experiences as a conscientious objector engaged in farm work during the First World War (see Jones in this volume). His early anti-colonial activism clearly had a formative impact on his political consciousness and operates on a continuum with his subsequent opposition to the war, founded, as he described in his 'Answers to Questions of Objection to Combatant Service', not on an opposition to violence or killing, but to enforced military service (Knights 108).

While this link between incipient Bloomsbury and Indian nationalism has been discussed by scholars working on South Asia, such as Elleke Boehmer, the implications of his involvement have not been investigated within the context of the Bloomsbury

Group more broadly. Garnett's collaboration, and the lengthy treatment and contextualization of the events in his autobiography, offers a corrective to accounts which emphasize either the imperialism or the apolitical nature of the group's members. It also offers another vantage point on potentially homogenizing accounts of the group. His narrativization of this period working with the India House revolutionaries is also illuminating for its constant shifting between identification and difference. The terms through which he understood his connection to Indian radicals speak to both imperialist 'othering', and a desire to oppose and violently overthrow imperial institutions. Writing decades after the event, he presents himself as ignorant of South Asian culture and history but in solidarity with the aims and means of his companions. Queer desire and Garnett's eroticized response to his Indian comrades provide another context of affiliation that also braids resistant and orientalizing modes. His friendships provide an important contemporary context for E. M. Forster's relationship with Syed Ross Masood and a prehistory for the later, interwar contexts of Asian Bloomsbury in the connections between, for example, Leonard Woolf with Mulk Raj Anand, or Aubrey Menen's involvement with queer Bloomsbury (Lytton Strachey, and Duncan Grant among others) in 1930s Fitzrovia.[5]

Garnett was no stranger to revolution given his parents' (Edward and Constance) association with Russian revolutionaries including Sergey Stepniak, who had assassinated General Mesentzoff in St Petersburg in 1878 and founded the Society of Friends of Russian Freedom in England. Indeed, shortly after David's birth, his mother travelled to Russia with Stepniak in order to advance her Russian translation work (Knights 8–9). Later, in 1909, by which time Constance was one of the leading translators of Russian fiction into English (see Bronstein in this volume), when David Garnett came into contact with a network of Indian revolutionaries, he would surely have had his parents' connections in mind.

While studying at the University Tutorial College in Red Lion Square, Garnett met Sukhasagan Dutt and was attracted by his 'luxuriant black ringlets' (Garnett 137). Dutt's elder brother was in prison for an assassination attempt in Midnapore in which two Englishwomen were killed (Garnett 140). Garnett 'was not in the least shocked' by this act of terrorism, but rather by his friend's repudiation of his brother's actions (141). He presents himself as entirely in sympathy with revolutionary activism: 'I had been brought up to accept acts of political murder and violence with sympathy bordering on admiration; I had known and respected at least two eminent assassins, and I should have thought it particularly disgraceful to resent the murder of Englishmen by Indians, since I was myself English and to some extent shared the guilt of British imperialism' (140). His attitude to empire sets him apart: 'I took for granted, without investigation, that British rule in India must be bad, exactly as most British boys of my age took for granted that it was good' (141).

But his initial response to Dutt is riven with assumptions gleaned from sensational Victorian fiction. When he learns of Dutt's Bengali identity, he remarks: 'I suppose that's somewhere in India, isn't it? ... I knew almost nothing about India except what I had picked up from Colonel Meadows Taylor's *The Confessions of a Thug*, and as I did not think thuggee was the best subject to start off with, I asked him if he would join me for lunch at the A.B.C. in Southampton Row' (137). The British focused much attention on the sensational nature of *thagi* – a secretive form of homicidal robbery – as a way of emphasizing the supposedly degenerate and innately violent nature of colonial subjects (see Tickell 32–7). Even though Garnett exhibits solidarity with Indian nationalism, his assumptions and reference points at this early stage emerge from the same place as imperialist characterizations.

Very quickly, however, Garnett sought to rectify his ignorance by working through a reading list offered him by his new comrades: he read translations of the Sanskrit drama, *Sakuntala*, the epics the *Mahabharata* and *Ramayana*, and he 'dipped into Upanishads' (143). Dutt became a close friend and 'one day, when Dutt came to tea with Constance and me in Hampstead, he suggested taking me on to meet some friends of his who lived in Highgate in a house called India House, which belonged to an old Mahratta called Krishnavarma ... regarded by the British authorities as the leader of a most dangerous, seditious movement' (143). As Garnett's friendship with Dutt developed, he was introduced to a wider circle of compatriots including Ashutosh Mitter, Narajan Pal, and his father, Bepin Chandra Pal, who was a well-known Indian orator, politician, and freedom fighter. Garnett was fascinated, indeed seduced, by one particular man, with 'a delicate aquiline nose, a sensitive, refined mouth and an extremely pale skin' (143). This was Vinayak Savarkar reading aloud, as Garnett realizes in hindsight, from his history of the Indian War of Independence to be published soon after in May 1909 (145). Garnett, then just seventeen, was unusual as an Englishman welcomed at India House. He writes at length about the exhilaration and opportunity he felt as a result of his difference: 'I rejoiced in the sense of freedom which it gave me ... I had embarked on an adventure of my own finding; there was nobody to guide me; nobody to feel ashamed of me. It was a new departure' (144). While mingling with the India House crowd, listening to speeches and Indian music on the gramophone, Garnett talks at one point with a 'tall young man' with a 'Byronic attitude' (146). A short while later, he recounts, 'One morning ... opening the paper, I read the news that Sir Curzon Wyllie had been assassinated at a soiree for Indian students at the Imperial Institute by a young Indian called Dhingra ... I thought it extremely probable that some of my acquaintances were implicated' (147). The young Byronic man was indeed Dhingra.

From this point on, Garnett became deeply involved in the aftermath of the assassination. When Dhingra was not permitted to read his statement in court, Savarkar asked Garnett to arrange publication, which he did, via his parents' friend Robert Lynd, the following day in the *Daily News* (August 1909). When India House was shut down, Savarkar went to live in Red Lion Passage, and lunched with Garnett most days. They often, he recalled, had to shake off a detective 'watching their lodgings or following them in the street' (148). On 13 March 1910, Savarkar was returning to London from Paris when he was arrested at Victoria Station for sedition in India. He was to be extradited to India to stand trial as the British authorities knew he would receive a harsher sentence there (153). Garnett visited him regularly in jail, raised money for his defence and wrote a letter, headed 'Past Offences', to the *Daily News* (3 May 1910) objecting to his extradition. Constance rallied to the cause, contacting sympathetic friends such as William Rothenstein and Henry Nevinson, writing letters of support and raising funds (R. Garnett 1991: 243).

The final stage of Garnett's involvement came when he assisted Savarkar in concocting an escape plan. After weeks of preparation which involved Garnett buying disguises, chartering boats and planning routes, as well as making contact with a network of collaborators including Sinn Fein members (via family friend, anarchist Florence Dryhurst) and Indian nationalists such as Vivendranath Chattopadhyaya (D. Garnett 154-8). 'Chatto' was to supply the 'rescuers', Garnett was to transport them from France and drive the getaway car. The plan was derailed, first by the man who failed to supply the boat and then by Garnett's father who arrived in Paris to escort his son home. Edward wrote to a friend: 'I am on my way to Paris. D. is there, engaged in a wild romantic scheme – which may have most serious consequences ... the poor boy is living in pure romantic cloudland: swept off his feet by his affection for S., and perhaps the tool of others' (qtd in R. Garnett 244). Garnett's involvement by this point was driven by personal attraction: he had 'imposed' himself on these 'enemies' of his country, he writes, for personal reasons. He was unable to bear the thought of Savarkar's imprisonment, a man of such 'intense vitality' (D. Garnett 157). Constance wrote to her husband expressing concern at her son's entanglement: 'he loves him with that first rush of romantic devotion and adoration – it is the first time he has felt this. Remember how you felt once – and what it would have meant to you at 18, if this awful thing had happened to the person you adored' (qtd in R. Garnett 243)

Savarkar was sentenced in December 1910 to life imprisonment on the Andaman Islands (although he only served fourteen years).[6] Garnett had no further contact with him and his autobiographical reflections on the episode indicate his sense that he 'had played a fool's part in the affair' (161). He writes: 'it was not my business to intervene ... what good could an English boy do by helping them? ... Nor did I believe in terrorism ... Why was I risking my future for a cause in which I did not believe' (161). He recognizes that his motivation was 'romantic and altruistic', a judgement borne out by a poem he wrote for Savarkar in 1910: 'You cannot change it, or destroy/The lasting image of a fiery boy./I gave my heart to free a man in chains' (D. Garnett 161 and 'To V.D.S.'; Knights 47). Despite the romance and adventure of his escapade, as his biographer notes, if Garnett had been arrested he could have been charged with high treason and given the death sentence, life imprisonment, or transportation under the Treason Felony Act (1848) (Knights 46–7).

Garnett's involvement illuminates the transracial lines of queer desire in this period as well as the transnational constellations of revolutionary and anarchist solidarity. The Garnetts' networks of Irish and Russian revolutionaries have been explored and delineated but these networks are rarely understood to include Indian individuals and organizations. But his participation in anti-colonial resistance also resonates with a rather different context: that of the Bloomsbury Group's performative engagement with race and empire in the prewar period. Just as he was, in his collaboration with Savarkar, metaphorically ventriloquizing or taking on the identity of the revolutionary, when Garnett first met members of the Bloomsbury Group, he was literally in Indian masquerade. In 1911, he was invited by James and Marjorie Strachey to join a group dressed as 'Nègres Enflammés' attending a charity ball for the Women's Suffrage Society (D. Garnett 1953: 206). He decided to attend dressed, instead, as a Rajput prince – borrowing clothing from 'a Rajput Kumar of my acquaintance' (206). Here he was introduced to Virginia Stephen (as she then was) and became reacquainted with her brother, Adrian. Very soon after this, at the home of J. A. Hobson, he met Duncan Grant, whose lover he later became (D. Garnett 211). The Stephens and Grant were known to him as 'heroes of the *Dreadnought* hoax', an event which 'shed glory on Adrian' and whose 'heroine' was Virginia Stephen (D. Garnett 211). The *Dreadnought* hoax, staged on 7 February 1910, coincided with the aftermath of the assassination and exploring these two events in conjunction highlights the shifting lines between political activism and masquerade in the Bloomsbury context. Not only that, they suggest the often contingent or contextual workings of resistance, or anti-imperialism, as we shall see.

THE *DREADNOUGHT* HOAX

The infamous *Dreadnought* hoax was masterminded by Anglo-Irishman Horace Cole, and involved a group of friends including Virginia Woolf, Duncan Grant and Adrian Stephen boarding HMS *Dreadnought* disguised as Abyssinian princes and their entourage: Virginia Stephen as Prince Sanganya; Anthony Buxton as Prince Makalen; Cole as Mr Herbert Cholmondely, a Foreign Office attaché; Duncan Grant as Prince Mandok; Guy Ridley as Prince Golen and Adrian Stephen as Herr George Kauffmann, a German interpreter. A telegram preceded the party's arrival at the Weymouth docks, but the Foreign Office neglected to verify its authenticity. The group were in blackface, complete with false beards and moustaches, courtesy of the famous costumier, Willy Clarkson (Stephen 18). Woolf's brother, Adrian, was the translator, and although they had purchased a Swahili grammar and attempted a few words in the train on the way down to the south coast, he resorted to Greek and Latin during the escapade. They were met by crowds, files of marines, Admiral May, and the Zanzibari anthem (Navy officials had not been able to source the Abyssinian anthem). They were toured around the ship and shown its intimate details from the newest wireless equipment to the officers' bathrooms. All went to plan, despite some precarious moments involving slipping moustaches. An extra frisson was provided by the presence of the Stephens' cousin, Willy Fisher, Flag Commander of the *Dreadnought*. The Stephens had long made fun of their respectable and conformist

"THE EMPEROR OF ABYSSINIA" AND HIS SUITE.
Names from left to right :
Virginia Stephen, Duncan Grant, Adrian Stephen, Anthony Buxton,
Guy Ridley, Horace Cole.

FIGURE 1. 'The Emperor of Abyssinia and His Suite', published in *The Dreadnought Hoax* by Adrian Stephen (Hogarth Press, 1936).

cousins; in fact, Fisher may have been one of the personal motivations behind the plan (Downer 95).

The hoax sent shock waves through the British establishment when the news broke on the front page of the *Daily Express* on February 12 with the headline: 'AMAZING NAVAL HOAX, Sham Abyssinian Princes Visit the Dreadnought'. An anonymous interview with Woolf, 'Lady Prince's Story', appeared in the *Daily Mirror* followed by a cartoon three days later (15 and 17 February). The *Mirror* article stressed the Navy's amusement: 'With that keen sense of humour which is one of the characteristics of the British naval service, they freely admit that the hoaxers scored heavily, and, far from bearing them any ill-will, they give them full credit for their successful and audacious trick' (15 February 1910, *Daily Mirror*: 5). Despite this response, the prank made a mockery of British naval security and ridiculed the might of the military at this politically sensitive, prewar moment, and its scandalous nature ensured worldwide newspaper coverage for months afterwards (see D. Jones 80). The prank's subversion underpinned its immediate iconicity: it quickly became a 'cultural touchstone' (Johnston 3). The event was memorialized on postcards and in a music hall song, performed at the Weymouth Pavilion (Barkway 21).[7] The *Express* had coined the catchphrase, 'bunga, bunga', supposedly the princes' response to their tour, and naval officers were taunted with the phrase in the street (Downer 124). When the real Emperor arrived two weeks later, Woolf recounts, he was met with this taunt (Johnston 31).

When, as late as 1940, Woolf delivered a talk on the escapade to her local Women's Institute (W.I.), she emphasized government and naval responses to the hoax. The prank was discussed in Parliament given the group's exposure to the interior of the battleship, including 'secret isntruments' [*sic*]: 'we might have been German spies' she noted (Johnston 27).[8] The German name of the translator was perhaps a satirical nod at this possibility. Bizarrely, Duncan Grant was subjected to a ritual caning by Navy officials, and Willy Fisher sought out the Stephens in Fitzroy Square and roared at them: 'Did we realise that we owed our lives to the British Navy? Did we realise that we were impertinent, idiotic? Did we realise that we ought to be whipped through the streets' (Johnston 28, 29). Her return to the experience three decades on indicates how deeply the hoax impacted on the young Virginia Stephen's consciousness and resonates with her subsequent iconic reference to 1910 as a watershed year. Her 1921 story, 'A Society', refers to the hoax and specifically satirizes the ritual caning intended to avenge the Navy. In 1936 after the death of Horace Cole, and the same year Adrian published his account, she took a trip down to Weymouth to revisit the site where she played her 'joke on the Dreadnought' (*Letters* 6: 17).

On one level, these events – hoax and assassination – are diametrically opposed: a prank, steeped in the appetite for performance and masquerade that characterized Bloomsbury, and an act of political violence. Cole was a well-known hoaxer and had already pulled off the 'Sultan of Zanzibar' hoax with Adrian in Cambridge in 1905. Cole and his accomplices enjoyed the time, funds, and self-assurance to concoct and carry out the plan; they had the luxury and security of a social position that alleviated concern about the hoax's outcome. They were undermining an aggressive, militaristic patriotism, while Dhingra was employing a self-sacrificial patriotism to oppose colonial rule in his homeland. The assassination drew on knowledge and support from a transnational network of revolutionaries to strike at an institution (the Imperial Institute) in the heart of imperial London which symbolized the erasure of the realities of British violence in India in favour of a discourse of friendship and mutual advantage.

The hoax, in its use of blackface and racial stereotype, relies on the hierarchies of empire which the India House revolutionaries were attempting to overturn. The prank, and its later narrativization, was an act of cultural appropriation born of racist ignorance and patronizing assumptions (see Sarker in this volume). The hoaxers drew on racial tropes familiar to their audiences via a long history of exhibition and spectacle in the heart of empire. Most importantly, minstrel shows and music hall acts involving racial masquerade were still readily available on London's stages in the early twentieth century. As Gretchen Holbrook Gerzina has argued, 'the performing of race was a "natural" and pervasive part of the London scene', hence the success of the hoax and Woolf's ease in participating: her position as 'much audience as performer' (Holbrook Gerzina 77). Racial masquerade was so pervasive that 'the authorities – accustomed to representations of Africans – were unable to see beyond the false presentations' (Holbrook Gerzina 80).[9] Furthermore, the racist depictions of bawdy, comedic and carefree individuals on the music hall stage both underpin and contrast with the hoaxers' performance of privilege and dignity as Abyssinian royalty. The *Express*'s report suggests the deep-rootedness of racist tropes in the imperial imagination, describing the actors' wigs as 'black woolly mats' and the false 'nigger lips' (Downer 123). Photographs belie this description; the newspaper was drawing on such racist stereotypes to further sensationalize the event. Audiences, including the Navy, had been trained to understand a homogenized construction of 'blackness' via these performances, so even such a self-consciously flawed performance was perceived as 'authentic'. Furthermore, of course, the visit itself conferred honour and status on the Navy and its vessels which further increased the will to believe.

However two aspects of the hoax – the *Dreadnought* battleship and the Abyssinian impersonation – trouble its dismissal as *merely* a joke and constitute its subversive element. Cole called the hoax his 'navy joke', and as so often in British modernism, that subversion was achieved through the tropes of a problematic primitivism. It is hard, however, to overestimate the topical power of the *Dreadnought* battleship as a choice of location for the hoax. As Richard Hough writes, 'never before or since has the construction of one man-of-war had such an effect on service opinion, domestic politics and international relations' (Hough 2). Launched on 10 February 1906 (four years before the hoax) and unprecedented for its speed, range and the size of its guns, the dreadnought inaugurated a 'new era in battleship development' (Roberts 7). The new ship immediately made obsolete its predecessors and 'was at once a powerful statement of British technological capability and strategic daring, and the unmistakeable embodiment of the Royal Navy's superiority, which changed the very rules of the naval game' (Blyth 2). The chosen name, as well as referencing a long history of British naval vessels, starting with the first *Dreadnought* in 1573, was also a statement of bravado. As Jan Rüger has explored, the launch also harnessed mass media modes of advertising and propaganda, including choreographed and spectacular fleet displays and a range of dreadnought products (9). The ship immediately began appearing in songs, films and poems: 'the very fact that members of Bloomsbury's literati chose the *Dreadnought* for their hoax underlined that the ship had become a cultural icon with undeniable symbolic status' (Rüger 11).

The enormous cost of the ships meant that the public had needed persuading and the shipbuilding scheme was not without controversy. Ironically, the new Liberal government, committed to reductions in defence spending, was forced to confront the need for upgrading the Navy and became responsible for 'the most deadly fighting machine ever launched' (Hough ix). In fact, the Dreadnought and naval defence was one of the key political issues of late Edwardian Britain, issues whose reach extended to the colonies.

H.M.S "DREADNOUGHT."

FIGURE 2. 'HMS *Dreadnought*', published in *The Dreadnought Hoax* by Adrian Stephen (Hogarth Press, 1936).

New Zealand, for example, pledged 'to defray the cost of two Dreadnoughts for England's use ... at the cost of some four million pounds' ('Notes of the Week' 1909: 454). Soon after her arrival in London in 1908, Katherine Mansfield attended the dockyard launch of one of the dreadnoughts, the HMS *Collingwood*, paid for by her country. Writing to Garnet Trowell about the ceremony, she describes the heightened emotion as the iron supports are broken down and 'the great bulk of her swept down its inclined plank into the sun – and the sky was full of gold – into the sea – which waited for her' (Mansfield 88). She focuses her attention on 'the builders of the ships – the rough men who had toiled at her' who 'stood silently on her deck' (88).

The timing and venue of the hoax sits at the heart of these debates chronologically and symbolically. In response to the 'Navy Scare' of 1909 – when alarming information about Germany's dreadnought building plans emerged – the Admiralty demanded eight new battleships. The battleship symbolized British military power in the face of increasing German aggression. Lloyd George's 1909 'People's' Budget, which included increased taxes on the wealthy to pay for the new ships, was rejected by the House of Lords, prompting the General Election of January 1910 (15 January–10 February) which coincided with the hoax (Downer 97). A constitutional crisis over the power of the House of Lords raged throughout that year and resulted in a second General Election (December 1910).

None of this was lost on Virginia Woolf and one can feel its presence in *The Voyage Out* (which she was working on in early 1910), whose anti-imperialism is very much centred on naval power and the sea routes of empire. In that novel, the narrator's description of passing warships as 'sinister grey vessels ... eyeless beasts seeking their prey' contrasts with Clarissa Dalloway's eroticized squeal of patriotic excitement: 'Warships, Dick! Over there! Look!' (61). After the ships pass, the travellers talk of 'valour and death, and the magnificent qualities of British admirals … Life on board a man-of-war was splendid, so they agreed' (62). Helen's remark that 'it seemed to her as wrong to keep sailors as to keep a Zoo … surely it was time we ceased to praise courage' is met with disapproval (62).

The hoaxers' performance, then, is a topical intervention into national debates about national security, taxation, and colonial responsibility, and its subversion is aimed directly at a hyper-masculine, jingoistic response to naval artillery and the machinery of war. In similar ways, the choice of location and target of the Wyllie assassination points not only to the broader question of Indian Home Rule, but also to the subversion of a particular narrative about imperial relations. The National Indian Association sought to 'befriend' and seek allegiances with Indians in London at the same time as the State was engaged in increased surveillance measures. The widespread impact of the hoax, too, emerged from exploitation of the 'danger within' narrative and the subversion of the Navy's supposed invincibility. The British Navy 'exuded a confidence higher than arrogance, an assurance' bred at Trafalgar and continuing for the century that followed (Massie xiv). The hoax aimed its subversion at a British institution under intense public scrutiny in this moment and used as its stage the most potent manifestation of both controversy and power. As Lucy Delap has explored, the iconography of the ship contravened conventional female associations of such vessels. The *Dreadnought* was quickly coded as epitomizing a heroic, aggressive masculinity, ripe for satirical subversion by the Bloomsbury pranksters. Pacifists and suffrage campaigners such as Helena Swanwick openly opposed the naval arms race and spending on dreadnoughts in periodicals such as the *Common Cause* (Delap 97– 101). Such understandings of the vessel account for the specific press attention to Woolf's cross-dressing and the particularly transgressive presence of a disguised woman on board the war ship (Delap 102–3). Attempts to homogenize the motivations of the hoaxers, and ignore Woolf's position as the only woman, risk muting aspects of the episode's charge. Clara Jones has made a similar argument in relation to Woolf's W.I. talk on the hoax. She was, in 1940, both gently mocking or challenging her host organization's patriotism during wartime but also finding affiliation with her female audience (through shifting pronouns) against the male privilege of the pranksters (C. Jones 169–76). Woolf's interest in the rituals, spectacles, and performances that buttress, protect, and perpetuate male power culminates in *Three Guineas* but persists throughout her oeuvre.

In relation to Abyssinia, too, the topical significance would have been clear to Woolf and her fellow pranksters and the general public, if not, seemingly, to the Navy. The hoax was an attack on aggressive military posturing made in the name of the only African state to have successfully fought off European colonial powers. For all the talk of Abyssinian royalty, the Emperor Menelik II (1844–1913) had suffered a stroke in 1909, so Anthony Buxton was actually playing Ras el Makalen, the emperor's cousin, supposedly in Britain to visit Eton as a possible school for the princes. Since the opening of the Suez Canal, the European powers had been battling each other over control of northern East Africa, but given Abyssinia's continued resistance to colonization, by 1910 the country was a powerful symbol of black pride and independence. This symbolism would, of course, intensify into the 1930s with Rastafarianism. In 1896, for instance, Menelik had defeated the Italians at the Battle of Adowa and in 1902, the British, pro-Italian, historian George F. H. Berkeley described the battle as 'a peculiar phenomenon … that a European army of about twenty thousand men should be annihilated by a native African race … it seems possible that it heralds the rise of a new power in Africa … The suggestion has even been made – absurd as it appears at present – that this is the first revolt of the Dark Continent against domineering Europe' (vii–viii). Later, in his lengthy chapter on Abyssinia in *Empire and Commerce in Africa* (1920), Leonard Woolf would note that 'The position of Abyssinia in Africa is peculiar. To-day it is the only native State which has retained even the semblance of independence' (140). We now know, too, details of the extensive research Virginia Woolf conducted, including on the history of European attempts to colonize Abyssinia, as preparation for this volume (see Barrett).

In her own writing of this period, too, Virginia Woolf made reference to Ethiopia and imperialism. In *The Voyage Out*, Ethiopia appears in the context of imperial Rome's designs on north Africa which echo those of contemporary Europe: 'His generals, in the early part of his reign, attempted the reduction of Aethiopia and Arabia Felix ... but the heat of the climate soon repelled the invaders and protected the unwarlike natives of those sequestered regions' (162). In the decade after the Adowa victory, Ethiopia's independence was secure, but in 1906 when Menelik suffered the first of a series of strokes concerns over succession led to intensified encroachments by European powers. The Tripartite Agreement with Britain, France, and Italy was signed in 1906 to protect their interests (against Germany) in the region (Zewde 114). At the time of the hoax, Germany's interventions in the region meant that Britain was seen as an ally (Downer 99). More broadly, the hoax's performance of diplomacy masks the history of violence and economic exploitation in relation to British rule in Africa. As Leonard Woolf would put it: 'the dealings of all European States with African kings is one of almost unredeemed treachery and breach of faith' (165). The assassination too had underscored this treachery and hypocrisy, although in a different colonial context.

The history of scholarship on the Bloomsbury Group has been uneven in its continued attention to the same 'celebrity' members – something this volume will surely begin to rectify. The recent biography of David Garnett will lead to renewed interest in his novels – remarkable, in particular, for their treatment of nonhuman identities. The flexibility of his diverse political engagements would also benefit from further scholarship by way of continuing the early focus here. This conjunction of assassination and hoax – via David Garnett – points to the multifarious expressions of anti-imperialism in late Edwardian London, as well the ways in which the heart of empire facilitated networks of revolutionaries and anarchists. It also highlights the history of particular spaces in Bloomsbury – here Red Lion Square – and the ways in which they afforded serendipitous connections.[10] Furthermore, for both Woolf and Garnett these episodes are about performance: the experimentation or identification with novel or transgressive identities, whether gendered or racial cross-dressing or via queer politics. Garnett's involvement is, on one level, a racial masquerade akin to the hoax, although with much more at stake. It is, in part, about his teenage adulation of resistance and racial otherness; his personal attraction to Savarkar enabled a solidarity or crossing over. It emerges, also, from an understanding of political activism inherited from his mother and networks of Russian émigrés in London. The jailbreak plot, in particular, develops into a more familiar novelistic or cinematic great escape narrative. Elements such as the 'female disguise consisting of a motoring hat and veil, then commonly worn by female motorists' bought by Garnett for Savarkar and the clandestine planning meetings with Chattopadhyaya in hired boats at the 'Kensington end of the Serpentine' make the escape plan, like the *Dreadnought* hoax, seem parodic and highly self-conscious (D. Garnett 155).

But what seems clear in relation to these events as they pertain to 'Bloomsbury' and empire is the contingent or intersectional approach required to take full account of their origins and effects. Actions and affiliations take on very different signification when viewed in relation to queer or Asian Bloomsbury, for example. Garnett's actions may appear surprising viewed backwards from the perspective of his later life, or in relation to accounts of Bloomsbury as apolitical or reactionary in its politics, but in the context of the Garnett's late nineteenth-century networks, the connection with revolutionary nationalism is rather less surprising. The collision of Bloomsbury and extremist nationalism that Garnett's life makes apparent underscores the need for a redrawing of the contours of modernist London to allow for a more flexible account of the collaborations between metropolitan and colonial writers, artists and radicals. The Bloomsbury Group, but also the spaces of Bloomsbury – home to so many anti-colonial organizations in this period – facilitated meetings and chance encounters which had surprising consequences. As the cultures of empire shifted and buckled, the unevenness of resistance in this period produced unexpected congruencies, and ones which our critical paradigms can at times obscure.

NOTES

1. For detailed accounts of this assassination and its contexts see Datta; Tickell (135–83); Visram (156–62).
2. See, for example, Houen (34–92).
3. See Tickell for further details of Indian radicals who stayed at India House between 1905 and 1910 (when it was closed by the police): these included revolutionary nationalists such as Lala Har Dayal (leader of the Ghadr party); political activist Virendranath Chattopadhyaya, brother of Sarojini Naidu and feminist and nationalist leader, Madame Bhikaji Cama. Nonviolent activists, including M. K. Gandhi, were also visitors to the hostel (Tickell 138–46).
4. Cf. Mr Vladimir's rationale for the Greenwich bomb in Conrad's *The Secret Agent*: 'What we want is to administer a tonic to the conference in Milan … Its deliberations upon international action for the suppression of political crime don't seem to get anywhere. England lags. This country is absurd with its sentimental regard for individual liberty' (23).
5. See, for example, Nasta and Menen.
6. See Islam, *Savarkar: Myths and Facts*, which argues for two distinct phases in his politics: his early revolutionary nationalism based in Hindu–Muslim unity and his shift, while in jail, to Hindu separatism and collaboration with British rule.
7. The song's lyrics were: 'When I went on board a Dreadnought Ship/Though I looked just like a costermonger/They said I was an Abyssinian Prince/Because I shouted "Bunga-Bunga"' (Lee 285).
8. See D. Jones for discussion of Woolf's narrativizing of the hoax for her W. I. talk and its context within wartime anxieties: 'she once again commandeered the deck of the *Dreadnought*', Jones argues, 'to challenge the theatre of war with a story of peace' (92).
9. The hoaxers' use of 'Abyssinian' denotes their supposed, specific national origins, but the slippage in usage between 'Ethiopia' and 'Abyssinia' in the early twentieth century also alludes to a wider history of white American blackface and African American performance. More specifically, 'Ethiopian', used to mean 'African', was a common, generic term for minstrel performers and venues following the popular, blackface group the 'Ethiopian Serenaders' who toured in England from 1846. By way of contrast, the adjective 'real' or 'original' was used to distinguish groups of African American performers. See B. Zewde for a fuller history of the terminology (1).
10. Red Lion Square's position as home to radical organizations and publishers intensified into the 1930s when it was home to Charles Lahr's Progressive Bookshop, Lawrence and Wishart, and the *Left Review*.

WORKS CITED

Barkway, Stephen. 'The "Dreadnought Hoax": The Aftermath for "Prince Sanganya" and "His" Cousins'. *Virginia Woolf Bulletin* 21 (2006): 20–28.

Barrett, Michele. 'Virginia Woolf's Research for *Empire and Commerce in Africa* (Leonard Woolf, 1920)', *Woolf Studies Annual* (2013): 83–122.

Berkeley, G. F. H. *The Campaign of Adowa and the Rise of Menelik*. London: Archibald Constable, 1902.

Blyth, Robert J. 'Introduction'. *The Dreadnought and the Edwardian Age*. Ed. Robert J. Blyth, Andrew Lambert and Jan Rüger. Farnham: Ashgate, 2011. 1–8.

Boehmer, Elleke. *Indian Arrivals 1870–1915: Networks of British Empire*. Oxford: Oxford UP, 2015.

Chirol, Valentine. *Indian Unrest*. London: Macmillan, 1910.

Conrad, Joseph. *The Secret Agent*. London: Penguin, 2012.

Datta, Vishwa Nath. *Madan Lal Dhingra and the Revolutionary Movement*. New Delhi: Vikas Publishing, 1978.

Delap, Lucy. 'Maritime Symbolism in Edwardian Gender Politics, *The Dreadnought and the Edwardian Age*'. Ed. Robert J. Blyth, Andrew Lambert and Jan Rüger. Farnham: Ashgate, 2011. 95–108.

Downer, Martyn. *The Sultan of Zanzibar: The Bizarre World and Spectacular Hoaxes of Horace De Vere Cole*. London: Blackspring Press, 2010.

Garnett, David. *The Golden Echo*. London: Chatto & Windus, 1953.

Garnett, Richard. *Constance Garnett: A Heroic Life*. London: Sinclair-Stevenson, 1991.

Gerzina, G. Holbrook. 'Virginia Woolf, Performing Race'. *The Edinburgh Companion to Virginia Woolf and the Arts*. Ed. Maggie Humm. Edinburgh: Edinburgh UP, 2010. 74–87.

Houen, Alex. *Terrorism and Modern Literature*. Oxford: Oxford UP, 2002.

Hough, Richard. *A History of the Modern Battleship Dreadnought*. London: George Allen and Unwin, 1968.

Islam, Shamsul. *Savarkar: Myths and Facts*. Delhi: Media House, 2004.

Johnston, Georgia. 'Virginia Woolf's Talk on the Dreadnought Hoax'. *Woolf Studies Annual* 15 (2009): 1–46.

Jones, Clara. *Virginia Woolf: Ambivalent Activist*. Edinburgh: Edinburgh UP, 2015.

Jones, Danell. 'The Dreadnought Hoax and the Theatres of War'. *Literature and History* 22.1 (2013): 80–94.

Knights, Sarah. *Bloomsbury Outsider: A Life of David Garnett*. London: Bloomsbury, 2015.

Lee, Hermoine. *Virginia Woolf*, London: Vintage, 1997.

Mansfield, Katherine. *The Collected Letters of Katherine Mansfield*, Vol. 1 1903–1917. Ed. Vincent O'Sullivan and Margaret Scott. Oxford: Clarendon Press, 1984.

Massie, Robert K. *Dreadnought: Britain, Germany and the Coming of the Great War*. London: Random House, 1991.

Menen, Aubrey. *The Space within the Heart*. London: Hamish Hamilton, 1970.

Nasta, Susheila. 'Negotiating a "New World Order": Mulk Raj Anand as Public Intellectual at the Heart of Empire (1925–1945)'. *South Asian Resistances in Britain 1858–1947*. Ed. Rehana Ahmed and Sumita Mukherjee. London: Continuum, 2012. 140–60.

'Notes of the Week'. *The New Age* 4.23 (1909): 454.

Owen, N. (2007), *The British Left and India: Metropolitan Anti-Imperialism 1885–1947*. Oxford: Oxford UP.

Roberts, John. *The Battleship Dreadnought*. London: Conway Maritime Press, 1992.

Rüger, Jan. 'The Symbolic Value of the *Dreadnought*'. *The Dreadnought and the Edwardian Age*. Ed. Robert J. Blyth, Andrew Lambert and Jan Rüger. Farnham: Ashgate, 2011. 9–18.

Stephen, Adrian. *The 'Dreadnought' Hoax*. London: Hogarth Press, 1936.

Tickell, Alex. *Terrorism, Insurgency and Indian-English Literature: 1830–1947*. New York: Routledge, 2012.

Visram, Rozina. *Asians in Britain: 400 Years of History*. London: Pluto Press, 2002.

Waraich, M. J. S. and K. Puri. *Tryst with Martyrdom: Trial of Madan Lal Dinghra*, Chandigarh: Unistar, 2003.

Woolf, Leonard. *Empire and Commerce in Africa*. London: Routledge, 1998.

Woolf, Virginia. *The Letters of Virginia Woolf, Vol. 6*. Ed. Nigel Nicolson and Joanne Trautmann. London: Chatto and Windus, 1983.

Woolf, Virginia. *The Voyage Out*. Ed. C. Ruth Miller and Lawrence Miller. Oxford: Blackwell, 1995.

Zewde, Bahru. *A History of Modern Ethiopia 1855–1991*. Oxford: James Currey, 2001.

CHAPTER FOUR

Bloomsbury and Feminism

LAUREN ELKIN

There is a test for films, TV shows, books, any narrative art really, called the Bechdel test, which asks: does this story meet one or more of the following criteria? If so, it may be considered a feminist work:

1. The movie has to have at least two women in it,
2. who talk to each other,
3. about something besides a man.

The test comes from a 1985 comic strip by Alison Bechdel called *Dykes to Watch Out For*, although Bechdel credits her friend Liz Wallace with developing the criteria, suggesting Wallace was thinking of a passage in Virginia Woolf's 1929 feminist essay *A Room of One's Own*:

> All these relationships between women, I thought, rapidly recalling the splendid gallery of fictitious women, are too simple ... And I tried to remember any case in the course of my reading where two women are represented as friends ... Almost without exception they are shown in their relation to men. It was strange to think that all the great women of fiction were, until Jane Austen's day, not only seen by the other sex, but seen *only in relation* to the other sex. And how small a part of a woman's life is that. (82, emphasis added)

Conversation, for Bechdel and for Woolf, appears to provide the basis for a feminist vision. There is something about women talking to each other about something other than men which would seem – informally speaking – to suggest the fullness, the complication of 'a woman's life'.

I wish to bring the notions of feminist relationality and exchange raised by the Bechdel test and *A Room of One's Own* to bear on the subject of Bloomsbury and feminism. While acknowledging that Bloomsbury is a 'kaleidoscopic' phenomenon, whose meaning is relative from moment to moment, and critic to critic, if we draw on what Bloomsbury had to say for itself, it essentially boils down to a group of friends who liked to talk to one another.[1] Many accounts by its participants bear this out: Clive Bell recalled that he and his contemporaries 'shared a taste for discussion in pursuit of truth and a contempt for conventional ways of thinking and feeling, contempt for conventional morals if you will' (119–20). Duncan Grant provided a description of what happened at the Thursday evening gatherings given by the Stephen siblings, where 'what has since been called "Bloomsbury" for good or ill came into being'; guests arrived around ten and lingered until two or three in the morning drinking whisky and cocoa and nibbling on buns. Above all, 'people talked to each other ... Conversation; that was all' (403–4). Frances Partridge recalls: 'What they enjoyed most was talk – talk of every description, from the most abstract to the most hilariously ribald and profane ... The Bloomsburies called spades spades and said what they thought' (76). And, not least, Virginia Woolf famously describes the liberating effect of their conversations with the young men who went to Cambridge with Thoby, who would come over and talk not of society but of ideas, and the liberating frankness when those conversations turned to sex, 'buggery', and seminal fluid: 'there was now nothing that one could not say, nothing that one could not do, at 46 Gordon Square' (196) (see Avery in this volume). But was there a specifically *feminist* politics of the Bloomsbury Group? Quentin Bell raises the question in his memoir, claiming the group is inherently 'feminist' because it was an early instance of a 'moral adventure ... in which women were on a completely equal footing with men': 'It was also more or less feminist in a wider and more usual sense ... I think that they were more persistent and more thoroughgoing than most, if not all, of their contemporaries in their rejection of the claims of authority to establish canons for men and women' (42–3).[2]

Bloomsbury came about because a group of young men who liked to talk to one another at Cambridge wanted to go on doing so in London. The Cambridge Apostles – whose ranks included Thoby Stephen, Lytton Strachey, John Maynard Keynes, and Leonard Woolf – were also called the Cambridge Conversazione Society. Ann Banfield has investigated its impact on Woolf's work through its members' reverence for the analytic philosophy of G. E. Moore and Bertrand Russell; in her introduction, she briefly considers what conversation might have meant to the women associated with Bloomsbury:

> Bloomsbury began, we recall, in Woolf's version, not simply with her and her sister's inclusion in the conversation, but with the pronouncing of an abstract term, a universal: whether the subject was 'beauty', 'good', or 'reality' ... It developed by logical argumentation: 'Never have I listened so intently to each step and half-step in an argument, ... never have I been at such pains to sharpen and launch my own little dart. And then what joy it was when one's own contribution was accepted. No praise has pleased me more than Saxon's saying ... that he thought I had argued my case very cleverly.' (33)

This was a far cry from the conversations the Stephen sisters were accustomed to keeping up back in Kensington, where 'we were not asked to use our brains much':

> One no longer had to endure that terrible inquisition after a party – and be told, 'You looked lovely'; Or, 'You did look plain.' Or, 'You must really learn to do your hair.' Or, 'Do try not to look so bored when you dance.' Or, 'You did make a conquest,' or, 'You were a failure.' All this seemed to have no meaning or existence in the world of Bell, Strachey, Hawtrey, and Sydney-Turner. In that world the only comment as we stretched ourselves after our guests had gone, was, 'I must say you made your point rather well'; 'I think you were talking rather through your hat.' It was an immense simplification. ('Old Bloomsbury' 52)

In her own retrospective essay, modestly titled 'Notes on Bloomsbury', Vanessa Bell describes the feeling of total liberation she and her siblings shared in the absence of elders looking over their shoulders: 'If you could say what you like about art, sex or religion, you could also talk freely and very likely dully about the ordinary doings of daily life. There was very little self-consciousness, I think, in those early gatherings, but life was exciting, terrible and amusing, and we had to explore it, thankful that one could do so freely' (105).

In Bell's reference to the 'stiff young ladies to whom it did not occur not to talk about the weather' we hear the story of the Stephens sisters' liberation – one they would probably not think of as 'feminist', but which almost certainly was, in the sense of two young women venturing to live life on their own terms without regard for convention or public judgment (104). Bell notes that when she and her sister began receiving the young men fresh from Cambridge, talking of G. E. Moore and the 'meaning of good', it seemed to her that 'the young men were perhaps not clear enough in their own heads to mind trying to get clearer by discussion with young women who might possibly see things from a different angle' (101). Conversation was a way of coming to terms with this new world, and both genders had much to learn by learning to take part in it.

It seems to me, then, that if conversation between women about subjects other than men is inherently feminist, and Bloomsbury was essentially about conversation, then the conversational exchanges between women within Bloomsbury might help us to better understand the relationship between Bloomsbury and feminism. But what did Bloomsbury, and the conversations it enabled, mean to its female members? How important did the female members find exchange with each other, not merely with male members of the group? Very, if we are to judge from the thematizing and valorizing of female conversation in their work. In her 1928 study of the women's movement *The Cause*, Ray Strachey describes women's claiming of political power as a transition from the kind of behind-the-scenes influence a few aristocratic women historically enjoyed, 'secured through the relationship, friendship, or love of the men who were conducting the business of government', to the growing influence women had over public policy once they began banding together to explicitly discuss their social circumstances (33). In other words, in order to gain political power, women had to stop speaking through their men, and start speaking to each other.

Strachey particularly describes the 'great years of the Women's Movement, when organized societies were expanding with incredible rapidity, when agitation was becoming an exact science', and when 'the meetings which multiplied in halls and drawing rooms, in schools and chapels, at street corners, and on village greens, did not seem like the dull and solemn stuff of politics; they were missionary meetings, filled with the fervour of a gospel, and each one brought new enthusiasts to the ranks'. Strachey observes how easily women's issues, especially suffrage, lent themselves to public and private debate:

> Everyone in the country felt an interest; everyone knew, or thought they knew, the fundamental differences between men and women, and consequently everyone was ready to have an opinion. No special learning, no abstruse facts nor formidable statistics were required. One could be 'for' or 'against' with the greatest certainty and ease, and find plenty of simple arguments on either side. One could say that 'women's place is the home', and feel that everything was disposed of; or one could say 'two heads are better than one' and feel equally triumphant; and all over the country people began to say one or other of these things. (302–3)

Place was incredibly important to the feminist movement, and Bloomsbury was a breeding ground for women's liberation. One major component of this was the fight for women's suffrage; another, more everyday kind of feminism was lived in the boarding houses and bedsits where young women could come and live independently. In a different context – that of early to mid-twentieth-century New York – Jane Jacobs has written of the importance of exchange in a neighbourhood; cities and people thrive on this contact. As Woolf's work frequently shows us, women not only need a room of their own in which to be creative; they also need the city, and specifically, a neighbourhood of their own, to enable contact between them.

There are deep connections between feminism and the London neighbourhood that gave the Bloomsbury Group their name. In order to examine how conversation became so important to the women in the group, I will mainly focus on the early years of the group, the formative moments for the Stephen sisters as individuals and artists in their own right, beginning with their move to Bloomsbury until the onset of the First World War; I will consider as bookends to this period Woolf's short story 'Phyllis and Rosamond' (1905) and Vanessa Bell's painting A Conversation (1913–15).

THE NEIGHBOURHOOD

Sara Blair has argued for the importance of understanding Bloomsbury as produced *by* and *in* Bloomsbury, of seeing it 'not as a movement or group or coterie or junta but as a local world' (814).[3] The Stephen sisters were part of a larger feminist reclaiming of Bloomsbury that operated through a use of social and conversational as well as architectural space. Although in the nineteenth century it had been a scruffily genteel middle-class neighbourhood, around the turn of the twentieth century, Bloomsbury became a haven for radical feminists and independent young women; a number of women's organizations were headquartered there, including the Women's Social and Political Union, the International Franchise Club, the Women's Freedom League, and the National Union of Women's Suffrage Societies – many of these in fact in the same building at 34 Mecklenburgh Square, which came to be nicknamed Reform House. This is where Woolf came to do clerical work for the People's Suffrage League, run by Margaret Llewelyn-Davis, where Janet Case served on the executive committee, and where she set the suffrage office where Mary Datchet works in *Night and Day* (1919). According to Naomi Black, she was also associated with the Women's Cooperative Guild and the National Union of Women's Suffrage Societies, and was therefore 'squarely in the middle of the organisational network of social feminism in Britain' (184). Barbara Green draws an explicit link between the fight for women's suffrage and Woolf's own feelings of emancipation in Bloomsbury: 'Virginia Woolf walked because the suffragettes marched' (38).[4]

The group's feminist conversations and commitments have their roots in Bloomsbury's local politics and social reconfigurations. Bloomsbury before the war was full of feminist activists; Kathryn Holland describes the many activities of the Strachey women in particular during this period, organizing marches, writing and editing suffragist papers, suggesting the Stracheys' activism may be productively read in the context of Woolf's feminist writing, and that, indeed, we may think of them as Woolf's 'principal feminist interlocutors' (75).[5] Many of these connections were forged or connected by the work the Woolfs did at the Hogarth Press (see Battershill in this volume), which published a series of eleven feminist pamphlets including texts by Willa Muir, Margaret Llewelyn Davies, and the Viscountess Rhondda, who founded the Six Point Group in 1921.[6] Ten years after Strachey wrote *The Cause*, the Woolfs would publish a collection of essays edited by Strachey called *Our Freedom and Its Results*, which looked at the impact of the women's movement on politics, morality, and daily life.

Late in life, Woolf evinced hostility to the words 'feminism' and 'the emancipation of women': 'none of these tags and labels express the real emotions that inspired' the women's movement (*Three Guineas* 137). Many critics have taken her satiric representations of the suffrage workers in *Night and Day* as early evidence of this suspicion; Alex Zwerdling, for instance, reads this as Woolf's impatience 'with the narrowly political focus the Suffragette agitation had created' (214). But in her recent study *Virginia Woolf: Ambivalent Activist*, Clara Jones nuances Woolf's relationship to politics, notably with regard to the suffragist campaigns of the 1900s and 1910s.[7] Jones focuses her study on what she calls Woolf's ambivalence about engaging in activism throughout her life, and shows us a writer who was a 'highly critical but nonetheless committed participant' in the kinds of organizations outlined above (3). 'Would it be any use if I spent an afternoon or two weekly in addressing envelopes for the Adult Suffragists?' Woolf writes in a 1910 letter to her former Greek tutor Janet Case, expressing a desire to help but doubt about whether that help would make a real contribution. 'The only way to better [the state of affairs] is to do some thing I suppose. How melancholy it is that conversation isn't enough!' (*Letters* 1: 421). Conversation may not be 'enough', but it is indispensable as a starting point for feminist change.

Woolf's 1905 short story 'Phyllis and Rosamond' examines the limitations of a certain kind of conversation in which women are trained, and it does so by contrasting the world Woolf and her siblings came from with the one they moved to. 'The stucco fronts, the irreproachable rows of Belgravia and South Kensington seemed to Phyllis the type of her lot; of a life trained to grow in an ugly pattern to match the staid ugliness of its fellows. But if one lived here in Bloomsbury', she goes on, 'one might grow up as one liked' (24). The story introduces the reader to the Tristram sisters, who are young, artistic, and free: mirror images for Phyllis and Rosamond (themselves modelled on Vanessa and Virginia Stephen), who are 'slaves' to their class and situation: 'We are daughters, until we become married women' (27). Unlike in Woolf's account of learning to talk to the Apostles, Phyllis can't access the conversation; everything she's been taught to talk about won't hold up there:

> The talk was of certain pictures then being shown, and their merits were discussed from a somewhat technical standpoint. Where was Phyllis to begin? She had seen them; but she knew that her platitudes would never stand the test of question and criticism to which they would be exposed. Nor, she knew, was there any scope here for those feminine graces which could veil so much. (25)

Phyllis and Rosamond have been taught to converse in a particular mode, one that is not informed by the critical discourse of an Oxbridge conversation society; their ways of discussing are invalid in Bloomsbury. As Melanie Tebbett points out in a very different context – her social history of London's working-class women and gossip – 'women's talk has traditionally been disparaged as an inferior form of conversation, lacking the significance of men's words, although their use of language has often been one of the few ways in which women could assert themselves ... The ideal mode of discourse for women was judged for many years to be silence' (7). Woolf is not asking us to see Phyllis's potential viewpoints on art as comparable to Jane Austen's engraving on a one-inch piece of ivory – but we can hear here an early instance of her argument in *A Room of One's Own* that women's talk is seen as 'trivial' (74). Phyllis and Rosamond 'held intellect in great reverence', but they have been raised to run homes, not to think for themselves (23). The form of conversation isn't enough, they find; content and style matter as well.

IN THE STUDIO

Another more everyday kind of feminism was being negotiated indoors: Bloomsbury was gaining a reputation for being a hotbed of progressive politics and a place where women could pursue independent lifestyles, living frugally but freely in boarding houses. In drawing rooms and studios, Bloomsbury women sought a space in which to talk to one another. The kinds of conversations and connections that were facilitated by these living arrangements sustained this everyday urban feminism, and a closer look needs to be taken between feminism, aesthetics, and the progressive feminist atmosphere of the neighbourhood that lent the group its name. Intimacy and connection were major ways in which the links between neighbourhood and group politics were developed.

In 1905, wanting to connect and exchange with other artists, Vanessa Bell founded the Friday Club, 'a place where artists could talk shop, listen to lectures, discuss their work and even from time to time hold exhibitions' (Shone 26; see also Humm in this volume). According to Isabelle Anscombe, the club's membership was mainly composed of women; Spalding mentions a few of Bell's friends from the Royal Academy, where she studied painting (Margery Snowden, Mary Creighton, and Sylvia Milman), some recruits from the Slade (Edna Clarke Hall and Claire Atwood) and 'certain of Vanessa's friends and relatives', including Katherine Cox, Marjorie Strachey, and Beatrice Mayor. Diane Gillespie quotes an unpublished typescript in which Bell admitted to feeling intimidated by a similar group, the New English Art Club, populated by men who 'seemed somehow to have the secret of the art universe within their grasp, a secret one was not worthy to learn, especially if one as that terrible low creature, a female painter' (36). 'Whatever the Friday Club achieved', writes Frances Spalding, 'its existence is a testimony to Vanessa's organisational prowess' (56). It is also a testimony to Bell's desire to create a context in which women painters could talk to one another without fear of being judged and found wanting: the Friday Club as a feminist alternative to Thursday night Bloomsbury gatherings.

Critics have especially studied the group's politics as it regards their aesthetic theories, arguing not only for the influence of Fry and Bell but the possibility of Bloomsbury women influencing each other. Simpson considers the 'feminist gift-sphere' within which Woolf moved, both inside and outside of Bloomsbury, and the female friendships that sustained her: Jane Harrison, Violet Dickinson, Janet Case, Vita Sackville-West, and Katherine Mansfield (172). Margery Snowden was a particular confidant of Bell's; in Bell's published letters, those which deal most explicitly with questions of art and aesthetics are to her.[8] Woolf had rich relationships with women, and an increasing body of criticism addresses the relationships among the women in and around the Bloomsbury Group. Mary Ann Caws's *Bloomsbury Women* puts Woolf, Bell, and Dora Carrington into conversation with each other through attentive readings of their letters and diaries, their incessant requests for talk and gossip, to 'Tell ... tell ... tell ...' (50). Diane F. Gillespie's *The Sisters' Arts* considers Woolf and Bell's mutual influence on each other, while Jane Dunn's *A Very Close Conspiracy: Vanessa Bell and Virginia Woolf* takes a more biographical approach.

Christopher Reed looks at the 1915–16 portraits Bell painted of the women in her circle – Iris Tree, Mary Hutchinson – in terms of their 'formal composition and geometric settings' (151), suggesting that the photos of Bell posing nude with Molly MacCarthy in Bell's studio at 46 Gordon Square assert an ambition to be at home the way the figures in modernist paintings inhabit their environments: sensuously, instinctively, free of conventional inhibitions, integrated harmoniously with settings perceived in terms of abstract color and form' (151). Colour could be radical, for male and female artists alike. Stansky notes that in the *Daily Herald* a contemporary critic, Christina Walsh, equated Post-Impressionism with the suffragettes: 'The Post-Impressionists are in the company of the Great Rebels of the World. In politics the only movements worth considering are Woman Suffrage and Socialism. They are both Post-Impressionist in their desire to scrap old decaying forms and find for themselves a new working ideal' (qtd in Stansky 7).[9]

We cannot really describe Bell as a 'Great Rebel of the World' as easily as perhaps some might refer to her sister. Her biographer, Frances Spalding, notes that she preferred the 'conversation and the company' of men; perhaps, as Woolf dramatizes in 'Phyllis and Rosamond', conversation between women must in some way call attention to the social hurdles which must be overcome for women to live and converse freely, whereas with men, she could simply talk as if those hurdles did not exist. But conversation among women was clearly important to her, given that she dedicated a large canvas to it in the middle of the decade (19). The monumentality of *A Conversation* (1913–16; reproduced on the front cover of this volume) suggests the extent to which Bell saw female conversation as key not only to women's self-actualization but to her own status as an artist.

CONVERSATION

Painted in 1913 and modified in 1916, the painting crowds three women in front of a curtained window, which frames a garden full of flowers. One woman speaks while the other two listen; the woman who speaks looks beseeching as she gestures with one hand, palm upward, fingers closed. The three women are drawn together by the hand, which almost touches the other woman's fur coat (Woolf perhaps unconsciously echoes this when Mary fingering Katherine's fur skirt-trim in *Night and Day*): just one of the many nonverbal ways in which the three figures overlap and make contact. It is a picture that is full of unresolved and unresolvable ambiguities; as Corin Sworn observes in her essay on the painting: '[Bell's] repeated refusal to depict specific positions for her figure and clearly demarcate the spaces around them allows her to enmesh roles and positions discursively' (172). Space itself becomes discursive in the painting, but it is through the relation of the female forms to each other that the importance of their conversation is concretized.

It seems inarguable that a model for the work was a painting by Henri Matisse, whose work featured heavily in the Second Post-Impressionist Exhibition. English audiences were much taken with the canvases Matisse showed, which included *Dance I*, *La Luxe I*, and *The Red Studio*; Richard Shone argues that Bell's 1912 painting *A Room* at the Second Post-Impressionist Exhibition was an 'homage' and 'a conscious echo' of Matisse's *The Red Studio*. Bell visited his Matisse's studio when she was in Paris in January 1914. One painting in particular that Fry included in the show speaks volumes about the importance of female conversation for Bell: a canvas called *The Conversation* (1908–12) depicts a man in his pyjamas and a woman talking in front of a window, with a vibrant blue background, and outside, patches of flowers (or possibly pools with flowers floating on them). Bell has taken Matisse's man and woman, and turned them into an all-female group. Indeed, Gillian Beer has even suggested that the woman on the right was originally painted as a man with a cane. While Bell was working on the painting, in January 1914, she visited Paris, and was taken to Matisse's studio.

And yet the modernist aesthetic theories with which Bell engaged – notably Clive Bell's theory of significant form and Roger Fry's ideas of vision and design – are more interested in the relationships between forms on the canvas rather than what they might point to beyond it (see Hussey in this volume). Thus, two figures like those in Matisse's painting might be said to be in 'conversation' with each other merely in terms of the relationship of their two forms. Lisa Tickner finds an example of this in a study for Bell's *Studland Beach* (1912–13); the relationship of the child's hat to the mother's 'bring[s] the figures into a different kind of emotional contact. Before, they seemed to look in easy companionship at the same distant vista. Now, the foreshortened boater tilts around and up in a direct address' (67).

The same could be said of the conversation genre more generally. Developed from portrait paintings in the Netherlands in the sixteenth century, and popularized in England by William Hogarth (a source with appropriately Woolfian resonance), it emerged out of the *sacra conversazione* genre of Italian Renaissance painting, depicting the Virgin and Child attended by saints.[10] No one speaks in these sacred conversation pieces; they communicate spiritually, wordlessly. Indeed, a later canvas by Matisse entitled *La conversation* (1938) would merely picture two women sitting beside one another, not speaking or even facing each other. Bell captures this in the relation of forms to one another: as Sue Roe says of *A Conversation*, 'their whole bodies are talking' (169). This was the painting that made Woolf write to Bell in 1928: 'I think you are a most remarkable painter. But I maintain you are into the bargain, a satirist, a conveyor of impressions about human life: a short story writer of great wit and able to bring odd a situation in a way that rouses my envy. I wonder if I could write the Three Women in prose' (*Letters* 3: 498–9).

According to Jane Goldman, however, we need to complicate Bell's relationship to the 'Bloomsbury aesthetic' of significant form. Goldman suggests, rather, that Bell's conception of colour is 'at odds with the theories of Fry and Clive Bell' (123). For Vanessa Bell, 'colour is in fact form', and colour – as Woolf reminds us in *Walter Sickert: A Conversation* – is laden with its own significance. Key to this point is the relationship between form and content in a painting; we tend to think of modernist or 'significant' form as creating life on the page, or canvas, rather than replicating some independent external reality – that is, imitating it. But 'instead of insisting that form can be significant only at the expense of context/subject matter, as Fry and Clive Bell do', Goldman argues that Vanessa Bell 'exploits the tension between the two, showing that form and content may cohere in a painting, without making it imitative' (146). The political content of a painting, therefore, cannot easily be divorced from its form, and strictly abstract work – like that Bell completed for the Omega workshop – cannot be said to be void of content or innocent of politics.

Bell thought of her painting again in 1918, when Woolf asked her to illustrate her short story 'Kew Gardens'. Reading the story, which is organized around four conversations overheard by a snail in a London park, Bell responded most enthusiastically to the third one, between 'two elderly women of the lower middle class, one stout and ponderous, the other rose cheeked and nimble', who are engaged in a 'very complicated dialogue':

'Nell, Bert, Lot, Cess, Phil, Pa, he says, I says, she says, I says, I says –'

'My Bert, Sis Bill, Grandad, the old man, sugar,

Sugar, four kippers, greens

Sugar, sugar, sugar'. (93)

In the end, she created a new woodcut for the story (see Diane Gillespie's account of the final design, 139), but it is telling that, as Laura Marcus observes, 'Bell was drawn to the only dialogue in the story that takes place between two women; point of view could thus be read in gendered terms':

> Bell is perhaps responding less to the class and intellectual superiority implicit in the way Woolf constructed the dialogue than to its potential for the depiction of women's community. Hence Bell's reference to *The Conversation* [*sic*] in this context, a painting whose lines encircle, or, in Woolfian terms, 'englobe' conversation between women. (140)

The conversation between the women makes sense only to them; they navigate its complex, laconic linguistics through familiarity and shorthand.

At a talk given at the Courtauld Institute in 2009, Gillian Beer suggested that Bell has even done away with perspective. This would explain why, in the painting, it seems unclear whether the green and brown blobs above the listening women's heads are hats or some kind of foliage outside. Without perspective, we can't 'place' the elements of the painting; the painting can dwell in a kind of ambiguity, similar to the dialogue we overhear in 'Kew Gardens'. But what a wonderful challenge to 'meaning' to omit perspective from a painting about conversation, in which the various points of view could be said to be the women's 'perspectives' on the subject at hand. In fact, Bell gives us a 'very complicated dialogue' which takes place entirely within the 'silent kingdom of paint'. The conversation is unlikely to be the sort of lofty inquiries into 'beauty' and 'the good' that was central to early Bloomsbury; but closer, perhaps, to the kinds of 'trivialities' Woolf makes a case for in *A Room of One's Own*. Perhaps even in the conversation itself, there is no 'perspective', only the informality of opinions. Placing women in relation to one another in this wordless, embodied conversation strips out the necessity for women's language to scan a certain way, to meet with approval; we strain to hear what they're saying, but it's only between them.

Across Virginia Woolf's work, conversation plays an important role in allowing people to air their diverse points of view. Her 1934 essay on Walter Sickert, which lays out the differences between writers and painters as the former's impulse to verbosity and the latter's withdrawal into the 'silent kingdom of paint', is entitled *A Conversation* (13). The essay could be said to function as a kind of window into the kinds of conversations the Bloomsbury Group engaged in. *The Common Reader* was originally meant to be a conversation, which she tried out in a piece for the *Nation and Athenaeum* in 1923 on Joseph Conrad. It did not turn out as she hoped, and she abandoned the plan to structure the essays as dialogues. Laura Marcus comments that this may have been born of a desire 'to reawaken classical aesthetic discourse, and in particular the Platonic or Socratic dialogue' (17).

Jane Dunn suggests Bell's *A Conversation* had an influence on *A Room of One's Own*: five months after Woolf saw the painting again at Bell's 1928 exhibition, she sent her sister the letter praising it, wondering if she could capture the painting in prose. Soon after, Woolf read the two papers on 'women and fiction' at Cambridge women's colleges that would be extended to become *A Room of One's Own* (157). Perhaps, as Marcus argues, the critical essay itself takes on this dialogical function for Woolf, becoming a 'conversation with the reader, in which the essayist becomes a mediating figure between reader and author, present and past' (18). Perhaps Woolf wrote the *Three Women* in prose every time she wrote an essay: if one imagines the reader and subject as well as the essayist as female, there are the three women.

The story we know Woolf wrote in response to *A Conversation* is 'A Society' (1921), in which a group of female friends discusses their ostensible purpose of being put on earth to bear children. They take it upon themselves to enquire as to the state of the world that the men have made, making themselves 'into a society for asking questions' (119). Judging from her letter to Bell, and this story, Woolf clearly reads *A Conversation* as satire; we might read it, suggests Jane Marcus, as 'Woolf's attempt ... to offer a parallel sisterhood of intellectual inquiry and social conscience' to rival the Apostles (91). The development from 'Phyllis and Rosamond' to *A Conversation* permits us to read conversation as a feminist trope of the revolutionary relationships between forms. Where Phyllis finds that the form of conversation isn't enough, but content and style matter as well, *A Conversation* finds that the form is enough; content isn't even necessary to represent. We don't know if it meets point three of the Bechdel test, but it certainly meets one and two. As Woolf later notes in 'Old Bloomsbury', 'Talk – even the talk which had such tremendous results upon the lives and characters of the two Miss Stephens – even talk of this interest and importance is as elusive as smoke' (165). The form of contact between women – their significant form – is as important as the content of their discussions.

As Marcus has shown, collective identity was important to Woolf: 'Virginia Woolf first learned to say "we" as a woman' (11). In *Three Guineas*, she also resorts to the device of the society to critique the world the men have made: the anonymous and secret Society of Outsiders is built on her refusal of patriotism and patriarchy. Only this time, the stakes are much higher: the Society of Outsiders is founded to 'prevent war ... by finding new words and creating new methods' (170). Those methods, ostensibly, will be found through discussion. Even when talk is just talk, and Woolf's or Bell's attitude towards their subjects is ambivalent at best – as we see for 'Phyllis and Rosamond', or as in *A Conversation* – it is a major way in which the women of Bloomsbury freed themselves from the constrictions of gender and class to create their new world, about which we have not yet tired of talking.

NOTES

1. On the term 'kaleidoscopic', see Simpson, who suggests that Bloomsbury 'may be understood as both a literal and metaphorical meeting point and as a multidisciplinary intellectual and artistic nexus for the sharing and debating of modern, unorthodox, avant-garde ideas (and, of course, the details of one another's personal lives)' (170).
2. In the plates in the middle of the book, Quentin Bell captions a photograph from 1911 of Clive Bell, Desmond MacCarthy, Marjorie Strachey, and Molly McCarthy at Studland by quoting Desmond MacCarthy looking at himself forty years later: ' "What a fine military-looking character," ... He referred to himself and not, as might be supposed, to the belligerent suffragette on his left.'
3. Blair is reacting to a suggestion by Tony Aldous that 'The term "Bloomsbury", whether used in approbation or in derision, had ... not all that much to do with the place as a place. The brilliant aura of Lytton Strachey, the Bells, [Roger] Fry, [Virginia] Woolf, and the rest might almost as easily have been attached to Marylebone or St John's Wood if two or three of them had happened to live there' (814).
4. For more on Woolf and the city, see Potts and Shahriari, Bradshaw, Neverow, Bowlby, Squier, Evans and Cornish, and Elkin.
5. See also Chapman and Manson.
6. And, of course, Virginia Woolf's *Three Guineas* (1938). See Laura Marcus ('Virginia Woolf and the Hogarth Press'). I would like to thank Francesca Wade for discussing Mecklenburgh Square with me and for pointing me in the direction of the Viscountess Rhondda.

7. For other critical work on Woolf and suffrage, see Snaith, Zwerdling, and Jane Marcus.
8. I am grateful to Sarah Milroy, co-curator of the recent Vanessa Bell retrospective at the Dulwich Picture Gallery in London (8 February–4 June 2017), for sharing these reflections with me. Private conversation, 16 January 2017.
9. Roger Fry rejected this outright: 'The accusation of anarchism was constantly made. From an aesthetic point of view this was, of course, the exact opposite of the truth' (qtd in Stansky 6). See Goldman for a fascinating discussion of colours and the suffrage campaign.
10. See Einberg and Egerton.

WORKS CITED

Allen, Judith. *Virginia Woolf and the Politics of Language*. Edinburgh: Edinburgh UP, 2010.

Banfield, Ann. *The Phantom Table: Woolf, Fry, Russell, and the Epistemology of Modernism*. Cambridge: Cambridge UP, 2000.

Bechdel, Alison. 'Testy'. *Dykes to Watch Out For*. 8 November 2013. www.dykestowatchoutfor. com/testy. Accessed 28 May 2017.

Beer, Gillian. 'On *A Conversation* by Vanessa Bell'. *The Guardian*, 26 November 2009. www. theguardian.com/artanddesign/audio/2009/feb/24/gillian-beer-vanessa-bell. Accessed 28 May 2017.

Bell, Clive. 'What Was Bloomsbury?' *The Bloomsbury Group: A Collection of Memoirs and Commentary*. Ed. S. P. Rosenbaum. Toronto: U of Toronto P, 1995. 115–23.

Bell, Quentin. *Bloomsbury*. London: Weidenfeld and Nicholson, 1968.

Bell, Vanessa. 'Notes on Bloomsbury'. *Sketches in Pen and Ink*. Ed. Lia Giachero. London: Hogarth Press, 1997.

Black, Naomi. *Virginia Woolf as Feminist*. Ithaca, NY: Cornell UP, 2003.

Black, Naomi. 'Virginia Woolf and the Women's Movement'. *Virginia Woolf: A Feminist Slant*. Ed. Jane Marcus. Lincoln: U of Nebraska P, 1983.

Blair, Sara. 'Local Modernity, Global Modernism: Bloomsbury and the Places of the Literary'. *ELH* 71.3 (2004): 813–38.

Bowlby, Rachel. 'Walking, Women, and Writing: Virginia Woolf as Flâneuse'. *Still Crazy after All These Years*. London: Routledge, 1992. 1–34.

Bradshaw, David. 'Woolf's London, London's Woolf'. *Virginia Woolf in* Context. Ed. Bryony Randall and Jane Goldman. Cambridge: Cambridge UP, 2012. 229–42.

Chapman, Wayne K. and Janet M. Manson. Eds. *Women in the Milieu of Leonard and Virginia Woolf: Peace, Politics, and Education*. New York: Pace UP, 1998.

Dunn, Jane. *A Very Close Conspiracy: Vanessa Bell and Virginia Woolf*. London: Jonathan Cape, 1990.

Einberg, Elizabeth and Judy Egerton. *The Age of Hogarth: British Painters Born 1675–1709*. London: Tate Gallery, 1988.

Elkin, Lauren. *Flâneuse: Women Walk the City*. London: Chatto & Windus, 2016.

Evans, Elisabeth F. and Sarah E. Cornish. Eds. *Woolf & the City: Selected Papers of the Nineteenth Annual Conference on Virginia Woolf*. Clemson: Clemson U Digital P, 2010.

Fry, Roger. 'The French Post-Impressionists'. Preface to the Catalog of the Second Post-Impressionist Exhibition (London, 1912), repr. in *Modern Art and Modernism: A Critical Anthology*. Ed. Francis Frascina, Charles Harrison and Deirdre Paul. London: Paul Chapman in association with the Open University, 1986. 89–91.

Gillespie, Diane F. *The Sisters' Arts: The Writing and Painting of Virginia Woolf and Vanessa Bell*. Syracuse, NY: Syracuse UP, 1991.

Goldman, Jane. *The Feminist Aesthetics of Virginia Woolf: Modernism, Post-Impressionism and the Politics of the Visual*. Cambridge: Cambridge UP, 2001.

Grant, Duncan. 'Virginia Woolf'. *Horizon* 2.18 (June 1941): 403–4.

Green, Barbara. *Spectacular Confessions: Autobiography, Performative Activism, and the Sites of Suffrage, 1905–1938*. Basingstoke: Macmillan, 1998.

Holland, Kathryn. 'The Strachey Women in *A Room of One's Own* and *Three Guineas*'. *Tulsa Studies in Women's Literature* 32.1 (Spring 2013): 75–98.

Jones, Clara. *Virginia Woolf: Ambivalent Activist*. Edinburgh: Edinburgh UP, 2016.

Marcus, Jane. 'Thinking Back Through Our Mothers'. *New Feminist Essays on Virginia Woolf*. Ed. Jane Marcus. Lincoln: U of Nebraska P, 1981. 1–30.

Marcus, Jane. *Virginia Woolf and the Languages of Patriarchy*. Bloomington: Indiana UP, 1987.

Marcus, Laura. 'Virginia Woolf and the Art of the Novel'. *Contemporary Woolf/ Woolf contemporaine*. Ed. Claire Davison-Pégon and Anne-Marie Smith-Di Biasio. Montpellier: Presses Universitaires de la Méditerranée, 2014. 15–32.

Marcus, Laura. 'Virginia Woolf and the Hogarth Press'. *Modernist Writers and the Marketplace*. Ed. Iain Willison, Warwick Gould and Warren Chernaik. Basingstoke: Macmillan, 1996. 124–50.

Neverow, Vara. 'Virginia Woolf and City Aesthetics'. *The Edinburgh Companion to Virginia Woolf and the Arts*. Ed. Maggie Humm. Edinburgh: Edinburgh UP, 2010. 88–103.

Partridge, Frances. *Memories*. London: Victor Gollancz, 1981.

Potts, Gina and Lisa Shahriari. Eds. *Virginia Woolf's Bloomsbury*, 2 vols. Basingstoke: Palgrave Macmillan, 2010.

Reed, Christopher. *Bloomsbury Rooms: Modernism, Subculture, and Domesticity*. New Haven: Yale UP, 2004.

Roe, Sue. 'The Impact of Post-Impressionism'. *The Cambridge Companion to Virginia Woolf*. Cambridge: Cambridge UP, 2000. 64–190.

Shone, Richard. *Bloomsbury Portraits: Vanessa Bell, Duncan Grant and Their Circle*. London: Phaidon, 2005.

Simpson, Kathryn. 'Woolf's Bloomsbury'. *Virginia Woolf in Context*. Ed. Bryony Randall and Jane Goldman. Cambridge: Cambridge UP, 2012. 170–82.

Snaith, Anna. *Virginia Woolf: Public and Private Negotiations*. Basingstoke: Palgrave, 2000.

Squier, Susan. *Virginia Woolf and London: The Sexual Politics of the City*. Chapel Hill: U of North Carolina P, 1983.

Stansky, Peter. *On or about December 1910*. Cambridge, MA: Harvard UP, 1997.

Strachey, Ray. *The Cause*. London: Virago, 1978.

Sworn, Corin. 'A Conversation'. *Vanessa Bell*, Catalog to Dulwich Picture Gallery Retrospective. Ed. Sarah J. Milroy and Ian A. C. Dejardin. London: Philip Wilson, 2017. 170–72.

Tebbutt, Melanie. *Women's Talk? A Social History of 'Gossip' in Working-Class Neighbourhoods, 1880–1960*. Aldershot: Scolar Press, 1995.

Tickner, Lisa. 'Vanessa Bell: Studland Beach, Domesticity, and "Significant Form"'. *Representations* 65 (Winter 1999): 63–92.

Woolf, Virginia. *The Complete Shorter Fiction*. Ed. Susan Dick. New York: Harcourt, 1985.

Woolf, Virginia. *The Letters of Virginia Woolf*, 6 vols. Ed. Nigel Nicholson and Joanne Trautman Banks. London: Hogarth Press, 1975–80.

Woolf, Virginia. 'Old Bloomsbury'. *Moments of Being*. Ed. Jeanne Schulkind. London: Pimlico, 2002.

Woolf, Virginia. *A Room of One's Own*. New York: Harcourt, 1981.

Woolf, Virginia. *Three Guineas*. Intro. Jane Marcus. New York: Harcourt, 2006.

Woolf, Virginia. *Walter Sickert: A Conversation*. London: Hogarth Press, 1934.

Zwerdling, Alex. *Virginia Woolf and the Real World*. Berkeley: U of California P, 1986.

Case Study: Bloomsbury, the Hogarth Press, and Feminist Organizations

CLAIRE BATTERSHILL

In 1918 Virginia and Leonard Woolf published Katherine Mansfield's short story *Prelude* as a stand-alone pamphlet at their newly founded independent publishing house, the Hogarth Press. These were still early days for a fledgling publisher: Mansfield's story was the Press's second literary publication. While the Woolfs were by this time professional writers with established reputations – Leonard Woolf's first novel *The Village in the Jungle* was published by Edward Arnold in 1913, and Virginia Woolf's *The Voyage Out* was published by Duckworth in 1915 and they both regularly wrote journalistic essays and book reviews – they were still very much amateur publishers learning their craft. Like most printers, as part of the production process they produced a quantity of unevenly inked, messy page proofs of their early hand-printed pamphlets. One such first proof, from *Prelude*, is printed on the back of a list of resolutions passed by the 'National Council for Adult Suffrage' in a 1 June 1917 meeting.

The resolutions listed on the document include approval, in principle, of the 'Representation of the People Bill' that appeared before parliament that same month. The meeting minutes record the objections of the group to aspects of the bill that would exclude certain women from democratic participation (for example those who were employed in industry and who were resident in Ireland). The Council's advocacy for equal adult suffrage was not fully successful until 1928, when what was also often called 'universal suffrage' was granted in Britain, but the 'Representation of the People Act' that was passed in February of 1918 was nevertheless a landmark in feminist history, since it granted more than 8.5 million women (those over the age of 30 who owned property) the vote.[1]

This kind of archival document, with a modernist short story one side and an activist group's response to a proposed piece of legislation on the other, demonstrates the habitual, everyday connections between Bloomsbury aesthetic and sociopolitical engagements. These links to the broader institutions of feminism supplement an understanding of the first-wave feminist theory arising from Bloomsbury circles (and particularly Virginia Woolf's own sense of the intertwined material, aesthetic, and financial elements of emancipation). Examining and analysing the artefacts of feminist participation challenges any notion of Bloomsbury's political detachment; and reveals

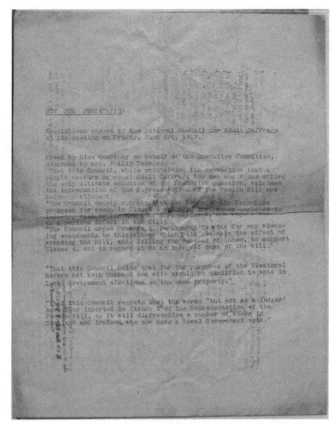

FIGURE 3. Typed minutes from a meeting of the National Council for Adult Suffrage. Image courtesy of the E. J. Pratt Library at Victoria University in the University of Toronto.

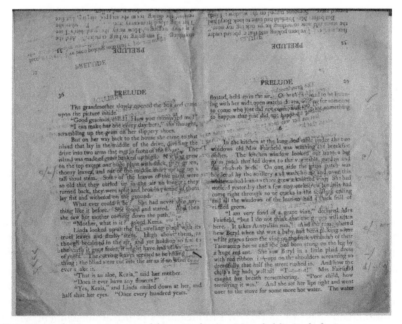

FIGURE 4. Hogarth Press page proof from Katherine Mansfield's *Prelude*. Image courtesy of the E. J. Pratt Library at Victoria University in the University of Toronto.

some of the overlapping textual, social, and political spaces that were central to feminist activism of the period.

What initially seems like an unlikely location – the back of a literary proof copy – for material documenting the history of suffrage is not so unlikely at all when the connections between the informal social gatherings for which Bloomsbury is known are combined with an analysis of the more formal organizations to which its members were connected. Both the activities of the Hogarth Press (and the act of publishing her own work and the work of other women writers like Mansfield) and Virginia Woolf's direct participation in the suffrage movement are important historical aspects of Bloomsbury feminism and have received sustained attention in recent feminist scholarship on Woolf.[2] The Mansfield proof is a textual and a political artefact showing how shifting legal structures are (sometimes literally) interleaved with modernist literary experiments, and indicating the complexity of material evidence: of moments when history and literature meet.

To understand the implications of the Mansfield proof itself, it is helpful to briefly address the well-documented connections between Bloomsbury and the formal organizations dedicated to advancing women's rights. The connections were, in part, geographical. Given the location of Bloomsbury as a neighbourhood that also housed the headquarters of the National Union of Women's Suffrage Societies, among other women's organizations, important feminist conversations were happening in and around the Bloomsbury gatherings occurring sometimes around a corner or across a street (see Elkin in this volume). As Anna Snaith argues – and as Sara Blair's work on the demographics of the neighbourhood itself affirms – it is reasonable to see 'Bloomsbury itself as a site of liberation and feminism' (27). I will return to Woolf in a moment, since the legacy of her feminist participation is so complex that it deserves sustained attention, but first I want to briefly address the participation of other Bloomsbury Group members – including Duncan Grant, Clive Bell, Leonard Woolf, John Maynard Keynes, and Lytton Strachey – in feminist institutions and organizations of the early twentieth century.

Much of Bloomsbury's early involvement with the suffrage movement came through the energetic Strachey family. Lytton Strachey's mother, Lady Jane Strachey, who lived at 51 Gordon Square, was elected to the Executive committee of the National Union of Women's Suffrage Societies in 1907, the largest umbrella organization of suffragists.[3] Lady Strachey, like the Woolfs, sought a publishing platform for writing consonant with her beliefs and with her cause, and she helped to found the suffragist journal, *The Englishwoman*, in an attempt to create a forum for serious discussion of feminist issues.[4] She, along with her daughter Pippa, organized the 'Mud March' that year, the first large public procession in support of suffrage comprising some 3,000 women walking together from Hyde Park to Exeter Hall.[5] John Maynard Keynes volunteered as a steward for the march.[6]

Beyond occasional participation in suffrage action, frequently at the behest of a Strachey, members of Bloomsbury also produced art and writing that engaged, both directly and indirectly, with the aesthetics and priorities of the suffrage movement. In 1909, Duncan Grant won a poster competition put on by the Artists' Suffrage League, and the image was used as propaganda for the National Union of Women's Suffrage Societies (Crawford 16). Grant's propaganda poster is a direct and straightforward example of the ways in which Bloomsbury art and activism could give rise to one another. However, suffrage posters also had broader aesthetic resonances in Bloomsbury art. Jessica Berman points out the affinities between radical suffrage art and the aesthetics of both Virginia Woolf and Vanessa Bell and argues that 'the connection between postimpressionism and political engagement has been obscured by the dominance of the concept of "significant form" and by our continuing assumption that modernist aesthetics of the sort Woolf espoused were antithetical to overt political engagement' (49; see Hussey in this volume on 'significant form').

Leonard's political interests have always remained an important part of his legacy. His involvement with the Fabian Society and his anti-imperialist politics following his time as a civil servant in Ceylon, however, have received much more critical attention than his feminism.[7] Nevertheless, Leonard Woolf's direct involvement in feminist activism and in organizations was earnest and long-lasting. He participated in adult suffrage campaigns but was particularly interested in the Women's Co-Operative Guild and in cooperatives more generally as economic and social models (Glendenning 146–7). He gave speeches at the Guild's conferences and assisted in advocating for women's participation in trade unions and advancement in the professions. In a 1913 letter to Margaret Llewelyn Davies, a friend of the Woolfs who was also the general secretary of the Guild from 1899 to 1921, Leonard wrote of his intense enjoyment of the Congress, which he and Virginia had attended in Newcastle that year: 'I feel we must thank you for the Congress. I don't know when I've enjoyed anything so much & Virginia feels the same ... I only hope you'll allow us to come again another year' (Spotts 381). Virginia Woolf added a note in her own hand to the letter confirming her enjoyment of the experience. Leonard Woolf made good on his promise and returned two years later to the 1915 Congress in Liverpool and his involvement with the Guild through talks and exchanges with Llewelyn Davies continued for many years. He was very impressed by Davies and invested in her organization. Assessing her legacy after her death, he writes: 'If [Margaret Llewelyn Davies] had been a man, her achievements would have filled probably half a page in *Who's Who*.' That she was not included at all was 'the kind of fact which made – and makes – feminism the belief or policy of all sensible men' (*Beginning Again* 101). While Leonard Woolf's rather earnest and straightforward view of feminism, however, is relatively easy to summarize, things were never quite so simple for Virginia Woolf.[8]

Pamela L. Caughie begins her recent essay 'Feminist Woolf' with a question that plagues anyone approaching Woolf's feminism now: 'What more can be said on the topic of Virginia Woolf and feminism?' (305). Woolf is the most prominent Bloomsbury feminist in part because the best known textual expressions of her feminism – *A Room of One's Own* and *Three Guineas* – are layered, complex, and meandering excursions in the field of women's history. In a refusal that seems retrospectively strange, at least at first blush, Woolf deliberately didn't use the word 'feminism' to describe her own work. She writes famously in *Three Guineas* of the obsolescence of the word:

> What more fitting than to destroy an old word, a vicious and corrupt word that has done much harm in its day and is now obsolete? The word 'feminist' is the word indicated. That word, according to the dictionary, means 'one who champions the rights of women'. Since the only right, the right to earn a living, has been won, the word no longer has a meaning. And a word without a meaning is a dead word, a corrupt word. Let us therefore celebrate this occasion by cremating the corpse. Let us write that word in large black letters on a sheet of foolscap; then solemnly

apply a match to the paper. Look, how it burns! What a light dances over the world! (179).

Sowon Park suggests that this 'bewildering' passage must be historicized and read in light of the associations between militant and violent suffragette action and the word 'feminism' (rather than the broader, more pacifist organizations with which Woolf was affiliated) (127). It is important to reiterate the fact that Woolf's distrust of the word 'feminism', as it was specifically used in the 1920s, did not extend to its broader implications: she is eloquent and insistent about the possibilities for female identity and expression in every aspect of her writing life from her novels to her occasional review essays. Furthermore, as Laura Marcus notes, subsequent readings of Woolf by feminists of the later twentieth century have come to tell their own story about the development and definition of feminism broadly writ: 'The preoccupations of post-war feminist literary and cultural criticism could, indeed, be traced through accounts of and approaches to Virginia Woolf' (142).[9] In other words, Woolf's prominent place among twentieth-century feminists is undisputed (despite her own repudiation of the word itself) and the body of scholarship and criticism tracing the specific character of her feminism is vast.

In perhaps the most frequently quoted passage in *A Room of One's Own*, the specific kind of feminism Woolf proposes is crucially material in nature, and naturally goes beyond democratic participation: 'a woman must have money and a room of her own if she is to write fiction' (3). As Anna Snaith points out in her recent introduction to the Oxford edition of *A Room of One's Own* and *Three Guineas*, 'with popularity comes simplification', and this phrase and variants on it have been so often repeated that they now risk standing in entirely for a more sophisticated and shifting feminism to which 'interconnection' (of politics and art, education and class, gender and society) is 'central' (xi). The relationship between Woolf's feminist aesthetics and the suffrage activities taking place in her own neighbourhood and among her friends and family was important but also vexed, and working out exactly what Woolf thought of the organized institutions of feminism remains a complicated task, even with a rich and diverse critical history to draw from.[10]

It is perfectly possible, of course, to be intimately acquainted with, interested in, and yet still suspicious of one's own neighbours (as Woolf was of women's societies busying themselves in the 'upstairs rooms' of Bloomsbury), even if they contribute to a sense of belonging and freedom in one's city and in society.[11] Snaith describes Woolf's 'ambivalence' (31) towards the suffrage movement as expressed through the character of Mary Datchet in her early novel *Night and Day*, who works in a suffrage office in Russell Square, as Woolf herself famously did stuffing envelopes for an organization now thought to be the People's Suffrage Federation in 1910. Clara Jones takes Woolf's 'ambivalence' in her activist participation as the primary character of her work as 'a highly critical but nonetheless committed participant' in women's activist causes (4). Jones's analysis of Woolf's participation in and thinking about formal feminist organizations including the Women's Institute, the Women's Co-Operative Movement and the People's Suffrage Organization, shows Woolf grappling with the complex relations between abstract ideals and actual participation in organized feminist activism. Ultimately Jones's careful and detailed analysis of Woolf's writings about activism show that her 'persistent feelings of ambivalence and uncertainty did not compromise her political practice in her life and writing – they instead formed an invaluable, constituent part of it' (98). Jones's is a convincing reading, and one that goes some way to explaining why when Woolf herself received the right to vote, she was non-plussed: 'I don't feel much more important', she wrote in her diary (1: 104). Alex Zwerdling's landmark analysis points out, however, that Woolf's scepticism about the efficacy of suffrage in truly gaining ground did not extend to the movement and she remained concerned with the broader social issues raised by attempts to secure the right to vote (214).

It is important to acknowledge, too, that Woolf has been read as an historical figure of importance in retrospectively analysing suffrage rhetoric. Jane Marcus, in her introduction to an historical volume on the Pankhursts, reads the suffrage context into Woolf's analysis of women's rights in *A Room of One's Own*:

> Virginia Woolf in 1928, the year women finally got the vote, the year Mrs. Pankhurst died, presented the world with a permanent literary tribute to the suffrage movement's giving voice to women. Constructed brilliantly around the literary tropes of interruption and absence, *A Room of One's Own* eloquently enacts the history of the struggle. The collective female narrator's voice of the victimized generic 'Marys' of the old ballad, the spoken text proceeds by interrupting itself to tell the tale of absences and gaps in literary history where women should be, eloquently articulating that absence by ellipses and in peroration calling on the voice of the absent working-class woman who is washing up the dishes to become 'Shakespeare's sister'. Woolf's figure of the pregnant suicide, Judith Shakespeare, is the literary equivalent of the abandoned pregnant servant girl who appears in all of Mrs. Pankhurst's speeches' (*Suffrage and the Pankhursts* 10).

I quote this passage at length in part to give a sense of the ways in which Woolf's feminist legacy has extended beyond and outside of Bloomsbury (significantly through Marcus's own forceful influence) and informed the broader narratives of female political participation. Sowon Park similarly suggests that Woolf's two polemical talks on feminism rose out of an atmosphere that was suffused with the very ideas she articulates so elegantly: 'A Room of One's Own and Three Guineas are so deeply rooted in the culture of suffrage that, far from being isolated ground-breaking pieces "irretrievably cut off from the actors" they are, in fact, firmly placed at the intellectual centre of the first-wave women's movement' (24). Even if Woolf's own direct connection with suffrage action stopped short of the more violent activism of the Pankhursts (placing her, as Zwerdling and Park note, firmly on the side of the pacifist suffra*gist* rather than the militant suffra*gette*), and even if being granted the vote left her cold, Marcus and Park draw convincing parallels that show suffragettes marching into Woolf's literary imagination and into her texts.[12]

If for Woolf, electoral rights for women, though crucial, seemed to offer a partial and even inadequate kind of emancipation, the establishment of 'A Press of One's Own' afforded her a freedom both creative and intellectual that even significant changes in social and legal structures could not provide.[13] The Hogarth Press, driven not only by Virginia Woolf but often more strongly by Leonard, published works directly concerned with structural changes that were occurring in national policy around women's rights and through organizations including the Women's Co-Operative Movement; political groups promoting suffrage and birth control; and women's educational groups. It was a feminist publishing operation from the start in the sense that it freed Woolf from obligations to editors and publishers, though Woolf's association of the word 'feminism' with a specific kind of violent militant protest, as I mentioned earlier, prevented her from ever describing it using exactly that term. Laura Marcus, finding Woolf's activist involvement in the form of occasional lectures for women's societies to be somewhat cursory, suggests that 'it may be that the place to look for Woolf's feminist activism is [not in suffrage organizations but] in other kinds of institution, such as the Hogarth Press, for which she wrote *Three Guineas* as part of a series on women and feminism' (para. 5). While a great deal of scholarly attention has turned to the Press over the past decade, its precise intervention into and relationship with the Woolfs' feminism has yet to be fully explored.

The story of the Hogarth Press usually begins with the Woolfs' first literary publication, *Two Stories*, which appeared in July of 1917. The 150 copies of the small pamphlet containing Virginia Woolf's 'The Mark on the Wall' and Leonard's 'Three Jews'[14] were not only authored by the Woolfs but also handmade by them: the text was typeset by Virginia, then printed (or, in printer's parlance, 'machined') by Leonard on their newly acquired hand press, and finally sewn by Virginia into colourful patterned paper covers (some red and some blue) using bright red thread.[15] Woodcuts by the artist Dora Carrington (who was associated with Bloomsbury through her long, intimate, tragic relationship with Lytton Strachey), adorned the stories. In an early undated circular distributed to prospective subscribers, the Woolfs laid out their purpose in starting the Press: 'to publish at low prices works of merit, in prose or poetry, which could not, because of their merits, appeal to a very large public'. They went on to describe the printing practices of their then tiny household operation: 'The whole process of printing and production (except in one instance) is done by ourselves, and the editions are necessarily small, not exceeding 300 copies' (1). The founding of the Hogarth Press saw the Woolfs taking the means of production for prose and poetry literally into their own hands. The tale of *Two Stories* (and of the ensuing development of the Hogarth Press, in the years that followed, from a homespun operation to a full-scale general publisher) is a familiar one at least in scholarly quarters, and has come to stand in metonymically for the Press's whole history and reputation, just as that room and those 500 pounds have become emblems of Woolf's feminist ethos.[16]

However, the Hogarth Press's feminist publications were not by any means limited to Woolf's own. The Press published eighty-five women writers between 1917 and 1946, when the business was sold to Chatto & Windus.[17] Their writings covered a variety of genres from light verse to serious political and sociological reportage. The women themselves included well-known and now-canonical authors such as Vita Sackville-West, Rebecca West, Gertrude Stein, as well as first-time authors including the teenaged poet Joan Adeney Easdale and the New Zealand novelist Anna D. Whyte. And, of course, there was Katherine Mansfield, with whom Virginia Woolf had a famously competitive literary friendship. In a recent reevaluation of Mansfield's relationship with the Bloomsbury Group, Todd Martin argues that adopting a network theory model when thinking about Bloomsbury can allow us to see the group's borders as more permeable and to understand how figures like Mansfield – adjacent to but not part of Bloomsbury – can inform our understandings of the group itself. Martin particularly argues for consideration of those, including Mansfield, who frequented Lady Ottoline Morrell's social occasions at Garsington in relation to the Bloomsbury Group. This framework proves fruitful when it comes to engagements with and understandings of suffrage and feminist participation. Mansfield's portrayals of suffragettes and the suffrage movement are unsympathetic: she was sceptical of the power of the vote to improve or change political circumstances for the better.[18]

A handful of Hogarth Press books deal directly with the women's institutions and organizations promoting feminist causes during the period. In 1925, Scottish novelist, essayist, and translator, Willa Muir published an extended meditation on social and sexual differentiation entitled *Woman: An Inquiry*. Muir's essay addresses the question of whether 'the division of the human race into men and women involves a division of spiritual as well as of sexual functions, so that the creative work of women is different in kind from the creative work of men' (11). Muir discusses several current understandings of the relationship between gender, morality, and creativity and proposes that women develop their own self-conscious method of producing art that better reflects their gendered worldview. She is careful to note that both men's work and women's work deserve to be included in creative and cultural traditions precisely because of their differences in kind. Another Hogarth Essay, published in 1928, the same year as *A Room of One's Own*, was *Leisured Women*, by Lady Rhondda (Margaret Mackworth), the editor of the feminist periodical *Time and Tide*,[19] which provides an incisive feminist critique of the pursuit of a traditional female homemaker role at the expense of political action and social participation. One of the important roles of the Hogarth Press was to examine the shifting and volatile status of particular social issues during the particularly tumultuous period of its operation. Part of the Woolfs' method for remaining current and for admitting and reflecting on social change was to produce pamphlets and anthologies dedicated to current cultural reflection. Both Lady Rhondda's and Willa Muir's pamphlets were produced in the 1920s as part of the Hogarth Essays series (Muir's in the First Series and Lady Rhondda's in the Second Series) and published first as self-contained stand-alone pamphlets. By the 1930s, the Press was contributing to what Maria DiCenzo describes as a culture in which 'feminists engaged in the process of "stock taking" on a regular basis; the exercise of reappraising the advancement of the movement was a feature of media produced by the suffrage campaign and remained a strong tendency on the part of feminist organisations after the war' (422). To that end, the Woolfs published *Our Freedom and Its Results* (1935) – a collection of five essays reflecting on aspects of life after emancipation by suffragists Eleanor F. Rathbone, Erna Reiss, Ray Strachey, Allison Neilans, and Mary Agnes Hamilton. In her essay, Ray Strachey offers an assessment of feminist cultural presence that also lends some additional context to Woolf's own rejection of the word 'feminism' in *Three Guineas*. She writes that the purpose of this habit of 'stock-taking' is to contextualize suffrage action for a postwar generation of women who 'show a strong hostility to the word 'feminism', and all which they imagine it to connote. They are, nevertheless, themselves the products of the women's movement' (10). While Woolf's own suffrage participation clearly pre-dated the war (and was connected through personal relationships directly with Strachey's own activism), her wariness of the word 'feminism' and its specific connotations was clearly a broader phenomenon in the 1930s.

The most overtly feminist Hogarth Press publication that has received the most critical attention is *Life as We Have Known It by Co-Operative Working Women* (1931). Brought to the Press by Margaret Llewelyn Davies after the long friendship with the Woolfs that I mentioned earlier, it had an 'Introductory Letter' written by Virginia Woolf that has been the subject of much debate: it has been interpreted in completely opposite ways as both an indication of her political detachment and her activism. Woolf's essay begins with a reflection on her experience attending the 1913 Congress in Newcastle and describes her own attempt to understand and to feel the importance of the Women's Co-Operative Movement. As Jones points out, the fact that the letter is addressed not to the public but to Davies herself has been taken as an indication of Woolf's detachment and snobbishness. However, an additional context for this mode of address is that it accords with the practice established by the Woolfs in the Hogarth

Letters series. The series offered writers the opportunity to write letters to recipients of their choosing (fictional or real, living or dead) and in doing so to think through and discuss contemporary aesthetic, social, and political concerns. That the Hogarth Letters series was conceived of and published by the Press in the early 1930s as Woolf was composing her 'Introductory Letter' to *Life as We Have Known It* suggests that she was adopting this rhetorical mode herself and choosing Llewelyn Davies as her addressee in just the way that E. M. Forster addresses 'Madan Blanchard' in his Hogarth Letter, or Rebecca West addresses 'a grandfather'. The letter itself demonstrates many of the self-conscious and reticent habits that Jones identifies as characteristic of Woolf's political engagement. Continuing on from her account of her experience at the 1913 Congress, she writes that the volume's autobiographical texts by working women might illuminate the characters themselves in order to humanize the organization's political actions: 'it might be that we should find these papers interesting; that if we read them the women would cease to be symbols and would become instead individuals' (xxxi). Woolf's essay goes on to show the ways in which the women's writings do challenge and complicate her own present-day assessment of her earlier activist experiences. Alice Wood argues in her detailed contextual reassessment of the introduction that while Woolf felt comfortable with her role as a publisher of these works (and thereby with the Hogarth Press as a publisher for working-class women's writing that would be unlikely to be published by a mainstream firm), she was uncomfortable with her own role in introducing the collection.[20] A Bloomsbury frame on a working-class collection could be seen as the kind of propagandist gesture of which Woolf was suspicious, and yet Woolf's commitment to the publication of women's life stories comes across clearly (see Simpson in this volume). The complicated and troubled history of the *Life as We Have Known It* essay confirms that Woolf's own uncertainties about her activist participation were grounded in reasonable fears about public reception.

Like the 'Introductory Letter' to *Life as We Have Known It*, the Mansfield proof copy embodies some of the complexities and ambivalences of Woolf's connections to formal feminist organizations. So how does one read this double-sided document? What, for instance, does it mean that we find the meeting minutes kept by the Woolfs only to be used as a piece of scrap paper? Analysing a printer's proof presents a variety of challenges inherent in the very form of the document itself. Producing proof copies was common printers' practice: as bibliographer Philip Gaskell writes, as a matter of course, 'proofs – trial prints – of newly-imposed formes were made [using hand-presses] so that any errors that had crept into the text in the process of setting the copy in type (and there were always some) might be discovered and rectified before the sheet was printed' (110). The Mansfield proof shows few corrections to the actual text: there are a few minor adjustments: replacing an 'x' with a 'z', for example, and a 'b' with a 'd' (these sorts of errors were called 'literals' by printers and would now colloquially be called 'typos': mistakes involving individual letters), but there are no significant textual emendations. The handwriting for the corrections appears to be Leonard's. The proofing practice itself, therefore, was quite straightforward. The use of recycled paper is also perhaps predictable: Gaskell notes that printers typically avoided wasting paper or materials wherever possible, and 'first proofs were pulled on one side only of a piece of defective or spoiled paper' (111). The Woolfs clearly followed this standard printer's practice of reusing scrap pieces of paper to check their typesetting, their inking, and the quality of their printing. In a recollection of visiting the later and by then more established Hogarth Press in the 1930s, Cecil Woolf remembers the care the Woolfs, like most printers, took not to waste anything: 'Leonard and Virginia were naturally frugal and my uncle undoubtedly carried this carefulness, this abhorrence of what he perceived as waste, to the point of eccentricity. I remember, for example, that in the lavatory printers' proofs were hung up for use as toilet paper' (1). While some discarded proofs may have been doubly reused in this unseemly fashion and were in this way lost to the historical record, some scrap pieces of paper always seem to survive against even the most unlikely odds.

So the proof was produced in a way that would have been common practice for printers using the kind of equipment the Woolfs did at the early Hogarth Press. Perhaps less usual is that this sheet appears to have been used not once but twice. Diagonally across the checked text, there are ghostly impressions of pages from *Prelude* in faint, smudged ink. The page appears to have been used more than once. It has been doubly recycled: first for proof correction and then perhaps for blotting extra ink from a forme at the end of the printing day. This additional use marks these page proofs as printer's extras: not textual documents to be pored over or substantively edited but proofs checked for correctness. This second gesture shows the Woolfs messily learning to print, and doing so as amateurs outside of the traditional publishing trade. Even if the doubling of institutional documentation and literary expression was unintentional, this suffrage document in the end met an appropriate fate: repurposed in the service of publishing a young woman's modernist writing.

Using a single archival document as a starting point, this essay has outlined some of the connections between Bloomsbury and feminist organizations and institutions of the early twentieth century. There were clearly real and meaningful connections between Bloomsbury aesthetics and feminist organizations, as the Mansfield proof illustrates. However, the nature and character of these connections was, as is often the case with Virginia Woolf, slippery and uncertain: the ink is often slightly smudged, and one text is nearly always laid over another. The Woolfs were at once invested in suffrage, in pacifist forms of feminist advocacy, in women's education, and in the activities of the Women's Co-Operative Guild, but were also conscious of the limitations of these organizations. One of the significant but often underrecognized institutions of feminism to emerge from Bloomsbury, however, was the Hogarth Press. Acknowledging the truly collaborative nature of that enterprise and the specific character of the material labour involved (with Virginia setting the type and binding the books and Leonard doing the printing) is to recognize, too, the importance of female labour in bringing new works into the world.[21] For, as Virginia Woolf wrote in her 1931 talk 'Professions for Women', social, legal, and structural changes are not enough: 'Even when the path is nominally open – when there is nothing to prevent a woman from being a doctor, a lawyer, a civil servant – there are many phantoms and obstacles, as I believe, looming in her way. To discuss and define them is I think of great value and importance; for thus only can the labour be shared, the difficulties be solved' (144).

NOTES

1. The text of the act can be accessed through the Parliamentary Archives online ('Representation of the People Act 1918').
2. Much of Woolf criticism in the past decade has focused on her political participation and on recuperating her social engagement rather than reading her as a fragile or isolated figure (see Clara Jones for the most recent sustained exploration of the developments in scholarship on Woolf as a more engaged political participant).

3. As Sowon Park points out, 'In 1914 the National Union had over 53,000 members and 46,000 "friends" who could not afford full membership, making it the largest suffrage society in Britain' (120).

4. Woolf wrote an obituary of Jane Strachey after her death in 1920 ('Papers of Jane Maria Strachey' GB 106 7JMS).

5. Jane Strachey has received relatively little biographical attention despite her activist participation, her connection to Bloomsbury circles, and her very interesting life. Ironically, she appears under her husband's entry in the Oxford Dictionary of National Biography (Vetch para. 1).

6. Elizabeth Crawford quotes a letter from Keynes to Lady Strachey as evidence of his participation in the march. She also notes that 'Keynes had long been exposed to the workings of the women's suffrage campaign; his mother was a practical exponent of "women's rights" and his father, a close friend of Henry Fawcett, had in 1888 been auditor of the Cambridge Women's Suffrage Association' (17).

7. For a recent reappraisal of Leonard Woolf's early colonial writings, see a recent special issue of the *Journal of Commonwealth Literature* devoted to his work edited by Elleke Bohemer.

8. For detailed readings of both Woolfs' involvement with the Women's Co-Operative Guild, see Alice Wood and Clara Jones.

9. On the intense conflict between feminist scholars of the 1970s and the Woolf's literary estate, see Marler. For more on the history of Woolf's feminist scholarly following see Marcus.

10. For a recent critical review essay on feminist scholarship about Woolf, see Caughie. Despite her speculation at the start of her essay about whether more feminist readings of Woolf can really add to an already crowded field, she ends on a note of hopefulness about the prospect of such work in the future: 'By continuing to write about Woolf's feminism, we keep it from hardening into a naturalized belief' (315).

11. For a theoretical approach to modernism that uses the metaphor of neighbourly relations as an epistemological and aesthetic trope, see Alexandra Peat and Sarah Copland.

12. Jones points out, however, that the lines between these groups were not always so clear: 'recent historians of the movement have made efforts to complicate a received narrative in which the distinctions between constitutional suffragist and militant suffragette are accepted' (68).

13. For another use of this phrase, see Kukil.

14. On the occasion of the hundredth anniversary of the publication of *Two Stories*, the Virginia Woolf Society of Great Britain published a facsimile edition of the publication replicating the typesetting quirks and even the red thread used by Virginia for the binding. The newly relaunched Hogarth Press imprint under Penguin Random House also published a new *Two Stories* in 2017, containing Virginia Woolf's 'The Mark on the Wall' and a newly commissioned story by Woolf enthusiast and fiction writer Mark Haddon.

15. For more on *Two Stories* see Sorensen.

16. The standard history of the Hogarth Press is Willis's. Scholarly work on the press over the past decade, coinciding with the rise of material modernisms as a dominant critical approach in the field and exemplified in Helen Southworth's edited collection has awakened a new interest in the Press's broader remit (considering for example its anti-colonial texts, its Russian translations, its poetry publications, its middlebrow novels and its religious offerings).

17. For more biographical and bibliographical detail on each of these women and their works, see Claire Battershill, Helen Southworth, Nicola Wilson, Alice Staveley, Elizabeth Willson Gordon and Mike Widner, 'The Modernist Archives Publishing Project'.

18. For a detailed treatment of Mansfield's relationship with suffrage politics and particularly with the individualist feminism of Dora Marsden, see Garver.

19. For more on *Time and Tide*'s feminist dimensions and cultural significance see
    Catherine Clay.
20. The critical reception of the 'Introductory Letter' has been complicated, too, by the
    existence of two distinct drafts (the second significantly revised, with some of what might
    be considered snobbish toned down). For more on the relationship between these drafts
    and the critical debates they have occasioned, see Jones (118).
21. An important and as yet underresearched aspect of the Press's labour history is the
    involvement of female Press workers in its later operations (including for example
    managers Barbara Hepworth and Aline Burch, and book traveller Alice Ritchie, among
    others). For the only article so far on labour beyond the Woolfs', Richard Kennedy's, and
    John Lehmann's at the Press, see Staveley on Norah Nicholls.

WORKS CITED

Battershill, Claire, Helen Southworth, Nicola Wilson, Alice Staveley, Elizabeth Willson
    Gordon and Mike Widner. The Modernist Archives Publishing Project (MAPP). www.
    modernistarchives.com. Accessed 17 August 2017.

Bell, Clive. *Art*. London: Chatto & Windus, 1914.

Black, Naomi. *Virginia Woolf as Feminist*. Ithaca, NY: Cornell UP, 2003.

Blair, Sara. 'Local Modernity, Global Modernism: Bloomsbury and the Places of the Literary'.
    ELH 71.3 (2004): 813–38.

Boehmer, Elleke. Ed. 'Intentional Dissonance: Leonard Woolf's *The Village in the Jungle*'.
    Journal of Commonwealth Literature 50.1 (2015).

Brown, Susan, Patricia Clements and Isobel Grundy. Ed. 'Willa Muir'. *Orlando: Women's
    Writing in the British Isles from the Beginnings to the Present*. Cambridge University Press
    Online, 2006. http://orlando.cambridge.org/. Accessed 9 July 2017.

Caughie, Pamela L. 'Feminist Woolf'. *A Companion to Virginia Woolf*. Ed. Jessica Berman.
    Oxford: Wiley-Blackwell, 2016. 305–17.

Clay, Catherine. '"The Modern Weekly for the Modern Woman": *Time and Tide*, Feminism,
    and Interwar Print Culture'. *Women: A Cultural Review* 27.4 (2016): 397–411.

Crawford, Elizabeth. *The Women's Suffrage Movement: A Reference Guide, 1866–1928*.
    London: Psychology Press, 1998.

Garver, Lee. 'The Political Mansfield'. *Modernism/Modernity* 8.2 (2001): 225–43.

Jones, Clara. *Virginia Woolf: Ambivalent Activist*. Edinburgh: Edinburgh UP, 2016.

Kukil, Karen. 'Woolf in the World: A Pen and a Press of One's Own'. Special Collections
    Exhibition. www.smith.edu/libraries/libs/rarebook/exhibitions/penandpress/case14b.htm.
    Accessed 5 February 2017.

Marcus, Laura. 'Woolf's Feminism and Feminism's Woolf'. *The Cambridge Companion to
    Virginia Woolf*. Ed. Susan Sellers. Cambridge: Cambridge UP, 2010. 142–79.

Marler, Regina. *Bloomsbury Pie: The Making of the Bloomsbury Boom*. New York: Henry
    Holt, 1997.

Martin, Todd. *Katherine Mansfield and Bloomsbury*. London: Bloomsbury, 2017.

Papers of Jane Maria Strachey. Women's Library Archives GB 106 7JMS. www.lse.ac.uk/
    Library/Collections/Collection-highlights/The-Womens-Library. Accessed 20 July 2017.

Park, Sowon S. 'Virginia Woolf and Suffrage: The Mass Behind the Single Voice'. *Review of
    English Studies* 56.223 (2005): 119–34.

Peat, Alexandra and Sarah Copland. 'Mending Walls and Making Neighbors: Spatial Metaphors
    in the New Modernist Studies'. *Intervalla*. Special issue on 'Modernist Currents', 2017.

www.fus.edu/intervalla/volume-4-modernist-currents/mending-walls-and-making-neighbors-spatial-metaphors-in-the-new-modernist-studies. Accessed 10 June 2017.

Representation of the People Act 1918. Parliamentary Archives. HL/PO/PU/1/1918/7&8G5c64. www.parliament.uk/about/living-heritage/transformingsociety/electionsvoting/womenvote/parliamentary-collections/collections-the-vote-and-after/representation-of-the-people-act-1918/. Accessed 2 May 2017.

Snaith, Anna. 'Introduction'. *A Room of One's Own and Three Guineas*. Oxford: Oxford UP, 2015.

Snaith, Anna. *Private and Public Negotiations*. Basingstoke: Palgrave Macmillan, 2000.

Sorenson, Jennifer Julia. *Modernist Experiments in Genre, Media, and Transatlantic Print Culture*. New York: Routledge, 2017.

Southworth, Helen. *Leonard and Virginia Woolf, the Hogarth Press and the Networks of Modernism*. Edinburgh: Edinburgh UP, 2010.

Staveley, Alice. 'Marketing Virginia Woolf: Women, War, and Public Relations in *Three Guineas*'. *Book History* 12 (2009): 295–332.

Vetch, R. H. 'Strachey, Sir Richard (1817–1908)', rev. Elizabeth Baigent. *Oxford Dictionary of National Biography*. Oxford: Oxford UP, 2004. www.oxforddnb.com/view/article/36341. Accessed 1 August 2017.

Willis, J. H. *Leonard and Virginia Woolf as Publishers: The Hogarth Press 1917–1941*. Charlottesville, VA: U of Virginia P, 1992.

Wood, Alice. 'Facing Life as We Have Known It: Virginia Woolf and the Women's Co-Operative Guild'. *Literature and History* 23.2 (2014): 18–34.

Woolf, Leonard. *Letters of Leonard Woolf*. Ed. Frederic Spotts. New York: Harcourt, Brace, Jovanovich, 1989.

Woolf, Virginia. 'Professions for Women'. *Selected Essays*. Ed. David Bradshaw. Oxford: Oxford UP, 2009.

Woolf, Virginia. *A Room of One's Own and Three Guineas*. Ed. Anna Snaith. Oxford: Oxford UP, 2015.

Woolf, Virginia and Leonard Woolf. *Two* Stories. London: Hogarth Press, 1917.

Woolf, Virginia and Leonard Woolf. *Two Stories*. Ed. Stephen Barkway. The Virginia Woolf Society of Great Britain, 2017.

Woolf, Virginia and Mark Haddon. *Two Stories*. London: Hogarth Press, 2017.

CHAPTER FIVE

Bloomsbury and Philosophy

BENJAMIN D. HAGEN

Philosophy clearly mattered to the Bloomsbury Group. 'So fundamental was philosophy to [its] development', S. P. Rosenbaum asserts, 'that a literary history of the group must be to some extent a philosophical history too' (*Victorian Bloomsbury* 161). Some matters are indisputable. For instance, that the Conversazione Society at Cambridge University – an exclusive discussion group also known as the Apostles – served as the initial setting of Bloomsbury's philosophical education. E. M. Forster, Desmond MacCarthy, Roger Fry, Leonard Woolf, Lytton Strachey, and John Maynard Keynes were all elected members. Between Fry and MacCarthy's respective elections in 1887 and 1896, Bertrand Russell and G. E. Moore also became Apostles and began their work – which continued well into the twentieth century – of opening (and encouraging) the disciplinary rift between analytic and continental methods of philosophical inquiry. Though the Bloomsbury Apostles did not officially read philosophy at university, many of them nevertheless had direct ties to a major *event* in its history: the emergence of an 'analytical empiricism', as Russell calls it, that incorporated a rigorous mathematics, developed 'a powerful logical technique', valued linguistic clarity and symbolic precision, and sought to 'achieve definite answers' to 'certain problems' – thus demonstrating 'the quality of science' (*The History* 834).

Rosenbaum, Ann Banfield, and others have illuminated this Cambridge–Bloomsbury connection, establishing through their research the (possible) influence of the epistemological and ethical innovations of Russell and Moore on the aesthetic, biographical, political, personal, and economical writings of Bloomsbury itself – including works by those who were not Apostles (e.g. Clive Bell) and those who did not attend Cambridge at all (e.g. Virginia Woolf).[1] It is now commonplace to assume the prominence of Moore's *Principia Ethica* (1903) in the intellectual development of the group and uncontroversial to assert that his essay, 'The Refutation of Idealism' (1903), and Russell's *The Problems of Philosophy* (1912), played key roles too. To research Bloomsbury and philosophy is thus, in contemporary modernist studies, to disclose the impact of specific disciplinary insights and interventions on the continuity and constitutive intimacies uniting these many nonphilosophers. Moore's distinction between means and ends,[2] for instance, as well as his related notion of organic wholes (*Principie Ethica* 36) and his emphasis on states of mind or feeling rather than codes of conduct[3] are said to have attracted the Bloomsbury Apostles who read his work and were affected (more importantly?) by his charm.[4]

Of greatest import, perhaps, is the philosophical realism developed by Russell and Moore as a revolt against the Idealism of George Berkeley. Idealism and realism share an infamous philosophical scandal as their point of departure: namely, the purportedly unbridgeable gulf between human perception and the physical world.[5] According to Russell, Berkeley 'consider[s] common objects, such as a tree', and then asserts that 'all we know when we "perceive" the tree consists of ideas ... Its being ... consists in being perceived' (*The Problems* 61). The Cambridge philosophers respond to this argument with an epistemology that accepts the limitation of human perception assumed by Idealism and yet (at the same time) affirms the independence of a reality that operates beyond (and even without) human perception. This unperceived reality is populated by logical constructs (the corresponding truths of which are not empirically observable in the world itself) as well as physical matter (things in themselves, *real* trees that exceed the mass aggregate of possible perspectives). Though there may still be a difference between perceptible objects (which can appear from myriad angles or distances) and real or logical objects (which are imperceptible), this solution becomes the philosophical condition of possibility, in a time of great advances across scientific fields, of 'knowledge beyond our own experience ... Far from being the focus of a problem, the unobserved becomes a necessary feature of the things knowledge arrives at, the essence of the reality Idealism denies' (Banfield 48).

This Cambridge realism echoes the work of Bloomsbury in a variety of ways, since much of their work attempts 'to catch [a] thing that they sometimes called "reality"' – that which cannot directly be sensed (Johnstone 37). While Cambridge–Bloomsbury scholars insist upon these (potential) correspondences as *actual* lines of influence or inspiration, however, this chapter develops lines between Bloomsbury and Philosophy a bit differently. The following sections explore, first, the difficulty of verifying the priority of Cambridge philosophy for understanding Bloomsbury's intellectual consistency before, second, reinterpreting what philosophy *is* for the philosophers whom Bloomsbury knew most intimately. In my final section, I turn to writings and artworks of Keynes, Strachey, Vanessa Bell, and Virginia Woolf. In focusing on figures whom one would and *would not* expect to find in a philosophical study of Bloomsbury (Vanessa Bell instead of Roger Fry?), I account for how these writers and artists *conceive* of philosophy by *working* philosophically – rather than merely producing works inertly influenced or inspired by prior philosophical sources.

CHALLENGING CAMBRIDGE PHILOSOPHY'S PRIORITY

As compelling and as clear as the Conversazione Society's presence in the intellectual development of many Bloomsbury men may be, several difficulties arise when one attempts to verify either the extent or the *priority* of Cambridge philosophy for understanding Bloomsbury philosophy. While one can assert and support through evidence of direct citation, allusion, formal education, or conceptual mutation that Kant mattered greatly to Hegel, that Husserl inspired Heidegger, and that Plato continues to feed the thought of nearly all philosophers, a critical project that seeks to establish the philosophical ground of a *non*philosophical group does not have the same evidence on which to draw in this case – because comparatively little of it exists. One cannot prove or presume, after all, that Bloomsbury read Russell, Moore, Plato, or Kant with the same rigor one would expect when writing an intellectual history across the lives and works of philosophers. Anecdotal evidence from letters, diaries, and journals may tell us that Fry read Russell's work[6] and that most of Bloomsbury (including Virginia Woolf) read *Principia Ethica*;[7] however, only Keynes was 'qualified to understand' the specialized writings of their Apostolic teachers – for example, 'Russell's discoveries in symbolic logic' (Rosenbaum, *Victorian Bloomsbury* 196).

To argue, for instance (as Rosenbaum does), that Forster 'knew his Moore better' than his biographers might think is *not*, after all, an argument that Forster knew his Moore *well* (Rosenbaum, '*The Longest Journey*' 33). *The Longest Journey* shows some familiarity with the Cambridge challenge to Idealism (something 'any educated person of this century' would have known [Furbank 45]), yet Forster neither demonstrates an awareness of Moore's arguments nor maintains his distinction between the epistemological and the ethical. Indeed, the biographer against whom Rosenbaum asserts the possibility of Moore's influence bluntly responds 'that Moore's rather "scholastic" and arithmetical way of talking of "organic unities" ... would have repelled [Forster] had he encountered it' (Furbank 45). Moreover, Rosenbaum's turn to an osmotic argument – that Forster was influenced indirectly, through discussions with friends – also raises the question of how well Forster's *friends* knew Moore's writings ('*The Longest Journey*' 32–3). In the case of Leonard Woolf, it is telling that he devotes more space in his autobiography to extoling the philosopher's charm, his gestures, idiosyncrasies, and greatness than to matters of doctrine or discipline. He states that 'Moore's distinction between things good ... as ends and things good merely as means ... answered our questions' about 'what justification there was for our belief that friendship or works of art ... were good'; however, Leonard Woolf neither explores nor demonstrates *how* Moore arrives at this influential position (148). Is this sufficient ground for insisting on the priority of the Cambridge–Apostolic influence on Bloomsbury? Is this attention to largely unverifiable osmotic processes and indirection the only way to investigate Bloomsbury and philosophy (or Bloomsbury's philosophy)?

This combination, in Cambridge–Bloomsbury scholarship, of bold correctives, scant evidence of rigorous engagement, yet plenty of anecdotal evidence of proximity, affection, and private conversation also characterizes Banfield's paratactic coordination of Russell, Fry, and Virginia Woolf; Berel Lang's isomorphic application of Moorian intuition to Keynes's writings on probability and Fry's formalism; Jaakko Hintikka's comparative analysis of significant form and sense-datum; and (more recently) Christine Reynier's assertion that Virginia Woolf's 'On Being Ill' (1930) develops a philosophical response to and qualification of Moore's interventions in the Victorian moral philosophy of Henry Sidgwick. This work collectively opens up lines of further inquiry, but it is often highly speculative – despite its regular claim to act as a historical corrective to other philosophically engaged scholarship.

Banfield seeks, specifically, to displace the scholarly tendency to apply continental philosophy to Bloomsbury writers, such as Virginia Woolf. While the argument across Banfield's magisterial book is compelling and her analyses persuasive, and while Russell is as much a *subject* of this work as Woolf is, his theory of knowledge nevertheless plays the familiar role of textbook 'literary theory'. His writings serve as a cipher or master language that translates and elucidates the 'otherwise unexplained obsessions of [Woolf's] novels which, in isolation, remain puzzling' (Banfield 4). However, it would be a mistake to claim that Woolf (or Fry, for that matter) did not have the same level of engagement with continental thought as they did with analytic philosophies and an even greater categorical mistake to assume that the consistency of their thought is best understood on the model of philosophical systems. Woolf read Dorothy Richardson and Marcel Proust, after all, for whom European traditions were more significant than those of Cambridge realism were. Furthermore, as Andrew McNeillie argues, 'it would certainly be ... to the point to consider ... [Woolf's] hellenic interests', her study of Renaissance literature, as well as 'the examples of Dostoevsky, Chekhov, and Turgenev ... on whom [she] wrote, as she never wrote on Moore' – or, we might add, Russell (13). We might also note that Woolf read and relished Michel de Montaigne – whose philosophical and classical insights into the conveyance, exploration, and discovery of the self or soul could be read in conjunction with any number of philosophies. Indeed, the philosophical basis of Woolf's thought (or the thought of any member of the group) might be better viewed as a nondisciplinary superposition of otherwise discordant concepts and ideas, which might help explain why Rosenbaum and Banfield's work on the Cambridge–Bloomsbury connection is as compelling and persuasive, say, as that of Mark Hussey, Stephen M. Barber, Derek Ryan, Laci Mattison, and others.[8]

Despite the excellence of scholarship that sounds out resonances between Woolf and other – that is, non-Cambridge – paradigms, it would still be wrong, I think, to completely deprioritize Cambridge philosophy in accounts of Bloomsbury's intellectual history or to displace Russell or Moore's realism in favour, say, of Maurice Merleau-Ponty's phenomenology of perception. In lieu of prioritizing this or that philosopher, I return instead to an old question, *What is philosophy?*, as a means to explore the conjunction 'Bloomsbury and Philosophy' otherwise. What is philosophy, after all, for Moore and Russell? What might it be for Keynes, Strachey, Vanessa Bell, and Virginia Woolf? I hope to show that philosophy *itself* is a problem (or a mode of problem making) for these thinkers – a way of knowing, doing, living, and loving that makes and *welcomes* problems.

THE PROBLEM OF PHILOSOPHY

The first lecture in Moore's *Some Main Problems of Philosophy* – delivered at Morley College in 1910 but not published until 1953 – takes the question, 'What Is Philosophy?', as its title. The first sentence of the lecture quickly rephrases and alters the question, however, smuggling in several assumptions under the veil of Moore's typically rigorous method of analysing *how* one uses words and what one really means by them. 'I want', he begins, 'as a start, to try to give you a general idea of what philosophy *is*: or, in other words, what sort of questions it is that philosophers are constantly engaged in discussing and trying to answer' (Moore, *Main Problems* 1). The equation between the question of philosophy's identity and the task of inventorying the problems it (whatever it is) attempts to solve suggests that philosophy is, for Moore, first and foremost a 'subject', an academic field of study, and that subjects in general are defined – more than that, *constituted* – by the questions they ask and try to answer. Philosophy here is transmuted into the disciplinary practice of human beings called philosophers. What these beings do, what they ask and try to answer thus constitutes the very essence of philosophy itself.

While this reverse engineering of philosophy as *whatever philosophers do* makes sense – Moore is delivering this lecture to nonspecialists, after all, whose primary concern might be what one should expect to learn or study in a course of philosophy – his second paragraph suggests that the question, *What problems comprise the subject of philosophy?*, is more difficult to answer than questions like, *What does one study in a course of history? Of ancient Greek? Of physics? Of mathematics?* Common sense might presume that one studies *what has happened and why* in History; *how to read poetry and drama* in ancient Greek; *how to manipulate numbers* in Mathematics. But in philosophy? Moore writes that it 'is not at all an easy thing' 'to give a description of the *whole* range of philosophy'; after all, 'philosophers have ... discussed an immense variety of different sorts of questions' that one would have to include in a 'general description' that 'arrange[s] them properly in relation to one another' (*Main Problems* 1). There's something forbidding about this hesitancy that launches an otherwise rather confident and accessible survey of philosophical problems and concepts. For philosophy is not just the sum of an inventory, for Moore, but a field of problematic relations that has no clear or obvious entrance and no definite pathway from simple or rudimentary to complex or professional. The difficulty of philosophy, then, is not so much a matter of obscure ideas, figures, systems, or questions but a matter of the struggle to sense its coherence, its beginning, and its vast range of seemingly unrelated concerns. What is the plane or territory, after all, on which the metaphysician, logician, and moral philosopher are all engaged in one 'subject' called philosophy (*Main Problems* 25–6)?

Moore does not answer this question directly and leaves the leap from *What is …?* to *What problems …?* unbridged. Yet perhaps there is a sense in which philosophy itself enjoys and shares with *the good* a privileged indefinability in Moore's writings. Perhaps what makes philosophy valuable or coherent is, counterintuitively, its vagueness as a subject; perhaps what philosophy *is*, for Moore, can only be shown or enacted.

Moore's explicit problematization of how to address philosophy's essence resonates with the aesthetic and literary problems in Forster and Woolf's fiction of beginning, arranging, and connecting forms, things, and human beings. 'One may as well begin', *Howards End* (1910) opens, 'with Helen's letters to her sister' (3). This sentence, which emphasizes its beginning *as* a beginning, implies that there is *no* proper beginning – no definite pathway or clear trajectory from Helen's brief affair to Margaret's ownership of Mrs. Wilcox's property. In a novel that sets out to teach readers *how* to connect ('Only connect!') and, thus, how to escape a life lived 'in fragments' (159), the characters, the narrator, and potentially Forster and his readers are nevertheless caught – like London itself (swiftly encroaching on Howards End) – in a 'tangle' of accidents, conspiracies, cruelties, misunderstandings and miscalculations (283, 287, 289).

From their disorienting beginnings, Woolf's novels also launch readers deep into tangles: for example, the maternal tangle of Helen Ambrose's painful separation from her children in *The Voyage Out* (later sublimated and complicated in the education of her niece) as well as Clarissa Dalloway's 'plunge' outdoors to 'buy the flowers herself', which doubles as a plunge into the past, amidst London's postwar amnesia, and (later) into an encounter with the suicide of a young man (3). As Woolf writes in 'Modern Fiction', life (much like philosophy) 'is not a series of gig lamps symmetrically arranged' but 'a luminous halo, a semi-transparent envelope' (160). There is neither a proper entrance to nor exit from this luminosity but only an aesthetic labour to connect pieces, arrange relations, and make problems. In Woolf's essay, then, fiction that aims to capture something of life could be said to be *philosophically* literary.

The philosophico-aesthetic efforts of Moore, Forster, and Woolf also characterize Martin Heidegger's approach to the question, 'What Is Metaphysics?' (1929). He foregoes a definition of metaphysics, however, and immerses his audience (and reader) directly into a question that we might take up when *doing* metaphysics. 'In this way', he writes, 'we will let ourselves be transposed directly into metaphysics. Only this way will we provide metaphysics the proper occasion to introduce itself' (93). For all the differences between Moore and Heidegger, they both introduce philosophy by avoiding the question, *What is it?* They answer the question, *What is philosophy?* not by establishing a definition but, rather, by attempting to demonstrate or activate it by modelling philosophical/

metaphysical inquiry. Woolf observes a similar ethos in Fry's style of lecturing. He did not merely share aesthetic theories with audience members or itemize what they should note on the slides he had prepared. He would model how to gaze 'afresh at [a] picture', performing with them what it is like to see, observe, and to be surprised by the details of a Poussin or Rembrandt or Cézanne 'as if for the first time' (*Roger Fry* 262).

Though Russell's *The Problems of Philosophy*, which owes its direction and some of its content to Moore's Morley College lectures, doesn't explicitly pose the question, 'What is philosophy?' his first chapter makes a more direct statement on what we are doing or how we *begin* to do philosophy. He asks, 'Is there any knowledge in the world which is so certain that no reasonable man could doubt it?' and continues about a sentence later,

> When we have realised the obstacles in the way of a straightforward and confident answer, we shall be well launched on the study of philosophy – for philosophy is merely the attempt to answer such ultimate questions ... after exploring all that makes such questions puzzling. (*The Problems* 9–10)

Russell will end this chapter's meditations on the phantom table by emphasizing and reinforcing what he says in this passage: namely, that philosophy's value is in *the attempt* to answer questions rather than in the specific answers philosophers themselves have developed. Its 'power [to ask] questions which increase the interest of the world, and show the strangeness and wonder lying just below the surface even in the commonest things of daily life' (*The Problems* 25) – this power comprises the most prominent feature of philosophizing: not solving or answering but asking, crafting, and posing problems. To *do* philosophy is to make and convey problems. To be a philosopher is, by extension, *to become* a problem, which is to say, to become critical, to learn to make puzzles and to make them visible or perceptible to others.

For a writer best remembered for his insistence on facts, his rejection of belief, and his theory of knowledge, this picture of philosophy demonstrates the pedagogical value of a practice sensitive to angles of vision, to the ground shifting beneath self-evident ideas and assumptions, to the satisfying affects and effects bound up with learning to welcome the very uncertainty and vagueness which Moore highlights in the introductory Morley College lecture as well. For Fry, visual art also accomplishes this work; aesthetic labour is itself, for him, a philosophical activity – that is, a matter of helping viewers to see differently. 'For our representative of common sense', Fry writes in 'The Philosophy of Impressionism' (1894), 'does not know how little he sees of *things* – how fluctuating, evanescent and fantastic are the actual visual impressions of objects, how they melt and glide into each other' (19). (These sentences precede and anticipate Moore and Russell's later complications of perception.) Indeed, as he argues, it is difficult for us now to recall 'what an outrage on the common sense' geometrical perspective must have been for viewers in the fifteenth century (14), how innovations in visual art necessarily interfere with ways of seeing 'that training or habit has prepared us for' (15). For these reasons, the post-Impressionists serve as an 'inestimable boon ... for future imaginations' – if only because of their explicit challenge to common sense and sight (Fry, 'Post Impressionism' 105). While Moore valued common sense as a way to demystify overly complicated philosophical arguments, both he and Russell fundamentally (and publicly) frame philosophy itself as a thinking, feeling, and seeing otherwise – a task also taken up by Bloomsbury's economist (Keynes), historian/biographer (Strachey), and sister artists (Vanessa Bell and Virginia Woolf).

PHILOSOPHICAL BLOOMSBURY

Following these versions of Moore and Russell, a new way to study Bloomsbury and philosophy emerges: if we conceptualize philosophy beyond its function as a doctrinal base and approach it, instead, as an activity – something one lives or becomes – what might we learn to see of such philosophy in Bloomsbury writings and art? In what ways might these nonphilosophers promote an activation, attachment, and attraction to problems – a love of wisdom that unsettles common sense and teaches others, through disturbance and delight, to see otherwise?

Keynes on the history of ideas and human being

In all of Bloomsbury's publications, Keynes's writings come closest to what we might call professional philosophy. Indeed, his early theories of probability emerge from agreements and disagreements with Moore's ethical writings, and his most learned essay, 'The End of Laissez-faire' (1926), tracks the hybridization of incompatible paradigms – Christianity, Darwinian evolution, individualism, socialism, and so on – that nevertheless popularized the conservative notion that 'the ... watchword of government', as Bentham puts it, 'ought to be – Be quiet' (qtd in Keynes 9: 278). The range of references in this later essay is impressive, but what makes the essay most *philosophical*, perhaps, is not Keynes's engagement with Locke, Hume, Paley, Bentham, Rousseau, Burke, Godwin, Darwin, and others. Rather, philosophy here functions in the pedagogical effort to help his listeners at Oxford in 1924 (present for the lecture version of this essay) and his later Hogarth Press readers to understand that laissez-faire is not simply one coherent idea among others – and certainly not the *fittest* idea surviving some sort of economico-philosophical struggle. Through composing a genealogical tapestry of principles and popular assumptions, Keynes shows that this idea is predicated on the outmoded writings of noneconomists, on the corrupt functioning of eighteenth-century governments, on the model of a vulgar Darwinian progressivism, on the emergence of the businessman as the new secular saviour of the poor in spirit, and on a host of groundless and falsifiable presumptions.

Keynes thus shows how a scientifically mediocre, conceptually incoherent, and theologically motivated doctrine has disseminated across British culture and society through educational and religious institutions (despite the objections of economists post-1870) (9: 280–88). Keynes also asserts that laissez-faire transubstantiates cruelty, cost, and inequality into the natural and healthy order of things (9: 284). To deny the welfare of the less fortunate *because* of one's faith in governmental noninvolvement and the self-adjusting market is to deny this welfare without intellectual ground, for the love of money, and in the service of 'the great captain of industry, the master-individualist, who [we are told] serves us in serving himself, just as any artist does' (Keynes 9: 286). Thus, Keynes levies powerful philosophical challenges in this essay to traditional notions of the human, of human history, and of the natural. The history of ideas, he argues, is not a dialectics of competing and self-sublating notions but a history of confusions, misprisions, unlikely hybridizations, and misapprehensions that have served as alibis for the translation of poverty and wealth into destiny and the divine right of the secular market.

Later, in a well-known assessment of Moore's influence on Bloomsbury, entitled 'My Early Beliefs' (1938), Keynes offers an autocritique of the group predicated, largely, on its mistaken tendency to think of history as a story of progress built on a notion of the human as an inherently rational creature. Though Moore may have helped the

Bloomsbury Apostles to extricate themselves from the utilitarian influence of Bentham, from the love of wealth, and from Christianity, he still thinks of his group as 'the last of the Utopians ... who believe[d] ... moral progress by virtue of which the human race already consist[ed] of reliable, rational, decent people, influenced by truth and objective standards' (10: 446). People, they mistakenly imagined, could 'be safely released from the outward restraints of convention ... and left ... to their sensible devices, pure motives, and reliable intuitions of the good'; Bloomsbury had not been aware, however, 'that civilisation was a thin and precarious crust erected by the personality and the will of a very few, and only maintained by rules and conventions skillfully put across and guilefully preserved' (10: 446). Whether Keynes's diagnosis of his coterie's belief in human rationality is accurate for all members, a philosophically consistent critique of human nature and human history links his earlier genealogy of the complex but confused notion of laissez-faire with this bit of autocritical life-writing. Both texts suggest that to bring powerful, effective, yet poisonous ideas to their ends requires not just debate or historical demystification but a widespread revision – a learning *to see* this history and human being itself anew. But how do we learn to see? How do I train my eye or the eyes of others – their minds, my mind – to intuit the relational flux that underlies inherited pictures of the human being, of its history, of nature?

Strachey on relational life and history

Strachey's *Eminent Victorians* resonates with – though it predates – Keynes's implicit reconceptualization of history and human being, taking up the modernist challenge to see them otherwise (and to teach others to do so as well). Todd Avery has situated this project within contemporary academic debates about whether history is a science or an art, pointing to Strachey's enthusiasm for Moore as the motivation for his nonacademic contribution (respecting science's capacity to gather facts but asserting the artfulness of historiography for shaping and conveying them). Whether Strachey had Moore in mind when beginning and completing his Victorian portraits, he departs in this work on a philosophical adventure of his own devising. The opening gambit of Strachey's bestseller – that there is too much *known* about the Victorian age to ever write a history of it (9) – may seem dubious a century later, but the provocation of his preface has less to do with the truth of this wry claim than with the promise of his reorientation toward history through compositional attention to singular lives. He portrays the past not as a chronological narrative but as a biographical sequence – what concept of history emerges here? He draws up 'little bucket[fuls]' of human life without prioritizing or fetishizing causal chains or accumulations of fact – what concept of 'a life' emerges here (9)?

Though Strachey's volume is a polemic against what he judged to be the age of Victorian moralism and antirationality, it is also a pedagogical work that potentially trains his readers to notice and problematize the bounds of a life and the historian's method of recording the impacts of specific lives on various circles (personal, institutional, national, imperial). His preface claims, after all, to look 'in unexpected places' and 'shoot a sudden, revealing searchlight into obscure recesses, hitherto undivined' (9). His concern is sight-oriented – 'to illustrate rather than to explain' – 'bring[ing] to the light of day' things kept at 'far depths', presenting 'some Victorian visions to the modern eye' (9). What appears *to* the eye, however, is more difficult to articulate. What are these 'human beings' whose 'value ... is eternal, and must be felt for its own sake' (10)? Where do they begin and end? What do we make of Strachey's composite angle of admiration and ridicule? And how does attention to them complicate engagements with the past – with the facts of what has happened?

The thought-adventure Strachey launches readers on has less to do with answering these questions than with learning to feel their significance and the critical edge of the uncertainties they cut into icons and myths. Strachey's particular deployment of purported truths and facts – of Florence Nightingale, Cardinal Manning, Dr Arnold, General Gordon, and the cast of major and minor characters who populate these accounts – encourages readerly curiosity about the fundamentally *relational* aspect of human being and action in history as well as the mythological abstraction that so often clouds and obscures this relationality. True history and biography, in other words, are at odds with the 'memory of the world' – which remembers heroes, legends, villains, champions, and despots (133). In the case of Nightingale, 'her Crimean triumphs' at Scutari determined her popular image, but for her it was 'a mere incident' launching her on five decades of 'unknown labor' (133). To attend robustly to a life, our vision of the biographical subject must expand not in facts but in lateral attentiveness; Nightingale's legend is impossible without her embeddedness in a specific class, without access to capital, without unique means of entreating and mobilizing power, without her allies (royal, professional, personal, public), and without her sarcasm and rage and (potentially pathological) attachment to problems – 'how could it be otherwise?'; 'what had women to do with war?'; 'would anything, after all, be done' to reform the order of things (114, 121, 143)? The Nightingale who emerges from Strachey's study is, no doubt, incomplete and (perhaps) inexact (even fudged) but the human being he prepares and presents is not eternally fixed but shockingly many, with edges that bleed and blur in and out of the lives of others. This shape of a life – this approach to biography – thus allows *a life* to become an optic through which to see *a history* of human beings and struggles – one life as a perspective from which to view the effects of war, the slowness of bureaucracy, the less agreeable sides of heroes, and the intellectual shortcomings of the powerful. Far more than a polemic against specific Victorians (who serve as symbols for Victorianism itself), *Eminent Victorians* tasks readers (delighting them all the while) to reassess the units of their judgments, accounts, and narratives and, thus, to wonder where else these units might bleed, what else they might touch, and what lights might be available to teach us to see these unknown relations.

Vanessa Bell and the perspective of emptiness

Vanessa Bell might very well be the least cited, studied, or even mentioned member of the Bloomsbury Group in literary and philosophical histories – primarily because intellectual history tends to privilege *writers* (thus the greater attention to her mentor/ lover, Roger Fry, as well as her sister and husband). Even so, her paintings and designs visualize philosophical problems bound up with how and what we see and, moreover, with challenges to move and rest our eyes and mind in unexpected ways.

Heidegger begins his *Introduction to Metaphysics* (1959) by asking, 'Why are there essents ... why is there anything at all, rather than nothing?' (1). This question, he asserts, 'is the first ... the most far reaching ... the deepest ... the widest of all questions' (1–2). Vanessa Bell's art certainly does not articulate such an overwhelming question in words, but her lines, colours, arrangements, textures, figures, and themes nevertheless invert and modify this familiar problem (one Moore also thought fundamental to philosophy [*Main Problems* 1]). Like Strachey's life sketches, her experiments direct the viewer's gaze to unexpected areas of her often bright and active canvases. Unlike Strachey's biographies, however, many of these spots initially reveal nothing, an emptiness of high visual gravity. Altering Heidegger's question, many of Bell's paintings prompt one to wonder, 'Why is there nothing – *here, where I am looking* – rather than something? Among all these things, how has *nothingness* crept in? What might nothing do when my gaze wanders from things, when figures no longer dominate the canvas, when the plane of composition encourages me to fix my eyes on the eyeless?' We might note such challenges in the diagonal band of sand in *Studland Beach* (1912); the separation between vessel and nude in *The Tub* (1917); the respective side-eye and facelessness of the Mary Hutchinson (1915) and Virginia Woolf (1911, 1912) portraits; the featureless, rusted wall that crowds the *Street Corner Conversation* (1913); the viewless views of *Apples: 46 Gordon Street* (1909–10) and *The Other Room* (late 1930s); the blackened doorway in the background of *Landscape with Haystack* (1926); and the empty chairs of *Interior with a Table* (1921), *The Artist's Desk* (1925), and *View into the Garden* (1926).

Perhaps the most remarkable encounter with emptiness appears in the distinctly Bellian work, *A Conversation* (1913–16; reproduced on the front cover of this volume). This painting – which captured the attention of her sister[9] – arranges three women in a circle, seated and leaning in toward one another. The black, purple dress of one figure, who is presumably speaking (or about to speak), dominates the bottom left quadrant of the canvas. Her face and body are caught in profile: orange hair, blue eyes, pale skin, bare neck extending almost horizontally above, slightly to the left, of the centre. The elbow of her right arm, bent and resting on her covered thigh, projects her forearm vertically, her right hand (mostly closed) bent back and palm up. Her cheeks appear flushed. Closest to the viewer is the first listener, whose brown dress covers the right side of the canvas. Her back turns to the foreground, her reddened (shadowed) face turned and tilted left in a skewed profile: eyes sharp, triangular, concentrating. This figure blocks the second listener, whose dark red dress is visible only over the first listener's left shoulder and behind the speaker's gesturing hand. The first listener's face overlaps the second's – whose face (though partial) is the most directly turned toward to the viewer. Visible between these faces, above the head of the speaker, and between white curtains suggesting a mid-ground window, is a garden of red, yellow, pink, and white flowers. Despite a distinction in colour between the bright outside/background and the darkened inside/foreground, 'the flatness of the design' dissolves the 'division suggested by the window' and unifies women and flowers 'in the same pictorial surface' (Goldman 148). For Corin Sworm, who describes the painting a bit differently, 'this visual vagueness catches the listeners [and viewers] between spaces – formally enmeshing them in the outside world while also anchoring them to the interior, framed by the window' (171). Moreover, the flowers outside/inside mirror the viewer, who seems let in on an intimate (or antagonistic?) conversation from which they are simultaneously barred (see Elkin in this volume).

The position of these figures does not draw our gaze toward their faces but toward the void at the centre of their circle: between the dark red dress and the empty hand of the speaker. What are we to make of this emptiness at the centre of this intimate busyness? Of figures caught in the midst of saying something – and thus rendered as saying nothing? Of the bright, eyeless flowers that reflect back to the viewer the impossibility of overhearing? Such questions, inspired by the centre of this stilled and frozen conversation, become an occasion to theorize the fragility of intimacy, the otherwise invisible relationships usually tucked away from majoritarian gazes, the 'structural necessity', as Derrida puts it, 'of the abyss' (163). We might also see here a becoming-philosophical in Bell's working through of what Jane Goldman reads – in Virginia Woolf's response to and repurposing of her sister's art – as a feminist aesthetics (150). Regarding *To the Lighthouse*, Goldman teaches us to read Woolf's famous riposte to Fry – 'I meant *nothing* by The Lighthouse' (*Letters* 3: 385) – as part of a larger prismatic recoding of silence, darkness, shadow, and absence into occasions for a 'moment of intimacy' between a feminine gaze and feminine object (Goldman 179). 'In telling Fry she "meant *nothing* by The Lighthouse,"' Goldman writes, 'Woolf may present to him a silence that in other contexts and from other perspectives may speak volumes' (167).

Though perhaps not part of a politically motivated feminism, Bell's attraction to emptiness might help us press Goldman's reading of Woolf (and her acceptance of Bell as a figure of social withdrawal [166]) even further. Indeed, *A Conversation* seems dead set in its refusal to signify, symbolize, figure, or apply a code – a gesture that repeats (with a difference) Woolf's denial that her lighthouse meant *anything* (let alone that it stood in for a phallus). 'One has to have a central line down the middle of the book', Woolf explains to Fry, 'to hold the design together' (*Letters* 3: 385). The lighthouse functions to sustain, shore up, or embrace the elements of the novel. Likewise, the emptiness of Bell's colour patches, views, and objects sustain her compositions. To mean *nothing* is, perhaps, the very point. The very vision.

The 'central line' of Woolf's lighthouse corresponds to the completion of Lily Briscoe's painting at the end of her novel ('she drew a line there, in the centre ... it was finished' [211]) and thus suggests that Lily's painting – like Bell's and like Mrs. Ramsay's restful and restorative solitude much earlier in the novel – means *nothing*. The line is a practice not of signification but, as in Bell's work, an effort to compose a perspective of emptiness. 'There was freedom', Mrs. Ramsay muses, 'there was peace, there was, most welcome of all, a summoning together, a resting on a platform of stability. Not as oneself ... but as a wedge of darkness' (65–6). Borrowing from Eve Kosofsky Sedgwick's late work, we might learn to read this darkness, which pervades Woolf's novel, alongside Bell's work as an occasion to practice an intimacy not with other human beings but, rather, with 'nonbeing' – an 'urgent and even exciting intimacy' that feels 'much less like dread or excitement or relief of any kind ... than like a kind of law of perspective, a strangely spacious framework of impermanence in which ideas, emotions, selves, and other phenomenon can arise in new relations' (Sedgwick 70–71).

Virginia Woolf's late philosophy

When Virginia Woolf uses the word 'philosophy' in her diaries and memoir, it initially seems to mean something like a personal belief or a sense about how the world or how existence works. It is at some remove, then, from references to theories of knowledge or ethics that mark works like *The Voyage Out* (1915) and (more famously) *To the Lighthouse*.[10] We might turn, for instance, to 'A Sketch of the Past' (1939–40) where reflections on the link between sudden, violent moments of being and her career as a writer prompt Woolf to

> reach what I might call a philosophy; at any rate it is a constant idea of mine; that behind the cotton wool [of daily life] is hidden a pattern; that we – I mean all human beings – are connected with this [pattern]; that the whole world is a work of art; that we are parts of the work of art. (72)

But we might also turn to the lesser known reference of Woolf to her 'philosophy of the free soul', which she now hopes (as she writes in her 1937 diary, just after the publication of *The Years*) to 'put ... into operation' (*Diary* 5: 68). Or her earlier 1933 entry, referencing perhaps the same idea, 'that [she has], at last laid hands upon [her] philosophy of anonymity' (*Diary* 4: 186). And there is also the much later reference to her 'tiny philosophy' in early 1940, which is 'to hug the present moment (in which the fire is going out)' (*Diary* 5: 262). And her private criticism later that same year of Herbert Read's review of Roger Fry's last lectures and of Read's autobiography, *Annals of Innocence and Experience* (1940), 'what is the value of a philosophy which has no power over life?' (*The Letters* 6: 340).

Though it may be poor form to generalize from such scant if tantalizing evidence of a late Woolfian philosophy (evidence spread across myriad days, weeks, months, years, and projects), 'philosophy' is clearly a word Woolf applies to herself and others with some care and caution ('tiny philosophy'; 'what I might call my philosophy'). In October 1932, after all, she reacts – as if allergically – to *The Selected Letters of D.H. Lawrence* (edited by Aldous Huxley): 'To me Lawrence is airless, confined: I dont want this, I go on saying. And the repetition of one idea. I dont want that either. I dont want "a philosophy" in the least; I dont believe in other people's reading of riddles' (*Diary* 4: 126). As in the previous diary entries – and the famous passage from 'A Sketch' – the word 'philosophy' in 1932 does not refer to an academic subject (or a field of study); unlike these other references, however, it refers to a claustrophobic system that restricts and restrains, that includes and excludes, 'a metaphysical system', Barber suggests, 'a fixed solution' that only works for some and reviles those for whom it does not (205). Recoiling from this sense of philosophy – one that might also refer to Hegel's, Kant's, or Berkeley's 'philosophy' – Woolf appeals to the dead Lawrence (and thus to herself), 'why not some system that includes the good? What a discovery that would be – a system that [does] not shut out' (*Diary* 4: 127). Here Woolf seems to gesture toward a concept of the good not so much at odds with Moore's indefinable virtue but, rather, one that is linked in a later work like *Three Guineas* (1938) to a practice, as Barber puts it, of introducing into systems and institutions 'possibilities for ethically inhabiting them so as to critically reconfigure them' (203).[11]

Woolf's later use of philosophy – while cautious – suggests a desire to reclaim it for other purposes: as a way to think her ethos or her relation to herself (her cultivation of independence from and indifference to coercive desires), as a way to convey her sharp focus on the here and now (not taking for granted, though striving for the possibility of, a future for her and others), as a way to articulate a creative ontology – an aesthetics of existence that extends beyond the art of life she admires in the writings of Montaigne. Moreover, these late references to philosophy exhibit a position, an orientation, a habitus, or a set of patient though persistent practices that invites, accepts, and affirms uncertainty, openness, and even vagueness – a quality these references share with the openings of Moore and Russell's respective inventories of philosophy's main problems. And these references also have everything to do with the connection between a love of wisdom and an urgency to learn to live, to survive, and (when necessary) to die. This may be a long way around to a thesis regarding Woolf's late philosophy as a way to read Cambridge philosophers who are so often invoked as a lens for interpreting Bloomsbury's coherence and consistency. Or, rather, perhaps a thesis regarding an adjacency – a radical one – of Woolf and her Bloomsbury intimates *beside* these philosophers.

Roger Fry: A Biography (1940) reorients the importance of this love of wisdom for the Bloomsbury Group. For while Woolf includes a chapter on Fry's academic and social life at Cambridge, the most extensive reference to philosophy comes in the last chapter, which maps the final decade of Fry's life. The episode to which I refer (which includes little commentary) concerns an account, written by Fry in French, of a woman whom he had befriended, who had (so her family assured him) treasured his companionship, but who (nonetheless) had killed herself suddenly. Woolf does not quote his narration of these events but, rather, a moving – even if somewhat crudely gendered – thesis on the coexistence of two contradictory principles: (1) the principle of a solid reality or world of definitive, eternal, indestructible substances and souls (which, he claims, one touches only through love) and (2) the principle of a completely relative reality in continuous flux. While love might manage to keep the chaos of this second principle – this second world – at bay, Fry concludes that the flux remains immanent, as indestructible as the substances of the first world. To make life under this second principle viable, Fry explains that he has learned the last and most enduring lesson of philosophy from the suicide of his friend – whom he names '*la sagesse*' (Woolf, *Roger Fry* 254). The pessimistic lesson, quite simply, is that of acquiescence to the inevitability of injustice, old age, and the failure of hope and ambition. If Fry's philosophy here sounds like an admixture of Platonic, Heraclitian, Spinozan, Bergsonian, and Russellian perspectives, there is a good reason, I think.[12] In this mishmash of philosophical grief – wedged rhetorically, by Woolf, between accounts of his travel and his public lectures – philosophy emerges (as it did for Woolf near the end of her life, as it does for Russell and Moore, though in more covert ways) not as a school subject or academic discipline but as a problem of learning to grapple with incommensurable experiences and existences, with learning to love this grappling, of learning to live with this wisdom so that one might, perhaps, also learn to die: the oldest definition, in some sense, of philosophy, which takes us from Socrates, through Cicero, up to Montaigne, to Cambridge, Moore, Russell, the Bloomsbury Group, and (finally) to ourselves.

NOTES

I would like to thank Laci Mattison for organizing a panel at the 2017 Louisville Conference on Literature and Culture since 1900, where I shared an early draft of this chapter. I would also like to thank her and Erik-John Fuhrer for presenting alongside me and for helping me strategize its elaboration here.

1. See Banfield; Johnstone; Levy; Regan; and Rosenbaum, *Victorian Bloomsbury* and *Edwardian Bloomsbury*.
2. For Moore, the 'fundamental question of Ethics' does not concern specific rules of conduct; rather, it asks, 'What things are goods or ends in themselves?' (*Principia Ethica* 184).
3. Here, Moore follows Plato, whose ethics 'are distinguished by upholding ... the view that intrinsic value belongs exclusively to those states of mind which consist in love of what is good or hatred of what is evil' (*Principia Ethica* 108, 178).
4. Leonard Woolf writes, 'George Moore was a great man, the only great man whom I have ever met or known in the world of ordinary, real life' (131).
5. On Kant's foundational articulation of this scandal, see Moore, 'Proof'.
6. Fry writes to Marie Mauron, 'Just now I am reading Bertrand Russell's books. He is one of the men of genius of our time. With help from others he is starting a real metaphysic based on fundamental ideas about mathematics' (*Letters* 2: 485).
7. An allusion to *Principia Ethica*, which Helen Ambrose is presumably reading, appears in Virginia Woolf's *The Voyage Out* (1915: 25, 65).

8. See Barber, 'Exit Woolf' and 'States of Emergency'; Hussey, *The Singing of the Real World*; Mattison, 'Virginia Woolf's Ethical Subjectivity'; Ryan, 'Woolf and Contemporary Philosophy' and *Virginia Woolf and the Materiality of Theory*.

9. In a letter to Bell about this painting, Woolf writes, 'I think you are a most remarkable painter. But I maintain you are [also] ... a short story writer of great wit and able to bring off a situation in a way that rouses my envy. I wonder if I could write the Three Women in prose' (*Letters* 3: 498).

10. For references to Moore's *Principia Ethica* in *The Voyage Out*, see note 7. In *To the Lighthouse*, Andrew Ramsay's description of his father's research seems to allude to Russell's example of the table in *The Problems of Philosophy*: '[Lily] asked [Andrew] what his father's books were about. "Subject and object and the nature of reality ... Think of a kitchen table ... when you're not there"' (26). See Banfield (65–75).

11. Despite his preference for systematic argumentation, Moore shares with Woolf a distaste for system building. Near the end of *Principia Ethica*, he writes, 'To search for "unity" and "system", at the expense of truth, is not, I take it, the proper business of philosophy, however universally it may have been the practice of philosophers' (222).

12. Spinoza is present, in a sense, at Fry's cremation in 1934. Woolf recounts that 'a paper ... was given to his friends' that included 'the words of Spinoza which ... [Fry] had said were the right words: "A free man thinks of death least of all things; and his wisdom is a meditation not of death but of life"' (*Roger Fry* 298). See Ryan, 'Entangled in Nature'.

WORKS CITED

Avery, Todd. '"The Historian of the Future": Lytton Strachey and Modernist Historiography between the Two Cultures'. *ELH* 77.4 (2010): 841–66.

Banfield, Ann. *The Phantom Table: Woolf, Fry, Russell and the Epistemology of Modernism*. Cambridge: Cambridge UP, 2000.

Barber, Stephen M. 'Exit Woolf'. *Feminism and the Final Foucault*. Ed. Dianna Taylor and Karen Vintges. Urbana and Chicago: U of Illinois P, 2004. 41–64.

Barber, Stephen M. 'States of Emergency, States of Freedom: Woolf, History, and the Novel'. *Novel: A Forum on Fiction* 42.2 (2009): 196–206.

Derrida, Jacques. *Of Grammatology*. Trans. Gayatri Chakravorty Spivak. Baltimore: Johns Hopkins UP, 1997 [1967].

Forster, E. M. *Howards End*. Intro. David Lodge. London: Penguin, 2000 [1910].

Fry, Roger. *Letters of Roger Fry*, 2 vols. Ed. Denys Sutton. London: Chatto & Windus, 1972.

Fry, Roger. 'The Philosophy of Impressionism'. *A Roger Fry Reader*. Ed. Christopher Reed. Chicago: U of Chicago P, 1996 [1894]. 12–20.

Fry, Roger. 'Post Impressionism'. *A Roger Fry Reader*. Ed. Christopher Reed. Chicago: U of Chicago P, 1996 [1911]. 99–110.

Furbank, P. N. 'The Philosophy of E.M. Forster'. *E.M. Forster: Centenary Revaluations*. Ed. Judith Scherer and Robert K. Martin. Toronto: U of Toronto P, 1982. 37–51.

Goldman, Jane. *The Feminist Aesthetics of Virginia Woolf: Modernism, Post-Impressionism, and the Politics of the Visual*. Cambridge: Cambridge UP, 2001.

Heidegger, Martin. *An Introduction to Metaphysics*. Trans. Ralph Manheim. New Haven: Yale UP, 1959.

Heidegger, Martin. 'What Is Metaphysics?' Trans. David Farrell Krell. *Basic Writings*. Ed. David Farrell Krell. New York: HarperCollins, 2008. 89–110.

Hintikka, Jaakko. 'The Longest Philosophical Journey: Quest of Reality as a Common Theme in Bloomsbury'. *The British Tradition in 20th-Century Philosophy: Proceedings of the*

17th International Wittgenstein Symposium. Ed. Jaakko Hintikka and Klaus Puhl. Vienna: Hölder-Pichler-Tempsky, 1995. 11–26.

Hussey, Mark. *The Singing of the Real World: The Philosophy of Virginia Woolf's Fiction*. Columbus: Ohio State UP, 1986.

Johnstone, J. K. *The Bloomsbury Group: A Study of E.M. Forster, Lytton Strachey, Virginia Woolf, and Their Circle*. New York: Noonday Press, 1963.

Keynes, John Maynard. *The Collected Writings of John Maynard Keynes*. Ed. Elizabeth Johnson and Donald Moggridge. Cambridge: Cambridge UP, 1989. 30 vols.

Lang, Berel. 'Intuition in Bloomsbury'. *Journal of the History of Ideas* 25 (1964): 292–302.

Levy, Paul. *Moore: G.E. Moore and the Cambridge Apostles*. New York: Rinehart & Winston, 1980.

Mattison, Laci. 'Virginia Woolf's Ethical Subjectivity: Deleuze and Guattari's Worlding and Bernard's "Becoming-Savage"'. *Deleuze Studies* 7.4 (2013): 562–80.

McNeillie, Andrew. 'Bloomsbury'. *The Cambridge Companion to Virginia Woolf* (2nd ed.). Ed. Susan Sellers. Cambridge: Cambridge UP, 2010. 1–28.

Moore, G. E. *Principia Ethica*. Cambridge: Cambridge UP, 1903.

Moore, G. E. 'Proof of an External World'. *Philosophical Papers*. New York: Collier Books, 1966. 126–48.

Moore, G. E. *Some Main Problems of Philosophy*. London: Allen & Unwin, 1953.

Regan, Tom. *Bloomsbury's Prophet: G.E. Moore and the Development of His Moral Philosophy*. Philadelphia: Temple UP, 1986.

Reynier, Christine. 'Virginia Woolf's Ethics and Victorian Moral Philosophy'. *Philosophy and Literature* 38.1 (2014): 128–41.

Rosenbaum, S. P. *Edwardian Bloomsbury: The Early History of the Bloomsbury Group*, Vol. 2. New York: St. Martin's Press, 1994.

Rosenbaum, S. P. '*The Longest Journey*: E. M. Forster's Refutation of Idealism'. *E. M. Forster: A Human Exploration*. Ed. G. K. Das and John Beer. London: Macmillan, 1979. 32–54.

Rosenbaum, S. P. *Victorian Bloomsbury: The Early History of the Bloomsbury Group*, Vol. 1. New York: St. Martin's Press, 1987.

Russell, Bertrand. *The History of Western Philosophy*. New York: Simon and Schuster, 1945.

Russell, Bertrand. *The Problems of Philosophy*. New York: H. Holt, 1912.

Ryan, Derek. 'Entangled in Nature: Deleuze's Modernism, Woolf's Philosophy, and Spinoza's Ethology'. *Understanding Deleuze, Understanding Modernism*. Ed. Paul Ardoin, S. E. Gontarski and Laci Mattison. London: Bloomsbury, 2014. 151–68.

Ryan, Derek. *Virginia Woolf and the Materiality of Theory: Sex, Animal, Life*. Edinburgh: Edinburgh UP, 2013.

Ryan, Derek. 'Woolf and Contemporary Philosophy'. *Woolf in Context*. Ed. Bryony Randall and Jane Goldman. Cambridge: Cambridge UP, 2012. 362–75.

Sedgwick, Eve Kosofsky. *The Weather in Proust*. Ed. Jonathan Goldberg. Durham, NC: Duke UP, 2011.

Strachey, Lytton. *Eminent Victorians*. Ed. Michael Holroyd. London: Penguin, 1986 [1918].

Sworn, Corin. 'A Conversation'. *Vanessa Bell*. Ed. Sarah Milroy and Ian A. C. Dejardin. Philip Wilson Publishers, Dulwich Picture Gallery, 2017. 171–8.

Woolf, Leonard. *Sowing: An Autobiography of the Years 1880–1904*. New York: Harcourt, 1960.

Woolf, Virginia. *The Diary of Virginia Woolf*, 5 vols. Ed. Anne Oliver Bell. New York: Harcourt Brace Jovanovich, 1977–84.

Woolf, Virginia. *The Letters of Virginia Woolf*, 6 vols. Ed. Nigel Nicholson and Joanne Trautmann. New York: Harcourt, 1975–80.

Woolf, Virginia. 'Modern Fiction'. *The Essays of Virginia Woolf*, Vol. 4: 1925–8. Ed. Andrew
    McNeillie. New York: Harcourt, 1994. 157–65.
Woolf, Virginia. *Mrs. Dalloway*. Ed. Bonnie Kime Scott. New York: Harcourt, 2005 [1925].
Woolf, Virginia. 'A Sketch of the Past'. *Moments of Being: A Collection of Autobiographical
    Writings* (2nd ed.). Ed. Jeanne Schulkind. New York: Harcourt, 1985. 64–159.
Woolf, Virginia. *To the Lighthouse*. Ed. Mark Hussey. New York: Harcourt, 2005 [1927].
Woolf, Virginia. *The Voyage Out*. Ed. Jane Wheare. London: Penguin, 1992 [1915].

Case Study: Bloomsbury, Mulk Raj Anand, and Henri Bergson

LACI MATTISON

Modernism has always been transnational, and Mulk Raj Anand's fiction and nonfiction exemplify this. It makes sense, then, that scholarly interest in Anand has increased exponentially, in step with the transnational turn in modernist studies. Anna Snaith, for instance, sees Anand as part of the 'anti-colonial networks' of Leonard and Virginia Woolf's Hogarth Press; Kristin Bluemel writes of Anand, in his connection to Orwell and his work at the BBC, as one of the 'radical eccentrics' important to 'intermodernism'; and Jessica Berman reads Anand alongside Joyce to emphasize 'the multidirectional flow of global literature and culture, where streams of discourse move not just from metropolis to colony, or even from colony back to metropolis, but also ... from colony to metropolis to another colony and back again' (93). As scholars like Snaith, Berman, Bluemel, Sara Blair, and others recognize in varying ways, Anand forged links between cultures and ideas in his fiction and nonfiction to reveal affiliations between East and West. In this chapter, I turn my attention to one such affiliation that has yet to be explored: how Anand brings together Hinduism and the philosophy of Henri Bergson. I argue that Anand triangulates Hinduism, modernist aesthetics, and Bergsonian philosophy to emphasize cross-cultural connections between modernism and Hinduism for his own revolutionary purposes, namely, the reformation of Orthodox Hinduism. In the process, I illuminate Anand's revisionist history of Bloomsbury, and of Bloomsbury and philosophy.

In what follows, I offer some background about Anand and modernism, particularly in his relationship to Bloomsbury; I then turn to a significant conversation Anand had with Virginia Woolf before addressing Anand's direct reference to Bergsonian *élan vital* in his late novel *Reflections on a White Elephant*. I conclude with an exploration of other Bergsonian aspects of Anand's first novel, *Untouchable* (1935), which showcase how his aesthetic interpretation of Bergson's philosophy progresses from the personal to the political. Anand thus demonstrates the relationship between the personal experience of Bergsonian intuition, which might allow one access to a perception of the *élan vital*, and its potential revolutionary aspects. With this move, Anand underscores the political aspects of Bergson's philosophy, which scholars in the twenty-first century are now also beginning to explore.[1]

ANAND AND BLOOMSBURY

Anand constantly works to connect Eastern and Western ideas and, moreover, to reveal the intimate affiliations that already exist among ideas that might seem, on the surface, to be culturally disparate. In his own words, he sees his work as 'a kind of bridge between India and the West' (qtd in Berry 40). This impulse is most apparent in his *Conversations in Bloomsbury*, published in 1981. In this book of linked personal essays, Anand recounts his interactions in the latter half of the 1920s with the writers and thinkers who we understand to be central to canonical modernism (members of the Bloomsbury Group but also others who were in and around Bloomsbury at the time, such as T. S. Eliot and D. H. Lawrence). *Conversations in Bloomsbury* does not, however, offer us as exact an account of Anand's time with the Bloomsbury Group as we might wish. Regina Marler, for instance, describes it as 'an inaccurate but lively account of his meetings with the Group' (135). Following Marler, Snaith notes one such inaccuracy regarding the proofs Anand mentions correcting for the Hogarth Press in *Conversations in Bloomsbury*, Theodora Bosanquet's *Henry James at Work*. Snaith writes that 'this essay ..., the only book in the Hogarth Essays Series to be hand-printed by the Woolfs, was published in 1924 before Anand arrived in Britain. A second impression was printed by the Garden City Press in 1927, but would not have required proof correction' ('Colonial Writers' 157). A more notable discrepancy occurs between the timeline recounted in *Conversations in Bloomsbury* and that in Marlene Fisher's book (based upon taped interviews with Anand in the 1970s). Fisher writes that 'it was during the years 1929–1932 while living at No. 5 and No. 7 Great Ormond Street that Mulk met E. M. Forster' who then introduced Anand to the Woolfs (36). Yet, in 'Tea and Empathy from Virginia Woolf', Woolf remarks that she is working on *Orlando* (published in October 1928). While one could dismiss Anand's account because of these inaccuracies, such a stance is counterproductive and counterintuitive to the very nature of creative nonfiction like *Conversations in Bloomsbury*. Rather, as this essay makes clear, we should look to Anand's nonfiction work as exemplary of how he crafts narrative encounters to present cross-cultural connections and to narrate his own writerly origin story within the context of Bloomsbury.

Anand's interactions with members of the Bloomsbury Group were obviously important for his formation as a writer, as he told Fisher:

> Bloomsbury was a fraternity ... It was not just a slogan or a name; it meant something very wonderful. They were joined together in the sense of receiving each other. Each person had an at-home evening. And I feel that the sharing of these values, ... the experimentation with ideas – all this was part of living together as an international fraternity. I think, frankly, if I hadn't gone to this school of creativeness, which I call the friendship of people, I may not have written novels. (qtd in Fisher 36)

This expression of gratitude for the generosity of spirit and communion Anand found in Bloomsbury is marked in his dedication of *Conversations in Bloomsbury* 'to the memory of Leonard and Virginia Woolf and E. M. Forster'.

The publication of Anand's first novel would likely not have been possible without this Bloomsbury 'fraternity' and, more specifically, without the offer from E. M. Forster to write the Preface. The manuscript had been turned down previously by nineteen different publishers, and the eventual publisher of *Untouchable* wrote to Anand that Forster's Preface would 'be the book's passport through the latent hostility of the ordinary reviewer' (cited in Cowasjee 45).[2] The 'latent hostility' refers to the very subject matter of the book, which would have been considered 'dirty' by English readers and reviewers. The narrative centers on the life of Bakha, a young dalit, who, because of his (lack of) position in the Hindu caste system, cleans the refuse of society and, because of this activity, is considered unclean. As Bakha says to his father: 'They think we are mere dirt because we clean their dirt' (79). Forster directly confronts this potential hostility to Anand's work in the opening paragraphs of his Preface: 'Is it a clean book or a dirty one? Some readers, especially those who consider themselves *all-white*, will go purple in the face with rage before they have finished a dozen pages, and will exclaim that they cannot trust themselves to speak' (my emphasis).

Forster's emphasis on racial prejudices in the Preface to *Untouchable* takes on further resonances when examined through the lens of Anand's own brown-bodied locatedness in Bloomsbury (and, on Forster's side, of his love for Syed Ross Masood). Anand's perspective – as a colonial subject and as narrated in *Conversations in Bloomsbury* – like the transnational turn in modernist studies, challenges a geographically and nationally specific image of the Bloomsbury Group. As Blair argues, Bloomsbury (both the location and the group) was 'a site of cultural contact and contestation where both canonical high modernisms and an emergent anticolonial modernism take shape' (814). Indeed, Blair positions Bloomsbury as the site from which Anand's 'ongoing project – colonial, postcolonial, aestheticist, and activist by turns – organically grows' (831). Anand is her exemplary figure of a writer whose work 'substantively extends our notion of the cultural work that gets done in and through the Bloomsburyness of "Bloomsbury"' (831). So while not 'Bloomsbury' in the way scholars have generally defined its members, Anand's connections to the group were not only productive for his genesis as a writer, but they also draw attention to his positionality as an *outsider within*, which requires us, as Blair suggests, to reconceive of Bloomsbury as not a static, closed circle but as a dynamic, rippling one.

Yet Anand's discussion of Bloomsbury is not without critique. Even though Anand celebrates Bloomsbury in his interview with Fisher (and elsewhere), he also remarks on the tensions between insider and outsider that he felt while in Bloomsbury. As *Conversations in Bloomsbury* demonstrates with every turn of the page, Anand was conscious of himself as 'still an outsider' (91). In his Preface to the Second Edition, Anand emphasizes the element of critique in the book:

> The writers of the Bloomsbury Group, and their affiliates in the Universities of Oxford and Cambridge were, of course, humane people, but like the exalted Mayfair-Kensington-Bayswater-Wimbledon-Kew Gardens middle sections, they remained enclosed in their precious worlds, without guilts about their status as aristocrats having been achieved by the labour of generations of industrial workers in Midlands and the colonies. (viii)

Even more searing than his picture of the members of the Bloomsbury Group floating around in their own little bubbles, silver spoons still in their mouths and disconnected from the real world, is his critique of what he considered to be a lack of political engagement (he excepts the 'protestants, Forster and [Leonard] Woolf' from this criticism [viii], but overlooks Keynes). As an outsider within Bloomsbury – rubbing shoulders with people who, with some exceptions, largely swallowed 'Kipling's jingoism' (8) without second thought and exclaim, unironically, 'Come, come, the British did give you roads – and justice!' (15) – Anand's cross-cultural connections serve as powerful correctives to the British misconception of having 'given' everything to the people they have colonized.

ANAND, WOOLF, AND SHIVA-SHAKTI

Beginning with Bloomsbury helps us position Anand as a significant contributor to the conversations about modernism in the moment of modernism and, for the focus of this chapter, also creates an important context for his Bergsonian affiliations via a conversation with Virginia Woolf about Shiva-Shakti. The afternoon Anand meets Woolf is recounted in the essay 'Tea and Empathy from Virginia Woolf', whereby the conversation about Shiva-Shakti begins with a question from Woolf: 'Isn't one of your Gods androgynous?' She later mentions that she is writing *Orlando* to express her 'feeling that we are male-female-male, perhaps more female than male' (111). Anand recounts the conversation as such:

> I bent my head to look for the meaning of the word. I guessed what she meant: 'Han!' I grunted, 'Shiva'.
>   'I think the Hindus were clever', said Virginia. 'They evolved an incarnation of the male and female and fused the two. Indeed some part of woman is man and man has woman in him – some more than others.'
>
>   . . .
>
>   'The myth of this image reconciles the opposites', I dared to explain. 'Shiva Shakti. From their union comes all creation.' (108)

Anand adjusts this claim later in the conversation when he says, 'Actually, the female is supposed to be the source of all life ... I know a Doctor Ramji here who can excite this power in himself and others. Shakti it is called' (109). Anand reveals that he has had the experience of Shakti 'in the Regent's Park Ashram of Doctor Ramji' (110). He describes it to Woolf as 'feeling the heat of this – energy. Nerves begin to tingle. The body is almost on fire. The spine becomes warm. Vibrations travel to the neck. The head becomes hot ... I saw rainbow colours before my closed eyes' (110). This transnational exchange presents a fascinating intersection between emerging modernist aesthetics – Woolf's investment in androgyny in *Orlando* and *A Room of One's Own* and her fashioning of what Pamela Caughie has called a 'transgenre' (502–3) – and Hindu religious experience. Anand and Woolf's reported discussion gains further resonance and weight, as I will show, in yet another connection Anand draws to Shakti: Bergson's philosophical explication of the vital life force.

In several other places, Anand explains how modernist aesthetics and philosophies are not entirely new in that they reiterate core aspects of Hinduism: 'the new truths of Freud ... had, of course, been anticipated in the branches of tantric philosophy' (qtd in Berry 35).[3] This affirmation is echoed in *Conversations in Bloomsbury*, most notably in a conversation between Anand, Catharine Carswell, and Nancy Cunard. Anand says, 'there are quite a few diggings down of our sages, which anticipate what Freud has found. In fact, some areas of the subconscious were anticipated. And Lawrence's search for the man–woman connection in the ecstasy of sex was already practised by certain secret cults' (38). These two examples showcase how Anand asserts his own presence in the space of Bloomsbury. In these conversations, he not only creates a 'bridge between India and the West', but also subtly addresses and corrects the British imperialist image of India as only progressing because of British rule. Anand shows how these philosophical concepts that are so new and exciting to Bloomsbury artists and thinkers, so productive for new modes of aesthetic experimentation, are already, in a way, 'old' in India.

The conversation with Virginia Woolf, however, stands out from other passages of this kind. In contrast to sections of Anand's *Conversations in Bloomsbury* where he links modernist philosophy and aesthetics to a Hindu precursor, Woolf (rather than Anand) generates this connection. Anand thus presents Woolf as someone who, like himself, looks for bridges between cultures, who seeks to create a space where a daughter of the British Empire and a colonial subject can share in a community of ideas. By presenting this affiliation between modernist aesthetics and Hinduism as Woolf's, Anand differentiates between Woolf and other Bloomsburians encountered in *Conversations*.

Anand's presentation of Woolf throughout 'Tea and Empathy' positions her as, like himself, an *outsider within*, particularly in contrast to Leonard Woolf, who is also present for this conversation. While discussing Hinduism, when Virginia expresses admiration that 'you Hindus have the advantage of always looking inwards. You people lift veil after veil – and some of you have seen', Leonard responds, 'I think they overdo it' (106). A moment later: 'And so the earth is hell', muttered Leonard Woolf. 'That is why some people here say you Indians should go on your upward path and leave the earth to us practical people' (107). Notably, Anand addresses this type of imperialist rhetoric at the end of *Untouchable*, when the poet Iqbal Nath Sarshar explains that the image of the Hindu people as disinterested in material, earthly matters relies on a misinterpretation of the *Upanishads*, particularly the mistranslation of the word *maya* as 'illusion'. According to the poet, who follows the recent translation by Ananda Coomaraswamy (likely referencing his 1933 *On Translation: Māyā, Deva, Tapas*), 'the word *maya* does not mean illusion, it means magic' (152). The poet's words offer a corrective to Leonard Woolf's: 'The Victorians misinterpreted us. It was as if, in order to give a philosophical background to their exploitation of India, they ingeniously concocted a nice little fairy story: "You don't believe in this world; to you all this is *maya*. Let us look after your country for you and you can dedicate yourself to achieving *Nirvana* (release from the trammels of existence)"' (153). Anand's presentation of Leonard, via this dialogue in 'Tea and Empathy', dramatically contrasts other sections of *Conversations in Bloomsbury*, where Leonard is generally cast as an exception to the imperialism present in Bloomsbury, described by Anand as different from other Englishmen because he 'had lived and worked in Ceylon and even resigned from the Civil Service, because he did not want to be a part of Imperialist rule' (23–4).

In this essay, however, Anand casts Leonard Woolf in a different light than he does elsewhere to emphasize Virginia Woolf's way of thinking about the world in contrast to that of Bloomsbury's men. In her response to Leonard's comments, Woolf refers to Bertrand Russell, who, along with G. E. Moore was and remains significant to any discussion of Bloomsbury and philosophy (see Hagen in this volume): '"But men and women are not all Bertie Russell's mathematics," Virginia Woolf said. "And the Hindus, well – they do seem to have a sense of the ... Unseen ... of the unfathomable."' Anand's interpretation of this comment is as follows:

> I felt that Virginia Woolf was insinuating a critique of the liberation ideas of the men around her, including her husband's, and she wanted to hint at her own obsession with feelings and in the chaos of the undermind. I had also allied myself with the in-between things beyond the big words. And I felt that she could be crazed by her loneliness in the midst of cynics like her husband and Lytton Strachey, Roger Fry, Clive Bell and John Maynard Keynes. (107)

While one might argue that Anand's comment about the 'cynics' of Bloomsbury is too broad-stroke, what is important here is how Anand positions his and Woolf's sensibilities about life as something that a mathematical or analytic way of knowing the world fundamentally misses.

Anand's interpretation of Woolf's position of difference in the Bloomsbury Group aligns with his reading of *Mrs. Dalloway* and his own sensibilities – as 'a young Indian philosopher' – which he hopes to share with Woolf (103). Anand writes of *Mrs. Dalloway*, 'I had sensed that in the shadows of her prose-poem she was looking for something she could not see', that 'she groped around looking for flashes in the dark' (103). Perhaps these 'in-between things' (107), for Anand, are not adequately addressed by the philosophies of Moore or Russell. Notably, Anand is reading *Principia Ethica* during this same period, and (as a student of philosophy studying under Professor George Dawes Hicks at University College) he went on to complete a dissertation in 1929 that is, in part, on Russell's philosophy (Innes 218). Yet he remarks that these philosophies lack insight that might be gained through writing or Shakti: 'I wanted to liberate the unconscious via the Shakti-Shakta Tantric thought and dig down to the depths. And I was finding far more *satisfaction* in the writing of my confession novel [*Seven Summers*] ... than in studying even the loose emotions of G. E. Moore's *Principia Ethica*' (162–3).

Anand finds the philosophical twin to Shakti not in the Bloomsbury philosophies of Moore or Russell but in Bergson. While Bergson was immensely popular in Britain in the early twentieth century,[4] his ideas stand in notable contrast to the analytic philosophies that have come to dominate discussions of the Bloomsbury Group.[5] And yet, perhaps the affinity Anand sees between himself and Woolf is of the same sort he sees between Bergson and Hinduism. As Ruth Gruber notes of *Mrs. Dalloway* in the first dissertation published on Woolf in 1935:

> It is Bergson's problem and solutions which modulate her thinking and with it her style. The poetic concept of reality, peculiar to the French philosopher, is the kernel of her writing. She is too innately creative, too inherently Bergsonian to be called Bergson's imitator. It is conceivable that she would have found the way without him; yet living in the Bergsonian atmosphere, she draws even unconsciously from the truths he had established. Life is to be understood, he had proclaimed, not through the brain or mechanical reason, but through poetic intuition ... Like Bergson, she denounces science in its attempt to explain mechanically the process of the mind and human consciousness. (109)

Gruber's point that Woolf cannot be 'called Bergson's imitator' might be extended. Like Anand's claim about the affinity between Bergson's philosophy and Hinduism – not as influence but as congruence – we see not a direct effect of Bergsonian ideas on Woolf's writing (she appears never to have read his work),[6] but a similarity of perceiving, thinking about, and being in the world. Her writing and Bergson's were parallel articulations of how one might illuminate a sensibility different from the intellectual one that 'cannot, without reversing its natural direction and twisting about on itself, think true continuity, real mobility, reciprocal penetration – in a word, that creative evolution which is life' (*Creative Evolution* 162).

SHAKTI AS BERGSONIAN *ÉLAN VITAL*

I do not suggest that Anand 'applies' Bergsonian philosophy to Hinduism, but rather that he shows how Bergsonian ideas accord with Hinduism. While scholars have addressed the significance of Bergson's philosophy to modernist ideas and in connection to canonical writers such as James Joyce, Virginia Woolf, William Faulkner, T. S. Eliot and Marcel Proust,[7] the connections to Bergson in Anand's work and the affiliations between Bergsonian philosophy and Hinduism that Anand brings to light have been overlooked. Anand's discussion of Shakti with Woolf in *Conversations in Bloomsbury* serves as a precursor to the more directly stated Bergsonian connection in *Reflections on a White Elephant*, where Anand links Shakti to modernist philosophy when one character exclaims: 'Shakti is like Henri Bergson's élan vital!' (100). Anand's reference to Bergson in this late novel, in turn, illuminates passages in the earlier *Untouchable* where his aesthetic experiments should be viewed not only in conversation with Joyce or Woolf, as they often are, but also alongside Henri Bergson's philosophy.

Élan vital is central to Bergson's revisionist thought, and in *Creative Evolution* (1907) he presents it as an alternative to explanations of evolution that rely on mechanism or finalism. Like all of Bergson's ideas – of the image, memory, free will, language, and so forth – his conception of evolution and the *élan vital* grows from and is thus intricately embedded within his theory of the nature of time (or *durée*), and all these concepts rely upon the method of intuition. The first chapter of *Creative Evolution* thus fittingly begins with an explanation of duration. For Bergson, a new understanding of time as despatialized and unordered by the intellect is necessary before a new understanding of evolution is possible. If we think of the future as prescribed by the past, or the present as moving toward a teleological end, we cannot think creative evolution but instead perceive change as already given – fated, determined – because, according to Bergson, we have spatialized the flow of real time, *durée*. We replace the experience of change with the image of a progression of static states, ending finally at an apex, *Homo sapiens*, although 'the line of evolution that ends in man is not the only one' (xii). As Bergson describes the 'false evolutionism of [Herbert] Spencer', such a conception of change 'consists in cutting up present reality, already evolved, into little bits no less evolved, and then recomposing it with these fragments, thus positing in advance everything that is to be explained' (xiii–xiv). Such an explanation, however, fails to understand the vital impetus, the creative life force, the *élan vital* – simply, the nature of life itself. As Paul Douglass explains it, the *élan vital* is 'an evolutionary power – protean, self-initiated change – [that] lies at the origin of the universe' (303). *Élan vital* is a creative, generative force. As such, it is the power of continual de- and regeneration, a dynamism that also shares congruencies with various strands of modernism.

Given Anand's investment in change – social, cultural, political, and religious – it is perhaps not so surprising that the *élan vital* is one of the concepts from Bergson's philosophy that he embeds in his work.[8] Before turning to Anand's reference to Bergson, some context is necessary. The narrative of *Reflections on a White Elephant* largely follows the struggle of Mahant Kalidas's installation as His Holiness in Mahakali after the death of his father. Mahant Kalidas was educated at Cambridge and spent a significant amount of time in Europe. He wishes to reform Hindu practices which he sees as outdated and unnecessarily violent. The underlying tension of the novel is between reformist and Orthodox Hinduism. In this way, *Reflections on a White Elephant* is congruent with Anand's larger project of religious, political, and social reform, and Anand's reference to *élan vital* in this context, in turn, highlights these same aspects of Bergsonian philosophy.

The direct reference to Bergson comes via Madeleine la Meri, Mahant Kalidas's former Parisian lover, whom he asks to visit Mahakali in order to assist with his installation as the new Holiness. As Berry notes, Anand typically includes 'a character whose role is to speak the 'wisdom' for which the novel is the vehicle' (73). While *Reflections* was not yet published when Berry wrote her study of Anand, Madeleine fits this trope. The reference to Bergson is embedded in a discussion of becoming instead of being, a dynamic process versus a static state, which might appear to be a coded reference to Bergson's process philosophy. Yet, Madeleine does not mean 'becoming' in a philosophically specific sense but as a node of connection between ideas of becoming that includes Bergson, as well as Heraclitus, Socrates, Buddha, and yoga (101–2).

Madeleine, as a speaker of wisdom, artfully synthesizes ideas as she pulls from various religious and philosophical traditions and thus models Anand's own knitting together of Hinduism and Bergsonism. In this conversation, Madeleine simultaneously links her ideas of becoming to the Hindu sages and offers a critique of the Hindu belief in transcendence, claiming that the Hindu priests want their followers 'to rise to [the] sky! To one God! But he is in you!' She continues, 'They all want to become Gods-Goddesses! ... They do not know that some of your ancestors wanted Shakti! ... Shakti is like Henri Bergson's Elan vital!' (101). Later in the novel, Madeleine returns to this idea (minus the reference to Bergson) when she claims, 'Vital energy is inside us!' (188). With these references, Madeleine highlights something that has been overcoded in Hinduism through a focus on the heavens over the earth, which, as the poet states at the end of *Untouchable*, relies on a misinterpretation of the word '*maya*' (as 'illusion' rather than 'magic'). The world, Madeleine affirms, is not illusion; and one doesn't need to ascend to the heavens to transcend, to reach *Nirvana*; one can transcend on earth. In this way, the connection to Bergsonian ideas allows Anand to put forward a revisionist Hinduism, which as he states in *Apology for Heroism*, he saw as 'more and more the social organism of caste and less and less a unified religion' (9).

ÉLAN VITAL AS AESTHETIC EXPERIENCE IN *UNTOUCHABLE*

The *élan vital* appears not only in direct reference in Anand's late novel *Reflections on a White Elephant* but also as an aesthetic experience of Bakha's in Anand's first novel, *Untouchable*. We know that Anand's interest in Bergson began when he was living in Bloomsbury. Fisher writes that Anand was 'eager to go to Paris to meet Henri Bergson', although 'Bergson was away' when he visited Paris in 1926 (17).[9] And, even though Anand's first novel was not published until 1935, references in *Conversations in Bloomsbury* make it clear that Anand was already conceptualizing *Untouchable* in the late 1920s. The main character of *Untouchable*, Bakha, appears in *Seven Summers* (32–4), which Anand was writing while in Bloomsbury, although it wasn't published until 1951. It is no great leap given these circumstances to suggest that what Anand states overtly in *Reflections on a White Elephant* might also be implied in *Untouchable*.

Bakha's personal, aesthetic experience of *élan vital* would not be possible without Bergsonian intuition. As Bergson makes clear, we typically and fundamentally misunderstand life, the *élan vital*, because we rely on intelligence, rather than accessing our capacity for a supraintellectual engagement with the world, which he calls intuition. We are, fundamentally, selective creatures, choosing out of all possible stimuli those to which we will attend. This selective capacity keeps us alive but, on the other hand, requires that we ignore the stimuli or perceptions that are not necessary for our everyday existence in the world. Such a functional curating is the tendency of the intellect: 'The essential function of intelligence is therefore to see the way out of a difficulty in any circumstances whatever, to find what is most suitable, what answers best the question asked. Hence it bears essentially on the relations between a given situation and the means of utilizing it' (*Creative Evolution* 150–51). Yet, this intellectual mode of being in the world, in overcoding stimuli and perceptions that are not useful to us at any given moment, cuts us off from *durée* and from intuition; it also presents change to us as a series of states, rather than a process. To conceive of the *élan vital*, then, we must move beyond a strictly intellectual conception of reality.

For Bergson, *durée* is a unified multiplicity, meaning that anything that exists in the universe does so within its own *durée*, and these various durations qualitatively compose the whole of the flow of real time. Given such a conception of time, intuition can not only allow us access to an experience of own duration, which we are generally not conscious of because we spatialize time through the intellect, but it can also allow us access to other durations. Bergson writes in *The Creative Mind* that

> the intuition of our duration, far from leaving us suspended in the void as pure analysis would do, puts us in contact with a whole continuity of durations which we should try to follow either downwardly or upwardly: in both cases we dilate ourselves indefinitely by a more and more rigorous effort, in both cases transcend ourselves. (158)

G. William Barnard, extending Bergson's own radio metaphors, describes these various durations as different 'frequencies' or 'vibrations' that we might 'tune into': 'According to Bergson there are multiple dimensions of experience, multiple levels of reality (e.g. quantum, molecular, mineral, vegetal, animal, and human), each possessing a unique, albeit ever-changing, temporal rhythm; there are countless levels of experience (and time) other than our own; there are countless "planes" or, if you will, "channels" of *durée*' ('Tuning into Other Worlds' 285–6). While we are generally unaware of these different vibrations of reality, intuition allows us access to these different 'channels': first, as Bergson notes, our own, then, potentially, to others. As Barnard makes clear, such a vision of the cosmos radically alters conceptions of identity: while 'we typically act as if we (and everyone else) are solid, bounded essentially unchanging beings', Bergson's theory of duration and the method of intuition that gives us access to the universe-in-process presents identity as 'constantly in flux' and 'intrinsically interactive. Who we are can be found, if anywhere, in the in-betweenness of the ongoing relations that take place between us and the various, equally constantly changing melodies of experience that surround and interpenetrate us' ('Pulsating with Life' 343). For Bergson, then, we are connected in a web of durations. The duration we inhabit is nested within the larger *durée* of the universe and interconnected with all other beings, both human and nonhuman.

Bergson's description of the intuition of *durée* resonates with Clarissa Dalloway's 'transcendental theory' (152–3) – her idea it is possible to be connected in a web of consciousness with other people and places – which appears with notable revision in Anand's presentation of Bakha in *Untouchable*. During this day-in-the-life novel, the protagonist Bakha has become aware of his position as a dalit – an untouchable – through various traumatic events. While Clarissa articulates this theory to Peter, Bakha's sensibilities remain unconscious to him, noted only by the narrator, 'for though he had the receptivity of the man who is willing to lend his senses to experience, he had an unenlightened will ... The cumulative influence of careful selection had imprisoned his free will in the shackles of slavery to the dreary routine of one occupational environment. He could not reach out from the narrow and limited personality he had inherited to his larger yearning' (94). Here, Anand highlights the fact that, because of Bakha's position as a dalit, his ability to, in Bergson's words, 'transcend [him]self' is hindered. And yet, Bakha's 'wealth of unconscious experience ... was extraordinary. It was a kind of crude sense of the world ... such as the peasant has who can do the job while the laboratory agriculturalist is scratching his head ... But it wanted the force and vivacity of thought to transmute his vague sense into the superior instinct of the *really* civilized man' (94–5). But, in the next sentence, the narrator tells us that '*a spark of some intuition* suddenly set him ablaze. He was fired with a desire to burst out from the shadow of silence and obscurity in which he lay enshrouded' (95, emphasis added).

At this moment, outside of the spaces where he labours – away from the latrines and outside the city streets – Bakha runs down a hill into a meadow and lies on his back in the grass beside a pool, where he 'lent himself to the stillness about him, making not the slightest stir'. This intuitional 'spark' enables Bakha to move beyond himself, as the narrator describes him as if his body has been evacuated of life, as if 'energy' has transferred between Bakha's body ('he lay as if dead') and the 'exuberant spaces about him' (95). The narrator states: 'In a moment or two his frame seemed to have sunk into insignificance, drowned as it were in a pit of silence, while the things on the sunny bank began to take life, each little stem of plant becoming a big leaf, distinct and important. The whole valley seemed to him aglow with life' (95). In this scene, Bakha experiences himself as part of the interconnected web of consciousness, the mesh of durations that make up the cosmos. Such a repositioning of Bakha implicitly critiques the Hindu caste system, in which groups of people are categorized and divided from each other (only one such example of a divisive religious, social, and cultural system that others groups of people). The narrator's description of Bakha intuiting the *élan vital* therefore presents a radical contrast to the way (most of) the caste Hindus in the novel see and treat Bakha.

The intuitional 'spark' that connects to a world beyond individual identity (and that therefore destabilizes caste as such) is contrasted in an earlier passage where a 'shock' underscores Bakha's separateness. The scene begins when he bumps into a man on the street, who states that Bakha, simply by touching him, has 'defiled' him and that he 'will have to go and take a bath to purify' himself (46). In what follows from this encounter, the man calls Bakha a 'dirty dog! Son of a bitch! The offspring of a pig!' (47); a crowd gathers and continues the verbal berating; an urchin child accuses Bakha of beating him (48); one person in the crowd says that 'they [the sweepers] ought to be wiped off the surface of the earth!' (49); and the man that Bakha touched strikes him (50). This encounter causes Bakha to question why the high-caste Hindus 'always abuse us'. He concludes: "Because we are sweepers. Because we touch dung ... For them I am a sweeper, sweeper – untouchable! Untouchable! Untouchable! That's the word! Untouchable! I am an Untouchable!" Like a ray of light shooting through the darkness, the recognition of his position, the significance of his lot dawned upon him' (52). This recognition is described in language that both parallels and contrasts that of the scene previously described:

> The contempt of those who came to the latrines daily and complained that there weren't any latrines clean, the sneers of the people in the outcastes' colony, the abuse of the crowd which had gathered round him this morning. It was all explicable now. *A shock* of which this was the name had passed through his perceptions, previously numb and torpid, and had sent a quiver into his being, stirred his nerves of sight, hearing, smell, touch and taste, all into a quickening. (52, emphasis added)

The 'shock', while enlivening his senses, marks his realization that he is an Untouchable and is therefore not only outside of this socioreligious system but also despised, but the later 'spark of some intuition' (95) enables Bakha's experience of the *élan vital*, his sense of the processual generation of the life force of which he is a part. While the 'shock' separates, the 'spark' connects.

CONCLUSION: THE POLITICAL POSSIBILITIES OF THE *ÉLAN VITAL*

Anand's embedding of a Bergsonian experience for Bakha begins to hint at the ways in which Bergson's philosophy offers a vision of social justice, which is, at the end of *Untouchable*, made explicit in a political conversation that Bakha overhears. In gesturing toward Bergson in this context, Anand contrasts at least one Bloomsburian thread of critique: Russell's concluding remarks in his 1912 'The Philosophy of Bergson', where he states

> Those to whom activity without purpose seems a sufficient good will find in Bergson's books a pleasing picture of the universe. But those to whom action, if it is to be of any value, must be inspired by some vision, by some imaginative foreshadowing of a world less painful, less unjust, less full of strife than the world of our every-day life, those, in a word, whose action is built on contemplation, will find in this philosophy nothing of what they seek, and will not regret that there is no reason to think it true. (347)

As scholars like Frédérick Worms and Alexandre Lefebvre show, such an interpretation does not hold for Bergson's later thought in *The Two Sources of Morality and Religion* (1932). In this book, Bergson puts forth an argument about our biological tendency toward a 'closed' morality, rather than an 'open' one, and, in parallel, 'static' religion, rather than 'dynamic' religion. The morality of a closed society is one of exclusion, of *us* versus *them*. While we could describe that of the open society as one of inclusion, the word does not quite suffice because it implies an outside. At the core of open morality is universal love that is, according to Lefebvre, 'the emotion from which human rights are born, and which they in turn disseminate' ('Human Rights' 33).

At the end of *Untouchable*, Anand offers a radically divergent interpretation of Bergsonian thought than Russell's, one that aligns with Bergson's theory of the open society and of dynamic religion. This conversation follows a speech that Mahatma Gandhi gives to a crowd that has gathered in Bakha's village about ending untouchability. Gandhi positions the treatment of Untouchables as an internal oppression parallel to British colonial rule: 'As you all know, while we are asking for freedom from the grip of a foreign nation, we have ourselves, for centuries, trampled underfoot millions of human beings without feeling the slightest remorse for our iniquity. For me the question of these people is moral and religious ... I regard untouchability ... as the greatest blot on Hinduism' (146). After this speech, Bakha overhears a conversation between the Oxford-educated Mr R. N. Bashir and the poet Iqbal Nath Sarshar that begins with Bashir criticizing Gandhi for what he sees as a hypocritical position: stating that untouchability should be ended while also affirming 'that he is an orthodox Hindu' (150). Bashir's comments, in addition to his claims that Gandhi is old-fashioned, suggest that one cannot reform Orthodox Hinduism while remaining part of the religion.

Sarshar's response to Bashir, on the other hand, positions India – and more specifically Hinduism – as already possessing everything that is necessary for social and religious reformation, and for freedom from oppression more broadly. In notably Bergsonian language, the poet states: 'We [meaning, Hindus] know life. We know its secret flow. We have danced to its rhythms ... We can feel new feelings. We can learn to be aware with a new awareness. We can envisage the possibility of creating new races from the latent heat in our dark brown bodies ... We can be trusted to see life steadily and see it whole' (153). A couple of pages later, the poet also affirms, 'all is in a flux, everything changes' and that 'the old mechanical formulas of our lives must go, the old stereotyped forms must give place to a new dynamism' (155). The words 'secret flow', 'flux', and 'new dynamism' all recall Bergsonian *élan vital*, as well as *durée*, but the message itself is also Bergsonian: if one reconceives of time as duration – flux, flow, perpetual change – freedom is possible, and the radically new can emerge if we stop conceiving of evolution within the 'old mechanical formulas' and begin to envision a 'new dynamism'. When Bashir states that he 'can't understand' Sarshar's points, Sarshar clarifies that the adoption of the machine and particularly of the toilet, can destroy caste (155). While 'new dynamism' and the implementation of the toilet seem entirely contradictory points, they are positioned as two sides of the same coin: that the potential to connect to the *élan vital* can incite very practical, social changes that will allow 'the sweepers [to] change their profession ... Then the sweepers can be free from the stigma of untouchability and assume the dignity of status that is their right as useful members of a casteless and classless society' (155).

The conclusion the poet offers resonates (almost uncannily) with Bergson's direct reference to Hinduism, which appears in *The Two Sources of Morality and Religion* and where he claims that the influx of Western industrialization in India has allowed the completion of the mystical experience for Hindus. Bergson argues that 'complete mysticism', defined as 'action, creation, love' (225) was not possible for the Hindus of ancient India because 'pessimism', resulting from a feeling of 'helplessness' in the face of starvation due to famine, 'prevented India from carrying her mysticism to its full conclusion, since complete mysticism is action' (226). However, with the introduction of the machine,

> which increased the yield of the land, and above all moved the products from place to place ... deliverance became possible in an entirely new sense; the mystical impulse, if operating anywhere with sufficient power, was no longer going to be stopped short by the impossibility of acting; it was no longer to be driven back into doctrines of renunciation or the systematic practice of ecstasy; instead of turning inwards and closing, the soul could open wide its gates to a universal love. (226–7)[10]

Bergson's comments on mysticism in *Two Sources* are a direct outgrowth of the earlier concept of the *élan vital*, which his definition of mysticism clarifies: 'the ultimate end of mysticism is the establishment of a contact, consequently of a partial coincidence, with the creative effort which life itself manifests. This effort is of God, if it is not God himself' (220–21). For Bergson, God *is* the *élan vital*, and our capacity for intuition can give us a direct connection to this vital life force.

In his reference to the *élan vital* as Shakti, in the dalit Bakha's intuitive experience of the *élan vital* which allows him to feel his connection in the vibratory web of the cosmos, and in the poet's Bergsonian-Hindu solution to oppression, Anand forges transnational connections in the moment of modernism. But beyond the interconnections between aesthetics, philosophy, and Hinduism, he also highlights how Bergson's philosophy presents not only aesthetic engagements with the world but political ones, as well. In this way, Anand's utilization of Bergson resonates with the aim of Bergson's *Two*

Sources, which positions love as 'a concrete and practical political force' (Lefebvre and White 9). As Lefebvre clarifies, what Bergson means by love is not a gushy feeling (for someone or something) or an obligation, but it is a 'word for the exaltation and intensity of being that comes through the immersion in life', 'the name he gives to the emotion (*sentiment*, in French) that accompanies our power to tap into and realize the essence of life itself: interconnection, mobility, creativity, and movement' ('Human Rights' 36). In drawing together Bloomsbury, Anand and Bergson, and in tracing one of Anand's aesthetic, philosophic, and religious triangulations, we find that such an intuitional experience of the *élan vital* is possible in places as distant as Clarissa's and Woolf's London and Bakha's Bulashah Hills.

NOTES

1. See, for example, Grosz; Lefebvre and White; Lefebvre, *Human Rights*; Marrati.
2. This letter is dated 30 November 1934.
3. This letter is cited as 'unpublished correspondence [between Berry and Anand] written between September 20, 1967, and April 30, 1968'.
4. See Gillies. She details Bergson's popularity in the second chapter, titled 'Bergson and British Culture'.
5. However, Woolf's sister-in-law, Karin Stephen, did write a book on Bergson, *The Misuse of Mind: A Study on Bergson's Attack of Intellectualism*, which was published in 1922. Ann Banfield notes that Woolf was present on 3 February 1913 when Karin Stephen presented her paper, 'What Bergson Means by "Interpenetration"' (35). See also Gillies's discussion of the congruencies between Bergsonian philosophy and Roger Fry's and Clive Bell's ideas about art (52–8, 107–31).
6. As she writes in a letter dated 16 August 1932, 'I may say that I have never read Bergson' (*Letters: Volume 5*, 91).
7. In addition to Gillies and Gruber, see Kumar. See also Ardoin, Gontarski, and Mattison.
8. See also the reference to Bergson's Metanoia in *Conversations in Bloomsbury* (22).
9. Fisher's account of this is cited as 'Taped conversation with MRA, Khandala, May 19, 1973'. This same trip to Paris is recounted in Cowasjee differently, with no mention of Bergson (11–12).
10. Bergson's examples of Hindu thinkers who have been able to achieve complete mysticism because of Western industrialization are the nineteenth-century mystic Sri Ramakrishna and his disciple Swami Vivekananda (226). For a fascinating account of Bergson's thought alongside that of Hindu scientists and philosophers, see Brown. Although she does not note Bergson's reference in her chapter on Swami Vivekananda, some interesting connections are drawn in her chapter on Sri Aurobindo Ghose.

WORKS CITED

Anand, Mulk Raj. *Apology for Heroism: A Brief Autobiography of Ideas*. New Delhi: Arnold-Heinemann, 1975.

Anand, Mulk Raj. *Conversations in Bloomsbury*. Oxford: Oxford UP, 1995.

Anand, Mulk Raj. *Reflections on a White Elephant*. New Delhi: Har-Anand, 2002.

Anand, Mulk Raj. *Seven Summers: A Memoir*. London: Penguin, 2005.

Anand, Mulk Raj. *Untouchable*. London: Penguin, 1940.

Ardoin, Paul, S. E. Gontarski and Laci Mattison. Eds. *Understanding Bergson, Understanding Modernism*. London: Bloomsbury, 2013.

Banfield, Ann. *The Phantom Table: Woolf, Fry, Russell and the Epistemology of Modernism*. Cambridge: Cambridge UP, 2000.

Barnard, G. William. 'Pulsating with Life: The Paradoxical Intuitions of Henri Bergson'. *The Participatory Turn: Spirituality, Mysticism, Religious Studies*. Ed. Jorge N. Ferrer and Jacob H. Sherman. Albany: State U of New York P, 2008. 321–48.

Barnard, G. William. 'Tuning into Other Worlds: Henri Bergson and the Radio Reception Theory of Consciousness'. *Bergson, Politics, and Religion*. Ed. Alexandre Lefebvre and Melanie White. Durham, NC: Duke UP, 2012. 281–98.

Bergson, Henri. *Creative Evolution*. Trans. Arthur Mitchell. New York: Dover, 1998.

Bergson, Henri. *The Creative Mind: An Introduction to Metaphysics*. Trans. Mabelle L. Andison. New York: Dover, 2007.

Bergson, Henri. *The Two Sources of Morality and Religion*. Trans. R. Ashley Audra and Cloudesley Brereton. Notre Dame, IN: U of Notre Dame P, 1977.

Berman, Jessica. *Modernist Commitments: Ethics, Politics, and Transnational Modernism*. New York: Columbia UP, 2011.

Berry, Margaret. *Mulk Raj Anand the Man and the Novelist*. Amsterdam: Oriental Press, 1971.

Blair, Sara. 'Local Modernity, Global Modernism: Bloomsbury and the Places of the Literary'. *ELH* 71.3 (2004): 813–38.

Bluemel, Kristin. *George Orwell and the Radical Eccentrics: Intermodernism in Literary London*. London: Palgrave, 2004.

Brown, C. Mackenzie. *Hindu Perspectives on Evolution: Darwin, Dharma, and Design*. London: Routledge, 2012.

Caughie, Pamela. 'The Temporality of Modernist Life Writing in the Era of Transsexualism: Virginia Woolf's *Orlando* and Einar Wegener's *Man into Woman*'. *Modern Fiction Studies* 29.3 (2013): 501–25.

Cowasjee, Saros. *So Many Freedoms: A Study of the Major Fiction of Mulk Raj Anand*. Oxford: Oxford UP, 1977.

Douglass, Paul. *Bergson, Eliot, and American Literature*. Lexington: UP of Kentucky, 1986.

Douglass, Paul. 'Bergson on *Élan Vital*'. *Understanding Bergson, Understanding Modernism*. Ed. Paul Ardoin, S. E. Gontarski and Laci Mattison. London: Bloomsbury, 2013. 303–4.

Fisher, Marlene. *The Wisdom of the Heart: A Study of the Works of Mulk Raj Anand*. New Delhi: Sterling, 1985.

Gillies, Mary Ann. *Henri Bergson and British Modernism*. Montreal and Kingston: McGill-Queen's UP, 1996.

Grosz, Elizabeth. *Time Travels: Feminism, Nature, Power*. Durham, NC: Duke UP, 2005.

Gruber, Ruth. *Virginia Woolf: The Will to Create as a Woman*. New York: Carroll & Graf, 2005.

Innes, C. L. *A History of Black and Asian Writing in Britain, 1700–2000*. Cambridge: Cambridge UP, 2002.

Kumar, Shiv. *Bergson and the Stream of Consciousness Novel*. London: Blackie, 1962.

Lefebvre, Alexandre. 'Human Rights and the Leap of Love'. *Journal of French and Francophone Philosophy* 24.2 (2016): 21–40.

Lefebvre, Alexandre. *Human Rights as a Way of Life: On Bergson's Political Philosophy*. Stanford, CA: Stanford UP, 2013.

Lefebvre, Alexandre and Melanie White. 'Introduction'. *Bergson, Politics, and Religion*. Ed. Lefebvre and White. Durham, NC: Duke UP, 2012.

Marler, Regina. *Bloomsbury Pie*. New York: Henry Holt, 1997.

Marrati, Paola. 'The Natural Cyborg: The Stakes of Bergson's Philosophy of Evolution'. *Southern Journal of Philosophy* 48 (2010): 3–17.

Snaith, Anna. '*Conversations in Bloomsbury*: Colonial Writers and the Hogarth Press'. *Virginia Woolf's Bloomsbury, Vol. 2: International Influence and Politics*. Ed. Lisa Shahriari and Gina Potts. Basingstoke: Palgrave, 2010. 138–57.

Snaith, Anna. 'The Hogarth Press and Networks of Anti-Colonialism'. *Leonard and Virginia Woolf, the Hogarth Press and the Networks of Modernism*. Ed. Helen Southworth. Edinburgh: Edinburgh UP, 2012. 103–27.

Woolf, Virginia. *The Letters of Virginia Woolf*, Vol. 5: 1932–5. Ed. Nigel Nicolson. London: Hogarth Press, 1979.

Woolf, Virginia. *Mrs. Dalloway*. New York: Harcourt, 1925.

Worms, Frédérick. '*The Two Sources of Morality and Religion*: A Distinction That Changes Everything'. Trans. Alexandre Lefebvre and Perri Ravon. *Bergson, Politics, and Religion*. Ed. Alexandre Lefebvre and Melanie White. Durham, NC: Duke UP, 2012. 25–39.

CHAPTER SIX

Bloomsbury and Class

KATHRYN SIMPSON

Even before the Stephen siblings relocated to Gordon Square and regular meetings of Thoby Stephen's friends and sisters brought the Bloomsbury Group into being, the geographical location of Bloomsbury was already characterized by political and ethnic diversity. It was a site of social tension and contradiction in being 'marginal and progressive ... class-defined and ... class-liberated' (Blair 821). Indeed, Sara Blair argues that it was Bloomsbury's significance as 'home to an economy of alternative cultural production' that the Bloomsbury Group drew on as 'a crucial resource in the elaboration of a "Bloomsbury" culture, politics, and style' (821). Critical assessments of the group's cultural production in the areas of political and literary writing, economic theory and artistic creativity return repeatedly and in complex ways to the entangled issues of class privilege and prejudice. Ann Banfield's observation that 'Bloomsbury' was the result of a geographical and intellectual 'displacement' of the Stephen siblings from Hyde Park Gate and Cambridge philosophy to London (8) also helps to productively conceptualize this group in terms of class. The Bloomsbury Group was an intellectual elite deliberately at odds with its social origins, 'a (civilizing) fraction', splintering (and displaced) from its 'provenance ... in the professional and highly educated sector of the English upper class' and critical of the institutions of this class as a whole, as Raymond Williams explains it (169, 162).[1] While Williams notes the group's 'remarkable record of political and organizational involvement' in social and reform movements, he asserts a lack of 'solidarity' and 'affiliation' on the part of its members, arguing that their motivation stemmed from a sense of 'social conscience' towards the 'helpless victims' of 'the cruelty and stupidity of the system' (155) (see Ayers in this volume). For others, however, the Bloomsbury Group's 'integration of the economic, political, and aesthetic dimensions of public life in its art and thought' and its commitment and contribution to the building of 'a democratic, economically egalitarian, international civilization' (Froula 4) was far more than 'a new *style*' that Williams sees the group as representing (Williams 154).

Yet style was an important and far from trivial part of the many ways in which the Bloomsbury Group engaged with issues of class – from the more open, liberal style of personal relations, to new styles in political, economic and aesthetic thinking, writing and creating, and in engaging with audiences and the 'masses'. Michael Whitworth explains that in the early twentieth century 'there were several competing systems of social categorization available', the two main ones being 'a tripartite division of society into upper, middle, and lower classes ... and a bipartite division into the "elite" and the "masses"', with these classifications further complicated by 'various subdivisions', overlaps and correspondences (52). Immersed in, interacting with and intervening in this period of dramatic social, political and economic change, the Bloomsbury Group's attitudes to and involvements in these complex issues of class were perhaps inevitably problematic and contradictory. Yet their sustained commitment to addressing these issues is evident in many ways and they were, as Leonard Woolf asserts, 'in the van of the builders of a new society', an energetic force in the political and artistic vanguard working 'to construct something new' (*Sowing* 161).

While Leonard Woolf was adamant that 'we [the Bloomsbury Group] had no common theory, system, or principles which we wanted to convert the world to; we were not proselytizers, missionaries, crusaders, or even propagandists' (*Beginning Again* 25), what he says of the three members he singles out in particular – John Maynard Keynes, Roger Fry, and Virginia Woolf – is significant in that they were all working in some ways against the grain, particularly the grain of Victorian traditions, values and ways of conceptualizing the world. Keynes's rewriting of economic theory, Fry's radical reassessments of art and aesthetics, Woolf's reconceptions of literary form and the literary marketplace, and Leonard Woolf's political writing and activism were significant ways in which 'Bloomsbury' challenged its Victorian inheritance, not least the rigid structures of class and established hierarchies of authority and influence.[2] All were acutely aware of the ways in which, as Virginia Woolf asserts in 'Character in Fiction', 'All human relations have shifted' in the early twentieth century, with the relationship between 'masters and servants' the first in Woolf's list (422). They worked, in their different spheres, to scrutinize middle-class values and authority and to shore up working-class political agency. They sought to recognize the needs, desires and beliefs of the individual in the face of a socioeconomic system that constrains experience, to ameliorate the impact of economic turbulence on 'the precarious life of the worker' (Keynes, qtd in Patinkin 704),[3] and to extend working-class access to intellectual ideas so as to promote a democratizing of high culture. Banfield argues that while 'the implicit *raison d'être* of Bloomsbury discussions was the extension of knowledge beyond the confines of the university elite', its 'co-education' within this group was 'preceded by various projects for the extension of knowledge' (17). These include giving lectures to working-class audiences (by Moore, Fry, Forster, and Virginia Woolf) and contributing to the Home University Library of Modern Knowledge, 'a series of small, inexpensive books' written by academics and intellectuals, the intended audience being 'shop assistants' and 'working men' (Banfield 17–18, 19).[4] Yet it is precisely the nature of these challenges and the group's influence and privilege, alongside the variety of contradictory and sometimes prejudiced attitudes expressed, that have provoked extreme responses. For those who see this group as overprivileged and snobbish, their work is perceived as indicative of an elitist outlook, one out of touch with the 'real' world, a view frequently accompanied by a sense of distrust, suspicion and anger. For others, the work of its central figures played a role in the destabilization of traditional hierarchies of class, value, and taste as they attempted to adapt the monetary economy and shape the literary marketplace into something more civilized, humane, and accessible.

In *Bloomsbury Pie: The Making of the Bloomsbury Boom*, Regina Marler charts the fall and rise in Bloomsbury's reputation as a cultural phenomenon, from its nadir in the 1930s when 'Bloomsbury' was 'a term of abuse' (11),[5] to its 'boom' from the 1960s onwards. What attracted some – the Bohemian lifestyle, the cultural ease and influence that class privilege confers, and the convention-defying edginess, summed up in the quip attributed to Dorothy Parker or Margaret Irwin that the Bloomsbury Group 'lived in squares, painted in circles and loved in triangles' – was for others the source of often fierce criticism. Q. D. Leavis's somewhat bitter review of Woolf's *Three Guineas* is indicative of what such privilege was seen to entail: social and intellectual elitism and isolation, class blindness and, therefore, a limited ability or willingness to engage with the 'realities of life' (415). This well-known swipe at Woolf and Bloomsbury encapsulates the vehement class-based attacks staged by the Leavises and others in the 1930s and 1940s. By the 1950s the group's class privilege had become more firmly the focus of criticism and an anti-Bloomsbury stance formed part of the class war being waged in the British literary sphere.

By the 1960s, however, the 'pendulum' of popularity began to 'swing … back in favour of Bloomsbury', a change Marler attributes to Leonard Woolf's decision to write and publish his autobiography, a move that enhanced his role as 'the bridge between Bloomsbury itself … and what would become the Bloomsbury industry' (34, 23). From then on Bloomsbury has thrived to become arguably the best known cultural group in the Western world, referenced across the cultural field of film, theatre, music, ballet, journalism, and in a vast and ever-increasing array of commodities. Yet Bloomsbury retains the allure of celebrity and daring, of innovation and creativity, of class and cultural distinction in both popular and academic contexts. As Jennifer Wicke suggests, what is 'remarkable' is that Bloomsbury was 'a rarified group [that] was both elite and emblematic' (9). It was privileged, intellectual yet also democratic, and the creative, practical, and theoretical work undertaken by its members sought to unsettle established conceptions of class and to promote greater equality in the spheres of politics and culture. Members of Bloomsbury sought to democratize modernist art and taste for all classes, to make it accessible to a wide audience through publications and publication practices, artistic processes and marketing strategies, and by making visible working-class issues. Enterprises such as the Omega Workshops and the Hogarth Press signal a desire to work at a tangent to the burgeoning commercialization of art and literature in the early twentieth century (see Humm and Battershill in this volume).

Yet this is not without the difficulties, limitations and contradictions inevitable during periods of change and transition, as attested by the fierce debates during the 1920s and 1930s, referred to as 'the Battle of the Brows', which served in many ways to reassert class-based hierarchies through a focus on taste and cultural hierarchy. This tension arose as a result of a number of factors, including the ongoing development of technologies that generated and made available a diversity of cultural production, and social and political changes that enabled greater access to culture. The emergence of modernist forms and their cultural ascendancy also produced not only a tension with existing realist mainstream art and literature and its increasing commercialization, but necessitated a demarcation of cultural boundaries and designation of mutually exclusive categories which the terms 'low', 'middle', and 'high' brow satisfied.[6] In BBC radio broadcasts and newspaper articles the battle lines were drawn in debates that revolved around distinctions based on class and education, taste and appreciation, intellectual response and aesthetic sensibility, art and the market, and the serious and 'frivolous' in literary works. Bloomsbury Group members Virginia and Leonard Woolf, Desmond MacCarthy, and Clive Bell were involved along with other writers and critics, such as J. B. Priestley and the Leavises. However, the battle lines were far from clearly or consistently drawn, even within the Bloomsbury Group itself. But these debates and battles reveal both the sense of society as clearly stratified (as the high, middle, and low brow designations were conflated with class identities) and, paradoxically, the greater complexity and commonalities that these reductively drawn designations seek to obscure (as Whitworth explains, 52–9). Brown and Grover problematize the battle lines still further and read the concept of 'middlebrow' and the 'battle' as being 'the product of powerful anxieties about cultural authority and processes of cultural transmission' in a landscape of increasing access to, and commercialization of, culture (1). They see in both the Woolfs' Hogarth Press and their opponents, the Leavises' journal, *Scrutiny*, antagonistic attitudes to the middlebrow and a desire to control 'access to cultural goods' opened up 'by commerce or the state' (8).

The work of critics such as Jennifer Wicke, Jane Garrity, Lawrence Rainey, Mark S. Morrisson, and Tim Armstrong in the 1990s and 2000s has also brought about a dramatic shift in the understanding of modernism's and the Bloomsbury Group's relationship with mass culture and the marketplace. Far from being remote from mass culture and commercial enterprise, Bloomsbury was revealed to be not only complicit in this, but also to exhibit a market savvy approach in making money while simultaneously promoting its values through modelling new ways of producing, marketing and selling not only art but a 'lifestyle' (Wicke 6). The rule-breaking Bloomsbury Group was influential in representing a 'life space' that was seen as better, freer, more creative and more democratic. It was in the business of 'selling culture to the civilized', as Jane Garrity puts it, and Wicke argues that Bloomsbury played a key role in shaping the market as we understand it today. Perceiving parallels and interconnections between Keynes's ground-breaking economic theories and Bloomsbury's aesthetics and modes of production and consumption, Wicke argues that the modernist thinking, art, and lifestyle of this group 'contributed profoundly to a sea-change in market consciousness' that 'changed the nature of modern markets for once and all' (5). In this 'Bloomsbury becomes a market in miniature' with individuals producing, consuming and recirculating their goods to each other and then to the wider market (12). It is a market ready to respond not only to Bloomsbury design but to the utopian and celebrity 'design for living' embodied and celebrated in the goods for sale (9). Wicke argues that Keynes's economic theory reconceptualized the market as chaotic and fluid, a 'sensitive organism' primed to respond to unpredictable and various stimuli rather than as 'a mathematical self-regulating machine' (11, 15). Like others in the group, he 'eschewed utilitarian explanations of human behaviour and did not take utilitarian ethics as a reasonable guide for behaviour or policy' (Backhouse and Bateman 718). Like them he shared 'a fascination with the emerging study of psychology and the varieties of human motivation' and 'us[es] psychological explanations of economic behaviours such as investment and consumption' (Backhouse and Bateman 718). As Blair sums it up, Keynes's conception of the space of the market was that of 'a dreamworld of desire and a social site of tension and collective action' (829) – a productive space in which and through which Bloomsbury could challenge dominant culture's hierarchies of value and social structures.

However, it is clear that while members of the Bloomsbury Group challenged the status quo and questioned established beliefs and notions of value, they were also complicit with certain dominant, class-based views and attitudes. For example Garrity's examination of the Bloomsbury Group's involvement in 1920's *Vogue* notably reveals not only the 'blurring of the boundary between high and low' culture through Bloomsbury's use of 'mass cultural forms to disseminate its values', but also its entanglement with the problematic politics of this mass market vehicle in relation to gender, class, race and nationality ('Selling Culture' 30, 34). As she states, '*Vogue*'s strategy of "marketing modernity"' in this context works to affirm 'British aristocratic values' which are synonymous with dominant and elitist cultural hierarchies of 'high' and 'low' and antagonistic to 'society's democratizing impulses' (32). Focusing specifically on Woolf's appearance in *Vogue* and other mass commercial vehicles she argues that 'Woolf's ... image ... create[s] a bridge between 'high' and 'low' culture, [but that] this is not in the service of eradicating the cultural hierarchy' ('Virginia Woolf' 187). Between 1924 and 1926 *Vogue* published a number of Woolf's reviews and essays and while some of these suggest Woolf's 'class bias', Garrity argues that the range of subjects covered signals Woolf's refusal of the magazine's 'economic or ideological imperatives' ('Virginia Woolf' 210, 209). Photographs of Woolf were also published, notably a photograph of Woolf wearing her mother's dress and looking down demurely which was published in *Vogue* twice, in May 1924 and May 1926. Garrity notes that this photograph recalls Woolf's 'literary and ancestral pedigree' and positions her in the roles of 'child and wife, firmly within the parameters of *Vogue*'s heterosexual economy' (202), but this image clearly also evokes her origins in the heart of the British cultural elite.[7]

This ambivalence and contradiction in attitudes, actions and ideological commitments is understandable and perhaps inevitable: Woolf and other Bloomsbury members were aware of the power of their 'cultural capital' and sought to make use of their education, social position, influence, authority and reputation to make an intervention, yet they were complicit in certain dominant, class-bound structures and systems of value that supported it. In promoting certain tastes in modernist art and culture and in selling the Bloomsbury 'lifestyle', they aim to diversify access to 'legitimate' highbrow culture and taste, but they do not question the value of such culture and taste and this has rightly led to accusations of class prejudice. Nonetheless, Fry's Omega Workshops and the Woolfs' Hogarth Press represent moves towards a more democratic access to the pleasures of artistic and literary appreciation and a greater intellectual independence. These enterprises sought to support living artists and to grow a market for modern art and literature, to provide a publication outlet for works not supported by larger commercial publishers, and to find ways to remove barriers to enable working-class voices to be heard. Their goal in this approach to life, artistic creativity, and markets is at a tangent from the norm[8] and aims to create new artistic-economic enclaves and to promote a 'living taste' for 'living art' (Woolf, 'Middlebrow' 158). For Fry, commercialization of art resulted in a culture rendered artistically bankrupt by the predominance of what he calls 'opifact[s]', a term he coined to define 'art' that is produced for commercial purposes, for ready consumption as a commodity, and used only to shore up the social prestige of the owner. Such objects stand in stark contrast to 'works of art' that provoke and inspire 'esthetic emotion' and enjoyment as they speak to the spirit and energize the soul, as Fry explains in 'Art and Commerce', published by the Hogarth Press 1926 (in Goodwin 112).

THE OMEGA WORKSHOPS' ARTISTIC-ECONOMIC EXPERIMENT

Opening in 1913, the Omega Workshops was an artistic-economic experiment intended to provide a physical space for producing, displaying, and marketing contemporary, innovative arts. It supported its artists financially and aimed to stimulate market demand for 'living art' through the cultivation of the aesthetic response and taste necessary for its appreciation. Run on collective lines, with work marked only with the sign of Omega (rather than with a personal signature), the Workshops were intent on sustaining 'the free functioning' of artists' 'creative power', as Fry says in 'Art and Socialism'[9] (in Goodwin 184), enabling them to work on specific commissions and to contribute, in Winifred Gill's phrase, to the 'bank of designs' (Gerstein 81) for customers to choose from. This structure and the insistence on anonymity partly reflects 'Fry's ideal of collaborative aesthetic production' (Reed, *Bloomsbury Rooms* 79). Crucially, it also sought to avoid the temptation to create only for remunerative rewards so as to evade the dangers of the marketplace that Fry saw as besetting works of art and artists themselves. It also sought to encourage customers to respond with (in Clive Bell's terms) 'aesthetic emotion' to the designs and to their 'significant form' (Bell 4, 8), rather than simply investing in the cultural capital signalled by the name of the artist or experiencing art only as expert opinion might dictate.

The Omega produced decorative, handmade arts for the domestic and everyday (furniture, textiles, pottery, clothing, rugs and books), generating a 'domestic modernism' that Reed argues not only marked Bloomsbury's difference from other 'mainstream modernist design', but was 'the basis of a new social and aesthetic order' (*Bloomsbury Rooms* 15, 14).[10] However, although the *Prospectus for the Omega* asserted the value of 'the things of daily life', high prices meant that few people could afford to buy such everyday objects (12). Indeed, the unique shopping experience at the Omega Workshops, bringing customers into direct contact with the artist-designers so as to foster the appreciation and understanding of modern art, was also an exclusive one. Although Woolf herself experienced the way that Fry's theories and interpretations of art could illuminate works she had not been able to appreciate before, she was scathing about his flattery of wealthy customers, 'wheedling' them 'to buy stuff' (*Diary* 1: 237). In working to woo wealthy patrons and by persuading them to buy, Fry hoped also to stimulate a wider interest but, in spite of these efforts, the Omega closed in 1919, its collectivist economic organization collapsing as artists took on individual commissions and earned independent income.

Fry realized 'that the function of art was to serve the imaginative lives of humans, and not their actual or biological lives' (Goodwin 18). Believing that art energizes the spirit, produces pleasure, and stimulates intellectual and aesthetic responses, Fry along with other members of Bloomsbury sought ways to enhance lived experience through an enlarged appreciation of art. He also sought to counter 'snobbism' – an 'intellectual and aesthetic pretence' which he saw as 'the almost universal parasite upon culture' and which shores up certain values and tastes at the cost of 'democratic equality' ('A Moral Lecture, or Perhaps an Immoral One' in Goodwin 141, 142). However, despite the democratic impulse underlying Fry's desire to foster aesthetic response in as wide an audience as possible,[11] and his belief that such a response can be trained, he also argues that relatively few people are sensitive enough to respond to 'the esthetic emotion [which is] an emotion about form', rather than to the 'racial and social emotion' that accrues to visual art and music and which resonates with experience in real life ('The Artist and Psycho-Analysis' in Goodwin 127, 128). Significantly, this innate sensibility and response to modern art can be found in people from all classes. In 'Retrospect', Fry considers the immediate response to the Post-Impressionist exhibitions and reflects that whereas 'the cultured public' failed to appreciate the art of Matisse and Cézanne because for them artistic appreciation is a marker of social status, he notes, 'one's maid' may have the 'sensibility' to respond to the form and aesthetics of this art 'by a mere haphazard gift of Providence' (in Goodwin 89, 90). Although in other of Fry's essays such democratic ideas are put into question, as Woolf enthusiastically notes in *Roger Fry*, for him, 'anyone's sensation – his cook's, his housemaid's – was worth having. Learning did not matter; it was the reality that was all-important' (132).

THE HOGARTH PRESS, CLASS, AND THE LITERARY MARKET

There can be no doubt that the Hogarth Press holds a cultural and literary importance for the Woolfs' own political and literary reputations and success, for diversifying the range of published writers and broadening its readership in relation to the literary mainstream, and for Bloomsbury and the literary world itself. While the Omega Workshops and the Hogarth Press are frequently perceived as 'kindred enterprises, springing from the same ground and in frequent interaction with each other' (Porter 7), the Press had greater success. As Laura Marcus notes, it played an important role in positioning Bloomsbury in 'a more central position in intellectual and cultural life' (129). Drew Shannon argues that the Woolfs 'could not possibly have known … that the writers they chose to publish would ultimately form a virtual roll-call of importance' (317), but others note the role that cultural privilege and, in particular, the Woolfs' literary connections, also played in its 'early success' (Barkway 236). Stephen Barkway's discussion of business negotiations between the Woolfs and Vita Sackville-West also makes clear that by the mid-1920s Virginia Woolf was well aware of the 'distinction' of being published by the Hogarth Press 'which, rightly has no price', as she explains in a letter to Sackville-West (cited in Barkway 237). However, opportunities to sell out to larger publishers, which would have made the Press more lucrative, were resisted since this would have compromised the Woolfs' freedom to publish what they chose. While the Woolfs were keen to make a profit, this was not to be at the expense of their aesthetic and political values. As Shannon asserts, the Hogarth Press 'list … speaks first and foremost of friendship, then of taste and discernment, then of marketability' (317).

Echoing some of the same aims and values as Omega and similarly occupying a marginal economic position (in being jointly owned and not entirely driven by the commercial goals of making a profit), the Press was shaped predominantly by more intrinsic motivations. As Leonard Woolf expresses it 'we were interested primarily in the immaterial inside of a book, what the author had to say and how he said it' rather than 'fine printing and fine binding' (*Downhill* 80). The Woolfs were both involved in activities focused on addressing questions of class inequality in practical and overtly political ways. Leonard's work in bringing about working-class political reforms as a political writer and his roles in the Cooperative Movement and the Labour Party seem most obvious, but, as Clara Jones has recently reiterated in *Virginia Woolf: Ambivalent Activist*, Virginia Woolf was also politically active (and indeed an 'activist') in a number of ways throughout her life. Woolf taught at Morley College and was involved with the People's Suffrage Federation in the early 1900s, attended Fabian Society and Labour Party Conferences alongside Leonard, took the role of secretary for the Branch of the Women's Cooperative Guild (1916–20) chairing monthly meetings at Hogarth House (Lee 360), and worked with the National Federation of Women's Institutes. Both Leonard and Virginia were concerned with opening up access to intellectual debate and with broadening the scope for this debate through the publication of writers and writing that would not find an outlet elsewhere. As Helen Southworth so convincingly argues, 'it seems clear that they intended to include those whose working-class origins or whose distance from London meant that they did not have the credentials or the networks available to their middle-class, metropolitan counterparts' (*Networks* 207). The Hogarth Press aimed to make visible working-class experience through publication of writing focused on 'domestic issues, and specifically the British mining and manufacturing industries', seeking the 'authenticity' of an insider's perspective, and enabling 'different' and working-class voices to be heard, providing 'a viable entry point onto the London scene for provincial and working-class writers' and simultaneously seeking 'to create a dialogue between the impoverished north of England and the more affluent south' (208).

In terms of literary publications too the Woolfs 'engaged in complex ways with questions related to the marketing and promotion of working-class writing' in their 'attempts to create a space via their press from where working-class fiction writers might speak for themselves' (Southworth, *Networks* 217).[12] As Froula suggests, the Woolfs were creating a public space for 'freedom of speech in the struggle for civilization' (10), fostering access to intellectual ideas and literature not only for the 'common reader' but creating spaces for the 'common writer' as well. Although critics have discussed 'a discourse of exclusivity regarding the Press productions' and their desirability as 'must have' objects denoting cultural value and style (Gordon 109, 107), the Woolfs worked towards making their Hogarth Press publications more affordable. The Press actually facilitated the entry of modernism into the more general literary marketplace (Willison et al xv) with the success of the Hogarth 'Uniform Editions' of Woolf's novels (begun in 1929) making Woolf's writing more affordable and enabling her to reach a wider public, which was important to her professionally, politically and personally (see Froula; Snaith, *Public and Private* 45). This is in keeping with the expansion of access to 'highbrow' modernist works for a broader class of 'common readers' at home and abroad through the Modern Library Series publications as explored by Lise Jaillant. She also discusses the influence of Woolf and other celebrity authors associated with Bloomsbury in opening up access to (and sales of) literary works through their introductions to Oxford World's Classics series, suggesting that the kudos of Bloomsbury and recognition of its writers 'by the lower middleclass, the self-educated and other readers of the World's Classics' played a role in broadening literary readership as it simultaneously further expanded the reputations of the authors themselves (53).

VIRGINIA WOOLF AND THE COMPLEXITY OF CLASS

Virginia Woolf has long been seen as the central figure of Bloomsbury and has been the focus for a reassessment of the group's class politics, beginning with Alex Zwerdling's influential *Virginia Woolf and the Real World* (1986) and followed in the 1990s by a number of critics examining Woolf's representations of class and her complex and contradictory perspectives (such as Caughie, Childers, Emery, and Tratner). In more recent assessments, Woolf, her membership of Bloomsbury, and her modernist aesthetics and feminist politics remain important concerns in considerations of her class politics (see Jones, Latham, Shiach, Snaith, and Wilson). As Laura Marcus argues, Woolf's role at the Press as co-owner, writer, and producer enabled her to occupy a liminal space, 'a space somewhere between the private, the coterie, and the public sphere' (145) which she found to be highly productive. However, this position has also been perceived as a 'slippery' one in terms of an understanding of Woolf's class politics. These are seen by some as prejudiced and even offensive, by others as contradictory and complex, and by others still as indicative of her status as a 'democratic highbrow' aiming to 'inculcate good reading practices' in her readers in the belief that 'an educated public is crucial to the success of democratic society' (Cuddy-Keane, *Virginia Woolf* 13, 2).[13] Her faith in her reader as a 'fellow-worker and accomplice' positions the reader as an active participant and co-producer, one able to approach books with an open mind as well as 'imagination, insight and judgement', as she argues in 'How Should One Read a Book?' (60, 68). Her 'common reader' is an astute and critical reader, alert to the ideological and political significance of literature, and able to assert independent judgments and to appreciate the significance of form and style in the generation of meaning and in the operation of power and authority. Through her essays and BBC broadcasts,[14] Woolf seems to seek to train her readers to fulfil this role, encouraging them to cultivate discernment and taste in their response to highbrow art and culture. However, the BBC debate, 'Are Too Many Books Written and Published?' that the Woolfs scripted and delivered, not only indicates that they could, as public intellectuals, successfully address a mass audience, but also confirms the values on which the Hogarth Press was based: an engagement with 'the practical, material problems of everyday life' and the belief that 'the value of a book [is] in its use, not its iconic status' (Cuddy-Keane, 'Are Too Many' 237). While the polarized positions the Woolfs assume in this debate are a requirement of the format, rather than indicating their actual views, Virginia Woolf's contribution confirms her 'emphasis on the expanding opportunities for writers and readers' and making books written by a greater diversity of authors available, thus extending publishing's 'potentially inclusive and democratic reach' (237). But she also sees 'the productive continuities between popular and "serious" reading' (237) and recognizes the value of more frivolous, 'low brow' writing, 'the sweets and cakes ... the easy books and the flashy books and the books that ask no trouble in reading', that will facilitate a greater maturity of critical response enabling those 'Millions' of readers to access more serious writing, 'interesting books, difficult books, histories, biographies, poetry' (242–3).

Woolf's ideas about access to literature and importantly the means by which culture is accessed (through a training of the intellectual capacity of the 'common reader' or via a commercialized cultural marketplace) also resonate with her somewhat ambivalent position in the 'Brows' debate, signalling again the 'slipperiness' of her attitudes to class distinctions. The letter she wrote but did not send to the editor of *The New Statesman and Nation*, 'Middlebrow', in part confirms her sense of a high/low polarity – with high brows associated with intense intellectual activity and displaying 'thoroughbred intelligence' and the low brows with bodily 'thoroughbred vitality' (152–3). It also seems to confirm a sense of hierarchy and a patronizing attitude to the low brow since, Woolf suggests, it is only the high brows that can 'show' the low brows 'what life looks like' (154). The satirical tone of the letter, however, mocks the reductive definitions and conceptions of high brows and low brows alike and also seeks to undermine distinctions – one marker of the highbrow, important to Woolf, is their 'vigour of language' which can belong both to the aristocracy and to charwomen (155). The list of 'low brows' whom she claims she 'love[s]' surprisingly includes stockbrokers, admirals, bank clerks and duchesses along with a wife and mother, bus conductors, miners, cooks, and prostitutes (154) and she sees high and low brows existing in a complementary relationship with each other. The real enemy in all this is the promoter of highbrow/lowbrow antagonism, the 'middlebrows', whose 'brows are betwixt and between' and who take Bloomsbury highbrows as their target in particular (155, 158).[15] In mockery of the designation of the place for the group (the postcode for the individual), Woolf also asserts that both high and low brows can 'live happily together on equal terms' in Bloomsbury where low rents deter the middlebrows from living (160).

While there is a sense in which Woolf was in tune with her contemporary moment in relation to this democratic agenda,[16] this has been seen as problematic in the light of the uneasy tensions of her own position as a feminist intellectual dependent on the work of servants, particularly working women, her class affiliations and complicity in class hierarchies, her attempts to explain her class attitudes, and in terms of her depictions of working-class characters and experience in her fiction. Her essay, 'Am I a Snob?', presented to the Memoir Club and the Letter she wrote by way of introduction to a collection of writings produced by members of the Women's Cooperative Guild, *Life as We Have Known It* (1931), are two sites of contention in this debate. The self-mocking, playful tone of her confession of a snobbish attraction for aristocratic ease and elegance makes her class views hard to pin down and highlights the complex perspective on class that is also evident in her more serious explanation of her position in relation to working women in the later publication, explanations which are also, as Alison Light argues, complicated by Woolf's self-critical attitude (*Mrs Woolf* xviii). In her 'Introductory Letter' Woolf explains that she admires working women and their campaigns for reform, but that she is unable to fully engage and sympathize with them, and indeed to represent them fully in her fiction, because she has not experienced the manual labour that informs their day-to-day experience and their thinking. For some, this introduction serves as a positive indication of Woolf's socialist and feminist commitment, but others as see it as an evasion and a refusal to face her own class prejudice. What seems significant is that Woolf here acknowledges that her middle-class perspective is not a superior one in this context but is, rather, a failing and she admits that her middle-class perspective limits and distorts her views, assumptions, and imaginative depictions of working-class life, it 'mak[es] the picture false' as she acknowledges ('Introductory Letter' xxiii). In other essays, Woolf also specifically addresses the 'silence' surrounding 'class distinctions' in literature and the 'disability' of 'birth' that affects a middle-class author, so that his or her 'social rank' precludes a realistic and genuine representation of the upper and lower classes ('Niece' 92, 94). She notes that this 'ignorance' is most obvious in relation to the working classes who, perceived as existing 'on the other side' of a 'gulf' of narrative interest (95, 93), rarely appear and then only in implausible and stereotyped ways (94). Her hope for 'a truly democratic age' when such class distinctions have disappeared (96) is echoed in her late essay, 'The Leaning Tower',[17] where she speculates on the possibility of an egalitarian 'common ground' in the postwar period, a world with 'no more towers [of social, economic and educational privilege] and no more classes' (121). However, while 'trespass[ing] freely' ('Leaning' 125) on cultural domains usually reserved for the elite few asserts a democratic impulse that some critics celebrate, for others who note Woolf's 'explicitly anti-democratic prejudices outside the sphere of reading', the focus only on 'a democratisation of reading, writing, and literary study' puts into question any fuller commitment to the 'ideal of common solidarity' (Ellis 148, 147).

Critical assessments of Woolf's representations of working-class characters and experience in her fiction often revolve around questions about her ideological commitment and genuine engagement. Critical perspectives are diverse and include a range of responses from accusations of class prejudice, to seeing her fictions as voicing a scathing critique of middle-class authority precariously reliant on rigid class hierarchies. Zwerdling argues that Woolf 'wrote about class and money with exceptional frankness at a time when these subjects were increasingly felt to be indecent' (88). Tratner suggests that, while working-class characters might be peripheral in Woolf's narratives (such as

Mrs McNab and Mrs Bast in *To the Lighthouse*), they carry significant political weight and bring to the surface anxieties about the stability of middle-class life in a changing social and political landscape. Some critics point out that the way Woolf engages with class has a detrimental impact on her work. Light, for example, argues that 'the figure of the servant and of the working woman haunts Woolf's experiments in literary modernism and sets a limit to what she can achieve' (*Mrs Woolf* xviii). Others analyse the aesthetics and formal qualities of Woolf's work as the very means through which challenges to class stereotypes and power hierarchies are made (see Snaith on *To the Lighthouse* and *Flush*; Wilson 2013).[18] Leonard Woolf's assessment of Virginia as 'highly sensitive to the atmosphere which surrounded her' and 'therefore the last person who could ignore the political menaces under which we all lived' (*Downhill* 27) chimes well with more recent critical trends which examine the complexities of Woolf's ambiguous engagement with class as nuanced by the broader historical and political context as well as by Woolf's specific personal and creative response to this.[19] While her representations of class, particularly the working classes, may be problematic in a number of ways,[20] as David Bradshaw asserts, 'obliquely but resonantly, Woolf's writing is flush with sympathy for the "lower orders"' (12). From Woolf's first individual publication with the Hogarth Press, 'Kew Gardens' (1919), where Trissie longs to follow a path other than the one her class and gender dictate, to *Between the Acts* (1941) where the working-class villagers' carnivalseque performance in the pageant shines a critical light on the behaviour of their so-called betters over the course of British history, there is a sustained and determined engagement with class issues in Woolf's fictional *oeuvre*.

As some members of the Bloomsbury Group have asserted, friendship rather than a specific set of principles or strategies for achieving certain goals was key to its formation and longevity. Reed argues that the cohesiveness of the group can be attributed to its working relations and collaborations, as well as to cohabitation and travelling together (*Bloomsbury Rooms* 6). Individuals pursued their own interests in different spheres and articulated their differing views on social and class issues. Significantly, they shared endeavours, such as the Omega Workshops and the Hogarth Press, which coalesced around the broad goals of creating a space and a market for contemporary art and literature which may not easily find an outlet in the mainstream. The Omega sought to ensure that innovative and challenging art could generate a living for its artists as it also sought to encourage and educate a wider public so as to overcome barriers to aesthetic appreciation and intellectual understanding of art as a central facet of civilized society. The Woolfs also worked towards promoting a more democratic access to the rich cultural repository of literature and 'serious' writing, opening up intellectual and political ideas and debates. They sought to make inroads into the cultural landscape they saw as beset by the damaging forces of commercialization and entrenched attitudes to class that constrained individual selves and expectations, and limited horizons. However, while the promotion of 'civilization' was a broadly shared goal for many members, there were differing ideas about how this may be attained, from the socialist and democratic approach favoured by the Woolfs to the conservative and elitist ideas of Clive Bell. Nonetheless, despite or possibly because of their complex and sometimes contradictory positions and engagements with class, the fact that certain Bloomsbury members, notably Keynes and Virginia Woolf, have long been recognized as influential figures demonstrates the wide reach of their achievements and challenges. While far from revolutionary, the change the Bloomsbury Group has achieved is evolutionary with a continuing, reverberating influence on notions of culture, class, and the individual.

NOTES

1. Indeed, he sees the group as 'a forerunner in a more general mutation' within this class bringing about a wider change 'in the English ruling class' longer term (Williams 163).
2. A number of critics have explored the Bloomsbury members' relationships with their Victorian past. See Steve Ellis, Jane de Gay, Simon Joyce, for example.
3. This is from Keynes's *The Tract on Monetary Reform* (1923).
4. Though Banfield notes that the audience for these books in reality included 'the women [who were] largely excluded from Cambridge' (19).
5. This can be seen in severe criticisms of the group, such as those voiced by D. H. Lawrence, for example, and in the fictions of their contemporaries who depict Bloomsbury Group members in satirical and severely critical ways. These include Marjorie Strachey's *The Counterfeits* (1927), Wyndham Lewis's *The Apes of God* (1930), Roy Campbell's 'The Georgiad' (1931).
6. As John Baxendale sums it up, 'A "Battle of the Brows" had been flaring up throughout the 1920s, fanned from one direction by the rise of modernist literature, art, and music, and from the other by the explosive growth of commercial popular culture. Each development was suspected of heralding the end of civilization, in a world knocked off its balance by the experience of the Great War' (71).
7. Cuddy-Keane and Garrity assess these appearances in relation to the ambivalence produced from the tension between Woolf's role as a woman writer and the ideological stance of *Vogue*. Cuddy-Keane notes that Woolf's of review of *The Letters of Walter Raleigh*, titled 'A Professor of Life', that sits alongside the second appearance of this photograph expresses Woolf's irritation at Raleigh's masculine posturing and denigration of literary appreciation as feminine (30), and Garrity that the evocation of Julia Stephen's role as 'the angel in the house' alongside Woolf's own identity as a writer and artist suggests the magazine's ambivalent and anxious stance in relation to conventional and conservative gender norms ('Virginia Woolf' 202, 204–5).
8. As Helen Southworth explains, for example, the Hogarth Press defied publishing norms with its 'hybrid operation' being 'unique in its successful combination of the risk-taking of a smaller press and the professional production work of a commercial press' (*Networks* 10). The Press's list was diverse, eclectic, and international, an indication of the Woolfs' '*complete* editorial freedom', responsiveness to their contemporary moment, and their commitment to publishing a wide variety of authors. In this the Press unsettled 'entrenched notions about class and culture' and 'functioned as a vibrant, dialogic space or network ... where class bias and cultural norms are continually interrogated' (18). This was in contrast to the literary mainstream which, as Nicola Humble explains, was dominated by middlebrow fiction from a range of genres that 'in the obsessive attention it paid to class markers and manners . . . was one of the spaces in which a new middle-class identity was forged, a site where the battle for hegemonic control of social modes and mores was closely fought by different factions of the newly dominant middle class' (5). Humble notes the interest of contemporary critics in the changes in 'literary culture', and specifically that their 'interests in codifying popular taste, and in taking the temperature of the nation's culture, provide some useful accounts of literary consumption' (15, 12). She mentions Q. D. Leavis's *Fiction and the Reading Public* (1932), George Orwell's essays, 'Bookshop Memories' and 'In Defence of the Novel' (1936) and Cyril Connolly's *Enemies of Promise* (1938) in this light. Clive Bloom confirms the popularity of genre fiction in the literary mainstream (from romance and country-house novel, to detective, imperial adventure and literary thriller, ghost tales, and science fiction) and notes the dramatic increase in the numbers of books published between 1914 and 1939 (13, 37).
9. This was first published 1912 and later in *Vision and Design* (1920) (Goodwin 44).

10. See also Rosner's exploration of modernism's relationship with the domestic.
11. Including, as Reed notes, his 'commitment to art education for children of all classes' (*Bloomsbury Rooms* 116).
12. These include novelists John Hampson Simpson and William Plomer, and poet Edwin Muir, with more 'proletarian fiction writers' becoming 'a regular feature of the Hogarth Press fiction list' following the return of John Lehmann to the Press in the late 1930s (Southworth, *Networks of Modernism* 228). See also Southworth 'Outside the Magic' and Lara Feigel.
13. Also see Friedman.
14. Such as the series of three BBC broadcasts, 'Are Too Many Books Written and Published' (July 1927), 'Beau Brummell' (November 1929) and 'Craftsmanship' (April 1937).
15. See also Beauman, Felski, Humble, and Light (*Forever England*) for further discussion of the middlebrow.
16. Some of the findings of the Mass-Observation Project, begun in 1937, for example, reveal that observers felt that they can be intellectuals regardless of a lower class status (Hubble 209). This project grew out of concerns about 'the gap that had opened up in the modern, mechanized society of the 1930s between the masses and the intellectual and cultural elite' and sought evidence from voluntary observers from all classes, 'all human types', in order that the real social environment can be understood and then transformed by creating a dialogue between artists and scientists and the 'masses' (205).
17. This was a lecture given to the Workers Educational Association in Brighton in 1940.
18. Snaith's analysis of Woolf's use of free indirect discourse in *To the Lighthouse* counters the authority of the middle class narrator and 'bring[s] Mrs McNab's consciousness to the fore' allowing her to present 'herself as a individual ... with her own vision, memory, imagination and anger' (*Public and Private* 78). She also examines the footnotes in *Flush* used to voice the 'unsaid' of power relations in relation to gender, class, and species ('Of Fanciers' 620). Mary Wilson examines what she terms the 'threshold aesthetic' in Woolf's writing through which servant labour is rendered visible and 'writ[ten] ... into the structure of the novel' (41, 54).
19. For example, Clara Jones's transcription and analysis of an incomplete and unpublished sketch, the 'Cook Sketch' written in 1931, examines the complexities of Woolf's 'sensitivity' to working-class realities in 'her historical moment' as well as 'her persistent anxieties about how she engaged with class in her writing' (14).
20. These may even be lost from published versions, as Jones notes in relation to Woolf's revised plans for *The Waves* ('Cook Sketch').

WORKS CITED

Armstrong, Tim. *Modernism: A Cultural History*. Cambridge: Polity Press, 2005.

Backhouse, Roger E. and Bradley W. Bateman. 'Keynes, John Maynard (New Perspectives)'. *The New Palgrave Dictionary of Economics*, Vol. 2 (2nd ed.). Ed. Steven N. Durlauf and Lawrence E. Blume. Basingstoke: Palgrave Macmillan, 2008. 716–25.

Banfield, Ann. *The Phantom Table: Woolf, Fry, Russell and the Epistemology of Modernism*. Cambridge: Cambridge UP, 2000.

Barkway, Stephen. '"Oh Lord What It Is to Publish a Bestseller": The Woolfs' Professional Relationship with Vita Sackville-West'. *Leonard and Virginia Woolf, The Hogarth Press and the Networks of Modernism*. Ed. Helen Southworth. Edinburgh: Edinburgh UP, 2010. 234–59.

Baxendale, John. 'Priestley and the Highbrows'. *Middlebrow Literary Cultures: The Battle of the Brows*. Ed. Erica Brown and Mary Grover. Basingstoke: Palgrave Macmillan, 2012. 69–81.

Beauman, Nicola. *A Very Great Profession: The Woman's Novel 1914–39*. London: Virago, 1983.

Bell, Clive. *Art*. London: Chatto and Windus, 1931.

Blair, Sara. 'Local Modernity, Global Modernism: Bloomsbury and the Places of the Literary'. *English Literary History* 71.3 (2004): 813–38.

Bloom, Clive. *Bestsellers: Popular Fiction since 1900*. Basingstoke: Palgrave Macmillan, 2002.

Bradshaw, David. 'The Blight of Class: Woolf and the "Lower Orders"'. Special Issue: Woolf and Materiality. Ed. Derek Ryan. *Virginia Woolf Miscellany* 85 (2014): 11–13.

Brown, Erica and Mary Grover. Eds. 'Introduction: Middlebrow Matters'. *Middlebrow Literary Cultures: The Battle of the Brows*. Basingstoke: Palgrave Macmillan, 2012. 1–25.

Caughie, Pamela L. 'Virginia Woolf and Postmodernism: Returning to the Lighthouse'. *Rereading the New: A Backward Glance at Modernism*. Ed. Kevin J. H. Dettmar. Ann Arbor: U of Michigan P, 1992. 297–323.

Childers, Mary M. 'Virginia Woolf on the Outside Looking Down: Reflections on the Class of Women'. *Modern Fiction Studies* 38.1 (1992): 61–79.

Cuddy-Keane, Melba. 'Are Too Many Books Written and Published?' Special Topic: The History of the Book and the Idea of Literature. *PMLA* 121.1 (2006): 235–44.

Cuddy-Keane, Melba. *Virginia Woolf, the Intellectual, and the Public Sphere*. Cambridge: Cambridge UP, 2003.

de Gay, Jane. *Virginia Woolf's Novels and the Literary Past*. Edinburgh: Edinburgh UP, 2006.

Ellis, Steve. *Virginia Woolf and the Victorians*. Cambridge: Cambridge UP, 2007.

Emery, Mary Lou. ' "Robbed of Meaning": The Work at the Center of *To the Lighthouse*'. *Modern Fiction Studies* 38.1 (1992): 217–34.

Feigel, Lara. 'Buggery and Montage: Birmingham and Bloomsbury in the 1930s'. *Woolfian Boundaries: Selected Papers from the Sixteenth Annual International Conference on Virginia Woolf*. Ed. Anna Burrells, Steve Ellis, Deborah Parsons and Kathryn Simpson. Clemson, SC: Clemson U Digital P, 2007. 51–7.

Felski, Rita. *The Gender of Modernity*. Cambridge: Harvard UP, 1995.

Friedman, Susan Stanford. 'Virginia Woolf's Pedagogical Scenes of Reading: *The Voyage Out*, The Common Reader and Her "Common Readers"'. *Modern Fiction Studies* 38.1 (1992): 101–25.

Froula, Christine. *Virginia Woolf and the Bloomsbury Avant-Garde*. New York: Columbia UP, 2005.

Garrity, Jane. 'Selling Culture to the "Civilized": Bloomsbury, British *Vogue*, and the Marketing of National Identity'. *Modernism/Modernity* 6.2 (1999): 29–58.

Garrity, Jane. 'Virginia Woolf, Intellectual Harlotry, and 1920s British *Vogue*'. *Virginia Woolf in the Age of Mechanical Reproduction*. Ed. Pamela L. Caughie. New York: Garland, 2000. 185–218.

Gerstein, Alexandra. Ed. 'Catalogue'. *Beyond Bloomsbury: Design of the Omega Workshops 1913–19*. London: Fontanka, 2009. 80–167.

Goodwin, Craufurd D. Ed. *Art and the Market: Roger Fry on Commerce in Art, Selected Writings*. Ann Arbor: U of Michigan P, 2001.

Goodwin, Craufurd D. 'Virginia Woolf as Policy Analyst'. *Virginia Woolf's Bloomsbury*, Vol. 2. Ed. Lisa Shahriari and Gina Potts. Basingstoke: Palgrave Macmillan, 2010. 66–87.

Gordon, Elizabeth Willson. 'How Should One Sell a Book? Production Methods, Material Objects and Marketing at the Hogarth Press'. *Virginia Woolf's Bloomsbury*, Vol. 2. Ed. Lisa Shahriari and Gina Potts. Basingstoke: Palgrave Macmillan, 2010. 107–23.

Hubble, Nick. 'Imagism, Realism, Surrealism: Middlebrow Transformations in the Mass-Observation Project'. *Middlebrow Literary Cultures: The Battle of the Brows, 1920–1960*. Ed. Erica Brown and Mary Grover. Basingstoke: Palgrave Macmillan, 2012. 202–17.

Humble, Nicola. *The Feminine Middlebrow Novel, 1920s to 1950s: Class, Domesticity, and Bohemianism*. Oxford: Oxford UP, 2001.

Jaillant, Lise. ' "Introductions by Eminent Writers": T.S. Eliot and Virginia Woolf in the Oxford World's Classics Series'. *The Book World: Selling and Distributing British Literature 1900–1940*. Ed. Nicola Wilson. Leiden: Brill, 2016. 52–80.

Jones, Clara. *Virginia Woolf: Ambivalent Activist*. Edinburgh: Edinburgh UP, 2016.

Jones, Clara. 'Virginia Woolf's "Cook Sketch" '. *Woolf Studies Annual* 20 (2014): 1–23.

Joyce, Simon. *The Victorians in the Rearview Mirror*. Athens: Ohio UP, 2007.

Latham, Sean. *'Am I a Snob?': Modernism and the Novel*. Ithaca, NY: Cornell UP, 2003.

Leavis, Q. D. 'Caterpillars of the Commonwealth Unite!' *Scrutiny*, 1938, *Virginia Woolf: The Critical Heritage*. Ed. Robin Majumdar and Allen Mclaurin. London: Routledge, 2014.

Lee, Hermione. *Virginia Woolf*. London: Chatto & Windus, 1996.

Light, Alison. *Forever England: Femininity, Literature and Conservatism between the Wars*. London: Routledge, 1991.

Light, Alison. *Mrs Woolf and the Servants: The Hidden Heart of Domestic Service*. London: Penguin, 2007.

Marcus, Laura. 'Virginia Woolf and the Hogarth Press'. *Modernist Writers and the Marketplace*. Ed. Ian Willison et al. Basingstoke: Macmillan, 1996. 24–50.

Marler, Regina. *Bloomsbury Pie: The Making of the Bloomsbury Boom*. New York: Holt, 1997.

Morrisson, Mark S. *The Public Face of Modernism: Little Magazines, Audiences and Reception 1905–1920*. Madison: U of Wisconsin P, 2001.

Patinkin, Don. 'Keynes, John Maynard (1883–1946)'. *The New Palgrave Dictionary of Economics*, Vol. 2 (2nd ed.). Ed. Steven N. Durlauf and Lawrence E. Blume. Basingstoke: Palgrave Macmillan, 2008. 687–716.

Porter, David H. *The Omega Workshops and the Hogarth Press: An Artful Fugue*. London: Cecil Woolf, 2008.

Rainey, Lawrence. *Institutions of Modernism: Literary Elites and Public Culture*, New Haven: Yale UP, 1998.

Reed, Christopher. *Bloomsbury Rooms: Modernism, Subculture, and Domesticity*. New Haven: Yale University Press, 2004.

Reed, Christopher. 'Introduction'. *Beyond Bloomsbury: Design of the Omega Workshops 1913–19*. Ed. Alexandra Gerstein. London: Fontanka, 2009. 11–15.

Rosner, Victoria. *Modernism and the Architecture of Private Life*. New York: Columbia UP, 2005.

Shannon, Drew Patrick. 'Woolf and Publishing: Why the Hogarth Press Matters'. *Virginia Woolf in Context*. Ed. Bryony Randall and Jane Goldman. Cambridge: Cambridge UP, 2012. 313–21.

Shiach, Morag. *Modernism, Labour and Selfhood in British Literature and Culture, 1890–1930*. Cambridge: Cambridge UP, 2004.

Snaith, Anna. 'Of Fanciers, Footnotes, and Fascism: Virginia Woolf's *Flush*'. *Modern Fiction Studies* 48.3 (2002): 614–36.

Snaith, Anna. *Virginia Woolf: Public and Private Negotiations*. Basingstoke: Macmillan Press, 2001.

Southworth, Helen. Ed. *Leonard and Virginia Woolf: The Hogarth Press and the Networks of Modernism*. Edinburgh: Edinburgh UP, 2010.

Southworth, Helen. ' "Outside the Magic (and Tyrannical) Triangle of London-Oxford-Cambridge": John Hampson, The Woolfs, and the Hogarth Press'. *Woolfian Boundaries: Selected Papers from the Sixteenth Annual International Conference on Virginia Woolf*. Ed. Anna Burrells, Steve Ellis, Deborah Parsons and Kathryn Simpson. Clemson, SC: Clemson U Digital P (2007): 43–50.

Tratner, Michael. *Modernism and Mass Politics: Joyce, Woolf, Eliot, Yeats*. Stanford, CA: Stanford UP, 1995.

Whitworth, Michael. *Virginia Woolf: Authors in Context*. Oxford: Oxford UP, 2005.

Wicke, Jennifer. 'Mrs Dalloway Goes to Market: Woolf, Keynes, and Modern Markets'. *Novel: A Forum on Fiction* 28.1 (1994): 5–23.

Williams, Raymond. 'The Bloomsbury Fraction'. *Culture and Materialism: Selected Essays*. London: Verso, 2005.

Willison, Ian, Warwick Gould and Warren Chernaik. Eds. *Modernist Writers and the Marketplace*. Basingstoke: Macmillan, 1996.

Wilson, Mary. *The Labors of Modernism: Domesticity, Servants, and Authorship in Modernist Fiction*. Farnham: Ashgate, 2013.

Woolf, Leonard. *Beginning Again: An Autobiography of the Years 1911–1918*. London: Hogarth Press, 1964.

Woolf, Leonard. *Downhill All the Way: An Autobiography of the Years 1919–1939*. London: Hogarth Press, 1967.

Woolf, Leonard. *Sowing: An Autobiography of the Years 1880–1904*. London: Hogarth Press, 1960.

Woolf, Virginia. 'Am I a Snob?' *Virginia Woolf: Moments of Being* (2nd ed.). Ed. Jeanne Schulkind. London: Grafton, 1989. 219–39.

Woolf, Virginia. 'Character in Fiction'. *The Essays of Virginia Woolf, Vol. 3*. Ed. Andrew McNeillie. London: Hogarth Press, 1988. 420–38.

Woolf, Virginia. *The Diary of Virginia Woolf, Vol. 1: 1915–19*. Ed. Anne Olivier Bell. London: Penguin, 1979.

Woolf, Virginia. 'How Should One Read a Book?' *The Crowded Dance of Modern Life: Selected Essays*. Ed. Rachel Bowlby. London: Penguin, 1993. 59–69.

Woolf, Virginia. 'Introductory Letter to Margaret Llewellyn Davies'. *Life as We Have Known It*. Ed. Margaret Llewellyn Davies. London: Virago, 1977. xvii–xxxxi.

Woolf, Virginia. 'Middlebrow'. *The Death of the Moth and Other Essays*. Ed. Leonard Woolf. London: Penguin, 1961. 152–160.

Woolf, Virginia. 'The Niece of an Earl'. *Crowded Dance of Modern Life: Selected Essays*. Ed. Rachel Bowlby. London: Penguin, 1993. 92–6.

Woolf, Virginia. *Roger Fry*. London: Penguin, 1979.

Zwerdling, Alex. *Virginia Woolf and the Real World*. Berkeley: U of California P, 1986.

Case Study: Bloomsbury's Rural Cross-Class Encounters

CLARA JONES

Named for the area of London in which they lived, the Bloomsbury Group has long been imaginatively identified with the urban. However, prominent members, including Leonard and Virginia Woolf, Vanessa Bell, Duncan Grant and John Maynard Keynes, lived much of their lives in East Sussex, in houses central to (the myth of) Bloomsbury sociability. Charleston Farmhouse, Vanessa Bell's home in Firle, and Monk's House, the Woolfs' home close by in Rodmell, have been read as rural retreats where artists could escape the social and psychic pressures of London. Frances Spalding describes the benefits of Charleston's 'isolation': 'A mile or two distant even from any nearby village, it encouraged an existence entirely free of the usual social pressures' (164). Hermione Lee suggests that Monk's House's location 'down at the end of the long village ... seemed to symbolise her [Virginia Woolf's] preference for apartness and seclusion' (427). Lee is also scrupulous in drawing attention to the fact that Rodmell was a 'busy, noisy, self-supporting community, with a pub, a mill and a forge' (429) and that in spite of Woolf's mixed feelings about her place in this community it was one with which both she and her husband came into daily contact. Likewise, while Vanessa Bell may have chosen Charleston for its relative seclusion, as we shall see, neither she nor her children were able to maintain complete separation from the wider community.

Taking my cue from Lee, I want to figure out what role the occupants of Charleston and Monk's House played in their Sussex communities and how class mediated in these relationships. Recent work in Virginia Woolf studies has drawn attention both to her relationship to the countryside and her class politics.[1] This chapter responds to this critical turn through a consideration of Bloomsbury's rural cross-class encounters during the interwar period. Drawing on primary sources, including local newspapers, Leonard Woolf's papers in the University of Sussex Special Collections and Vanessa Bell's letters at the Tate, this chapter clarifies the extent of their interactions with their communities and the distinctly mixed feelings Bloomsbury had about their neighbours – 'villagers' and gentry alike.

CHARLESTON FARMHOUSE – FIRLE

As is well known, Vanessa Bell sublet Charleston Farmhouse in 1916 in order to establish a base for Duncan Grant and David Garnett while they worked as labourers at local New House Farm. After a series of tribunals and appeals, Garnett and Grant had secured non-combatant status as conscientious objectors to the First World War. However, their running of a fruit farm at Wissett Lodge in Suffolk was not judged to be work of 'national importance' – a stipulation of their exemption.[2] Spalding describes how Bell assumed responsibility for securing both men work as farm labourers, making contact with Mr Hecks, farmer at New House Farm (155). The move to Charleston then, although inspired by instrumentalism in extraordinary circumstances, was driven by the need to participate in rural society rather than escape it.

Social class is also important to the story of the move to Charleston. The curious hybridity of Grant and Garnett's status as gentlemen-farm-labourers invites questions about who they may have come into contact with and how this activity may have influenced Bloomsbury's position in local class structures. Bloomsbury biographers have traditionally focused on the physical challenges such work entailed. In her biography of Garnett, Sarah Knights comments:

> He soon discovered that working for someone else was entirely different to working for oneself. He was employed pulling mangles, a grueling and back-breaking job involving hours stooping in muddy fields. Although Hecks was only four years Bunny's [Garnett's] senior, their relations remained formal. Whilst Bunny was clearly 'a gentleman', Heck's attitude was that of a yeoman farmer towards his labourer. (123)

Knights suggests that some of the restraint on Hecks's part may have been on account of his anxiety about hiring a conscientious objector (CO) at a time of such popular hostility towards objectors. Perhaps Hecks's restraint was also due to Garnett's status, 'clearly a "gentleman"'. Was it Grant's and Garnett's muddying of class distinctions that was the difficulty?

Garnett was taken aback at the nature of his work, as Knights points out: 'Having expected to learn farming, Bunny was surprised to be allocated the most unskilled manual work, including dung-carting' (125–6). The *Sussex Express* reports of exemptions for local workers casts light on why Grant and Garnett may have been allocated such work. In a short passage titled 'Firle Farmer Exempted' in April 1916 we find 'Reginald George Hecks, New House Farm, Firle, a young farmer, was granted conditional exemption' (*Sussex Express*, 14 April 1916).[3] Subsequent reports show that 'on the application of R. G. Hecks' conditional exemption was granted to cowman, Arthur Stephen Howness and to foreman and head cowman, William Henry Boys (*Sussex Express*, 21 July 1916 and 20 April 1917). It is significant that all three men were granted only 'conditional exemptions'. As these exemptions could have been revoked at any time, it would have been essential for Hecks to be able to go on proving to his local tribunal that he and his exempted employees were performing skilled work that no one else could (particularly not women).[4] Garnett and Grant's presence on the farm, and Garnett's eagerness to engage in more skilled work, must have been a source of anxiety for Howness and Boys.

The local context of Garnett and Grant's war work has not interested their biographers and existing accounts make no reference to other men or women undertaking such work. In her assessment of the longevity of Grant's friendship with John Maynard Keynes, Spalding is dismissive of this farm work and effaces the other people who undertook it alongside Grant and Garnett: 'their long-standing friendship rested on a bond untouched by the ructions of daily life. While Maynard hobnobbed with political leaders, Duncan worked alongside the ill-assorted individuals left behind as farm labourers' (*Duncan Grant* 195). It is not clear what made these individuals 'ill-assorted'. We may hazard that Spalding's infelicitous phrase aims at capturing the mixed class make-up of Hecks's employees, or perhaps she assumes anyone 'left behind' will have been either old or infirm.[5] The *Sussex Express* tribunal reports contribute to our understanding of the conditions of Garnett's and Grant's farm work and show that their fellow workers were not merely 'left behind' but had to live and work under the strain of temporary exemption.

We move now from one end of the rural social order to the other, from farm labourer to squire of the manor. Vanessa Bell's letters of the interwar period reveal that life at Charleston was not sealed off from intrusions from the local community and she adopts a pragmatic if ironical attitude to those of Viscount Gage of Firle Place, of whose estate Charleston Farmhouse was a part. Bell and Grant and the other sometime residents of Charleston were not in frequent contact with Lord Gage as he left the 'management of the estate to his agents' and so had 'little need to meet his tenants' (*Duncan Grant* 335). Spalding suggests this by way of explaining Quentin Bell's recollection of an early visit paid by Gage to Charleston when he was mistaken by Roger Fry for a plumber and directed to the bathroom (140). This anecdote, featuring off-hand treatment of an aristocrat, is of a type central to the popular idea(l) of Bloomsbury and its disregard for social norms and hierarchies. It also subtly preserves a version of Charleston as cut off from the Sussex community in which they lived.

This is not quite borne out by Vanessa Bell's interwar letters. Lord Gage is a recurring, humorous figure, and one whose identity is often mistaken. In 1932 Vanessa Bell writes to her husband Clive:

> Julian is still at Charleston where he had a visit from Lord Gage who turned up on Sunday afternoon just as Julian was entertaining a Labour party meeting in the drawing room! J of <u>course</u> didn't recognise Grubby for some time & when he did kept him talking outside the house never even offering him a drink. I hope he's getting used to us. (Tate Gallery Archive, VB to CB, 24 February 1932, 8010/2/264)

A number of things are striking here, not least Bell's unflattering nickname for Gage, 'Grubby'. This pet name identifies Gage with the earth and land, and is perhaps fitting for a country squire. It also undercuts his aristocratic status, instead associating him with the 'unwashed' peasantry, particularly with Bell's sometime gardener, Walter Higgins, whom Bell referred to as 'the Dolt'. Such an ignominious nickname combined with the running joke of Gage's not being recognized or being mistaken for someone else, frequently of a lower class, makes him an interesting, anxious figure for rural Bloomsbury. Bell clearly takes pleasure in Julian's show of bad manners in this anecdote and in the humorous asymmetry of an aristocrat stumbling upon a local Labour Party meeting. Julian's inhospitable behaviour and the Labour presence in the house suggest Charleston's local allegiances did not lie with the gentry.

During the 1930s Julian and Quentin Bell became involved in Labour politics and Vanessa Bell's letters to her husband in 1931 and 1932 detail their activities with their East Sussex constituencies. In 1931 Vanessa Bell writes: 'we are getting swamped in politics here. Julian drives canvassers all over the country at all hours & has his car plastered with Labour placards' (VB to CB, 20 October 1931, TGA 8010/2/257). In another letter she remarks: 'He [Julian] seems to be collecting a large communist party in the parishes of Firle and Glynde' (VB to CB, 8 February 1932, TGA 8010/2/262). The potential for friction caused by her sons' activism informs Bell's references to Gage; in another letter she writes: 'Grubby laughed at Julian's bearded activities in the district' (VB to CB, 14 January 1932, TGA 8010/2/261). As Bloomsbury biographer, Quentin Bell characterizes his mother as apolitical, even less interested in current affairs than her sister (37). While Vanessa Bell presents herself as bipartisan, 'keeping an open mind' (VB to CB, 20 October 1931, TGA 8010/2/257) in her letters to Clive Bell, this may have been a diplomatic decision made to avoid frustrating her Liberal-voting husband. Later, in the days following the 1931 General Election, Bell admits to voting Labour in a letter to Clive (VB to CB, 1 November 1931, TGA 8010/2/224). I will treat the subject of Bloomsbury's Labour politics in more detail later but for now I note some familiar tropes in Virginia Woolf's record of her encounters with Lord Gage. A September 1928 diary entry recording a dinner at the Keynes's to which Gage was invited is striking:

> found him with his flat face & Circassian blood, more of a character that I expected. Clive with inverse snobbery had run him down. We talked about the King, & he snubbed me by saying that he remarked an odd fact – everyone talks to him about the King. Every class, every kind of person, is interested to know what the king has for dinner. And here was I, the intellectual, the labour woman, doing just the same thing. (*Diary* 3: 198–9)

Woolf's appraisal of Clive Bell's 'inverse snobbery' is consistent with the various snubs issued to Gage at Charleston. Woolf's account of her own 'snubbing' and the way class operates here is suggestive. One can imagine Gage's comments about interest in royal gossip cutting across class lines bringing Woolf up short. She was self-conscious in the company of aristocrats and this conversation focused on class clearly encouraged her to reflect on her own status in relation to her noble dinner companion. Her characterization of herself here as 'the intellectual, the labour woman' registers a mixture of rebellious self-assertion and discomfort. She attempts to see herself through Gage's eyes. Her self-identification as a 'labour woman' is intriguing and holds echoes of the way Vanessa Bell reports her sons' political activities. This claim of allegiance to Labour is peculiar because it appears to contradict a statement Woolf makes earlier in the same diary entry: 'We don't belong to any "class", we thinkers' (*Diary* 3: 198). In response to the aristocratic person of Lord Gage, both Virginia Woolf and Vanessa Bell reach for Labour politics to announce their difference and possibly their opposition to his class.

While Bloomsbury may have felt ambivalent about their neighbours, keen to keep their distance from the local landed gentry, this was not how everyone saw it. Mistaken identity continued to be a keynote of Bloomsbury relations with Lord Gage when in 1931 *Daily Telegraph* society columnist Marianne Mayfayre wrote a short piece entitled 'Farmhouse Homes' to mark Gage's recent marriage:

> Lord and Lady Gage, whose wedding was an important event of the summer season, have some very interesting neighbours at Firle, Lord Gage's lovely old Sussex home in the Downs.
>
> In two farmhouses nestling in the folds of the Downs near by live respectively Mrs Maynard Keynes (Lydia Lopokova) and Mrs Duncan Grant (Vanessa Bell).
>
> At Cobbe Place, anther converted farmhouse, are Mr and the Hon Mrs Ponsonby.
>
> At Glyndebourne is Mr John Christie, the millionaire, whose organ is the envy of all his friends, and who enlivens the dinner parties of the neighbourhood occasionally

by wearing Swiss national costume instead of a dinner jacket. (*Daily Telegraph*, Wednesday, 2 September 1931, 7)

Mayfayre reads Bloomsbury as part of rural high society and a community of fashionable residents. Being linked to Gage in so public a forum and identified in this way with local grandees again encourages us to reconsider the orthodox view of Charleston as a closed and isolated community apart from the rural social order. Vanessa Bell contemplated a pragmatic take on the muddle with her name. To Clive Bell she wrote:

> I am told by Leonard & Bunny that a solicitor could get a large sum out of them [the *Daily Telegraph*] & I think of trying – After all why not – if they hand over 100 rather than run the mill of being had up for libel I dont see why one shouldnt take advantage of it ... Meanwhile photographers write daily to Mrs Duncan Grant to ask for sittings. (VB to CB, 8 September 1931, TGA 8010/2/251)

In the end it appears these plans went nowhere, but Mayfayre did apologize for her mistake in a subsequent column: 'Vanessa Bell, the famous woman painter, is, of course, Mrs Clive Bell, and I regret that by a slip of the pen she should have been incorrectly described' (*Daily Telegraph*, Wednesday, 16 September 1931, 7). Whether this 'slip of the pen' was a genuine mistake or a deliberate and mischievous reference to Bell's relationship with Grant is impossible to say. Bell's response is valuable for showing she herself was aware of the way rural Bloomsbury was interpreted and was willing to capitalize on their notoriety.

Local newspapers also took an interest in Charleston and its residents. In a 1938 letter to Clive Bell, Vanessa Bell records a summer village fete:

> We got 1st prize for our usual red eating apples & 2nd prize for [raddish?] & 3rd for something else – so the dolt feels very proud of himself. Angelica went to the show and was photographed with two other beauties for a local paper. (VB to CB, 28 August 1938, TGA 8010/2/301)

Bell's account of Charleston's success, social and otherwise, at this quintessentially local and rural occasion is characterized by both pride and disinterest. It is no surprise that Bell seems pleased with Angelica's social success – her delight in her daughter's appearance and others' recognition of this runs throughout her letters. Although she appears dismissive of her garden's wins in the fruit and vegetable contests, urbanely mocking Walter Higgens for taking such things seriously, her reference to 'our usual red eating apples' reveals a familiarity with the protocols of these events, so important to rural community calendars. While it may suggest that these are the apples Charleston put forward every year in the hope of bagging a prize, it may also register complacency; these are the apples that are regularly awarded first prize, perhaps out of deference to their growers' superior position in the village hierarchy. Such gestures occurred frequently – Virginia Woolf's election as Treasurer of her village Women's Institute (WI) is one such example – and Bell's letter gives us an insight into the freighted nature of local events as apparently innocuous as village fetes. Charleston's prize-winning produce, grown by Higgens for the credit of the house and its residents, and Angelica's status as local beauty, implies a more complicated level of involvement with their community than has been recognized.

Quentin Bell's decorations for the Rodmell Village Hall are an example of community involvement that appears to have been driven by a more straightforward participatory impulse. Vanessa Bell writes to Julian in 1937: 'We went over & saw Q's village hall decorations at Rodmell – they will be very successful when the walls [around?] are painted I think. At present they're too small & isolated & the hall still full of Christmas decorations which make them difficult to see' (VB to JB, 10 January 1937, TGA 9311/75). In 1937 Rodmell's 'village hall' was a single meeting room appended to the Rectory.[6] (The present village hall was opened in 1960 by Leonard Woolf.) As Jeremy Burchardt (2012) and Keith Grieves (1999) have observed, the interwar period was characterized by increasing popular demand for new village halls and clubrooms to act as common meeting and leisure spaces for the whole village. Grieves discusses how the egalitarian impulse behind this campaigning in East Sussex after the First World War led to disputes with the Church and local landowners. The call for 'undenominational social centres' (Grieves 171), run by the community rather than the Church, threatened clerical hold on local activities. A number of Grieves's case studies demonstrate the difficulty communities encountered in getting these projects off the ground due to resistance from wealthy local families unwilling to support such ventures by supplying land or offering subscriptions (Grieves 176). While there was a desire for these spaces to be 'managed by self-help in the interests of everybody' in practice they often remained under some level of 'ecclesiastical control' (Grieves 173). This was clearly the case with the Rodmell meeting room, which was physically attached to the Rectory. (This perhaps explains why WI and Rodmell Social Club meetings took place there but not local Labour Party meetings, which, as I shall discuss later, met at Monk's House.)

Bell's decorations should be read in the context of the village hall movement and the tensions this gave rise to in interwar rural communities. Vanessa Bell's account of them is not much to go on but it is interesting that they are described as vying for position with Christmas decorations. Given Julian and Quentin's enthusiastic support for various local Labour groups across East Sussex at this time, we can assume they would have been in sympathy with the village hall movement's desire to challenge 'old elite structures' (Grieves 173). These decorations participate in an effort to lay claim to public space for leisure in the village and are evidence that the aesthetic project of Charleston did not have, by its very nature, to take place apart from or against the workings of the wider community. These decorations, painted for Rodmell residents by a resident of Charleston, also draw attention to the relationship between these two Bloomsbury rural bases and the degree to which they collaborated and drew each other into their community activities. This will become especially clear in my discussion of the Rodmell Labour Party that follows.

MONK'S HOUSE – RODMELL

The situation of Monk's House in a village meant the Woolfs had less choice about participating in rural community life than their relatives and friends at Charleston. This was also a matter of inclination. They were on pleasant, if rather distant, terms with their neighbours, including Major and Diana Gardner, Mrs Chavasse, and Mr Fears, the postman. They made visits and financial gifts to the local elderly, (*Diary* 4: 124–5) and attended village weddings (*Letters* 4: 338) and 'festivals' (*Letters* 4: 176). Virginia Woolf also kept a beady eye on village gossip, reporting the 'violent quarrels and incessant intrigues' (*Letters* 6: 391) of Rodmell in letters and diaries. The bulk of the Woolfs' interactions with Rodmell came about as a result of participation in local groups and boards. Leonard Woolf was an enthusiastic committee member, so his involvement with the local Labour Party and role on the village school board is not surprising. As I have suggested elsewhere, in spite of her mixed feelings about the efficacy of such activities, Virginia Woolf also chose to associate with a range of political and social organizations throughout her life.

In *Virginia Woolf: Ambivalent Activist* I explore Woolf's fractious but tender relationship with the Rodmell WI, with whom she organized village plays and for a time acted as Treasurer. This WI work was the most substantial she undertook in the village. Rodmell village reports in the *Sussex Express* show that from the mid-1930s Virginia Woolf was also captain of the village stoolball team, a game with significant implications in terms of both class and gender. Stoolball is a bat and ball game, often supposed to be a precursor to cricket, with its origins in medieval England. Popular throughout the seventeenth and eighteenth centuries with both men and women, stoolball has traditionally been identified with female, working-class players – the stool of the name is supposed to be derived from the milkmaid's three-legged milking stool (Lowerson 410). By the nineteenth century the game was less widely played but remained popular among female villagers in Kent and Sussex. The class dynamics of the mid-Victorian revival in the game are suggestive in terms of Woolf's captaincy: 'female members of the gentry, landowners and Anglican clergy, anxious to *preserve* village life, started clubs for local women … Thereafter the game spread, largely because of the *social maternalism* of upper-class female patronage: "There is no doubt that the countryside would be merrier if there were a stool-ball club for women in every village. They cannot very well be left to organize it for themselves"' (Lowerson 410).[7]

Virginia Woolf's captaincy of the Rodmell stoolball team is less surprising than it first appears when read in terms of the classed history of the sport. Her role was likely an honorific one, bestowed in deference to her class position in the village. As Hermione Lee notes and her interactions with her village WI testify, this local identification of Woolf with Rodmell's 'middle-class gentry' (431) is one she resented. In an August 1935 letter to John Lehmann, Woolf writes: 'The village is playing stoolball, and I must go and sit on the grass and watch' (*Letters* 5: 422). Woolf makes no mention of her role in the village team and this reference is characterized by the language of duty, betraying Woolf's awareness of the distance between herself and 'the village' and the degree to which class coloured such interactions.

Yet Woolf also felt ill at ease with the local gentry and landowners – witness her interactions with Lord Gage – and her thinking about village life throughout the interwar period and into the Second World War shows her loyalties oddly split. In an unpublished letter to the press written in 1931 called 'The Villa Jones' Woolf attempts to solve the problem of unsightly building on the Downs with a scheme that will benefit local people:

> Why not tax the view values of all new houses; & [tax those] who build & let the villagers {access/assess} the tax. For {assuredly} the villagers are going to suffer. The rich are not going to come to the country in order to see the Villa Jones. (Jones 95)

While this extract shows an awareness of how rural life is defined by relations between classes – here upper and working classes – the logic of Woolf's letter-writer is not altogether clear. The suggestion appears to be that unsightly building will put 'the rich' off visiting the countryside, and that 'the villagers' will lose out financially as a result. Woolf perhaps had tourism in mind here. The interwar period was a moment of renewed enthusiasm for the rural and this may be a nod to the economic benefits small businesses, such as village tearooms, might have derived as a result of middle and upper-class leisure drivers. But surely 'villagers' were more likely to suffer from unregulated private building developments because the houses that were being built were unlikely to be affordable? So while 'The Villa Jones' shows an awareness of the classed nature of village life it also characterized by a failure of understanding. The very language of 'suffering' villagers dependent in one way or another on 'the rich' reveals a feudal logic to Woolf's thinking about the countryside and class.

The divide between 'rich' and 'villager' Woolf creates here leaves us wondering where she might fit. As an upper-middle-class relative newcomer to the village she occupies the same liminal position as Vanessa Bell at Charleston. Another unsent letter from the period, later published as 'Middlebrow', gives us some insight into Woolf's contradictory feelings about her position in the village. In this letter Woolf famously describes middlebrows as 'betwixt and between', neither one thing nor the other. The middlebrow's offence is conceived spatially – they live in South Kensington on neither high nor low ground. Although much of the letter takes its geographical markers from London, there is a significant shift mid-way through. After a diatribe about the influx of middlebrows to the countryside, the narrator reflects:

> Such are the thoughts, such are the fancies that visit 'cultured invalidish ladies with private means' (see advt.) when they stroll in their suburban gardens and look at the cabbages and at the red brick villas that have been built by middlebrows so that middlebrows may look at the view. (V. Woolf 119)

Although the writer of the 'Middlebrow' letter is a self-proclaimed highbrow, this passage betrays some uncomfortable overlap between the letter-writer and her middlebrow neighbours. Woolf's decision for her highbrow to be the owner of a suburban garden, close to so many middlebrows, may reflect Woolf's contemporary anxiety that the East Sussex countryside was fast becoming 'a suburb of Brighton' (*Letters* 4: 380). It might also reveal her awareness of her own 'betweeness' and an uneasy parity between herself and the loathed middlebrow.

The Woolfs' activity with the Rodmell Labour Party, which met in Monk's House from 1931, involved them in village life and Virginia Woolf refers to this activity in her letters and diaries. She writes to Lady Simon: 'We live in the heart of the lower village world, to whom Leonard lectures on potatoes and politics. The gentry dont call' (*Letters* 6: 464). Here we find Woolf showing off her rural credentials. Her playful claim of kinship with the 'lower village' and off-hand reference to the inattentive 'gentry' suggest the Woolfs' loyalties lie with the former. The reference to the 'heart of the lower village world' gestures literally to the location of Monk's House in the furthest end of the village but also metaphorically announces their solidarity with 'the villagers'. Woolf makes similar manoeuvres in other references to Labour Party meetings. In 1938 she writes in her diary: 'The village cabal against us is roused by the L.P.' (*Letters* 6: 162). And in 1940: 'We're thought red hot revolutionaries because the Labour party meets in our dining room' (*Letters* 6: 391). However, the message of the original passage remains ambiguous. It is telling that Leonard lectures 'to' their neighbours on 'potatoes and politics'. The power dynamics are pronounced and this imbalance is borne out in the minutes of the Rodmell Labour Party.

This minute book, held in the Leonard Woolf Papers, includes reports of the monthly meetings held at Monk's House from 1931 onwards and records of attendance. While scholars have referred to these meetings in passing little detailed attention has been paid to the minutes themselves and what they reveal about the character and make-up of the Rodmell group. Alison Light, one of the few exceptions, has written interestingly about the minutes. Light notes the small membership of the Rodmell branch and draws attention to the fact that a number of those who attended meetings were the Woolfs' employees – Annie Thompsett and then Louie Meyer acted as secretary – and suggests 'the Woolfs could hardly be on an equal footing with the villagers' (239–40). Members of the Rodmell branch would be unlikely to encounter the 'politicized language of class antagonism' (240) that they have found at larger meetings, Light suggests.

Diana Gardner, who, according to the minute book, attended meetings first as a 'visitor' in July 1937 and later, from August 1939, as a member, offers an account of the Rodmell branch in her memoir of 1930s Rodmell (Rodmell Labour Party Minute Book, SxMs-13/2/I/4/I). She describes how she came to look forward to the branch meetings as 'a central point of interest and ideas' (Gardner 28). Gardner writes: 'the atmosphere was almost always friendly and free', in contrast to her experiences as a delegate at a larger Labour meeting in Brighton where she was dismayed at the 'general prejudice and vehemence' she encountered (28). She does not remember a visit from two Trade Unionists to the Rodmell Branch fondly: 'I felt that, to them, I was an abhorred member of the bourgeoisie who should be dispatched hence!' (28). In 1945 Gardner realized her sympathies were actually Liberal rather than Labour, having always had misgivings about 'Socialism – which was the declared aim of the Labour Party in those days' (19).

Gardner's memories of the Labour Party meetings in Rodmell confirm Light's analysis of the branch. Her characterization of the meetings as a forum for ideas and her hostility to class thinking, which she interprets as 'prejudice', suggests the meetings were perhaps light on politics. The fact that Gardner only started coming to meetings in order to meet the Woolfs (18) certainly suggests she saw these meetings more as a social than a political occasion. The admittance of 'visitors' to branch meetings goes some way to confirming this social dimension too. The minutes of a meeting in April 1932 record: 'It was proposed & carried that we should hold Discussions at these meetings and if we found any person who was interested to bring them along' (SxMs-13/2/I/4/I). Looking at the small number of members present at this meeting – 'Messrs Woolf, Bell, Hancock, Fears, Kennard & Mrs Thompsett' – we can also realistically read this drive to include visitors as a way of reaching out to new members. Judging by the familiar names recorded in subsequent meetings and the fact in February 1935 it was decided 'that each member should bring a friend' to the next meeting, it appears this drive was not entirely successful.

Leonard Woolf's austere approach to his role as Chair might have had something to do with this. Gardner writes: 'He might express a point of view and find it challenged by an opposite point of view. He would sit silently, his face hard and unsmiling' (28). This autocratic bent is evidenced by Leonard Woolf's contributions and emendations to the minute book. He is scrupulous in checking and signing off the minutes of previous meetings and on occasion makes corrections. For instance, the record of his talk on 'the colonial question' at the February 1936 meeting written by Mrs Everest, branch secretary, have been corrected by Leonard. The original reads: 'Mr Woolf gave a discussion on Colonial question and read a very interesting pamphlet.' Leonard has changed this to 'Mr Woolf delivered an address on the colonial question and a very good discussion followed' (SxMs-13/2/I/4/I). Although it is the chair's role to correct minutes, these corrections are high-handed – particularly the change from the slightly inaccurate but simple 'gave a discussion' to the rather grand 'delivered an address'. It is also interesting that the reading of a pamphlet in the secretary's version is replaced with a 'good discussion'. These emendations support Gardner's account of Leonard's unyielding and even combative style as chair of the branch. It is difficult not to read a level of contempt in these changes to the secretary's wording, perhaps a manifestation of a Fabian confidence in the importance of middle-class, educated leadership of the working class. In his autobiography Leonard Woolf comments on his years of committee work for the Labour Party and the Fabians:

> I am not a good committee man unless I am chairman or secretary; as an ordinary member, I tend either to become exasperated by what seems to me inefficiency and waste of time or to sink into a coma from which at long intervals I rouse myself to sudden, irritated energy. (349)

Leonard Woolf's behaviour towards his comrades in the Rodmell branch is consistent with his own appraisal of his approach in meetings. Judging by the minutes, it appears that something about this particular committee, perhaps its class make-up, led to what appears to be an extreme manifestation of this behaviour.

If Leonard's manner in these meetings was overbearing, Virginia Woolf's seems to have been the opposite. In his biography of Woolf, Quentin Bell remembers his frustration at the way his aunt behaved at Rodmell Labour Party meetings:

> I was trying to get the party to pass resolutions urging the formation of a United Front – or something equally urgent, vital and important – and Virginia managed to turn the debate in such a way that it developed into an exchange of Rodmell gossip. In this way of course she was much nearer to the feelings of the masses, if one may thus describe the six or seven members of the Rodmell Labour Party, than I was. I wanted to talk politics, the masses wanted to talk about the vicar's wife. (*Virginia Woolf* 186)

Bell may well have found his aunt's efforts to bring the discussion round to local issues revealing of her taste for gossip and mundane in comparison to the 'urgent, vital and important' questions he thought the proper stuff of Labour meetings. There are a number of reasons, themselves political, why Woolf may have felt the need to steer the meetings in this way. This 'domestic' approach would have acted as a necessary counter to Leonard's behaviour in meetings, and may be read as a diplomatic move on Woolf's part. The distinction Bell sets up in this passage between 'politics' and 'gossip' is misleading and he half acknowledges this by admitting that Woolf 'was much nearer the feelings of the masses' than himself. What goes unacknowledged here is the reason why rural working people might understand the vicar's wife politically. Mrs Ebbs, wife of Rodmell's vicar, was unpopular in the village; in a letter to her sister from October 1938 Woolf reports Rodmell's unenthusiastic reception of news of Chamberlain's agreement with Hitler at Munich:

> here at Rodmell a service was hastily got up ... Mrs Ebbs in vain tried to whip up the villagers to some excitement; but one and all they remained perfectly sure that it was a dirty business; and meant only another war when we should be unable to resist. (*Letters* 6: 280)

Mrs Ebbs's prominence here and her inability to convince 'the villagers' to celebrate Hitler's appeasement is significant in terms of local politics and suggests there may have been legitimate reasons for her to be discussed during a debate about a United Front at a Rodmell Labour Party meeting.

Earlier in this chapter I outlined the aims of the village hall movement and touched on the threat this posed to the dominance of the Church in the life of the village. In Rodmell, Mrs Ebbs was for a time the president of the local WI and active on the board of the village school. Given Mrs Ebbs's prominence in village organizations and the dislike she inspired in the village, it is significant that the Rodmell Labour Party met at Monk's House and not in the village hall appended to the Rectory. As Light suggests, holding meetings at Monk's House was bound to have caused inhibitions and risked perpetuating traditions of deference and patronage associated with the 'Big House'. This may have represented the lesser of two evils, if meeting at the village hall might have risked clerical interference. The fact that the Rodmell branch met at Monk's House even when the Woolfs were not themselves present, suggest it was not for reasons of their convenience alone that the group met there.[8]

The 1932 decision for 'discussions' to make up part of the group's meetings mean that, as Light suggests, these meetings sometimes took on the character of an 'adult education class' (280). Discussions, which were introduced by a member or Labour visitor, covered a range of topics but many were closely related to Labour issues. In September 1932 a Mr Aves visited to speak on the subject of 'Why socialists should be co-operatives?', in November 1932 Mr Hancock spoke on the 'agricultural worker', in August 1936 Quentin Bell introduced a discussion on 'the Popular Front' and in May 1940 Mrs Penfold spoke on the Budget (SxMs-13/2/I/4/I). The minutes also record the party business and branch administration that made up a part of each meeting. In June 1936 the branch agreed to take '100 copies of "Country Folk" magazine from divisional party' and in September 1937 it was decided that the Rodmell delegate at the General Meeting should 'vote in favour of a resolution condemning the *Daily Herald*' (SxMs-13/2/I/4/I). At a meeting in March 1939, the minutes record the membership's decision for their delegate to propose a motion at the next Divisional Party Meeting proposing that 'the delegate of the Lewes Divisional Party to the annual Conference of the Labour Party be instructed to support any proposal at the Conference which has as its object the return of Sir Stafford Cripps to the party' (SxMs-13/2/I/4/I).[9]

These meetings took place in the 1930s as the political situation in Europe became more frighteningly unstable and the threat of fascism more striking (see Foster in this volume). The Popular Front and the war in Spain recur as topics of discussion, and in December 1936 the branch decide to send a contribution for an ambulance to the international column in Spain (SxMs-13/2/I/4/I). As we have seen, Julian and Quentin Bell were active in East Sussex Labour through their branches in Firle and Glynde, and from early 1932 Quentin Bell also attended the Rodmell meetings. Angelica Bell and Vanessa Bell also start attending from September 1938. Vanessa Bell's presence can be read in the context of a letter she wrote to her sister in March:

> Please tell Leonard that if he can find any use for an incompetent like myself in the political world I am willing to be used, but I know it's not much good. At the same time, when things have got to such a pass, I don't see how the least politically minded can keep out of it. I can read and write and even type-write and have no pride. (*Letters* 444)

This diffident but moving letter is a startling echo of one Woolf herself wrote to Janet Case in 1910, when still Virginia Stephen, offering her help to the adult suffrage cause: 'I could neither do sums or argue, or speak, but I could do the humbler work if that is any good. You impressed me so much the other night with the wrongness of the present state of affairs that I feel that action is necessary' (*Letters* 1: 421). Both women stress their ineptitude but also their commitment to action.

A willingness to participate in the political life of their rural communities brought two generations of the Bloomsbury Group – Quentin and Vanessa Bell and Leonard and Virginia Woolf – to a meeting of the Rodmell Labour Party in August 1939 where Louie Everest 'opened a discussion on Education and the school leaving age' (SxMs-13/2/I/4/I). Virginia Woolf wrote to her niece Judith Stephen, who would herself attend a Rodmell Labour meeting and talk about education the following year: 'A large Labour Party meeting [at Rodmell] discussed education two nights ago; Louis [Everest] read a paper; even Nessa gave tongue. But I mustn't drivel on; and there's so much to say I'm stopped like a bottle held upside down' (*Letters* 6: 353). It is ironic that just as she tantalizingly reveals that 'even Nessa gave tongue' at this meeting Woolf cuts herself off, pleading 'there's so much to say'.

This chapter has lingered over ephemeral materials – local newspapers, society columns, minute books – unpublished sketches and throwaway references in letters rather than works of the Bloomsbury canon. This archival approach is born of a conviction that the communities surrounding Monk's House and Charleston, the villages of Firle and Rodmell, should be recognized both as rich contexts for and significant influences on Bloomsbury's identity and values during these years. The familiar story of Bloomsbury's 'escape' to the East Sussex countryside looks less convincing in light of this material that locates them as, albeit bemused, ambivalent or autocratic, prize-winning apple growers, stoolball captains and branch committee chairs. Bloomsbury's relationships to their local communities were not straightforward, and scrutinizing them we become more aware of the complicated and often contradictory ways in which its members thought about the class of others as well as their own.

NOTES

1. Work on Woolf and the rural has tended to focus on her final novel, *Between the Acts,* the only of her works to be set entirely in the countryside, including Esty (85–107) and Joannou. Also see Alt, Scott, and Harris.
2. The farmer from the Board of Agriculture who conducted the assessment insisted they find work on an established farm, scuppering their plan to remain self-employed (Knights 119).
3. I am very grateful to Ciaran Bermingham for drawing my attention to these newspaper reports and for discussing the politics of exemption with me.
4. For more on exemptions for skilled farm labourers during the First World War, see Horn (76–7).
5. Horn points out that while in the early days of the war farmers were able to 'make up a considerable part of the deficiency by the use of retired workers and those invalided out of the forces' (73) it soon became obvious this approach was unsustainable.
6. I am grateful to Catriona Grant of the Rodmell Village Society for being so generous with her time and discussing the history of the village hall with me.
7. It is also worth noting that stoolball experienced a minor renaissance in the wake of the First World War. This was mainly driven by the efforts of W. W. Grantham who promoted the game as a less strenuous alternative to rugby and cricket for men returning injured from the war. See Grantham.
8. For example in February and March 1932 and March 1933. Leonard Woolf Papers, Rodmell Labour Party Minute Book, SxMs-13/2/I/4/I.
9. This final example casts the politics of the Rodmell branch as more to the left of the party than Light suggests. Stafford Cripps was expelled from the Labour Party in early 1939 as a result of his commitment to the Popular Front and his willingness to collaborate with the Communist Party.

WORKS CITED

Alt, Christina. *Virginia Woolf and the Study of Nature*. Cambridge: Cambridge UP, 2010.

Bell, Quentin. *Virginia Woolf*. London: Hogarth Press, 1972.

Bell, Quentin. *Bloomsbury Recalled*. New York: Columbia UP, 1995.

Bell, Vanessa. *Selected Letters of Vanessa Bell*. Ed. Regina Marler. London: Bloomsbury, 1994.

Burchardt, Jeremy. 'State and Society in the English Countryside: The Rural Community Movement, 1918–39'. *Rural History* 23.1 (2012): 81–106.

Daily Telegraph, Wednesday, 16 September 1931.

Daily Telegraph, Wednesday, 2 September 1931.

Esty, Jed. *A Shrinking Island: Modernism and National Culture in England*. Princeton: Princeton UP, 2004.

Falmer. The Keep. Leonard Woolf Papers. Rodmell Labour Party Minute Book. SxMs-13/2/I/4/I.

Gardner, Diana, *The Rodmell Papers: Reminiscences of Virginia and Leonard Woolf by a Sussex Neighbour*. London: Cecil Woolf, 2008.

Grantham, W. W. *Stoolball and How to Play It*. London: Tattersall, 1931.

Grieves, Keith. 'Common Meeting Places and the Brightening of Rural Life: Local Debates on Village Halls in Sussex after the First World War'. *Rural History* 10.2 (1999): 171–92.

Harris, Alexandra. *Romantic Moderns: English Writers, Artists and the Imagination from Virginia Woolf to John Piper*. London: Thames & Hudson, 2010.

Horn, Pamela. *Rural Life in England in the First World War*. New York: St Martin's Press, 1984.

Joannou, Maroula. *Women's Writing, Englishness and National and Cultural Identity: The Mobile Woman and the Migrant Voice, 1938–62*. Basingstoke: Palgrave, 2012.

Jones, Clara. *Virginia Woolf: Ambivalent Activist*. Edinburgh: Edinburgh UP, 2016.

Jones, Clara. 'Virginia Woolf and "The Villa Jones"'. *Woolf Studies Annual* 22 (2016): 75–95.

Knights, Sarah. *Bloomsbury's Outsider: A Life of Bunny Garnett*. London: Bloomsbury, 2015.

Lee, Hermione. *Virginia Woolf*. London: Vintage, 1997.

Light, Alison. *Mrs Woolf and the Servants*. London: Penguin, 2007.

Lowerson, John. 'Stoolball and the Manufacture of Englishness'. *ISHPES Studies* 1 (1993): 410–12.

Scott, Bonnie Kime. *In the Hollow of the Wave: Virginia Woolf and Modernist Uses of Nature*. Charlottesville: U of Virginia P, 2012.

Spalding, Frances. *Duncan Grant: A Biography*. London: Chatto & Windus, 1997.

Spalding, Frances. *Vanessa Bell: Portrait of the Bloomsbury Artist*. London: Tauris: 2015.

Sussex Express, 14 April 1916.

Sussex Express, 21 July 1916 and 20 April 2017.

Tate Gallery Archive. Charleston Trust, TGA 8010.

Tate Gallery Archive. Julian Bell Collection. TGA 9311.

Woolf, Leonard. *Downhill All the Way*. Oxford: Oxford UP, 1980.

Woolf, Virginia. *The Death of the Moth and Other Essays*. London: Hogarth Press, 1942.

Woolf, Virginia. *The Diary of Virginia Woolf*, 5 vols. Ed. Anne Olivier Bell and Andrew McNeillie. New York: Harcourt Brace Jovanovich, 1977–84.

Woolf, Virginia. *The Essays of Virginia Woolf, Vol. 6: 1933–1941*. Ed. Stuart N. Clarke. London: Chatto & Windus, 2012.

Woolf, Virginia. *The Letters of Virginia Woolf*, 6 vols. Ed. Nigel Nicolson and Joanne Trautmann. London: Hogarth Press, 1975–80.

CHAPTER SEVEN

Bloomsbury and Jewishness

SUSAN WEGENER

In the forum on 'Virginia Woolf and Jews' in the 2013 *Woolf Studies Annual*, David Eberly observes how critical characterizations of Woolf's antisemitism have been contradictory, and the oppositions in the forum itself demonstrate that instability ('Responses' 17). While this chapter examines Jewishness in the Bloomsbury Group broadly, looking at the dissention in Woolf scholarship alone is a good place to start a discussion on Jewishness and Bloomsbury. Any study of Jewishness in the Bloomsbury Group must acknowledge that antisemitism is deeply intertwined with their philosophies, and has had real consequences. Almost every member made offhand or pointed remarks that created a hostile environment for Jews; no Jewish person could be part of the group – or even enter the periphery – without being identified, labelled, and constantly reminded of their outsider status. As a result, this artistically influential group left a legacy that includes antisemitism.

The tendency of some critics has been to apologize for the antisemitic remarks and argue that historical context justifies some prejudices. However, Maren Linett declares: 'it is time to move beyond … apologies and excuses … and continue the important work of exploring what her antisemitism meant to Woolf, and how it functioned for her personally, politically, and … aesthetically' ('Responses' 19). Historicizing is necessary, but when attempting to contextualize antisemitism verges too closely on apologizing for it, we must look not only at antisemitism in its particular historical context, but also at the effects – perhaps unconscious – that it has had on current readers. This chapter argues that the members of the Bloomsbury Group deliberately separated Bloomsbury from Jewishness by repeating antisemitic stereotypes and frequently invoking Jewishness (particularly Leonard Woolf's) in negative ways. This divide enabled the Bloomsbury artists to develop their tastes and artistic philosophies in opposition to that which they defined as Jewish. The mere mention of Jews or Jewishness is not necessarily antisemitic, but for the most part, only Leonard Woolf referred to Jewish people, the idea of Jewishness, and Judaism with any kind of curiosity or attempt to understand the Jew's lived experience. While antisemitism influenced their ideas about art, and the group members made a point to identify and oppose that which they considered to be Jewish, their artistic productions also worked to ignore and erase authentic Jewishness from British artistic culture. Attempting to erase Jewishness from art and literature is not the same as Hitler's elimination of Jewish people in Nazi Germany and beyond. But acknowledging that antisemitism played a part in the development of Bloomsbury artistic philosophies allows us to better understand the ways in which literary and artistic movements in England created a climate that permitted the spread of Nazism.

When Virginia Stephen accepted Leonard Woolf's marriage proposal, she stated her objections to his Jewishness: 'I feel angry sometimes at the strength of your desire. Possibly your being a Jew comes in at this point. You seem so foreign' (*Letters* 1: 496–7). Certainly Leonard's family seemed foreign to Virginia when she first encountered the realities of Jewish life, such as keeping kosher. After meeting Leonard's family for tea, Virginia satirized her experience in a letter to Janet Case in which she was shocked that the Woolfs did not eat ham or shellfish (502–3). She described Leonard's mother Marie as 'vampire like & vast in her demand for my entire attention & sympathy' and Woolf family parties as unbearable (*Diary* 3: 321). The Woolfs' cultural Jewishness was unfamiliar to Virginia, and she reacted badly to these differences. While Virginia called Leonard a 'penniless Jew' and was concerned with the realities of his class and Jewish heritage, she was mostly critical about his family's Jewishness, rather than about any way that he looked or acted (*Letters* 1: 500–501). Leonard himself was assimilated and did not seem to be particularly foreign, but it is significant that his Bloomsbury friends insisted upon this label. Natania Rosenfeld rightly notes that Virginia labels Leonard a foreign Jew and allows that to trump any of his specific qualities: 'Virginia makes it essential *what* Leonard is, and not *how* he is' (59 original italics). When the Jew does not have identifiably Jewish characteristics, the antisemite creates them. Rather than commenting on Leonard's name, looks, accent, mannerisms, or anything tangible that might have identified him as Jewish, Virginia (and others) created a narrative that marked the Jew and reduced him to a stereotype, usually a romantic wanderer or a vulgar outsider.

Even before Virginia met Leonard, she was intrigued by her brother Thoby's descriptions of his Jewish classmate, and turned him into an almost mythical creature: 'I was of course inspired with the deepest interest in that violent trembling misanthropic Jew who had already shaken his fist at civilization and was about to disappear into the tropics so that we should none of us ever see him again' ('Old Bloomsbury' 188). Leonard was exotic because Virginia hadn't met anyone with his background, but she was already casting him in antisemitic terms. Lytton Strachey and Vanessa Bell also reduced Leonard to stereotype, even after they had grown close to him. Leonard was often good natured about his friends' language, as evidenced by his amused response to Lytton referring to a Jewish family as 'utterly vulgar with the sort of placid easy-flowing vulgarity of *your* race' (*Letters* 95). Vanessa was also casually antisemitic when comparing her brother in law to a corrupt Jewish moneylender: 'I think I owe you a letter and I'm afraid of getting in trouble if I don't pay what I owe to the Jews' (qtd in Lee 308). Presumably Leonard took this as a joke.

In part Lytton, Vanessa, and the others imposed antisemitic stereotypes upon Leonard so that they could attempt to make sense of a man who was outside their frame of reference. But this was also a defence mechanism practised by those who were wary of integrating someone who was different specifically because he was Jewish. Jewish assimilation in early twentieth century England meant that there was less Jewish difference that people like Virginia Woolf found so foreign. But this meant that a person could never be sure if she was in the presence of a Jew, and risked being mistaken for a Jew herself. Janice Ho writes: 'The possibility of Jews passing as British ... while seeming to confirm the successful universality of liberal principles, also fuelled anti-Semitic anxieties about the undetected infiltration of the nation' (717). The idea of the Jew who was basically indistinguishable from non-Jewish English citizens truly threatened the purity of Englishness. The need to maintain a divide between Bloomsbury and Jewishness was one reason why Virginia referred to Leonard as 'the Jew' and 'my Jew', even years after their marriage. Likewise, when Lytton called Leonard 'the Rabbi' it was an affectionate title in school, but one meant to verify Leonard's status as the only Jewish person in his group at Trinity College (Glendinning 38). Calling a Jewish person 'Jew' held him at a distance and ensured that he was always identifiable. While we might brush this off as playful banter, this type of language is a sinister guarantee that Leonard would never pass as an English gentile, whether or not he was trying to do so.

Hermione Lee, citing antisemitic slurs made by Clive Bell, Vanessa, and Virginia, attempts to brush them off as harmless jokes. She calls these casual remarks 'marital habits' that 'were not cause for offence' (308–9). But this was not simply a private language between wife and husband. Rather, all the members of Bloomsbury spoke to Leonard this way, and Virginia felt free to deride her husband (under the guise of a joke) in front of their friends and family. Perhaps Leonard truly did not object, although his refusal to answer a question when being called 'the Jew' by Virginia suggests that this kind of treatment did not sit well with him, and his usual tolerance had its limits (*Letters* 470). While Leonard's feelings are important, of course, the issue is more complicated than whether or not Leonard was offended. This kind of language established an antisemitic climate that allowed everyone in the group to distance themselves from Jewishness. To maintain the divide between Bloomsbury and Jewishness they only had to identify who was Jewish and who was not. A Jewish person's specific characteristics were important in marking them as a Jew, but they need not be invoked. While some Jewish people might be identified by a particular look or style, there was a so-called Jewish essence that came through no matter how assimilated a person was.

It is difficult to determine Leonard's feelings about antisemitism in the Bloomsbury Group. His inconsistent statements over the years suggest that he was ambivalent about his Jewishness and the way the group treated him. In 1968, after publishing the final volume of his autobiography, he said that he had 'always been conscious of being primarily British and have lived among people who without question accepted me as such ... [antisemitism] has not touched me personally and only very peripherally' (*Leonard Woolf* 429). Yet Jewish suffering was a consistent theme in his writing, both in the five volumes of his autobiography and in his novels. Leonard's daily dealings with antisemitism and the way he spoke about Jewishness in personal interactions were different than how he characterized it in his writing. Victoria Glendinning suggests that the group did not talk about Leonard's reactions to antisemitism. In a parenthetical aside, she observes that 'no one liked to inquire what he felt about the expressions of anti-Semitism in his wife's fiction' (236). It certainly does seem that Leonard's denial or gracious willingness to overlook the antisemitism in his environment was necessary. If he felt that there was nothing he could do about it, focusing on his anxiety or attempting to challenge the rest of the group would only exacerbate the situation. And as Ho points out, perhaps his tactic of ignoring or tolerating antisemitism was part of his belief that to be born Jewish meant inevitable suffering.

In *The Journey Not the Arrival Matters*, Leonard aligns himself with Jews who have been oppressed for thousands of years:

I have my full share of the inveterate, the immemorial fatalism of the Jew, which he has learned from his own history beginning 3,428 years ago – so they say – under the taskmasters of Pharaoh in Egypt ... and so on through the diaspora and the lessons of centuries of pogroms and ghettoes down to the lessons of the gas chambers and Hitler. Thus it is we have learned that we cannot escape fate. (127–8)

If Leonard believed that to be Jewish was to suffer, it is hard to accept that he did not mind the antisemitism in his environment. Critics are divided on this subject as well. Lee writes that Leonard knew that he was the target of antisemitic jokes and accepted these without resentment, although 'when it came to his family, [Virginia's] prejudices *were* offensive, and may have offended him' (308–9).

While Lee seems to suggest that Leonard's resignation means he did not feel persecuted, Ho writes that Leonard's account of Jewish suffering in *The Wise Virgins* is an attempt to convey the suffering that he felt as the only Jew in the Bloomsbury Group. For example, when Harry is involved in a conversation with Arthur, Katharine, and Camilla about love and whether Jews feel emotions differently than Christians, Harry censors his responses. When Arthur says: 'You don't mind my saying so, but it's a characteristic of your race – they've intellect and not emotion; they don't feel things', Harry feels compelled to stifle his feelings: 'He thought to himself that he did not answer because if he did he would show that he was suffering and had lost his temper' (107). Similarly, Harry resents that Camilla and her group do not accept him the way he is and want him to change in order to fit in (130). Ho points out that even though Leonard writes that Jewish suffering is inevitable – everyone born a Jew will suffer – this is not some kind of biological or cultural trait. 'Suffering ... is not merely a natural or religious occurrence, but is produced through the exercise of sovereign power' (730). Jews suffer from social and political oppression by those in the cultural or religious majority, and they are suffering even if they never articulate their pain or challenge their oppressors.

Did Leonard suffer in the Bloomsbury Group? It seemed that no matter how well he fit in, he was first and foremost a Jew. Rupert Brooke referred to Leonard and Virginia as 'the Jew and his wife' (Delany 187) and when Dora Carrington was dating the Jewish painter Mark Gertler, Lytton wrote to ask if she was 'in the Jew's arms at the present moment' (Holroyd 371). This kind of identification meant not just naming Jews, but also attaching so-called Jewish characteristics to the person to mark them further. The details of heritage and experience did not always matter; in fact, it was often necessary to ignore that reality in order to uphold the idea of Jewish difference. To ask Leonard about his background and attempt to understand his Jewish perspective would mean acknowledging Jewish diversity and lived experience.[1] Since the Bloomsbury Group's artistic philosophy depended in part on defining itself against what it was not – Jewish – then there had to be a stereotypical Jewishness that was unchanging and applicable to all Jews.

Some of the basic, most enduring Jewish stereotypes and characteristics attributed to Jews have to do with money, the body, male effeminacy, emotional and physical excess, gaudiness in dress and taste, the city, wandering, nervousness, and blurred boundaries. Linett observes that the stereotypes are often contradictory or unstable; Jews are connected with modern, crowded, city spaces/ghettoes, but also ancient worlds and desert wandering (*Modernism* 4–8). One of Virginia Woolf's frequently quoted antisemitic statements is a backhanded compliment that invokes the idea of Jewish vulgarity and potency:

> How I hated marrying a Jew – how I hated their nasal voices, and their oriental jewellery, and their noses and their wattles – what a snob I was: for they have immense vitality, and I think I like that quality best of all. They can't die – they exist on a handful of rice and a thimble of water – their flesh dries on their bones but still they pullulate, copulate, and amass. (*Letters* 4: 195–6)

Rosenfeld states that even Leonard Woolf's short story 'Three Jews' suggests that British Jews in particular cannot completely assimilate because of their 'distinct, almost laughable ... even pathetic ... lack of magnetism in British ways' (83). The members of the group reproduced many of these associations, but the idea of a Jewish form or taste seemed to especially resonate with the Bloomsbury artists.

When Roger Fry's ideas about visual aesthetics began to influence the group, conversations often turned to art. Vanessa writes to Virginia about these discussions with Roger, Clive Bell, and Duncan Grant, and notes that 'none of us really agree with Leonard ... so your husband had better reconsider his position, I think' (137). This kind of debate and disagreement was typical of the group, but it is worth mentioning as an example of Leonard's differences, particularly when it comes to the ways in which they understood art and Jewishness. Leonard's parody of the Bloomsbury Group in *The Wise Virgins* hits close to home in a scene where the characters Wilton and Arthur evaluate Harry Davis, who is a painter:

> 'There has never been a good Jew artist, and there never will be.'
> 'Why not?'
> 'They're too like Davis – too cold and clammy and hard. They're just like crabs or lobsters. They give me the creeps.' (113)

For the Bloomsbury Group, Jewish form or taste was synonymous with stereotypes, particularly the idea that Jews overdressed, wore gaudy jewellery, and had exaggerated facial features. Lytton's descriptions of Jewish party guests often reduced Jews to comic material based on appearance. He writes about the publisher William Heinemann as 'a fascinating figure ... [a] more absolute jew face couldn't be imagined – bald-headed, goggle-eyed, thick-lipped; a fat short figure, with small legs ... a voice hardly English ... and all the time somehow, an element of the grotesque' (Holroyd 436). Virginia also focused on voice when she declared: 'I do not like the Jewish voice; I do not like the Jewish laugh' (*Diary* 1: 6).[2] The physical form, dress, and so-called voice of Jewishness was an affront to Bloomsbury sensibility.[3]

To the members of the Bloomsbury Group, if Jews did not adhere to stereotypical conceptions of Jewishness, they were out of place. In 'Jews', Woolf described Mrs. Loeb as having an essence that put her out of place in the socialite lifestyle. 'She might be behind a counter', Woolf wrote, instead of entertaining upper-class English guests (*Carlyle's House* 14). Lytton criticized *The Wise Virgins*, telling Henry Lamb that Leonard did not have the natural talent to be a novelist, and instead should 'be a camel merchant, slowly driving his beasts to market' (Glendinning, Foreword xiii). The members of the Bloomsbury Group repeated ideas of Jews as greedy shopkeepers or ancient wanderers, but they had a particular issue with the way that Jewishness encroached upon their ideas about art. Jewishness was equal to bad taste, and the idea of Jewish people as artists was somewhat absurd. This is in part because the conception of good art was intertwined with an idea of Englishness.

Leena Kore Schröder invokes Sartre's ideas about ingrained national antisemitism and points out that 'one does not have to espouse antisemitic opinions in order to be an antisemite; it is always already part of one's cultural and political unconscious' (30). Schröder analyses how Woolf's writing evinces a set of ideological values about England and Englishness of which, according to Schröder, Woolf is unaware. When Woolf writes nostalgically about the English countryside, Schröder argues, she reveals a 'conception of nation ... [that] also contains deep spaces of implicit antisemitism' (31). Schröder demonstrates these ideas by contrasting two stereotyped characters created by Woolf: Mrs. Loeb, who is Jewish, foreign and grotesque, with English Lady Bruton, who is refined and comfortable in her London home and the English countryside.

While Schröder claims that Woolf was not aware of the ways in which ideological values about Englishness peppered her work, I argue that she did begin to think about how attitudes about Jewishness affected art and culture. In introducing British culture to new artistic concepts about form, the Bloomsbury artists invited viewers to attach nostalgic associations about Englishness with good art. If these cultural values are already infused with antisemitism they may produce a negative association with non-English, or more specifically, Jewish form. Perpetuating English stereotypes in artistic form reinforces antisemitic conceptions of Jewishness, but it also works to erase any realistic Jewish perspective from new artistic movements, and by extension, from social consciousness. In other words, Bloomsbury art contributed to a climate of cultural antisemitism that allowed Nazism to flourish.

By the time she wrote *The Years*, Woolf considered her own writing and its relation to Jewishness and antisemitism, perhaps the way that E. M. Forster does in 'Jew-Consciousness'. His essay, published in 1939, amusedly studies the casual antisemite and reflects upon the antisemitism that he witnessed throughout his life. It also seems to be an acknowledgement of his own casual antisemitism. While the tone of the essay is somewhat light-hearted – the figure of the antisemite is humorous, and he refers to antisemitism as 'silliness' – Forster warns that '[antisemitism] is destroying much more than the Jews; it is assailing the human mind at its source, and inviting it to create false categories before exercising judgement' (12–14). Because Forster is writing to his peers and telling them how to take an intellectual approach to fighting prejudice, we might assume that the members of the Bloomsbury Group are among his intended audience. Were they ever motivated to examine their prejudices and acknowledge the connection between their attitudes and rise of Nazism? It does seem that by 1937 when Virginia Woolf published *The Years*, she was reflecting upon her own antisemitism.

Critics have identified tension in the ways in which Woolf wrote and spoke about Jews and Jewishness in the late 1930s. Again, Eberly observes how even in a brief forum on Woolf and Jews, scholars disagree about whether Woolf's antisemitism waned or intensified in the late thirties ('Responses' 17). As the Second World War and the threat of Nazism approached, Woolf did contemplate the reality of the life of a Jew in interwar Britain, and even identified with Jewishness and reflected upon her own antisemitism. But self-examination did not result in a more enlightened understanding of Jewishness. Rather, this analysis seemed to confirm the imperative to maintain a barrier between British Jews and gentiles, and resulted in Woolf's continued projection of negative thoughts and feelings onto the figure of the Jew and the idea of Jewishness. The most overt example of this is in *The Years*, when Sara and North Pargiter have an antisemitic conversation about Sara's Jewish neighbour Abrahamson. Linett observes that Woolf associates the body with Jews/Jewishness, and this physicality is opposed to the life of the mind ('Jews, Nazis' 2). In this scene, Sara connects having to share a bath with her Jewish neighbour to feeling forced to sacrifice her artistic integrity by joining the workforce and writing for money. Linett reads Sara's disgust toward Abrahamson's body as a reflection of Woolf's own resentment of Leonard, whose Jewishness was a liability as Nazism continued to spread ('The Jew in the Bath').

Woolf thinks about the ways in which being married to a Jew negatively affect her and expose her to danger. But it seems that she, like Forster, also broadly contemplates the connections between casual antisemitism in Britain and the rise of Nazism. In representing Sara as an antisemite who is coded as Jewish, Woolf uses Jewishness to represent her fears and express her disgust, but she also examines those feelings. She reflects upon the nature of antisemitism and how casual remarks that stem from ingrained prejudice are directly connected to Nazism.[4] In the scene, Sara and North both vilify Jews, but Sara and Abrahamson are also joined as mutual victims of North's gaze. His revulsion toward Abrahamson's Jewish body mirrors the contempt and disgust that he also feels for Sara. It is important that North is in the military; his conversation with Sara seems to be casually antisemitic, but the language and attitudes conveyed through his soldierly mannerisms imply state sanctioned and militarily enforced antisemitism.

Many critics have identified Sara as Woolf's surrogate and a way for Woolf to express antisemitic views that would otherwise be socially unacceptable, while others read Sara's attitudes as Woolf's attempt to distance herself from antisemitism.[5] Because Sara is an antisemite who is also aligned with Jewishness, it seems that Woolf uses Sara to voice Woolf's own antisemitism, but simultaneously distances herself in order to examine that behaviour. North's impression of Sara – that she hasn't changed and that 'she looked neither young nor old; but shabby' – recalls Woolf's comments about Jewish longevity and stubborn existence quoted earlier in this chapter. Linett notes that Woolf connects Jewishness to vitality and admires this quality, but also feels that there is something unnatural about it (*Modernism* 186). When North sees Sara for the first time after his return from Africa he is often uneasy in her presence, yet he seems to appreciate that although he had expected her to have aged she has not, for 'a plain face scarcely changed' (*The Years* 313). North again focuses on Sara's face when he realizes that she has a smudge on the side of her nose, a mark that may identify her with Jewishness (317).[6] While North contemplates possible reasons for why Sara never married and whether men have ever found her desirable, Sara refuses to look in the mirror and proceeds to conduct their dinner leaving the smudge in place. Not only does the presence of this greasy mark on Sara's face anticipate the conversation she is about to have with North about Abrahamson, the Jewish tallow trade worker who will leave 'a line of grease round the bath', but it also directly connects her to Abrahamson's smudged body, whose Jewishness marks him as an outsider just as Sara's status as an unmarried woman writer ostracizes her (339).

Again, Linett observes that Woolf connects Jewishness to bodily repulsiveness 'via images of vulgarity, fat, food, and heat' (*Modernism* 184). In the dinner scene, North does seem to dwell on the heat and low lighting in the room and on the nastiness of the meal that Sara provides, from the cheap table settings to the unappealing food, greasy tablecloth, and ornate pudding. Even before Abrahamson becomes a topic of conversation, Woolf invokes Jewishness. Sara's lodging house serves bloody mutton that night:

> They sat down and she took the carving-knife and made a long incision. A thin trickle of red juice ran out; it was underdone. She looked at it. 'Mutton oughtn't to be like that,' she said. 'Beef – but not mutton.' They watched the red juice running down into the well of the dish ... the rather stringy disagreeable object ... was still bleeding into the well. The willow-pattern plate was daubed with gory streaks. (*The Years* 318–21)

This recalls Woolf's description of the Jewish aristocrat Victor Rothschild as 'too butcher like in his red flesh, too thick cut, underdone, assertive' (*Diary* 4: 189–90). Lara Trubowitz thoroughly analyses Woolf's sketches of Rothschild and demonstrates how Woolf uses them to mark differences between Jewishness and Englishness: 'She depicts his flesh as red by evoking not only the blood-soaked clothing of the butcher's trade, but also the butcher's blood-soaked beef, which is now figuratively equated with Rothschild's own 'red' or butchered body' (126). To Woolf, Jewishness is coarse, monstrous, and animal-like, in contrast to refined, clean Englishness (see also Tromanhauser in this volume).

Although North likes Sara and has remained close with her throughout his travels in Africa, he cannot seem to separate her from the revulsion he feels for the way she eats, dresses, and resides. This detailed denigration of Sara makes her ensuing attack on Abrahamson seem almost ironic. To be sure, Sara is bigoted and cruel but North's judgments are also mean-spirited and hateful. There is no excuse for Sara's antisemitic reduction of Abrahamson to 'the Jew': '"The Jew," she murmured. "The Jew?" he said ... "The Jew having a bath" she said ... "And tomorrow there'll be a line of grease around the bath," she said. "Damn the Jew!" he exclaimed' (339). Sara and North agree in their objections to the Jewish body and their desire to dissociate from the Jew. But at the same time North is thinking about how Abrahamson's hairs in the bath repulse him, he says to himself: 'Hairs in food, hairs on basins, other people's hairs make him feel physically sick' (340). The immediate conversation is about the Jew, but the meal North just shared was with Sara, whose 'manner irritated him' and whose food, although not necessarily hair-infested was sickening enough with its yellowed, gravy-stained tablecloth and its 'slabbed-down mass of cabbage in one oozing green water' (314–38). North looks at the way Sara eats a 'fly-blown' banana and describes the fruit as 'the finger of a glove that had been ripped open' (322–3). North's repulsion with the meal and anger toward Sara not only echoes the feelings about Abrahamson, but also joins Sara and Abrahamson as the objects of North's contempt.

Again, Sara and North express hate and disgust in this scene, but they react differently to these feelings. North has been angry since he arrived; he is repulsed by Sara's impoverished lifestyle and annoyed by the interruptions to their conversation. He curses several times, viciously kicks the heat fender, and tries to control his temper when Sara becomes distracted while telling the story of her interview with the man in the newspaper office. She gets side-tracked and trails off, lost in her thoughts: '"But the Jew's in my bath, I said – the Jew ... the Jew..." She stopped suddenly and emptied her glass.' As a character, Sara has a tendency to be a bit flighty, but at this moment she is thoughtful and reflecting upon her words. North watches her and thinks:

> Yes ... there's the voice; there's the attitude; and the reflection in other people's faces; but then there's something true – in the silence perhaps ... 'How much of that was true?' he asked her. But she had lapsed into silence. The actual words he supposed ... had created yet another person; another semblance, which one must solidify into one whole' (342).

Because she is already aligned with Jewishness, Sara's contemplation of what she is saying about 'the Jew' suggests that these 'actual words ... [that] had created yet another person' were two sides of Sara – one who makes antisemitic remarks, and one who connects with Jews and Jewishness. Sara and North love each other and think similarly, but Sara is also vulnerable to North's anger and contempt. While both characters speak the same antisemitic slurs, the text implies that Sara feels the effects of the very prejudice she espouses, while North brings those attitudes to his position in the military where he (in theory) has the power to inflict them upon others.

It is the contrast between Sara's casual antisemitism and North's military presence that suggests a moment of self-reflection about how the English citizen's offhand remarks about Jews might relate to fascist oppression. Woolf identifies with Sara, and it makes sense that she would reflect upon the complexity of her feelings about Jewishness during a time in which she was beginning to understand what it was like to be Jewish. Her diary entries reveal her close attention to Hitler's progress and to her awareness of the Woolf family's anxieties about their position as Jews: 'Jews persecuted, only just over the Channel ... The Jews obsess' (*Diary 5*: 189, 191). When the Woolfs travelled through Europe in 1935 they were advised by the British foreign office to avoid Nazi processions in case Leonard was identified as Jewish (Trubowitz 113–14). In making Sara an antisemitic English woman who is also coded as a Jewish victim of North's hatred, Woolf is thinking about how English attitudes toward Jews contributed to the spread of Nazi violence. Like Forster, Woolf had begun to reflect upon the antisemitism in her personal environment and its broader effect on the nation. But because she went no further in making this connection, and never made a definitive statement condemning it, she only verified the connection between Bloomsbury and antisemitism.

Perhaps, as Phyllis Lassner claims, Woolf abandoned any sympathy for and disavowed any personal identification with the Jewish outsider when the violent realities of war threatened that alliance (135). Maybe the members of the Bloomsbury Group could not renounce antisemitism because their artistic philosophies depended too much on opposing Jewishness, or perhaps their nostalgia for pure Englishness meant that they accepted their prejudices as part of their identity. Asking these questions allows us to better understand the pervasiveness of antisemitism and hostility to Jewishness in the Bloomsbury Group and consider how their philosophies shaped their art and contributed to their legacy.

NOTES

1. Again, Virginia, Lytton, and Vanessa knew that Leonard, who assimilated, was a different type of Jewish person than his mother, who did not necessarily practice Judaism but was culturally Jewish.
2. See Linett for analysis of how Woolf describes Jewish form in her writing, particularly Mrs. Loeb in 'Jews' (*Modernism* 184).
3. Jewishness itself may have been considered bad form and aesthetically unpleasant, but Jews could appreciate (and afford) good art. The Bloomsbury painters respected Gertrude Stein's opinion and admired her collection, along with the collections of her brothers Leo and Michael. Marie Woolf attended art shows all over London, and Vanessa wrote to Duncan, who was looking to sell his work: 'I suppose you had better see Lady H. de W. [Margherita, Lady Howard de Walden] Roger doesn't know her. He thinks she's a Jew, in which case she may have good taste' (*Letters* 206). It seems that some Jews had the taste to recognize and purchase high-quality art, but could not inspire or produce it.
4. David Bradshaw also argues that Sara is coded as Jewish in 'Hyams Place'.
5. Including Bradshaw, who claims that Woolf uses Sara to vilify antisemitism and distance Sara's views from her own, whereas Linett argues that Woolf uses Sara as a mouthpiece for her own antisemitism.
6. The smudge is noticeably on the side of Sara's nose, an image which calls to mind Oliver Bacon from 'The Duchess and the Jeweller'. 'When he pass[ed] through the knots of jewellers in the hot evening who were discussing prices ... one of them would lay a finger to the side of his nose and murmur, "Hum – m – m," as he passed. It was no more than a murmur ... a finger on the nose' (248–9). Trubowitz parses this passage and offers several possibilities for the gesture, including 'the non-Jew's code or shorthand for Bacon's Jewishness ... when the jeweler 'lay[s] a finger' on his own nose, he is informing his fellow non-Jewish jewelers that a Jew is in their midst' (116–17).

WORKS CITED

Bell, Vanessa. *Selected Letters of Vanessa Bell*. Ed. Regina Marler. New York: Pantheon
     Books, 1993.

Blair, Sara. 'Local Modernity, Global Modernism: Bloomsbury and the Places of the Literary'.
     English Literary History 71.3 (2004): 813–38.

Bradshaw, David. 'Hyams Place: *The Years*, the Jews and the British Union of Fascists'.
     Women Writers of the 1930s: Gender, Politics and History. Ed. Maroula Joannou.
     Edinburgh: Edinburgh UP, 1999. 179–91.

Delany, Paul. *The Neo-Pagans: Rupert Brooke and the Ordeal of Youth*. New York: Free
     Press, 1987.

Eberly, David. Forum: Virginia Woolf and Jews. *Woolf Studies Annual* 19 (2013): 17–18.

Forster, E. M. 'Jew-Consciousness'. *Two Cheers for Democracy*. London: Edward Arnold,
     1972. 12–14.

Glendinning, Victoria. 'Foreword'. *The Wise Virgins* by Leonard Woolf. New Haven: Yale UP,
     2007. vii–xiv.

Glendinning, Victoria. *Leonard Woolf: A Biography*. New York: Free Press, 2006.

Ho, Janice. 'Jewishness in the Colonies of Leonard Woolf's *The Village in the Jungle*'. *Modern
     Fiction Studies* 59.4 (2013): 713–41.

Holroyd, Michael. *Lytton Strachey: The New Biography*. New York: Farrar, Straus, &
     Giroux, 1995.

Lassner, Phyllis. '"The Milk of Our Mother's Kindness Has Ceased to Flow": Virginia
     Woolf, Stevie Smith, and the Representation of the Jew'. *Between 'Race' and
     Culture: Representations of 'the Jew' in English and American Literature*. Ed. Bryan
     Cheyette. Stanford: Stanford UP, 1996. 129–44.

Lee, Hermione. *Virginia Woolf*. New York: Knopf, 1997.

Linett, Maren. 'The Jew in the Bath: Imperiled Imagination in Woolf's *The Years*'. *Modern
     Fiction Studies* 48.2 (2005): 341–61.

Linett, Maren. *Modernism, Feminism, and Jewishness*. Cambridge: Cambridge UP, 2007.

Linett, Maren. '"What'll He Gobble Next?" Jews, Nazis and Bodily Excess in Virginia Woolf's
     1930s Writing'. Forum: Virginia Woolf and Jews. *Woolf Studies Annual* 19 (2013): 1–3.

Rosenfeld, Natania. *Outsiders Together: Virginia and Leonard Woolf*. New Jersey: Princeton
     UP, 2000.

Schröder, Leena Kore. '"A Question Is Asked Which Is Never Answered": Virginia Woolf,
     Englishness, and Antisemitism'. *Woolf Studies Annual* 19 (2013): 27–57.

Trubowitz, Lara. *Civil Antisemitism, Modernism, and British Culture, 1902–1939*.
     New York: Palgrave Macmillan, 2012.

Trubowitz, Lara, David Eberly, Alice Keane, Maren Linett, Beth C. Rosenberg, Christina L.
     Svendsen, Natania Rosenfeld. 'Responses'. Forum: Virginia Woolf and Jews. *Woolf Studies
     Annual* 19 (2013): 16–25.

Woolf, Leonard. *The Journey Not the Arrival Matters: An Autobiography of the Years 1939–
     1969*. New York: Harcourt Brace Jovanovich, 1989.

Woolf, Leonard. *Letters of Leonard Woolf*. Ed. Frederic Spotts. San Diego: Harcourt Brace
     Jovanovich, 1989.

Woolf, Leonard. *The Wise Virgins*. New Haven: Yale UP, 2007.

Woolf, Virginia. *Carlyle's House and Other Sketches*. Ed. David Bradshaw. London: Hesperus
     Press, 2003.

Woolf, Virginia. *The Diary of Virginia Woolf*, 5 vols. Ed. Anne Olivier Bell. San Diego: Harcourt Brace, 1977–84.

Woolf, Virginia. 'The Duchess and the Jeweller'. *The Complete Shorter Fiction of Virginia Woolf*. Ed. and Intro. Susan Dick. San Diego: Harcourt Brace, 1989. 248–53.

Woolf, Virginia. *The Letters of Virginia Woolf*, 6 vols. Ed. Nigel Nicolson and Joanne Trautmann. New York: Harcourt Brace Jovanovich, 1975–80.

Woolf, Virginia. *Moments of Being*. Ed. Jeanne Schulkind. New York: Mariner Books, 1985.

Woolf, Virginia. *The Years*. New York: Harcourt, Brace, 1937.

Case Study: Leonard Woolf and John Maynard Keynes: Palestine, Zionism, and the State of Israel

STEVEN PUTZEL

The second of November 2017 marked the hundredth anniversary of the 'Balfour Declaration', which paved the way for 'the establishment in Palestine of a national home for the Jewish people'. In a mere 125 words, this document profoundly affected the outcome of the First World War, the ill-fated Treaty of Versailles, decades of British and French policy in former Ottoman Empire territory, the eventual formation of the state of Israel, and the ongoing conflict between Israelis and the Palestinians. Leonard Woolf and John Maynard Keynes were deeply involved in the question of Palestine, though not always in agreement with each other. Their writings on Jewishness, Palestine, and Zionism provide a glimpse into Bloomsbury's complex views of race, religion, and geopolitical decisions that would reshape the Middle East and lead to conflicts still raging today. Keynes, arguably the most influential economist of the twentieth century, was notoriously antisemitic, yet supported the Balfour Declaration and Zionism. Woolf, though Jewish himself, saw the Declaration as dangerous and ill-advised, and identified himself as non-Zionist. Keynes and Woolf would be among the most eloquent voices for progressive ideas in the decades following the Balfour agreement, though Keynes would remain faithful to the Liberal Party, while Woolf worked behind the scenes to forge Labour's international policies. After the Conservatives defeated the minority Labour government and left the Liberal Party devastated in the 1924 elections, Woolf told Lydia Lopokova, 'Maynard must become Labour' (Hill 243). Keynes responded with an article in the Nation and Athenaeum (1925), 'Am I a Liberal', in which he rejects the Conservatives but fears that Labour is controlled by Leftists whom he labels, 'the party of catastrophe' (Collected 9: 297). Both Woolf and Keynes believed in internationalism over nationalism – Woolf through his strong support of the League of Nations and Keynes through his Economic Consequences of the Peace (1919) (see Ayers and Goldman in this volume) and the voluminous political and economic treatises that followed.

Political economists have long struggled to reconcile the Keynes who privately employed Shylock stereotypes, used terms such as 'Jew-boy', 'imps', and 'serving devils' (Collected 10: 382–4) with the progressive economist who collaborated with Zionists after the First World War and helped Jewish intellectuals flee Germany before the second. Melvin Reder in 'The Anti-Semitism of Some Eminent Economists' includes Keynes along with Joseph Schumpeter and Friedrich von Hayek, dismissing the oft-repeated defence that 'their disparaging comments about Jews were a product of the time and place of utterance and should not be judged by the more delicate sensibilities of educated people in the early twenty-first century' (Reder 849). Instead he argues that Keynes's antisemitism was endemic, expressing a deeply seated class hatred. Leonard Woolf was acceptable as a 'marriage partner for Virginia Stephen' and as a member of the Apostles because he did not fit the stereotype and because his non-Jewish education at St. Paul's and Cambridge made him an exception (840–41). As we will see, Woolf learned early in life to suppress, though not deny, his 'Jewishness', to thrive and win acceptance at Cambridge and in Bloomsbury, though he would always see himself as an outsider, self-identified as the wandering Jew.

A history of Keynes's antisemitism begins long before Bloomsbury soirees or even his interaction with the Cambridge Apostles. An essay examining 'The Differences between East and West: Will They Ever Disappear', penned when he was a seventeen-year-old at Eton, disparages the 'Orientals', that is, Jews and Chinese. It is difficult for anyone with any sensibilities whether delicate or not to read: 'It is not that the Jews are traditionally the accursed race that makes anti-semites [sic], it is because they have in them deep-rooted instincts that are antagonistic and therefore repulsive to the European, and their presence amongst us is a living example of the insurmountable difficulties, in making cats love dogs' (Chandavarkar 1619).

Keynes never outgrew this visceral dislike of Jewishness, though, Jews, like Leonard Woolf, who did not fit the stereotype, could be acceptable, even laudable. For example, writing about fellow participants of the Versailles Peace Conference of 1919 in his essay 'Dr. Melchior: a Defeated Enemy', Keynes speaks glowingly of the German, Carl Melchior: 'this Jew, for such, though not by appearance, I afterwards learnt him to be, and he only, upheld the dignity of defeat' (*Collected* 10: 403). He adds that he understood 'what a precisian he was, a strict and upright moralist, a worshipper of the Tablets of the Law, a Rabbi' (*Collected* 10:428). In the same memoir Keynes describes Klotz, the French minister of finance as 'a short, plump, heavy-moustached Jew … prating of his "goold"' and who projected 'the image of a hideous Jew clutching a money bag' (10: 422). S. P. Rosenbaum briefly mentions 'Leonard Woolf sitting among his auditors at the Memoir Club' (93) listening to these antisemitic remarks, but there is no record of any response.

A selection of letters between Keynes and Lydia Lopokova between 1918 and 1925 provides a candid view of the couple's casual antisemitism. On 27 April 1922 Lydia responds to a letter from Keynes not included in the volume: 'What a description of Litvinoff, and Jews are Jews, very funny' (Hill 40). On 25 October 1923 Lydia writes: 'Do you like to hear quotations? "Jew: a man who kills 2 birds with 1 stone and then wants the stone back"' (Hill 115). On 16 November 1924 Maynard writes that he is 'a little sad at the death of Edwin Montagu', his Cambridge mentor to whom Keynes owed 'nearly all [his] steps up in life'. After a moving eulogy, Keynes adds 'But he had a big talent in his way; one of the Jews of divided nature – half artist and lover, and half consumed with extravagant desires and ambitions' (Hill 256). Even when eulogizing this friend and mentor, Keynes finds it necessary to demonstrate that Montagu deserves praise *despite* his unpleasant Jewish physiognomy and mannerisms. In her reply to Keynes's Montagu letter, Lydia mentions a meeting with Virginia and Leonard noting affectionately that Leonard is the 'sensible man in Bloomsbury' (Hill 257). Despite their common banter targeting Jews and Jewishness, neither Keynes nor Lydia notes Leonard's Jewishness. He, like Montagu, is the exceptionable Jew. Although Lydia's slurs usually are not particularly political, one observation she makes on 4 November 1923 directly relates to Palestine and the implementation of the Balfour Declaration: 'also we spoke about the zionist [sic] movement, how unjust it was towards the arabs [sic] and that English government should clear out or send a pure English man but not a Jew. I agreed' (Hill 121). In other words, a British diplomat who is Jewish is not entirely English.

Perhaps the most controversial and thus most commonly quoted criticism of what some perceive as Keynes's virulent antisemitism stems from Keynes's short character sketch of Albert Einstein. The sketch, written for presentation to the Memoir Club, was found among his papers under the title 'My Visit to Berlin, 22 June 1926', first published 'in the *New Statesman* in the 21 October 1933 edition' (Weintraub 43) and later included in the *Collected Writings* under the title 'Einstein'. The sketch begins:

> I, who have seen Einstein, have to record something apparently – perhaps not really different – that is 'a naughty boy', a naughty Jew-boy, covered with ink, pulling a long nose as the world kicks his bottom; a sweet imp, pure and giggling. It is obvious that literally he has had his bottom many times kicked, that he expects it.

Keynes adds, 'He is that kind of Jew – the kind which rarely has its head above water, the sweet, tender imps who have not sublimated immortality into compound interest' (*Collected* 10: 382–3). We can sense the Bloomsbury Memoir Club audience relishing both the expected Jewish stereotypes and the playful homoeroticism of Keynes's language. Before concluding that 'he was the nicest, and the only talented person I saw in all Berlin', he interjects 'I had indeed had a little flirt with him' (10: 383). If Keynes had left his memoir there, perhaps commentators would dismiss the antisemitism has harmless playfulness, but Keynes comes back to Einstein's Jewishness, linking him to three other German Jews, Carl Fürstenberg, Kurt Singer, and Carl Melchior – all of whom Keynes liked and respected. He adds:

> Yet if I lived there, I felt I might turn anti-Semite. For the poor Prussian is too slow and heavy on his legs for the other kind of Jews, the ones who are not imps but serving devils, with small horns, pitch forks, and oily tails. It is not agreeable to see a civilisation so under the ugly thumbs of its impure Jews who have all the money and the power and the brains. (10: 384)

Leonard Woolf would have been spared this performance since he and Virginia were visiting Ottoline Morrell in Garsington, Oxfordshire (V. Woolf, *Letters* 3: 278). Weintraub quotes from a correspondence between Keynes's biographer, Robert Skidelsky, and the economist Don Patinkin to condemn Keynes's use of the term 'Jew-boy' as well as his perpetuation of antisemitic stereotypes. We can hear the fury in Patinkin's words:

> If your interpretation of Keynes's *New Statesman* article is correct, then it is really scandalous for by October 1933, the dictatorial and violently anti-Semitic nature of the Nazi regime was evident for all to see. After all, why had Einstein left Germany for England? ... So I think this article is even worse than Keynes's morally insensitive preface to the German edition of the *General Theory*. (Weintraub 45)

The problem with this line of attack is that Patinkin, Skidelsky, Weintraub, and others never bothered reading Keynes's actual *New Statesman* article, relying instead on Keynes's 1926 essay for the Memoir Club, an essay Keynes never himself published.

When asked to provide a word-sketch to accompany David Low's caricature of Einstein for *The New Statesmen*, Keynes obviously went back to his Memoir Club essay. But 1933 was not 1926, the Nazis were ascendant in Germany, Jews like Einstein and Freud were fleeing to countries willing to take them, and Keynes was writing in a public forum, rather than to his fellow Bloomsburians. Gone is the term 'Jew-boy', and gone are the ugly stereotypes. Here is part of what Keynes actually wrote for the *New Statesmen*:

> The boys, who cannot grow up to adult human nature, are beating the prophets of the ancient race – Marx, Freud, Einstein – who have been tearing at our social, personal and intellectual roots, tearing them with an objectivity which to the healthy animal seems morbid, depriving everything, as it seems, of warmth of natural feeling ... So it is not an accident that the Nazi lads vent a particular fury against him. He does truly stand for what they most dislike, the opposite of the blond beast – intellectualist, individualist, supernationalist, pacifist, inky, plump. ('Einstein' 481)

What accounts for a 180-degree change in tone and substance – from the blatantly antisemitic 1926 memoir to the eloquently anti-Nazi? Partly this is the difference between Keynes the Bloomsburian, perpetuating the antisemitic British middle-class prejudice and stereotypes and Keynes the world-renowned economist and public figure. The starkness of the change, however, reflects the stark changes occurring in Europe in the seven intervening years.

Arguing that Keynes was actually a 'Zionist Philo-Semite', Anand Chandavarkar points out the irony that though Keynes's antisemitic remarks have received wide dissemination, his 'support for Zionism has been completely ignored', adding

> it is hardly known that Keynes was the only non-Jewish member of a high-powered advisory committee under the chairmanship of Herbert Samuel which prepared the preliminary draft report for presentation of the Zionist case for a Jewish national home in Palestine, for the Peace Conference in Paris on February 23, 1919 ... Keynes's acceptance of the membership of a high-powered Zionist committee, which prepared the ground for the Balfour Declaration is prima facie testimony of his sympathy for the Zionist cause, long before it became fashionable with the advent of institutionalised persecution of Jews in Germany and Austria. (Chandavarkar 1622)

This would be impressive if it were true. Chandavarkar and others drawing on his article were misled by Chaim Weizmann's inclusion of Keynes's name on the advisory committee that drafted the Zionist Commission's 'case for the Peace Conference' (Weizmann 243). Keynes did not participate in drafting the Balfour Declaration – a complex two-year process of US–British negotiation. Keynes was, of course, a British representative to the Paris Peace Conference of 1919. After he resigned from the British Delegation he accepted Herbert Samuel's invitation to join the Financial Advisory Committee, a subcommittee of Samuel's 1919 Advisory Committee on Economic Development, but Keynes attended only two of the six meetings, although he did sign the final report. His main contribution seems to have been to support Samuel's idea that the Zionist banks be under the control of the World Zionist Organization and the establishment of a Mortgage Bank of Palestine (Gross 15).

Keynes's *Economic Consequences of the Peace* (1919) is a powerful indictment of the Paris treaty, especially the terms of German reparations, but it says nothing about the break-up of the Ottoman Empire and the Mandatory system that made the League of Nations responsible for overseeing Palestine and the rest of the Middle East. Keynes represented the British Treasury at the Paris Peace Conference until he resigned in protest over the terms of reparation. In a 30 November 1918 diary entry Virginia enthusiastically writes: 'But the real news of the past week is of a confidential nature. [Gilbert] Murray has asked L. to be his secretary if, as is possible, he is chosen to represent England on the League of Nations Committee at the Peace Conference. This would mean a visit to Paris. More than this need not be said; but it is an important possibility' (*Diary* 1: 221). Murray was not a delegate, though he was later Chairman of the Executive Committee of the League. Though he did not attend the Peace Conference, and Virginia did not get her trip to Paris, Leonard was just as involved with the aftermath of the war as Keynes. Woolf's position as Secretary to the Labour Party Committee on Imperial Affairs and the Committee on International Affairs, his dedication to the League of Nations and the concept of international government, his research for his book *Framework of a Lasting Peace* (1917), and his position as editor of *The International Review*, *The Contemporary Review*, and *Political Quarterly*, as well as his regular contributions to *The New Statesman and Nation* – not to mention that he was Jewish himself – kept him close to the problem of Palestine throughout his life. Woolf remained deeply concerned with Palestine and Israel into the 1960s.

For Woolf, the debate over the fate of Palestine began in the early years of the First World War with Jewish intellectuals and political activists split into two main groups, Assimilationists and Zionists. The Ottoman Empire, which belatedly joined the Axis Powers, controlled the Middle East. Consequently, the British government viewed both Arab groups and international Jewish groups as essential allies in the war against Turkey. In May 1916 France and Great Britain signed the secret Sykes-Picot Treaty, which stipulated that after the war France would control Syria and much of what is now Lebanon while Britain would control central and southern Mesopotamia. Palestine would be under international administration. Chaim Weizmann established a political committee that included the foreign office's Mark Sykes, co-author of the Franco British treaty, Norman Bentwich (Leonard Woolf's old St. Paul's schoolmate), two representatives of the Rothschild banking dynasty, and other prominent international Zionist intellectuals.

On 18 July 1917, they presented a draft declaration to Lord Arthur Balfour. Keynes's mentor Edwin Montagu, Secretary of State for India, who, like Woolf, was an assimilationist Jew, convinced Balfour and the committee to amend the wording. Both versions recognize Palestine as the 'National Home' for the Jewish people, but the draft would grant 'internal autonomy to the Jewish nationality in Palestine, freedom of immigration for Jews, and the establishment of a Jewish National Colonizing Corporation [under the direction of the Zionist Organization] for the re-establishment and economic development of the country' (Weizmann 203). The final Declaration, issued 17 November 1917, stated that the British government would 'use their best endeavours to facilitate the achievement' of this Jewish national home, but with the key caveat: 'it being clearly understood that nothing shall be done which may prejudice the civil and religious rights of existing non-Jewish communities in Palestine, or the rights and political status enjoyed by Jews in any other country' (Schneer 341). For Woolf, as for Montagu and Keynes, it was essential that implementation of the Balfour Declaration would neither interfere with the assimilation of European Jews nor reduce the rights of the Arab majority population of Palestine. Both Woolf and Keynes would, in their own ways, see Britain's failure to fulfil this promise of Arab rights as a cause of the intractable conflict between Arabs and Jews throughout the Mandate years and after.

At the end of the war the British military occupied the former Ottoman-controlled Palestine, until the Council of the League of Nations officially created the British Mandatory of Palestine in July 1922, which was to set up limited self-governance and implement the terms of the Balfour Declaration. Woolf's pamphlet *Scope of the Mandates Under the League of Nations* (1920) outlines and analyses Article 22 of Part I of the Treaty of Peace with Germany, and demonstrates that the implicit imperialism of the wartime Sykes-Picot Agreement which outlined Britain's determination to control the region's oil reserves would make implementation of the Balfour Declaration impossible. The pamphlet stipulates that the Mandatory system 'makes a complete break with the previous methods of Imperialism and the old status of subject races' (*Scope* 3). In other words, the Mandatories, when named, would be trustees of the League of Nations and would serve the territories rather than their own self-interests. Article 22 makes clear that in the case of the Ottoman territories 'their existence as independent nations' is to be 'provisionally recognized subject to the rendering of administrative advice and assistance by a Mandatory' (*Scope* 7). Woolf certainly has Palestine in mind when he adds:

> If the idea behind these Class A mandates were loyally worked out, there might be a fair hope of prosperity and peace in the Near East. The Near East is inhabited by many races, but ... they are torn by racial animosities and by reaction against European penetration and exploitation ... They desire to be recognized as independent nations. (*Scope* 7)

Woolf's 1 May 1920 essay 'Article XXII' in the *New Statesman*, written after the United Kingdom was named Mandatory for Palestine, recognizes the 'dangerous character of the Middle Eastern problem' and that the UK's violation of at least one of the provisions of the Article already endangered the future of the region. Britain was meant to offer administrative 'advice and assistance' to Palestine as an 'independent nation', but Palestine was not meant to become 'the pawn of the predatory imperialisms' ('Article XXII' 94). The victorious British and French governments, Woolf tells us, intended to apply the Sykes-Picot Agreement of 1916 that would give Britain access to and control over the oil in the region – thus rendering Article 22 meaningless. Woolf warns that if the British do not abide by the League's Mandatory system, there will be 'perpetual trouble, ending possibly, or probably, in a blaze which it will tax all our military resources to extinguish' ('Article XXII' 95).

We get a clearer understanding of Woolf's view of Palestine and its people – both Arab and Jew – with his description in *Beginning Again* of the Russian translator and Ukrainian Jew, S. S. Koteliansky (Kot), whom he met at the 1917 Labour Party Conference. When Leonard and Virginia invited Kot along with the Jewish painter Mark Gertler to Asheham the topic of discussion was 'Jews, Judaism, the relation of Jews to other people, their differences, their faults, and virtues' (Glendinning 198). Some of this talk finds its way into the autobiography. For example: 'There are some Jews who, though their ancestors have lived for centuries in European ghettoes, are born with certain characteristics which the sun and sand of the desert beat into the bodies and minds of Semites' (*Beginning* 249). Woolf adds, 'I have felt the same qualities of steely, repressed, purged passion, burnt into a Semite by sun and sand, in an ordinary Arab pearl diver from the Persian Gulf.' Woolf listened as this man eulogized a dead comrade, noting, 'it was in Arabic and I did not understand a word, and yet I understood every word. It was Isaiah and Jeremiah and Job – and Kot' (*Beginning* 249–50). In other words, Arabs and Jews are Semitic cousins, a truth that was at the core of Leonard's hope for Palestine.

The question of Palestine and Zionism and the relationship between Arabs and Jews was not a major discussion point in Bloomsbury's Memoir Club, but it certainly was in the 1917 Club, founded by Leonard Woolf, Ramsay MacDonald, Oliver Strachey, and other socialists and Labour Party members (*Beginning* 215). Dozens of references in Virginia's diaries and letters demonstrate that this was a favourite haunt of Bloomsbury artists and writers. Though a Liberal, Keynes, too, frequented the club (*Diary* 1: 139); Glendinning even claims that Keynes partly financed the Gerrard Street (Soho) premises (192). Two years before his first stint as Prime Minister, MacDonald published *A Socialist in Palestine* (1922), in which he describes his own experience in Palestine and outlines a view almost identical to Woolf's. Both recognize the inevitability of 'friction in adjusting Arab and Jew into one community', adding, 'a policy which, whilst keeping Palestine open to a Jewish "return", not only protects an Arab in his rights but sees that he shares amply in the increased prosperity of the country, is certainly not doomed to failure' (MacDonald 21).

Although Leonard Woolf avoided reference to his own Jewishness in his Labour Party work, his comments on his friend Kot, the autobiographical nature of *The Wise Virgins* (1914), his identification with 'the Wandering Jew', and his story 'Three Jews' (1917) demonstrate that he was fully aware of his position as outsider in the rarefied waspish atmosphere of Bloomsbury (see Wegener in this volume). In reference to her interview with Trekkie Parsons, Leonard's long-term companion and executrix, Freema Gottlieb writes: 'Mrs. Parsons told me that Leonard had often confessed to her that his Jewishness had only really began to matter to him, in a negative way, because of Virginia's antisemitism in the early days of their marriage' (Gottlieb 25). In the last volume of his autobiography Woolf recalled the antisemitism he experienced at St. Paul's where he first 'heard the word "swot", – "he's a bloody" or "he's a dirty swot"' (*Journey* 129).[1] Anthony Julius cites examples of representative Bloomsbury Jewish insults: 'In general chatter, at a Bloomsbury circle gathering, a question was asked, addressed to all those assembled. A pause. And then, loudly, Virginia Woolf instructed, pointing to her husband, Leonard: "Let the Jew answer." To which Leonard replied: "I won't until you ask properly"' (Julius 365). Gottlieb and many others have explored Woolf's *roman à clef, The Wise Virgins* (1914), with its unflattering portrait of his mother (Mrs. Davis) and its ambivalent attitude towards Harry, Woolf's antiheroic counterpart. Harry's passive-aggressive presentation of his 'Jewishness' to his lovers Camilla and Gwen is particularly notable in relation to Woolf's own courtship of Virginia. According to Harry, Jews 'wait hunched up, always ready and alert, for the moment to spring on what is worth while, then we let ourselves go' (*Wise Virgins* 110). When Camilla asks him what is worthwhile, his answer is racial caricature. ' "Money," he said, "money, of course. That's the first article of our creed – money, and out of money, power. That's elementary. Then knowledge, intelligence, taste"' (111). During his less enthusiastic courtship of Gwen (whom he eventually marries) Harry identifies himself as 'the wandering Jew, the everlasting Jew' (194). When Gwen tells him she doesn't like him calling himself 'that', he responds, 'Jew? Why not? I am one, and proud of it too. And the everlasting one. And the point of him is, you know, that there never is any kingdom for him to find' (195). Although the novel may seem to perpetuate the very Jewish stereotypes that Woolf encountered at St. Paul's and later in Bloomsbury, Harry voices the frustrations, loneliness, and pride of the educated semi-assimilated Jew in Britain – something Woolf would not express directly until he wrote his autobiography.

As the debate between Zionists and Assimilationists raged, Woolf wrote 'Three Jews' (1917). Although Leena Kore-Schröder places 'Three Jews' in the context of antisemitism in Britain during the First World War, and in the context of Woolf's marriage to a non-Jew (314), what may be more directly significant to our understanding of this short story is Woolf's involvement with Labour Party politics, the wartime coalition government's flirtation with both Jewish Assimilationists and Zionists, and the resulting 1917 Balfour Declaration. In Leonard's story, the second Jew, who, like the first, is a religious sceptic, notes that the beautiful English day in Kew Gardens 'doesn't belong to us', adding 'we belong to Palestine still, but I'm not sure that it doesn't belong to us for all that' ('Three Jews' 5). This line takes on a more topical, political resonance when we remember that the negotiations that would result in the Balfour Declaration were already well underway. This one line, with its intentional ambiguity, gets to the heart of the Zionist debate, to the relationship between Jews of the diaspora and the holy land. Is Palestine a future homeland or is Palestine at the core of every wandering Jew?

Throughout the 1920s Woolf remained adamantly non-Zionist. Looking back in *The Journey Not the Arrival Matters*, Woolf recalls a two-hour meeting in 1921 with the influential and persuasive Chaim Weizmann, President of the World Zionist Organization (185). As head of the British Admiralty laboratories during the First Word War, Weizmann had developed the process of industrial fermentation to cheaply produce large quantities of acetone, a key ingredient in the cordite used in munitions (Weizmann 172). This work helped Weizmann gain access to David Lloyd George, Prime Minister of the Wartime Coalition Government, as well as to President Wilson. Woolf explains that even Weizmann could not 'convert' him:

> I think that the whole of history shows that the savage xenophobia of human beings is so great that the introduction into any populated country of a large racial, economic, religious, or cultured minority always leads to hatred, violence, and political and social disaster. ... That was why I thought originally that the Balfour Declaration and the introduction of a Jewish minority and a Jewish state in a country inhabited by a large Arab population was politically dangerous. (*Journey* 185–6)

Weizmann had, in fact, co-opted and redefined the concept of Zionism. As Noam Pianko demonstrates in *Zionism: The Roads Not Taken*, Zionism was historically an intellectual, religious, cultural, and internationalist idea, rather than a fanatically nationalistic political movement exclusively focused on creating a Jewish homeland in Palestine. In other words, Jews like Woolf who disagree with Weizmann's narrowly nationalistic Zionism, as well as antisemitic or philosemitic non-Jews like Keynes could support this broader view of Zionism. Pianko analyses Zionism as defined by Simon Rawidowicz, Mordecai Kaplan, and Hans Kohn, demonstrating its deep moral, scholarly, and global roots. Kaplan, in particular, was critical of Weizmann's linkage of Jewishness with national sovereignty, criticizing his 'imperialistic attitude' and his reference to the Mediterranean as 'a Jewish sea' (Pianko 128). Kaplan, like Woolf, blamed Weizmann's brand of Zionism for the Arab riots of 1929, lamenting that the Balfour Declaration 'has been like a foreign body in the system of Jewish revival, causing irritation and liable to set up a dangerous poison' (Pianko 128). Weizmann successfully redefined non-Zionism as anti-Zionism and rendered 'assimilationist', a category in which he placed Leonard Woolf, a pejorative term. By 2010, Anthony Julius, in his monumental *Trials of the Diaspora*, comes very close to equating 'the new Anti-Zionist' with antisemitism.[2]

In the first British census of Palestine (1922) the population was 757,182 with 11 per cent of the population Jewish, in 1930 it was 1,035,154 with 17 per cent Jewish. The estimated population in 1948 was nearly 2,000,000 with 33 per cent Jewish. After the

UN-sponsored partition granting about 56 per cent of the former Mandatory of Palestine to Israel and 43 per cent to the Arabs (Jerusalem was international), the population of Israel was 873,000, 82 per cent of which was Jewish. Considering these statistics, it is not surprising that the British Mandate spelled trouble from the start. After the 1929 Arab riots, the British government began recommending limitations on Jewish immigration. In 1930, during the second Labour government, Ramsay MacDonald's Secretary of State for the Colonies, Lord Passfield (Sidney Webb), issued 'The Passfield White Paper' (1930) limiting Jewish immigration and thus preserving the Arab majority in Palestine. After heavy protest from the international Jewish community, the Prime Minister wrote what came to be known as 'The MacDonald Letter' to Chaim Weizmann (1931), insuring that Jews who could find work would be allowed to immigrate. Arabs were now furious, dubbing it the 'Black Letter'. Woolf, as Secretary of the Labour advisory committees on foreign and imperial affairs supported Webb's White Paper and favoured some restrictions on Jewish immigration. Woolf makes his views on this controversy clear in a 1932 *Political Quarterly* book review. After praising Norman Bentwich's factual history of the British occupation and the subsequent Mandate, he cites his own views:

> with a little more honesty and firmness of purpose the British politicians and Palestinian administrators might have avoided many of the disastrous and shameful events which have accompanied our administration. I have myself always been very doubtful of the wisdom of the Zionist ideal. The world is already suffering not from too little, but from too much nationalism ... That Palestine should be the territory which had to be converted into the home for this new Jewish nationalism was peculiarly unfortunate, in view of the exacerbated condition of indigenous nationalism everywhere in the Near East immediately after the war.

He claims that in the first years of the Mandate 'a *modus vivendi* between the Arabs and Jews might have been secured', if not for 'Moslem [sic] extremists' and 'the British Government's disingenuous and vacillating attitude after the riots and massacres of 1930' ('England in Palestine' 299–300).

As a reaction to Arab protests against the Mandatory in the thirties, the Peel Commission of 1937 recommended just what Woolf did not want – the partition of Palestine into Jewish and Arab areas. Arabs rejected this, while the Zionists under Weizmann accepted for purposes of negotiation. In 1939, the British rejected partition and proposed creating an independent Palestine to be governed by Palestinian Arabs and Jews in proportion to their numbers in the population in 1939, that is, 70 per cent Arab to 30 per cent Jewish. It also severely restricted Jewish immigration.

The rise of fascism in Europe in the 1930s, the Second World War, and the Holocaust changed the nature of the discussion. Keynes, all of Bloomsbury, and most of the world agreed with Woolf that when Hitler began killing the Jews Zionism and anti-Zionism began to become irrelevant (*Journey* 186). In fact, the main argument for Keynes being pro-Zionist includes references to his support of German-Jewish scholars after the rise of the Nazis in 1932. He was, for example, among the forty-one original members of the Academic Assistance Council (AAC), initiated in May 1933, little more than one month after Germany passed the *Gesetz zur Wiederherstellung des Berufsbeamtentums*, 'aimed at removing racially and politically undesirable persons from the civil service', as the result of which, 'something like a quarter of the academic staff at German universities and research institutes were dismissed' (Grenville). The AAC was dedicated to raising funds and finding work opportunities for the 'Many eminent scholars and men of science and University teachers of all grades and in all faculties [who] are being obliged to relinquish their posts in the Universities of Germany. ... The issue raised at the moment is not a Jewish one alone; many who have suffered or are threatened have no Jewish connection.'[3] Although Jewish academics were subject to Nazi purges as early as 1932, the AAC recognized that other ethnic and religious groups as well homosexuals were also subject to dismissal. On 12 March 1938 Germany annexed Austria and it was absolutely clear to Keynes that no Jew in Germany or Austria was safe. In an article for the *New Statesman* entitled 'A Positive Peace Programme', published barely two weeks after the annexation, Keynes makes it clear that it is not only German scholars who are endangered and require the world's attention: 'There should be an offer to Germany to make organised arrangements for all German and Austrian Jews who wish to migrate and be naturalised elsewhere' (510). It should be noted that Keynes never advocated that these scholars be relocated to Palestine. The war and Holocaust, however, did little to curb Keynes's antisemitic language. In a letter to Lord Halifax shortly before his death in 1946, Keynes criticizes the American 'conception of international affairs' partly because of their 'Jewish economic advisers (who, like so many Jews, are either Nazi or Communist at heart)' – hardly benign. These are among Keynes's last words on Jews and Jewishness (*Collected* 24: 626).

Woolf saw the link between Nazism and the Palestine controversy in a different light. In fact, he felt that without the threat of Nazism in Europe Jewish culture would soon be fully assimilated. In 1940, a year after the war had begun, Woolf wrote a review of Arthur Ruppin's *The Jewish Fate and Future* – a statistical analysis of Jewish population trends in Europe, America, and in Palestine. Ruppin argues that assimilation in Eastern Europe was the greatest threat to cultural Zionism and would lead to 'loss of religious beliefs, habits, and traditions, and frequency of mixed marriages' ('Jews' 707). At the end of the review it is difficult to determine whether Woolf is echoing Ruppin or speaking for himself (or a bit of both) when he writes 'If the fanatical anti-semitism of the Nazi spreads, the Jew will survive; he will survive if Palestine really becomes a National Home or a Jewish state' (707).

About the same time that he reviewed Ruppin's book, Woolf wrote a long article for *Political Quarterly*, 'Utopia and Reality', in which he discusses the failure of the League of Nations to prevent another world war and seems to anticipate Michel Foucault on power, force, and violence: 'The phenomenon [of Power] is not confined to the relations between states; it can be observed within states in the relation between government and individuals and between individual and individual' (167). The article examines the concept of *'realpolitick'*, arguing that the 'reality in power and conflict' does not obviate international cooperation (177). Woolf concedes that the majority Arabs have the power 'to shoot Jewish immigrants', but that they also have the 'power to co-operate' with the Jew, concluding that 'the attainability of the Zionist policy will depend upon whether Arabs and Jews pursue their separate interests by conflict or whether they pursue their common interests by co-operation' (178). He goes on to apply this analysis to the war in Europe and to argue that the idea of international government is not necessarily a utopian dream that should fade away with the failure of the League of Nations.

Woolf had the dubious honour of writing the 1941 Labour Advisory Committee on Imperial Questions Draft Report on Palestine, in which he realized 'that it is not possible to reconcile promises made originally to the two communities' (L. Woolf, *Letters* 428–9). But he also recognized that the war had changed the equation. He tells his readers that 'The aim should be to establish a regime which will give time and opportunity for healing the breach and composing the difference between the two communities and which, when that has been accomplished, will make it possible for Jews and Arabs to co-operate peacefully in a self-governing Palestine' (429). Crucially, he rejects all proposals to partition Palestine, calling it 'a policy of despair and, under existing circumstances, is so desperate as to be almost inevitably disastrous'. He was adamant that immigration and land sales must be reasonably restricted to preserve the Arab majority and to 'safeguard the Arab cultivator and small owner' (430).

Perhaps Woolf's clearest articulation of his position is his 1942 article 'The Tangle in Palestine', in which he reviews Albert M. Hyamson's *Palestine: A Policy* – a book that echoes Woolf's own misgivings with the contradictory promises in the Balfour Declaration and the Mandate back in 1918 and 1920. Jews were promised a 'Home for the Jewish people' and Arabs that nothing would be done 'which might prejudice the civil and religious rights of existing non-Jewish communities in Palestine' (260). Woolf explains to his readers that Hyamson's 'sympathies are clearly with the Jewish "moderates" and with the interpretation of the National Home as a cultural rather than a political home; he stands therefore with Ahad Ha'Am rather than with Dr. Weizmann' (260).[4] Woolf shows himself to be more practical than Hyamson, recognizing the reality that if Jews are not allowed to immigrate to Palestine it will be 'neither a home nor national' (260). Woolf agrees with the author that the only practical solution is a Palestinian state that is not Arab or Jewish: 'Given a reasonable limitation of immigration, and a cautious but honest attempt to create a bi-national state, it is possible that the fears and passions of the two communities may die down, in which case some of the difficulties in the way of making Palestine a real National Home for the Jews, now insoluble, would vanish' (261).

Reviewing Richard Grossman's *Palestine Mission* in 1947, just one year before the creation of the State of Israel, Woolf echoes his 1940 views, though the war, Nazi atrocities, and the violent Zionist insurgence against British control of Israel had changed the context. 'Both protagonists,' he tells his *Political Quarterly* readers, 'are right and both wrong, and the blind, unreasoning passions with which they are both afflicted make any reasonable or civilized settlement impossible' (367). His outrage becomes more pointed: 'the self-righteous sadism of both sides and of their supporters, masquerading in the hypocritical cloak of misery, patriotism, or impartiality, is revolting' (367). In 1949, one year after the partition of Palestine, against which Woolf had railed, he reviews *Trial and Error: The Autobiography of Chaim Weizmann*, who by that time was the first president of the new State of Israel. What is most fascinating is that Woolf in the same article reviews a new biography of Mahatma Gandhi, and Gandhi's own autobiographical account of his early years. Dismissing the obvious dissimilarities between these two nationalists, Woolf sees 'a remarkable resemblance in their aims, their methods, and their achievements' (284). Woolf praises both men and characterizes British domination of India and worldwide persecution of Jews as 'unmitigated evils'. He adds, 'But I cannot accept the implicit assumption of these two great men that freedom and nationalism are intrinsically good and must be pursued irrespective of consequences' (285). He ends his review unequivocally: 'I do not believe that the freedom of India or of Israel is going to be of much account so long as people in either country believe that a dead or starving Muslim is of less account than a dead or starving Hindu, or that a dead or starving Arab is of less account than a dead or starving Jew' (285).

In his work for the Labour Party, and as co-editor of *Political Quarterly* from 1930 to 1959 (sole editor in the war years), Woolf was fully immersed in the politics of Palestine, including the 1936–9 Arab Revolt, the 1937 Peel Commission which recommended partition of Palestine, the 1939 British White Paper restricting Jewish land acquisition and immigration, Zionist insurgencies against the Mandate in 1939 and 1944, the 1947 UN General Assembly recommendation to partition of Mandatory Palestine, the establishment of the Jewish State of Israel in 1948, the first Arab–Israeli war that followed, and the 1949 cease-fire and partition of Palestine that left Israel with unrestricted immigration and a Jewish majority. As editor of the *Political Quarterly*, Woolf included articles both critical and supportive of Jewish Palestine. For example, Norman Bentwich's 'The Present and Future of Palestine' notes that although millions of pounds in contributions from Jewish people around the world had kept *Eretz Israel* solvent, there was little money for Arab resettlement. Bentwich quotes George Eliot's vision of 'A new Judea poised between east and west [that] will be a covenant of reconciliation between peoples' (256). No utopian, Woolf would have agreed that such an outcome would be a miracle in the land of miracles, but he would not have been surprised that the side-lining of the internationalist Cultural Zionism of Bentwich and Ahad Ha'am and the dominance of ultranationalism and religious fervour would keep the region waiting for the miracle. What is clear from all of these articles is that despite impressive Jewish economic success, the dwindling Arab population remained in poverty, and the promise of the Balfour Declaration to insure their rights remained unfulfilled. Keynes, too, wrote extensively on Palestine, though virtually every reference has to do with its currency reserve and its effect on the British economy. He is also impressed with the economic success of Jewish Palestine, but seems unconcerned about the plight of the Arab minority.[5]

In *Downhill all the Way* (1967), ostensibly discussing his journey to Manchester to deliver a speech in his failed run for Parliament, Woolf goes off on a tangent describing zoos he has visited, including his 1957 visit to the Jerusalem zoo. He compares the ramshackle zoo and its longhaired monkeys to the 'ramshackle suburb frequented by those unshaven, long-haired orthodox Jews' whose 'self-conscious, self-righteous hair and orthodoxy fill [him] with despair' (43). The monkeys, he says, 'gazed at one ... with the self-satisfaction of all the orthodox who have learned eternal truth from the primeval monkey, all the scribes and pharisees who spend their lives making mountains of pernicious stupidity out of molehills of nonsense' (43). He contrasts the Orthodox in Jerusalem to the energetic, more secular Israeli majority in Tel Aviv, Haifa, and Tiberias. This leads him into a page-long diatribe against what he calls 'the horrifying' influence of 'Orthodox Judaism' in Israeli politics, reminding him of 'how much evil religion has induced human beings to do!' (44). This description sounds as antisemitic as Maynard and Lydia Keynes at their worst, but Woolf's point is that a homeland for Jewish people is not the same as a homeland for an orthodox religion. It is the secular, inclusive, internationalist Israel that impressed both Woolf and Keynes.

Woolf's tone and word choice is reminiscent of his rendering of other wandering Jews, Harry in *The Wise Virgins* and Samuel Jacoby, Woolf's most positive character in his play *The Hotel* (1963). Asked if he believes in God, Jacoby answers 'You can't believe in the old gentleman with the beard ... there are so many fools and knaves whom one can see all round one turning the world into hell that there's no point in taking the trouble to invent an invisible super-fool or super-knave in order to put the blame on him' (*The Hotel* 89). In his autobiography Woolf mocks those who believe in the 'old bearded Jehovah sitting up there on Mount Sinai amid the thunder and lightning and once in three thousand years showing his backside to a favoured Moses' (*Downhill* 44). Though this language is disturbing and clearly offensive to many religious Jews, Woolf at the same time recognizes that 'the books which we call *Job, Ecclesiastes,* and *Micah* had laid the foundations of a civilized morality and a sceptical, rational theism' that would in time become '"the religion of all sensible men" – agnosticism or atheism' (44). Woolf, Keynes, and many of the original Bloomsbury Group were 'Cambridge Apostles' – followers of the philosopher G. E. Moore – who inspired 'not with the religious voice of Jehovah from Mount Sinai ... but with the more divine voice of plain common-sense' (*Sowing* 148). Woolf saw that Palestine could be the homeland for Semitic people, both Arab and Jew, if it were not for the 'religious and philosophical nightmares, delusions, hallucinations, in which Jehovah, Christ, and St. Paul, Plato, Kant, and Hegel had entangled us' (147).

In *The Journey, Not the Arrival, Matters*, Woolf provides a more detailed account of his 1951 visit to Israel, conceding that his early dream of a united Palestine has given way to late twentieth-century *Realpolitik*. 'When the Jewish National Home and hundreds of thousands of Jews had been established in Palestine, when Hitler was killing millions of Jews in Europe, when the independent sovereign state of Israel had been created, when the Arabs proclaimed their intention of destroying Israel and the Israelis, Zionism and anti-Zionism had become irrelevant' (186). The *kibbutzim* impress him, and he sees the Israeli attitude towards Nazareth, which has been called the Arab capital of Israel, as positive and hopeful. Woolf might not be pleased to know that today, old Nazareth, though still predominantly Arab, is now part of Greater Nazareth, ringed by the ever-encroaching Jewish suburban development.

Quentin Bell observed about his uncle that 'Although he had never been a Zionist, and had foreseen the disasters that would arise when a Jewish state was created in what had been an Arab country, he fell in love with Palestine and its inhabitants and he met a taxi driver who ... agreed with Leonard and Lucretius in thinking that religion is a great trouble maker' (Bell 127). The taxi driver was an Arab, Quentin still calls the area 'Palestine', and what Leonard fell in love with was the social experiment of the *kibbutzim*, and the vitality of the young multicultural country.

A letter to the editor of *The Times* dated 25 March 1968 and subsequent letters to Lord Fisher are Leonard's last words on Israel and the problem of Palestine. Lord Fisher's wife had written a letter to *The Times* in which she decries an Israeli reprisal against Arab insurgents, likening the Arabs to the French Resistance fighters of Second World War:

> Sir, Lady Fisher of Lambeth says that the Arabs attacking Israelis from Jordan are not terrorists or saboteurs, but heroes and brave men. The act of sabotage for which the Israelis staged the reprisal (which personally I do not defend) was to blow up a bus containing children. I wonder whether the late Archbishop of Canterbury or Jesus Christ would agree with Lady Fisher of Lambeth. (*Letters* 253)

In his correspondence with an irate Lord Fisher, Woolf summarizes his view of the Middle East troubles. 'From the first moment of the Balfour Declaration I was against Zionism on the ground that to introduce Jews into an Arab occupied territory with the ultimate prospect of establishing an independent Jewish state would lead to racial trouble' (*Letters* 454). In subsequent letters the 87-year-old Leonard Woolf demonstrates a keen understanding of the complex and terrible situation between Arabs and Israelis, the new realities wrought by the Holocaust, and the 'enormous increase in the Israeli population', adding 'there is now an established Israeli state with a large and immensely energetic population'. Woolf then quotes New Testament scripture to the Archbishop, reminding him of Christ's 'uncompromising attitude towards violence and cruelty' (*Letters* 455). Though Woolf was, in the end, a strong defender of Israel, he saw both Arabs and Jews as Semitic protagonists, and he was deeply saddened that a homeland for some descendants of Abraham has meant exile for others. Woolf cuts off the seven-month correspondence with 'I think that for anyone anywhere at any time to shoot a policeman in the back or kill a child because he is acting for his own country and homeland when it is under the heel of a conqueror is unjustifiable and morally wrong. The end does not justify the means.' As some, like the UK Prime Minister, celebrate the centennial of the Balfour Declaration and others excoriate it, as debates over sanctions rage, as rockets rain down on Israeli cities, and as the death toll in Gaza mounts, we realize just how prescient Leonard Woolf had been.

NOTES

1. In *The Journey Not the Arrival Matters*, Woolf briefly discusses the difficulty of being Jewish at St. Paul's claiming that his 'stiffnecked and pigheaded' nature as well as his 'being fairly good at games' mitigated the antisemitism (129). For a clearer idea of what life was like for Jewish boys at St. Paul's see Norman Bentwich's account in *My 77 Years* (9–10).
2. See Anthony Julius, 'Contemporary Secular Anti-Zionists', chap. 7 of *Trials of the Diaspora* (441–531).
3. The original draft announcement of the AAC dated 22 May 1933 is in the Leo Szilard Papers, mms 32, Special Collections and Archives, UC San Diego Library. It was widely distributed in such outlets as the *Times, Science, Nature*, and the *British Medical Journal*. The Council successfully resettled over 2,000 mostly German-Jewish scholars before the Second World War had ended. In 1936, it was reconstituted as the Society for the Protection of Science and Learning. It still exists as the Council for At-Risk Academics (CARA). Much of CARA's work is now helping displaced academics in the Middle East. Ironically, their linked publications name Israel as a major offender for 'hundreds of incidents of attacks on education …, restrictions on movement, curfews, denial of building permits and the issuing of demolition orders against schools, settler attacks on schools and universities, and actions of Israeli military forces'. http://www.protectingeducation.org/education-under-attack-2014, 150.
4. Ahad Ha'am, meaning 'one of the people', is the penname of Asher Zvi Hirsch Ginsberg, founder of Cultural Zionism, of the Haifa *Technikum*, and mentor to Chaim Weizmann.
5. Keynes provides advice about the currency reserves of Palestine (*Collected* 24:380) speaks of writing down their balances (24:286), the land lease program (24:287), and many other aspects of Palestinian finances just before the creation of Israel (24: 42, 140, 618, and 627).

WORKS CITED

Bell, Quentin. *Bloomsbury Recalled*. New York: Columbia UP, 1995.

Bentwich, Norman. *My 77 Years: An Account of My Life and Times 1883–1960*. Philadelphia, PA: Jewish Publication Society of America, 1961.

Bentwich, Norman. 'The Present and Future of Palestine'. *Political Quarterly* 20.3 (July 1949): 247–56.

Chandavarkar, Anand. 'Was Keynes an Anti-Semite?' *Economic and Political Weekly* 35.19 (6 May 2000), 1619–24.

Glendinning, Victoria. *Leonard Woolf: A Biography*. New York: Free Press, 2006.

Gottlieb, Freema. 'Leonard Woolf: The Pride, The Shame'. *European Judaism: A Journal for the New Europe* 10.1 (23–30). www.jstor.org/stable/41442488c

Grenville, Anthony. 'The Rescue of Refugee Scholars'. *Association of Jewish Refugees Newsletter* 9.2 (2009): 1–2. www.ajr.org.uk/journalpdf/2009_february.pdf.

Gross, Nachum T. 'Herbert Samuel's Advisory Committee of 1919'. *Journal of Israeli History* 19.1 (1998): 5–21

Hill, Polly and Richard Keynes. Eds. *The Letters of Lydia Lopokova and John Maynard Keynes.* New York: Scribner, 1989.

Julius, Anthony. *Trials of the Diaspora: A History of Anti-Semitism in England.* Oxford: Oxford UP, 2010.

Keynes, John Maynard. *Collected Writings of John Maynard Keynes,* 30 vols. Ed. Elizabeth Johnson and Donald Moggridge. Royal Economic Society, 1978. Cambridge Core, 2012.

Keynes, John Maynard. 'Einstein'. *New Statesman and Nation,* 21 October 1933, 481.

Keynes, John Maynard. 'A Positive Peace Programme'. *The New Statesman and Nation* 15.370 (26 March 1939): 509–10. proquest.com.ezaccess.libraries.psu.edu/docview/1306875120/fulltextPDF/3B8B23B78A5943EDPQ/5?accountid=13158

MacDonald, Ramsay. *A Socialist in Palestine.* Wentworth Press, 2016 [1922].

Moggridge, D. E. *Maynard Keynes: An Economist's Biography.* London: Routledge, 1992.

Pianko, Noam. *Zionism: The Roads Not Taken.* Bloomington: Indiana UP, 2010.

Reder, Melvin W. 'The Anti-Semitism of Some Eminent Economists'. *History of Political Economy* 32.4 (2000): 833–56.

Rosenbaum, S. P. *The Bloomsbury Group Memoir Club.* Basingstoke: Palgrave Macmillan, 2014.

Schneer, Jonathan. *The Balfour Declaration: The Origins of the Arab-Israeli Conflict.* New York: Random House, 2010.

Schröder, Leena Kore. 'Tales of Abjection and Miscegenation: Virginia Woolf's and Leonard Woolf's "Jewish" Stories'. *Twentieth Century Literature* 49.3 (2003): 298–327.

Weintraub, E. Roy. 'Keynesian Historiography and the Anti-Semitism Question'. *History of Political Economy* 44.1 (2012): 41–67.

Weizmann, Chaim. *Trial and Error: The Autobiography of Chaim Weizmann.* New York: Harper, 1949.

Woolf, Leonard. 'Article XXII'. *The New Statesman* 15.368 (1 May 1920): 94–5. proquest.com.ezaccess.libraries.psu.edu/docview/1306847417/fulltextPDF/D99C3D60510141AAPQ/4?accountid=13158.

Woolf, Leonard. *Beginning Again: An Autobiography of the Years 1911–1918.* London: Hogarth, 1964.

Woolf, Leonard. *Downhill All the Way: An Autobiography of the Years 1919 to 1939.* London: Hogarth, 1967.

Woolf, Leonard. Ed. *Framework for a Lasting Peace.* London: George Allen, 1917.

Woolf, Leonard. *The Hotel.* New York: Dial Press, 1963 [1939].

Woolf, Leonard. 'Jews and Their Future'. Review of *The Jewish Fate and Future* by Arthur Ruppin. *New Statesman and Nation* 19.484 (1 June 1940): 706–7. search.proquest.com.ezaccess.libraries.psu.edu/docview/1306881439/fulltextPDF/ C477908750804672PQ/21?accountid=13158

Woolf, Leonard. *The Journey Not the Arrival Matters: An Autobiography of the Years 1939–1969.* London: Hogarth Press, 1970.

Woolf, Leonard. *Letters of Leonard Woolf.* Ed. Frederic Spotts. New York: Harcourt, 1989.

Woolf, Leonard. 'Review of *England in Palestine*'. *Political Quarterly* 3.2 (1932): 298–300.

Woolf, Leonard. 'Review of *Palestine Mission* by Richard Grossman'. *Political Quarterly* 18.4 (1947): 367.

Woolf, Leonard. 'Review of *Trial and Error* by Chaim Weizmann, *Mahatma Gandhi* by H. S. L Polk, et. al., and *The Story of My Experiments with Truth* by Mahatma Gandhi'. *Political Quarterly* 20.3 (1949): 284–5.

Woolf, Leonard. *Scope of the Mandates under the League of Nations*. London: C.
    F. Roworth, 1919.
Woolf, Leonard. *Sowing: An Autobiography of the Years 1880–1904*. London: Hogarth
    Press, 1960.
Woolf, Leonard. 'The Tangle in Palestine'. Review of *Palestine: A Policy* by Albert M. Hyamson.
    New Statesman and Nation 23.582 (18 April 1942): 260–61. search.proquest.com.
    ezaccess.libraries.psu.edu/docview/1306888103/fulltextPDF/ C6EC8312E6CB4174PQ/
    18?accountid=13158.
Woolf, Leonard. 'Three Jews'. *Virginia Woolf Bulletin* 5 (2000 [1917]): 4–11.
Woolf, Leonard. 'Utopia and Reality'. *Political Quarterly* 11.2 (1940): 167–82.
Woolf, Leonard. *The Wise Virgins*. New York: Harcourt, 1979 [1914].
Woolf, Virginia. *The Diary of Virginia Woolf*, 5 vols. Ed. Anne Oliver Bell. New York: Harcourt
    Brace Jovanovich, 1977–84.
Woolf, Virginia. *The Letters of Virginia Woolf*, 6 vols. Ed. Nigel Nicolson and Joanne
    Trautmann. New York: Harcourt Brace Jovanovich, 1975–80.

CHAPTER EIGHT

Bloomsbury and Nature

PETER ADKINS

> Supposing, then, that we are able to isolate in a work of art this purely aesthetic
> quality to which Mr Clive Bell gives the name of 'significant form'. Of what
> nature is it?
>
> (Fry, *Vision* 236)

In Roger Fry's 'Retrospect', the coda to his works of criticism collected in *Vision and
Design* (1920), he looks back over the theory of aesthetics that has emerged since the
1910 'Manet and the Post-Impressionists' exhibition and confronts us with the problem
we necessarily encounter if we want to think about Bloomsbury and Nature: 'Of what
nature is it?' Of *what* nature are we speaking, invoking or, perhaps, even challenging
or disregarding when we speak of Bloomsbury and Nature? For Fry, reassessing the
formalism of the 1910s, the question 'of what nature is it?' is directed not only towards
the inherent properties of art (the nature *of* art) but its representational relation to the
natural world (the *nature* of art). It was in this second sense that, as Fry understood,
formalism posed a radical challenge to ideas of nature and aesthetics. If the history of
modern European art could be defined by the faithful 'representation of nature', formalist
theorists of nonmimetic aesthetics announced that 'no single fact, or set of facts, about
nature' need any longer be 'obligatory' for the modern artist (Fry, *Vision* 231). Chief
among these formalist theories was Clive Bell's idea of 'significant form', a term he
coined in describing the paintings at the Second Post-Impressionist Exhibition in 1912
and subsequently fleshed out in detail two years later in *Art* (1914). An artwork's formal
unity, Bell asserted, resided not in its ability to represent a given subject from nature
but in 'lines and colours combined in a particular way' that give rise to 'certain forms
and relations of forms, [that] stir our aesthetic emotions' (*Art* 8). Art no longer needs
to represent nature but should rather *present* these 'pure forms', as Bell goes onto to
characterize them, of shape and colour (*Art* 53; see also Hussey in this volume). As Fry
recognized in 'Retrospect', significant form entailed the notion that the 'representation of
nature was entirely irrelevant' and that a 'picture might be completely non-representative'
(*Vision* 231).

Fry's anxieties around the nature of modern art foregrounds the slipperiness of
the word 'nature', a word which Raymond Williams famously defined as 'perhaps the
most complex' in the English language since its different meanings are 'variable and at
times even opposed' (184). For Fry and Bell, and for other members of the Bloomsbury
Group, the concept of 'nature' is put to work in two ostensible ways. Firstly, 'nature'
(or variations of the word) denotes the nonhuman world from which the artist or writer
takes his or her subject: this is the world of 'natural forms' as Fry calls it (*Vision* 39) or the

'physical universe' in Bell's preferred term (*Art* 16). 'Nature' here is understood to mean the artwork's site of referentiality, the world of natural objects outside of the canvas, in line with Williams's definition that one understanding of nature is 'the material world itself' (184). This is the nature that, as will be described below, was not only the subject of dispute regarding artistic representation but was also undergoing reconfiguration in science and politics. The second manner in which 'nature' is invoked by members of Bloomsbury is in a narrower, generic sense to mean the set of aesthetic ideals that have been established through cultural representations of the countryside. Here, 'nature' invokes pastoral or romantic traditions in art and literature, evident in Fry's description of the seventeenth century painter Claude Lorrain's 'studies from nature' in which the 'shifting patterns of foliage and sky ... arrange themselves in some beautifully significant pattern' (*Vision* 183) or Virginia Woolf's description of 'the nature worship' of poets such as William Wordsworth and Alfred Tennyson for whom rural life is 'the sanctuary of moral excellence' ('Pastons and Chaucer' 9). Nature, in this sense, carriers an ideological weight which, as Timothy Morton writes, establishes it as an aesthetic 'object "over there"' implicitly or explicitly contrasted to the urban or the cultural (*Ecology* 125).[1] Moreover, these two distinct but closely related usages are not infrequently conflated with one another. Fry's assertion that Claude Monet's paintings are the work of an artist who has 'really *looked* ... at nature' and revealed 'what things really look like' to a public who are 'gradually [brought] round to admitting truths which a single walk in the country with purely unbiased vision would have established' moves seamlessly from a usage of nature to apparently signify material reality to the pastoral ideal of the countryside (*Vision* 30). As this chapter will explore, this unresolved tension between nature in its broadest sense to mean the nonhuman world and in its narrower aesthetic sense becomes both central and problematic to formalism's assertion that the 'representation of nature [is] entirely irrelevant' and the Bloomsbury Group's approach to nature more generally (*Vision* 231).

Fry and Bell's theorizing of art and nature was symptomatic of a wider cultural crisis around ideas of the natural world at the turn of the twentieth century. Fry's interest in the relationship between nature and aesthetics dated back to his studies at Cambridge in the 1880s, where he had taken a degree in natural sciences while also advancing his interests in art and architecture. During this period he developed a friendship with the radical socialist and early homosexual activist, Edward Carpenter, whose books such as *Civilisation: Its Cause and Cure* (1889) drew attention to the environmental cost of industrialized capitalism. Carpenter championed a quasimystical and aesthetically minded 'return to nature' that has since been characterized as contributing to the 'most ... important period of green politics before 1980' (Carpenter 58–9; Gould viii). As Virginia Woolf recounts in her biography of Fry, Carpenter created a 'great impression' on Fry's emergent ideas of 'democracy and the future of England', and would visit Carpenter at his self-sustaining market garden farm in Yorkshire where he was putting his anticapitalist 'return to nature' theory into practice (*Fry* 46–7). As I detail below, Fry's writings in later years on Post-Impressionism's presentation of nature bear the traces of Carpenter's socially transgressive ideas of nature. Furthermore, the influence of Carpenter's proto-environmentalism on the Bloomsbury Group extends beyond Fry. The literary output of E. M. Forster, who, like Fry, had read and later befriended Carpenter (see Wolfe in this volume) similarly reveals an indebtedness to Carpenter's politicized understanding of nature. 'The Machine Stops', Forster's 1909 speculative narrative of a future human population who exist beneath the destroyed surface of the earth, offers a fictional expression of the threat of irreversible environmental degradation so clearly articulated in Carpenter's books. Indeed Kelly Sultzbach has argued that Forster's entire oeuvre should be read back through its politically complex engagement with nature and, more specifically, the pastoral tradition. As Sultzbach charts, Forster's portrayal of the natural world develops from the Edwardian pastoralism of his early stories to the 'anti-pastoral[ism]' of 'The Machine Stops' and eventually arrives at the 'postpastoral' *A Passage To India* (1924), where ethno- and anthropocentric racism is troubled by Forster's portrayal of the vast Marabar Caves, whose echoes 'resonate with multiple valences of subjective human experience, nonhuman or prelinguistic communication, and alternate forms of knowledge' (Sultzbach 40–43, 71).

The question 'of what nature is it?' not only speaks to the political uncertainties around nature that were being addressed by figures such as Carpenter and Forster but advances within the sciences which, as Fry recognized, were having 'an important bearing on the new movement in art' (*Vision* 21). Ann Banfield has examined how Post-Impressionism's revaluation of aesthetics and nature was shaped by Fry's interests in the philosophical implications of modern physics, in which the wave theory of light and kinetic accounts of gases had revealed nature's unperceivable inner workings (12–14). If, for Fry, physics exposed the limitations of the human senses in perceiving nature's true forms, then, on one level, Post-Impressionism and formalism were an attempt to register this fact in the arts. Moreover, the implications of discoveries in other branches of science were radically decentring and destabilizing the human in different ways. The inhuman sense of scale that attended nineteenth-century evolutionary and geological theories, which extended the earth's prehistory far beyond earlier estimates, challenged a cultural imaginary that placed the locus of all meaning within the human. The dethroning of the human, as one species among many on an inhuman planet that long predates it, emerges as a recurrent anxiety in the fiction penned by the Bloomsbury Group. David Garnett's fantastical narrative of species metamorphosis, *Lady into Fox* (1922), for instance, speaks not only to the ways in which emergent questions of interspecies relationality threatened the way we conceive other animals (most clearly in the novel's bloody portrayal of hunting) but science's limitations in offering any definitive answers to such questions. As Garnett's narrator states, the events of the novel cannot be 'explain[ed] … away by any natural philosophy. The materialism of our age will not help us here' (2). As in his subsequent novel, *A Man in the Zoo* (1924), in which a human voluntarily moves into a Large Ape-House enclosure and subjects himself to the taxonomical spectacle that other species endure, Garnett's writing registers the ongoing reverberations of Darwinian theory within the twentieth century. The ambivalent primitivism of Leonard Woolf's anti-imperialist novel, *The Village in the Jungle* (1913), is similarly informed by the absorption of evolutionary theory into the cultural imagination. In Woolf's novel, the spectre of a prehistoric nature haunts the narrative. The Sri Lankan jungle figures as 'a strange world … of bare and brutal facts … a world of trees and the perpetual twilight of the shade' pregnant with dangers of atavism and meaninglessness, a parallel to the South American coastal setting of Virginia Woolf's first novel, *The Voyage Out* (1915) where an 'immense forest … vast and dark' similarly threatens to claim the narrative's characters (Woolf, *Village* 22; Woolf, *Voyage* 403).

Of all the Bloomsbury Group, Virginia Woolf emerges as the figure whose engagement with the crisis of nature in the early twentieth century is both the most sustained and experimental, and whose writing has been the subject of the most critical inquiries around the topic of nature. As critics such as Christina Alt and Bonnie Kime Scott have noted, Woolf's writing is characterized by a longstanding preoccupation with changes in scientific understandings of nature and the implications that these new understandings bring to bear on literature (Alt 3–5; Scott 42–4). Indeed, Sultzbach has argued that Woolf's modernist writing is predicated on developing literary techniques that convey the radical alterity of the nonhuman world, a world which always exceeds our perceptions and ideas of it (126). Furthermore, for Woolf, enquiries into nature are never separable from questions of the human. As Derek Ryan has shown, Woolf creates textual frameworks in which humans are firmly embedded within the materiality of the world and in which the human is always already entangled with the nonhuman (*Virginia Woolf* 77). For Ryan, Woolf's writing demonstrates the way in which emergent ideas of nature bring into crisis the concept of the human as a discrete, fully individuated subject. The human is revealed to be an assemblage of material and immaterial processes whose boundaries are as porous as they are well defined; the human is, in more than one sense, inhuman (*Virginia Woolf* 182–3).

This chapter will focus on the points of connection, influence, and divergence within the Bloomsbury Group's reassessment of nature. Beginning with Fry and Clive Bell's formalist recasting of nature, it will go on to consider how their theories appear to have influenced the presentation of the natural world in the fiction of Virginia Woolf. Yet, Woolf's nature is not the same nature as imagined by Fry and Bell. Jane Goldman's revisionary assessment of Woolf and Post-Impressionism, an account that foregrounds the influence of Vanessa Bell on Woolf's modernism, draws attention to the fact that within the aesthetic theories of the early twentieth century, 'Nature' and the 'object world' were usually gendered feminine (*Feminist* 125). As this chapter will examine in the writing of both Woolf and Vita Sackville-West, a figure often positioned at the periphery of the Bloomsbury Group, the reimagining of nature also necessarily involves a contesting of gender and sexuality.

THE NATURE OF POST-IMPRESSIONISM

In the unsigned introduction to the catalogue for the 1910 'Manet and the Post-Impressionists' exhibition, written by Desmond McCarthy under the instruction of Roger Fry, there is a description of an imagined dialogue between the artists being exhibited at the Grafton Galleries and the generation of Impressionist painters before them: 'You have explored nature in every direction and all honour to you; but your methods and principles have hindered artists from exploring and expressing that emotional significance which lies in things, and is the most important subject matter of art' (*Manet* 9). The exhibition's artworks, which included paintings by Édouard Manet, Paul Cézanne, Vincent Van Gogh, and Paul Gauguin as well as early pieces by Henri Matisse and Pablo Picasso (see Humm in this volume), were, the catalogue explained, predicated on a break with 'the close imitation of nature' that had become 'dogma' in the nineteenth century (*Manet* 8). This disavowal of art's reliance on naturalism was central to the 'Post' prefix of Fry's term 'Post-Impressionism'. Where Impressionism had 'encouraged an artist to paint a tree as it appeared to him at the moment under particular circumstance', Post-Impressionism strove to elicit the ' "treeness" of the tree', that is to say, 'the emotions and associations as trees may be made to convey in poetry' (*Manet* 9). Nature is not represented on the canvas in a Post-Impressionist painting, so much as its '-ness', or essence, is presented. A work of art, McCarthy and Fry go so far as to suggest, might be more truthful to its subject by being less naturalistic, in the same way that 'a good rocking-horse often has

more of the true horse about it than an instantaneous photograph of a Derby winner'
(*Manet* 9).

The 1910 exhibition, then, insisted on a renewed understanding of art's relation
to nature, as opposed to claiming a clean break with representation. As the exhibition
catalogue pronounced, Post-Impressionism cut through culturally received notions of
nature not so as to disavow the referential world but to return to its true grounding in
'emotions and associations'. The implicit romanticism in such an idea was evident in the
paintings on show. An attempt to return to a primitive vision of nature was discernible in
Van Gogh's landscapes, Cézanne's still lives, and Gauguin's exotic Polynesian portraits.
As Maurice Merleau-Ponty would later state in his analysis of Cézanne's paintings,
the Post-Impressionists attempted to capture the 'primordial world' before 'the human
organisation of ideas and science' (13). This presentation of nature in primitive,
sensuous terms was understood to challenge not only aesthetic norms but civilized
societal ideals, as reflected in the scandalized reception the exhibition received from
critics and attendees. Indeed, the Bloomsbury Group consciously exploited the socially
transgressive potential of this primitivist aesthetic. Virginia Woolf (then Stephen) and
Vanessa Bell's arrival at the Post-Impressionist Ball as 'bare-shouldered bare-legged
Gauguin girls, almost – as it seemed to the indignant ladies who swept out in protest –
almost naked' underscored both the radical implications of the art on display, as well
as the orientalist undercurrents informing such renderings of nature (Bell, *Virginia
Woolf* 170).

If the 1910 exhibition pivoted around a contestation of naturalism that gave rise to
a romantic formalism, then the Second Post-Impressionist Exhibition in 1912 marked
another departure. This time it was abstract formalism that predominated, especially
Cubism, reflecting the direction in which Fry and Clive Bell's theories had moved in the
intervening years (Goldman, *Modernism* 45). Fry, as Frances Spalding notes, had been
increasingly drawn to the idea that complete freedom from 'illusionistic imitation' could
only be expressed through abstract art (151). Yet the question of nature remained at stake.
As Fry writes in the catalogue for the second exhibition, it is 'equivalence, not a likeness,
of nature that is sought', an equivalence that Bell also gestures to in his contribution to
the exhibition catalogue, asserting that the painter now occupies the same position as the
'literary artist who wishes to express what he feels for a forest [and who] thinks himself
under no obligation to give an account of its flora and fauna' (Fry, *Vision* 190–91; Bell,
'English' 193).[2] Post-Impressionism, at least in this second definition of it, aims not to
represent nature but to establish a sense of relationality to it through nonmimetic use of
form, colour, and emotion. The paintings, Fry explains, 'aim not at illusion, but at reality'
(*Vision* 190).

Fry's notion that modern art should not represent nature so much as reveal reality
itself is boldly articulated in Bell's *Art*. Bell's assessment of nature and aesthetics asserts
that art might cut through natural forms to the universal reality undergirding material
appearances. To 'see objects as pure forms', Bell explains in *Art*, 'is to see them as ends in
themselves'. He continues:

All of us, I imagine, from time to time, get a vision of material objects as pure
forms ... Who has not, once at least in his life, had a sudden vision of landscape as
pure form? For once, instead of seeing it as fields and cottages, he has felt it as lines and
colours. In that moment has he not won from material beauty a thrill indistinguishable
from that which art gives? (52–3)

Here, as in Fry's aforementioned assessment of Monet, Bell appears to conflate nature in its broad sense with a narrower aestheticized understanding. In Bell's example, the world of material objects is typified through the pastoral features of a landscape painting (fields and cottages) and then subjected to a moment of visionary abstraction in which it reveals its underlying pure forms. Bell's example of a penetrating vision is not just an aesthetic judgement against the history of representational art but an assertion that when viewed with the defamiliarizing 'eye of an artist' the pastoral ideal of the countryside is comprised of precisely the lines and colours found in avant-garde paintings (*Art* 53). For Bell, an artwork no longer beholden to nature's outward forms might express the 'ultimate reality' found 'behind' appearances (*Art* 54). Yet, at this juncture, there emerges an important contrast between Fry and Bell's respective formalisms. Even within Fry's avowal of abstract formalism in the 1912 exhibition catalogue, he is anxious to clarify that the idea that art should 'give up all resemblance to natural form' remained a 'logical extreme' on which it is 'too early to be dogmatic' (*Vision* 190). By 1920, his assessment of significant form is clearer: Bell has 'go[ne] too far' in the direction of abstraction, since 'even the slightest suggestion, of the third dimension in a picture must be due to some element of representation' (*Vision* 231).

Fry's hesitance to disavow *all* representation of nature can be seen in the products produced in the Omega Workshop (1913–19) he ran with Vanessa Bell and Duncan Grant, which as Scott highlights, incorporated natural motifs and landscapes within their textile prints and furniture designs (Scott 126). Similarly, the paintings produced by Grant and Vanessa Bell in their Charleston farmhouse in rural Sussex exhibit a reimagining, rather than rejection, of subjects from the natural world. The landscapes and still lives of Vanessa Bell, whose work was displayed at the 1912 exhibition, succeed in conveying, as Goldman states, 'the sensual pleasure of artistic form' *and* the 'forms and movements' found in nature (*Feminist* 147). What Fry identifies as Clive Bell's inability to fully resolve the opposition between the 'material' world of 'objects' and the 'ultimate reality' of 'pure form' becomes in Vanessa Bell's art a productive means of reassembling art's relation to nature and revising pastoral traditions (Bell, *Art* 54–5). For Virginia Woolf, literature similarly could reveal formalism's blind spots when it came to abstract universalism. For Woolf, the advances of formalism, particularly its mode of defamiliarization that challenged the mimetic authority of realism, posed clear potential for the development of a new literary aesthetics. In 'The Mark on the Wall' (1917), the narrator fixes her gaze on an ambiguous 'mark' on her sitting room wall and lets her 'thoughts swarm upon [the] new object' (*Haunted* 76). In a manner akin to Clive Bell's defamiliarizing eye of the artist, Woolf's narrator attempts to perceive the mark in all its nonhuman alterity. Following a series of associative thoughts that take her to the imaginative limit of her ability to 'understand Nature's game', the narrator paradoxically envisages those inhuman entities that exist *outside* the purview of the human, imagining trees growing at imperceptibly slow speeds or standing unseen 'on winter's nights' in 'empty fields' (*Haunted* 82–3). Here the relation between perception and the object world, central to Fry and Bell's reformulating of art and nature, is couched within the processes of human cognition and insists upon the temporal, embodied acts of seeing and imagining that always shape the perception of those forms. Moreover, the story's domestic setting and comic revelation that the mark is 'a snail' underscores the defamiliarizing potential to even the most commonplace, least romantic of objects (*Haunted* 82–3).[3]

The conclusion to Woolf's story also denotes an important difference between her fiction and the aesthetic theories of Fry and Bell, where in the latter we often find natural objects dematerialize into ahistorical forms. Goldman suggests that Woolf is sympathetic to Vanessa Bell's approach to aesthetics where 'instead of insisting that form can be significant only at the expense of content/subject matter ... Bell exploits the tension between the two, showing that form and content may cohere ... without making it imitative' (*Feminist* 146–50). As in 'The Mark on the Wall', Woolf's writing refuses to isolate either form or content and instead deploys formalist techniques of defamiliarization within narratives shaped by time and history. While Fry proposed in a 1913 letter that Woolf cites in her biography of him that one should consider 'poetry [as] analogous to the things represented in painting' since, for both, content is 'merely directive' of an 'abstract and universal' pure form, for Woolf literature is a mode wherein the abstractions of formalism become subject to the specificities of history (*Fry* 183). In Woolf's fiction the question of nature is never an abstract problem to be solved through art theory but, as in Vanessa Bell's art, a reimagining of the human's relation to the nonhuman world.

POST-IMPRESSIONIST FICTION
AND INHUMAN NATURE

To the Lighthouse (1927) marks Woolf's most explicit engagement with Post-Impressionism, not only in its portrayal of Lily's formalist composition and what Mary Ann Caws identifies as the influence of Post-Impressionism on the novel's 'visual and rhythmic' formal qualities (139) but in the thematic centrality of the relationship between the human and the nonhuman. The opening section of the novel, 'The Window', establishes Mr and Mrs Ramsay's internal conflict with what they perceive to be the perpetual threat of nature's meaninglessness. Mrs Ramsay, perhaps unconsciously recalling Grimm's fairy-tale 'The Fisherman and His Wife' that she read to James earlier that day, is haunted by the way in which 'nature' can one moment seem to murmur 'I am guarding you – I am your support' and then 'suddenly and unexpectedly' threaten to bring about 'the destruction of the island and its engulfment in the sea' (*Lighthouse* 17). Her horror that nature's providence might be an illusion concealing a destructive chaos produces an 'impulse of terror' at the 'ephemeral[ity]' of human life (*Lighthouse* 17). In a later passage, she seeks refuge from the terror of nature's inhuman vicissitudes by attempting to locate the 'coherence in things, a stability, something ... immune from change', paralleling her husband's desire for a linear series of logical philosophical propositions arranged 'like the alphabet ... twenty-six letters all in order' that will provide the skeleton key to 'the nature of reality' (*Lighthouse* 85, 30, 22). In turn, the intellectual turmoil that Mr Ramsay experiences in not being able to reach the letter R, which Banfield suggests stands in for 'reality', manifests itself in a strikingly similar fear of oceanic deluge (Banfield 47).[4] Woolf writes:

> It was his fate ... to come out thus on a spit of land which the sea is slowly eating away, and there to stand, like a desolate seabird, alone. It was his power, his gift, suddenly to shed all superfluities, to shrink and diminish so that he looked barer and felt sparer, even physically, yet lost none of his intensity of mind, and so to stand on his little ledge facing the dark of human ignorance, how we know nothing and the sea eats away the ground we stand on – that was his fate, his gift (*Lighthouse* 38).

The free indirect discourse of the passage conveys a tension between the brute fact of the external world which 'diminish[es]' Mr Ramsay's sense of self and the processes of meaning-making he relies upon for self-presence and mastery over his environment. While he might be 'fate[d]' to look out to sea, he remains ever able to return inward to his 'gift' of philosophy, where the 'intensity' of his mind can logically reduce the inhuman scale of the ocean to an epistemology in which the human mind, as that against which nature is implicitly measured, remains the locus of meaning. Evoking Matthew Arnold's 'Dover Beach' (1867), in which the speaker's harmonious vision of the glimmering English Channel is threatened by the 'long, withdrawing roar' of religious faith he hears in the breaking waves and a Victorian anxiety that the world is being revealed to be an indifferent 'darkling plain' (*Poems* 240–43), Mr Ramsay attempts to restore a threatened order through the meaning-making processes of the human mind. Yet, as in Arnold's poem where anxieties about nature remains unresolved, there is a sense that both the ocean and the 'dark[ness] of human ignorance' can be stymied for only so long (*Lighthouse* 38).

Gillian Beer has argued the inhuman sense of scale that oceans instil in Woolf's characters captures the cultural anxiety that attended scientific advances in the nineteenth century, particularly the way in which geological and evolutionary discoveries introduced a prehistory that challenged settled ideas of culture and morality (27). In the inner lives of Mr and Mrs Ramsay Woolf portrays a late Victorian impulse of terror produced by science's decentring of the human. In the Ramsays' parallel attempts to construct coherence and meaning in the face of a world revealed to be inhuman, Woolf portrays a historical moment in which new cultural constructions of nature were being forged. In this respect *To the Lighthouse* self-reflexively historicizes the very uncertainties that gave rise to the investigations in science, philosophy, and aesthetics that influenced the Post-Impressionist exhibitions, and, by extension, Woolf's novel itself.

Yet, the Ramsays' attempts to rationalize nature do not coincide with Woolf's own portrayal of the nonhuman world. Towards the end of the novel, Cam Ramsay senses 'slumbrous shapes in her mind, shapes of a world not realized but turning in their darkness', and in the 'Time Passes' section Woolf similarly imagines a world in which the human is no longer centred (*Lighthouse* 154). The house, 'deserted' by the Ramsays and vulnerable to the inhuman processes of nature, is 'left like a shell on a sand-hill to fill with dry salt grains', with Woolf's memorable description of mouldering books, thistles thrusting through the larder tiles, and the long wavering grass of the lawn correlating to Mr and Mrs Ramsay's fears of nature's destructive amorality (*Lighthouse* 112–13). Like the narrator in 'The Mark on the Wall' who imagines unseen trees growing at imperceptible rates, 'Time Passes' reverses the conventional scales of fiction in which temporal units are dictated by human action for a narrative which operates at a nonhuman scale. Important human events, such as the deaths of principal characters, are relegated to only parenthetical inclusion, while the human drama of the First World War is, in an ironic reversal of pathetic fallacy, registered only as distant thunder. Conventional scales of time, moral significance, and meaning are overturned; the human is effectively decentred. Unlike Mr Ramsay's retreat into the anthropocentric unity of philosophical logic, 'Time Passes' risks a nonanthropocentric imagining of that which cannot be seen or experienced by the human.

The distinction between anthropocentrism and anthropomorphism, especially as regards aesthetics, comes sharply into focus during the course of *To the Lighthouse*. If anthropomorphism, understood as the conscious or unconscious projecting of human meaning onto nonhuman entities, is to a certain extent inescapable, the novel shows that it does not follow that anthropomorphism necessarily always works towards anthropocentrism. Ryan identifies in Woolf's writing what he describes as a willingness to engage with 'the risk of anthropomorphism' since while Woolf offers depictions of nature that are 'not centred on humans' her writing also tacitly acknowledges 'that some anthropomorphism [is] necessary' to make sense of the world ('Snakes' 294–5). What Ryan describes as the potential for 'nonanthropocentric anthropomorphism' in Woolf's practices as a writer ('Snakes' 294) can also be seen in Lily Briscoe's activities as a Post-Impressionist artist. In contrast to the Impressionism of the painter Mr Paunceforte whose earlier trip to the Isle of Skye has left a legacy of visiting artists all painting the same 'lemon-coloured sailing boats, and pink women on the beach' (*Lighthouse* 14), Lily looks to depart from what McCarthy and Fry described as Impressionism's 'receptive, passive attitude towards the appearance of things' (*Manet* 8–9). Instead, she intends that her painting of the garden will reveal the underlying 'shape' in 'the midst of chaos', echoing Bell's radical Post-Impressionist avowal of a landscape reduced to pure form (*Lighthouse* 132–3). Yet, while Bell's aesthetic theory tends towards a dematerialized formalism that empties nature of its content in its pursuit of an ultimate reality, Lily's artistic practice is informed by a nonanthropocentric vision of the materiality of nature itself. Her active perception of the nonhuman world guides and influences the brush strokes in ways that seem to exceed her own individual, human agency:

> She began precariously dipping among the blues and umbers, moving her brush hither and thither, but it was now heavier and went slower, *as if* it had fallen in with some rhythm which was dictated to her (she kept looking at the hedge, at the canvas) by what she saw, so that while her hand quivered with life, this rhythm was strong enough to bear her along with it on its current (*Lighthouse* 131–2; emphasis added).

The use of 'as if', a connective which Ryan points out is conducive to nonanthropocentric anthropomorphism in its implications of conditionality and contingency ('Snakes' 295), presents Lily in a dynamic interrelation with the environment she feels to be dictating her movements. It becomes unclear whether the 'life' with which her hand quivers is her own or that of the nonhuman rhythms she has become attuned to. Subsequently losing 'consciousness of outer things, and her name, and her personality and her appearance', Lily is presented as entering an intuitive relation with the external world that heightens her sense of embodiment but which also enacts a moment of depersonalization (*Lighthouse* 132). If Bell's account implicitly situates nature in passive terms as something which is worked on by the artist's interrogative eye, Woolf's portrayal of artistic composition foregrounds the nonhuman world's agency over the artist. As opposed to the Ramsays' sense of impending darkness and blindness, Lily's openness to the continuity between the human and the nonhuman is precisely what facilitates her sense of having had her 'vision' at the novel's end (*Lighthouse* 170).

VITA, VIRGINIA, AND QUEER NATURE

While Lily's vision involves an experience of depersonalization, in the broader context of the narrative her bodily identity as an artist is emphasized and presented as inseparable from discourses of gender. As Goldman states, Lily's 'aesthetic contemplation' is informed as much by her 'social and political ... struggle' with Charles Tansley and Mr Ramsay as it is by abstract questions of form. Moreover, within this politicized dimension to Lily's composition the question of nature remains prescient. As Goldman writes, the erasure of the tree's centrality in Lily's second painting is a rejection of a pastoral tradition in which the tree is a 'natural, unifying sign of an old-order status quo' (*Feminist* 170). While

Lily is receptive to the world of nonhuman objects and rhythms, she is simultaneously critical of the patriarchal cultural associations through which nature has historically been aestheticized. In contrast to Bell and Fry's writing on aesthetics, Woolf's novel critically engages with the relationship between the coconstitutive discourses of nature and gender. We might, in this respect, detect an influence other than Post-Impressionism on *To the Lighthouse*: her sexual and literary relationship with Vita Sackville-West.

Sackville-West's place within the Bloomsbury Group is often contested. Quentin Bell omits her almost completely from *Bloomsbury* (1968), describing her only in passing as 'in some respects a "Bloomsbury" figure' (68). More recently, Victoria Rosner has defined Sackville-West as a 'key associate' rather than a member, since she does not fit Rosner's working definition that the 'Bloomsbury Group's members either originated or made foundational contributions to British Post-Impressionist painting, literary modernism, the field of macroeconomics, and a new direction for public taste in art' (3). Indeed, Sackville-West herself did not feel entirely at ease in the company of Bloomsbury, despite her relationship with Virginia Woolf and the fact that she also knew both Clive Bell and Leonard Woolf. Declining Virginia Woolf's invitation to visit Hampton Court with Duncan Grant, Vanessa and Clive Bell in 1927, she writes: 'I don't relish the idea of butting in where I'm not wanted' (*Letters* 235–6). Nonetheless, in both Sackville-West's correspondence with Woolf and the influence of her poetry on Woolf's portrayal of nature there is a sense in which she *does* butt in, providing a queer counterpoint to the influence of Fry and Bell's formalism.

In the summer of 1925, as Woolf began to work on an early draft of what would become *To the Lighthouse*, her relationship with Vita Sackville-West was similarly taking form. While, by the end of the year, their growing affection for one another would culminate in a sexual encounter at Sackville-West's house at Long Barn, the letters sent to each other during the summer exhibit a developing literary relationship in which questions of nature are frequently discussed. Sackville-West, then working on her long georgic poem of Kentish rural life, *The Land* (1926), explained to Woolf that she believed modern poetics needed 'the prosaic' rather than 'purple poetry' when portraying the countryside, wryly adding that she was confident that 'you could run a small-holding from the information supplied' in her poem's detailing of 'exactly how and when to cut hay, cereals and beans' (*Letters* 67–8). For Woolf, in response, the 'test of poetry' was that 'without saying things, indeed saying the opposite, it conveys things', giving the example of the 'fens, marshes, shingle, the East Coast, rivers with a few ships, coarse smelling weeds ... a whole landscape in short' that she associates with the poetry of George Crabbe, despite there being 'nothing of the sort' in Crabbe's poems themselves (Leaska and DeSalvo 69). Woolf's observation to Sackville-West that nature poetry 'conveys things' without explicitly 'saying' them offers an indication of what Leslie Hankins has characterized as the way in which both their published work *and* their correspondence encodes lesbian desire (186). The classical overtones and lesbian undertones to what Woolf describes in a letter as a 'romantic ... vision' of Sackville-West 'stamping out the hops in a great vat in Kent – stark naked, brown as a satyr, and very beautiful' finds a published response in Sackville-West in *The Land* (Woolf, *Letters* 198). For Sackville-West, the traditional pastoral subject of 'the tillage, and the reaping' of the countryside also accommodates a self-defined female sexuality (*Land* 1). In her deployment of suggestive imagery, such as the spring fritillaries that 'scarfed in dull purple like Egyptian girls' emit 'an ancient snaring spell' or the 'tall and airy world' of 'women and woods, with shadowed aisles profound | That none explore', the poem teases at a same-sex desire that transgresses the poem's conservative form (*Land* 44, 85).

Critics such as Suzanne Raitt have highlighted how Sackville-West's poem is representative of a 1920s English homosexual literary subculture defined by a retreat into the relative freedoms of the countryside (12). It is a literary impulse which Woolf satirizes in *Orlando* (1927), where the novel's sexually metamorphosing protagonist spends several hundred years writing a poem entitled 'The Oak Tree', at one point, directly quoting the 'Egyptian girls' lines from *The Land* (183). Yet, Sackville-West's poem not only establishes a space for human lesbian desire but offers a momentary glimpse of the potential for a queer reading of nature itself. While in certain passages the poem deploys tropes of pastoral fecundity that endorse and even naturalize patriarchy and heteronormativity, such as in the description of the farmer who 'mates up his beasts' every winter according to what is later described as 'natural law', elsewhere the poem suggests the *un*naturalness of such practices (*Land* 19, 34, 1). In the poem's clearest engagement with modernist ideas, Sackville-West describes human perception of nature as 'fragmentary', broken off from 'a whole' which we do not have access to, and that, as such, the perceiving human and the perceived natural world should be understood as 'entangled in strange mesh' (*Land* 49). In contrast to a personified or feminized nature portrayed elsewhere in the poem, this understanding of nature's wholeness as a 'strange mesh' signifies a materiality that resists symbolism or appropriation since there is always 'some relation we may not adjust' to our own ends (*Land* 49). If literary tropes elsewhere frame nature within heteronormative narratives of fecundity and fertility, the 'strange mesh' signifies that which escapes such narratives. It is what remains when 'all else dies' (*Land* 49). This is nature understood not through cyclical paradigms of reproduction but rather as a remainder or materiality that exceeds a life and death binary. Indeed, Sackville-West's imagery foreshadows contemporary theories of queer nature in this instance, finding a parallel with Timothy Morton's assertion that a 'queer ecology' unconstrained by heteronormativity 'requires a vocabulary' that recognizes that 'life-forms constitute a *mesh*, a nontotalizable, open-ended concatenation of interrelations that blur and confound boundaries' (*Queer* 275). Sackville-West's 'strange mesh' opens up a momentary space that does not look to attach queer ideas to nature so much as recognize that, as Morton specifies, 'ecology is queer' (*Queer* 277).

Woolf, who had read a near completed manuscript of *The Land* in late 1925, portrays Lily in *To the Lighthouse* as arriving at a strikingly similar conclusion (Glendinning 152). For Lily, looking out across the garden to the sea and sky, the air presents itself as if 'a fine gauze ... held things and kept them softly in its mesh' (*Lighthouse* 152). In contrast to Mr Ramsay's perception of the sea earlier in the novel, Lily's anthropomorphic vision of how 'the cliffs looked as if they were conscious of the ships' imagines nature as an entanglement of human and nonhuman entities. The nonhuman world that makes Lily quiver with life as she paints is a mesh of 'external passing and flowing' in which relationality is foregrounded and desire untethered (*Lighthouse* 133). Christina Froula has argued that Lily's artistic vision is informed by an intensity of desire not only for the mourned object of Mrs Ramsay but for 'a world teeming ... with grass, ants, plantains, canvas, brush, so many lives – the everyday world of things in themselves' (133). In Lily's vision of nature as a soft mesh in which the human is intractably entangled, Woolf goes further than Sackville-West's portrayal of a queer nature, presenting the act of composition as a site of aesthetics, politics and sexuality that not only exceeds heteronormativity but exceeds the human itself.

Woolf's *To the Lighthouse* synthesizes a variety of answers to Fry's question, 'of what nature is it?' The novel not only presents the reader with the same aesthetic reimagining of the relationship between nature and artistic forms which fuelled Post-Impressionism and its formalist legacies but returns that vision (or re-vision) of nature to its political roots. While the formalism penned by Fry and Clive Bell in the decade after the Post-Impressionist exhibitions worked towards framing art and nature in terms of underlying order and pure forms, Woolf's polite rebuttal in a letter to Fry that there is no 'symbolism' in *To the Lighthouse* implicitly situates her literary formalism as neither universal nor ahistorical (Woolf, *Letters* 3: 385). Instead, in foregrounding both the historical conditions and more-than-human desires that guide Lily's vision, Woolf's novel articulates a clear feminist agency in relation to questions of art and nature. Regulated by conventions of neither aesthetics nor sexuality, Woolf's novel speaks to a network of Bloomsbury influences that include Sackville-West and Vanessa Bell, as well as Fry and Clive Bell. In its portrayal of desire and queerness, it returns in many respects to Edward Carpenter. If Fry's radical ideas about nature and aesthetics had first been awoken by Carpenter, for whom a return to nature was coterminous with a departure from heteronormativity, then Woolf's historicizing and queering of nature similarly insists on foregrounding the sexual politics of modernist aesthetics.

Banfield describes Fry's excitement at the prospect for 'a new way of seeing nature' in the early twentieth century thanks to intellectual advance that he described in a letter to Marie Mauron as moving beyond 'systems [of thought that are] entirely anthropocentric' (Banfield 250). In Woolf's writing, we find an articulation of that possibility, not within systematic thought but literary aesthetics. In the short, twelfth chapter in 'The Lighthouse' section of *To the Lighthouse*, entirely enclosed within the square brackets that earlier denoted nonanthropocentricism, Lily looks out over the bay and sees that the boat with the Ramsay family aboard has been 'swallowed up ... they had become part of the nature of things' (*Lighthouse* 154). If, for Fry, the question 'of what nature is it?' drew attention to the slippage between 'nature' as signifying the inherent properties of an object and as a noun denoting the nonhuman world, Lily's vision collapses both distinctions into one. In Woolf's novel, the question of nature no longer implies a distance between the human subject and the nonhuman world; it extracts the 'and' from the equation of 'Bloomsbury and Nature'. Instead, what we find in the legacy of Fry's Post-Impressionism, Bell's significant form, Sackville-West's pastoral poetry and Woolf's prose is Bloomsbury Nature.

NOTES

1. For Morton, the two usages of nature I have outlined are inseparable since nature is always a 'transcendental term in a material mask' (*Ecology* 14). See Terry Gifford's *Pastoral* for a comprehensive overview of how pastoral aesthetics have developed alongside changing conceptions of nature.
2. Bell's sentiment echoes Fry's 1909 defence of the pathetic fallacy, where he asserts that the artist should 'arrange the sensuous presentment of objects' so that 'the emotional elements are elicited with an order and appropriateness' that nature, 'heartlessly indifferent to the needs of the imaginative life', does not provide (*Vision* 38).
3. Diane Swanson locates a 'Copernican shift' in Woolf's experimental short fiction of the late 1910s, arguing that these early stories foreshadowed and enabled her 'reframing and defamiliarizing of the human world in her later novels' (71).

4. Banfield argues that, in this respect, Mr Ramsay mirrors Leslie Stephen's interest in 'the classic problem' of the applicability of logic to facts. In an alternative account of Stephen's influence on Mr Ramsay and nature, Scott draws parallels between the novel and Stephen's activities as a mountaineer (Scott 135–6).

WORKS CITED

Alt, Christina. *Virginia Woolf and the Study of Nature*. Cambridge: Cambridge UP, 2010.

Arnold, Matthew. *The Poems of Matthew Arnold*. Ed. Kenneth Allott.
    London: Longsmans, 1965.

Banfield, Ann. *The Phantom Table: Woolf, Fry, Russell and the Epistemology of Modernism*.
    Cambridge: Cambridge UP, 2000.

Beer, Gillian. *Virginia Woolf: The Common Ground*. Edinburgh: Edinburgh UP, 1996.

Bell, Clive. *Art*. London: Chatto and Windus, 1931.

Bell, Clive. 'The English Group'. *Modernism: An Anthology of Sources and Documents*.
    Ed. Vassiliki Kolocotroni, Jane Goldman and Olga Taxidou. Edinburgh: Edinburgh UP,
    2011. 192–4.

Bell, Quentin. *Bloomsbury*. London: Futura, 1976.

Bell, Quentin. *Virginia Woolf: A Biography: Vol. 1, Virginia Stephen 1882–1912*.
    London: Hogarth Press, 1970.

Carpenter, Edward. *Civilisation: Its Cause and Cure and Other Essays*. London: George
    Allen, 1921.

Caws, Mary Ann. 'Pens and Paintbrushes'. *The Cambridge Companion to the Bloomsbury
    Group*. Ed. Victoria Rosner. Cambridge: Cambridge UP, 2014. 131–43.

Froula, Christine. *Virginia Woolf and the Bloomsbury Avant-Garde: War, Civilization,
    Modernity*. New York: Columbia UP, 2005.

Fry, Roger. *A Roger Fry Reader*. Ed. Christopher Reed. Chicago: U of Chicago P, 1996.

Fry, Roger. *Vision and Design*. London: Penguin Books, 1961.

Garnett, David. *Lady into Fox and A Man in the Zoo*. London: Hogarth Press, 1985.

Gifford, Terry. *Pastoral*. London: Routledge, 1999.

Glendinning, Victoria. *Vita: The Life of Vita Sackville-West*. London: Penguin Books, 1984.

Goldman, Jane. *The Feminist Aesthetics of Virginia Woolf: Modernism, Post-Impressionism and
    the Politics of the Visual*. Cambridge: Cambridge UP, 1998.

Goldman, Jane. *Modernism, 1910–1945: Image to Apocalypse*. Basingstoke: Palgrave
    Macmillan, 2004.

Gould, Peter C. *Early Green Politics: Back to Nature, Back to the Land, and Socialism in
    Britain, 1880–1900*. Brighton: Harvester Press, 1988.

Hankins, Leslie Kathleen. 'Orlando: "A Precipice Marked V" between "A Miracle of Discretion"
    and "Lovemaking Unbelievable: Indiscretions Incredible"'. *Virginia Woolf: Lesbian Readings*.
    Ed. Eileen Barrett and Patricia Morgane Cramer. New York: New York UP, 1997. 181–202.

Manet and the Post-Impressionists. Exhibition Catalogue. Grafton Galleries.
    London: Ballantyne, 1910. 7–13.

Merleau-Ponty, Maurice. *Sense and Non-Sense*. Trans. Herbert L. Dreyfus and Patricia Allen.
    Evanston: Northwestern UP, 1964.

Mitchell A. Leaska and Louise A. DeSalvo. Eds. *The Letters of Vita Sackville-West to Virginia
    Woolf*. London: Virago Press, 1984.

Morton, Timothy. *Ecology Without Nature: Rethinking Environmental Aesthetics*.
    Cambridge: Harvard UP, 2009.

Morton, Timothy. 'Queer Ecology'. *PMLA* 125.2 (2010): 273–82.

Raitt, Suzanne. *Vita & Virginia: The Work and Friendship of V. Sackville-West and Virginia Woolf*. Oxford: Oxford UP, 1993.

Rosner, Victoria. 'Introduction'. *The Cambridge Companion to the Bloomsbury Group*. Ed. Victoria Rosner. Cambridge: Cambridge UP, 2014. 1–15.

Ryan, Derek. 'Following Snakes and Moths: Modernist Ethics and Posthumanism'. *Twentieth-Century Literature* 61.3 (2015): 287–304.

Ryan, Derek. *Virginia Woolf and the Materiality of Theory*. Edinburgh: Edinburgh UP, 2013.

Sackville-West, Vita. *The Land*. London: William Heinemann, 1939.

Scott, Bonnie Kime. *In the Hollow of the Wave: Virginia Woolf and Modernist Uses of Nature*. Charlottesville: U of Virginia P, 2012.

Spalding, Frances. *Roger Fry: Art and Life*. Norwich: Black Dog Books, 1999.

Sultzbach, Kelly. *Ecocriticism in the Modernist Imagination: Forster, Woolf, and Auden*. Cambridge: Cambridge UP, 2016.

Swanson, Diana L. 'Woolf's Copernican Shift: Nonhuman Nature in Virginia Woolf's Short Fiction'. *Woolf Studies Annual* 18 (2012): 53–74.

Williams, Raymond. *Keywords: A Vocabulary of Culture and Society*. Abingdon: Routledge, 2011.

Woolf, Leonard. *The Village in the Jungle*. London: Hogarth Press, 1971.

Woolf, Virginia. *A Haunted House: The Complete Shorter Fiction*. Ed. Susan Dick. London: Vintage Books, 2003.

Woolf, Virginia. *The Letters of Virginia Woolf*, 6 vols. Ed. Nigel Nicolson and Joanne Trautmann. London: Hogarth, 1975–80.

Woolf, Virginia. *Orlando: A Biography*. Ed. Brenda Lyons. London: Penguin Books, 1993.

Woolf, Virginia. 'The Pastons and Chaucer'. *The Essays of Virginia Woolf: Vol. 3*. Ed. Andrew McNeillie. London: Hogarth Press, 1988.

Woolf, Virginia. *Roger Fry: A Biography*. New York: Harcourt, Brace, 1940.

Woolf, Virginia. *To the Lighthouse*. Ed. David Bradshaw. Oxford: Oxford UP, 2008.

Woolf, Virginia. *The Voyage Out*. Ed. Lorna Sage. Oxford: Oxford UP, 2009.

Case Study: Eating Animals and the Aesthetics of Meat in Virginia Woolf's *The Years*

VICKI TROMANHAUSER

Thinking through and with meat can help us to make sense of the formal challenges we see in Woolf's return to realism in the 1930s. Woolf conceived of her novel, *The Years* (1937), as unwanted flesh, and finishing it brought physical relief, as if a 'bony excrescence [or] bag of muscle – were cut out of my brain' (*Diary* 5: 3). The tremendous strain of writing and revising the family chronicle of the Pargiters, which spans roughly fifty years from 1880 to the 'Present Day', pressed Woolf up against her own mental and physical limits. Yet what had been so taxing about the novel also proved in retrospect one of its strengths; comparing it favourably against her more overtly experimental novels, she suspected that *The Years* 'has I think more "real" life in it; more blood & bone' (*Diary* 5: 38). Whether succulent or unsavoury, the novel's meals become sites of unexpected vibrancy and life through which Woolf makes the matter of the meat matter. The many occasions in which meat is served spoiled, stringy, or underdone expose the ways in which cultural processes once deemed natural appear raw or 'off' in the interwar period. The fleshy realities of meat's disguised source reassert themselves in the meaty fug of Martin's City chophouse, the undercooked joint Sara serves North, and the spoiled fish Kitty endures at the Lodge in Oxford.

In depicting these meals, Woolf represents the meat of the matter in such a way as to engage with a long Western cultural and intellectual tradition of depriving animals of the capacity for self-reflective thinking and of the kind of critical reflection that affords humans memory and the ability to order events into thoughtful narrative. Animals, according to this tradition, stay on the surface of life without the capacity for intellectual transcendence and thus remain poor in world, thought, and selfhood. As Ron Broglio explains in *Surface Encounters: Thinking with Animals and Art*: 'Animals are said to live on the surface of things. Surfaces are seen as fleeting appearances, mere shadows, lacking the substantiality found in the "depth" of human interiority' (xvi). Therefore, for Broglio, eating meat is the ultimate means by which humans incorporate and appropriate the other both physically and epistemologically – taking what is outside, alien, and unknown and converting it into the self-same substance of our bodies and our thought:

> Meat is the moment when what remained hidden to us is opened up. The animal's insides become outsides. Its depth of form becomes a surface, and its depth of being becomes the thin lifelessness of an object exposed. Meat makes the animal insides visible, and through sight the animal body becomes knowable. And while meat serves as a means for us to take in the animal visually and intellectually, it also marks the moment when the animal becomes physically consumable. (1)

In its visceral materiality, meat marks a moment of transformation, a kind of alchemical metamorphosis of living being into lifeless flesh, of sentient subject into inert object, of obscure animal interior into fully exposed exterior, and of opacity into intelligibility. By exposing insides as 'visually accessible exteriors', meat, as Broglio explains, provides 'a means by which human interiority can think itself' (14).

It is tempting to turn this description back on Woolf's diary entry about *The Years* as a 'bony excrescence [or] bag of muscle' cut out of her brain. Given the symmetry of Woolf's representation of meaty writing as interiors made exterior with Broglio's transformative effect of living flesh becoming exposed meat, we might consider the best way to take these surfaces seriously. How might the surface as a conceptual space we typically assign to the animal present an occasion for thinking differently? In spite of our overinvestment in the depth of human interiority and the metaphysical peaks of cultural knowledge, how might we see the supposed noninteriority of the animal as productive of value and meaning? As Pamela Caughie has argued, the form of *The Years* plays upon the 'dichotomy between what is surface, superficial, and conventional and what is deep, significant, and natural' in order to challenge our evaluative associations with those terms (95). 'At stake in this text, then', she explains, 'is not freeing the true nature from conventional forms but exposing the seemingly natural as conventional and disclosing our tendency to accept certain conventions as natural and normative' (99). Not only does *The Years* insist that we take surfaces seriously, but it turns insides out, converting repressed interiors into sensually legible and perhaps more intelligible exteriors.

It is important to recall that Woolf's literary depictions of meat took shape amidst shifting conceptions of carnivory in English dietary culture. Isaac Harris's *Diet and High Blood Pressure*, published by the Hogarth Press the same year as *The Years*, for example, reflects the extent to which gastronomical values had shifted in the interwar period. A physician and dietary reformist, Harris reflects a changing culinary culture that was devoting increased attention to what Britons were eating and how they were preparing their food, including a National Food Inquiry in the mid-1930s which surveyed the British public about its culinary practices (Humble 57). Having absorbed the lessons in nutrition occasioned by the food rationing of the war years, his recommendations (supplemented by sample dietary regimens) are nutritional rather than epicurean, and questions of health trump considerations of custom and tradition, status and fashion. Eating, he insists in Spartan terms, is a matter of 'replenish[ing] energy and replac[ing] tissue wastage' (104).

Harris replaces the formal seven- or eight-course Victorian meal with a series of smaller meals and recognizes the importance of vegetables as more than just garnishments to meat. The shifts away from the formal, multicourse meal and away from the meat-concentrated diet of which it consisted are not only nutritionally desirable, but also socially advantageous. While Harris stops short of recommending a diet that is strictly vegetarian or vegan (he includes daily regimens for lacto-vegetarians), he nevertheless anticipates a future of reduced protein consumption and reliance upon animal protein alone, a change in dietary practice he connects with a larger program of social reform. Linking gluttony for animal flesh with the symbolic anthropophagy we witness in entrenched social inequities, he argues, 'the relentless fury with which man has persecuted his fellow creatures will remain an indelible stain on our present civilization, and a day will come when killing an animal for food will inspire the horror which cannibalism excites at present' (100). Along with its dietary recommendations, the book makes a plea for the reorganization of English society on a 'cooperative basis' (92) as a means of overcoming class disparities and creating 'conditions under which it will be possible for every individual to lead a healthy and care-free existence' (93), values which would have appealed to Leonard Woolf, who read and commented on the proofs (12). 'It is quite true we do not put human flesh in a pot, cook it and serve it out for dinner,' Harris remarks, 'but thousands and thousands of human beings are broken on the juggernaut wheel of our civilization. We do not feed on the corpses of our victims, but large numbers of persons die as a result of conditions brought about by our present mode of living... Is this not cannibalism in the strictest sense of the term?' (90). What Harris calls 'the civilization machine' 'has turned against us, is crushing us' (90).

If the Woolfs never contemplated a meatless diet themselves, changes to their domestic staff in the mid-1930s brought Virginia closer to the preparation of food. She dismissed their cook Nellie Boxall (who had been notoriously proprietary about her kitchen) in 1934, and inherited Mabel Haskins, cook for the vegetarian sister of Roger Fry, Margery, while Nellie Boxall went on to work for another Bohemian couple in Bloomsbury, the vegetarian film and screen star Elsa Lanchester and her husband Charles Laughton (Light 229, 236, 212). Then in Rodmell the Woolfs hired Louie Everest as their daily cook, whom Woolf wrote into a fictional sketch about a London butcher while she was revising the manuscript of *The Years*. One of Woolf's lives of the obscure, 'Ode Written Partly in Prose on Seeing the Name of Cutbush Above a Butcher's Shop in Pentonville', a typescript dated 28 October 1934, brings the story of the tradesman to the surface from the otherwise invisible depths of his shop. Woolf's ode, which can do no more than sing the poetry of the butcher's life 'partly in prose', reads as an allegory of how to bear the gravity of immanence. John Cutbush's life seems doomed from the start when he stands 'glum' between his parents who in selecting a profession for him decide his fate, not unlike a meat animal destined for the slaughter: 'Shall John be florist or butcher?' (237). Cutbush struggles under the crushing state of affairs that Harris diagnosed in his monograph on dietary reform. Even where the sketch's parodic edge introduces levity, tragedy exercises its generic pull: a competitor opens a shop opposite diminishing his profits, he loses a son, and his daughter is a worry for always chasing after boys.

The choice between butchery and floristry represents two competing aesthetic impulses in the ode. Woolf's homage is as strewn with animal carcasses as it is with flowers, the light and lovely stuff of poesy. A hint of this alternate life enchants his story, and flowers mark the moments in which the butcher aspires and romances: 'lovely are the willows / and lilies sliding and twitching' by the pond where he courts Louie (237), who lounges on 'earth laid over with buds and bulbs' (238), and when the young apprentice decides to open his own shop, 'he sees the violets and the asphodel and the / naked swimmers on the bank' (239). But if Cutbush dreams and woos in poetry, he must ply his trade in prose. The stuff of his trade permeates every aspect of their lives – 'meat smells everywhere'

(240) – and Woolf's descriptions repeatedly emphasize its bulk and heft, which seems increasingly to adhere to the butcher, weighting him down, tethering him to the material circumstances of his life hawking carcasses. Rising at 'chill dawn', he sees 'the cold meat / shrouded in white nets borne on men's shoulders' and deals all day long in 'the stark and frozen corpses that shall lie like / mummies in the ice house till the Sunday fire revives / them' (238). Woolf is keen to illuminate the social conditions that freeze life, that chill, curtail, and amputate it like so much expendable flesh.

John Cutbush may dream of Byron's *Don Juan* and swimming in the Hellespont, but he can't escape the weight of the hog and bullock cadavers he carts across London and is figuratively ground under the wheels himself in the eternal sausage grinder of the English social system: 'But time has run its wheels over him. So many million miles / have the trams passed; so many million hogs and / bullocks have been sliced and tossed; so many bags / bulged. His face is red; his eyes bleared; / staring at the flares so many nights' (240). Woolf's anaphoric phrasing and pronounced alliteration beat out a pattern of nearly iambic lines. The more Woolf bends the genre of life writing toward writing the life of meat, the more her language gravitates toward the rhythms of verse. The heft of the carcasses doesn't crush the poetic impulse, but invites it, becomes its beating source.

In perhaps the ode's most arresting image, butchery and the botanical overlap as Woolf grafts one upon the other. The shop window frames the bullock meat like artwork in a gallery: 'The sides of oxen are patterned with flower leaves in the pink flesh. Knives slice' (239). Like Cutbush's very name, which runs the cuts of meat he hocks into the romantic vegetation of his courting days on Primrose Hill, the flower leaves impressed upon raw pink flesh presents a spectacle suspended between animate and inanimate, gruesome thing and object of sacred sublimity. The image allegorizes the operations of the ode, where aesthetics makes a surprising appearance in places we least expect to find it, in an inert animal carcass and in the life of its handler, who elsewhere in British fiction would disappear into his environment, into the undifferentiable proletarian mass and the inscrutable depths of the lower orders.[1] It is as if Woolf is testing the extent to which she can creatively make a bisected animal carcass, an utterly abject object, over into a thing of beauty, not unlike finding the poetry in a butcher's brutal work.

A related process of aestheticizing meat as social and political commentary infuses the scenes of eating in Woolf's novel. In *The Years* the fleshy realities of meat's concealed source reassert themselves as a way of coming to terms with a period of history so thick with violence as to become saturated with it. Consider the scene where Martin Pargiter invites his cousin Sara to enjoy the 'admirable mutton' of his regular City chophouse (217). A heavy air of 'smoke mixed with the smell of meat' signals their entry into this professional masculine establishment, where Martin can enjoy the fantasy of being his servant 'Crosby's God', 'Almighty, all-powerful Mr. Martin!' (220, 218). The enchanting properties of Martin's inflated personal mythos and of his favoured restaurant fare (flesh dressed up in the euphemistic language of gastronomy) are brought up short by the disenchanting language of Sara's interjections, which insistently bring into focus the bodies that are injured and dismembered in the business of sustaining patriarchal authority and imperial power. Mutton, as Allie Glenny explains, was 'the great staple of Victorian patriarchy', and in the Stephen household Leslie enjoyed his daily mutton chop for lunch (Glenny 185). As a dandy who dines off the financial and social privilege made possible by his father's hefty inheritance, itself the product of his years in the service of empire, Martin deflects attention from himself by attempting to draw Sara out, about her mother and her past, but the prospect of other people listening in prevents any meaningful exchange.

In the spring of 1914, just months before the outbreak of the First World War, the sumptuous abundance of 'A vast brownish-yellow joint [that] was being trundled from table to table on a lorry' (216) doubles as an unmistakable reference to the mutilated body of a fallen soldier and its dubious chances of recovery and regeneration. Woolf suggests that Martin and an entire class that has made good on the investments of its military pensions are dining on the carnage of the war to come. The enchanted image of animal flesh roasted into a gustatory sensation is here enlisted to perform the disenchanting work of unmasking violence and exposing the casualties of military aggression, patriarchal authority, and the exploitative drive for profit. Martin repeatedly hushes his inebriated cousin and her indecorous references to such brutality, which unsettle his sense of 'the drowsy benevolence which waits on a good dinner and a glass of wine' or 'the generalised sensation of universal well-being' he reads in Sara's flushed cheeks (219, 218). Sara pantomimes Martin's sister Rose, who has been imprisoned for her militant suffragism, and conjuring the force-feeding of the hunger-strikers, exclaims, 'sitting on a three-legged stool having meat crammed down her throat!' Then brandishing her fork, Sara shouts, 'I don't believe in force!' (220). For such outbursts, Martin places his hand over the mouth of the bottle to silence her inebriated speech. From mutton to soldier's corpse to instrument of force, the chop house scene creates a chain of reference that unsettles the prevailing textual pattern of deflection, indirection, and distance, the very strategies that characterize Martin's preferred conversational mode and its tendency to conceal the casualties of institutional power. 'A damned unpleasant thing', Martin says evasively of his sister's imprisonment and the coercive tactics that silence women's dissenting political voice (219).

By the end of the scene, 'the fug, the warm meaty smell of the City chophouse, had suddenly become intolerable' (221). And Martin apologizes to Sara, 'I oughtn't to have taken you there. It's a beastly hole' (221). The chop house scene opens a hole in the text, a kind of wound that leaks into the complacency of Martin's consciousness, one that for Woolf proves emblematic of the delusional exuberance of the prewar spring with its atmosphere of 'lighthearted and irresponsible' ease (213). The sudden intolerability of the 'fug' registers retrospective disgust at the consequences of this delusion, just as the meat symbolizes patriarchal authority crammed down the throats of its victims.

If true to their name the Pargiters as plasterers display a special aptitude for concealment, for masking and the deft deployment of surfaces, then carving becomes an insistent strategy in the text for penetrating those guises and bringing their concealed interiors, the 'blood & bone' of being, into view (*Diary* 5: 38). Carving, as etiquette and household manuals of the day maintained, was a delicate art requiring precision and training, at once exemplary of its humanizing function in distinguishing man from beast and calibrated to mark subtle gradations of social class and standing (Visser 227–42). Mrs. Beeton devotes extensive discussion in her *Book of Household Management* to the proper carving of various meat animals (respectively cow, lamb, fish, etc.) and Emily Post, observing that the disappearance of the custom of carving meat at table had passed out of vogue by the 1920s, advises that the untrained hand would best leave the carving to the experienced cook in the kitchen.

In the 1917 air-raid episode, Renny, the husband of Maggie Pargiter, expresses some reluctance at taking up this hallowed masculine tradition, when Sara, cousin Eleanor, and the Polish homosexual Nicholas Pomjalovsky gather at his house for a dinner party. As

Allie Glenny acutely observes, Renny 'carves with a glazed, almost shellshocked refusal of feeling', which extends analogously to his work manufacturing arms (Glenny 189):

> 'Yes. Isn't it natural…' she began. 'Could you allow the Germans to invade England and do nothing?' she said, turning to Renny. She was sorry she had spoken; and the words were not the ones she had meant to use. There was an expression of suffering, or was it anger? on his face.
>
> 'I?' he said. 'I help them to make shells.'
>
> Maggie stood behind him. She had brought in the meat. 'Carve', she said. He was staring at the meat which she had put down in front of him. He took up the knife and began to carve mechanically.
>
> 'Now, Nurse', she reminded him. He cut another helping. (271)

Renny's reluctance to carve the unspecified 'meat' handed him by Maggie implicitly addresses Eleanor's question of whether war is 'natural' to the human species, written into our biological being, while it expresses his aversion to a model of Victorian patriarchy and militarism exemplified in the likes of Captain Abel Pargiter, whose talent for 'flicking cutlets dexterously on to plates' as head of table is unimpeded by his having lost two fingers in the Indian Mutiny of 1857 – quelling resistance to English imperial sovereignty – and expresses to his admiring daughter Delia 'his decision, his common sense' (34). Renny's work as a munitions manufacturer, and the wholesale slaughter of soldiers on the battlefield that such work makes possible, folds into carving animal flesh, a task he carries out 'mechanically' but not 'dexterously', as though relinquishing agency in the very act that for prior generations conferred singular prestige, privilege and rank.

From one angle, human history, like the Pargiter chronicle, might be read as the repression of flesh, with its stink of mortality, vulnerability, animality, and thingness. Edibility, as much as animality, forms a limit upon which humanness constructs itself. The immanence of the animal body is precisely what, for Georges Bataille, guarantees human exceptionality by virtue of its place in the ontological food chain – *prêt à manger*, animal life presents itself to us as always having been a thing, potentially edible matter upon which the transcendental human nourishes itself (39–40). Yet the substitution of animal for human meat, which for Freud was requisite for the foundation of civilization and ritually commemorated in the totem meal, is one that, as Jacques Derrida argues, has been at best only partially or imperfectly realized, since 'the so-called non-anthropophagic cultures practice symbolic anthropophagy and even construct their most elevated socius, indeed the sublimity of their morality, their politics, and their right, on this anthropophagy' (Derrida 114). As Anne Anlin Cheng explains, 'we have to be willing to eat ourselves and others in order to be the privileged humans that we are… Consumption makes otherness our own, but it also opens us up to an unruly sociality where what is our 'own' becomes food for the other' (Cheng n.p.).

Renny grimly apprehends this 'unruly sociality' in the spectacle of civilian survival. It was precisely the mechanized and technologized nature of modern warfare, like industrial manufacturing, that explained the catastrophic proportions of human carnage in the First World War and that rendered the human form itself indistinguishable from its animal others, reduced to a mere tangle of flesh on the battlefield as an enlarged abattoir. What Renny performs when he carves at table, as Eleanor's question about the naturalness of war so disconcertingly reminds him, is his complicity in a larger project of disarticulating or unmaking bodies, of transmuting the proper form of life (human or animal body) to flesh (edible or wasted matter).[2] Renny's ambivalence betrays an uncertainty about whose flesh he is carving and, as warplanes bombard the city overhead, expresses a deep discomfort about our own status as flesh – a consubstance with animals that conjures the unwelcome family resemblance Delia feels when looking at her father of being 'too much alike' (35).

The sirens sounding the all-clear bring little comfort; and Renny's savage quip, 'they're only killing other people', concedes his own family's potential status as flesh in his almost casual resignation to the losses of those less immediately privileged in the raid (277). While Woolf deleted many overt references to the war in successive revisions of the novel, from the holograph draft through the galley proofs (Levenback 114–53), the text moves the Front metaphorically into Maggie's cellar. Under the singing bombs overhead the characters descend into the 'crypt-like' coal cellar (274), mummified in wraps and blankets against the chill, and into what Sara calls 'a cave of mud and dung' (277) – a phrase she recalls from her reading of *Antigone*, thus overlaying the trenches onto the ancient heroine's live burial and edging the diners themselves closer to the interred corpse. This family basement-trench-Antigonian tomb takes us deep into the repressed underside of the family meal and occasions questions for the characters about their internal consistency – how 'we don't know ourselves, ordinary people' (266) – in their failure to realize their species-specific mandate as *homo sapiens*.

The more the Pargiters attempt to sequester themselves from the animosity and primal aggression in the world outside, the more thoroughly such forces pierce the rind of human immunity: 'A little blur had come round the edges of things. It was the wine; it was the war. Things seemed to have lost their skins' (272). All kinds of skins and ontological boundaries are discomfitingly shed in the scene. The characters relish the loss of Victorian decorum as they dine free of servants (or nearly so, since they employ a charwoman to clean) and tables in the coal cellar, instead balancing plates upon their laps. But in flouting such decorum they take on the perilous pose of soldiers crouched in the trenches: 'I have spent the evening sitting in a coal cellar while other people try to kill each other over my head,' Renny quips (279). His barbed outbursts about the killing taking place overhead, like his expressed ambivalence about carving the meat, offer a dark gloss on Eleanor's and Nicholas's optimistic discussion of improving the soul and forming 'new combinations', continually threatening to drag their utopian hopes down under the weight of materiality (280). As Eleanor protests, 'but you must let us think of something else' (277). The entire air-raid scene is delicately and uncertainly pitched between two visions of the world to come: Renny's anxieties of annihilation, informed by reports of battles and casualty figures he reads in the daily papers, 'history in the raw' (*Three Guineas* 9), and Eleanor's and Nicholas's aspirations for a 'New World'. If the Pargiter family, and indeed the very family of humanity, is to survive, it must discover new forms of kinship based not on consanguinity with its jealous and proprietary relations, but, as Eleanor and Nicholas suggest, on difference, freedom, equality, and cooperation – the Bloomsbury values in which Woolf cautiously continued to place her hope in the thirties.

Difference, however, has its sharp edges. Near the dinner's end, Sara observes that Nicholas 'ought to be in prison' because he loves 'the other sex' (281–2). Eleanor feels chafed by Sara's candid disclosure: 'For a second a sharp shiver of repugnance passed over Eleanor's skin as if a knife had sliced it… Underneath was – what? She looked at Nicholas. He was watching her' (282). And she realizes: 'All the evening, off and on, she had been feeling about him; this, that, and the other; but now all the feelings came together and made one feeling, one whole – liking' (282). Eleanor's 'sharp shiver' in the face of difference quickly recognizes 'liking' and likeness. Neither the unmarried Eleanor nor the homosexual Nicholas here will enlarge the Pargiter clan by biologically reproducing. Eleanor feels her own permeability in connection with the penetrability of other borders thought to be fixed, necessary, and, to borrow her word, 'natural': gendered, national, sexually orientated, and speciated. The Polish Nicholas's nickname 'Brown' additionally racializes him as a foreigner in a way that the heterosexual Frenchman René or 'Renny' is not. The discovery of Nicholas's otherness here brings the surprise not of difference, but intimacy. The queer bond forged between them in this moment of lacerating exposure on both sides, a surgical scrutiny of other and self as Eleanor looks at Nicholas and finds herself examined by him in return, suggests new ways of imagining kinship. Injury and disfigurement, as Sarah Cole and Abbie Garrington have crucially pointed out, run through the novel and emphasize the extent to which the characters are woundable, whether by the hands of others or their own: Abel's right hand was mangled in the Indian Mutiny of 1857; Sara was dropped as a baby, leaving one shoulder higher than the other; Morris has a 'white scar' on his hand (104); and Rose, too, bears a 'thin white scar' (150) on her hand presumably from an attempted suicide (see Cole 256–8; Garrington 123–31). And if in *The Years* female, foreign, queer, and animal bodies appear particularly vulnerable to the knife's sharp point and to being constituted as edible, it is also from this place of extreme vulnerability in realizing the capacity to be sliced that the novel opens up new possibilities for affiliation and affinity and ventures alternative conceptions of the family.

The 1917 chapter ends with another curious exposure when Eleanor meets the 'rheumy, twinkling' eyes of an old man on the omnibus who is eating his supper out of a paper bag (285). 'Like to see what I've got for supper, lady?' he entreats her with cocked eyebrow, and then 'he held out for her inspection a hunk of bread on which was laid a slice of cold meat or sausage' (285). This closing image of a meal-on-the-go traveling through London along with the 'cadaverous' omnibus passengers (an uncanny description with which Woolf opens and closes the chapter) is an unsavoury double of the admirable mutton trundled among the tables of Martin's chop house and suggestively incarnates the city, figuratively dispersing cold meat through its blacked-out streets in a grim portent of the First World War's posthumous geography as, in 1937, the prospect of an even worse sequel seemed increasingly likely (264, 284). From one vantage, the old man's lude invitation to Eleanor represents a disturbing echo of the young Rose's traumatic confrontation with the male exhibitionist in the street in the 1880 chapter, another scene of a man and his meat which pits masculine sexual aggression against socially enforced female sexual passivity and muteness. Yet surely at 61, Eleanor, who has travelled extensively through the city's diverse neighbourhoods in her philanthropic work, is in a better position to hold her own in the company of a strange man than the ten-year-old Rose. And so alternatively, the twinkle in the old man's eye might playfully be read in the spirit of Eleanor's and Nicholas's toast to a 'New World' and the 'new combinations' it promises as an overture to queer intimacy based upon their shared vulnerability in 1917, 'the year in which civilian endurance was most severely tested' (Levenback 118).

Madelyn Detloff and Brenda Helt argue that more than just a synonym for gay, lesbian, bisexual or trans identity, queerness constitutes a 'critical/epistemological predisposition' at odds with presumptions about 'the naturalness of identity, of sex, of gender, or of desire' (1). Given this queer disposition, the metaphysics of digestion as social integration within the body politic deserve further thought. Can eating as consumption be queered? Kyla Wazana Tompkins identifies the alimentary as a prominent mode for exploring precluded forms of identity that resist normative discourses of desire and sexual, gender or racial affiliations. She employs the term 'queer alimentary' to describe the way in which the mouth and its oral pleasures provide a stage on which 'nonnormative desires can be played out' (5, 185). As part of this queer alimentary practice, Eleanor, the old man, and cold meat make their way together through London's darkened streets via public transportation (just as the omnibus had promised female emancipation for Elizabeth in *Mrs. Dalloway*) as a 'new combination', like the 'nuptials' or 'marriage of opposites' Woolf celebrates at the end of *A Room of One's Own* (95, 103) when the narrator observes a girl and a young man climb into a taxi-cab.

What proves most striking and subversive about the novel's encounters with meat, even as it is carved up to be served, is the way that instead of articulating and clarifying the limits of human and animal, consuming subject and edible object, interiority and exteriority, they hold such distinctions in suspension. At the heart of the omnivore's dilemma is the problem of the confusion of fleshes that an indiscriminate diet produces. Even our most refined culinary arts can produce the dizzying sense that sophisticate and primitive, edible meat and nonedible body, aesthetic object and bare flesh are, in Delia's words, 'too much alike'. Eating raw intensifies the paradoxes that surround the consumption of meat. In the case of eating sushi, as Anne Anlin Cheng explains, the 'inherent, flickering imbrication between 'meat' and 'flesh' ... both instantiates and disproves human exceptionality', since sushi 'symbolizes the supposedly exclusively human value for aesthetic experience – even as a raw food it transgresses the protocols of civility' (n.p.). And Cheng warns us, the 'failure of that distinction reflects back on our own *fresh* and *dying* flesh' and thus exposes 'a curious, glaring gap between our biological attachment to yet ontological detachment from our own meatness' (n.p.). This confusion of fleshes elicits the 'negative capability' at work in what Cheng dubs 'the sushi principle': that is, 'the double delirium of knowing my own animalness even as I partake in the social-aesthetic ritual designed to disguise (but never quite fully) the rawness, vibrancy, violence, and naturalness of that eating' (n.p.). Eating raw flesh reflects dubiously back on its consumer, threatening the clarity of borders between interiority and exteriority, subject and object, lifeless thing and lively being and thus making our own objecthood, fleshness, and edibility distressingly visible.

When Sara invites her younger cousin North to a lunch of undercooked mutton in the novel's 'Present Day' section, the strangely invigorated meat engages the lives on both sides of the meal. Sara's reduced financial circumstances in the postwar period leave her unable to reproduce the opulence of Martin's prewar chophouse. The bleeding joint Sara's maid serves – which, she observes, is acceptable for beef, but not for mutton – appears further evidence of Mrs Malone's diagnosis of the deplorable state of English culinary affairs earlier in the novel, where she decries the outrage to culinary decency that results from the democratization of education and a dinner of spoiled fish. Sara and North find themselves under the influence of Cheng's 'sushi principle' as the strange vitality of the meat, the not-quite-dead flesh bleeding into the plate, introduces the queasy prospect of food coming to life. When Sara cuts into the leg of mutton, she seems to be performing a surgical incision rather than carving meat at table: 'A thin trickle of red juice ran out; it was underdone' (302).

'Another cut off the joint?' she asked.

'No, thank you,' he said, looking at the rather stringy disagreeable object which was still bleeding into the well. The willow-pattern plate was daubed with gory streaks. (304)

The plate's tasteful and delicate 'willow-pattern' is blotted out by the 'gory streaks' that ooze gruesomely from that 'stringy disagreeable object'. The conspicuously textured descriptions of the food's material substance present us with a remainder that cannot be fully digested or absorbed, with flesh that resists metabolic transformation into the self-same substance of those who would eat it.

Among the meal's horrors are the vegetable dishes, which feature 'a slabbed-down mass of cabbage in one oozing green water; in the other, yellow potatoes that looked hard' (302). The cadaverous vegetables suggest gangrenous limbs and rigor mortis, and topping them off for desert is a rather gaudy affair, 'an ornate pudding, semi-transparent, pink, ornamented with blobs of cream' whose 'quivering mass' resembles flesh that is uncannily both alive and dead (304, 305). Sara's oddly fleshy pudding resonates with the saturated consciousness that was for Woolf the hallmark of literary modernism – itself 'a luminous halo, a *semi-transparent* envelope surrounding us from the beginning of consciousness to the end' ('Modern Fiction' 160; emphasis added). In her modernist manifesto 'Modern Fiction' (1925), Woolf famously pits the conventional 'materialist' writers (Wells, Bennett, and Galsworthy) against the modernist 'spiritualists' (Chekhov and Joyce), whose task is to turn away from the body and from air-tight sequential narrative in order to capture, instead, the 'quick of the mind' in its continually shifting impressions, which Woolf represents in mystical, metaphysical terms as the proper 'stuff' of fiction that has eluded the realism of materialist writers (160). But in what Melba Cuddy-Keane has identified as Woolf's 'trope of the twist' or 'turn & turn about method' after a June 1923 diary entry, Woolf characteristically revises the values of such oppositional terms. By praising the 'spiritual' in the decomposing corpses of the cemetery episode in James Joyce's *Ulysses*, Woolf parts ways with 'the transcendent and rarefied consciousness with which [she] is so aligned', Cuddy-Keane argues, and 'embraces not only a physical subject matter but a metaphysics that locates the spiritual in the physical self' (191).

The lodging house table performs something like its hostess's talent for ventriloquy, making vividly present the textures of absent bodies and substances. 'There are things he hadn't told her', North acknowledges, as Woolf's novel doesn't disclose to readers, about his military exploits in Africa on behalf of king and empire. In his tactful omission of the grisly details of the violence of combat and colonial expansion, North participates in a code of manly, heroic conduct that conceals from the civilian population back home the horrors of war's violence and the agony of suffering bodies. Yet these elisions, both from North's communications to his cousin and from the novel's representation of the colonial and global wars that form part of the public history of its 'years', find expression in the text's descriptions of the food. The garish fluids that leak from the meat, the lurid textures of the stringy mutton, and the 'quivering mass' of the pink pudding provide a textual means of making visible the undisclosed violence of North's African campaigns and of bringing that concealed narrative of brutality into view. Moreover, the scene's careful staging – the parlour maid lifting the great metal cover from the dish to reveal the mutton underneath, Sara's 'long incision' with the carving-knife into the leg, and North 'cutting his mutton into strips' (302) – comes to figure the novel's own stylistics, its preoccupation with surfaces, with the act of exposing interior depths and thus transforming invisible insides into visible and intelligible outsides. These conspicuous descriptions of the meal's material substance disturb narrative pacing, disrupting the flow of the characters' conversation and the scene's development of renewed intimacy between estranged cousins. North's lunch with his cousin Sara late in the novel creates its own trail of reference that bleeds into other analogous scenes and unsettles them. As we follow the trail of meat and mutton, we can trace it back to its source in North's colonial sheep farm in Africa, follow it to the table in the chop house or lodging-house, and even witness its greasy remains in the stain left on the bathtub wall by Sara's Jewish neighbour Abrahamson in the tallow trade (see Wegener in this volume). (In my own rendering, it's convenient to imagine they all derive from the same sheep, rather like Mrs. Ramsay's eternally returning rooks Joseph and Mary in *To the Lighthouse*.)

The text brings two forms of rendering into alignment. Just as Sara's Jewish neighbour in the tallow trade converts animal waste (fat, grease) into a material of value (tallow), so Woolf works the shocks of war and force into the continuous weave of her multigenerational story of the Pargiters. Rendering is a dirty business, as *The Years* reminds us by insistently presenting us with the ugliness, the unappealing and gruesome qualities of the matter of our meat, of substance that resists being converted into a thing of beauty or recruited for culturally productive or redemptive ends. There is a gravitational force to such moments, where Woolf's unstinting, graphic language pulls us down into the immediacy of the stuff on the table and refuses us the comforts of abstraction.

The evident danger of contamination and infection that undercooked meat poses to the wary consumer, and that our reflex of disgust is biologically programmed to elicit, also helps to figure the porousness of hierarchies and classificatory structures that govern human sociality and order the natural world. Bonnie Kime Scott (42–70) and Christina Alt (72–105) have significantly shown how Woolf's writing persistently challenges the taxonomizing imagination that informs English culture and institutions, from the class system and public schools to the imperial civil service and professions. Whether it runs red juice or oozes green water or quivers pinkly, the food on Sara's table is anything but content to stay in its place and manages to exude, if not quite agency, animacy. The ontological food chain so prevalent in Western culture, as Mel Chen has recently argued, rests upon an 'animacy hierarchy', a linguistic principle she employs to describe the conceptual arrangement of 'human life, disabled life, animal life, plant life, and forms of nonliving material in orders of value and priority' (13). As a 'scale of relative sentience that places humans at the very top' and declines by degrees into the animal, vegetable, and mineral, such a hierarchy operates as a kind of ecology, in which interrelations between types, like the divisions within them, can shift according to context (89). Since the effects of animacy need not require intentionality or choice (54–5), what Chen's heuristic model helps us to see are the ways in which immanence or animality, the 'stuff' that adheres to the nonhuman animal, 'sometimes bleeds back onto textures of humanness' and thus impels certain figures towards states of lesser being or even nonbeing (89). Yet animacy, as Chen shows us, itself can operate in queer ways. Recognizing how categories as diverse as disability, womanhood, nonnormative sexuality, animality, the vegetal, and the inanimate have traditionally operated as the support for a humanness that disavows them, Chen argues, can alternatively open up possibilities for forging queer kinships that might unfix the conventional ordering of life.

Crucial to the mystery of what the future holds in store is the question of how one eats, especially as it bears upon whom one counts as kin. When Milly and Hugh Gibbs, Edward Pargiter's former Oxford colleague, arrive at Delia's party in the 'Present Day' section, their human form is almost unrecognizable beneath their tremendous girth. They have grown 'substantial' over the years – landed, wealthy, and plump; Milly's fat arms remind North of 'pale asparagus' and the flesh has grown over her diamond rings (355, 354). The pressure of the values they project (heterosexual, familial and clannish, landed and proprietary, nationalist and imperial) figure to North as a great set of devouring tentacles ('long white tentacles that amorphous bodies leave floating so that they can catch their food'), the conceptually grasping human hand devolved into a monstrous, inhuman sucking appendage (358). Here we might recall the way the text measures Hugh's scholarly and intellectual deficiencies at Oxford against the superior erudition of Edward by way of their hands when Hugh extends a 'great red paw' that resembles 'a piece of meat' to accept Edward's proffered port – the master of 'cubbing' indiscernible from his chosen prey (49). In a queer twist, the hand Edward opposes to Hugh's is neither muscular nor masculine, but 'finicky' and 'girl[ish]' (49), a surer sign of his mind's incandescence by incorporating difference. Hugh's hand, 'bound round with raw beef-steak', is a sign of mindless flesh incapable of checking its 'natural' urges or restraining its brute impulses (357).

The amplitude of Milly and Hugh Gibbs' voracious, reproductive bodies threatens to collapse into the very edible matter they would devour, even as they fasten upon their nephew as the next potential food gobbet, weighing him for digestive processing:

> That was what it came to – thirty years of being husband and wife – tut-tut-tut – and chew-chew-chew. It sounded like the half-inarticulate munchings of animals in a stall. Tut-tut-tut, and chew-chew-chew – as they trod out the soft steamy straw in the stable; as they wallowed in the primeval swamp, prolific, profuse, half-conscious, he thought; listening vaguely to the good-humoured patter, which suddenly fastened itself upon him.
> 'What d'you weigh, North?' his uncle was asking, sizing him up. (356)

Though they represent throwbacks to Abel's prolific generation, North's vision of the Gibbs' domestic life is a far cry from the dining room of Abercorn Terrace, plunging them instead into the stables where they wallow in 'soft steamy' droppings as if all that their familial life yields is summed up in the rectum, rather than its 'pastoral other', the mouth (Tompkins 185). The 'disgust' elicited by their corpulent bodies – 'gross, obese, shapeless' (360) – leads North reactively to entertain fantasies of dynamite, a reprise of his experience in the trenches as he envisions exploding those profuse flanks like 'dumps of heavy earth' (356).

By contrast, their hostess revels in breaking with alimentary custom. Holding the dinner party in the rented rooms of an office building, Delia delights in the loss of the central table of her childhood: 'People were sitting on the floor, on chairs, on office stools. Long office tables, little typewriting tables, had been pressed into use' (377). The novel arrangement allows for spontaneous mingling and movement, and, waving her hand 'promiscuously', Delia encourages her guests to break ranks and communicate freely across the old social barriers (377). Faced with a dearth of soup spoons, she mentally divides her guests into those who insist upon them, whom she pejoratively dubs 'English', and those, with whom she affiliates herself, willing to flout convention by foregoing spoons. At the end of the dinner, Delia dredges up the caretaker's children from the basement to offer them their slice of the cake (which she cuts especially large) and they then sing in cockney accents, amidst smeared plates, empty wine glasses and bread crumbs, a dissonant chorus: 'There was something horrible in the noise they made. It was so shrill, so discordant, and so meaningless' (408). Although readers may chafe at Woolf's depiction of the working class's distortion of language (see Simpson in this volume), sound without meaning, as 'noise' and 'shriek', imposes itself upon the Pargiters with almost palpable force, abrading the senses and jangling the nerves (408). But ultimately such disruptions to varnished social convention and revisions to the guest list might be, Eleanor ventures inquisitively, 'beautiful?' in their hint of 'another life, here and now' (408, 405).

Central to the ethics of eating well is the question of where literally and epistemologically we would make the cut: between eater and eaten, human subject and inhuman thing, living and nonliving, who and what, and between those to whom we extend ethical consideration and those from whom we withhold it. Since, as Derrida admonishes us, we may not be able 'to "cut" once and for all where we would in general like to cut', it is a question we must revisit with every meal (Derrida 117). If, as Woolf maintained, the 'appalling narrative business of the realist' is a matter of 'getting on from lunch to dinner' (*Diary* 3: 209), *The Years* turns the business of the realist back upon itself to expose, as one of Woolf's contemporary reviewers put it, 'the blood and marrow of history' (Howard Spring in the *Evening Standard*; Majumdar and McLaurin 377). The new materially grounded realism we see in Woolf's fiction advocates proximity over distance, surface over depth, as a way of releasing us from the repressive social structures that conceal violence and suffering in the name of a privileged class – or even species.

NOTES

1. A butcher appears briefly in *David Copperfield* (1850) as 'the terror of the youth of Canterbury', a young pugilist who anoints his hair with beef suet and challenges schoolboys to fight (Dickens 230). Although David loses the first fight, he later revels in the defeat of his butcher-nemesis, who loses his front tooth in the skirmish. D. H. Lawrence, who once kept the accounts for a pork butcher in Eastwood, also introduces a butcher as a foil to Tom Brangwen and his efforts at self-cultivation in *The Rainbow* (1915). Tom's older brother Frank runs a butchery connected with the family farm, dismisses education, and noisily airs his grievances against the world at the pub.
2. Despite the mechanization of the First World War, several million nonhuman animals joined that abattoir. A recent exhibition at the British Library dedicated to animals in the Great War, curated by Matthew Shaw, details the military reliance by all sides upon horses, mules, oxen, and camels to transport munitions, food, and the wounded, and the recruitment of trained dogs and carrier pigeons to relay messages between the front lines and headquarters (Shaw n.p.).

WORKS CITED

Alt, Christina. *Virginia Woolf and the Study of Nature*. Cambridge: Cambridge UP, 2010.

Bataille, Georges. *Theory of Religion*. Trans. Robert Hurley. New York: Zone Books, 1992.

Broglio, Ron. *Surface Encounters: Thinking with Animals and Art*. Minneapolis: U of Minnesota P, 2011.

Caughie, Pamela. *Virginia Woolf and Postmodernism: Literature in Quest and Question of Itself*. Chicago: U of Chicago P, 1991.

Chen, Mel Y. *Animacies: Biopolitics, Racial Mattering, and Queer Affect*. Durham: Duke UP, 2012.

Cheng, Anne Anlin. 'Sushi, Otters, Mermaids: Race at the Intersection of Food and Animal; or David Wong's "Louie's Sushi Principle"'. *Resilience: A Journal of the Environmental Humanities* 2.1 (May 2015).

Cole, Sarah. *At the Violet Hour: Modernism and Violence in England and Ireland*. Oxford: Oxford UP, 2012.

Cuddy-Keane, Melba. *Virginia Woolf, the Intellectual, and the Public Sphere*.
    Cambridge: Cambridge UP, 2003.
Derrida, Jacques. '"Eating Well", Or the Calculation of the Subject'. Trans. Peter Connor and
    Avital Ronell. *Who Comes after the Subject?* Ed. Eduardo Cadava, Peter Connor and Jean-
    Luc Nancy. New York: Routledge, 1991. 96–119.
Detloff, Madelyn and Brenda Helt. 'Queering Woolf – An Introduction'. *Virginia Woolf
    Miscellany* 82 (2012): 1–4.
Dickens, Charles. *David Copperfield*. Hertfordshire: Wordsworth Classics, 2000 [1850].
Garrington, Abbie. *Haptic Modernism: Touch and the Tactile in Modernist Writing*.
    Edinburgh: Edinburgh UP, 2013.
Glenny, Allie. *Ravenous Identity: Eating and Eating Distress in the Life and Work of Virginia
    Woolf*. New York: St. Martin's Press, 2000.
Harris, Isaac. *Diet and High Blood Pressure*. London: Hogarth Press, 1937.
Humble, Nicola. *Culinary Pleasures: Cookbooks and the Transformation of British Food*.
    London: Faber & Faber, 2005.
Levenback, Karen L. *Virginia Woolf and the Great War*. Syracuse: Syracuse UP, 1999.
Light, Alison. *Mrs. Woolf and the Servants: An Intimate History of Domestic Life in
    Bloomsbury*. London: Bloomsbury, 2008.
Majumdar, Robin and Allen McLaurin. Eds. *Virginia Woolf: The Critical Heritage*.
    New York: Routledge, 1975.
Scott, Bonnie Kime. *In the Hollow of the Wave: Virginia Woolf and Modernist Uses of Nature*.
    Charlottesville: U of Virginia P, 2012.
Shaw, Matthew. 'Animals and War'. 29 January 2014. www.bl.uk/world-war-one/articles/
    animals-and-war
Tompkins, Kyla Wazana. *Racial Indigestion: Eating Bodies in the Nineteenth Century*.
    New York: New York UP, 2012.
Visser, Margaret. *The Rituals of Dinner: The Origins, Evolution, Eccentricities, and Meaning of
    Table Manners*. New York: Grove Weidenfeld, 1991.
Woolf, Virginia. *The Diary of Virginia Woolf*, 5 vols. Ed. Anne Olivier Bell and Andrew
    McNeillie. San Diego: Harcourt, 1977–84.
Woolf, Virginia. 'Modern Fiction'. *The Essays of Virginia Woolf*. Vol. 4. Ed. Andrew McNeillie.
    New York: Harcourt, 1994 [1925].
Woolf, Virginia. 'Ode Written Partly in Prose on Seeing the Name of Cutbush above a Butcher's
    Shop in Pentonville'. *The Complete Shorter Fiction of Virginia Woolf*. Ed. Susan Dick.
    New York: Harcourt, 1989.
Woolf, Virginia. *A Room of One's Own*. Ed. Susan Gubar. New York: Harcourt, 2005 [1929].
Woolf, Virginia. *Three Guineas*. Ed. Jane Marcus. New York: Harcourt, 2006 [1938].
Woolf, Virginia. *The Years*. Ed. Eleanor McNees. New York: Harcourt, 2008 [1937].

CHAPTER NINE

Bloomsbury and Politics

DAVID AYERS

Any discussion of Bloomsbury and politics is confronted not only by the fact that the members of the group had differing political views and commitments in terms of the landscape of the period, which was dominated by the rise of socialism, but also by the manner in which study of the group has shifted with changes in the politics of criticism. These changes have been themselves political and institutional in character but also, as Bloomsbury has become increasingly an object of international appropriation, subject to a network of critical relations stretched across geographies and periods, with America as a dominant force. This increasingly decentred Bloomsbury has a political geography quite different to the apparent geographical localism which the group's name seems to imply. Yet this is not to say that the critical accretions can be brushed away and the original politics of Bloomsbury revealed, since our very sense of how we might construe those past politics is never an entirely historiographical question.

One turning point in the critical construction of the politics of Bloomsbury is found in Raymond Williams' famous essay, 'The Bloomsbury Fraction', which made its first appearance as a talk given at the University of Kent in 1978 and is best known in what has become its definitive version in *Problems in Materialism and Culture* (1980). The moment of its appearance marks a point in the British context of the reception of ideas from France and the United States which could be considered the intellectual form of what Marxism – in an entirely different context – has labelled 'combined and uneven development'. This was a point at which Althusserian theory – the principal object of all demands for theory in cultural studies at the time – was putting one form of pressure on the British brand of lightly theorized Marxism-socialism, while imported US identity politics were increasingly challenging the native forms of feminism and of workerism more generally, forms that were conditioned by that same brand of Marxist socialism. Williams' lecture came as inflation dominated the British economy – as it dominated the world at that time – and just as the famous Winter of Discontent of 1978–9 took shape as a confrontation between the powerful trades unions across the public sector services and the nationalized industries (mining, steel, motor manufacture and so on) and the minority Labour government led by James Callaghan.

By the time that 'The Bloomsbury Fraction' appeared in *Problems in Materialism and Culture* the political landscape had changed significantly since its first appearance as the 1978 lecture. Callaghan's government had lost a vote of no confidence in the house over its handling of industrial relations and the wave of strikes of the Winter of Discontent, and the British electorate, disgruntled by inflation, strikes and a weakening economy which saw the UK labelled as the 'sick man of Europe', returned a Conservative majority government under Margaret Thatcher. Among the many, often colossal shifts which followed in the three successive terms won by the Conservatives (in the elections of 1979, 1983, and 1987) was a move away from the Keynesian approach, which advocated stimulation of demand by government intervention during periods of recession, towards the contrasting macroeconomic model of monetarism, advocated by Milton Friedman – adviser to Margaret Thatcher and to Ronald Reagan – which argued that money supply should be tightly controlled and that the levels of government borrowing demanded by the Keynesian approach (and applied worldwide in the period after the Second World War) were inflationary and ultimately damaging to growth.

The controls on monetary policy were just part of the confrontation with the socialist and Marxist-dominated trades unions engineered by the Thatcher government in the 1980s. This was a period of defeat both for all stripes of socialism – the ameliorative Keynesian approach, intended to stabilize capitalism and maintain high levels of employment, and the Marxist or state-socialist approach which had emphasized public ownership and workers' control. At the point where Williams sets out his position on Bloomsbury at a conference on Keynes held at the University of Kent college which bears his name, the turn against the postwar Keynesian consensus is just beginning to take place, although Williams does not anticipate this or address it. Nevertheless, Keynes's influence on the postwar order – enhanced through the reception of *The General Theory of Employment, Interest and Money* (1936) – can be construed, on any orthodox measure, as the height of the political influence of Bloomsbury in the form of 'Keynesianism'. The turn to monetarism, while it arguably represented an extension of the discipline of macroeconomics of which Keynes was the principal founder, could be understood as a setback for the more socially ameliorative approach integral to Keynesianism.

This political turn was not Williams' starting point in 'The Bloomsbury Fraction', although – once we include its American dimension – it can be recognized as an important marker in a shift from economic to cultural leftism in the Anglophone world. Even though he presented the work at a conference about Keynes, Williams' essay was already aimed at the literary and cultural context. It reflected a moment at which the notion of the 'political' in cultural-critical discourse was subject to various pressures. The claim on which Williams' essay hinges – that the 'Bloomsbury Group' were 'a true *fraction* of the existing English upper class' (156) – appears after several pages, only after Williams has acknowledged the 'extraordinary grouping of talents', the importance of the modality of 'friendship' (151) in Bloomsbury, and given credit to the group principally for ushering in 'the new critical frankness', especially in relation to sexually explicit discourse (154). Williams is operating under the shadow of the structural Marxism of Althusser and his disciple in Britain, Terry Eagleton, a tendency which had the habit of assigning cultural phenomena to identifiable levels or groupings. Althusser analysed ideology in terms of its institutional locatedness and its function as an apparatus, and in the same spirit Williams defines Bloomsbury as a class fraction in order to retain the identification of Bloomsbury with its class even as it constituted itself as an ideological subgroup within that class (see Simpson in this volume). This intentionally bald characterization sets what is intended to be a politically firm context for Williams' comments about the 'structure of feeling' of Bloomsbury, revisiting the nebulous phrase which Williams had coined in the pre-structural Marxism era and chosen to retain despite its apparent looseness.[1] Williams uses the term to frame his discussion of what he argues is the political stamp of Bloomsbury, its association with 'social conscience'. Contradicting what he takes perhaps to be the casual leftist dismissal at that time of the Bloomsbury Group as 'aesthetes', Williams reminds his audience not only of Leonard Woolf's work for the Labour Party, on the theory of the

League of Nations, and his writing on imperialism, but also of Virginia Woolf's regular hosting of meetings of the Women's Cooperative Guild (WCG) at her home.

Williams does this though not in the spirit of more recent commentary which often seeks to redeem the politics of cultural figures supposed to be in some way transgressive and claim them for contemporary identity politics, but in order to assert with more apparent justice his central claim that Bloomsbury – presenting itself as a casual 'group of friends' but in fact representing a sect of Cambridge associates who came out of the circle of the Cambridge Apostles and of G. E. Moore – were the ideological harbingers of 'social conscience':

> It might come as a surprise, to Bloomsbury and to those formed in its image, to set a mark on 'social conscience'. The phrase itself, from just this period, has become widely naturalized, and it is then very difficult to question it. One way to do so is to note its widespread association with that other significant phrase, 'concern for the underdog'. For what has been most carefully defined is the specific association of what are really quite unchanged class feelings – a persistent sense of a quite clear line between an upper and a lower class – with very strong and effective feelings of sympathy with the lower class as victims. Thus political action is directed towards systematic reform at a ruling-class level ... It is a matter of social conscience to go on explaining and proposing, at official levels, and at the same time to help in organizing and educating the victims ... [This] is the precise formulation of a particular social position, in which a fraction of an upper class, breaking from its dominant majority, relates to a lower class *as a matter of conscience*; not in solidarity, nor in affiliation but as an extension of what are still felt as personal or small-group obligations, at once against the cruelty and stupidity of the system and towards its otherwise relatively hapless victims. ('The Bloomsbury Fraction' 155)

Williams' formulation is a counsel against taking Bloomsbury on its own terms, but also a statement which in its moment articulates a confrontation between a Marxist or at least workerist position that advocates the political education of the working class, and a reformist and antirevolutionary position, such as that advocated by the Fabians within the Labour Party. That revolutionary politics would be increasingly in abeyance from that time forward, and that something like a culturally centred identity politics, owing more to American than to British experience, would come to dominate cultural studies, was not quite visible to Williams in the moment in which he wrote.

Williams located Bloomsbury in reformism, and the implicit question ever since has been how far something called 'Bloomsbury' can be mined for any politics which might escape this categorization – although it has never adopted the form of a theoretical debate about the comparative merits of reform versus revolution which might properly be thought to be at the heart of the question, rather than the question of the mode of evaluating the status of a handful of favoured cultural figures. Williams offers no examples, and does not even demonstrate that the phrases 'social conscience' or 'concern for the underdog' formed any part of the Bloomsbury vocabulary – did Keynes use these phrases? Or the Woolfs? Or the Stracheys? Whether the group had a collective antirevolutionary position is debatable. Leonard supported the first Russian Revolution of February 1917, which saw the overthrow of the Tsar and the installation of a more liberal parliament promising free elections. He lost enthusiasm following the Bolshevik takeover in October of that year, but opposed the British intervention against the Bolsheviks in 1918 and continued to argue against it even as he encountered censorship, although his position was not one of support for Bolshevism and did not match that of communist and socialist trades unionists at the time, who expressed solidarity with Lenin's government. His main points were to question the anti-Bolshevik ideology of politicians such as Churchill and press organs such as the *Times* ('They encourage ... a crusade against what?') and to wonder out loud whether the 'idea' behind Bolshevism might 'with good will' have been more widely experimented with as 'a usable form of government', suspecting that Allied intervention would lead to the effective destruction of the 'idea of Communism'.[2] Woolf continued to explore the ideas of Communism and report on them to readers of his column in *Contemporary Review*, so his position cannot be described as anticommunist, yet while the Russian Revolution had brought questions of the possibilities of socialism very much to the fore, it had also served to focus discussion more on the means of achieving socialism than on its application.

The question of revolution was very much in the air in the wake of 1917, and in Britain culminated in the General Strike of 1926 which in effect demonstrated the weakness of the trades unions and of the revolutionary elements within them, a shift from the more unstable position of the years 1918–20. The Bolsheviks of course were the firm advocates of revolution, and Leon Trotsky's *Where Is Britain Going?* (1926), one of several of his works to be published by a mainstream London publisher in the nineteen twenties, was met by a barrage of responses from the reformist left. Trotsky begins his attack on the British reformist approach by referring to a speech by the British Conservative Prime Minister, Stanley Baldwin, given in Leeds in March 1925, in which Baldwin had called for 'gradualness' in social reform and criticized Trotsky by name (Middlemas and Barnes 299). Trotsky defends revolutionary violence, reminding the British that their own imperial history showed that they entirely recognized the value of violence when it suited their own interests, criticizing the reformist Fabians, and pointing to Cromwell and the English Civil war, and to the history of Chartism, to demonstrate that violence had indeed been a key feature of British political history, despite the assertion of Conservatives and Fabians that it was not the British way (*Where Is Britain Going?* 15–37). The book drew critical replies from the philosopher Bertrand Russell, the Labour leader Ramsay MacDonald, and the later Labour leader George Lansbury (*Leon Trotsky on Britain* 211–45). Maynard Keynes also weighed in mercilessly. He described Trotsky's book as 'a turbid stream with a hectoring gurgle', finding its 'flashes of insight' to be offset by 'inevitable ignorance'. Keynes dismisses Trotsky's rhetoric as that of the 'brigand-statesmen to whom Action means War', but makes a serious examination of Trotsky's claim that socialism must inevitably come about through revolution, criticizing his attention to means over ends, denouncing the 'empty-headedness of Force at the present stage of human affairs', and asserting, against Trotsky's appeal to 'theological' Marxism, that at this moment 'we lack more than usual a coherent scheme of progress, a tangible ideal' ('Trotsky on England' 84, 86, 90–91). Keynes was firmly committed to a 'middle way' and took a dim view of even the reformist element within the Labour Party. While he distinguished them from the Bolsheviks – whom he called the 'Party of Catastrophe' – he considered the Labour Party to be conditioned by 'malignity, jealousy [and] hatred of those who have wealth and power'. While the Labour Party spoke for its own sectional class interests, Keynes declared that he would speak for his own: 'the *class* war will find me on the side of the educated *bourgeoisie*' ('Am I a Liberal?' 324, 328).

The notion that the class enemy was motivated by resentment against the wealthy, and also against the superior cultural grace of the wealthy and educated, is a recurrent trope in Virginia Woolf's fiction. In *Night and Day* (1919), the relationship between Katharine

Hilbery and Ralph Denham is shaped by his resentment of her superior social rank. He derides her lack of professional life and the ease of access which wealth confers: 'it's all been done for you. You'll never know the pleasure of buying things after saving up for them' (12). His resentment is said to be such that 'his will-power was rigidly set upon a single object – that Miss Hilbery should obey him' (48). This novel is a romance, which draws on Woolf's own relationship with her social inferior Leonard. While it deals only with the resentment of the professional class for the possessors of inherited wealth, the theme of resentment is clearly signalled. In *Mrs Dalloway* (1925), Miss Kilman, the philanthropist and recent convert to Christianity is depicted as a baleful influence on the daughter of Clarissa Dalloway, wife of a Conservative politician. The figure of Miss Kilman is far from a persuasive or rounded portrait but seems to develop the observation on the psychology of class resentment in *Night and Day* into something more closely resembling the contemporaneous position of Keynes on the psychology of socialist resentment. Woolf's novel implies that the hatred of the internationalist Miss Kilman is based on a resentment of the ruling class which derives from a repressed identification:

> Miss Kilman did not hate Mrs Dalloway ... Observing her small pink face, her delicate body, her air of freshness and fashion, ... there arose in her an overmastering desire to overcome her; to unmask her. If she could have felled her it would have eased her. (137)

This vocabulary of unmasking and felling repeats that of *Night and Day*, where Denham experiences a similar desire in relation to Katharine: 'The vitality and composure of her attitude, as of a bright-plumed bird poised easily before further flights, roused him to show her the limitations of her lot' (12); while it is Katharine who imagines having a profession and 'trampling' other people (46). Although it had been Nietzsche who, in *On the Genealogy of Morality*, advanced the term *ressentiment* to characterize the resentful attitude of the slaves towards the masters, and the Christian and socialist philosophies which derived from it, this Bloomsbury version does not appear to be underpinned by Nietzsche, although it finds a strong echo in Moore's condemnation of the 'great evil' in which a 'cognition of what is good or beautiful' is 'accompanied by an inappropriate emotion', the 'hatred of what is good or beautiful', 'envy and contempt' (260). In fact, Woolf's *Mrs Dalloway* is entirely ordered around the question of upper class political alignment according to an analysis not so much of the politics of Miss Kilman, the outsider, but those of Peter Walsh, a socialist just slightly inferior in social rank to the successful Tory Dalloway, whom Clarissa had chosen to marry in preference to Walsh.

Walsh is of an inferior family to that of Dalloway, described as Anglo-Indian, meaning that they have been part of the imperial administration in India but not at the centre of government in London. Walsh has an anti-imperial attitude, but one which is compromised by his acquired and now involuntary identification with British militarism. This is given complex voicing in the episode which finds Walsh in Whitehall reflecting on himself – 'He had been a Socialist – in some sense a failure – true' – and admiring a parade of young soldiers – 'One had to respect it; one might laugh; but one had to respect it, he thought' (55, 56).[3] So while Williams had raised a question of the 'structure of feeling' involved in what he identified as the Bloomsbury brand of reformism, and while Keynes spoke acidly about Labour class resentment and expressed identification with his own class position, Woolf offers a complementary take on the likely ineffective ambivalence of the governing class but second-tier socialist, Peter Walsh, the 'failed' insider who is set against the resentful outsider, Miss Kilman, a Christian internationalist in turn motivated not simply by hatred but by a complex identification with the ruling class, a form of love such as that which grows in Denham, indissociable from his resentment of Katharine's social superiority and the grace that goes with it.

If we decide to take *Mrs Dalloway* as proposing an analysis, it would be that socialism and internationalism are not to be considered in terms of their desirability or justice or rationality, but that they are the product of deformed psychologies – of the comfortable irony of the upper class socialist, who identifies with the thing he laughs at, or the resentment of the outsider, whose identification with her object takes a directly destructive form. Whether or not this is the position that can properly be modelled as the novelistic ideology, it is clear that the question of the politics of Bloomsbury has historically acquired most urgency in relation to the figure of the author, Virginia Woolf. Woolf's ideas on women's authorship and education in works such as *A Room of One's Own* (1929) have been considered by many commentators to 'anticipate the concerns of feminists in the future' (see Elkin in this volume).[4] The future's political claim on Woolf has occasioned much critical manoeuvring. Julia Briggs, for example, is keen to set evidence of the Woolfs' combined political commitment alongside honest documentation of Virginia's distance from and lack of any real interest in working women. Her biography gives the Woolfs' friendship with Margaret Llewelyn Davies significant space, and explains that the Woolfs were drawn into her work for the WCG, 'an organized body of 32,000 working women' (Briggs 91). Yet Davies' impact seems mostly to have been on Leonard, whom she introduced to Fabian politics, and Virginia's involvement seems to have been attendance at the Guild's 1913 conference in Newcastle, where she was 'impressed by the courage and commitment of the speakers' but 'felt herself excluded', in her own words, 'irretrievably cut off from the actors … an outcast from the flock' (91). Woolf's class position is repeatedly visited in the Woolf commentary. Woolf declared herself a 'snob' (Briggs 167) and despite having a Jewish husband was given to using antisemitic stereotypes (Briggs 308–9), but it is this question of class in the context of feminism which has attracted most attention.

The question of Woolf's class politics, and in general of her appropriation by recent and contemporary forms of identity politics, are commonplaces of the critical literature. Reviewing Woolf's work of the 1930s, marked by Woolf's pacifism and critique of patriarchy, Alice Wood notes her 'refusal to deal with or depict the social and economic problems facing the lower classes' in her late works (13). Examining Woolf's connection with the WCG, Evelyn Tsz Yan Chan discusses the WCG's activism on the issue of maternity care for working-class women, mentions Woolf's support for the publication of their letters (*Maternity*) but goes no further than claiming that 'Woolf would not likely have disagreed' with their arguments, noting that there is only a 'limited engagement with the topic in her writing' (Chan finds two passing examples) and concludes either that Woolf simply took a 'middle-class perspective' as she had in *Mrs Dalloway* and *Three Guineas* or, more hopefully, that Woolf had 'a tendency to deal with the issue from a broader and less politically restrictive perspective' and was 'more concerned with the possible overall results, relevant across all classes', of reforms in maternity care (44–6). These questions about lack of identification with the working class have always been framed by a discussion of the Woolfs' relative income. Making the calculation recently, Elena Gualtieri concludes that Virginia's inherited wealth generated income of £400 per annum, and that the Woolfs lived 'frugally for members of their class' but were 'certainly not poor', clocking in at about £156,000 per annum in terms of 2012 relative values (184). Even such a recent study as that of Clara Jones, framed as a proper documentation of

Woolf's activism rather than an extrapolation of her feminism from her published works, is predicated on acknowledging her 'reticence' and 'ambivalence' about her activities (6). As well as this question of class and relative income, some critics have recently sought to draw Woolf away from her appropriation by identity politics. Madelyn Detloff, for example, has argued that criticism of 1980s and 1990s was 'very certain about Woolf's identity as a lesbian' with all that follows in terms of conclusions about its centrality for her, but that there is danger in substituting the 'frigid mad genius' of Quentin Bell's early account with 'an ideal image of Woolf the lesbian feminist', suggesting that this claim should be reduced, and that it would be better 'simply to acknowledge that she desired other women in a sexual way' without going further (343). Reviewing even recent queer scholarship, Detloff argues that:

> Woolf's 'queering' extends beyond her own sexuality, or her attitudes towards others' gender or sexual performances, or her depiction of such in her writing. That said, she was clearly interested in these subjects, and was especially scathing in her critique of Victorian hypocrisy about sex and gender roles. (347)

Brenda Silver, in her study of the appropriation of Woolf as an icon across many cultural contexts highlights the tendency to a 'continuing invocation of an "authentic" Virginia Woolf' alongside the translation of this authenticity 'into descriptions and prescriptions for gender and sexuality during the "post-feminist" or queer movement of the early 1990s' (31).

Some questions related to Woolf's politics remain to be tackled, notably the pacifism expressed in *Three Guineas* at the time of the Spanish Civil War. Though usually celebrated as a critique of patriarchy (see Foster in this volume) it is clear that Woolf distanced herself from the socialist and antifascist politics of her nephew, Julian Bell, who was killed in that war, and from the attitude of her husband, and of many of her literary contemporaries. In all of this what is notable is the very high degree of expectation around Woolf – that she can stand for a universal and feminist politics of one kind or another – and the very strong need then to account for her class identification, most especially, and also the exact nature and extent of her experience of same-sex desire. It is hard to think of an author whose class identification has provoked so much scholarly comment, or indeed of an activist whose commitment has so exercised her commentators – activist contemporaries of Woolf such as Sylvia Pankhurst or Nadezdha Krupskaya have never provoked the same questions.

In such an overdetermined critical climate a more neutral approach might find it easier simply to document the facts of Bloomsbury politics. Keynes's unequivocal statements of class loyalty are widely reported, but in Woolf's case the history of the use of Woolf as a feminist icon is harder to repudiate than Woolf's actual politics which are more or less clearly discernible and, were she almost anyone else, might be examined with less burden of expectation. American second-wave feminism developed in most cases with little reference to the politics of socialist and Marxist feminism. The struggle between what was termed 'bourgeois feminism' and socialist feminism was strongly articulated in Britain but not in the United States, and it was in America that early adopters of Woolf grasped her potential significance for feminism and – both because of their distance from socialism and their ignorance of or indifference to British class politics both of Woolf's period and of their own – were able to found the Woolf industry, which eventually became the cornerstone of the Bloomsbury industry. When the pioneering feminist scholars Sandra Gilbert and Susan Gubar turned their attention to Woolf in *No Man's Land* (1988–9) they found in Clarissa Dalloway a 'queen' and a source of regeneration in the postwar world (Gilbert and Gubar 317). The term 'queen' functions here in much the same way that the term 'princess' can do for children, unrelated to any awareness of the social structure of monarchies and their historical evolutions, let alone to the specifics of the question of the British monarchy and its postwar role in underpinning the declining authority of class rule as Labour settled in as the decisive alternative to Toryism following the extension of the franchise in 1918. This extension had in turn been a response to growing trade union power and awareness of the potential threat presented by large numbers of men who had recently been under arms – the examples of the Russian Revolution and attempts at revolution in Germany and elsewhere were very fresh. This situation of the ruling class is basically what *Mrs Dalloway* attempts to deal with, as most commentators by now have figured out, but the earlier feminist and American construction of Woolf could see little of it.

It has become a commonplace of recent more populist intellectual discourse to describe any position or modelling as a construct. In this rhetorical and generally unanalysed use of the fundamental concept of social constructivism, it is usually models or positions rejected by the commentator which are labelled as 'constructs', without any attempt to deal with the issue that the claim that the supposed construct is also a construct, and that a kind of *mise-en-abyme* results. Bruno Latour, who later abandoned the position of social constructivism, once argued that 'the result of the *construction* of a fact is that it appears unconstructed by anyone', as part of a structure of adoption in which '*circumstances* simply vanish from accounts, being far better left to political analysis than to an appreciation of the hard and solid world of facts' (Latour and Woolgar 240). Latour and Woolgar sought to focus on the circumstances – viewed anthropologically – which created the apparently stable objects of science, and concluded that the institutional practices of science itself created these only apparently stable objects. If their account was subject to easy rebuttal in the context of the natural sciences, the questions they set in play have much relevance to the human sciences, where the very evident *in*stability of objects is plainly linked to a whole series of institutional and extrainstitutional variables. This may be true to different degrees depending both on the object and on the contemporary states of play in the construction of that object, but it is clear that the modelling of Bloomsbury is subject to such rapidly shifting political variables – variables which include contestations about the nature of the political itself – and that as an object it is shaped by sets of considerations which go beyond any simple consideration of fact.

Writing in 1978, Raymond Williams seems almost unaware of the modulation of Bloomsbury was about to take into queer politics (see Avery in this volume), even as his identification of the issues of 'friendship' and 'frankness' seem to lean in that direction. Williams' account draws on Leonard Woolf's attempt in his autobiography to contest received notions of 'the Bloomsbury Group' and substitute his own model of an informal circle of 'friends', in doing so entering a process of historical claim and counterclaim which had already begun.[5] Writing in 2016, art historian Christopher Reed was able to situate the republication of his 1991 essay, 'Bloomsbury Bashing', at the cusp of a struggle between Woolfians and advocates of Bloomsbury in which the desire to rescue Woolf from the charge of being an 'aesthete' (which Williams also mentions at that time) had resulted in the 'bashing' of Bloomsbury sexual mores which were thought somehow to have got in the way of Woolf's reputation as a political novelist. So while Williams had focussed on the politics of 'friendship' in the group, albeit without any direct discussion of same-sex relationships, and probably mainly with a view to getting a set of Marxist ducks in a row, Reed documents from quite a different perspective his own earlier reading of Woolf – he began with *Orlando* and was delighted by its 'gender-bending wit' – as part of an attempt at Columbia to claim a prominent place for Woolf in the male-dominated canon. What he found as he investigated Woolf though was 'contempt for Woolf and her Bloomsbury colleagues ... in scholarship that supposedly celebrated transgression, aesthetic and/or political', finding himself particularly unnerved by the 'gay-bashing' strand in much feminist scholarship (36–7). Reed recounts that he was disappointed at the time by responses to his article, especially that of feminist critic Jane Marcus who, Reed thinks facetiously, pleaded 'guilty' to the charge of Bloomsbury-bashing, claimed that it had been done to defend Woolf from the reputation of Bloomsbury, and that 'anyway it was fun' (qtd in Reed 38). That was something over twenty years ago, and marks a contestation in the realm of a principally US-mediated conflict over queer politics which is quite different than the struggle over class politics which Williams had joined in Britain a decade earlier. As he looks back to the eighties, Reed marks one of the questions on which the issue of the politics of Bloomsbury hinges. Is it correct to assert, as Reed does apropos of Lytton Strachey's now famous question to Vanessa Bell as to whether she had semen on her dress ('Semen? Can one really say it?'), that 'the disruptive power of laughter' can deauthorize established social dynamics? Or might we question, as Reed reminds us that Foucault did, whether 'gay sex or gay identity were in themselves counter-hegemonic' (Reed 38)? This question though moves silently past the question of the class status of Bloomsbury and past Woolf's question whether laughter itself was a complicit mode of resistance to capitalism.

It is here, in relation to the question of politics, that modes and types of the political jarringly meet. In a fine essay, Dominic Janes convincingly maps Bloomsbury 'queerness' on to Maynard Keynes' *The Economic Consequences of the Peace* (1919). Janes argues that Keynes's friendship with Strachey, who 'was ostentatiously out of kilter with contemporary standards of manliness', and his knowledge of the queering readings of prominent British figures in Strachey's *Eminent Victorians*, both conditioned his portrayal of the British leadership at the 1919 Paris Peace Conference. Influenced by Strachey's 'deliberately camp' style (21), Keynes portrayed the Prime Minister of France, Georges Clemenceau, as a 'dandy' (25), and Prime Minister of Britain, Lloyd George, as a 'supernatural diplomat in drag' (Harries 149, qtd in Janes 27). Janes concludes that 'the presentation in *The Economic Consequences of the Peace* of the peculiar personal performances of the Allied leaders at the Paris Conference played a powerful role in discrediting processes of political leadership and alleging the mismanagement not only of the war but also of the peace' (29). Setting aside the logic of the claim here – that queering the European leaders would discredit them – this account seems to bypass the stated political aims of Keynes' text: a revision of the Treaty, especially regarding the Covenant of the League of Nations; a reduction of reparations demanded by the Allies from Germany; an abandonment of Allied demands for options in coal to reimburse France; the cancellation of Allied indebtedness to the United States and of other inter-Allied indebtedness; the creation of massive loans from the United States to enable European economic regeneration (see Goldman in this volume). On this last point Keynes notes that America is unlikely to lend to a Europe still wed to 'hatred and nationalism' until and unless it turns to 'the thoughts and hopes of the happiness and solidarity of the European family' (*Economic Consequences* 267). Finally, in order to stabilize the 'present essentially middle-class Government of Germany' and resist 'a victory of Spartacism in Germany' which 'might well be the prelude to Revolution everywhere', 'precipitate the dreaded union of Germany and Russia' and put an end to the hopes of the Treaty, Germany should be allowed to lead a renewal of trade with Russia, bringing Russian grain into Europe in exchange for German technology, while Britain should abandon its policy of military interventionism (270–71). All of Keynes' 'remedies' point to economic regeneration as a means of assuring that revolution shall not spread beyond Russia, although what he sees ahead is not so much revolution, which 'offers no prospect of improvement', but the 'bankruptcy and decay of Europe' (277). The shape of Keynes' argument – that only massive economic stimulus would avert decay and the possibility at least of widespread revolution – is politically fairly explicit and seems to lead straight back into the realm of economics and of class interests which Williams sought to foreground. This is not quite the agenda of undermining democratic leadership which Janes describes. Are there then multiple 'political' Bloomsburies, each created by the sectional interest which models it – Marxist, feminist, or queer? Perhaps not. Probably no one now has strong reason to dissent from the bare bones of Williams' identification of Bloomsbury as a 'class fraction' – that much seems inscribed in some of its principal texts – but equally no one takes this to mean that Bloomsbury should no longer speak to those aspects of politics on which it opened early vistas.

NOTES

1. On this much-discussed term, see, for example, Matthews.
2. On this period of Woolf's life see Wilson (144–51). The quoted phrases are from 'Europe's Doom', Woolf's September 1919 article for *International Review*, qtd in Wilson (149–50).
3. And see Ayers (78–88).
4. See Barrett 'Introduction' to *A Room of One's Own* and *Three Guineas*, x.
5. Williams refers to passages *Sowing* (160–1), and especially *Beginning Again* (21–3 and 74–5).

WORKS CITED

Althusser, Louis. 'Ideology and Ideological State Apparatuses (Notes towards an Investigation)'. *Lenin and Philosophy and Other Essays*. Trans. Ben Brewster. New York: Monthly Review Press, 2001. 85–125.

Ayers, David. *English Literature of the 1920s*. Edinburgh: Edinburgh UP, 1999.

Briggs, Julia. *Virginia Woolf: An Inner Life*. London: Allen Lane, 2005.

Chan, Evelyn Tsz Yan. *Virginia Woolf and the Professions*. Cambridge: Cambridge UP, 2014.

Detloff, Madelyn. 'Woolf and Lesbian Culture: Queering Woolf's Queering'. Ed. Bryony Randall and Jane Goldman. *Virginia Woolf in Context*. Cambridge: Cambridge UP, 2012. 342–532.

Gilbert, Sandra M. and Susan Gubar. *No Man's Land: The Place of the Woman Writer in the Twentieth Century. Vol. II: Sexchanges*. New Haven: Yale UP, 1989.

Gualteri, Elena. 'Woolf, Economics and Class Politics'. Ed. Bryony Randall and Jane Goldman. *Virginia Woolf in Context*. Cambridge UP, 2012. 183–92.

Harries, Martin. *Scare Quotes from Shakespeare: Marx, Keynes, and the Language of Reenchantment*. Stanford, CA: Stanford UP, 2000.

Janes, Dominic. 'Eminent Victorians, Bloomsbury Queerness and John Maynard Keynes' *The Economic Consequences of the Peace* (1919)'. *Literature and History* 23.1 (2014): 19–32.

Keynes, John Maynard. 'Am I a Liberal?' *Essays in Persuasion*. London: Macmillan, 1933. 323–38.

Keynes, John Maynard. *The Economic Consequences of the Peace*. London: Macmillan, 1920.

Keynes, John Maynard. 'Trotsky on England'. *Essays in Biography*. London: Macmillan, 1933. 84–91.

Latour, Bruno and Steve Woolgar. *Laboratory Life: The Social Construction of Scientific Facts*. Intro. Jonas Salk. Beverly Hills and London: Sage, 1979.

Matthews, Sean. 'Change and Theory in Raymond Williams's Structure of Feeling'. *Pretexts: Literary and Cultural Studies* 10.2 (2001): 279–94.

Middlemas, Keith and John Barnes. *Baldwin: A Biography*. London: Weidenfeld and Nicolson, 1969.

Moore, G. E. *Principia Ethica*. Rev. ed. Ed. Thomas Baldwin. Cambridge: Cambridge UP, 1993.

Nietzsche, Friedrich. *On the Genealogy of Morality and Other Writings*. Ed. Keith Ansell Pearson. Trans. Carol Diethe. Cambridge: Cambridge UP, 1994.

Reed, Christopher. 'Bloomsbury Bashing: Homophobia and the Politics of Criticism in the Eighties'. *Queer Bloomsbury*. Ed. Brenda Helt and Madelyn Detloff. Edinburgh: Edinburgh UP, 2016. 36–63.

Silver, Brenda R. *Virginia Woolf Icon*. Chicago: U of Chicago P, 1999.

Trotsky, Leon. *Leon Trotsky on Britain*. Intro. George Novak. New York: Monad, 1973.

Trotsky, Leon. *Where Is Britain Going?* Intro. H. N. Brailsford. London: George, Allen and Unwin, 1926.

Williams, Raymond. 'The Bloomsbury Fraction'. *Problems in Materialism and Culture: Selected Essays*. London: Verso, 1997. 148–69.

Williams, Raymond. 'The Significance of "Bloomsbury" as a Social and Cultural Group'. *Keynes and the Bloomsbury Group: The Fourth Keynes Seminar Held at the University of Kent at Canterbury 1978*. Ed. Derek Crabtree and A. P. Thirlwall. London: Macmillan, 1980. 40–67.

Wilson, Duncan. *Leonard Woolf: A Political Biography*. London: Hogarth Press, 1978.

Wood, Alice. *Virginia Woolf's Late Cultural Criticism: The Genesis of* The Years, Three Guineas, *and* Between the Acts. London: Bloomsbury, 2013.

Woolf, Leonard. *Beginning Again: An Autobiography of the Years 1911–1918*. London: Hogarth Press, 1964.

Woolf, Leonard. *Sowing: An Autobiography of the Years 1880–1904*. London: Hogarth Press, 1960.

Woolf, Virginia. *Mrs Dalloway*. Ed. Stella McNichol. Intro. and notes Elaine Showalter. London: Penguin, 1992.

Woolf, Virginia. *Night and Day*. Ed. Julia Briggs. London: Penguin, 1992.

Woolf, Virginia. *A Room of One's Own* and *Three Guineas*. Ed. Michèle Barrett. London: Penguin, 1993.

Case Study: From Bolshevism to Bloomsbury: The Garnett Translations and Russian Politics in England

MICHAELA BRONSTEIN

Politics, like humour, is notoriously difficult to translate. Indeed, sometimes the political seems to be precisely what *fails* to translate. This is one of the subtexts of Emily Apter's argument in *Against World Literature*: the politics of translation, she says, is an 'entrepreneurial … drive to anthologize and curricularize the world's cultural resources' (3). In this vision, the politics of translation is a politics of domination. Translation seeks to profit from the cultural resources of other nations, erasing local contexts and commitments. Translation, in this view, works in service of a global ideology, that of 'world literature', or Pascale Casanova's 'world republic of letters' – a vision of transnational literary space in which friction between national literatures constitutes a mere temporary obstacle to various forms of hegemonic power constituted by apparently apolitical visions of literary prestige.

Yet we can all think of numerous examples of political texts aimed at a specific social context in one country and one language that have travelled well, have gained political significance in new contexts rather than losing it.[1] This chapter is about the forms in which politics *does* translate. My case study is the politics of one of the most influential translation projects in the history of the novel – Constance Garnett's efforts to bring Russian literature to the Anglophone public in the early twentieth century. From 1893 onwards, a river of pages flowed from her pen. Apter's case is against 'world literature' in its modern form, of which the giants of nineteenth-century Russia certainly constitute lofty examples today; Garnett's work, rendering an entire national tradition in one British voice, is certainly a foundational moment for any later-day conception of the ways national classics begin to seem to belong to the world.

Yet at the time no one anticipated a transnational project of canon formation; rather, the work of translating was deeply embedded in local politics, and in the frictions and gaps between languages and cultures. Readers and translators alike never lost sight of the distance between themselves and original audience who had received the work; they were very aware that these works had not been intended for them. Claire Davison associates Bloomsbury's collaborative translation projects with a resistance to nationalism: Woolf, Mansfield, and others collaborated with S. S. Koteliansky in order to translate 'not as an authority who knew but as an amateur keen to find out, using translation to stand outside their own traditions, habits and established hierarchies' (177). The results of such gestures were diverse: some figures stood outside their own traditions in order to look back at them with a critical eye, others to turn towards other nations. Regardless, the group of people surrounding Garnett became not just consumers of translations but theorists of its uses as well, fashioning arguments based on her work about what the political uses of transnational literature might be. Garnett and her husband Edward sat at the intersection between Bloomsbury and several other worlds – the early twentieth-century Russian émigrés, as well as an earlier generation of modernism. Their son David was one of the youngest of the Bloomsbury set; Edward was Conrad's friend and publisher, as well as an editor to D. H. Lawrence. And as Constance translated, the members of their circle developed different hopes and guesses about what the purpose of translating the Russians was, all of which in some way take for granted a friction between languages and cultures.

Neither Garnett's translations nor the initial Bloomsbury response to the Russian novelists are highly regarded today. And yet, the terms in which they are critiqued seem contradictory: on the one hand, Garnett's translations are deemed to have smoothed out the rough edges of Russian stylists' prose, making them dully appealing to British readers of the time. On the other hand, the reception of these novelists seems, equally infuriatingly, to have exoticized them, to have made them incomprehensible emissaries of an irremediably foreign Russia. Early twentieth-century British reception of Russian literature, it seems to more knowing critics today, somehow both erases and glamorizes difference. This tension at the time had to do with the way the work of translating was bound up in politics – with the way Russian literature was called upon to do work for either Russian or British political causes. Garnett's translations began as a project about bringing British attention to Russia; by the time of their greatest popularity, as Bloomsbury fell under the spell of the 'Dostoevsky cult', Russian literature became a tool with which English thinkers intervened in English cultural politics.[2]

The most common critiques of Garnett's translations describe her as 'domesticating or "taming" the works to English tastes' (May 38). According to this analysis, she reduced the strange stylistic tics of each author, made them all into the same 'smooth lawn mowed in the English manner' (Chukovsky 221). These comparative studies offer testimony to the ways her translations simplify aspects of Dostoevsky's style especially. Historically some of her thinking bears this out: she and her husband Edward Garnett very much feared Russian literature would be perceived as incomprehensibly foreign; they put tremendous thought and care into determining how best to introduce the books to a presumptively sceptical British audience.[3]

And yet if Garnett might be said to erase differences between authors, the authors remained exceedingly strange to their British readers. Garnett invented a voice of Russian literature that was not necessarily faithful, but it certainly didn't strike its audience as a familiar English style. Peter Kaye, describing the responses of a wide array of modernist writers, refers to 'Dostoevsky's intrusion into the English house of fiction' (10) – a phrase which usefully captures an outsider status. The most famous (infamous?) effect of Garnett's project was a particular fascination with Dostoevsky as mystic seer. Virginia Woolf's invocations in 'The Russian Point of View', a 1925 essay, are both well known and representative: 'The novels of Dostoevsky are seething whirlpools, gyrating sandstorms, waterspouts which hiss and boil and suck us in. They are composed purely and wholly of the stuff of the soul' (186). Woolf's emphasis on the shocking strangeness of the Russian novels is typical. Those whirlpools are far from the picturesque lawn Garnett's detractors allege.[4] Scholars critique Garnett's translations for failing to be precisely what their reception at the time saw them as: Chukovsky's discussion of the original Russian ('convulsions … nervous tremblings … a volcano'; 221) sounds not too distant from Woolf's hissing waterspouts.[5]

Woolf's vision, of course, seems to see the novels as apolitical: they are a natural – or perhaps supernatural? – force; they tell us something new about the human soul, or maybe just about novel writing. But they seem to have no political context – certainly not a Russian one. (Note that 'the stuff of the soul' is not particularly a 'Russian soul'.) In 'The Russian Point of View', she even suggests that the apparent strangeness of Russian literature is due to the limitations of translation: it seems strange not because it makes Russian writers sound falsely British, but because it makes them scandalously unconventional: 'They have lost their clothes, we say, in some terrible catastrophe … We become aware and self-conscious' (182–3). Translation strips away the social smoothness whereby idioms sound natural and familiar rather than strangely sincere; its readers feel their own trespass into an audience in which they are neither invited nor anticipated. Rather than Kaye's figure of Dostoevsky as the intruder, this image suggests that reading a translation constitutes a kind of violation; the gaze of British readers upon translated works of literature strips bare what ought to remain veiled. Translation makes its readers aware of their own social norms and niceties. It is, in ways I'll discuss later, political – but the politics is domestic and local.

The majority of commentary on English reception of Russian literature pushes in the opposite direction, taking its cue from critiques like May's and Chukovsky's, whereby Garnett is supposed to have made Russian literature too clear to an English audience. Rebecca Beasley and Philip Ross Bullock trace this idea back to Matthew Arnold's discussion of 'transparency' as a central virtue for translations (288–9). This is not an erroneous impression, as numerous comparisons of Garnett's translations to the originals have demonstrated.[6] Yet it's equally notable how nontransparent, how little like windows onto a clearly realist world, the Russian novelists appeared to a Bloomsbury audience. In the final section of this essay, I'll show how one moment in which Garnett is markedly *less* transparent than other translators had far-reaching consequences.

Understanding the political implications of these translations, then, has to start from the opposite point to the readings of Garnett as a domesticating translator: she does not make Russian matters into familiar English ones; she makes a British audience perceive Russian characters and society as shockingly foreign and strange. Yet – paradoxically – the consequence of this foreign contrast was closer attention to domestic social change.

THE ENGLISH DOMESTICATION
OF RUSSIAN POLITICS

The broad arc of the reception of Garnett's translations as they moved into the British public sphere is a shift from thinking of translation as a project about educating British readers about real events and ideas in Russia, to translating for domestic purposes, for the benefit of British society. Constance, along with some of the Russian figures associated with her, had the former idea. An incident from 1917 particularly highlights this: upon being asked if Constance had any translations of Russian news articles, Edward forwarded a translation done by someone else of an article Constance found counter-revolutionary. She wrote to him with outrage, explaining that she deliberately *hadn't* translated that particular article:

> I think it is a sin to publish at this time anything likely to damage the Russian revolutionary movement, to cheapen & belittle it, & to confirm the stupid contempt for it in English & American readers. I think it is treachery – & I should have thought you would understand that & share my feeling.[7]

Sin, treachery: these are strong terms. The scorn she feels for a public that doesn't side with the revolution is palpable. Russian translation, here, is a political mission, held to particular ideological standards. On the same page in the *Daily News* as one review of *The Brothers Karamazov* in 1912, there appeared an appeal for the Russian Famine Fund – a cause for which Constance herself wrote a letter to the *Times* (R. Garnett 261–2). In other words, for her, the relevant context for Russian literature was Russian politics.

In this, Constance differed to some extent from Edward. As Helen Smith says,

> the Russian émigrés hoped that the promotion of their national literature would marshal British public opinion against the absolutist government; [Edward] Garnett believed Russian writing offered authors at home a new set of 'ancestors' capable of revivifying the British novel, and that it could force Anglo-Saxon readers to face up to some unpalatable truths about themselves and their own national culture. (305–6)

Constance firmly sided with the émigrés – and, as the letter to Edward shows, this had an effect on her translations. In 1917, she chose her news article translations carefully, in part to support the cause of revolution in Russia – or at least not to damage it. The same tension goes back to her earlier literary translations, particularly in their prefatory material. When Constance tells the literary history of nineteenth-century Russia, it becomes a parade of cruel censorship and excitingly radical ideological movements in response. For instance, in the preface to her first Dostoevsky translation, *The Brothers Karamazov* in 1912, she dwells on his youthful revolutionary sympathy and effaces all evidence of the more reactionary, Slavophilic beliefs he held by the time of his major fiction. She implies, for instance, that his journal *Epoch* ceased publication because it 'was … prohibited' by censors (vi), rather than that it closed due to mounting debts. (Censorship had closed a previous Dostoevsky journal; at *Epoch*, it only affected individual articles.) A reader of *The Brothers Karamazov* who begins the novel through the lens of her preface would think of Dostoevsky as a voice of the oppressed Russian masses crying out for revolutionary freedom.

This purpose is most publicly evident, however, in the Turgenev translations, which were her first major success and for which she attempted to obtain prefaces by her close friend Sergei Stepniak. Stepniak's friendship had led her to learn Russian in the first place; he was the Garnetts' main point of contact within radical émigré circles. Stepniak was also likely responsible for an assassination that may have provided Conrad with inspiration for *Under Western Eyes*.[8] Stepniak died unexpectedly, so only two prefaces of his were published. They are careful explanations of Russian politics, distinguishing radicals and Slavophiles. The preface to *A House of Gentlefolk* ends: 'It is the poem of the youth of the Russian democracy, the birth of which Turgenev has discovered and hailed in this fresh and pathetic story' (xvii). The literary praise comes in as an awkward afterthought to a more forceful political point.

Given all this, how did Russian literature become whirlpools of the nebulous soul? The beginnings are apparent in Edward's divergence from Constance (and from Stepniak). Edward wrote the rest of the Turgenev prefaces after Stepniak's death. In some cases, he sounds a note similar to Stepniak's: for *Virgin Soil*, for instance, he offers the reader a lengthy introduction to 'the Nihilist party of the seventies' (xiii). In other instances, however, Edward's prefaces retain a strong interest in the politics while rewriting why that politics might matter. No longer are the radicals explicitly Russian figures; they happen to come from Russia, but they belong to the world – or maybe just to England. Take, for instance, his 1895 preface to *Fathers and Children*:

> Bazarov, in whom the comfortable compromising English mind sees only a man of bad form, bad taste, bad manners and overwhelming conceit; finally, Bazarov stands for Humanity awakened from century-old superstitions and the long dragging oppressive dream of tradition. Naked he stands under a deaf, indifferent sky, but he feels and knows that he has the strong brown earth beneath his feet. (xv)

There's something almost Lawrentian about that last image. You can see an important transition here: Edward sees the novels as political, but the politics is universal: Russia has given the nihilist to the world, and so now Bazarov confronts not complacent Russian liberals but the universal sky. And Edward's vision of this politics is starkly heroic. This is less a careful accounting for the historical roots of Russian revolutionaries, and closer to familiar modernist affects valorizing heroic defiance of convention. This Bazarov might be at home among the manifestoes of *Blast*.

The Russian radical, in other words, is turning into a symbol of what English modernism already desired. Stepniak's preface invoked a dream of democracy; Edward, by contrast, opposes Bazarov to 'The Crowd, the ungrateful Crowd, though for it Bazarov has wrested much from effete or corrupt hands, and has fought and weakened despotic and bureaucratic what power, what has its opinion or memory to do with his brave heroic figure?' (xvii). Revolution on behalf of the people has become denigration of the masses. Notably, Bazarov in the novel, a medical student, poorly fits Edward's descriptions. He 'wrests' nothing from powerful hands but the occasional success at dinner table argument: at the end of the novel, he dies because (distracted by a love affair), he performs an autopsy carelessly and contracts an infection. At one point he and Arkady *lie* on the earth, but the 'brave, heroic figure' Edward offers is his own.

The power of this image becomes visible in light of the response it called out of Joseph Conrad, who was published by Edward Garnett and read Constance's Turgenev translations. While Conrad thought more highly of Turgenev than he did the other Russian novelists, he did not share the Garnetts' revolutionary leanings, and almost perfectly inverts Edward's image. His 1907 novel *The Secret Agent* features a nihilist: his Professor is, however, 'lost in the crowd, miserable and undersized' (67). Despite their political differences, Conrad and Edward Garnett both make the nihilist into a general challenge to social interactions and norms, distinctive in part because of the nonnational blankness of his political views. Garnett sees a hero, Conrad a nightmarish villain; but they agree in seeing an alien force: alien not *because* he is Russian (Conrad's Professor is not), but because of the threat he presents to an orderly British society.

Even within his initial Russian context, Bazarov's importance had always stemmed in part from his malleability: part of the notoriety of *Fathers and Sons* in Russia and abroad was the ambiguity of its central figure. With Bazarov, Turgenev outraged all sides of the debate: he seemed a harsh satire to many on the left, but by contrast appeared to conservatives as a glorification of radicalism.[9] In a sense, Edward's repurposing is a fair inheritance of this tradition. Turgenev's character, from the beginning, exemplified the way political characters could be made to serve a variety of causes.

The melodramatic glamour of Edward's reading of Bazarov, stripped of any particular Russian history, does have a particular purpose. Edward might not have seen Russian literature for its actual Russian politics, but he did have a specific sense of what the Russians could offer English cultural politics. For instance, an early piece on Dostoevsky uses him to diagnose the failings of British society:

> I was delighted to find in the *Spectator* some years back a criticism on Mr. W. D. Howells's novels which defines our insular apprehensions in the naivest fashion. 'Mr. Howells,' said the critic, 'is a standing proof that subtlety of analysis need not involve the slightest sacrifice of wholesomeness.' The sentence conjures up a comforting little picture of idyllic, wholesome surroundings, say a vicarage lawn, where the pleasant clatter of tea-things is punctuated by the vicar's voice rising sonorously amid the cries of 'deuce' and 'vantage' from the sunk tennis-court. Dostoievsky would be a strange and ironical guest here, nor is he in place in a London club, hotel, in any well-to-do house or suburban villa residence. ('A Literary Causerie' 202)

That familiar, oh-so-conventional English lawn reappears once more, but again it is held in contrast to Russian literature. When Garnett exhorted his English readers to consider Dostoevsky as a connoisseur of 'diseased' minds, his point was that such 'unwholesomeness' was precisely what the English literary scene needed. Dostoevsky, the 'strange and ironical guest', clearly offers the same provocation to English norms as Bazarov, the 'man of bad form'.

Dostoevsky, Garnett goes on to say, offers 'that broad human tolerance and fraternal feeling peculiar to the Russian soul' (203). ('Soul', here, holds on to the 'Russian' modifier it would later lose in Woolf's essay.) It's easy to laugh at any cliché about 'the Russian soul'; nevertheless, Garnett's point is not to essentialize Russia but to offer a critique of British complacency and close-minded moral condemnation. This point could be rephrased in terms we might find more amenable: he is arguing, in the end, that Russian novelists have a different and more broad-minded standard of literary decorum. More beguilingly, it's worth noting that his language anticipates one of the most influential points made by Bakhtin decades later about Dostoevsky: in the British context, among vicars and tennis, Garnett implies, Dostoevsky would cause a *scandal* scene.[10]

This is Russian literature domesticated in two senses: made to serve a particular national purpose within England; and also, now, primarily dealing in matters of personal morality. Yet Edward is still invested in social, interactive settings of literary politics: the lawn, the country house. There remains one further turn yet to Bloomsbury's reception, anticipated by Edward's image of Bazarov's confrontation with the sky. That is, rather than shock British society, these novels might just shock an individual soul. David Garnett, for instance, turns the politics of Russian literature entirely inward. In a lengthy letter to his mother, in which he tries to convey (against her anticipated doubts) the importance of her work to a new generation: 'I think the publication of the Idiot has probably done more ~~violence~~ to alter the morals of my generation than the war or anything that happened to them in the war' (undated; David Garnett Collection, container 9.1). This is itself a stunning declaration – the fact that he appeared to begin by writing 'more *violence* to the morals of my generation' before thinking better of it heightens the intensity of the claim. There's an explicit substitution of moral alteration for real political violence.

One of the most important of the Woolf-Koteliansky translations has the same effect, reinterpreting Russian politics through the lens of personal morality. This was the suppressed chapter of *Demons*, 'At Tikhon's', which was published under the title *Stavrogin's Confession*, and had not appeared in Constance's edition.[11] The chapter is about Stavrogin's assault of a young girl; it reveals a transgression of sexual morality to have been the intended heart of Dostoevsky's most political novel, and it was censored in Russia when the novel first appeared. By bringing it to the English reading public, the Hogarth Press associated Russian political literature even more closely with the questions of sexual morality and personal freedom implied by Edward's desire to see British literature scandalized.

This vision of Dostoevsky as a revolutionary in the field of personal morality is, finally, the source of the more extreme aspects of his reputation. John Middleton Murry, whose friendship with D. H. Lawrence broke down in part over Murry's love for Dostoevsky, declared in his 1916 study that Dostoevsky was 'more than an unwilling part of life, he was a lover of all life; perhaps only those whose minds are driven to the desolation of ineffectual rebellion against life, are its true lovers' (42). This is Dostoevsky as prophet of human vitality.[12]

As the Russian writers exit the realm of Constance's émigré circle, then, they enter a particularly British cultural dialogue. Dostoevsky becomes an agent of provocation not just to standards of decorum but to moral values themselves. Roughly, we have three models of the way politics translates here: Constance's desire to translate without transposing Russian politics, to attend to what was happening in Russia; Edward's use of Russian political archetypes to make points about English society and norms; and finally, the stripping of the public dimension out – the vision of intense personal encounter, where the text allows the reader to confront the bare fact of human alienation like the characters described.

In their own time, the differences between these three approaches were, on some level, masked by the intensity with which their partisans experienced Russian literature as foreign. The sign of its alienness could refer to the awful political circumstances of life in Tsarist Russia; to its sharp challenge to English conventions; or to its vision of the rebellious individual confronting the abstract. Thus, the Bloomsbury theories of political translation are also theories of the untranslatable, of irreducible difference. They share, too, a frankness about instrumentalizing the literary texts in question. Smith even describes Edward Garnett's criticism as committed to a 'belief in the power of literature to change humanity' (311). The question of translation places the politics of texts in the light not of what the texts mean but of the relationships they form with their readers. The texts are no longer clear in their referents: articles about the revolution matter less for their accuracy and more for their effects on the British public; a character's nationality or role in a plot becomes fuzzy or obscure. The very presence of these works in the English language starts to resemble that of the scandalous characters of Dostoevsky novels, and equally have the potential to do violence. Bloomsbury *does* efface the original context of Russian literature. But the result is a different kind of local politics.

Critics of the time found the apparent 'foreignness' of these writers useful as a provocation to England – but they also recognized some of the startling elements of Russian literature as tactical. Percy Lubbock says that Dostoevsky might give the impression of artless 'indignation' over his characters' failings, but in fact 'kept himself far more disengaged from his story than we had thought' ('Dostoevsky' 269). In *The Craft of Fiction* Dostoevsky appears only to offer a few examples of well-chosen formal strategies.[13]

Woolf's work, too, dramatizes the process whereby the impression of strangeness and confusion turns out to be locally useful. 'Mr Bennett and Mrs Brown' emphasizes the unfamiliarity of Russian literature: its characters draw us into 'some enormous cavern. Lights swing about; we hear the boom of the sea; it is all dark, terrible, and uncharted' (386). In this 1923 essay, we can detect the beginnings of the strangeness she herself would attempt to evoke with the strange sonic landscape of *The Waves* in 1931, where Susan declares: 'Here in this vast station everything echoes and booms hollowly' (43). In Lubbock, the apparent chaos and emotional intensity of Dostoevsky is a considered artistic effect; in Woolf, the very strangeness of Russian literature is a prompt to thought, to further creative effort, and to the representation of ordinary lived English experience.

GARNETT'S TRANSLATIONS BEYOND BLOOMSBURY

Some of these interpreters missed something important – about the underlying nineteenth-century political debates in Russian literature, about Constance's attempt to draw attention to Russian politics in the present. But the domestications of Russian politics revealed something new – both about politics and about art – to English writers. What then, can we do, confronted with these theories of political translation? On one level, it might seem to be merely eccentric family gossip. What do the differing motives of the Garnetts matter, on one level, given that, after all, we have such clear evidence of the broader reception of Russian literature? At the time, the idea of the novel as a challenge to British moral respectability – represented by Edward, by David, by Murry, by Woolf, and more – won out. Why recover Constance's political dreams when no one noticed them at the time?

But Constance's translations travelled beyond the circumstances of her immediate reception. And her politics, I'd argue, did have an effect not just on her selection of articles and introductory materials, but in the way she translated the major texts themselves. The novels missed their moment in 1917. But analogous later movements found uses for them, because, in part, of her project. At many points, for instance, she interprets or makes more explicit what is understated in the original text. A. N. Nikoliukin writes about this general pattern, but it's notable that several of his examples are moments where she explicates or even heightens the political context at work – making explicit a reference to the Decembrist revolt (209), for instance. He also points out how her glossing of meanings can actually warp dialogue in a more political direction than the Russian texts warrants: adding an explanatory reference to revolution in one line of dialogue necessitates a corresponding response from another character whose dialogue in the original contained nothing on the subject, for instance (210).[14]

They aren't tendentious translations. But the *tone* of the translations accords with the sense of moral seriousness (remember her framing of denigrating the revolution as 'sin') she accords to the political situation in Russia. When critics argue that she didn't understand Dostoevsky's humour, they respond to a real difference between her work and many of her successors. She sucks much of the satirical energy out of a novel like *The Possessed*. But in doing so, she leaves those fictional revolutionaries a little of their dignity. They are a little less belittled and treated with a little less contempt. For instance, one of the members of a meeting in *Demons* is, according to Pevear and Volokhonsky 'that same nasty boy, dissipated beyond his years' (393). In Garnett he's 'that unpleasant and prematurely exhausted youth' (367). The translations are similar, though Pevear and Volokhonsky choose English idioms that match the Russian syntax more closely.[15] But there is a slight relaxing of the condemnation and the satire in Garnett: *unpleasant* is less visceral than *nasty*. And 'prematurely exhausted' holds much more sympathy than 'dissipated beyond his years'. He's not dissipated; he's just worn out. Here, Garnett's sympathy for the suffering Russian people converges with the Bloomsbury emphasis on personal morality: she refuses to let this become a conventional condemnation of vice.

The reasons for differences like these are probably impossible to reconstruct at this distance. I don't, for instance, believe that she was deliberately manipulating her portrayal only of identifiably radical characters: in her translations, the humour is softened for everyone, the psychological stakes made more alien. But moments like this suggest she saw what she wanted to see in the language – a suffering country full of sincere people. Woolf says of Russian literature as a whole that it is marked by 'the assumption that in a world bursting with misery the chief call upon us is to understand our fellow-sufferers' ('Russian Point' 183). If Garnett's style – felicities and infelicities alike – has a particular tone, it is this moral and ethical commitment, rather than the contradictory scale from domestication to exoticization on which critics and defenders alike have attempted to place her. This is part of why so many critics note the way the differences between authors' voices and between characters within the novels disappear in Garnett: her investment in contemporary Russian politics dwarfed her attention to the differences between a previous generations of Russian thinkers.

Regardless of the motives behind her word choices, the consequences are vast. The majority of Anglophone readers and commentators on Dostoevsky and Turgenev in English throughout the twentieth century read Garnett; her choices multiply out beyond her own text.[16] Her translations were unable to rally British people in 1917 to Russia. But they've rallied readers to other causes since. Take one word, Garnett's choice for translating the Russian *надрыв* in Dostoevsky. The word is noteworthy because it's extremely prominent, especially in *The Brothers Karamazov*, where it titles a volume and several chapters, as well as appearing in characters' dialogue: its many contexts are a challenge to the translator. The literal meaning is *tear* or *rent*, with a common usage referring to forms of psychological suffering or instability; it's translated by others as *anguish* (Leatherbarrow's choice, translating Nikoliukin 210), *strain* (Pevear and Volokhonsky), or *crack-up* (McDuff). *Strain* has the advantage of making some smoothly idiomatic phrases in English in its various contexts: for instance, 'нервный надрыв' (10.202) becomes 'nervous strain' in Pevear and Volokhonsky (*Demons* 254); another translator, similarly seeking English familiarity, tries 'overwrought nerves' (Maguire 282).

Garnett uses *laceration*, with results that often look strange in English. One chapter title in *The Brothers Karamazov*, for instance, becomes 'A laceration in the drawing-room': suggestive of some grotesque accident with a butter knife, perhaps. She has 'laceration of the nerves' (237) instead of 'overwrought nerves' or 'nervous strain'. Notably, *laceration* is the most visceral and graphic option taken by any translator I've found. It is also the least natural in English. *Strain* suggests social comedy and awkwardness; *crack-up* helps put some distance between the reader and the process of a mind breaking down or in anguish. Garnett's *laceration* makes it an open wound: the reader has to do all the work of transforming a physical meaning to a psychological one, while the other translators do the work for you. Her translation evokes the literal, rather than metaphorical, meaning of *надрыв*. But the English *laceration*, unlike the Russian, has no common figurative usage referring to mental states; the metaphor is very much still alive. The obvious effect of *laceration* is to contribute to the familiar elements of the Dostoevsky cult – bizarre characters using tortuous speech to describe incomprehensibly strange psychology. But *laceration* is always, definitively, *serious*: it is not a mere social unease (strain); a laceration of the nerves sounds more serious than overwrought nerves. *Laceration* is more sympathetic to those who suffer it.

In the pantheon of Dostoevskyan politically fraught psychological phenomena, *laceration* is far from the most directly political. But *laceration* is one of the phrases that clearly came from Garnett's Dostoevsky and gained political significance in later reception. Ralph Ellison, for instance, owned mostly Garnett translations of Dostoevsky, and the word multiplies across his writing.[17] In a letter to Richard Wright, he declared, 'Part of my life, Dick, has been a lacerating experience and I have my share of bitterness. But I have learned to keep the bitterness submerged so that my vision might be kept clear; so that those passions which could so easily be criminal might be socially useful' (3 November 1941; Ralph Ellison Papers, Folder 1.76.5).

Ellison – still a Communist at this time – is talking about the ways the various brutalities of American racism give him impulses that might be destructive – or could be channelled to revolutionary purposes. Dostoevsky was on his mind during the writing of the letter; a few lines later in the same letter he talks about 'memories which must be kept underground'. Garnett's language becomes a tool for expressing the violence of his experience. *Laceration* is a word that implies an active cause of the wound: if one is psychologically lacerated, someone or something had to make the cuts. *Strain, anguish, crack-up*, and *overwrought* all suggest an internal source for the suffering. Garnett's word helps Ellison to analyse his life not just through the lens of interior stress but as the product of external factors: racist American life lacerates him; he's not a mere victim of overwrought nerves or social strain.

Elsewhere, Ellison explicitly restores the term to its Russian political context. He liked to copy out passages from novelists that appealed to him; one handwritten example is the passage on 'laceration of the nerves' in *The Possessed*, which is about a character's choice of an unconventional marriage: 'It was a lacerating [*sic*] of the nerves. Defiance of common sense was too tempting' (Ralph Ellison Papers, Folder 1.112.5). On the one hand this highlights the same features of Dostoevsky as Edward Garnett, the perverse psychology and social scandal. Yet, after the quotation, he analyses the character in the novel as a reflection on the anarchist Mikhail Bakunin. Ellison is reexcavating the direct line between the domestic, personal elements of plotting and the most explicit problems of historical politics. Moments in the Bloomsbury reception like David Garnett's comments, or Murry's, disaggregated what in the original novels is headily mixed: matters of politics and of religion, of sex and of soul. Ellison's use reunites the disparate strands. He also finds a use for that persistent feeling of foreign and nontransparent psychology: Garnett's word, which refuses to let its readers assimilate the psychological landscapes of Dostoevsky's characters to familiar English social contexts, is able to carry the weight of representing what American racial violence does to its dispossessed black citizens. *Crack-up, anguish, strain*: none of these would do justice to the feelings he's describing. Garnett's translations don't just shape twentieth-century literature by their ubiquity; their very foreignness makes them useful in political worlds where other translations have no language.

Theories of the politics of translation often tend to be systemic in scope: they look at it as a reflection of a global world, whether in the sense of a global capitalistic economy or a more idealistic vision of communication across national boundaries. 'Comparative literature,' writes Apter,

> has often functioned as the humanities arm of Enlightenment diplomacy. It has been dedicated to producing complexly cultured, linguistically proficient citizens of the world who foster global understanding and the pragmatic conviction that universal consensus ... is achievable through an enhanced linguistic commons. (128)

Yet if translation and the reading of texts from other languages is diplomacy, I would suggest that its diplomatic effects are more immediate than the ideological superstructures Apter lists. The history of the Garnett translations suggests, above all, that translation is *tactical* – Garnett didn't translate to produce 'citizens of the world'; she translated to get a particular political response from a British audience. And the reception and use of her work is similarly specific in its aims: Edward, Murry, Woolf, et al., offer less ideas of the transnational than *uses* of the transnational, strategic deployments of the feel of foreignness as one more rhetorical weapon in British debates. Translation promotes ideologies, here, but the ideologies are not neatly represented by the act of translation itself.

And texts, like any tactics, find diverse, unpredictable audiences and uses far beyond the immediate purposes for which they are crafted. In Ellison's talk of passions and the underground, the psychological waterspouts of the Bloomsbury Dostoevsky are reunited with the political force of Constance's revolutionary dreams. She wanted to see change in the present; like any utopia, the future was waiting.

NOTES

1. To take an example close to the topic of this paper, Dostoevsky's *Notes from Underground* – a work deeply enmeshed in contemporary polemics that are now familiar to only a few of its global readers – not only has been read around the world, but has been rewritten and reimagined, in each new form becoming a tool for intervening in contemporary political discourses. The American tradition can be traced easily: Ralph Ellison and Richard Wright both reimagined the Underground Man (in *Invisible Man* and the short story 'The Man Who Lived Underground', respectively). The 2015 Pulitzer Prize winner *The Sympathizer*, by Viet Thanh Nguyen, rewrites Ellison's famous allusion to think about post-Vietnam War Vietnamese immigrant experiences in America, and in doing so also rewrites Dostoevsky.
2. The first major analysis of the 'Dostoevsky cult' is that of Helen Mucnic (73).
3. See Richard Garnett for their debates on the most appealing order in which to publish Dostoevsky's novels (263–5).
4. In Percy Lubbock's 1912 review of *Brothers Karamazov* he gestures towards the mowed lawn, but only to apply it to Turgenev: distinguishing between Dostoevsky, Tolstoy, and Turgenev, he says is as easy as 'between a crowded street, an illimitable plain, and a shaven lawn of grass' ('Dostoevsky' 269).
5. It's possible that Woolf's image in fact specifically derives from a *Russian* tradition of Dostoevsky reception; Davison compares her imagery to that of a Brodsky essay she cotranslated shortly before writing 'The Russian Point of View' (39–41).
6. For substantive comparisons, see May, Chukovsky, and Nikoliukin. Mucnic provides an earlier comparison.
7. Constance Garnett to Edward Garnett, 27 June 1917; Garnett Collection, Eton College. All archival research referenced in this article was supported by Harvard's Milton Fund.
8. See Moser for the history of Stepniak with the Garnetts, and Conrad's possible use of it.

9. For Bazarov's ambiguity and the complex publics of Russian literature, see Todd 420.
10. For the *locus classicus* of Bakhtin's discussion of the Dostoevskyan scandal scene, see 117–18.
11. See Davison 68–78 for an analysis of this translation.
12. Murry shares with Edward Garnett the tendency to find in Russian literature an endless source of images of the heroic figure standing up and facing – something. (It varies between a mob, the earth, the abyss, the future, etc.) Of Stavrogin of *Demons*, for instance, Murry says, he 'has looked upon the frozen waste of eternity' (161).
13. The well-known misapprehension that Dostoevsky was a poor or careless craftsman is not salient in the Bloomsbury readings. It tends to appear a bit later: see, for example, Nabokov (98).
14. It is worth noting that, according to David, Constance was well aware of the difficulty of translating Dostoevsky's obscurity, and struggled to keep the English as ambiguous or challenging as the original (Richard Garnett 266). Beasley and Bullock argue that Garnett clarified and simplified deliberately, on the basis of the following statement in an interview she gave in 1945: 'Dostoievsky is so obscure and so careless a writer that one can scarcely help clarifying him – sometimes it needs some penetration to see what he trying to say' (qtd in Beasley and Bullock 287). Struggling to *understand* Dostoevsky, however, doesn't need to imply a philosophical commitment to clarifying; indeed, clarification seems here an unfortunate inevitability ('one can scarcely help') rather than a symptom of Garnett's 'values' as a translator (Beasley and Bullock 288).
15. Dostoevsky's original is 'тот самый скверный мальчишка, истаскавшийся не по летам' (10.304).
16. Part of the reason for her ubiquity is the sheer scale of her achievement; even if translations of individual works could compete with hers (e.g. the Maudes' *War and Peace*), no one else translated so *much* of the Russian canon. The 1950s and 1960s saw many new translators as the death of Stalin brought more knowledge and specialists to Western audiences, but not all of the new efforts were of high quality, and Garnett, May points out, is consistently described throughout the period as an 'old reliable' standard and 'conscientious' option (45). Not until the Pevear and Volokhonsky Dostoevskys of the 1990s did the default choice of the public begin to shift; and Pevear and Volokhonsky at the time perceived the widespread acceptance of Garnett as the biggest obstacle to their project (Remnick 101).
17. Ellison's library is in the Rare Book Room at the Library of Congress; he did not typically annotate novels, so his Garnett translations are for the most part unmarked.

WORKS CITED

Apter, Emily. *Against World Literature: On the Politics of Untranslatability*. London: Verso, 2013.

Bakhtin, Mikhail. *Problems of Dostoevsky's Poetics*. Trans. Caryl Emerson. Minneapolis: U of Minnesota P, 1984.

Beasley, Rebecca and Philip Ross Bullock. 'Introduction: The Illusion of Transparency'. *Translation and Literature* 20 (2011): 283–300.

Chukovsky, Kornei. *A High Art*. Trans. Lauren G. Leighton. Knoxville: U of Tennessee P, 1984.

Conrad, Joseph. *The Secret Agent*. Ed. Bruce Harkness and S. W. Reid. Cambridge: Cambridge UP, 1990.

David Garnett Collection. Harry Ransom Center, University of Texas at Austin.

Davison, Claire. *Virginia Woolf, Katherine Mansfield and S. S. Koteliansky*. Edinburgh: Edinburgh UP, 2014.

Dostoevsky, Fyodor. *The Brothers Karamazov*. Trans. Constance Garnett. New York: Macmillan, 1912.

Dostoevsky, Fyodor. *The Brothers Karamazov*. Trans. David McDuff. London: Penguin, 2003.

Dostoevsky, Fyodor. *Demons*. Trans. Richard Pevear and Larissa Volokhonsky. New York: Everyman's Library, 2000.

Dostoevsky, Fyodor. *Demons*. Trans. Robert A. Maguire. London: Penguin, 2008.

Dostoevsky, Fyodor. *The Possessed*. Trans. Constance Garnett. London: Heinemann, 1913.

Dostoevsky, Fyodor. *Бесы*. Vol. 10. Leningrad: Nauka, 1974. Garnett Collection. Eton College.

Garnett, Edward. 'A Literary Causerie: Dostoievsky'. *The Academy* (1 September 1906): 202–3.

Garnett, Richard. *Constance Garnett: A Heroic Life*. London: Faber & Faber, 2009.

Kaye, Peter. *Dostoevsky and English Modernism, 1900–1930*. Cambridge: Cambridge UP, 1999.

Lubbock, Percy. 'Dostoevsky'. *Times Literary Supplement* (4 July 1912): 269–70.

May, Rachel. *The Translator in the Text: On Reading Russian Literature in English*. Evanston: Northwestern UP, 1994.

Moser, Thomas C. 'An English Context for Conrad's Russian Characters: Sergey Stepniak and the Diary of Olive Garnett'. *Journal of Modern Literature* 11.1 (March 1984): 3–44.

Mucnic, Helen. *Dostoevsky's English Reputation (1881–1936)*. New York: Octagon Books, 1938–9 (repr. 1969).

Murry, J. Middleton. *Fyodor Dostoevsky: A Critical Study*. London: Martin Secker, 1916.

Nabokov, Vladimir. *Lectures on Russian Literature*. Ed. Fredson Bowers. New York: Harvest, 1981.

Nikoliukin, A. N. 'Dostoevskii in Constance Garnett's Translation'. Trans. W. J. Leatherbarrow. *Dostoevskii and Britain*. Ed. W. J. Leatherbarrow. Oxford: Berg, 1995: 207–27.

Ralph Ellison Collection. Rare Book & Special Collections Division, Library of Congress, Washington, DC.

Ralph Ellison Papers, 1890–2005. Manuscript Division, Library of Congress, Washington, DC.

Remnick, David. 'The Translation Wars'. *The New Yorker*, 7 November 2005: 98–109.

Smith, Helen. 'Edward Garnett: Interpreting the Russians'. *Translation and Literature* 20 (2011): 301–13.

Todd, William Mills III. 'The Ruse of the Russian Novel'. *The Novel*. Ed. Franco Moretti. Volume 1 of 2. Princeton: Princeton UP, 2007. 401–23.

Turgenev, Ivan. *Fathers and Children*. Trans. Constance Garnett. Intro. Edward Garnett. London: Heinemann, 1906.

Turgenev, Ivan. *The House of Gentlefolk*. Trans. Constance Garnett. Intro. Sergei Stepniak. London: Heinemann, 1906.

Turgenev, Ivan. *Virgin Soil*. Trans. Constance Garnett. Intro. Edward Garnett. London: Heinemann, 1906.

Woolf, Virginia. 'The Russian Point of View'. *The Essays of Virginia Woolf*, vol. 4. Ed. Andrew McNeillie. San Diego: Harcourt, 1994.

Woolf, Virginia. *The Waves*. Ed. Molly Hite and Mark Hussey. Orlando: Harcourt, 2006.

CHAPTER TEN

Bloomsbury and War

J. ASHLEY FOSTER

Upon Julian Bell's death as a volunteer ambulance driver in the Spanish Civil War in 1937, his aunt Virginia Woolf writes in her account of his life, 'I suppose it's a fever in the blood of the younger generation which we cant [*sic*] possibly understand. I have never known anyone of my generation to have that feeling about a war. We were all C.O.'s [Conscientious Objectors] in the Great War' (*Platform* 28). These words mark the Bloomsbury Group's renowned internationalist pacifism, which was an integral part of their lives and informed their art, aesthetics, and writing.[1] In art and writing, Bloomsbury sought an alternative to war, not as a way to hermetically ignore the world, but as a way to theorize and formulate visions of peace – visions which were echoed in actions across the many public and private spheres of their lives. This chapter forges a historical arc of Bloomsbury's responses to national conflict, situating the group's members as key players within what I call an 'intersectional pacifism' of the modernist era. Though the space allotted does not allow for an exhaustive account, this chapter provides an overview of how Bloomsbury writings and actions put forth multivariate theories of peace that were engaged with feminist, socialist, antifascist, anti-colonial, and social justice movements through particular choice examples from Roger Fry, Leonard Woolf, Vanessa Bell, Duncan Grant, Mulk Raj Anand, and Virginia Woolf.

The Bloomsbury Group responded to war largely with a variety of intersectional visions for peace,[2] and in doing so made important contributions to the cultural conversations surrounding war and peace of their time, as well as to current discussions in social justice movements and peace studies today. Exploring Bloomsbury thought helps us to answer a call for peace studies put out by Paul Diehl, which maintains that 'studying peace requires, first and foremost, broader conceptions of peace. These include considerations of justice, human rights, and other aspects of human security' (9). The various Bloomsbury pacifisms, as Jean Mills and Grace Brockington have pointed out in their respective works on positive peace, reveal that peace, indeed, is more than just an absence of war. The theory of 'positive peace' maintains that peace is an active creation of a 'world in which the structural roots of conflict are supplanted by pro-peace values and practices' (Amster 473).

Addressing this need for an expanded concept of pacifism, I move to employ the logic that Paul Saint-Amour – informed by a distinguished lineage of theory – uses in *Tense Future* to formulate modernism and advocate for a 'weak' pacifism. In opposition to a 'strong'[3] definition of pacifism, a 'weak' notion of pacifism would, applying Saint-Amour's words on modernism, be 'associative instead of definitional, probabilistic instead of binary; to borrow a phrase, "connotative rather than denotative"' (38), a pacifism that 'functions in local and provisional ways' (38), to indicate concerns, preoccupations, and works for peace. Indeed, Charles Andrews shows that ' "pacifism" is not a static or homogenous category but instead names a range of antiwar convictions derived from various humanitarian, religious, affective, or philosophical bases' (5). A notion of 'weak' pacifism allows us to explore how pacifism and visions for peace in the Spanish Civil War and the Second World War responded and adjusted to the ethical challenges that the slaughter of civilians presented. And, a 'weak' pacifism, I argue, opens onto a theory of intersectional pacifism(s) by allowing the signifier of peace, and its companion 'pacifist', to encapsulate a range of practical, lived expressions and social activist alliances, challenging the discourses that portray the 'peace movement as simplistic, childish, or "intellectually primitive" ' (Andrews 51).

The First World War, with its transnational pacifist organizations, woman's movement for peace, and extensive relief work effort, sowed the seeds for an intersectional pacifism that took on a number of expressions in the interwar era as the 1930s gave way to more war. Initially coined by Kimberlé Crenshaw, 'Intersectionality', according to Patricia Hill Collins and Sirma Bilge, is a wide-spanning term that can signify 'a *heuristic*, a problem-solving or analytic tool' that recognizes the interconnection between the 'major axes of social divisions in a given society at a given time, for example, race, class, gender, sexuality, dis/ability, and age' and how they 'build on each other and work together' across 'intersecting categories of social division' (4). Reading Bloomsbury pacifism as intersectional, then, illuminates that the members of the group understood peace-making as an issue embedded in social structures and power dynamics. It reveals that for Bloomsbury, pacifism was not a single-issue cause. The members theorized ways in which the world could support peace by addressing systemic inequalities among nations, classes, genders, and races and through interlocking social structures. Bloomsbury projects offer an array of theoretical formulations about peace and the construction of a war-free world; not all of them are nonviolent; not all of them disavow mobilization under all circumstances. However, linking them under a 'weak' pacifist terminology allows us to elucidate the ways that these theories together create intersectional and unique tapestries of a more just, equitable world without war, and how they speak to each other and ourselves today.

THE FIRST WORLD WAR

A little-known manuscript by Roger Fry called 'The Friends Work for War Victims in France' (1915) shows the elements of imagination and action involved in creating a climate of peace.[4] It also exemplifies how First World War pacifism laid the groundwork for the revolutionary and intersectional pacifisms of the 1930s by bringing together war resistance and social justice action. In the spring of 1915, Fry travelled to the Marne to join his sister Margery and the Society of Friends in the work of reconstruction in those zones terrorized by the war, 'building temporary huts to house the inhabitants, giving them seeds and mending their agricultural implements' (*Letters* 384). 'The Friends Work' offers an account of this effort, a mission which David Garnett was also involved ('War Victims' Relief'). Written for *The Nation* (Caws and Wright 165), the manuscript was never published during Fry's lifetime.[5]

The volunteer work in France demonstrates the desire for international cooperation in the creation of goodwill. Ruth Fry, Roger Fry's sister, writes about the sentiment behind the relief work: 'Friendliness and love in us kindle their like in others ... If this be true of personal relations, we believe it to be true equally of civic and international ones' (xvii).

Farah Mendlesohn, throughout *Quaker Relief Work in the Spanish Civil War*, contends that the Society of Friends in the modernist era more and more progressively merged their social justice and peace testimonies. What had started as historically a testimony against war – and note these words – became, in the twentieth century, the peace testimony, which works at the crossroads of peace, social justice, and human rights as an intersectional activist endeavour.

'The Friends Work' extends Fry's pacifism and promotes peace on two registers: it facilitates the contemplative space to think upon the horrors of war juxtaposed with the constructive work of peace and it documents the positive effects of the relief work, illuminating a social justice pacifism based on preserving human life and dignity in the time of war. This is to say that the manuscript performs the activist pacifism it records. The kind of emotional processing Fry outlines in his seminal 1909 'Essay on Aesthetics' occurs within the pages of this document.[6] For Fry, art is the place where imagination is not only expressed, but educated. Art allows the emotions to be experienced and analysed in ways that 'actual life' eclipses, as 'life' demands immediate action (*Vision and Design* 15). Through art, we gain a new way of seeing and a 'clarified sense of perception' (18) that allows one to analyse emotions, recognize elements of the world that would be missed in real time, and harness the emotional and imaginative lives. Through these elements of contemplation, 'The Friends Work' inspires a revulsion of war and orientation towards peace in the reader.

The manuscript contains vivid images of destruction and ruins that are offset by painterly descriptions of the land and the effort of reconstruction. In 'An Essay in Aesthetics', Fry itemizes certain techniques to attain 'emotional elements of design': rhythm, mass, space, light and shade, colour, and the 'inclination to the eye of a plane' (23–4) which surfaces here in his writing (consciously or not) and results in a vivid, aestheticized language. Starting with a peaceful and poetic prose, Fry's syntactic rhythm describes the expansive plains, dappled with little hills, where the reader is introduced to a scene from a Post-Impressionist painting: 'Under the April sky pale with a North Easterly breeze the plains of the Marne and the low chalk hills that envelope them are at their loveliest. The poplars are violet dusted with gold and only here and there a spot of green accentuates the harmony' ('Friends Work' 1). Fry invokes the mixture of colour, space, rhythm, light, and shade, lulling the reader into contemplative harmony with the landscape. This harmony, the beauty, is then interrupted: 'Suddenly the boom of distant guns echoes gently' (1). Remarking upon the surreal nature of war, that 'seems to belong to the legendary and mythical' (1), Fry recounts, 'this destruction is total irremediable and complete. As one looks down the street the central chimney of each house sticks its blackened finger up against the sky, the rest is one heap of indistinguishable and irrelevant rubbish' (2–3). Continuing on down the road, Fry proceeds with his narrative of desecration in the village of Sommeilles: 'The church is standing though shattered here and there with the gaping holes made by shell [*sic*] ... The rest of the hillside is one long line of ruin' (3). Through these stylized descriptions based on the juxtaposition between war and peace, Fry offers the reader the opportunity to observe the destruction from battle contrasted alongside the serenity of the April sky and land.

Fry notes the utter devastation of the French towns, but also the work the Friends are undertaking to relieve the civilian population from the conditions of war. One homeless civilian expresses to Fry that the 'Friends' Mission were going to build her a wooden house and her life would begin again' (8). Fry continues later in the text, 'and so day by day the strange landscape of Sermaize les bains changes perceptibly and here and there the little wooden huts with their curtained windows push up their red-tiled or tar-felted roofs through the tumbled rubbish heap like fungusses [*sic*] that shoot up at once on some piece of burnt or wasted land' (9). Invoking images of mushrooms, the language here stresses a certain organic healing over the 'burnt or wasted' land. Fry's manuscript illuminates a restorative pacifism based, most literally, on rebuilding and constructive energies.

Leonard Woolf also represents Bloomsbury internationalism, albeit in a very different way. Deeply ingrained in pacifist activist networks, Woolf's actions and theories poignantly invite the argument for a 'weak' formulation of pacifism because, though he worked consistently for peace, he never fully disavows the possibility of force. He served in the Ceylon Civil Service 1904–11 (see Sarker in this volume), but when the First World War broke out, Woolf was prepared to register as a Conscientious Objector, which ultimately proved unnecessary because he was offered an exemption (Reed, *Rooms* 182). During the war years, Woolf was an active member of the Fabian Society, for whom he wrote the reports that were published as *International Government* in 1916, a 400-plus-page study, the last section drafted collaboratively with the Fabians. Through the 1920s, he was on the executive committee of the League of Nations Society, which became the League of Nations Union (Froula 100), was 'a secretary of the Labour Party Advisory Committees on International and Imperial Affairs', and ran for Parliament (*Downhill* 33).

Woolf's unique brand of 'weak' pacifism, which would resemble most closely Martin Ceadel's definition of *pacificism*, might best be described in Christine Froula's terms as 'preemptive peace' (Froula 97). His international theories also fall under the rubric of positive peace, which accents peace-making through a deliberate structural building or rebuilding. Consistently throughout *International Government* and *The Framework of a Lasting Peace* (1917), Woolf avers that a strong international government will stabilize relations between nations and pave the path to peace. For Woolf, 'the problem of war and peace is a problem of the relations of human groups' (*Framework* 12), and these groups, that is, 'States or nations' (12), can and should be regulated in their relations through government. *International Government* is a modernist text in that it strongly responds to the evolution of modernity and the interconnected conditions that it has brought about, showing how the development of trade, travel, communication, and economic interdependence puts out an ethical call for peace and global governance.

Though he never completely eliminates the possibility of force, Woolf's commitment to creating a future peace is radically emphasized in his 'declaration of political faith' (*Downhill* 36) of 1922:

> This country must stand out in Europe and the world as a sincere supporter of a policy of peace and international co-operation. The pivot of its programme must therefore be (1) a real League of Nations, inclusive of all nations, the members of which undertake a definite obligation not to go to war; (2) disarmament, beginning with drastic limitation of naval and military armaments, coupled with a general guarantee against aggression. (*Downhill* 38)

Woolf's speech goes on to demand, among other things, a more 'equitable settlement' between Germany and France, 'complete abandonment of the policy of imperialism', self-rule for India and Ceylon, and Egyptian independence (38–9). From these priorities, coupled with Woolf's First World War writings, a few salient elements stand out. Woolf consistently emphasizes the creation of peace in his thought and action, and his 'weak' and intersectional pacifism takes the form of an internationalism that manifests in the building of large-scale worldwide governing structures. The challenges he introduces to 'strong' pacifist discourses by speculating about when force is necessary, such as the clauses in *International Government* allowing for a state collective military action against an aggressive state (409–10), should encourage us to work through these ideas more carefully, and open room for wider debate and a further constellation between peace theories, political action, and international relations. His focus on the root structures of governance, the interrelationship between states, the movement towards an 'inter-State Socialism' (181), and anti-colonialism as essential to peace all open onto an intersectional pacifism that contends with the world as it is while maintaining the belief that humans are capable of living together without war.

On a more local and interpersonal register, Vanessa Bell's creation of a domestic centre in conversation with her art and politics allows us to read Bloomsbury lifestyle as a form of pacifist activism in and of itself. During the First World War, Bell moved to the countryside with Duncan Grant and David Garnett in order to facilitate their Conscientious Objection by allowing them to perform nonmilitary government service through farming. Bell and Grant famously turned their country house Charleston into a modernist masterpiece, decorating the majority of surfaces. Roger Fry's and Clive Bell's formalist aesthetics, which insist on the autonomy of 'art' from 'life', might tempt scholars to read all of Bloomsbury through this lens and lead them to erroneously believe Vanessa Bell's rural move, and the continued Bloomsbury production of art that more often than not failed to directly reference the war, was a form of isolated retreat (see Jones in this volume). However, Goldman treats at length the tension between the formalist theories and the integrated artistic practices of Bloomsbury and shows that these practices were received as politically radical within their time. This allows her to argue,

> However apologetic, revisionist, and ultimately rather dull, Bloomsbury formalist theories became, Bloomsbury artistic, political, social and sexual practices may be considered avant-garde nevertheless. And Bloomsbury formalism, of course, remains implicated in these practices. Notorious for its heady mix of sexual frankness and experimentalism, promiscuity, bawdiness, homosexuality, pacifism, feminism, liberalism and aestheticism' (*Modernism* 48)

Goldman continues on to cite Hermione Lee as observing that these transgressive practices should be read as a form of protest against the Victorian system that stressed them as taboo. Mary Ann Caws, likewise, has emphasized the 'interrelation in their thinking, living, and creating' (*Companion* 138).

Vanessa Bell's decision, then, to relocate to the country, create beauty and promote creativity and friendship amidst destruction and chaos, to spread values such as love and personal freedom, and to live in an unorthodox manner with untraditional sexual relationships, was an important political element in a larger challenge to the system that had, in the first place, created war. As Virginia Woolf shows in *Three Guineas,* the 'public and private worlds are inseparably connected' (168), and Bell combatted the public world of war with the private world of pacifist lifestyle. Brockington argues that 'art and aestheticism were central to the Bloomsbury Group's principled, political opposition to the war' (*Battlefield* 30) and a gesture of positive peace. Christopher Reed notes that 'Bell established rural outposts where Bloomsbury could protect its values and preserve its hope' (*Rooms* 169). He coins the term 'aesthetic of conscientious objection' intended to 'stress the often-overlooked continuities between Bloomsbury's political and aesthetic resistance to a war that threatened what the group saw as modernism's fundamental principles' (213). Putting these critical discussions in dialogue reveals Vanessa Bell as a committed pacifist whose painting and domestic art was an essential materialization of that commitment.

Bell's most explicitly antiwar work, *Triple Alliance* (1914), demonstrates the intersection of art, domesticity, and activism. Collaged newspaper articles reporting on the war 'intersperse patriotic fervour with accounts of casualties' (Brockington, *Battlefield* 81) and create a wallpaper-like background with bits of 'torn' maps, 'alluding to Europe's disintegration' (81). A table shaped by paint and newsprint holds a lamp made from the same material and two bottles, one of which is pastiched out of cancelled checks. This work's 'effect is to subordinate news of war to an image of domestic comfort' (Reed 171), where 'it brings out the tensions between art and war, public and private ... the domestic subject matter of the painting jars with, even ridicules, the military sense of its title' (Brockington, *Battlefield* 78). Brockington likens this collage to Picasso's famous *Bottle of Suze* (1912), and unfolds the political and aesthetic sympathies between the two works (*Battlefield* 80–81). Patricia Leighten has shown that Picasso's early *papier collé*, especially *Bottle of Suze*, reveals his lifelong pacifism (*Reordering* 124–5). Here, then, Bell's quotation of Picasso marks the pacifist transmissions in modernist circles and the way in which modernist aesthetics were engaged to promote pacifist ideals.

Invoking the form of collage carries with it the pacifist transmissions that emanate from Picasso's *papier collé*, the blurring of boundaries between life and art, and the inherently radical gesture of creating beauty and images of peace in a time of war. A little-known collage by Bell hidden in the Charleston Attic echoes these concerns. Now called *Angel,* and estimated by the Attic to have been created c. 1915, an angel painted in rich pastels kneels down to pray. Constructed from paper, paint, and the end of a pew, the form of the wings follows the top of the wooden plank, sloping downwards to her head encased between her steepled hands. Goldman writes that Bell, in describing Picasso's techniques, shows 'awareness of the way collage, in decorating frames while at the same time introducing external, three-dimensional materials into the painting, confuses the boundaries between art and life, and this sense of interpenetration itself may be understood as both formalist, in its sense of self-consciousness, and avant-garde in its sense of transgression' (56). *Angel's* transgression is to repurpose the materials of 'life' into a peaceful vision of beauty and harmony. Is it possible the angel is praying for Europe in a time of war?

THE SPANISH CIVIL WAR

With the sustained use of aerial bombardment against civilian populations during the Spanish Civil War as Francisco Franco – with the help of Germany and Italy – tried to overtake the democratic Republican Spain on a fascist platform between 1936 and 1939, however, pacifist ideals progressively worked in intersectional cooperation with radical social justice movements, particularly antifascism.[7] Spain caused Bloomsbury deep personal loss when Vanessa and Clive Bell's son Julian died as a volunteer ambulance driver from shrapnel wounds (Spalding 297–8). In protest of a spreading fascism and the slaughter of civilians, Spain became a site of transnational artistic and modernist production and Bloomsbury was absorbed in this global cause. Virginia Woolf wrote publicly against the fascist invasion in Spain, donated manuscript pages to sell on behalf of refugees, and attended the *Spain & Culture* meeting on 24 June 1937, where she and

Leonard sat behind speakers at the podium. The rally raised money for Basque refugee children, and renowned modernists, including Virginia, E. M. Forster, Vanessa Bell, and Duncan Grant were listed on the promotional materials (see Foster 65–8).

The Artists International Association (AIA) British chapter, for whom Virginia Woolf wrote 'Why Art Today Follows Politics', was a pacifist organization of which Quentin Bell, Vanessa Bell, and Duncan Grant were active members. From the very committed literature of the AIA, we can see how this pacifist activism operated intersectionally with socialism and antifascism. A pamphlet advertises the AIA's mission as one for 'peace, democracy, and cultural development', and cautions that artists' freedom is 'menaced by the threat of war and fascism'. It announces proudly AIA's collaboration with other pacifist and socialist organizations, among them the Left Theatre, the Left Review, and the International Peace Campaign. The AIA became involved in advocating for Spanish Relief when one of their members, Felecia Browne, died early in the conflict in the summer of 1936 (Radford 49) and put together a benefit exhibition of Browne's drawings, the Foreword for which was written by Duncan Grant ('Drawings of Felecia Browne'). In the following years, the AIA set up a number of fundraising events, including a 1936 exhibition 'Artists Help Spain' (Radford 52–3) and a portrait campaign where patrons commissioned portraits from famous British Artists, the proceeds of which went to Spain, including work from Quentin Bell and Duncan Grant (Portraits for Spain).

Duncan Grant, and Vanessa, Quentin, and Angelica Bell are attributed with having designed posters for the Spanish Medical Aid Committee (Martin 44; Foster 68), a subset of the National Joint Committee for Spanish Relief (NJC). The Charleston Trust in

FIGURE 5. Duncan Grant, design for poster Spanish Civil War, with handwritten annotation 'Save 50,000 Spanish children'. Image courtesy of the Charleston Trust. © Estate of Duncan Grant. All rights reserved, DACS, London / ARS, New York / DACS, London.

England has recently uncovered five studies by Duncan Grant for posters for the larger umbrella organization the NJC. One study features a bull with a somewhat human looking face drafted under the pencilled words 'Save 50,000 Spanish Children'. Under this image is a sketch of the outline of a bull with horns. The distinction between these two bulls is striking; the first, part of a larger picture of relief and request for donations, has a pleasant human face and expression; the second draws the viewer's eye to a set of sharp horns (see Figure 5). As the studies develop, these early stages morph into a bull stampeding into a crowd of children, with a human figure flayed in its horns (see Figure 6). The cowering, frightened children are being led away by a female figure, perhaps a governess or relief worker. The symbolism here is distressing – the bull, a classical signifier for Spain, is attacking its young and putting a generation under duress through the trauma of war.[8] This image, created approximately six months before Picasso's famous depiction of the bombing of the Basque town Guernica,[9] anticipates what many critics have considered to be his use of the bull as a threatening nationalist symbol. Three of the other studies all focus on variations of the same image. To the right of the paper, a family in the corner protects two children, while to the left a boat, hopefully filled with food, floats up to a dock (see Figure 7). The words announce, 'SPAIN FIGHTS ON SEND FOOD NOW/ FREE TRADE FOR SPAIN/ SAVE 50.000/ CHILDREN/ DONATIONS TO/ NATIONAL J C FOR/ SPANISH RELIEF.' These images are intended to spur the viewer to action and straddle the boundaries between art, activism, and propaganda. The family shown here needs help to feed their children. As the studies become more detailed, the male adult figure takes on more stereotypically popular front apparel, wearing a beret and holding what could be a bayonet or farming tool, indicating the AIA's partisan support of the Republican and antifascist factions of the war. Indeed, a sketch from Duncan Grant's trip to Spain in early 1936 reveals a potential source of inspiration for the poster study (see Figure 8); the man in the sketch looks remarkably like the man with his family as Grant fills in his features (see Figure 9). The viewer imagines that there are many families like these, starving from the conditions of war, and that if fascism goes unchecked, war and force might spread throughout Europe – a fear that inspired many, writers and artists included, to join or support the International Brigades, volunteers who fought for the Republic from around the globe.

Mulk Raj Anand was one of the many writers who went to Spain intending to combat fascism on the front lines. He enlisted in the International Brigades, but after confronting the moral demands of his unique brand of 'weak' pacifism, became a journalist ('Reminiscences' 14). Like the other Bloomsbury members, Anand uses artistic craft as a form of political intervention and for the creation of a peaceful world. Anand worked for Leonard and Virginia Woolf at the Hogarth Press and was a familiar figure in Bloomsbury circles, which he describes in *Conversations in Bloomsbury* (1981; see Mattison in this volume). One of the discourses that Anand challenges is Bloomsbury's own; he consistently shows that while many British intellectuals fancied themselves progressive, at bottom they 'believed in Pax Britannica', and were 'allergic to Gandhi, because he only wore a loincloth' (*Conversations* 8). Anand represents the pejorative interactions and constant microaggressions he experiences in Bloomsbury as powering his political radicalization: 'The humiliation for being inferior seemed like a wound in my soul, which would never heal ... And I decided in my mind that I would fight for the freedom of my country forever' (24). For Anand, fighting for freedom meant writing and creating new narratives about India. His brilliant First World War Trilogy, which includes the novels

FIGURE 6. Duncan Grant, design for poster Spanish Civil War, 'Save 50,000 children; Donations, etc'. Image courtesy of the Charleston Trust. © Estate of Duncan Grant. All rights reserved, DACS, London / ARS, New York / DACS, London.

FIGURE 7. Duncan Grant, design for poster Spanish Civil War, 'Spain Fights On'. Image courtesy of the Charleston Trust. © Estate of Duncan Grant. All rights reserved, DACS, London / ARS, New York / DACS, London.

FIGURE 8. Duncan Grant, portrait of an older man in beret labelled 'Seville'. Image courtesy of the Charleston Trust. © Estate of Duncan Grant. All rights reserved, DACS, London / ARS, New York / DACS, London.

FIGURE 9. Duncan Grant, design for poster Spanish Civil War (detail). Image courtesy of the Charleston Trust. © Estate of Duncan Grant. All rights reserved, DACS, London / ARS, New York / DACS, London.

The Village (1939), *Across the Black Waters* (1940), and *The Sword and the Sickle* (1942), shows that a true, sustainable peace requires social, political, and economic revolution.

The Trilogy offers a striking example of Anand's global perspective and advocacy for peace, human rights, and social justice. The middle of the three novels, *Across the Black Waters*, was drafted in Madrid and Barcelona while Anand was a journalist in Spain in 1937, and is informed by his time on the front (Cowasjee 108). The Trilogy also demonstrates how, for many, the Spanish Civil War morphed into the Second World War, as its writing and publication spans both wars. The Trilogy traces the growth of a young Sikh protagonist, Lal Singh, nicknamed Lalu. A peasant farmer on the verge of being arrested for falling in love with the landlord's daughter, Lalu joins the British Army. At the outbreak of the First World War, Lalu is transported *Across the Black Waters*, where he fights in France against Germany, losing all of his comrades in the trenches, and is wounded and taken as a prisoner of war. Years later, he is released and send home to India, where he sees the effects of the war on the countryside, which 'though it did not happen in India, it seemed ... to have happened to India' (*Sword* 11). Lalu is radicalized by the state of India, with a ' "money famine" spreading all over the country' (32) and becomes a union organizer to galvanize the peasantry into advocating for themselves against the landlords, which ultimately proves unsuccessful.

Anand, like Leonard Woolf, calls for a consideration of 'weak' pacifism due to his lifetime of humanitarian and pacifist activism (which was manifested by both his literary works and his attendance of numerous international conferences and allegiance to many causes, including the cofounding of the Progressive Writer's Association). Though Anand cannot be considered an absolutist pacifist, his peaceful leanings do keep him from being able to fight and kill in Spain ('Reminiscences' 15) and underwrite many of the concerns he has in literature and life. The *Sword and the Sickle* in particular brings to the front many of Anand's contributions to both thinking peace and resisting war. Here, I concentrate on one long passage from the text that conveys the intersectionality in Anand's work between war resistance, anti-colonialism, and social justice. Lalu sits on a train, thinking. Exemplifying Anand's global, humanitarian perspective, with a Marxist inflection, Lalu muses, 'everywhere it was the same ... there were no black or white people, no yellow or brown people ... but there were only two races and two religions in the world, the rich and the poor' (85). As Lalu gazes out the window, he remembers Europe:

> And a heavy cloud seemed still to hover over the lives of people in every land, broken lives, maimed by the war ... For a moment he could see the long vista of the ghosts of the dead strung on barbed wire across no-man's land. And the heaps of bodies which spread on the land where green fields had been. (85–6)

This is followed by Anand's equally strong condemnation of empire, for as long as imperial oppression continues war is inevitable: 'He had hesitated to believe Verma when the Professor said that all the madness had been brought about in the world by the lust of a few for Empire, and yet, from the changes on the map of the world, it appeared to be so' (86).

Here we see the intersectionality of socialism, anti-colonialism, and war resistance come together. Only through a more even distribution of goods and global equality can a sustainable peace last. The *Sword and the Sickle* challenges readers to imagine strategies for obtaining freedom and equality through cameo appearances of both Indian National Congress leaders Jawaharlal Nehru (249–53) and Mahatma Gandhi (though Anand expresses a fair amount of ambivalence about Gandhi) (201–9), celebrating civil dissent (50–55), creating a commune where everyone lives together in new and better housing (229, 346), offering improvements and strategies for more efficient farming and introducing technologies that will alleviate the striking class differences (160), and many more.[10] Through these writings, Anand contributes an important anti-colonial and antifascist vision for peace to Bloomsbury discourses.

THE SECOND WORLD WAR

As Anand argues that 'fascism is the twin brother of imperialism' (*Letters on India* 145), Virginia Woolf shows that oppression and inequality are at the heart of war and violence. *Three Guineas*, Woolf's pacifist response to the Spanish Civil War marks her 'as an important European theorist of feminism, pacifism, and socialism' (Marcus xxxv). In *Three Guineas,* she outlines numerous activities that women can undertake – from their position as 'Outsiders' to the war-making system – to build a transnational peace and develops an intersectional feminist pacifism. These politics likewise run through her Second World War essay 'Thoughts on Peace in an Air Raid', and *Between the Acts*, featuring a day in the English countryside when the town is putting on a pageant staged by Miss La Trobe. While I cannot do justice here either to the texts or the rich variety of Woolf criticism, I will instead focus on one point that brings together these three works: the interplay between the precarity of life and the interconnectedness of being. In each case, the texts engage a historical materialism that critiques war, capitalism, and the patriarchal system while putting forth visions for peace that contain a concern for and focus on ethics.[11]

Judith Butler offers a critical language through which to approach these themes of Woolf's later texts. For Butler, precariousness is an ontological state that both signals and results from our metaphysical and material interconnectedness: 'In a way, we all live with this particular vulnerability, a vulnerability to the other that is part of bodily life, a vulnerability to a sudden address from elsewhere that we cannot preempt' (*Precarious Life* 29). This is the precariousness of life: an individual's being puts out an ethical call to be respected, supported, and sustained. It is both personal and structural – we rely on others to treat us well, as we rely on sewage systems, electricity lines, and roads and bridges to keep us safe and healthy. In times of crisis or heightened vulnerability (like war), the call gets louder. This vulnerability signals how we are all interconnected: 'the shared condition of precariousness implies that the body is constitutively social and interdependent' (*Frames of War* 31). Woolf's texts show us that a war-making society heightens our vulnerability instead of protecting it, that the structures for being are interconnected and therefore peace must be a transnational movement, and calls for a rethinking of society along the lines of our interdependence.

The heightened precarity and the ensuing violation of ethics that Woolf writes about is gendered; she shows that, far from making women safer, men in conflict pose an intensified threat to women's bodies. In doing so, she challenges the narratives of protection and defence that a militarized society proclaims. *Three Guineas* fiercely states: '"Our" country denies me the means of protecting myself, forces me to pay others a very large sum annually to protect me, and is so little able, even so, to protect me that Air Raid precautions are written on the wall' (128). Indeed, the twinned themes of women's increased vulnerability and military force is at the heart of *Between the Acts*. Sarah Cole emphasizes that 'it is a novel build around the idea of precariousness' (343). The ethical call that the body puts out to be respected is violated by war and military conquest; Isa

Oliver meditates on this throughout the novel. She is haunted by a story she encountered in the daily paper about a woman who had been raped by troopers (Woolf, *Between* 15). In this story, as in Isa's thoughts, military prowess and violence against women converge, casting the precarity of life into full relief and the way in which violence is iterative – what manifests globally will occur locally.

While Woolf demonstrates how war increases vulnerability and is a violation of ethics, she also asks that, in Butler's words, we formulate 'another way of imagining community', one that 'affirms relationality' and 'one in which we are compelled to take stock of our interdependence' (*Precarious Life* 27). In 'Thoughts on Peace', Woolf ascertains that peace must be a global movement, asking the rhetorical question 'but what is the use of freeing the young Englishman [from the war machine] if the young German and the young Italian remain slaves [to war]?' (219). She demonstrates that we must 'think peace into existence' on all fronts for the effort to be successful (216).

For Woolf, art has the potential to help predispose an ethical way of being towards the world and to unify us in our difference. She argues that giving men 'access to the creative feelings' (219) will 'create more honourable activities for those who try to conquer in themselves their fighting instinct, their subconscious Hitlerism' (218). In *Three Guineas*, she gestures towards 'the voices of the poets ... to discuss with you the capacity of the human spirit to overflow boundaries and make unity out of multiplicity' (169). And Miss La Trobe's modernist play in *Between the Acts* reflects the audience's metaphysical interconnection and role in the creation of life, art, and war. The players gather on the stage with all sorts of reflective surfaces so that 'the audience saw themselves, not whole by any means, but at any rate sitting still' (133). A voice-over from the bushes demands, 'consider the gun slayers, bomb droppers – here or there. They do openly what we do slyly' (134). After the voice-over, the gramophone shifts to music, and the scene leaves the audience asking, 'was that voice our selves? Scraps, orts and fragments, are we, also, that' (136)? Emily Hinnov has claimed that the play facilitates a 'choran community', which she defines as 'textual instances that communicate the possibility of a genuine interface between self and other which also implies an awareness of the larger, interconnective community' that allows characters to 'rebuild a sense of communal unity'. The idea of 'choran community' reiterates that Woolf implies a rethinking of community in terms of interconnectedness and that this is an important element in the work towards sustainable peace.

Though Leonard Woolf's paradoxically titled *The War for Peace* (1940) advocates mobilizing against Hitler, we can read this as a 'weak' pacifist text because he keeps the aim for peace alive while emphatically critiquing war. For Woolf, though war is wrong, he believes that there is a 'nasty choice between two immense evils' (49). He explains: 'This vast, ramshackle old house which we call Europe is on fire, and we are all faced with the ugly choice of staying where we are with the probability of being later burnt alive or of jumping out of the window with the probability of breaking our necks' (48–9). However, he criticizes the system of war by reversing the standard narratives around 'political utopias and political realities' (58) throughout this book. Through examples, Woolf continues the argument that he started in *The Framework of a Lasting Peace*, namely that all the ideals we hold, including the elimination of slavery and the creation of democracy started as 'utopian' ideals: 'Everything is Utopian until it is tried' (*Framework* 58). In Woolf's analysis peace becomes the sanest, most practical and 'realistic' course of action, and the continuation of war an emotional and irrational choice. He uses what would now be considered an intersectional lens to work through the ways in which small and large states interact: 'These problems of government ... are simply a question of how the relations between individuals and groups shall be ordered and controlled – relations between individual and individual, between classes, nations, and races, between groups living in villages, town, districts, states, or continents' (*War for Peace* 80), accounting for the complexity of global interactions and connections. Throughout the text, Woolf reminds us that war is little more than 'an organized effort by vast numbers of human beings to kill one another' (4), and that there is nothing inevitable about it. While, for Woolf, there 'will always remain certain conflicting interests between states' there is 'no reason why they should be settled by power and war' (182). Instead he argues that if individuals can have primarily civil relations without violence, there is little reason why states cannot. In making world peace a necessity for international relationships and the progress of civilization, *The War for Peace* brings pacifist ambitions to the political area. Holding the space for a future peace in a world at war is in and of itself a great pacifist service.

HOLDING SPACE FOR PEACE

Each of these very disparate Bloomsbury projects for peace offers us a different element in the construction of what it would take to create a more just, sustainable world, employing modernist techniques and engaging modernist thought to stage an intervention in the mass militarization of the era. While their differences at times pull against each other and introduce tension into any 'strong' definition of pacifism, or even render it impossible, a 'weak' notion of pacifism allows us to weave an elaborate dialogue among texts and to read a variety of formulations for peace. This dialogue opens onto a theory of intersectional pacifism for it shows that all of these formulations for peace are in active interplay with a multiplicity of social, political, and structural concerns. For Bloomsbury, the First World War witnessed a restorative pacifism which emphasized relief work that promoted social justice and tried to mitigate the effects of war, the development of an internationalist pacifism that looked to global governance structures, a turn to domesticity as a form of dissent, and a mode of Conscientious Objection that was deeply ingrained in aestheticism. The 1920s and 1930s saw a pacifism that developed an intersectionality with antifascist, anti-colonialist, socialist, and feminist causes, and a pacifism that at times, paradoxically, argued war as the best path to peace. What Bloomsbury shows us is that abstaining from war, while one element of pacifism, is not the most important nor even the most difficult part. Their intersectional pacifisms were rooted in a complex manifold of issues of power, human society and organization, and individual agency. Bloomsbury radical pacifisms propose a number of possibilities for reform and revolution. And at those times when nonviolence fails (and here I am thinking particularly about the Spanish Civil War and the Second World War, and also about all the global tensions today), a belief in peace and a vision for peace is still needed to recover from war once the fighting stops. These projects offer us ways to hold that vision.

NOTES

1. Much gratitude goes to the Charleston Trust, especially Vanessa L. Jones, Darren Clarke, and Diana Wilkins for providing me information and images from afar and arranging an insightful visit to the Attic. My conversations with Vanessa were particularly inspiring and informed the readings of Duncan Grant here. An early draft of this paper was read

at the Modernist Studies Association Conference in 2016, and those who attended the panel 'Modernist Counter-Cultures of Peace in Times of Total War' assisted in refining the analysis of Roger Fry. Many thanks also to Jane Goldman for a generative ongoing dialogue and to Derek Ryan and Stephen Ross for their assiduous edits.

2. The distinctive nature and variety of reactions to the First World War is a central theme of Atkin's book, where he argues that 'anti-war reaction existed . . . through a far more widespread variety of individual experience than was generally assumed to be the case' (5).

3. For an example of a 'strong' definition of pacifism, see Martin Ceadel, who separates out differing pacifist philosophies, claiming an extreme, absolutist, unwavering pacifism as the only 'true' pacifism. In his definition, pacifism 'is the belief that all war is *always wrong* and should never be resorted to, whatever the consequences' (3). This is juxtaposed with a return to the antiquated term for pacifism, *pacificism*, which here delineates 'the assumption that war, though *sometimes necessary,* is always an irrational and inhumane way to solve disputes' (3). Under his indexing, the Bloomsbury Group are relegated to 'elitist' (46) 'quasi-pacifists' (45) because not all of them at all times hold a 'universalizeable, principled objection to all war' (9).

4. For a reading of this document that discusses Fry's familiarity with the war and trauma, see Brockington, *Above the Battlefield* (82–4).

5. It was printed in 1995 by the *Charleston Magazine.*

6. It is important to note that Fry himself would not approve of using his theories of art as an analytic for a document that transcribes 'actual life', or to imply that one would use aesthetics to illicit a particular ethical orientation. Though Fry argues admirably for the separation between aesthetic imagination and moral action, there are tensions throughout his writings that pull against this distinction, as Christopher Reed has noted. For Reed, 'Fry's sense of social mission was present from his earliest writings on art' (*Fry Reader* 3). See also Goldman (*Modernism* 42–8), who works through the tension between Bloomsbury's political theories and politics.

7. For further study of authors' involvement in the antifascist movement, see Bradshaw.

8. The *Charleston Attic* writes: 'This design differs to the others we have found in the attic, taking this symbol of Spanish nationality and transforming it into a threat to its own people. It brings the fighting itself into the frame. Here women and children recoil helplessly from the scene of a man being thrown by the bull.'

9. Spalding mentions Grant's and Bell's working on poster designs for Spain in the fall of 1936 (291–2).

10. For further analysis and foundational criticism on the Trilogy that addresses its revolutionary anti-colonialism and disdain of war, which intersects at several points with the reading presented here, see Cowasjee.

11. For further reading on Woolf and 'intimate ethics', see Berman.

WORKS CITED

Archive collections

Bell, Vanessa (c. 1915). *Angel*. Paint and paper on wood, 92 cm × 43 cm. The Charleston Trust, Charleston, England.

Grant, Duncan (c. 1936). Designs for Poster, Spanish Civil War, CHA/P/2258, CHA/P/2291, CHA/P/2303, CHA/P/2354, CHA/P/4120.

Grant, Duncan (1936). Sketch from Spanish Series 4174.

Papers of the International Artists Association, Tate Archive, London, TGA 7043.

The Papers of Roger Eliot Fry, The Archive Centre, King's College, England, REF/122.

Printed sources

Amster, Randall. 'Toward a Climate of Peace', *Peace Review: Journal of Social Justice* 25.4 (2013): 473–9.

Andrews, Charles. *Writing against War: Literature, Activism, and the British Peace Movement.* Evanston: Northwestern UP, 2017

Anand, Mulk Raj. *Conversations in Bloomsbury*, Oxford: Oxford UP, 1995.

Anand, Mulk Raj. *Letters on India.* London: Labour Book Service, 1942.

Anand, Mulk Raj. 'Reminiscences of Faiz Ahmad Faiz', *Indian Literature* 28.2 (1985): 9–22.

Anand, Mulk Raj. *The Sword and the Sickle.* Bombay: Kutub, 1955.

Artists International Association. *Unity of Artists for Peace, Democracy, and Cultural Development.* Papers of the International Artists Association, Tate Archive, London.

Atkin, Jonathan. *A War of Individuals: Bloomsbury Attitudes to the Great War.* Manchester: Manchester UP, 2002.

Berman, Jessica. *Modernist Commitments: Ethics, Politics, and Transnational Modernism.* New York: Columbia UP, 2012.

Bradshaw, David. 'British Writers and Anti-Fascism in the 1930s', Part I. *Woolf Studies Annual* 3 (1997): 3–27; Part II. *Woolf Studies Annual* 4 (1998): 41–66.

Brockington, Grace. *Above the Battlefield: Modernism and the Peace Movement in Britain, 1900–1918.* New Haven and London: Yale UP, 2010.

Butler, Judith. *Frames of War: When Is Life Grievable?* London: Verso, 2009.

Butler, Judith. *Precarious Life: The Power of Mourning and Violence.* London: Verso, 2004.

Caws, Mary Ann. 'Pens and Paintbrushes'. *The Cambridge Companion to the Bloomsbury Group.* Ed. Victoria Rosner. Cambridge: Cambridge UP, 2014. 131–43.

Caws, Mary Ann and Sarah Bird Wright. *Bloomsbury and France.* Oxford and New York: Oxford UP, 2000.

Ceadel, Martin. *Pacifism in Britain 1914–1945: The Defining of a Faith.* Oxford: Oxford UP, 1980.

Cole, Sarah. 'Woolf, War, Violence, History, and … Peace'. *A Companion to Virginia Woolf.* Ed. Jessica Berman. Chichester: Wiley Blackwell, 2016. 333–45.

Collins, Patricia Hill and Sirma Bilge. *Intersectionality.* Cambridge: Polity Press, 2016.

Cowasjee, Saros. *So Many Freedoms: A Study of the Major Fiction of Mulk Raj Anand.* Delhi: Oxford UP, 1977. 98–124.

Diehl Paul F. 'Exploring Peace: Looking beyond War and Negative Peace'. *International Studies Quarterly* 60 (2016): 1–10.

Drawings of Felecia Browne. Forward by Duncan Grant. Papers of the International Artists Association, Tate Archive, London, c. 1936.

Foster, J. Ashley. 'Recovering Pacifisms Past: Modernist Networks, the Society of Friends, and the Peace Movement of the Spanish Civil War'. *Quakers in Literature.* Ed. James W. Hood. Philadelphia: Friends Association for Higher Education, 2016. 47–79.

Froula, Christine. 'War, Peace, and Internationalism'. *The Cambridge Companion to the Bloomsbury Group.* Cambridge: Cambridge UP, 2014. 93–111.

Fry, Roger. *Letters Vol. II 1913–1934.* Ed. Denys Sutton. New York: Random House, 1972.

Fry, Roger. *Vision and Design.* Mineola: Dover, 1998.

Fry, Ruth A. *A Quaker Adventure.* New York: Frank Maurice, c. 1927.

Garnett, David. 'War Victims' Relief'. *We Did Not Fight: 1914–1918 Experiences of War Resisters.* Ed. Julian Bell. London: Cobden-Sanderson, 1935. 129–40.

Goldman, Jane. *Modernism. 1910–1945: Image to Apocalypse.* New York: Palgrave Macmillan, 2004.

Hinnov, Emily M. "'Each Is Part of the Whole: We Act Different Parts But Are the Same": From Fragment to Choran Community in the Late Work of Virginia Woolf'. *Woolf Studies Annual* 13 (2007): 1–23.

Leighten, Patricia. *Re-ordering the Universe: Picasso and Anarchism, 1897–1914.* Princeton: Princeton UP, 1989.

Marcus, Jane. 'Introduction' by Virginia Woolf. *Three Guineas.* Ed. Mark Hussey. Orlando: Harcourt, 2006.

Martin, Simon. *Conscience and Conflict: British Artists and the Spanish Civil War,* London: Lund Humphries, 2014.

Mendlesohn, Farah. *Quaker Relief in the Spanish Civil War.* Lewiston and Lampeter: Edwin Mellon Press, 2002.

Mills, Jean. *Virginia Woolf, Jane Ellen Harrison, and the Spirit of Modernist Classicism.* Columbus: Ohio State UP, 2014.

Portraits for Spain. Papers of the International Artists Association, Tate Archive, London.

Radford, Robert. *Art for a Purpose: The Artists' International Association, 1933–1953.* Hampshire: Winchester School of Art Press, 1987.

Reed, Christopher. *Bloomsbury Rooms: Modernism, Subculture, and Domesticity.* New Haven and London: Yale UP, 2004.

Reed, Christopher. Ed. *A Roger Fry Reader.* Chicago and London: Chicago UP, 1996.

Saint-Amour, Paul. *Tense Future: Modernism, Total War, Encyclopedic Form.* Oxford: Oxford UP, 2015.

'Spain Fights On'. https://thecharlestonattic.wordpress.com/2015/11/11/spain-fights-on/.

Spalding, Frances. *Vanessa Bell,* London: Weidenfeld and Nicolson, 1983.

Woolf, Leonard. *Downhill All the Way: An Autobiography of the Years 1919 to 1939.* New York and London: Harcourt, 1967.

Woolf, Leonard. *The Framework of a Lasting Peace.* New York and London: Garland, 1971.

Woolf, Leonard. *The War for Peace.* New York: Garland, 1972.

Woolf, Virginia. *Between the Acts.* Ed. Mark Hussey. Cambridge: Cambridge UP, 2011.

Woolf, Virginia. *The Platform of Time: Memoirs of Family and Friends.* Ed. S. P. Rosenbaum. London: Hesperus Press, 2008.

Woolf, Virginia. 'Thoughts on Peace in an Air Raid'. *Selected Essays.* Ed. David Bradshaw. Oxford and New York: Oxford UP, 2008. 216–19.

Woolf, Virginia. *Three Guineas.* Intro. and notes Jane Marcus. Ed. Mark Hussey. Orlando: Harcourt, 2006.

Woolf, Leonard and the Fabian Society. *International Government.* New York: Bretano's, 1916.

Case Study: Bloomsbury's Pacifist Aesthetics: Woolf, Keynes, Rodker

JANE GOLDMAN

11.30, Nov. 11th [Armistice Day, 1918]

Dearest,

The guns have been going off for half an hour, and the sirens whistling; so
I suppose we are at peace ... I see we are not going to be allowed any quiet all day.
— Virginia Woolf to Vanessa Bell (*Letters* 2: 290)

Woolf's letter on the morning of Armistice Day to her sister, whose home had been a refuge for conscientious objectors, encapsulates the semantic tensions in the term 'peace' for a Bloomsbury pacifist also seeking some 'quiet' at the official moment of the cessation of the hostilities of the Great War. Bloomsbury famously created domestic interiors as a kind of staging of a peace – a concept of peace, I argue below, that comes close to the classical concept of *otium*, which allows for a pacifist thinking and activism liberated from the toxic binary – generated by acute crisis – of 'peace' as meaning merely the absence of war (see Foster in this volume). Peace, a word so multifariously deployed in the first half of the twentieth century, is enmeshed not only in its Enlightenment and Romantic usages and cognate terms but in its more immediate usages and cognates, not least, for example, 'the Peace' and 'the Armistice'. Charleston, indeed, the 'home for pacifism and conscientious objection', and a 'tenancy rooted in queerness' (Clarke 156) by Vanessa Bell, Clive Bell, Duncan Grant, David Garnett, and frequented by fellow pacifists and conscientious objectors, Virginia Woolf, Leonard Woolf et al, was also the habitus in which John Maynard Keynes wrote *The Economic Consequences of the Peace* (1919).

Bloomsbury's record of pacifism and conscientious objection is in most standard accounts of the group. To briefly recap, Keynes was exempted during the war because of his work for the Treasury, but in equivocation over this role he nevertheless made, but did not follow up on, an application to the tribunal for exemption on grounds of conscientious objection (*ODNB*), resigning himself to working 'for a government I despise for ends I think criminal', as he told Duncan Grant who spent the war doing farm work at Charleston as a conscientious objector. Lytton Strachey, on the other hand, considered himself 'a conscientious objector but not a pacifist', and was 'finally declared unfit for service on medical rather than moral grounds' (*ODNB*). Clive Bell, author of the pamphlet *Peace at Once* (1915), which was seized, prosecuted and burnt by the authorities, was an unwavering pacifist in both World Wars, who laboured as a farmworker for most of the Great War at Garsington, the Oxfordshire home of Philip and Lady Ottoline Morrell, another Bloomsbury refuge for conscientious objectors. Leonard Woolf's tremor preempted his pursuit of formal conscientious objection. Desmond MacCarthy, on the other hand, served with the Red Cross before joining naval intelligence.

Yet at the fringes of Bloomsbury circles, and known by most in its inner circles, is a conscientious objector who was actually imprisoned for his militant pacifist stance, and who furthermore wrote a stunning experimental novel based on his experiences which has been rightly termed 'the most achieved of all pacifist writings' (Pattison 310) – the avant-garde poet, publisher, and translator, John Rodker, whose pacifist novel, *Memoirs of Other Fronts*, was published anonymously in 1932. Rodker, who in 1919 took over from Ezra Pound as London editor of *The Little Review*, founded his Ovid Press the following year, publishing, under this and other imprints, key avant-garde works by T. S. Eliot, Ezra Pound, Wyndham Lewis, Henri Gaudier-Brzeska, Le Corbusier, Paul Valéry et al. In 1937, Virginia Woolf records Rodker's 'nibbles' and 'offers' to buy into the Hogarth Press (*Diary 5*: 105, 106, 121). Rodker was one of the 'Whitechapel boys', a group of London Jewish artists and writers, including Mark Gertler, Isaac Rosenberg, and David Bomberg, all in various forms of contact with Bloomsbury Group members over decades.

In what follows I will sample the writing of both Keynes and Rodker alongside Woolf's for some insight into Bloomsbury's pacifist aesthetics through close attention to the deployment of the word 'peace' and related terms, tracing a rich nexus of pacifist aesthetics, increasingly suspicious, nevertheless, of the word 'peace' itself.

PEACE AND QUIET: VIRGINIA WOOLF

At last they came to the waterfall, to the grove of trees.

Then all Dorothy's powers fell upon the sight, searching out its character, noting its resemblances and its differences and taking it to her heart with all the ardour of a discoverer, with all the rapture of a lover. She had seen it at last – she had laid it up in her mind for ever. It had become one of those 'inner visions' which she could call to mind at any time in their distinctness and particularity. It would come back to her long years afterwards when she was old and her mind had failed her; it would come back stilled and heightened and mixed with all the happiest memories of her past – with Racedown and Alfoxden and Coleridge reading Christabel and her beloved, her brother William. It would bring with it what no human being could give, consolation and peace. (Woolf, 'Dorothy Wordsworth' 118)

What does Virginia Woolf mean by 'peace' here in her short essay, 'Dorothy Wordsworth' (1929), which reflects on the diaries of the sister of the Romantic poet, William Wordsworth? These journals offer a sisterly provenance and insight into his celebrated 'spots of time', which, 'scattered everywhere, taking their date/ From our first childhood' (*The Prelude* XI l.258, 275–6, 212), bring a 'renovating virtue' to 'depressed' minds, a 'virtue, by which pleasure is enhanced,/ That penetrates, enables us to mount,/ When high, more high, and lifts us up when fallen' (*The Prelude* XI. l.210, 216–18, 212). The term 'inner visions' cited here has direct provenance in Dorothy Wordsworth's journals where she talks of her 'dear recollections the bridge, the little waterspout, the steep hill, the church' in the village of Wensley as 'among the most vivid of my own inner visions, for they were the first objects that I saw after we were left to ourselves, and had turned our whole hearts to Grasmere as a home in which we were to rest' (Dorothy Wordsworth [VI] 151–2). But her brother's many 'inner' references in *The Prelude* (1805) along with his poem, 'The Inner Vision' (1833), would be perhaps more familiar echoes for Woolf's readers. In the latter, Wordsworth celebrates pacing 'the ground' with 'unuplifted eyes', accessing 'some happy tone/ Of meditation, slipping in between/ The beauty coming and the beauty gone', finding poetic inspiration in 'Whate'er the senses take or may refuse, – / The Mind's internal heaven' ('The Inner Vision' 1–4). If William Wordsworth seeks an aesthetic of retreat, slipping from the realm of the senses to an interior bliss, his sister retains 'vivid' 'recollections' of 'objects' as her 'own inner visions' per se. Over a century later, Woolf articulates in 'A Sketch of the Past' (c. 1940), 'the strongest pleasure known to me ... the rapture I get when in writing', derived from her experiences of 'sudden violent shock', that is of 'something [that] happened so violently that I have remembered it all my life' (Woolf, 'A Sketch' 72).

The first instance she gives is of physical sibling combat, and perhaps a familial and private origin of what became known in later adult public arenas as Bloomsbury pacifism:

> I was fighting with Thoby on the lawn. We were pommelling each other with our fists. Just as I raised my fist to hit him, I felt: why hurt another person? I dropped my hand instantly, and stood there, and let him beat me. I remember the feeling. It was a feeling of hopeless sadness. It was as if I became aware of something terrible; and of my own powerlessness. I slunk off alone, feeling horribly depressed. (71)

Woolf's socialized ethical awakening in the midst of fisticuffs with her brother contrasts with William Wordsworth's famously solitary moral tutelage under the 'ministry' of 'Ye presences of Nature' (*The Prelude* I.373, 493; 11, 14). Woolf's second kind of shock is a euphoric one, and more in keeping with Dorothy Wordsworth's 'inner visions':

> The second instance was also in the garden at St. Ives. I was looking at the flower bed by the front door; 'That is the whole', I said. I was looking at a plant with a spread of leaves; and it seemed suddenly plain that the flower itself was a part of the earth; that a ring enclosed what was the flower; and that was the real flower; part earth; part flower. It was a thought I put away as being likely to be very useful to me later. (Woolf, 'A Sketch' 71)

Unlike the speaker of William Wordsworth's 'The Inner Vision', Woolf describes not merely pacing the ground with 'unuplifted eyes' that may as well be fully closed, but actually focusing intently on it. She does not simply walk on the ground, she looks at it, grasping the contiguity of flower and earth as a 'whole' and by extension their contiguity with her embodied self. The memory of the shock of grasping relations between these elements feeds her sense of 'the rapture I get when in writing I seem to be discovering what belongs to what; making a scene come right; making a character come together' (72). And it is from this that she reaches 'what I might call a philosophy; at any rate it is a constant idea of mine; that behind the cotton wool is hidden a pattern; that we – I mean all human beings – are connected with this; that the whole world is a work of art; that we are part of the work of art' (72).

Woolf was reading Dorothy Wordsworth in February 1921, and returned to her in May 1929 in order to write her short article for the *Nation & Athenaeum* (12 October

1929) ('Dorothy Wordsworth' 119n1), which she describes as 'nine pages close pressed. How can one get it all in?' (*Letters* 4: 80). And Woolf's account is indeed a highly compressed piece of writing that collapses and simplifies numerous scenes and spots of time from the *Journals of Dorothy Wordsworth* (1897) into something of her own that bridges from Wordsworthian 'spots of time' to a developing Woolfian notion of 'moments of being'. Any reader interested in how Woolf turns the brother poet's most famous and enduring trope of Romantic subjective transcendence – via the prose jottings of the overshadowed sister diarist – to what is now understood as a modern(ist) or avant-garde feminist, materialist, and nontranscendent modern, perhaps existential, concept of 'the moment' must therefore carefully attend to Woolf's reworking of her source text. Woolf closes this closing paragraph of her essay by making Dorothy Wordsworth answer in materialist, phenomenological and affective mode, the 'passionate cry of Mary Wollstonecraft', which if it 'had reached her ears':

> 'Surely something resides in this heart that is not perishable – and life is more than a dream,' she would have no doubt whatever as to her answer. She would have said, quite simply, 'We looked about us, and we felt that we were happy.' ('Dorothy Wordsworth' 118)

The attentive act of looking 'about us', that is actively scrutinizing the particular ground on which we stand, in all its particularity, brings a bliss that prefigures Woolf's euphoric moment of 'shock' at the flower bed.

Attention to Woolf's revision and compression of Dorothy Wordsworth's writing becomes crucial where the restorative and enhancing powers of the process of recollection of 'the waterfall' (itself a compression of a number of waterfalls in the journal) mixed with memories of companions and of reading, that she ascribes to the workings of Dorothy Wordsworth's mind are summarized by Woolf as bringing 'what no human being could give, consolation and peace' (118). What does Woolf mean here by 'peace'? Is this Dorothy Wordsworth's own term? And why, we must ask, does Woolf, three years later when she comes to revise this essay as the final part of 'Four Figures' in her collection *The Common Reader: Second Series* (1932), cross out the word 'peace' ('Dorothy Wordsworth' 118) and replace it with the word 'quiet' ('Four Figures' 483)?

Before getting to that crucial replacement of 'peace' with 'quiet', there are other revisions and expansions too to the passage following the waterfall. In her account of 'all Dorothy's powers' Woolf turns her verbs from present participle to past historic so that 'searching out its character, noting its resemblances and its differences and taking it to her heart with all the ardour of a discoverer, with all the rapture of a lover' has become 'she searched out its character, she noted its resemblances, she defined its differences, with all the ardour of a discoverer, with all the exactness of a naturalist, with all the rapture of a lover' (483). There is a sense of increased exactitude in such revisions along with the insertion of a further power of 'the exactness of a naturalist'. The repetition of 'she' as the active agent of these particular activities distinguishes sister from brother and marks her listed achievements as historic events in the real world. The pluperfect of an act of seeing – 'She had seen it at last' ('Dorothy Wordsworth' 118) – becomes the perfect of an act of possession: 'She possessed it at last' ('Four Figures' 483). The second version of the paragraph now continues precisely as the first until the intrusion of 'quiet' over 'peace': 'It would bring with it what no human being could give, what no human relation could offer – consolation and quiet' (483). The achievement of either 'consolation and peace' or 'consolation of quiet' rests on considerable and energetic physical and mental activity, even more so in the revised version, at the scene remembered, at the scenes of remembering, at the scenes of writing and reading, rewriting and rereading.

William Wordsworth begins *The Prelude* with the prospect of a 'peace' available in the material present world rather than the afterlife, which offers merely the kind of deathly 'peace' of 'R.I.P.', the prayer for the dead – 'Requiescat in Pace'/ 'Rest in Peace':

Long months of peace (if such bold word accord
With any promises of human life),
Long months of ease and undisturbed delight
Are mine in prospect (*The Prelude* I.26–9)

The chilling kind of peace associated with the burial rites of the devout certainly hung over the Bloomsbury generation who grew up in the Victorian era, obsessed as it was with elaborate mourning the dead, and exemplified by Woolf's albeit atheist father Sir Leslie Stephen in his mawkish uxorial bereavement memoir, *The Mausoleum Book*. In the twentieth century the Bloomsbury Group's assault on the mores of the Victorians certainly included their death cult, which extended its grip into the era of the Great War and its aftermath, to what David Bradshaw calls 'the necrolatry of the state' (107). It is against the mass military state necrolatry of the war and postwar era that Bloomsbury's queer pacifism and conscientious objection are first joyously and heroically pitched. And by then, as we will explore below, there were powerful and huge new cultural and political dimensions and semantics attached to the word peace, and its cognates 'The Peace' and 'The Armistice', factors that in 1932 might well have informed Woolf's replacement, in her discussion of Dorothy Wordsworth's journal, of the word 'peace' with the word 'quiet'.

It is 'bold' indeed to claim 'peace' for a fallen historical human world rather than an eternal divine realm. Wordsworth's finessing of it into 'ease and undisturbed delight' moves the 'bold word', 'peace', closer to the pagan, classical Latin term *otium*, a now rare borrowing in English, which means 'leisure, vacant time, freedom from business … ease, inactivity, idle life' (Lewis and Short 1285). *Otium* most certainly 'does not all mean idle time', whereas *Neg-otium*, according to Bernard Stiegler, 'constitutes an economy which is internalizable via an accounting … of what is calculable for a businessman, and negotiable on a market, all sense of measure … being reduced to this calculation' (Stiegler 54). And war, with all its and economic consequences and industrial scale procurements, may well be a classic state of *Neg-otium*. *Otium* can also mean 'rest, repose, quiet, peace (opp. *bellum*)', that is a state contrary to war, originally designating and deriving from free time in military life. The related term, *vacuum* means more straightforwardly 'disengaged, unoccupied, idle' (Lewis and Short 1951). For the Roman republic, there are different degrees of *otium*, active to inactive, and the interrelated but distinct terms for peace – *pax, tranquillitas, otium*, and *concordia* – carry a range of considerable political and personal forces, public and private, which permeate through to modern day law and letters, underpinned certainly in the formal education of Bloomsbury members, steeped in Cicero, Tacitus, Ovid et al.

Although it seems to define idleness, repose and inactivity, *otium*, then, may be understood paradoxically as a state of energetic, engaged productivity, particularly artistic, literary, and intellectual, and so much so that *otium* and *otia* can mean the fruit and fruits of leisure and idleness as in Ovid's *otia nostra* ('my poems'). The *Oxford English Dictionary* shows that it is in this latter sense that otium has been used in English, at least into the late nineteenth century:

1815 T. Chalmers *Let.* in W. Hanna *Mem. T. Chalmers* (1851) II. 21 A life of intellectual leisure, with the *otium* of literary pursuits.

1850 Thackeray *Pendennis* II. xxx. 306 Mr. Morgan was enjoying his *otium* in a dignified manner, surveying the evening fog, and smoking a cigar.

1877 L. W. M. Lockhart *Mine is Thine* v. 55 Life cannot be meant to be passed in literary *otium* or philosophical speculation. (*OED*)

Wordsworth's 'ease' perhaps has less of the self-conscious force and satiric bite of Samuel Johnson's tour de force in *otium*, *The Idler*, but they both belong to the same otiose continuum to which Woolf and her Bloomsbury colleagues bring their own twentieth-century otiose turns and practices. Johnson, who stands behind Woolf's 'common reader' and whom she read voraciously, cites Horace in his first *Idler* essay (Saturday, 15 April 1758): '*Vacui sub umbra Lusimus.* ["At leisure we have sported under the shade"] – Hor. Lib. i. Ode xxxii. 1.' Play and sport may in themselves be strenuous activities but nevertheless count as forms of idleness and leisure.

Johnson defines the idler as a universal and levelling figure of noncombative, peaceful humanity:

> The *Idler*, who habituates himself to be satisfied with what he can most easily obtain, not only escapes labours which are often fruitless, but sometimes succeeds better than those who despise all that is within their reach, and think every thing more valuable as it is harder to be acquired ... Every man is, or hopes to be, an *Idler*. Even those who seem to differ most from us are hastening to increase our fraternity; as peace is the end of war, so to be idle is the ultimate purpose of the busy ... The *Idler* has no rivals or enemies. The man of business forgets him; the man of enterprise despises him; and though such as tread the same track of life fall commonly into jealousy and discord, *Idlers* are always found to associate in peace; and he who is most famed for doing nothing, is glad to meet another as idle as himself. (1)

The purposive business of the idler resembles the 'efforts, beyond the time of employment' that Bernard Steigler shows to 'belong within the realm of what the Romans cultivated as *otium*, a word which ... translates as "*studious leisure*"' (Stiegler 52–3, citing André 177). And Johnson marks out both writers and readers as quintessential idlers:

> There is perhaps no appellation by which a writer can better denote his kindred to the human species. It has been found hard to describe man by an adequate definition. Some philosophers have called him a reasonable animal; but others have considered reason as a quality of which many creatures partake. He has been termed likewise a laughing animal; but it is said that some men have never laughed. Perhaps man may be more properly distinguished as an idle animal; for there is no man who is not sometimes idle. It is at least a definition from which none that shall find it in this paper can be excepted; for who can be more idle than the reader of the *Idler*? (1)

Again the paradox of *otium* is exposed, since the idler 'sacrifices duty or pleasure to the love of ease', yet this ease is not the eschewal of activity per se, for the

> *Idler*, though sluggish, is yet alive, and may sometimes be stimulated to vigour and activity. He may descend into profoundness, or tower into sublimity; for the diligence of an *Idler* is rapid and impetuous, as ponderous bodies forced into velocity move with violence proportionate to their weight. (1)

Otium, more starkly put by Stiegler (recalling Roland Barthes' love of piano practice as true musical appreciation), 'is work', and 'work always involves an instrument, and hence ... so too does *otium*' (Stiegler 64). *The Idler* likewise demands *work* – an economy of writing style that requires considerable writerly diligence, and the deployment of energies devoted to pithy compositional restraint, to revision and excision, to the effectiveness of silence over verbal bluster:

> only let him that writes to the *Idler* remember, that his letters must not be long; no words are to be squandered in declarations of esteem, or confessions of inability; conscious dulness has little right to be prolix, and praise is not so welcome to the *Idler* as quiet. (Johnson 1)

Quiet here is not without force and sound, nor peace without volatility.

Dorothy Wordsworth mentions in her journals a church her brother saw in Rydale as 'an image of peace' upon which 'Wm. wrote some lines' (Dorothy Wordsworth [IV] 64). But she more often uses the term 'peaceful', and nowhere more notably than in the passage Woolf herself cites earlier in her essay (both versions) where she describes how Dorothy and William 'take the old cloak and lie in John's grove out of doors together':

> William heard me breathing, and rustling now and then, but we both lay still and unseen by one another. He thought that it would be sweet thus to lie in the grave, to hear the peaceful sounds of the earth, and just to know that our dear friends were near. The lake was still; there was a boat out. ('Four Figures' 481; cf. 'Dorothy Wordsworth' 116–17; Dorothy Wordsworth [V] 114)

Here the unspoken transcendent peace of the eternally silent grave (of their brother), its implicit sign R.I.P., is displaced by the living, noisy siblings' desire to hear the 'peaceful sounds of the earth'. How much further does Woolf take such celebrations of earthly living sonics in her own secular hymns, for example, to the urban 'roar of London' (*The Waves* 135). Here too in the heart of modern city life, Woolf's writing testifies, is a form of peace. Here too in the open-ended activities of writing and reading is a form of peace.

Woolf follows the extract on 'the peaceful sounds of the earth' with a comment on the 'strange love' shared by the Wordsworth siblings, and wrangles the aquatic associations of lake and boat into a metaphor for their creative collaboration and murky division of writerly labours:

> profound, almost dumb, as if brother and sister had grown together and shared not the speech but the mood, so that they hardly knew which felt, which spoke, which saw the daffodils or the sleeping city; only Dorothy stored the mood in prose, and later William came and bathed in it and made it into poetry. But one could not act without the other. ('Four Figures' 481)

Here Woolf's exercising of her own collaborative imagination in response to the *Journals of Dorothy Wordsworth* seems to be following her own advice in 'How Should One Read a Book?', the final essay in *The Common Reader: Second Series*: 'Do not dictate to your author; try to become him. Be his fellow-worker and accomplice' (573). She urges us to read with 'another aim' to 'refresh and exercise our own creative powers', and to recognize 'that is the time to read poetry when we are most able to write it' (576, 577). The kind of busy attentive peace that reading as the writer's fellow-worker and accomplice brings is described by Woolf at the close of her essay in terms that blatantly challenge to the Christian myth of a heavenly afterlife of eternal peace for the righteous and devout:

> Yet who reads to bring about an end, however desirable? Are there not some pursuits that we practise because they are good in themselves, and some pleasures that are final? And is not this among them? I have sometimes dreamt, at least, that when the Day of Judgment dawns and the great conquerors and lawyers and statesmen come to receive their rewards – their crowns, their laurels, their names carved indelibly upon imperishable marble – the Almighty will turn to Peter and will say, not without a certain envy when he sees us coming with our books under our arms, 'Look, these need no reward. We have nothing to give them here. They have loved reading.' (582)

Writers and readers are understood as happy and busy fellow-idlers, embodied in a material, secular world where books always and already give access to the lived, historically situated, and mortal pleasures that inform the peace that is more properly understood as *otium*.

THE PEACE AND THE ARMISTICE: JOHN MAYNARD KEYNES

The word 'peace' undergoes considerable semantic and connotative revisions in the context of the end of the Great War, the Armistice, and the Treaty of Peace with Germany. John Maynard Keynes, Bloomsbury's famous economist, was 'temporarily attached to the British Treasury during the war and was their official representative at the Paris Peace Conference up to June 7, 1919; he also sat as deputy for the Chancellor of the Exchequer on the Supreme Economic Council', according to the Preface to his now landmark book: 'He resigned from these positions when it became evident that hope could no longer be entertained of substantial modification in the draft Terms of Peace' (v). This book underpins why Bloomsbury pacifism is not only of interest because of its stance against the Great War, but because of its objections too to 'the Peace' that followed. It gives chapter and verse for later readers on why the terms of the peace led inevitably to the rise of fascism and Nazism in Europe, to the Spanish Civil War and to the Second World War. This book is a candid account of 'the destructive significance of the Peace of Paris': 'If the European Civil war is to end with France and Italy abusing their momentary victorious power to destroy Germany and Austria-Hungary now prostrate, they invite their own destruction also, being so deeply and inextricably intertwined with their victims by hidden psychic and economic bonds' (Keynes 3).

Before we can understand the Peace, we must consider the Armistice: 'Many persons believe that the Armistice Terms constituted the first Contract concluded between the Allied and Associative Powers and the German Government, and that we entered the Conference with our hands free, except so far as these Armistice Terms might bind us. This is not the case' (52). Hot on the heels of Lenin's 'Decree on Peace' of October 1917, President Woodrow Wilson's 'Fourteen Points' formed the optimistic basis for the German capitulation ten months later on the cessation of hostilities on 11 November 1918, Armistice Day, but, as Keynes painstakingly documents in his book, they did not in fact come to be embodied 'in an actual Treaty of Peace' (39). Instead the Treaty of Versailles emerged, after months spent in 'the weaving of that web of sophistry and Jesuitical exegesis that was finally to clothe with insincerity the language and substance of the whole Treaty' (47), in effect a slow-motion 'legerdemain', as 'the Carthaginian Peace' (32), pressing the most brutal and crushing terms on the defeated, a peace that Keynes insists 'is not *practically* right or possible' (33), a peace built on linguistic chicanery. The longest chapter in his book is the fifth on 'Reparation' (103–210), detailing just how punitive and impossible were the Reparation payments demanded of Germany by the Allies. Keynes departs from 'economic facts' at the close to emphasize

> the policy of reducing Germany to servitude for a generation, of degrading the lives of millions of human beings, and of depriving a whole nation of happiness should be abhorrent and detestable, – abhorrent and detestable even if it were possible, even if it enriched ourselves, even if it did not sow the decay of the whole civilised life of Europe. (209)

In his next chapter 'on the present situation of Europe, as the War and the Peace have made it' in which he no longer attempts to 'distinguish between the inevitable fruits of the War and the avoidable misfortunes of the Peace' (212), Keynes cites the 'Report of the German Economic Commission charged with the study of the effect of the conditions of Peace on the situation of the German population' (213): 'Those who sign this Treaty will sign the death sentence of many millions of German men, women, and children' (215). The chapter concludes ominously:

> As I write, the flames of Russian Bolshevism seem, for the moment at least, to have burnt themselves out, and the peoples of central and Eastern Europe are held in a dreadful torpor. The lately gathered harvest keeps off the worst privations, and Peace has been declared at Paris. But winter approaches. Men will have nothing to look forward to or to nourish hopes on. There will be little fuel to moderate the rigours of the season or to comfort the starved bodies of the town-dwellers.
> But who can say how much is endurable, or in what direction men will seek at last to escape from their misfortunes? (235)

Reading Keynes' coruscating irony ('and Peace has been declared at Paris'), who can now read or undersign that word 'Peace' with any faith in its signification even of a basic pax or cessation of hostilities, let alone of actual meaningful peace or quiet or ease or leisure or *otium*? The ill-conceived Peace Treaty of Versailles becomes here tantamount, then, to a declaration of war.

The word peace appears only three times in *Jacob's Room* (1922), published three years after *The Economic Consequences of the Peace*, all in the space of two paragraphs in chapter 4, and four if we count the adverb in chapter 2 where we find 'green summer waves, **peace**fully, amiably, swaying round the iron pillars of the pier' (*Jacob's Room* 26; emphasis added), an ominous boyhood scene in Scarborough that prefigures the later chapter's equally foreboding account of the youthful sea-borne Jacob's view of the Cornish coast:

> Strangely enough, you could smell violets, or if violets were impossible in July, they must grow something very pungent on the mainland then. The mainland, not so very far off – you could see clefts in the cliffs, white cottages, smoke going up – wore an extraordinary look of calm, of sunny **peace**, as if wisdom and piety had descended upon the dwellers there. Now a cry sounded, as of a man calling pilchards in a main street. It wore an extraordinary look of piety and **peace**, as if old men smoked by the door, and girls stood, hands on hips, at the well, and horses stood; as if the end of the

world had come, and cabbage fields and stone walls, and coast-guard stations, and, above all, the white sand bays with the waves breaking unseen by any one, rose to heaven in a kind of ecstasy.

But imperceptibly the cottage smoke droops, has the look of a mourning emblem, a flag floating its caress over a grave. The gulls, making their broad flight and then riding at **peace**, seem to mark the grave. (76–7; emphasis added)

Just as the earlier instance's adverb 'peacefully' moves 'green summer waves' almost imperceptibly through the mobile syntax toward the sinister, militaristic 'iron pillars', so too the triple accretion of the word 'peace' in the above passage sinisterly shifts the mood of changing appearances from the 'extraordinary look of calm, of sunny peace' via the simile of a state of 'wisdom and piety' to the metaphoric 'extraordinary look of piety and peace', begging the question *why* are calm and peace, piety and peace so repeatedly extraordinary? An answer comes in the next string of similes: 'as if the end of the world had come' and these objects lovingly detailed, almost in the manner of a Stanley Spencer painting, *The Resurrection, Cookham* (1924–7), undergo divine rapture – 'rose to heaven in a kind of ecstasy'. Apocalypse now! Surely the second coming is at hand? The third use of 'peace' occurs in the next paragraph's satiric prolepsis signalling the coming war that will extinguish Jacob for the moment gulled by the very 'gulls, making their broad flight and then riding at peace', that 'seem to mark the grave' (77). Notice how in this slippery chain of signifiers that ends in the self-conscious signifier of a 'mourning emblem, flag', how 'the grave' solidifies with a definite article at the close of this sentence from out of the merely seeming and illusory 'grave' with indefinite article, conjured itself in the previous sentence by the real smoke's figurative semblance to 'a mourning emblem, a flag floating its caress over a grave'. Here is inscribed a warlike signature of peace that underwrites the dead of the Great War – a 'peace' engendered war which ends in the inevitably war-engendering peace of 'the Peace'. In effect Woolf shows the peace going up in smoke before the Great War has even started.

PEACE VIBRATIONS: JOHN RODKER

Lytton has had his exemption taken away by the Tribunal, and is going to appeal. Rodker has been arrested, and declared insane (but something may have happened later). So far, nothing has been done to us. I collected this at dinner last night with Alix and Carrington, where there was also a most singular speckly eyed young man – Aldous Huxley – who owing to Ka [Cox], has got put into a government office. I warned him of what might happen to his soul; however, he spends his time translating French poetry. (VW to VB 26 April 1917, *Letters* 2: 150)

It is a scandal to discover that the avant-garde poet, experimental prose writer, translator and publisher, John Rodker (1894–1955) is only mentioned in the *Oxford Dictionary of National Biography* under the entry for the writer Mary Butts (1890–1937), as her husband from 1918 to 1926.[1] His visceral choric poems, many of which are written out of conscientious objection, and his pacifist novel, *Memoirs of Another Front* (1932), itself a reworking of an earlier poem, 'A C.O.'s Biography' (1916–17), are beginning to receive more critical attention. But my focus here is his deployment of the word 'peace' in his short and louche, avant-garde and phantasmagoric prose work, *Adolphe 1920*, published by the Aquila Press in 1929.[2]

More like a sustained prose poem than a novella, it is written in eight unnumbered sections of astonishing free indirect speech that trace an intoxicated eight hour period, from day to night, in the life of its protagonist. Dick, a writer, appears to be visiting in an hallucinogenic state, with 'mist laden mind' (10), an arena by turns enchanting and nauseating, headily perfumed on 'swooning mist' (5) and nauseatingly miasmic, a possibly Parisian, postwar fairground 'city of booths' (7), populated by exotic and grotesque beings and objects, animals and machines, lures and exhibits, and gathering and dispersing crowds of spectators who themselves become spectacle. All the while Dick is caught up in amorous triangles, in pursuit of one lover, Angela, and in flight from another, Monica, while also arranging a rendezvous with a third, a 'showwoman' performing with a boa-constrictor (22–3). The war is never overtly mentioned, but nevertheless hangs thickly over the scene. We cannot ignore the date, 1920, in the title, and the dates on the last page, 'Dec 1925 – May 1926' (131). And the war dead seem to haunt the piece.

From the very first sentences, the reader is never sure, like Dick himself, whether the protagonist is awake or dreaming as he unfolds 'his prose' (49): 'What had slit up his sleep? His eyes opened but the mind closed again. Piercing sweet the dawn star pierced him, his bowels shivering round it' (5). The reader becomes co-investigator with Dick of all that follows in his mental and physical unravelling, anaesthetized one moment, ecstatic the next, chasing one lover, fleeing another, through this fairground in the viscous 'shimmer of darkening air' (33), 'vacillating in light in dark' (132), caught between infernal and heavenly modes, where the 'sickly incense' (21) of the fair seems like the deadly gas of the trenches one moment and the next the mythopoeic vapours of a chthonic, Delphic pythian goddess. The heady prose of *Adolphe 1920* itself shimmers, trembles and vibrates with an eddying discourse of rising and falling vibration and motion:

> In the booth the half light was thick in the corners and under the cases. The air was throbbing into the afternoon, the frames wavered in it, and their waxy contents vibrated and lived. And the air trembled and lived too, and a vague population flitted batlike from the walls so that the air was full of it. Solemn faces shuffled from behind cases, disappeared, their faces swimming into wax. (32–3)

The pervasive sense of light and air as heavy and viscous simultaneously communicates modern physics and mythopoeic inferno, both repellent and attractive, and a common trope of modernist poetry. It is in this long paragraph that the word 'peace' makes its first of four appearances in *Adolphe 1920*. And peace arrives in an access of vibration that moves through air and liquid, solid and desolidifying objects, and through crowds and barely distinguished individuals, and the writing protagonist himself 'too':

> The wax rose and lived and the life of the place ebbed and flowed on a deep stertorous breath. The shimmer of darkening air confused his eyes, made them water. Blind wings were beating his head, his own being was confused and tenuous and his mind was ceasing to think. He too vibrated to the life of the place. His lethargy, the lethargy of all who now stood in the tent, alarmed Monica, and frightened, feeling she was trapped, she seized his arm and dragged him into the air. He was still at **peace** and his last vibrations faded in the street. The light was leaving the sky. The lamps had a bright dewy look, the air was brighter, thinner; the movement slowed, was loitering, as though all nature expected some shrill call to echo down the street, tear the air to brighter tatters, deliver an awaited message. There was a thudding in his ears. He thought it was the silence and his heart, but it was a steam engine generating power. (32–3; emphasis added)

The question of agency is suddenly forced by the switch of point of view in mid-sentence from Dick's to that of Monica, the scorned lover, who is alarmed by his succumbing to the collective lethargy that is trapping her, just as her 'feeling she was trapped' is a clause itself trapped mid-sentence. But while that sentence has 'dragged' Dick from 'lethargy' to 'air', the next seems to mourn that lost state of lethargy: 'He was still at peace and his last vibrations faded in the street.' Peace comes as a surprise here, and more so the term 'at peace', a common euphemism for the dead. Yet 'peace' here is, as the pun underlines, far from deathly 'still' since its ebbing but defining quality seems to be one of 'vibrations'. This sort of 'lethargy' is not so lethargic, more lotharious. Is this some allegory of coitus and forced withdrawal, where 'peace' is a state of orgasm, the little death? Dick has earlier been watching peep-show pornography courtesy of 'a man-eating one-leg' into which he 'slipped a penny' immediately following which payment a 'warm light moistened its eyes, lit up his chest' (18) and with 'his eyes on its eyes, his heart on its heart' he finds 'the excitement of beating air thrilled him' (18). Is this the same trope of light now permeating from the dewy lamps, the same thudding reifying machinic erotics that make Dick confuse a steam engine for his heart? There is a lesson here not only in love but in industrial labour relations from this 'steam engine generating power'.

What kind of 'peace' is Rodker, the conscientious objector, inscribing in the very city that hosted the postwar Treaty of the Peace? The second occurrence of this loaded word in *Adolphe 1920* is in a passage where Dick is reflecting on the status of his relationship with Angela, and seems to signify a precarious erotic equilibrium, satisfactory to Dick, but not so his restless lover:

> They had got to Camomile. Who said that women, despite themselves, before they notice, have reduced to camomile all love that starts champagne. It was too true, and stupidly he had thought it was himself slowed down their love with thinking, now its settling into what I want. No more late nights, **peace** only, friendship. Yet despite herself and conscious she herself had changed that brew, she thought it was the story of the horse. He had got her down to but one straw a day. That was too little or too much. She must have saved that up for some time. Now the old short cycle of her life would begin again as so often before. The intoxication of love, wine, moony nights, talk and talk and a new face opposite her, remote, flying, to be pursued, drowning her in words till gasping she could come up again and cling to it.
>
> What was his prose to her? Of course he loved. She knew it and was grateful, but that was not it. (49; emphasis added)

Dick's preference for the camomile of a settled erotic (or possibly nonerotic) life over the champagne phase of the chase is expressed in the telegraphic verbless sentence: 'No more late nights, peace only, friendship.' The compressed but mobile syntax and ambiguous punctuation invite multiple readings. Is it a statement of present fact or of future wish? What can 'peace only' mean here, squeezed between lost 'late nights' and 'friendship'? Do 'late nights' mean sexual activity, an erotic pleasure that is now 'no more'? Does peace, whatever it means, attach to 'late nights' and therefore is like them also 'no more', a thing of the past? Or is peace, whatever it means, the 'only' surviving state? Does 'only' attach to 'peace' in retrospect or in advance to 'friendship'? Does 'friendship' imply a falling off of erotic relations into a sexless companionship? Yet it is possible to understand that a bond of friendship is sustained by a peaceful erotic life, where peace is understood as a kind of sexual ease or *otium*. And this otiose existence is linked to Dick's literary production, something his restless muse apparently cares less about: 'What was his prose to her'?

The 'truth' about 'late nights' is then revealed as taken up with champagne rather than sedating camomile, not with sex so much as drink:

> The truth was he was bored with late nights. He did not want to drink and he had used all his tricks. When he was drunk he heard the clock, and she was that clock, ticking away his life, nothing, nothing; and if he did not remember what he had said, he was ashamed. But it was then her mind took wings, her anaesthesia weakened, her thoughts lived with darting presences, a host of faces came to their board speaking through her, mimicking, grimacing, alien. And there were dead among them.
>
>   But the population inside him had mournfully withdrawn, veiling its face. (49)

Angela, drunk, is less sedated and becomes a medium or Ouija board for 'darting presences', speaking faces, including 'the dead', and presumably the war dead. In drink, Dick's 'population' of 'darting presences', on the other hand, 'had mournfully withdrawn'. Camomile or champagne? Perhaps they should call the whole thing off. How can they strike the right mood for 'peace', for 'love', for otium in the postwar era of 'the Peace', as they wrestle with its libidinal economic consequences? And what is Dick actually writing about? In a startling elegiac paragraph towards the close of the book, Dick is writing about forgetting and about cinematic powers of resurrection of the (war) dead, something that seems to trigger memories of now iconic received images of a temporary Christmas truce or peace where opposing forces lay down weapons to play football in the snow:

> Yet he forgot too. The brains [sic] secretion a slime, oozing over, preserving, but deep hiding. In polar wastes among furious icy winds, a man kicks a ball, is alive, and for a moment some lens etches him, and makes him live again as often as a screen projects him to his fellows squatting in London or New York. He lives again among the young, the lovely, their tears of pity the blood his thirsting shade drinks to live again. That is now his life? (125)

No films exist, and very few photographs, to document the legendary Western Front Christmas football truce of 1914, yet the playful sporting figures of this temporary peace are for ever projecting in the surviving memories and imaginations of the living. The living, meanwhile, find themselves like Dick and Angela suddenly and hilariously in a taxi with 'the snake woman' and her snake, all four 'later' finding themselves in a 'dim, low room ... like other low rooms':

> They sat against the wall and Angela was by his side. In his **peace** he had half forgotten she was with him. The snake hung round her neck and she could not keep her hands from it till its owner in sudden jealousy took it from her. The waiter came back, hesitated, came nearer, took their order, went away again. (100; emphasis added)

Like the waiter on seeing the snake, Rodker's readers might well hesitate over his use of 'peace' here. It seems close to an edifying state of (post) erotic bliss for the semiconscious, lucky Dick, at least.

And the living meanwhile also find themselves in fairground booths watching peep-shows and cabarets: 'More girls came on stage. They were pink, smiling in straw hats, white shoes and white suits' (107). By now Monica has acquired a new 'escort' (101) whom she also polices, plucking him out of the dancers' theatrical charm to which he has gladly succumbed:

Monicas [*sic*] man stood up, swaying, green; yelled and was among them, shuffling with them, his hands fluttering, his face floating, his senses swaying in their emanations and the room rose to its feet shouting encouragement at him, but the spell was broken and Monica walked quietly down the room and dragged him back to his seat. (107)

This quiet movement by Monica ushers in the final usage of the word 'peace' in Rodker's book, as the watching Dick reports on his own mood:

His own **peace** grew deeper, stupefying. The air was heavy, warm, and he could not breathe. He went out of the room into the lavabos. He came out and Angela stood there trembling. (107; emphasis added)

While conventional peace may well be understood to deepen, how shocking to find peace 'stupefying' here. Dick's self-delivery from his ensuing sense of suffocation is rewarded after his toilet visit with the reappearance of Angela whose 'trembling' suggests she is finally in tune with Dick's own vibrations. Are the two lovers approaching 'the condition [of] *otium*' that Giorgio Agamben identifies in Titian's *Nymph and Shepherd*, a condition he also terms 'workless [*senz'opera*]' (Agamben 87)? Are they about to become such lovers 'who have lost their mystery', who 'mutually forgive each other', and who 'contemplate a human nature rendered perfectly inoperative' (Agamben 87)? Possibly so; possibly not. If this louche postwar demi-monde that Dick and Angela inhabit seems to resemble the official brothels frequented by soldiers on leave from the front, enjoying their military *otium*, then Rodker's pointed repeated use of 'peace' as some kind of anaesthetizing erotic signifier may well serve as another Keynesian indictment of 'the Peace'. On the other hand, Dick, like Rodker himself and Woolf herself, nevertheless caught between *otium* and *neg-otium*, is not a soldier on leave about to return to the trenches of war, but a writer conscientiously fighting on other fronts entirely.

NOTES

1. See the entry on Rodker in Birch; Pattison (310–11); and Goldman (124–32).
2. My page references are to this 1929 edition.

WORKS CITED

Agamben, Giorgio. *The Open: Man and Animal*. Trans. Kenneth Attell. Stanford, CA: Stanford UP, 2004.

André, Jean-Marie. *L'otium dans la vie morale et intellectualle romaine des origins à l'époque augustéenne*. Paris: PUF, 1965.

Birch, Dinah. Ed. *The Oxford Companion to English Literature* (7th ed.). Oxford: Oxford UP, 2009.

Bradshaw, David. '"Vanished like leaves": The Military, Elegy and Italy in *Mrs. Dalloway*'. *Woolf Studies Annual* 8 (2002): 107–26.

Clarke, Darren. 'Duncan Grant and Charleston's Queer Arcadia'. *Queer Bloomsbury*. Ed. Brenda Helt and Madelyn Detloff. Edinburgh: Edinburgh UP, 2016.

Goldman, Jane. *Modernism, 1910–1945: Image to Apocalypse*. Basingstoke: Palgrave, 2004.

Johnson, Samuel. 'The Idler No. 1'. 1758. *Quotidiana*. Ed. Patrick Madden. 14 January 2008. http://essays.quotidiana.org/johnson/idler_no_1/. Accessed 16 September 2017.

Keynes, John Maynard. *The Economic Consequences of the Peace*. London: Macmillan, 1919.

Lewis, Charleton T. and Charles Short. *A Latin Dictionary*. Oxford: Oxford UP, 1933.

Pattison, Iain. 'Pacifists and Conscientious Objectors'. *The Edinburgh Companion to Twentieth-Century British War Literature*. Ed. Adam Piette and Mark Rawlinson. Edinburgh: Edinburgh UP, 2012.

Rodker, John. *Adolphe 1920*. London: Aquila Press, 1929.

Rodker, John. *Memoirs of Other Fronts*. London: Putnam, 1932 [1926; published anonymously].

Rodker, John. *Poems & Adolphe, 1920*. Ed. Andrew Crozier. Manchester: Carcanet, 1996.

Stephen, Leslie. *The Mausoleum Book*. Oxford: Clarendon, 1977.

Stiegler, Bernard. *For a New Critique of Political Economy*. Trans. Daniel Ross. Cambridge: Polity Press, 2013.

Woolf, Virginia. *The Diary of Virginia Woolf*, 5 vols. Ed. Anne Olivier Bell and Andrew McNeillie. London: Hogarth Press, 1977–84.

Woolf, Virginia. *The Essays of Virginia Woolf*, 6 vols. Ed. Andrew McNeillie (vols 1–4) and Stuart N. Clarke (vols 5–6). London: Hogarth Press, 1986–2011.

Woolf, Virginia. *Jacob's Room*. London: Hogarth Press, 1922.

Woolf, Virginia. *The Letters of Virginia Woolf*, 6 vols. Ed. Nigel Nicolson and Joanne Trautmann. London: Hogarth Press, 1975–80.

Woolf, Virginia. 'A Sketch of the Past'. *Moments of Being* (2nd ed.). Ed. Jeanne Schulkind. London: Hogarth Press, 1982.

Woolf, Virginia. *The Waves*. London: Hogarth Press, 1931.

Wordsworth, Dorothy. *The Journals of Dorothy Wordsworth*. Ed. William Knight. London: Macmillan, 1904 [1894].

Wordsworth, William. *The Prelude* (1805). DjVu edition (2001). http://triggs.djvu.org/djvu-editions.com/WORDSWORTH/PRELUDE1805/Download.pdf

Wordsworth, William. *The Works of William Wordsworth*. London: Macmillan, 1889.

INDEX